Binominal Lexemes in Cross-Linguistic Perspective

Empirical Approaches to Language Typology

Edited by
Georg Bossong
Kristine A. Hildebrandt
Jean-Christophe Verstraete

Volume 62

Binominal Lexemes in Cross-Linguistic Perspective

Towards a Typology of Complex Lexemes

Edited by
Steve Pepper, Francesca Masini and Simone Mattiola

DE GRUYTER
MOUTON

ISBN 978-3-11-163165-3
e-ISBN (PDF) 978-3-11-067349-4
e-ISBN (EPUB) 978-3-11-067352-4
ISSN 0933-761X

Library of Congress Control Number: 2022941451

Bibliographic information published by the Deutsche Nationalbibliothek
The Deutsche Nationalbibliothek lists this publication in the Deutsche Nationalbibliografie; detailed bibliographic data are available on the internet at http://dnb.dnb.de.

Chapter "Exploring complex lexemes cross-linguistically" © Francesca Masini, Simone Mattiola and Steve Pepper; Chapters "Defining and typologizing binominal lexemes", "Hatcher-Bourque: Towards a reusable classification of semantic relations" © Steve Pepper

© 2024 Walter de Gruyter GmbH, Berlin/Boston
This volume is text- and page-identical with the hardback published in 2023.
Typesetting: Integra Software Services Pvt. Ltd.

www.degruyter.com

Contents

Francesca Masini, Simone Mattiola and Steve Pepper
Exploring complex lexemes cross-linguistically —— 1

Part 1: Form (morphosyntactic strategies)

Steve Pepper
Defining and typologizing binominal lexemes —— 23

Denis Creissels
Binominals and construct marking —— 73

Jakob Lesage
Compounds and other nominal modifier constructions in Pama-Nyungan languages —— 103

Marie-Elaine van Egmond
New types of binominal lexeme in Anindilyakwa (Australia) —— 153

Åshild Næss
Binominals in Äiwoo: Compounds, possessive constructions, and transitional cases —— 181

Bożena Cetnarowska
NN.GEN and NAREL juxtapositions in Polish: Syntactic schemas employed in building phrasal nouns —— 213

Françoise Rose and An Van linden
The derivational use of classifiers in Western Amazonia —— 237

Chiara Naccarato and Shanshan Huang
Binominals denoting instruments: A contrastive perspective —— 277

Part 2: Meaning (semantic relations)

Steve Pepper
Hatcher-Bourque: Towards a reusable classification of semantic relations —— 305

László Károly
Binominal strategies and semantic correlations in Turkic languages —— 355

Aslı Gürer
A classification of compounds in Karachay-Balkar —— 381

Polina Pleshak
Binominal lexemes in Moksha and Hill Mari —— 401

Part 3: **Acquisition**

Maria Rosenberg
Binominals and potential competitors in language development: Evidence from Swedish —— 431

List of contributors —— 463

Index of Subjects —— 465

Index of Languages —— 471

lexical typology, as also argued by Koptjevskaja-Tamm & Veselinova (2020). Taking into greater consideration word-formation processes and multi-word expressions is paramount to get a more truthful and comprehensive picture of vocabularies across languages. Indeed, both complex words and at least a section of multi-word expressions, viz. phrasal lexemes, are employed to create new complex lexical items, sometimes co-existing within one and the same language, where they may compete with each other, or compensate for one another in the expression of lexico-conceptual meanings (Masini 2009b).

The success of a 'unified' typological approach to complex lexemes depends on two conditions: (i) a supporting theoretical background; and (ii) clear definitions for cross-linguistic comparison.

As for (i), we believe that Construction Grammar approaches (Goldberg 1995; 2006; 2019; Hoffmann & Trousdale 2013; Hilpert 2014) may be the answer, for at least two reasons.

On the one hand, Construction Grammar has proved to be well-equipped to deal with cross-linguistic explorations, both contrastive studies (e.g. Hilpert & Östman 2014) and typology (Croft 2001). Crucially, regarding constructions (i.e., form-function pairings) as the basic units of linguistic analysis overcomes the traditional subdivision into levels of analysis, especially between syntax and the lexicon, thus accommodating quite straightforwardly a wide array of 'intermediate' structures like idioms and multi-word expressions (cf. the syntax-lexicon continuum as depicted by Croft 2001: 17; Goldberg 2013: 17). Studies within Construction Morphology (Booij 2010; Masini & Audring 2019) are also explicit about including multi-word expressions into the picture, allowing for a unified treatment of 'lexemes', namely constructions with a concept-naming function, independently of their structural complexity and internal composition (simple words, complex words, multi-word units, etc.). In short, a constructionist view 'licenses' an onomasiological approach to lexemes in general, and more specifically to 'complex lexemes', namely non-basic lexemes which reflect speakers' creativity along with their need to label new categories using previously existing, meaningful linguistic material (much in the vein of Martinet's 1949 'primary articulation').

Incidentally, since constructions may have different levels of schematicity or abstractness, we can take into consideration both lexically specified constructions (for instance, existing complex lexemes like *earthquake*) and more abstract constructions (for instance, NN compounding) that function as templates for the creation of new complex lexemes, since both are regarded as constructions or 'signs'. Assessing the productivity of lexical constructions may not be easy (especially in large-scale typological studies, which often must rely on data elicitation or descriptive grammars). However, despite the practical challenges it poses, productivity may be an important factor when it comes to understanding the inter-

This separation is a reflection of the traditional divide between morphology and syntax that has characterized linguistics since structuralism. The wealth of literature on the word/phrase (and compound/phrase, e.g. Lieber & Štekauer 2009b) distinction is symptomatic in this respect. However, when your goal is to understand how complex concept naming works, it is quite clear that *all* these strategies should be considered and kept together, for the simple reason that, potentially, *all* of them may express complex concepts. Suffice it to consider the crosslinguistic variation we encounter, in terms of morphosyntactic strategies, when we translate terms from one language to another. A trivial illustration follows for 'earthquake' in a few (related and unrelated) languages:[2]

(1) a. English [ENG]
         earthquake   NN compound
     b. Italian [ITA]
         sisma   simple N
     c. French [FRA]
         tremblement de terre (quake of earth)   NPrepN phrasal lexeme
     d. Polish [POL]
         trzęsienie ziemi (quake earth.GEN)   NN$_{GEN}$ phrasal lexeme
     e   Hebrew [HEB]
         רעידת אדמה [re'idat adama] (quake.CS earth)   construct state
     f. Arabic [ARA]
         زلزال [zalzāl]   (non-concatenative) derivation

Different strategies may surface in one and the same language (cf. French *tremblement de terre* vs. *séisme*, a simple word), possibly competing with one another, making the whole picture even more complicated.

Masini (2019a) discusses the relationship between word-formation and multi-word expressions and makes the case for a unified approach to these domains – both in theoretical linguistics and in typology – by virtue of their common function. She also advocates for a more active inclusion of multi-word expressions within

---

[2] List of abbreviations used in this chapter: ADJZ = adjectivizer; CLF = classifier; CON = connective; CS = construct state; GEN = genitive; NMLZ = nominalizer; OBL = oblique; PREP = preposition; REP = reported. As for language classification, we decided not to include genealogical information for the languages cited in this introduction, and in the whole volume, since there is no general agreement in the linguistic community about genealogical classification and language names. Rather, we decided to provide the ISO-code 639-3 (or the Glottocode, where no ISO-code exists) for each language when first introduced.

investigations (beyond European languages, cf. Müller et al. 2015–2016) despite some laudable initial attempts (see Štekauer, Valera & Körtvélyessy 2012), with the result that gaining comparable data on word-formation processes is not an easy task. Possibly as a consequence of this lack of typological studies, word-formation is under-represented in major typological online resources. Take, for instance, WALS Online (Dryer & Haspelmath 2013), where few features (13 out of 192) pertain to the "Lexicon" and where the "Morphology" area is entirely devoted to inflection, word-formation being basically absent, with the notable exception of reduplication (Rubino 2013). A similar picture emerges consulting APiCS Online (Michaelis et al. 2013).

On the other hand, the rise of lexical typology in the last couple of decades (Koch 2001; Brown 2001; Koptjevskaja-Tamm 2008; Koptjevskaja-Tamm, Rakhilina & Vanhove 2015) has contributed to bringing the lexicon back to typologists' attention. So far, however, these studies have mostly focused – quite understandably – on (simple) words and on lexical semantics (e.g. Vanhove 2008), rather than complex words and the devices that create them. Still, the latter issue falls within the scope of the field and would definitely deserve to be explored more fully, as Koptjevskaja-Tamm & Veselinova (2020: §2.2.3) have recently argued: "word formation is the research domain where the overlap between the lexical typology and morphology is particularly salient. However, systematic cross-linguistic research on word-formation strategies and their functions has so far been modest. This is all the more surprising given the abundance of data on word formation in individual languages and in individual language families". The authors advocate for a deeper interaction between the fields of morphology and lexical typology ("a huge, still very much unexplored domain"), and report, more generally, that "there is still no methodology that paves the way for a systematic comparison of the vocabularies of different languages".

Still another issue that arises for complex concept naming is the array of formal strategies that may perform this function, the different status these strategies may have in different research traditions, and the frequent lack of connection in the literature between different strategies. In morphology, the main mechanisms for creating complex words are derivation and compounding (Lieber & Štekauer 2009a; 2014; Štekauer, Valera & Körtvélyessy 2012), to which a variety of other mechanisms can be added, from reduplication to incorporation, from conversion to subtraction, from blending to clipping, and so on. Of course, simple words may convey a complex concept, too. And some types of multi-word expressions (cf. Baldwin & Kim 2010; Hüning & Schlücker 2015), like 'phrasal lexemes' (Booij 2009; Masini 2009), also perform a clearly concept-naming function. However, they are generally not considered as part of morphology, being objects beyond the word level (whatever the boundary may be).

Francesca Masini, Simone Mattiola and Steve Pepper
Exploring complex lexemes cross-linguistically
Editors' introduction

1 Towards a typology of complex lexemes

Concept-naming is one of the most fundamental activities performed by speakers, who need either ready-made labels to talk about entities or devices to build new labels (be they rules or processes, schemas or analogical mechanisms). Knowing how languages perform the basic function of creating labels to name concepts, especially complex concepts, is crucial to understanding their creative potential in building new (potentially stable) categories and, more generally, to understanding how they (may) categorize reality, and refer to it. What are the strategies employed by languages for naming complex concepts? How do they differ cross-linguistically, and what are the limits of their variation? Are there strategies that are more widespread than others, or even universal?[1]

These are questions for lexical typology and/or word-formation typology, but what we know about the typology of complex concept naming is very limited compared to what we know about domains like word order or inflectional morphology. There may be different reasons behind this state-of-affairs. Analysing all of them falls outside the scope of the present introduction: we will just discuss some factors that we deem relevant for our current purposes.

Complex concept naming is definitely related to word-formation. The domain of word-formation can count on an extremely rich and ever-growing body of literature, which would be impossible to credit here (suffice it to mention the collections edited by Booij, Lehmann & Mugdan 2000; 2004; Lieber & Štekauer 2009a; 2014; Müller et al. 2015; Lieber et al. 2021). However, quite surprisingly, word-formation has rarely been the subject of large-scale, thorough typological

---

[1] We wish to thank the many anonymous referees who generously agreed to review the chapters included in this volume, including this introduction: their insightful comments significantly improved the quality of the volume. Heartfelt thanks are also due to Jean-Christophe Verstraete for his guidance and constant support, which were essential to bring this project to conclusion. We are also grateful to the audience of the *When "noun" meets "noun"* workshop at the 50th Annual Meeting of the Societas Linguistica Europaea (Zurich, 10–13 September 2017). The usual disclaimers apply.

Note: Open Access for this chapter was granted by Alma Mater Studiorum – Università di Bologna.

Open Access. © 2023 Francesca Masini et al., published by De Gruyter. This work is licensed under the Creative Commons Attribution-NonCommercial-NoDerivatives 4.0 International License.
https://doi.org/10.1515/9783110673494-001

play between the strategies actually available in a language (family) to convey new lexico-conceptual meanings.

As for (ii), the comparability of linguistic structures is one of the most often debated questions in linguistic typology. Although this is a well-known problem dating back at least to the first modern descriptions of languages of Native North America (Boas 1911), the last couple of decades have witnessed an intense debate in the typological literature. Starting from Dryer (1997) and Croft (2001), and more recently Haspelmath (2007; 2010) and Cristofaro (2009), grammatical categories have come to be conceived as specific entities of single languages (*language-specific*) or even of specific constructions (*construction-specific*). It is by now widely assumed that cross-linguistic comparison should not be based on pre-established linguistic categories: "The most important consequence of the non-existence of pre-established categories for language typology is that cross-linguistic comparison cannot be category-based, but must be substance-based, because substance (unlike categories) is universal" (Haspelmath 2007: 124). Instead, cross-linguistic comparison should be conducted via comparative concepts, namely "concepts created by comparative linguists for the specific purpose of crosslinguistic comparison. Unlike descriptive categories, they are not part of particular language systems and are not needed by descriptive linguists or speakers. They are not psychologically real, and they cannot be right or wrong. They can only be more or less well suited to the task of permitting crosslinguistic comparison. They are often labeled in the same way as descriptive categories, but they stand in a many-to-many relationship with them [...]. Comparative concepts are universally applicable, and they are defined on the basis of other universally applicable concepts: universal conceptual-semantic concepts, general formal concepts, and other comparative concepts" (Haspelmath 2010: 665).

Applying this to the problem of complex lexemes, we are by now aware that 'word' is a cross-linguistically unreliable and tricky concept (cf. among many others, Ramat 1990; Haspelmath 2011; Arkadiev & Klamer 2019). But, most importantly, it is the wrong concept for the goal we are pursuing here, namely a typology of 'complex lexemes' intended as non-basic lexemes which also include objects that are *not* morphological 'words' (definable according to language-specific criteria).

What we would like to propose at this point is to consider 'complex lexeme' as a comparative concept. A first (admittedly tentative) definition of this category could be the following:

(2) A complex lexeme (CL) is a concept-naming unit, with a (potentially) stable denotation in a language, which combines at least two formatives or is the result of a (non-concatenative) formal operation over a formative, and which combines at least two concepts entertaining some semantic relation.

This definition appears broad enough to encompass complex words of various types, multi-word expressions and possibly other naming units a language may display that do not fall within these two classes, leaving their formal demarcation and definition to language-specific criteria which are simply not relevant for their inclusion into the CL category. However, this definition also poses some questions. Some clarifications are therefore in order.

One concerns the word 'potentially'. According to the definition in (2), a CL should have a concept-naming, labelling function, which is at least *potentially* stable in the system: nonce expressions, formed on the spur of the moment according to some template of lexeme creation, are not stable by definition, but have the potential to become conventionalized signs, given the appropriate conditions. So the word 'potentially' merely serves to keep nonce formations into the picture.

Another relates with the word 'unit', which is used here to express that CLs should be endowed with some degree of internal cohesion, to be ascertained and defined according to language-specific criteria.

Still another issue is 'complexity'. According to the definition in (2), the complexity of CLs is twofold, regarding both its formal and its functional side. On the formal side, we include items which are either the combination of two or more formatives (affixes, words, clitics, classifiers, etc.) or the result of the application of some other type of operation which does not involve the addition of morphosyntactic material (think of clipping or conversion). On the functional side, our definition states that CLs should combine at least two concepts. This may be a weak point of the definition because it seems to imply an iconic relation between form and function which is far from real. As a matter of fact, the world's languages display both basic (formally simple) lexical items that 'conflate' (Talmy 2007) two or more concepts (see Italian *sisma* in (3)), and formally complex lexical items that convey basic notions, as pointed out by Koptjevskaja-Tamm & Veselinova (2020). These facts should obviously be taken into account when trying to answer the wider question, raised by lexical typologists, of which meanings can/cannot be conveyed by simple/basic items or by complex/non-basic items. However, we think it might be fruitful to restrict CLs to items that are both formally and conceptually complex, partly for sheer convenience, partly because this restriction might help to focus on the task at hand: what are the strategies employed by languages for naming complex concepts (we already know simple words are one of these but we are far from having a full and typologically-informed picture of everything else) and what are the principles behind their cross-linguistic variation and distribution.

Obviously, a far-reaching typology of CLs as defined above is much easier to conceive than to actually build. The domain to be covered is vast indeed. However, it looks more feasible if one constrains the domain of investigation to something more manageable in terms of coverage, by creating (ad hoc) 'daughter comparative concepts' from the more general 'complex lexeme' comparative concept proposed in (2). For instance, the definition in (2) may be constrained in terms of the kind of formatives one wants to focus on (affixes vs. words, prefixes vs. affixes), the kind of processes involved (concatenative vs. non-concatenative), the nature of concepts being combined, or a combination of these factors.

This is the choice we have made in this volume, by putting the spotlight on a specific kind of CL, namely 'binominal lexemes', which will be introduced and defined in Section 2 (and Chapter 2). With this 'case-study', we would like to make the case that, by delimiting the range of possible combinations of concepts and formatives, in either structural or functional terms, doing 'complex lexeme typology' becomes an enterprise wihin the bounds of possibility.

2 Focus on binominal lexemes

The act of naming a (new) complex concept through the combination of two existing concepts can be seen most clearly in determinative noun-noun compounds, such as those in (3), all of which denote the meaning 'railway'.

(3)   a.   German [DEU] *Eisenbahn* [iron.way]
      b.   Mandarin Chinese [CMN] 铁路 *tie3 lu4* [iron road]
      c.   Mapudungun [ARN] *trenrüpü* [train.way]
      d.   Saramaccan [SRM] *talán fútu* [train foot]

In each of these examples, the first constituent (the 'modifier') serves to restrict the extension of the class of objects denoted by the second (the 'head'): a railway is conceptualized as a kind of way (or road) that is somehow related to the concept IRON (3a)-(3b) or TRAIN (3c), or as a kind of foot that is related to the concept TRAIN (3d).[3] They are all instances of nominal modification constructions (Croft 2001; 2022).

Now, one of the most interesting aspects of such compounds is precisely the fact that the relationship between the two combining concepts is not stated explicitly: the motivation for combining the two concepts in question must be inferred by the user. In the case of (3a)-(3b), the choice of concepts is clearly motivated by a conceptualization of 'railway' as a way that is MADE OF iron; in

---

[3] Naturally, these conceptualizations are particularly relevant during the coining and adoption of the new expression, and less so once it has become conventionalized.

(3c) a railway is conceptualized as a way that is USED BY trains; and in (3d) it is conceptualized metaphorically as a 'foot' that belongs to, or is PART OF a train.

Investigations into the range of semantic relations exhibited by determinative noun-noun compounds have the potential to reveal interesting insights into the associative nature of human thought (e.g., what are the most salient relationships, which ones are used for which kinds of complex concepts, what differences can be found across languages, etc.).

However, if *Eisenbahn* (3a) provides interesting evidence in this regard, so too do the complex lexemes in (4), all of which again denote the meaning 'railway'.

(4) a. French *chemin de fer* [track PREP iron]
　　 b. Russian [RUS] железная дорога *železnaja doroga* [iron.ADJZ road]
　　 c. Modern Hebrew מסילת ברזל *mesilat barzel* [track.CS iron]
　　 d. Bezhta [KAP] *kilos hino* [iron.OBL.GEN way]

The four complex lexemes in (4) are all functionally equivalent to those in (3) in that they all combine items denoting two concepts to denote the new (complex) concept 'railway'; in fact, the same two concepts as in (3a) and (3b): IRON and WAY.

But are they compounds? The answer to that question varies with the linguistic tradition of each individual language:
- For French, Floricic (2016) makes a distinction between compounds *stricto sensu* (or "compounds proper") and a subtype dubbed 'synapsie', a term which traces back to Benveniste (1966), "which is syntactic in essence and consists of a group of lexemes connected by a linker: *pomme de terre* 'potato; lit. apple of earth', *chemin de fer* 'railway; lit. way of iron', etc.".
- Uluhanov's (2016) discussion of word-formation in Russian makes no mention at all of the use of relational adjectives (like *železnaja*) in the formation of complex lexemes, let alone including them under 'Composition'.
- Levi's (1976) paper on Hebrew "compound nominals" of the type exemplified by (4c) generally avoids the term 'compound' itself, preferring the label traditionally used in Hebrew linguistics '*smixut* construction' (namely, construct state construction).
- Finally, Khalilov & Khalilova's (2016) coverage of composition in Bezhta allows that compounds "can also be based on the oblique nominal stem combined with a noun in the genitive case", as is the case in (4d).

What this tells us is that 'compound' is not a suitable term for use in cross-linguistic comparison, and it is precisely for this reason that we introduce the comparative concept 'binominal lexeme'. Informally, a binominal lexeme is simply a *noun-*

noun compound or its functional equivalent. (See Pepper, this volume, a for formal definitions, further examples and a typology of binominal lexemes.)

The term binominal lexeme covers all the examples in (3) and (4), despite the fact that they exhibit a range of morphosyntactic strategies (compounding, juxtaposition, prepositional, adjectival, construct and genitival). Given the onomasiological definition briefly introduced here and further developed in Chapter 2, it also covers the examples in (5), which clearly are not compounds.

(5) a. Slovak [SLK] *železnica* [iron.ADJZ.NMLZ] 'railway'
  b. Murui Hitoto [HUU] *ui.tɨraɨ* [eye.CLF(hair)] 'eyelash'[4]

(5a) is a denominal derivation that parallels the Russian example in (4b), except that it employs a nominalizing suffix (-*ica*) with the general meaning 'thing' instead of a head noun meaning 'road' (*doroga*). (5b) is an example of a classifier construction in which the classifier *tɨraɨ* has a derivational rather than a classificatory function. The former embodies the MADE OF relation, like (3a), (3b) and (4); and the latter embodies the PART OF relation, like (3d).

With this new comparative concept it becomes possible to study one of the most important types of complex lexeme formation found in the world's languages: that in which two object (or "nominal") concepts are combined to denote a new meaning.

The contents of the present volume show that binominal lexemes can be studied from a variety of perspectives:

- **Morphosyntactic strategies.** The formal mechanisms employed in creating binominals can be investigated:
  - cross-linguistically and in their totality, with the aim of exploring a particular typological classification (see Pepper 2020; this volume, a);
  - with a cross-linguistic focus on one particular strategy (see Creissels, this volume);
  - in their totality within a language family (see Lesage, this volume) or within a particular language (see van Egmond, this volume; Næss, this volume);
  - via a selection of strategies in a particular language (see Cetnarowska, this volume);

---

[4] Not surprisingly, speakers of the Amazonian language Murui Hitoto do not have a word for 'railway'. If they needed one, it might conceivably be *yoezo* [metal.CLF.REP:path], parallel to *yoeya* [metal.CLF:craft] 'boat made of iron, metal', with the repeater -*zo* 'path' used instead of the classifier -*ya* 'craft', cf. Wojtylak (2017: 194).

- contrastively, between unrelated languages (see Rose and Van linden, this volume);
- within a particular semantic domain (see Naccarato and Huang, this volume).

- **Semantic relations.** Again, these can be investigated cross-linguistically, for example, with a view to developing a unified classification (see Pepper 2020; this volume, b); within a language family (see Károly, this volume) or a particular language (see Gürer, this volume); or contrastively (see Pleshak, this volume).

- **Language acquisition.** The acquisition of binominals and competition between different binominal strategies can be investigated within individual languages or cross-linguistically (see Rosenberg, this volume).

These contributions, each of which could serve as a model for further work, will be introduced in more detail in the next section. The point to be made here is the diversity of research questions that they embody. However, there are many other potential paths of investigation that are not represented in the present volume. It will suffice here to mention two:

- **Correlations between form and meaning.** It might be expected that there is some kind of correlation between morphosyntactic strategies and the semantic relations found in binominals. According to Pepper (2020: §7.3) this is not the case from a typological perspective. However, such correlations are likely to be found in many specific languages, as first demonstrated for Nizaa (SGI) by Pepper (2010). This is clearly an area that needs more research (see Pepper 2020: §7.3.1 for a list of 22 languages from his sample of 106 that he finds worthy of further research in this respect).

- **Lexico-constructional patterns**: The choice of which two concepts to combine in order to denote a complex concept – in other words, to create a complex lexeme – varies across languages, and is influenced by both language contact, cultural considerations and language-internal resources. As an example, Figure 1 shows how concepts are combined to denote 'railway' in a sample of 57 languages (Pepper 2018a).

In short, the comparative concept of binominal lexeme – a suitably restricted and more manageable 'daughter comparative concept' of the more general 'complex lexeme' – offers rich scope for investigations into the nature of the (complex) lexicon. It can also serve as a model for further 'sibling' comparative concepts, such as those that involve property modification or action modification rather than object modificaton.

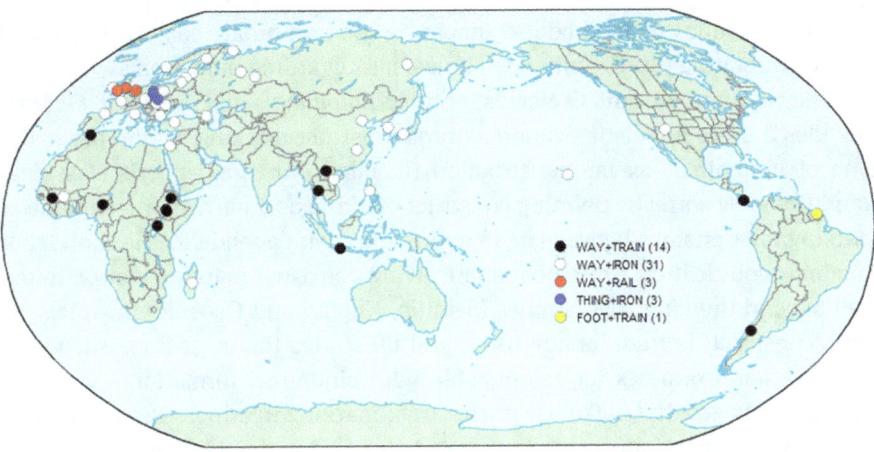

Figure 1: Lexico-constructional patterns for 'railway'.

3 What this volume is about

The present volume is divided into three parts: the first consists of typological, contrastive and descriptive studies that focus primarily on morphosyntactic strategies; the second on studies that focus primarily on semantic relations; and the third on acquisition. There is overlap, of course – several papers in the first part include a discussion of semantics, and those in the second make reference to morphosyntactic strategies – but the groupings show a certain coherence.

Following this introduction, the volume itself opens with the first of two contributions by **Steve Pepper**, entitled *Defining and typologizing binominal lexemes*. The goal of this chapter is "to provide a general introduction to binominals", and he starts by offering four different definitions of binominal lexeme. Although couched in a variety of terms, based on different theoretical frameworks, these have essentially identical extensions. He then presents a nine-way classification of binominals based on the morphosyntactic strategies employed in the world's languages. These nine 'binominal types' are arranged on a two-dimensional grid that also captures the number of grammatical markers, the locus of marking, and the degree of fusion. In addition, the grid reveals two strategies that are theoretically possible, but so far unattested. After discussing these "missing types", the paper turns to the question of grammaticalization and examines both gradient binominal phenomena and the relationship between binominals and possessive constructions. In order to evaluate the latter relationship quantitatively, he describes an innovate method for comparing two non-binary constructions, and he ends by stating two Greenbergian universals regarding binominals.

The chapter by **Denis Creissels**, entitled *Binominals and construct marking*, provides a cross-linguistic examination of construct marking as one particular type of binominal lexeme construction (labelled **con**[5] in Pepper's classification). Creissels starts by defining construct marking as a particular technique of marking relationships between head nouns and their dependents. He shows that nominal modification constructions involving construct marking can be found well beyond the language families (Semitic, Nilotic, and Oceanic) in which the term 'construct' is traditionally used, and illustrates the cross-linguistic variation. He then examines the relationship with binominal formation and shows that in languages that make use of construct marking in adpossessive constructions, it is common for construct markers to be used more or less productively in the formation of binominals.

In his contribution, *Compounds and other nominal modifier constructions in Pama-Nyungan languages*, **Jakob Lesage** develops his own set of comparative concepts that differs in two ways from those used in the rest of this volume. Firstly, he extends the concept of nominal modification to include (some) property modification constructions, on the grounds that "it is not possible to clearly distinguish nouns and adjectives in various languages of [his] sample and, where this may be possible, not all grammars provide enough data or analysis to make such a distinction". Secondly, his subdivision is made along functional lines rather than in terms of morphosyntactic strategies: he distinguishes between 'binominal compounds' (where the modifier has a classifying function rather than a qualifying function); 'descriptive phrases' (where the modifier has a qualifying function); 'generic-specific constructions' (combinations of a generic noun and a specific noun, between which there is a relation of hyponymy); and 'inalienable (attributive) possession constructions' (where the relation is meronymic).

Marie-Elaine van Egmond's chapter, *New types of binominal lexeme in Anindilyakwa (Australia)*, provides an intriguing description of four types of binominal lexeme in the polysynthetic Gunwinyguan language Anindilyakwa. The constructions involved are two possession constructions, one expressing inalienable possession and one indicating alienable possession, plus a proprietive suffix which has a 'having, being equipped with' meaning, and a privative construction that contributes a meaning of 'without'. In Van Egmond's analysis

---

5 The mnemonics for the nine types in Pepper's classification are **jxt, cmp, der, cls; prp, gen, adj, con;** and **dbl**. They are indicative of the morphosyntactic strategies employed but should not be taken literally (see Pepper, this volume, a).

three of these constructions are regarded as type **adj** in Pepper's classification, while the fourth (inalienable possession) is claimed to be an instance of Pepper's "missing type" **nml**. This analysis differs from that in Pepper (2020: 474) who classifies them as **gen** and **con**, respectively. The difference hinges on whether the affixes in question are regarded as transpositional or not (see Pepper, this volume, a: §2.3.2 for further discussion). Be this as it may, there is no disputing van Egmond's conclusion, that the study of typologically lesser-known languages may shed new light on the typology of binominals, as access to new data broadens the scope of the typological generalizations that we can achieve.

Åshild Næss' chapter, *Binominals in Äiwoo: Compounds, possessive constructions, and transitional cases*, describes the different morphosyntactic strategies available to form binominal lexemes in the Oceanic language Äiwoo, and the semantic relations that characterise the different construction types. The Äiwoo data show examples of two or three distinct types in Pepper's classification. Næss shows that in all but unambiguous compounding constructions, possessor indexing plays an important role. It is found on the head in the direct possessive construction, on the possessive classifier in the indirect possessive construction, and on the relational prepositions. In most of the ambiguous or transitional cases, the key question is whether possessor indexing is present and where it is located. Thus, Äiwoo shows a complex picture that cannot be fully accounted for in Pepper's typology: relational morphemes such as possessive classifiers and relational prepositions may also carry possessive marking, and it is in these cases that problems arise in assigning the Äiwoo constructions to appropriate types.

Bożena Cetnarowska's chapter, *NN.GEN and NAREL juxtapositions in Polish: Syntactic schemas employed in building phrasal nouns*, analyzes some multiword unit structures of Polish. More specifically, the author focuses on two types of what is called 'juxtaposition' in the Polish grammatical tradition, that is, noun + genitive noun (NN.GEN) and noun + relational adjective (NAREL). Both of these structures are binominal lexemes according to the definition adopted in the present volume (**gen** and **adj** types respectively). Since these are considered as phrasal units, Cetnarowska also compares them with another competing binominal, morphological compounds (or *compound proper*) (**cmp**). The main difference that emerges lies in their semantics: while **gen** and **adj** are endocentric, **cmp** is exocentric.

The chapter by **Françoise Rose** and **An Van Linden** (*The derivational use of classifiers in Western Amazonia*) investigates the distinction between two different types of binominal lexeme, that is, classifier derived nouns (**cls**) and noun-noun compounds (**cmp**), in two Western Amazonian languages, Mojeño Trinitario and Harakmbut, that are not genetically related or in contact with each other. This topic is particularly relevant since in several South American languages classifiers and nouns are not always easily distinguishable. For example, in Mojeño Trinitario the two categories share the same syntactic distribution but are formally different, while in Harakmbut they are formally identical but have different syntactic distributions. Having analysed **cls** and **cmp** types in the two languages, the two authors propose some criteria that help in distinguishing them. They conclude by presenting some historical considerations regarding the diachronic relationship between classifiers and nouns in Western Amazonian languages that are relevant for the general theory of classifiers.

Chiara Naccarato and **Shanshan Huang**'s chapter, entitled *Binominals denoting instruments: A contrastive perspective*, focuses on a contrastive analysis of complex nominals referring to instruments pertaining the semantic field of cooking in four typologically distant languages: Italian, Russian, Mandarin Chinese, and Japanese. Adopting an onomasiological approach to word-formation, the authors investigate the morphosyntactic strategies adopted by the four languages to create instrumental nouns, which kinds of instrument are more often expressed through binominal lexemes, and what are the semantic relations between the two constituents. They conclude by observing the existence of a possible correlation between the "onomasiological type" (as proposed by Štekauer 1998 and revised by Pepper 2018b) and the type of instrument denoted. From a formal point of view, Italian and Russian more often use derivational processes (**der**) and adjectival (**adj**) or prepositional (**prp**) constructions, while Chinese and Japanese only employ noun-noun compounding (**cmp**).

Steve Pepper's second contribution, *Hatcher-Bourque: Towards a reusable classification of semantic relations*, introduces the second part of this volume, in which the focus is on the unstated (or underspecified) semantic relation that pertains between the two nominal constituents of a binominal. Pepper proposes a 'reusable' classification based on a synthesis of Anna Granville Hatcher's high-level, four-way classification of 'non-appositional' relations (which he extends to also cover appositional relations) and Yves Bourque's low-level classification of 25 relations (extended to 29 by Pepper). The resulting, two-level 'Hatcher-Bourque' classification is proposed as the basis for further collaborative work in the domain of semantic relations, together with a freely available Excel-based tool for computer-assisted annotation of binominals (Pepper 2021).

László Károly's chapter discusses *Binominal strategies and semantic correlations in Turkic languages* based on data from five different branches of the Turkic family: Turkish, Kazakh, Uigur, Khakas and Yakut. The paper focuses on the question how the derivational strategy (**der**) and compounding (understood broadly as including the **con**, **jxt**, **adj** and **gen** strategies) are related to one another in terms of their semantic capacity, interchangeability and competitiveness. His thorough analysis of 201 semantic concepts in the five languages demonstrates that compounding is an active and frequently used word-formation strategy in Turkic that may significantly surpass derivation in terms of productivity in certain domains of the lexicon. Some minimal examples show that derivation and compounding are interchangeable, and thus that they are in competition. Károly's application for the first time in Turkic studies of Štekauer's (1998) onomasiological theory of word-formation is found to be an adequate framework for the systematic comparison of derivation and compounding.

The chapter *A classification of compounds in Karachay-Balkar* by **Aslı Gürer** provides an analysis of compounds in an understudied Turkic language belonging to the Kipchak group, Karachay-Balkar. More specifically, the author compares noun-noun compounds (**jxt**) with the *izafet* type, in which a marker occurs on the head of the construction (**con**). The latter is a common strategy in Turkish. The analysis shows that the distribution of the "linking element" (i.e. the *izafet* marker) is not optional but rather signals an argument relation between the head and the dependent, that is, its distribution overlaps with that of "transitive" (i.e. relational) nouns. The analysis furthermore indicates that the **con** strategy tends to be found in endocentric subordinate compounds.

Polina Pleshak's paper on *Binominal lexemes in Moksha and Hill Mari* describes the syntax and semantics of binominal lexemes in two Finno-Ugric languages spoken in the Volga Region: Moksha and Hill Mari. She shows that Moksha and Hill Mari demonstrate competition between two types of nominal modification construction, juxtaposed structures (**jxt**) and genitival constructions (**gen**) that do not express core possessive relations. In addition, she shows that the Finno-Ugric genitive has noncanonical attributive functions in certain contexts, and shares morphosyntactic properties with attributivizers. As regards compounds, she notes that binominals denoting similar relations are present in the dictionary as (fused) one-word and as two-word compounds, suggesting that this difference is not significant. Rather, the difference between more lexicalized one-word and more compositional two-word compounds is more relevant as it affects morphophonology and syntax. Whereas one-word compounds (**cmp**) are strict lexical units, compounds consisting of two or more words (**jxt**) can have more complex syntactic properties, which have to be taken into consideration in the classification.

Maria Rosenberg's chapter *Binominals and potential competitors in language development: Evidence from Swedish* deals with a specific type of binominal lexeme, noun-noun compounds (**cmp**). Employing Swedish production data from five children between 1 and 3 years old and taking an onomasiological approach, the author investigates some potentially competing constructions used to express semantic relations that are usually encoded by binominal lexemes in cross-linguistic perspective. Rosenberg concludes that competing structures have a narrower semantic scope than noun-noun compounds in Swedish, thus making them the strategy most used by children to express the relevant semantic relations. This can be cognitively explained given that juxtaposition is the preferred option because of its "structural accessibility", while some other structurally more complex strategies (e.g. prepositional structures) are acquired later.

References

Arkadiev, Peter & Marian Klamer. 2019. Morphological theory, language description and typology. In Jenny Audring & Francesca Masini (eds.), *The Oxford handbook of morphological theory*. Oxford: Oxford University Press.

Baldwin, Timothy & Su Nam Kim. 2010. Multiword expressions. In Nitin Indurkhya & Fred J. Damerau (eds.), *Handbook of natural language processing*, 267–292. Boca Raton, FL: CRC Press.

Benveniste, Émile. 1966. Différentes formes de la composition nominale en français. *Bulletin de la Société de Linguistique de Paris* 61(1). 82–95.

Boas, Franz (ed.). 1911. *Handbook of American Indian languages*. Washington, D.C.: Bureau of American Ethnology.

Booij, Geert. 2009. Phrasal names: A constructionist analysis. *Word Structure* 2(2). 219–240. https://doi.org/10.3366/E1750124509000427.

Booij, Geert. 2010. *Construction Morphology*. Oxford: Oxford University Press.

Booij, Geert E., Christian Lehmann & Joachim Mugdan (eds.). 2000. *Morphologie: ein internationales Handbuch zur Flexion und Wortbildung*. Vol. 1. Berlin: Mouton de Gruyter.

Booij, Geert E., Christian Lehmann & Joachim Mugdan (eds.). 2004. *Morphologie: ein internationales Handbuch zur Flexion und Wortbildung*. Vol. 2. Berlin: Mouton de Gruyter.

Brown, Cecil H. 2001. Lexical typology from an anthropological point of view. In Martin Haspelmath, Ekkehard König, Wolfgang Oesterreicher & Wolfgang Raible (eds.), *Language typology and language universals: An international handbook*, 1178–1190. Berlin: Mouton de Gruyter.

Cristofaro, Sonia. 2009. Grammatical categories and relations: Universality vs. language-specificity and construction-specificity. *Language and Linguistics Compass* 3(1). 441–479.

Croft, William. 2001. *Radical Construction Grammar: Syntactic theory in typological perspective*. Oxford: Oxford University Press.

Croft, William. 2022. *Morphosyntax: Constructions of the world's languages*. Cambridge: Cambridge University Press.

Dryer, Matthew S. 1997. Are grammatical relations universal? In Joan L. Bybee, John Haiman & Sandra A. Thompson (eds.), *Essays on language function and language type. Dedicated to T. Givón*, 115–143. Amsterdam: John Benjamins.

Dryer, Matthew S. & Martin Haspelmath (eds.). 2013. *The World Atlas of Language Structures Online*. Leipzig: Max Planck Institute for Evolutionary Anthropology. http://wals.info/ (22 February, 2018).

Floricic, Franck. 2016. French. In Peter O. Müller, Ingeborg Ohnheiser, Susan Olsen & Franz Rainer (eds.), *Word-formation: An international handbook of the languages of Europe. Vol. 4*, 2661–2682. Berlin: Mouton de Gruyter.
Goldberg, Adele E. 1995. *Constructions: A construction grammar approach to argument structure*. Chicago: The University of Chicago Press.
Goldberg, Adele E. 2006. *Constructions at work: The nature of generalization in language*. Oxford: Oxford University Press.
Goldberg, Adele E. 2013. Constructionist approaches. In Thomas Hoffmann & Graeme Trousdale (eds.), *The Oxford handbook of Construction Grammar*. Oxford: Oxford University Press.
Goldberg, Adele E. 2019. *Explain me this*. Princeton: Princeton University Press.
Haspelmath, Martin. 2007. Pre-established categories don't exist: Consequences for language description and typology. *Linguistic Typology* 11(1). 119–132. https://doi.org/10.1515/LINGTY.2007.011.
Haspelmath, Martin. 2010. Comparative concepts and descriptive categories in crosslinguistic studies. *Language* 86(3). 663–687.
Haspelmath, Martin. 2011. The indeterminacy of word segmentation and the nature of morphology and syntax. *Folia Linguistica* 45(1). 31–80. https://doi.org/10.1515/flin.2011.002.
Hilpert, Martin. 2014. *Construction grammar and its application to English*. Edinburgh: Edinburgh University Press.
Hilpert, Martin & Jan-Ola Östman (eds.). 2014. Reflections on constructions across grammars. *Constructions and frames* 6(2). Special Issue.
Hoffmann, Thomas & Graeme Trousdale (eds.). 2013. *The Oxford handbook of Construction Grammar*. Oxford: Oxford University Press.
Hüning, Matthias & Barbara Schlücker. 2015. Multi-word expressions. In Peter O. Müller, Ingeborg Ohnheiser, Susan Olsen & Franz Rainer (eds.), *Word-formation: An international handbook of the languages of Europe. Vol. 1*, 450–467. Berlin: Mouton de Gruyter.
Khalilov, Madzhid & Zaira Khalilova. 2016. Bezhta. In Peter O. Müller, Ingeborg Ohnheiser, Susan Olsen & Franz Rainer (eds.), *Word-formation: An international handbook of the languages of Europe. Vol. 5*, 3658–3678. Berlin: Mouton de Gruyter.
Koch, Peter. 2001. Lexical typology from a cognitive and linguistic point of view. In Martin Haspelmath, Ekkehard König, Wolfgang Oesterreicher & Wolfgang Raible (eds.), *Language typology and language universals: An international handbook*, 1142–1178. Berlin: Mouton de Gruyter.
Koptjevskaja-Tamm, Maria. 2008. Approaching lexical typology. In Martine Vanhove (ed.), *From polysemy to semantic change: Towards a typology of lexical semantic associations*, 3–52. Amsterdam: John Benjamins.
Koptjevskaja-Tamm, Maria, Ekaterina Rakhilina & Martine Vanhove. 2015. The semantics of lexical typology. In Nick Riemer (ed.), *The Routledge handbook of semantics*, 434–454. Abingdon: Routledge.
Koptjevskaja-Tamm, Maria & Ljuba N. Veselinova. 2020. Lexical Typology in morphology. In *Oxford research encyclopedia of linguistics*. Oxford: Oxford University Press. https://doi.org/10.1093/acrefore/9780199384655.013.522.
Levi, Judith N. 1976. A semantic analysis of Hebrew complex nominals. In Peter Cole (ed.), *Studies in modern Hebrew syntax and semantics: The transformational-generative approach*, 9–55. Amsterdam: North-Holland.

Lieber, Rochelle, Sabine Arndt-Lappe, Antonio Fábregas, Christina L. Gagné & Francesca Masini (eds.). 2021. *The Oxford encyclopedia of morphology*. 3 vols. Oxford: Oxford University Press.
Lieber, Rochelle & Pavol Štekauer (eds.). 2009a. *The Oxford handbook of compounding*. Oxford: Oxford University Press.
Lieber, Rochelle & Pavol Štekauer. 2009b. Introduction: Status and definition of compounding. In Rochelle Lieber & Pavol Štekauer (eds.), *The Oxford handbook of compounding*, 3–18. Oxford: Oxford University Press.
Lieber, Rochelle & Pavol Štekauer (eds.). 2014. *The Oxford handbook of derivational morphology*. Oxford: Oxford University Press.
Martinet, André. 1949. La double articulation linguistique. *Travaux du Cercle linguistique de Copenhague* 5. 30–37.
Masini, Francesca. 2009. Phrasal lexemes, compounds and phrases: A constructionist perspective. *Word Structure* 2(2). 254–271.
Masini, Francesca. 2019a. Multi-word expressions and morphology. In *Oxford research encyclopedia of linguistics*. Oxford: Oxford University Press. https://doi.org/10.1093/acrefore/9780199384655.013.611.
Masini, Francesca. 2019b. Competition between morphological words and multiword expressions. In Franz Rainer, Francesco Gardani, Wolfgang U. Dressler & Hans Christian Luschützky (eds.), *Competition in inflection and word-formation*, 281–305. Cham: Springer.
Masini, Francesca & Jenny Audring. 2019. Construction morphology. In Jenny Audring & Francesca Masini (eds.), *The Oxford handbook of morphological theory*, 365–389. Oxford: Oxford University Press.
Michaelis, Susanne Maria, Philippe Maurer, Martin Haspelmath & Magnus Huber (eds.). 2013. *APiCS Online*. Leipzig: Max Planck Institute for Evolutionary Anthropology. https://apics-online.info/.
Müller, Peter O., Ingeborg Ohnheiser, Susan Olsen & Franz Rainer (eds.). 2015. *Word-formation: An international handbook of the languages of Europe*. 5 vols. Berlin: Mouton de Gruyter.
Pepper, Steve. 2010. *Nominal compounding in Nizaa: A cognitive perspective*. SOAS University of London Master's thesis.
Pepper, Steve. 2018a. Lexico-constructional patterns in binominal lexemes. Paper presented at SLE Summer School 2018, Tartu. https://www.academia.edu/50523906/.
Pepper, Steve. 2018b. Onomasiological types and the typology of binominal lexemes. Paper presented at the *Typology and Universals in Word-Formation IV* conference, Košice. https://www.academia.edu/38060850.
Pepper, Steve. 2020. *The typology and semantics of binominal lexemes: Noun-noun compounds and their functional equivalents*. Oslo: University of Oslo PhD dissertation. https://www.academia.edu/42935602.
Pepper, Steve. 2021. *The Bourquifier: An application for applying the Hatcher-Bourque classification*. MS Excel. http://folk.uio.no/stevepe/Bourquifier.xlsx.
Pepper, Steve. This volume, a. Defining and typologizing binominal lexemes. In Steve Pepper, Francesca Masini & Simone Mattiola (eds.), *Binominal lexemes in cross-linguistic perspective*. Berlin: Mouton de Gruyter.
Pepper, Steve. This volume, b. Hatcher-Bourque: Towards a reusable classification of semantic relations. In Steve Pepper, Francesca Masini & Simone Mattiola (eds.), *Binominal lexemes in cross-linguistic perspective*. Berlin: Mouton de Gruyter.

Ramat, Paolo. 1990. Definizione di "parola" e sua tipologia. In Monica Berretta, Piera Molinelli & Ada Valentini (eds.), *Parallela 4: Morfologia, Atti del V incontro Italo – Austriaco della Società di linguistica italiana, Bergamo ottobre 2–4, 1989*, 3–15. Tübingen: Narr.

Rubino, Carl. 2013. Reduplication. In Matthew S. Dryer & Martin Haspelmath (eds.), *The World Atlas of Language Structures Online*. Leipzig: Max Planck Institute for Evolutionary Anthropology. http://wals.info/chapter/27 (22 February, 2018).

Štekauer, Pavol. 1998. *An onomasiological theory of English word-formation*. Amsterdam: John Benjamins.

Štekauer, Pavol, Salvador Valera & Lívia Körtvélyessy. 2012. *Word-formation in the world's languages: A typological survey*. Cambridge: Cambridge University Press.

Talmy, Leonard. 2007. Lexical typologies. In Timothy Shopen (ed.), *Language typology and syntactic description. Vol. 3: Grammatical categories and the lexicon*, 66–168. 2nd ed. Cambridge: Cambridge University Press.

Uluhanov, Igor' S. 2016. Russian. In Peter O. Müller, Ingeborg Ohnheiser, Susan Olsen & Franz Rainer (eds.), *Word-formation: An international handbook of the languages of Europe. Vol. 4*, 2953–2978. Berlin: Mouton de Gruyter.

Vanhove, Martine (ed.). 2008. *From polysemy to semantic change: Towards a typology of lexical semantic associations*. Amsterdam: John Benjamins.

Wojtylak, Katarzyna I. 2017. *A Grammar of Murui (Bue): A Witotoan language of Northwest Amazonia*. Cairns: James Cook University PhD dissertation.

Part 1: **Form (morphosyntactic strategies)**

Steve Pepper
Defining and typologizing binominal lexemes

Abstract: This chapter starts by demonstrating the need for the comparative concept 'binominal lexeme' in order to cover both 'noun-noun compounds' and their 'functional equivalents' (§1). To complement this informal definition, four different, but compatible definitions of binominal lexeme are developed: functional, onomasiological, formal and typological (§2). Although couched in a variety of terms based on different theoretical frameworks, these have essentially identical extensions.

In §3 a nine-way classification of binominal strategies is presented, together with the mnemonics used throughout this volume: **jxt**, **cmp**, **der**, **cls**; **prp**, **gen**, **adj**, **con**, and **dbl**. These nine types are represented on a two-dimensional grid that captures the number of markers, the locus of marking and the degree of fusion. The grid reveals two lacunae or "missing types": **prn** and **nml**. Whereas the first of these probably exists somewhere in the world's languages, the second seems to be a logical impossibility.

§4 discusses types that are intermediate between the nine main types and the grammaticalization pathways that produce them. It then goes on to examine the relationship between binominal constructions and adnominal possessives, and introduces a new methodology, based on the Pwav scale, for comparing two non-binary constructions. This leads to the formulation of two Greenbergian universals concerning binominals and nominal modification.[1]

1 Introduction

'Word-formation' – one of the two branches of 'morphology' (the other being 'inflection') – has traditionally been subdivided into 'compounding' and 'derivation'. Recent research, however, has shown these distinctions to be grossly over-simplified and misleading (Bauer 2005), to the point that many important linguistic phenomena that fall between the two stools tend to be overlooked. This chapter provides an overview of one such phenomenon: the process of forming new lexemes by combining two (or more) existing lexemes that denote nominal concepts.

---

1 For language names, ISO codes and genealogical classifications, as well as sources for all language examples, see Pepper (2020).

Note: This chapter has been made Open Access *in memoriam* my parents Harry Pepper (1926–1996) and Edna Pepper (1932–2022).

∂ Open Access. © 2023 Steve Pepper, published by De Gruyter. This work is licensed under the Creative Commons Attribution-NonCommercial-NoDerivatives 4.0 International License.
https://doi.org/10.1515/9783110673494-002

The most well-studied strategy for this kind of lexeme formation is the kind of noun-noun compounding found in Germanic languages (1).

(1) German (DEU) *Eisenbahn* [iron.way] 'railway'

Crosslinguistically, however, there are many other strategies, including, among much else, the use of a **preposition** (2a), an **adjectivizer** (2b) a **dependent-marking affix** (2c), and a **head-marking affix** (2d).

(2) a. French (FRA) *chemin de fer* [way PREP iron]
     b. Russian (RUS) *železnaja doroga* [iron.ADJZ road]
     c. Bezhta (KAP) *kilos hino* [iron.OBL.GEN way]
     d. Turkish (TUR) *demir yolu* [iron road.3SG]

Like *Eisenbahn*, all the examples in (2) combine the concepts IRON and WAY in order to denote the meaning 'railway', but they do so using quite different morphosyntactic strategies. However, since they are all "phrasal" in nature, they fall outside the domain of 'morphology', and consequently also 'word-formation', as traditionally understood. And since they are lexical, they tend to fall outside the domain of 'syntax' as well. They fall between two stools.

To cite a few examples from the otherwise excellent five-volume handbook of word-formation in the languages of Europe (Müller et al. 2015): Floricic (2016) limits his coverage of the prepositional type (*chemin de fer*) – by far the most common way to form new lexemes in French – to a single sentence. Uluhanov (2016) makes no mention at all of the adjectival type (*železnaja doroga*) in Russian (relational adjectives are only mentioned in the context of denominal derivation). Nor do Khalilov and Khalilova (2016) mention the genitival type (*kilos hino*) in Bezhta.

In contrast, Wilkens (2016: 3370) treats the Turkish type (*demir yolu*) under "composition" (i.e., compounding), showing how *ev kapısı* [house door.3SG] 'front-door' "displays one basic feature of Turkish composition with the compound marker -(s)I (3rd person singular possessive suffix)".

This uneven treatment is the result of two unhappy circumstances: the division of grammar into 'syntax' and 'morphology', and the use of language-specific categories for the purpose of cross-linguistic comparison. What is clearly a compound in German (1), and equally clearly a compound (according to the local tradition) in Turkish (2d), is marginal at best in French (2a), of unclear status in Bezhta (2c) and can in no way be considered a compound in Russian (2b). And yet all five forms are functionally and semantically equivalent: they all consist basically of two nouns – one of which modifies the other, which denote the concepts IRON and WAY respectively, and they all denote the same "complex concept" (see

Masini, Mattiola & Pepper, this volume): RAILWAY. They differ only in the morphosyntactic strategy employed to combine the two nominal roots.

It is in order to bring these five strategies (along with others) under a single umbrella that the comparative concept 'binominal lexeme' was developed (Pepper 2020). Informally, binominal lexemes (or 'binominals' for short) are *noun-noun compounds or their functional equivalents*.

The goal of this chapter is to provide a general introduction to binominals. Section 2 offers four different definitions of binominal lexeme. Although couched in a variety of terms, based on different theoretical frameworks, these have essentially identical extensions. Section 3 then presents a nine-way classification of binominals based on the morphosyntactic strategies that they employ in the world's languages. Five of these were exemplified in (1) and (2), and four more will be introduced in §3.2. These nine 'binominal types' are arranged on a novel two-dimensional grid that also captures the number of grammatical markers, the locus of marking, and the degree of fusion. In addition, the grid reveals two theoretically possible, but unattested strategies, which are discussed in §3.3. Finally, section 3 discusses binominals in the context of grammaticalization, both in terms of gradient binominal phenomena (§4.1) and the relationship between binominals and adnominal possessives, or – more generally – nominal modification constructions (§4.2). In order to do so, it describes an innovate general method for comparing two non-binary constructions.

2 Defining binominal lexemes

While fairly accurate, the preliminary definition of binominal lexeme given above – as a noun-noun compound or its functional equivalent – is too imprecise for cross-linguistic comparison. In this section I offer more precise definitions that can be broadly characterized as functional (§2.1), onomasiological (§2.2), formal (§2.3) and typological (§2.4).

2.1 The functional definition

We may start by asking, what in fact *is* the function of a noun-noun compound? The answer, it would seem, is to name a new concept through combined reference to two existing nominal concepts. This is a 'comparative concept' (Haspelmath 2010) that is suitable for cross-linguistic comparison, since it is based solely on functional and semantic, rather than formal, criteria.

The naming function is important, since this is what distinguishes a binominal, such as *chemin de fer*, from an adnominal possessive, or 'adpossessive', such as Fr. *la plume de ma tante* 'the pen of my aunt'.

Specifying that the two combining concepts are nominal serves to exclude adjective-noun combinations like Eng. *blackbird*, and verb-noun combinations like It. *lavapiatti* 'dishwasher' [lit. 'wash dishes'], which are clearly not noun-noun compounds. The term 'nominal' is used here in the extralinguistic sense of pertaining to an object, as opposed to an action or a property.) However, it has further significance, in that it excludes forms like Eng. *walking stick* and *dishwasher* – i.e. so-called synthetic compounds, which are usually regarded as noun-noun compounds. In each of these, one of the combining concepts (represented by the modifying and modified elements, respectively) refers to an action (walking, washing) rather than an object.

The reason for excluding synthetic compounds and the like from the category 'binominal lexeme', is the suspicion that they may exhibit deviant behaviour, and that their inclusion could potentially "muddy the waters" of the analysis. One way in which they clearly *do* differ from binominals is the following. In binominals, the relationship between the two combining concepts is unstated (or at least underspecified): the motivation for combining the concepts WAY and IRON in *chemin de fer* is because a railway is regarded as a 'way' that is *made (or composed) of* iron. However, that relationship is not stated explicitly. In *dishwasher* (and *lavapiatti*), on the other hand, the relationship between the instrument (denoted by the suffix -*er*) and the dishes is explicit: it is a washing relation.

This leads us to the first, purely *functional* definition of binominal lexeme:[2]

(3) **A binominal lexeme is a naming unit that is based on two nominal concepts one of which modifies the other.**

This functional definition can be expressed more formally in three different ways.

2.2 The onomasiological definition

We start with the onomasiological definition, because Štekauer's (1998) system of 'onomasiological types' (OTs) was seminal to the development of the comparative

---

[2] The rationale for including the qualification "one of which modifies the other" is explained below.

concept of binominal lexeme (see Pepper 2020: §1.2.3).³ Štekauer's classification is largely unfamiliar to mainstream linguistics (less so in Europe than elsewhere), primarily because it employs "non-standard" terminology that has its roots in the Prague School of Linguistics, in particular, the work of Miloš Dokulil (1962; 1966; 1994), most of which is available only in Czech (CES).⁴ This lack of familiarity is to be regretted, since Štekauer's work contains many interesting insights of interest to morphologists and typologists. To help rectify this unfortunate state of affairs, this section will attempt to "translate" Štekauer's theory into more familiar terms.

The onomasiological typology is based on the recognition of four 'conceptual categories': SUBSTANCE, ACTION, QUALITY, and CONCOMITANT CIRCUMSTANCE (Štekauer 1998: 9). The first three of these are directly equivalent to Croft's semantic classes OBJECT, ACTION and PROPERTY (Croft 2022, cf. also many earlier works); the latter terms are more familiar and will therefore be used here in preference to Štekauer's.⁵ Furthermore, Štekauer's exposition pertains to the linguistic sign in general, of which complex nominals are but a subtype; in line with the focus of the present volume, and since most of Štekauer's examples are in fact complex nominals, the present discussion is restricted to the latter.

The semantic structure of a complex nominal consists, in principle, of two parts: "an *onomasiological base* denoting a class, gender, species, etc., to which the object belongs", and "an *onomasiological mark* which specifies the base" (Štekauer 1998: 9). These terms translate directly into 'head' and 'modifier', respectively. Both of these elements represent one of the above-mentioned conceptual categories. In the case of complex nominals, the head almost always represents an object (or 'substance').

The modifier can be either simple or complex. A simple modifier represents a property, e.g. *black* in *blackbird*. A fully specified complex modifier consists of a verbal ('actional') part and an argument to the verb; following Dokulil, Štekauer calls these the 'determined' and the 'determining' constituents. In *man-eating tiger* the modifier *man-eating* consists of a determined constituent *eat* and the determining constituent *man* (that which is eaten). These equate to Croft's (2022) 'property modification construction' and 'action modification construction',

---

3 Štekauer's classification is embedded in a broader theory of word-formation that is interesting in its own right but not directly relevant to the present discussion.
4 Note, however that the 1962 work contains a 31-page summary in English, and that the 1966 and 1994 papers are in German and English, respectively.
5 Langacker (e.g. 2008), Haspelmath (e.g. 2012) and many others use the term 'thing' instead of 'object'. CONCOMITANT CIRCUMSTANCE covers Place, Time, Manner, etc. See §2.4 for more details on Croft's model.

respectively (see §2.4), and they constitute two of Štekauer's onomasiological types (see Table 1).

Now, in the act of word-formation, when this semantic structure is given linguistic form, part of a complex modifier, either the determined (actional) part or the determining part, may be omitted. In *spinning wheel* there is no determining element, and in *summer house* there is no determined (actional) element. These constitute two more onomasiological types.

Table 1: Onomasiological types 1–4.

Onomasiological type (OT)	Example	Modifier			Head
		Simple	Complex		
			Determined	Determiner	
OT1	*man-eating tiger*	n/a	EAT	MAN	TIGER
OT2	*spinning wheel*	n/a	SPIN	–	WHEEL
OT3	*summer house*	n/a	–	SUMMER	HOUSE
OT4	*blackbird*	BLACK	n/a	n/a	BIRD

There is a fifth onomasiological type, OT5, which is characterized by "an unstructured onomasiological level" (Štekauer 2005: 221) and covers cases of conversion, such as $time_N$ ~ $time_V$. This type is not relevant to the present discussion.[6]

Based on the preceding, it is clear that binominals correspond to Onomasiological Type 3. In Štekauer's terms, our original example (1), *Eisenbahn*, is a naming unit that consists of the onomasiological base (*Bahn*) and the determining element of the (complex) onomasiological mark (*Eisen*). Expressed in more familiar terms, *Eisenbahn* is a complex nominal that consists of a head (*Bahn*) and a (conceptually complex) modifier consisting of a determining element (*Eisen*); the determined element, representing the semantic relation between the two, is unstated.

We can thus formulate the following *onomasiological* definition of binominal lexeme:

(4) **A binominal lexeme is an Onomasiological Type 3 naming unit.**

The adoption of an onomasiological perspective has important implications for the interpretation of the functional definition (3). This is because the onomasiological

---

[6] For a more in-depth presentation, critique and revision of the system of onomasiological types, see Pepper (2018; in prep.).

model accords the same status to derivational affixes and lexical roots. In theory, an affix can represent any of the elements of the onomasiological structure:
- In *house-keeping*, the nominalizing suffix *-ing* denotes a process and represents the onomasiological base (i.e., the head), *keep* is the determined element of the mark (i.e., the modifier), and is *house* the determining element of the mark; so this form is OT1.
- In *writer*, the agentive suffix *-er* represents the base and *write* the determined element of the mark; so this is OT2.
- And in *novelist*, the agentive suffix *-ist* represents the base and *novel* the determining element of the mark; so this is OT3 – and consequently also a binominal.

Now, so far in this chapter, every example of a binominal lexeme has consisted of two nouns (in addition, sometimes, to additional grammatical material, such as the preposition *de* in *chemin de fer*). The consequence of adopting the onomasiological perspective is that a binominal lexeme may be comprised not only of two nouns, but of a noun and a nominalizer.

Furthermore, a binominal may consist of a combination of a noun and a noun classifier or noun class marker, as in Bora (BOA) *túúheju* [nose.CLF:hole] 'nostril' (Urban 2012: 127), Harakmbut (AMR) *siro-pi* [metal-CLF:stick] 'knife' (Rose and Van linden, this volume) or Bandial (BQJ) *jijamen* [CL:ji.goat] 'kid' (Watson 2015). However, this applies only when the classifier or class marker in question has a derivational function; if the function is merely classificatory, as in Bandial *ejamen* [CL:e.goat] 'goat', the form is not considered to be a binominal lexeme (see the discussion of the **cls** type in §3.2.1.4 below and Rose and Van linden, this volume).

2.3 The formal definition

It is possible to develop a further definition of binominal lexeme, one that may be more accessible for some linguists, in the following way. If we (provisionally) ignore the refinement of the notion of binominal to include denominal derivations (e.g. *novelist*) and certain noun classifier constructions (e.g. *siro-pi*), a simple definition of binominal would be "a naming unit consisting of two nouns, and possible additional grammatical material". However, in addition to being incomplete, this definition suffers from the problem that 'noun' is not a well-defined cross-linguistic comparative concept (Haspelmath 2012). The latter issue can be addressed using Haspelmath's term 'thing-root' (defined as "a root that denotes a physical object (animate or inanimate)") instead of 'noun', but this would still not encompass forms like *novelist* and *siro-pi*, since neither *-ist* nor *-pi* are roots. In addition to the term 'thing-root', we therefore require the notion of 'thing-affix', defined as "an affix that denotes a physical object (animate or inanimate)"; this would cover both nominalizers like -*ist* and classifiers like -*pi*.[7]

Since roots and affixes are both morphs (Haspelmath 2020), a suitable cover term for thing-root and thing-affix is 'thing-morph', defined as "a morph that denotes a thing (prototypically a physical object, animate or inanimate)".[8]

Now, a binominal lexeme by its very nature involves an unstated (or underspecified) relation R between the two nominal concepts: the MADE OF relation in *chemin de fer* and *siro-pi*; the PART OF relation in *túúheju*; the CREATOR OF relation in *novelist*; etc. (see Pepper, this volume, b for further discussion). This semantic relation constitutes the motivation for combining the two concepts in question: just as a railway is conceptualized as a way that is made of iron, a knife is a stick made of iron, a nostril is a hole that is part of a nose, and a novelist is someone who writes (or more generally, ceates) novels.

This aspect of binominals can be usefully incorporated into its definition (5):

(5) **A binominal lexeme is a naming unit that consists primarily of two thing-morphs, and possibly additional grammatical material, formed by combining two concepts between which there is an unstated (or underspecified) relation of modification.**

In a sense the reference to the unstated relation is redundant, since every naming unit consisting of two thing-morphs involves such a relation. However, it serves to exclude so-called 'co-compounds' (Wälchli 2005), in which the relation between the two constituents is one of coordination rather than modification. In addition, it highlights the existence of the semantic relation, and it explicitly excludes forms such as Viet. *bữa ăn sáng* [meal eat morning] 'breakfast', in which the additional material (over and above the thing-morphs *bữa* and *sáng*) denotes an action, EAT, making this an instance of Onomasiological Type 1 (see §2.2 above).

In conclusion, a binominal lexeme can take any of the following forms:
- two nouns (e.g. *rail.way*) – possibly with additional grammatical material (e.g. *chemin de fer*);
- a noun and a nominalizing affix (e.g. *novel.ist*) – possibly with additional grammatical material (e.g. Slovak (SLK) *želez.n.ica* [iron.ADJZ.NMLZ] 'railway');

---

[7] This assumes, of course, that the definition of affix covers classifiers and class markers, but we leave that issue aside here.
[8] The addition of the qualifying "prototypically" allows for the extension of Haspelmath's concepts to also cover abstract 'objects', such as LOVE.

- a noun and a classifier (e.g. *siro-pi*) – possibly with additional grammatical material (e.g. Harakmbut w<u>ã</u>-õh-wẽ [NPF-nose-CLF:liquid] 'nostril';
- arguably, two nominal affixes, as in neoclassical compounds, e.g. *hydromancy* < water + divination (see §3.2.1.3).

One might argue that this definition is unnecessarily restrictive, in that it excludes not just synthetic compounds and coordinate compounds, but also forms consisting of three (or more) thing-morphs denoting just two concepts (one complex concept, denoted by a binominal, and one simple concept, denoted by a thing-morph). Indonesian *jalan keréta api* 'railway' is a case in point, consisting as it does of *jalan* 'road' and *keréta api* [carriage fire] 'train'. However, the definition is more than sufficient for the purpose of the present volume.

2.4 The typological definition

As a comparative concept, the binominal lexeme construction can also be defined in terms of Croft's (1991: 67; 2001: 88; 1990: 185; 2022) model of basic cross-linguistic constructions. This model, the Scapa Grid,[9] is shown in Table 2. The model is based on Croft's insight that constructions can, indeed *must*, be defined cross-linguistically in terms of two parameters: semantics and "information packaging" (Croft 2022). In the Scapa Grid, these are realised as semantic classes and propositional acts, respectively.

Table 2: Croft's Scapa Grid of cross-linguistic constructions.

Semantic Class	Propositional Act		
	reference	modification	predication
object	UNMARKED NOUNS	genitive, adjectivizations, PPs on nouns	predicate nominals
property	deadjectival nouns	UNMARKED ADJECTIVES	predicate adjectives
action	action nominals, complements, infinitives, gerunds	participles, relative clauses	UNMARKED VERBS

---

[9] Croft has used this table for over 30 years but has never given it a name. It is called here the "Scapa Grid", since the cells are at the intersection of three **S**emantic **C**lasses (object, property and action) **A**nd three **P**ropositional **A**cts (reference, modification and predication).

In terms of this model, binominal lexemes fit neatly into the cell **object + modification**, and since 'modification' for Croft always means modification of an object concept, this equates to what other linguists (e.g. Bauer & Tarasova 2013: 10) call "adnominal nominal modification". Croft (2022) himself adopts the term 'nominal modification construction' (see §4.2 below).

What distinguishes binominal lexeme constructions from other nominal modification constructions, such as the possessive (modification) construction, is that the former involve lexicalization (see §4.2). On this basis, the following *typological* definition can be stated:

(6) **A binominal lexeme is an instance of a lexicalized nominal modification construction.**

All of the preceding definitions – functional (3), onomasiological (4), formal (5), and typological (6) – have the same extension. They all include both denominal nominal derivations and they all exclude synthetic compounds. They also all exclude coordinate compounds: the onomasiological definition does so because Onomasiological Type 3 involves an onomasiological base (i.e., a head) and a determining element (i.e., a modifier), and the typological definition states clearly that the relation between the two elements is one of modification, which again implies a head and a modifier. The two other definitions, however, require the qualifications regarding the nature of the relation noted above.

Having now defined binominal lexemes in four different, but compatible ways, we can proceed to how they may be classified on the basis of the morphosyntactic strategies that they exhibit: the typology of binominal lexemes.

3 Classifying binominal lexemes

In this section we present the classification of binominals based on morphosyntactic strategies (Croft 2022) that was originally developed by Pepper (2020) and is used throughout the present volume.

3.1 Pepper's (2020) nine-way typology

Intuitively, binominal lexemes are closely related to possessive constructions, or more precisely, those that express adnominal possession – as opposed to predicative possession and external-possessive constructions (Koptjevskaja-Tamm

2002). Attention has already been drawn (in §2.1) to the role of French *de* 'of' in both the binominal *chemin de fer* and the possessive noun phrase (PNP) *la plume de ma tante*. The structure [A *de* B] is common to both French constructions, with A denoting the head or possessum and B denoting the modifier or possessor. Similarly, in Germanic languages the formative *-s-* can be either a binominal linking element or a genitive marker. (It is somewhat rare in Modern English binominals, but examples such as *women's magazine, ladies' man, dog's breakfast* and *wolf's bane* show that it does exist.)

In Russian binominals there is a strong tendency to incorporate an adjectivizer, as in *železnaja doroga* [iron.ADJZ road] 'railway', whereas most adnominal possessives utilize the genitive case. However, examples of Russian binominals that use the genitive do exist (e.g. *palec nogi* [digit foot.GEN] 'toe'), as do Russian adnominal possessives that utilize adjectivizers, as in *mojeho bratrowe dieci* [1SG:M.GEN brother.ADJZ.PL child.PL] 'my brother's children' (Corbett 1987: 300).

This sharing of the same morpheme in binominals and possessives is found in languages all across the world, as witnessed by the fact that Pepper's (2020) database of 3,738 binominals contains over 400 instances in which the gloss includes one of the abbreviations 3SG, POSS, AL and INAL (which by no means exhausts the list of possessive morphemes).

Other evidence for the close relationship between binominals and adnominal possessives includes a significant overlap between the kinds of semantic relation exhibited by the two (Pepper 2010; 2016), and the existence of a bidirectional word order universal **Poss-N ≡ Mod-N** between possessives and compounds in Bauer's (2001) data, drawn from a genetically and areally balanced sample of 36 languages (Pepper 2020: 27).

All of this evidence suggests the hypothesis that a binominal lexeme construction will often have grammaticalized out of an adnominal possessive construction. That being the case, it makes sense to base a typology of binominals on that of possessive constructions, since it will facilitate investigation of the grammaticalization hypothesis.

The most comprehensive typological work on adnominal possession is Koptjevskaja-Tamm's (2002; 2003; 2004) survey of possessive noun phrases (PNPs) in Europe, in which she develops the typological classification shown in Figure 1.

PNPs are here subdivided on the basis of fusion (synthetic vs. analytic), with juxtaposition in between. Synthetic PNPs are further subdivided by the locus of marking (on the head, the dependent, or both), and analytic PNPs are subdivided into those that employ prepositions and those that employ linking pronouns. The classification is actually more extensive than this, since mention is also made (2002: 144) of a seventh type, possessive compounding, which is "mainly

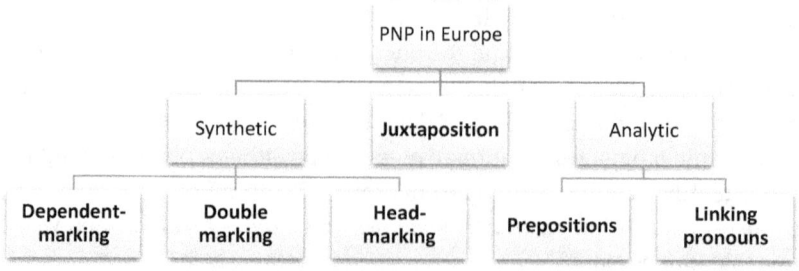

Typology of possessive NPs in Europe

Figure 1: Koptjevskaja-Tamm's typology of ossessive noun phrases.

restricted to Northern Swedish". In addition, derived (relational) adjectives are mentioned in passing (2002: 157) but not included explicitly in the classification.[10]

Of Koptjevskaja-Tamm's eight types, seven are found in Pepper's (2020) binominals data. Linking pronouns are not found (but see below under *Unattested strategies*, §3.3.1). In addition, Pepper identifies two strategies for creating binominal lexemes that are not used for attributive possession: denominal derivation (e.g. *novelist*; cf. Pol. *wiatr.ak* [wind.NMLZ] 'windmill') and the derivational use of noun classifiers (e.g. *siro-pi*; *jijamen*).

In all, nine strategies were identified by Pepper. They are listed in Table 3, together with examples of each strategy, labels, and three-letter codes that will be used extensively, both in the following presentation (which discusses each type in detail) and throughout this volume.[11] Note that the three-letter codes and labels are simply mnemonics and should not be taken literally: they are intended to suggest the prototype of each category rather than its full generality. Thus, **prp**, for example, denotes a type in which the additional marker can be any independent lexeme that forms a constituent with the modifier (for example, a postposition, connector, linker or determiner) and not just a preposition. Similarly, the additional, non-transpositional (i.e. non-word-class changing) affix attached to the modifier in a **gen** strategy need not necessarily be a genitive marker (although this is the prototypical case).

In addition, types are grouped according to the degree of grammatical marking that they involve. Four strategies (**jxt**, **cmp**, **cls** and **der**) involve no additional linguistic material, over and above the two main constituents; another four (**adj**, **gen**,

---

10 Whether this is because they are also considered marginal, or because they can be subsumed under dependent-marking, is unclear.

11 Strategies marked with an asterisk (*) are mentioned by Koptjevskaja-Tamm but not included in her six-way classification; those marked with a dagger (†) are new.

Table 3: Nine binominal strategies (Pepper 2020).

Marking	Strategy	Code	Example
0	juxtaposition	jxt	VIE *đường sắt* [road iron] RAILWAY
	compounding *	cmp	DEU *eisen.bahn* [iron.way] RAILWAY
	classifier †	cls	BOA *túú.heju* [nose.CL(HOLE)] NOSTRIL
	derivational †	der	SLO *želez.nica* [iron.NMLZ] RAILWAY
1	adjectival *	adj	RUS *želez.naja doroga* [iron.ADJZ.NMLZ] RAILWAY
	genitival	gen	KAP *kil.os hino* [iron.GEN road] RAILWAY
	adpositional	prp	FRA *chemin de fer* [way PREP iron] RAILWAY
	construct	con	PLT *lala.m.by* [road.PER.iron] RAILWAY
2	double	dbl	TBC *-emo.li sakila.li* [nose.POSS aperture.POSS] NOSTRIL

prp and **con**) involve marking on either the head or the modifier; and one (**dbl**) involves marking on both the head and the modifier.

The original version of this typology, which was presented to contributors of the present volume at SLE 2016 in Zürich and is reflected in some of the contributions to the present volume, consisted of eight types instead of nine: juxtaposition (**jxt**) and compounding (**cmp**) were not distinguished, on the grounds that the presence or absence of a space between the two constituent nouns (or the use of a hyphen) is merely an orthographic convention – as witness the variable spelling in English of a binominal like *flowerpot ~ flower-pot ~ flower pot*, and the alternative ways of transliterating a Japanese binominal like 蜘蛛の巣 SPIDER WEB as either *kumo no su* [spider GEN web] or *kumonoso*.

However, this was inconsistent with the decision to recognise **prp** and **gen** as separate strategies, since these differ only in whether the additional relational marker is a separate word or an affix. Instead of merging these two strategies, which would obscure important facts in languages that exhibit both types, the **jxt** type was added to the typology – despite the well-known fact that there is no accepted cross-linguistic definition of the notion of word (Haspelmath 2011). This is justified by the fact that every language appears to have such a notion, or, as Bauer (2000: 255) puts it, "all languages have a unit which falls between the minimal sign and the phrase". As Koptjevskaja-Tamm (2004: 175) says:

> *Juxtaposition or compounding* The border between juxtaposition and compounding is notoriously difficult to draw, and much more research is needed for determining to what degree this distinction makes sense cross-linguistically. Until then in many cases we have to rely on the local tradition. Thus, Mordvin is traditionally described as resorting to juxtaposition for cases like *tuma lopa* 'an oak leaf' or *ved' vedra* 'a water pail', while their English correspondents are normally treated as compounds. Also, as well known, combinations of head nomi-

nals with genitive-marked dependents and even with prepositional dependents, like Fr. *un chemin de fer* 'railway' (lit. 'a road of iron'), often border on compounds, and the absence of consensus on the treatment of cases like *women's magazine* and *boys' school* testifies to this.

In the absence of more robust criteria, we adopt Koptjevskaja-Tamm's policy of relying on the "local tradition". Given the nature of his data, Pepper (2020) employs the orthographic heuristic that a word space or hyphen signals juxtaposition (**jxt**), whereas the lack of either signals compounding (**cmp**). Pepper (2020: 257) found that this heuristic is actually sufficiently robust to reveal at least one interesting universal, viz. that two nouns are significantly more likely to fuse when the head is on the right.[12]

In addition, the original version of the typology did not stipulate how to handle cases in which multiple morphemes occur on one of the two main constituents. This is clarified by Pepper (2020: 142) as follows:[13]

> In order not to complicate the typology unnecessarily, two or more consecutive morphs attached to either the modifier or the head are counted as a single morph. For example Bezhta *kil.o.s hino* [iron.OBL.GEN way] RAILWAY is simplified to *kil.os hino* [iron.GEN way] and treated as having just one additional morph. In this I follow Nichols (1992: 62), who found such a simplification necessary "because the precise amount of multiple case marking in the constructions I am surveying is generally not made clear in grammars, so no consistent count could be made". A further reason is that there are too few examples of this phenomenon in my data to justify defining separate types to cater for them.

It is possible to arrange the resulting nine binominal types (or strategies) hierarchically, but to do so requires choosing between a grouping based on degree of fusion (i.e. analytical vs. synthetic, as in Figure 1), or one based on locus of marking (i.e. head, dependent, both or none), both of which would obscure important facts. Koptjevskaja-Tamm's decision to use the former obscures the fact that her category 'prepositional' is also a dependent-marking strategy, and the fact that markers on the head or dependent may be pronominal in nature. Similarly, a decision to use the latter would obscure other important facts.

In order to avoid such issues, the nine binominal types are arranged on a two-dimensional grid (Figure 2) which incorporates three different parameters: number of marked elements, locus of marking, and degree of fusion. It also allows

---

[12] In Pepper's database, binominals of type **jxt** are evenly divided (in a ratio of 1:1) between right-headed and left-headed, whereas those of type **cmp** favour right-headedness by a ratio of more than 4:1.

[13] This stipulation is particularly important in order to deal with polysynthetic languages like Anindilyakwa (see van Egmond, this volume).

for the addition of a second plane (or third dimension) if one wishes to capture the order of elements.

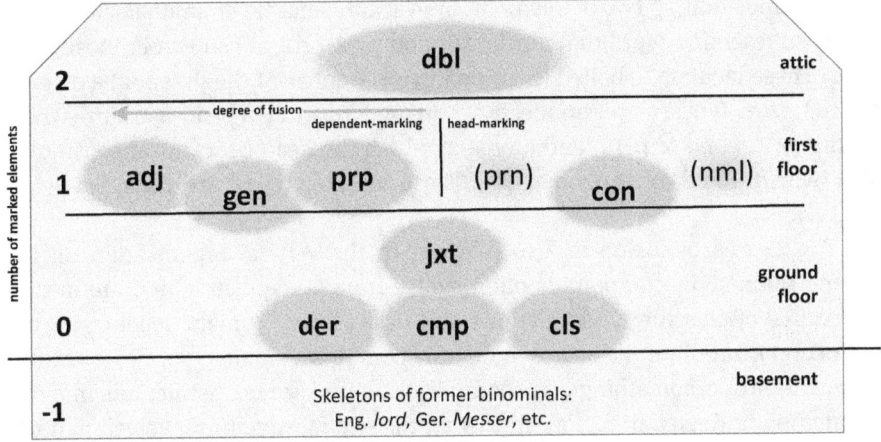

Figure 2: Visualization of the nine strategies on a grid.

The figure may be thought of as a two-storey house with an attic and a basement. On the ground floor (level 0) we find the four types that consist of just the two primary constituents and no additional grammatical material. On the first floor (level 1) are the four types which have an additional morpheme associated with one of the two primary constituents. (There are two apartments on this floor, one for head-marking and one for dependent-marking.) In the attic (level 2) there is just one type, with additional morphemes attached to each of the primary constituents. Finally, there is a basement containing the skeletons of former binominals such as Eng. *lord* and Ger. *Messer* (see §4.1.1).

The vertical dimension thus represents the *degree of marking* (0, 1 or 2 marked elements) and, on level 1, the horizontal dimension represents the *locus of marking* (head or dependent). In addition, the positioning of the three types in the left-hand apartment on level 1 (dependent-marking) represents the *degree of fusion*. The latter, illustrated in Figure 3, is a continuum that ranges, in Bybee's (1985: 12) words, from "the most highly fused means of expression, lexical expression", to "the most loosely joined means of expression, syntactic or periphrastic expression".

lexical --- derivational --- inflectional --- free grammatical --- syntactic
◄───
greater degree of fusion

Figure 3: Degree of fusion (Bybee 1985).

The occupied room, **con**, in the right-hand apartment on the first floor (head-marking) is positioned in the middle in order to mirror **gen**, with which it shares the feature of involving a non-transpositional affix (as opposed to a transpositional affix or adposition).[14] Two of the rooms are vacant; since no binominals have been found representing types that mirror **adj** and **prp**, gaps are shown in those positions. These lacunae, labelled (**prn**) and (**nml**), represent the potential existence of two further types, as yet unattested:[15] an analytic form of head-marking (which would correspond to **prp**), and a type in which the head bears a transpositional affix (which would correspond to **adj**). These "missing types" are discussed below in §3.2.4.

The degree of fusion is also relevant to the vertical organisation on the ground floor, since compounds often evolve from juxtaposition and are in turn the source of classifier constructions and derivations. It might seem irrelevant to the organization of the attic, which only contains a single type. However, this is because **dbl** is something of a catch-all, which makes no distinctions in terms of function or degree of fusion. In theory, the two morphemes involved in a **dbl** construction could be a combination of any of the types found elsewhere in the model: freestanding or affixed, transpositional or non-transpositional, and a more fine-grained classification based on more data remains to be done.

The use of ovals with gradient fill rather than the boxes with sharp outlines found in more traditional representations (including Koptjevskaja-Tamm's) is intended to convey the fact that the types are not clearly defined categories but rather points within a multidimensional space at which phenomena tend to cluster. This enables the representation of overlaps, grammaticalization pathways and various "in-between" or gradient phenomena, as will be seen in §4.

One parameter that is not catered for in the basic typology is the order of elements or, as it is usually called in studies of compounding, the position of the head. Such a parameter is required to differentiate between left- and right-headed binominals of the same type within a particular language, such as the existence of both Head-Mod and Mod-Head **jxt** binominals in Vietnamese (VIE) (7a); and of both Head-Mod.ADJZ and Mod.ADJZ-Head **adj** binominals in Polish (POL) (7b). This parameter is orthogonal to those shown in Figure 2 and can be thought of as an additional plane that mirrors the one depicted in Figure 2. The additional

---

14 The parallel between these two types is underscored by the fact that the term 'genitive' is sometimes applied to possessive markers that attach to the head, as in Malagasy *lalandrà* [road. GEN.blood] 'vein or artery' (Adelaar 2009). Dixon (2010: 268) advocates the use of the term 'pertensive' for possessive markers on the possessum, but we follow Creissels (2017; this volume) in adopting the term 'construct (case)'.
15 But see van Egmond (this volume) and §3.3.2.

parameter extends the nine-way classification into an 18-way classification, with labels such as **jxtL, jxtR, adjL, adjR**, etc.

(7) a. Vietnamese
 xe lửa [vehicle fire] TRAIN – **Head Mod** (native form)
 hoả xa [fire vehicle] TRAIN – **Mod Head** (loan from Sinitic)
 b. Polish
 kolej żelaz.na [course iron.ADJZ] RAILWAY (arch.) – **Head Mod.ADJZ**
 pchl.i targ [flea.ADJZ market] FLEA MARKET – **Mod.ADJZ Head**

In the following sections, each of the nine binominal types is described and exemplified in more detail.[16]

3.2 The nine morphosyntactic strategies

3.2.1 No additional marking: jxt, cmp, der and cls

The ground floor (level 0) of the taxonomy contains four types, **jxt, cmp, der** and **cls**, each of which has exactly two components: the two thing-morphs that are the primary constituents of a binominal. There is no additional grammatical material.

3.2.1.1 jxt

The **jxt** ("juxtaposition") strategy involves a head and a modifier, both of which are thing-roots. There is no additional grammatical material and little or no fusion between the two constituents, which are treated as separate words.

The **jxt** type is found in 22% of the binominals in Pepper's database (Pepper 2020). It occurs in 76 of the 106 languages and is a significant word-formation type (accounting for at least 10% of binominals) in 53 of these. It accounts for the majority of binominals in 22 languages and is the only binominal word-formation strategy in Ceq Wong (CWG), Datooga (TCC), Imbabura Quechua (QVI), Seychelles Creole (CRS), Vietnamese and Walman (VAN).

Examples of the **jxt** strategy (all with the meaning RAILWAY) are given in (8):

---

[16] All the examples, language names and glosses are as in Pepper (2020), where also the sources can be found

(8) a. Vietnamese *đường sắt* [road iron]
    b. Saramaccan (SRM) *talán fútu* [train foot]
    c. Western Farsi (PES) *rāh āhan* [way iron]
    d. Kildin Sami (SJD) *rūvv't čuekas* [iron road]
    e. Ho-Chunk (WIN) *mąąs nąągu* [metal road]
    f. Cabécar (CJP) *kóbäkã̌ ñala* [train road]

3.2.1.2 cmp

The **cmp** ("compounding") strategy involves a head and a modifier, both of which are thing-roots. There is no additional grammatical material, but a high degree of fusion between the two constituents, such that the binominal constitutes a single word.

The **cmp** type is the most frequent type in Pepper's data set, accounting for almost 30% of all binominals. It occurs in 67 of the 106 languages and is a significant word-formation type (accounting for at least 10% of binominals) in 48 of these. Furthermore, it accounts for the majority of binominals in 24 languages and is the only binominal word-formation strategy in Caijia (caij1234) and Tuwari (TWW). The paradigm case of this type is the noun-noun compound, in which two nouns are simply concatenated. Examples of the **cmp** type (again, all with the meaning RAILWAY) are given in (9).

(9) a. Baa (KWB) *kràkísà* [road.train]
    b. Bambara (BAM) *tɛrɛnsira* [train.road]
    c. German *Eisenbahn* [iron.way]
    d. Hawaiian (HAW) *alahao* [path.iron]
    e. Mapudungun (ARN) *trenrüpü* [train.way]
    f. Welsh (CYM) *rheilffordd* [rail.road]

Less prototypical examples of the **cmp** type are compounds that contain a linking element; these are discussed below in §4.1.4 in the context of gradient phenomena.

3.2.1.3 der

The **der** ("derivation") strategy involves a thing-root and a thing-affix. Less prototypically it can consist of two thing-affixes, as in neoclassical compounds.

The **der** type is found in just 432 of the 3,738 binominals in Pepper's database (12%), but it is attested in 60 of the 106 languages (57%). It is the preferred strategy in seven languages: Central Yupik (ESU), Croatian (HRV), Lithuanian (LIT), Oroqen (ORH), Polish, Puyuma (PYU) and Slovak, and the dominant strategy in two of these: Central Yupik and Puyuma.[17]

Some typical examples of the **der** type are listed in (10).

(10) a. Central Yupik *tallir.aq* [arm.AQ3] BRACELET
 b. Puyuma *ka-ḷauk-an* [TMP-lunch-LOC] MIDDAY
 c. Polish *wiatrak* [wind.NMLZ] WINDMILL
 d. Czech *kůzle* [goat.DIM] KID
 e. Hausa (HAU) *sàráunìyáa* [king.F] QUEEN
 f. Gawwada (GWD) *sintitte* [nose.SG:F] NOSTRIL

Only affixes that contribute some tangible semantic content are considered in scope. The meaning contribution may be very general (THING, 10c) or it may be more specific (LOCATION 10b). Note that the gloss provides only a rough indication of the meaning contribution of the affix and is not claimed to be consistent. For one thing, the exact meaning of many derivational affixes is hard to pin down and may exhibit considerable variation; in addition, sources vary in terms of the degree of specificity used in glosses. As a case in point, Nagórko (2016: 2839) highlights the instrumental nature of the Polish suffix *-ak*, whereas it is glossed more generally as NMLZ in the binominals database (10c)

Diminutives are deemed to bear the meaning contribution SMALL THING. They can denote a small version of the entity denoted by the base (10d) or something small that is related in some way to the base entity (10a). Combinations of a thing-root and a gender-denoting affix are only considered to be binominals when the affix marks a clear semantic alternation. Thus, in (10e–f) QUEEN alternates with KING and NOSTRIL with NOSE. On the other hand, Gawwada *xarrap. atte* [spider_web.SG:F] SPIDER WEB is not regarded as a binominal since the suffix does not appear to derive a new meaning through gender alternation.

Neoclassical compounds constitute a non-prototypical variant of **der**. A word like *hydromancy*, is clearly a binominal but it consists of a prefix (*hydro-* 'water') and a suffix (*-mancy* 'divination'): in other words, of two thing-affixes.

---

[17] Note, however, that the data set from Puyuma is very sparse and contains just three binominals, two of which are of type **der**. Most complex nouns in Puyuma, such as *pu-a-ḷima* [put-PJ-hand] GLOVE, have an actional component (often, as here, including a Projective Marker) and thus do not qualify as binominals.

3.2.1.4 cls

The **cls** ("classifier") strategy involves a thing-root and a noun classifier (thing-root or -affix). The denotatum of the binominal differs from that of the base, i.e., the classifier is used to derive a new meaning rather than for classification.

The **cls** type is the least frequent in Pepper's database, accounting for a mere 37 of the 3,738 binominals (1%). It is the preferred strategy in two of the 106 languages: Murui Huitoto (HUU, 11 out of 18 instances) and Trinitario (TRN, 12 out of 25). In addition it is found in Äiwoo (NFL), Bandial, Harakmbut and Swahili (SWA). It therefore requires much more detailed study. In order to facilitate further work, this section contains somewhat more detail than the others (see also Rose and Van linden, this volume, and Næss, this volume).

This type is motivated by the existence of forms such those in (11) and (12), which clearly qualify as binominals (examples from Urban 2012: 126–127).

(11) Arabela (ARL)
 a. *quitiaaca* [breast/teat.CL(liquid)] MILK
 b. *namijiaca* [eye.CL(liquid)] TEAR

(12) Bora
 a. *ííñuhéju* [earth.CL(hole)] CAVE
 b. *túúheju* [nose.CL(hole)] NOSTRIL

The classifier morphemes in these examples (*-aca* and *-héju*) have exactly the same function as the corresponding head constituents of, say, the Thai compounds, *náamtaa* [water.eye] TEAR and *ruucamùuk* [hole.nose] NOSTRIL. However, they cannot be used in isolation, so they are not thing-roots, and thus these binominals do not belong in the **cmp** type. These classifiers also constitute a closed class, which sets them off from the typical nominal constituents of **cmp** binominals. In both respects they are more like thing-affixes, so they could be classified under **der**. But classifiers differ markedly from affixes in having very precise semantics. This does not, in and of itself, constitute sufficient reason to separate them off from the **der** type, but the matter does not end there.

Aikhenvald (2000; 2017), citing criteria articulated earlier by Allan (1977), defines classifiers as "morphemes which occur in surface structures under specifiable conditions, denoting some salient semantic characteristics of the entity to which an associated noun refers". The examples from Arabela (11) and Bora (12) belong to one of seven subtypes of classifier in Aikhenvald's typology, which she calls noun classifiers,[18] and are characterized by the fact that they "occur with a noun independently of any other constituent of a noun phrase or a clause". They can be affixes to nouns, as above, but they can also be "independent words with generic semantics" (13).

(13) Minangkabau (MIN) (Aikhenvald 2000)
   a. *batang limau* [CL(tree) lemon] LEMON-TREE
   b. *buah limau* [CL(fruit) lemon] LEMON-FRUIT

If the Arabela and Bora examples were to be classified as binominals of type **der**, then (13) must be classified as binominals of type **jxt**, and noun classifiers as a group would then be split across two binominal types. That is not necessarily a problem, but it suggests that a better solution – one that would make it possible to investigate the classifier phenomenon more closely – is to define a separate subtype **cls**.

The question is, how to define this type? Examples that parallel those from Minangkabau are also found in Atlantic-Congo languages. In (14) pairs of singular and plural noun class prefixes, *m-/mi-* and *Ø-/ma-*, distinguish trees from fruits, in just the same way as the Minangkabau classifiers *batang* and *buah*. If the Minangkabau words qualify as binominals, so too should the Swahili forms.

(14) Swahili (Russell 2003)
   a. *mlimau / milimau* [CL3.lemon / CL4.lemon] LEMON TREE/S
   b. *limau / malimau* [CL5:lemon / CL6.lemon] LEMON FRUIT/S

And so should the Bandial examples in (15), where the noun class prefixes serve, among much else, to distinguish between animals and their offspring (cf. the Czech diminutive suffix in 10d, above.

(15) Bandial (Watson 2015)
   a. *jijamen* [CL(ji).goat] KID
   b. *ejamen* [CL(e).goat] GOAT

Such noun class prefixes are not noun classifiers in Aikhenvald's typology. Instead they are classified under subtype (i) 'genders and noun classes' (see foot-

---

18 The seven subtypes identified by Aikhenvald are: (i) genders and noun classes, (ii) noun classifiers, (iii) numeral classifiers, (iv) classifiers in possessive constructions, (v) verbal classifiers, (vi) locative classifiers and (vii) deictic classifiers.

note 18 on page 17). One of the major differences between these two subtypes, according to Aikhenvald, is that in a noun class language every noun belongs to a noun class, whereas in noun classifier languages, every noun does not have to take a classifier.[19] Consequently, there would be a very substantial cost to admitting words like (15a, b) to the pantheon of binominals: Every noun in Swahili and Bandial would qualify as a binominal of type **cls** and, as a result, the data from noun class languages would swamp those from noun classifier languages and give a distorted overall impression of the **cls** type. That problem may not be insurmountable provided one remains aware of it, but unfortunately the issue is yet more complicated. Consider (16).

(16) Gawwada
    a. *pi?atte* [kid.SG:F] KID
    b. *xarrapatte* [spider_web.SG:F] SPIDER WEB

If the Bandial examples are regarded as binominals, why not also the Gawwada? After all, the only real difference between a two- or three-gender system (like the one in Gawwada and many Indo-European languages) and a noun class system of the Atlantic-Congo type is the size of the system: Aikhenvald groups them under the same subtype. And yet, the Gawwada examples cannot by any stretch of the imagination be regarded as the functional equivalents of noun-noun compounds. Moreover, recognizing them as binominals would lead to the kinds of construction we are interested in in this volume being completely lost from sight. Somewhere on this slippery slope a line has to be drawn.

That line could be drawn between Aikhenvald's two subtypes; it would amount to defining noun classifiers, but not noun class markers, as thing-morphs. (11)–(13) would then be categorized as binominals, while (14)–(16) would not. This would have the unfortunate consequence that (13) and (14), which really are parallel in every way, would be accorded different treatments. The line could also be drawn by contriving a distinction between noun class languages and gender languages based on the size of the system: say, more than three for noun class languages and two to three for gender languages. The line would then go between (15) and (16). Not only would this be somewhat arbitrary, it would also result in the aforementioned imbalance between noun class languages and noun classifier languages.

---

[19] In addition, agreement is a necessary feature of noun class/gender systems but not of noun classifier systems. However, this does not impinge on the present discussion.

The solution adopted here is to draw the line instead between (15a) and (15b). The basis for making such a distinction is that in (15a) the denotatum of the whole (KID) is different from that of the base (GOAT), whereas in (15b) they are the same (GOAT and GOAT). In (15a) the noun classifier contributes a meaning component that *changes the denotatum*, i.e. its function is *derivational*. In (15b) this is not the case; nor is it in the two examples from Gawwada (16). Hence the qualification in the definition given above that the function of the classifier be derivational rather than classificatory.[20]

3.2.2 Marking on the head or modifier: prp, gen, adj and con

The first floor (level 1) of the binominal taxonomy also contains four types. What they have in common is that they contain one additional (grammatical) morpheme, over and above the two primary constituents. Three of the four (**prp, gen** and **adj**) share an apartment because the additional marker forms a constituent with the modifier; the fourth (**con**) lives alone, since the marker forms a constituent with the head.

3.2.2.1 prp

The **prp** ("prepositional") strategy involves a head and a modifier, both of which are thing-roots, and another independent lexeme that forms a constituent with the modifier.

The **prp** type accounts for 245 of the binominals in Pepper's database (6.5%), distributed across 27 languages, and it is the preferred strategy in eight of these: Barain, French, Italian (ITA), Maltese (MLT), Romanian (RON), Swahili, Tagalog (TGL) and Tarifit (RIF).

In the typical case, exemplified in (17a–c), the additional lexeme is a preposition (hence the choice of mnemonic for this type), but it may also be a postposition (17d) or a particle named according to a language-specific descriptive category, such as a connector (17e) or linker (17f).

(17)   a.   French *chemin de fer* [road of iron] RAILWAY
      b.   French *moulin à vent* [mill to wind] WINDMILL
      c.   Welsh *papur lle chwech* [paper for toilet] TOILET PAPER

---

[20] See Pepper (2020: 148–154) and Rose and Van linden (this volume) for further discussion.

    d. Hindi (HIN) *dāṃt kā braś* [tooth GEN brush] TOOTHBRUSH
    e. Lingala *nzela ya masini** [way CON train] RAILWAY (* no relation)
    f. Tagalog *butas ng ilong* [hole LK nose] NOSTRIL

While prepositions are fairly common, postpositions are rare and can be problematic, in that they can often be analysed as case affixes (i.e. **gen**) rather than adpositions (**prp**). The Hindi example (17d) is a case in point. It is glossed using the abbreviation GEN in the database (as decided by the contributor), but *ka* is also commonly regarded as a postposition (§4.1.5).

The most commonly used adpositions are those whose function also includes to indicate possession, such as the French *de* (17a) and the Hindi *ka* (17d), but some languages permit other prepositions to be used as well, such as a locative (17b) or purposive (17c). In other languages, the particle has a more general, associative meaning that is used for a wide variety of relations and not solely for possession. Examples include the Lingala Connective *-a* (17e) and the Tagalog Linker *ng* (17f).

In French, more than one preposition is available for use in binominal word-formation (17a-b). This suggests that the present typology may be too coarse-grained for certain kinds of investigation, for example, into the semantics of French prepositional compounds – or that it should be used in conjunction with a classification of semantic relations like Hatcher-Bourque (see Pepper, b, this volume).

3.2.2.2 gen

The **gen** ("genitival") strategy involves a head and a modifier, both of them thing-roots, with an additional, non-transpositional affix or segmental marker attached to the modifier.

There are 484 instances of the **gen** type in Pepper's database (13%), making it the third most frequent strategy in absolute terms (after **cmp** and **jxt**). It is also ranked third in terms of the number of languages in which it is found (55 out of 106, i.e. 52%). It is the preferred strategy in 15 of those languages: Amharic (AMH), Archi (AQC), Assamese (ASM), Bezhta, Estonian (EST), Gawwada, Greek (ELL), Irish (GLE), Kambaata (KTB), Kanuri (KAU), Latvian (LAV), Nepali (NEP), Sidamo (SID), Wawa (WWW) and Zinacantán Tzotzil (TZO).

Typically, the additional affix indicates the genitive case (18a-c) or possessive function (18d), but other cases occur as well, including the dative (18e).

(18) a. Bezhta *kilos hino* [iron.GEN road] RAILWAY
 b. Irish *muileann gaoithe* [mill wind:GEN] WINDMILL
 c. Kanuri *súwúlí kə́nzàbè* [opening nose.GEN] NOSTRIL
 d. Takia (TBC) *graŋen tatu* [side.3SG bone] RIB
 e. Gurinji *yawartawu marru* [horse.DAT house] STABLE OR STALL
 f. Tarifit *tisi ufus* [bottom STC.hand] PALM OF HAND

The Tarifit example (18f) illustrates the kind of confusion that arises if one assumes that descriptive categories are the same across languages. Here the *modifier*, 'hand', normally *fus*, is in what some Berber linguists call the "construct state" (hence the gloss, *status constructus*). The very same term is used in Semitic linguistics to describe a special form of the *head* in adnominal constructions. Consequently, Berber words glossed with STC belong to the type **gen** (dependent-marked) whereas Semitic words glossed with STC belong to the type **con** (head-marked), cf. (23e) below.

3.2.2.3 adj

The **adj** ("adjectival") strategy involves a head and a modifier, both of them thing-roots, with an additional, transpositional morpheme attached to the modifier.

The binominals database contains 196 instances of the type **adj** (5%) and it occurs in 28 languages (26%). The great majority of these are European languages, either Indo-European or Uralic (19). The six Slavic languages (Croatian, Czech, Lower Sorbian, Polish, Russian and Slovak) account for 130 of them alone. Whether this is because adjective as a productive lexical category is more frequent in Europe than elsewhere is a question for further research.

(19) a. Italian *via lattea* [way milk.ADJZ] MILKY WAY
 b. Lithuanian *geležinkelis* [iron.ADJZ.way] RAILWAY
 c. Polish *kolej żelazna* [course iron.ADJZ] RAILWAY (arch.)
 d. Polish *złoty pierścionek* [gold.ADJZ ring] GOLD RING
 e. Russian *železnaja doroga* [iron.ADJZ road] RAILWAY
 f. Kildin Sami *mājjtjes' lījjhm* [milk.ATTR cow] DAIRY COW
 g. Hungarian (HUN) *északi fény* [north.ADJZ light] ARCTIC LIGHTS
 h. Hungarian *képeslap* [picture.PROP.card] POSTCARD

The most common descriptive category for the additional morpheme is adjectivizer, but the terms attributivizer and proprietive are also found. Polish and Hungarian are notable for having two distinct constructions of this type. In Polish the same construction can be either head initial (19c) or head-final (19d). In Hungarian there are two different adjectival suffixes (19g-h): *-i* (labelled ADJZ) and *-s* (labelled PROP), both of which can be attached to a wide variety of nouns (Kiefer 2009).

Other examples are found scattered across the globe in Africa (20a), the Caucasus (20b), Asia (20c-e), New Guinea (20f) and Central America (20g).

(20) a. Kanuri *kámú nyìyáà* [woman marriage.ADJZ] MARRIED WOMAN
 b. Bezhta *kaƛ'ako tormoz* [hand.OBL.SUP.ATTR brake] HAND BRAKE
 c. Western Farsi *asiyāb bādi* [mill wind.ADJZ] WINDMILL
 d. Ket *soltu təqol* [gold.ADJZ finger.covering] GOLD RING
 e. Yakut (SAH) *tualetnay kuma:yi* [toilet.ADJZ paper] TOILET PAPER
 f. Kalamang (KGV) *sontum warten* [person sorcery.ADJZ] SORCERER OR WITCH
 g. Kekchí (KEK) *k'imal kab'l* [straw.ADJZ house] THATCH

3.2.2.4 con

The **con** ("construct") strategy involves a head and a modifier, both of them thing-roots, with an additional, non-transpositional affix or segmental marker on the head.

The type **con** accounts for 351 of the binominals in Pepper's database (9%) and is found in 24 of the 106 languages (23%). It is the preferred strategy in 10 of these: Anindilyakwa (AOI), Hausa, Hebrew (HEB), Iraqw (IRK), Kekchí, Kupsabiny (KPZ), Turkish, Western Farsi, Wolof (WOL) and Yakut; and it accounts for over 75% of all binominals in Hausa, Hebrew, Kupsabiny and Wolof.

The term 'construct' is traditionally used in Semitic linguistics but has been extended by Creissels (2017; this volume) to cover any obligatory marking on a noun that fulfils the role of head in nominal modifier constructions, provided it does not cross-reference features of the modifier that condition its use. Because of the latter proviso, example (22b) is a clear case of a binominal of type **con** that is not an instance of construct marking according to his definition, "since *x-* is an uncontroversial 3rd person singular prefix" (p.c.). Apart from this proviso, Creissel's term 'construct' covers every instance in the binominal database of the type **con**.

Binominals of this type are glossed in a variety of ways (21–23). Labels used in traditions other than Semitic include linker, possessive, genitive and pertensive.[21]

---

[21] In addition, Haspelmath (2009) proposes the term "anti-genitive".

The latter term, proposed by Dixon (2010b), is restricted to possessive constructions (unlike Creissels' construct), but does permit cross-referencing.

The type **con** covers what Croft (2003; 2022) terms 'linkers' and 'special forms' (to the extent that these occur on the head), as well as his 'indexical' strategies. Croft subdivides the latter according to whether or not they encode the category of person, into 'person indexation' and 'nonperson indexation'. Koptjevskaja-Tamm (2003: 645) makes what appears to be a similar distinction, albeit using different terminology, between two subtypes of head-marking:
1. **relators**, whereby the form of the head signals the presence of the dependent in the same NP, without, however, specifying its features;
2. **indexers**, whereby the form of the head varies according to the properties of the dependent.

Koptjevskaja-Tamm's relators correspond to Croft's linkers and special forms, since they do not exhibit contrast, whereas her indexers may involve either person indexation or nonperson indexation. Examples of the latter are found in Barain (21a-b) and Hausa (21c-d), where the markers are *-ji/-(g)eti* and *-r/-n*, respectively, depending on the gender of the dependent.

(21) a. Barain *sinja guma-geti* [nose$_F$ hole-POSS:3SG:F] NOSTRIL
     b. Barain *nokuno non-ji* [goat$_M$ child-POSS:3SG:M] KID
     c. Hausa *kàfá-r háncìi* [orifice$_F$-LK nose] NOSTRIL
     d. Hausa *dóokì-n kárfèe* [horse$_M$-LK metal] BICYCLE

On the other hand, the glossing of (22a-d), all of which make reference to the third person, suggests that these are indexers in Koptjevskaja-Tamm's scheme and examples of person indexation in Croft's.

(22) a. Kalamang *kanggir pul-un* [eye skin-3POSS] EYELID
     b. Kekchí *x-na'aj xam* [3ERG-place fire] FIREPLACE
     c. Takia *su mala-n* [breast eye-3SG] NIPPLE OR TEAT
     d. Yakut *χaraχ uː-ta* [eye water-3SG] TEAR

Lastly, the invariant possessive affixes in Kupsabiny (23a) and Malagasy (PLT) (23b) are relators for Koptjevskaja-Tamm but linkers for Croft. So too are the Galibi Carib (CAR) possessive suffix *-li* and its allomorph *-yɨ* (23c-d) since their distributions are phonologically determined and not conditioned by features of either the head or the modifier. The form of the Hebrew construct case (23e) is determined by the gender of the head, so it is a Koptjevskaja-Tamm relator, whereas it is a special form for Croft. Despite this variation, I regard all of the examples in this section as binominals of type **con**.

(23) a. Kupsabiny *kariit-aap maata* [car-POSS fire] TRAIN
b. Malagasy *lala-m-by* [road-PER-iron] RAILWAY
c. Galibi Carib *manati poti-li* [breast tip-POSS] NIPPLE OR TEAT
d. Galibi Carib *upupo kuwai-yɨ* [head calabash-POSS] SKULL
e. Hebrew *mesila-t barzel* [track-STC iron] RAILWAY

3.2.3 Marking on the head and modifier: dbl

In the attic (level 2) of the binominal house there is just one type: **dbl**. Like most attics, the contents are somewhat untidy, as will be explained shortly.

3.2.3.1 dbl

The **dbl** ("double") strategy involves a head and a modifier, both of them thing-roots, with additional morphemes attached to both.

There are just 37 instances of the **dbl** type in Pepper's database, a mere 1% of the total. They are distributed across 15 languages: Akkadian (AKK), Barain, Central Yupik, Galibi Carib, Hebrew, Kekchí, Maltese, Oroqen, Puyuma, Romanian, Seri, Somali (SOM), Takia, Trinitario and Western Farsi, in four of which they are the preferred binominal strategy: Akkadian, Seri (SEI), Somali and Takia.

(24) a. Galibi Carib *emo-li sakɨla-li* [nose-POSS aperture-POSS] NOSTRIL
b. Takia *patu-n kdabog-an* [egg-3SG yellow-3SG] YOLK
c. Oroqen *dalay-ŋi ŋə:kə-n* [sea-GEN bank-3SG:POSS] SHORE
d. Somali *bam-ka biyo-ha* [pump-DEF water-DEF] WATER PUMP
e. Maltese *l-isfar tal-bajda* [DEF-yellow of:DEF-egg] YOLK
f. Akkadian *piliš app-im* [hole:STC nose-GEN] NOSTRIL
g. Kambaata *qiissann-a wodar-u* [spider-F:GEN line-M:GEN] SPIDER WEB

As the examples in (24) demonstrate, there is considerable variation in terms of the kinds of markers (case, definiteness, possession, construct), and the ways in which they are combined. Sometimes it is the same affix that attaches to both major constituents (24a-b). In some languages the markers appear to cross-reference each other (24b), in others the affix on the head cross-references the modifier (24c). Somali exhibits two definiteness markers (24d) and Maltese a combination of definite marker and definite preposition (24e). Finally, Akkadian (24f) exhibits an older form of the Semitic construct state with the modifier in the oblique case, while in Kambaata (24g) both elements have genitive markers. The variety encountered here suggests that a more fine-grained classification would be possible. However, the binominals database contains too little data for this to be feasible. With more data these could be analysed in terms of combinations (one from each apartment) of the types found on level 1, and perhaps also Croft's distinction between relators, indexes and linkers.

3.2.4 Summary of binominal strategies

For ease of reference we conclude this section with a summary table of the nine binominal strategies, with their mnemonics, definitions and examples (of either RAILWAY or NOSTRIL).

3.3 Unattested strategies

As noted above and shown in Figure 2 on page 37), level 1 of the classification is divided into two "apartments", with dependent-marking strategies to the left and head-marking strategies to the right. The three dependent-marking strategies (**prp**, **gen** and **adj**) are situated from right to left, in that order, such as to reflect Bybee's (1985) scale based on degree of fusion. The single head-marking strategy (**con**) is situated in the middle of the right-hand section in order to highlight its symmetrical relation to **gen**, since **gen** is a non-transpositional affixing strategy associated with the dependent, and **con** is a non-transpositional affixing strategy associated with the head. Once the nine types are laid out in this manner, two gaps are revealed, labelled (**prn**) and (**nml**). These are the head-marking correlates of **prp** and **adj**, respectively. In this section we discuss possible explanations for these lacunae.

3.3.1 (prn)

The first missing type is the head-marking correlate of **prp**, which we have labelled (**prn**) for reasons that will become apparent. For such a type to exist, it must consist of a head, a modifier and another independent lexeme that forms a co-constituent with the head, e.g. **Mod {X Head}**.

Table 4: Summary of binominal strategies.

Mnemonic	Markers	Definition	Example
jxt	0	The **jxt** ("juxtaposition") strategy involves a head and a modifier, both of which are thing-roots. There is no additional grammatical material and little or no fusion between the two constituents, which are treated as separate words.	Saramaccan (SRM) *talán fútu* [train foot] RAILWAY
cmp		The **cmp** ("compounding") strategy involves a head and a modifier, both of which are thing-roots. There is no additional grammatical material, but a high degree of fusion between the two constituents, such that the binominal constitutes a single word.	German (DEU) *Eisenbahn* [iron.way] RAILWAY
der		The **der** ("derivation") strategy involves a thing-root and a thing-affix. Less prototypically it can consist of two thing-affixes, as in neoclassical compounds.	Gawwada (GWD) *sintitte* [nose.SG:F] NOSTRIL
cls		The **cls** ("classifier") strategy involves a thing-root and a noun classifier (thing-root or -affix). The denotatum of the binominal differs from that of the base; i.e., the classifier is used to derive a new meaning rather than for classification.	Bora (BOA) *túúheju* [nose.CL(hole)] NOSTRIL
prp	1 (modifier)	The **prp** ("prepositional") strategy involves a head and a modifier, both of which are thing-roots, and another independent lexeme that forms a constituent with the modifier.	French (FRA) *chemin de fer* [road of iron] RAILWAY
gen		The **gen** ("genitival") strategy involves a head and a modifier, both of them thing-roots, with an additional, non-transpositional affix or segmental marker attached to the modifier.	Amharic (AMH) *yebaburi ḥādīdi* [GEN.train way] RAILWAY
adj		The **adj** ("adjectival") strategy involves a head and a modifier, both of them thing-roots, with an additional, transpositional morpheme attached to the modifier.	Russian (RUS) *železnaja doroga* [iron.ADJZ road] RAILWAY
con	1 (head)	The **con** ("construct") strategy involves a head and a modifier, both of them thing-roots, with an additional, non-transpositional affix or segmental marker on the head.	Malagasy (PLT) *lalamby* [road.PER.iron] RAILWAY
dbl	2 (head and modifier)	The **dbl** ("double") strategy involves a head and a modifier, both of them thing-roots, with additional morphemes attached to both.	Akkadian (AKK) *piliš appim* [hole:STC nose.GEN] NOSTRIL

So what kind of item might be a candidate for the role of X? One way to approach this question is to look for a relation **prn** ↔ **con** that is isomorphic with the relation **prp** ↔ **gen**. Now, it is well-established that adpositions (**prp**) are a common source of case markers (**gen**): "Diachronically, case affixes arise from adpositions that become affixed to the noun" (Croft 1990: 34). The missing type **prn** could thus be whatever is the source of **con**.

According to Croft (2003: 35–36), "bound indexation markers", such as those in binominals of type **con**, develop out of (i) pronouns (in the case of person indexation) and (ii) articles (in the case of nonperson indexation). An example of the former is the Hausa (construct state) suffix -*n* (plural or masculine singular) or -*ř* (feminine singular), which attaches to the head in possessive constructions (25a, c). This suffix also occurs in the **Head.LK Mod** construction responsible for 40 of the 43 Hausa binominals in the database used in the present study (cf. examples 21c-d on page 22). According to Creissels (2009), this suffix results from the cliticization of a pronoun *na/ta* that is co-referent with the head noun in the synonymous construction illustrated by (25b, d).[22]

(25) Hausa (cf. *kàree* 'dog', *saanìyaa* 'cow')
    a. *kàre.n Daudà* [dog$_M$.CSTR:SG:M Dauda] 'Dauda's dog'
    b. *kàree na Daudà* [dog$_M$ that one (SG:M) of Dauda] 'Dauda's dog'
    c. *saanìya.ř Daudà* [cow$_F$.CSTR:SG:F Dauda] 'Dauda's cow'
    d. *saanìyaa ta Daudà* [cow$_F$ that one (SG:F) of Dauda] 'Dauda's cow'

In other words, the source of **Head.LK Mod** is **Head, PRON Mod**. The latter construction would be considered an instance of the missing type **prn** if the pronoun formed a constituent with the head (i.e., {**Head PRON**} **Mod**), but that is not the case. Instead, the pronoun forms a constituent with the modifier (**Head** {**PRON Mod**}), which means that (25b) and (25d), if they were binominals (which they are not, because they do not have a naming function), would be instances of **prp**, not **prn**. This is an example of reanalysis, in which an element preposed to the modifier in a head-initial construction is reinterpreted as a postposed marker on the head (26).

(26) *kàree {na Daudà}* Head, PRON Mod ➔ *{kàre.n} Daudà* Head.LK Mod

---

22 Newman (2000: 300) calls *na/ta* a (free) (genitive) linker. It can combine with personal pronouns, but is not itself a pronoun, according to him.

Clearly, constituency must be taken into consideration when looking for examples of the missing type **prn**. There are six logical possibilities (27). The component X might be a pronoun or an article, but it must form a constituent with the head. This means that constructions (27c) and (27d) are highly unlikely: they could only occur in a non-configurational language.

(27)   a. **{X Head} Mod**   b. **{Head X} Mod**   c. ~~Head {Mod} X~~
       d. ~~X {Mod} Head~~   e. **Mod {X Head}**   f. **Mod {Head X}**

An example of (e), in which a pronoun copy of the dependent (*ha* 'he') is preposed to the head, is provided by Nichols (1992: 79) from Atakapa (AQP, extinct isolate), together with a schematic English rendition (28a,b).

(28)   a.   *yukhiti icak kau ha tal*
           Indian man dead he skin
           'the skin of a dead Atakapa'
      b. [[the man] [he skin]] 'the man's skin'

(28a) is, of course, a possessive construction, not a binominal, so it does not count as an instance of the missing binominal type **prn**. However, since binominals often recruit their morphosyntactic strategies from possessive constructions (see below), it is perfectly possible that the type does exist somewhere. Were it to be found, it would correspond to Koptjevskaja-Tamm's "linking pronoun", the one type in her PNP classification that was not found in Pepper's binominal data. While the linking pronoun type of PNP is rare in European languages, its status across the world's language is unknown and it seems eminently possible that the binominal type **prn** could exist somewhere. Finding it, however, must remain a topic for further research.

3.3.2 (nml)

The second missing type is the head-marking correlate of **adj**, labelled **nml**. If such a type exists, it must consist of a head, a modifier and a transpositional (i.e., word class changing) morpheme attached to the head, just as **adj** consists of a head, a modifier and a transpositional morpheme attached to the modifier, cf. the Russian example *železnaja doroga* [iron.ADJZ road] RAILWAY. There are two logical possibilities:
- Either the additional morpheme is a nominalizer – that is to say, **Mod Head. NMLZ**, in which case the head element would not be a thing-root;

Defining and typologizing binominal lexemes — 55

- or it derives some other word class – as for example in **Mod Head.ADJZ**, in which case the resulting construction would not denote an object, but rather a property.

In neither case would the form in question be regarded as a binominal. In other words, **nml** as a type of binominal appears to be a logical impossibility, at least as long as one thinks in terms of major word classes; it is not found in the data for a good reason.

Having said that, van Egmond (this volume) proposes the INALP construction in Anindilyakwa as a possible candidate for the **nml** type. Her argument is that the Anindilyakwa Inalienable Possession (INALP) construction is used to denote

> parts of inanimate objects, plants, animals, and to components of body parts. The 'part' noun [i.e. the head] is marked for INALP and maintains its intrinsic noun class prefix, as this is frozen to the stem. The derived nominal behaves like an adjective in that it is now flexible and can take any pronominal/gender/noun class prefix to agree with the independent noun [i.e. the modifier] that represents the 'whole'. (page 164)

Van Egmond represents the structure as in (29a) and provides examples like (29b):

(29) a. [NCx-(G-)INALP-NCy.Head (NCx.Mod)]
  b. *ma-m-ayarrka mukayuwa*
    VEG-INALP-NEUT.hand VEG.dillybag
    'handle of dillybag'

In (29b), *ayarrka* 'hand' is used metonymically to denote a handle and is thus the head of a construction in which the modifier is *mukayuwa* 'dillybag'. Both of these are thing-morphs, and there is no actional element, so this is clearly a binominal. Now, *ayarrka* belongs to the neuter noun class and *mukayuwa* to the vegetable noun class. They cannot simply be juxtaposed because there is obligatory agreement throughout the clause in Anindilyakwa. So what happens is that an INALP prefix *m(a)-* is added to the head constituent, thereby permitting the VEG noun class prefix required by the modifier (*ma-*) to be attached to the head.

In van Egmond's analysis, this is tantamount to changing *ayarrka* into an Anindilyakwa Adjective (a property word); the process is transpositional (word-class changing) and since the marker is associated with the head, we therefore have an instance of the missing type **nml**. However, it is not the case that *ayarrka* ('hand') qualifies *mukayuwa* ('dillybag'); it is the reverse. The situation is thus no different in principle from the Hausa examples (21c-d) in which the form of the morpheme attached to the head is governed by the gender of the modifier. Like the Hausa binominals, the Anindilyakwa Inalienable Possession construction must therefore be classified as **con** in the binominal typology proposed here.

In conclusion, binominals consisting of two thing-roots and a transpositional morpheme attached to the head (i.e. **nml**) have not yet been discovered, and given the current definition, they would appear to be a logical impossibility.

4 Binominals and grammaticalization

4.1 Grammaticalization pathways

The two-dimensional representation of the typology of binominal lexemes was developed in order to account for gradient phenomena. This section discusses instances of constructions that fall in between the nine major types. It is based primarily on the data collected by Pepper (2020) but includes some examples from other sources. Each subsection refers to one of the numbered items in Figure 4.

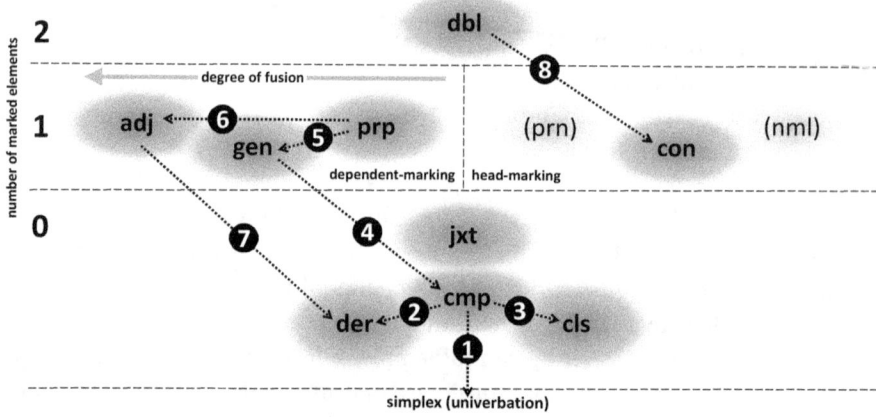

Figure 4: Formal classification showing gradient phenomena.

4.1.1 Univerbation (cmp ➔ simplex) ❶

Univerbation is the term given to the historical process by which an (analysable) item consisting of two or more morphemes develops into an (unanalysable) item consisting of a single morpheme. Examples of such simplex forms belong in the basement of the binominal house, i.e. level -1, but since they would not be binominals (by definition), such a level is not required for the classification.

However, since univerbation is a gradual process, it is only to be expected that there will be partially analysable items that are intermediate between the types on level 0 (**der, jxt, cmp, cls**) and that lower level. Two examples are given in (30). Eng. *nostril* (30a) was originally a compound but is no longer identifiable as such, despite the first constituent being recognisable as 'nose'. In Eng. *lord* (30b) and Ger. *Messer* (30c), on the other hand, the process of univerbation has reached its end-point: What started out as prototypical binominals of type **cmp** are today completely opaque to lay speakers.

(30) a. Eng. *nostril* < *nose* + *thirl* ('hole')
 b. Eng. *lord* < *hlāf* ('bread') + *weard* ('guardian')
 c. Ger. *Messer* 'knife' < Proto-Ger. **matiz* 'food' + **sahsą* 'knife, dagger'

4.1.2 Affixoids (cmp ➔ der) ❷

The difference between **cmp** and **der** is that the former consists of two thing-roots whereas the latter consists of a thing-root and a thing-affix. However, the distinction between a root and an affix is not clear-cut; the two exist as end-points on a continuum that can be defined in terms of autonomy versus dependence (Tuggy 1992). Between these two end-points one finds phenomena called affixoids that are neither fully autonomous nor fully dependent. Booij (2010) gives a number of examples from Dutch in which a noun acquires a specialized meaning when used as the head of a compound (31).

(31) *baron* 'baron' > rich dealer: *afval-baron* [trash-baron] 'rich dealer in trash'
 boer 'farmer' > seller: *sigaren-boer* [cigar-farmer] 'cigar seller'
 man 'man' > seller: *bladen-man* [magazine-man] 'magazine seller'
 marathon 'marathon' > long-session: *jazz-marathon* 'jazz marathon'

In English *postman* and many other compounds whose second constituent is *man*, phonological reduction of the second element *-man* from /mæn/ to /mən/ indicates a status intermediate between root and affix, even though it may not yet have "broken away from MAN, becoming a lexical formative on its own" (Matthews 1991: 94).

4.1.3 Bound nouns (cmp ➔ cls) ❸

As pointed out in §3.2.1.4, the type **cls** ("classifier") is the least well-defined and the most poorly represented in the database. If terminology is anything to go by, it consists of a number of somewhat disparate phenomena, as witnessed by the many transitional cases in Äiwoo (Næss, this volume). One of the strategies found in this language uses a "bound noun", a term suggestive of something intermediate between a noun and a classifier, which would in turn give rise to binominals mid-way between **cmp** and **cls**. The distinction between classifiers and bound nouns is discussed in detail by Rose and Van linden (this volume) in their description of the Western Amazonian languages Trinitario and Harakmbut, and they note "the analytical problem" of distinguishing between the types **cmp** and **cls**.

4.1.4 Linking elements (gen ➔ cmp) ❹

In many languages noun-noun compounds involve linking elements. Almost all the examples in Pepper's database are from Indo-European languages (32a-d), the only exceptions being from Korean (KOR) (32e), where it is found in what Yeon & Brown (2011) describe as "compounds in which the two elements are linked together by the addition of the so-called 'genitive s'" (p. 31). The latter, which causes tensing (or reinforcement) on the following plain consonant, is best regarded as a linking element in the modern language. Bauer (2001) cites an example from Cambodian (KHM) (32f) and mentions Yoruba (YOR) as having a "purely phonological" linking element that involves prolongation of the final vowel, while W. Bauer (1993) mentions a type of compounding involving a linking element -*aa*- "which is being increasingly used at present" in Maori (MRI) (32g).

(32)   a.   German *Nasenloch* [nose.LE.hole] NOSTRIL
        b.   Greek *siδiroδromos* [iron.LE.road] RAILWAY
        c.   Lithuanian *voratinklis* [spider.LE.web] SPIDER WEB
        d.   Russian *golenostop* [shank.LE.foot] ANKLE
        e.   Korean *khoskwumeng* [nose.GEN.hole] NOSTRIL
        f.   Cambodian *yianəthaan* [vehicle.LK.place] GARAGE
        g.   Maori *waiata-aa-ringa* [song-LK-hand] ACTION SONG

Many elements of this kind have their origin in case and/or number suffixes that have become semantically bleached and now often conflict with the grammar. For example, in the German *Regierungschef* [government.LE.head] 'head of government' the linking element *-s-*, a reflex of the masculine genitive, is here attached to a feminine noun. The Greek linking element *-o-* (32b) originates in an ancient thematic vowel but today functions solely as a compounding marker (Ralli 2013). Binominals such as these can be said to occupy the space between **gen** and **cmp** but are arguably closer to the latter. Other linking elements, like those in Yoruba and Cambodian, may only ever have had a phonological role.

Binominals with linking elements thus present a challenge when coding the data: classifying them consistently as either **cmp** or **gen** could obscure important distinctions in Germanic and Greek respectively. The solution adopted by Pepper (2020: 166) is to classify them in such a way as to bring out any contrasts that might be relevant in each individual language. Thus Germanic binominals with linking elements are coded as **gen** (to contrast with the **cmp** strategy otherwise found in those languages) and as **cmp** in Greek (to contrast with the "true" **gen** strategy).

4.1.5 Adpositions or case affixes? (prp → gen) ◐

As noted above (§3.3.1), case affixes often arise from adpositions that become attached to the noun. As a result, the status of some binominals as either **prp** or **gen** can be hard to determine. A classic example is the Japanese *no* construction which some linguists analyse as a genitive suffix (33a) and others as a postposition (33b). The orthography offers no clue since the particle *no* is written in Hiragana (の) while the other words are written in Kanji (蜘蛛の巣). In order to facilitate comparison with Korean, in which the equivalent possessive particle 의 (*-uy*) is always written as a suffix, Pepper took the decision to classify the Japanese forms as **gen** rather than **prp**.

(33) Japanese
    a. *kumonosu* [spider.GEN.web] SPIDER WEB
    b. *kumo no su* [spider POSTP web] SPIDER WEB

The orthography used in Maltese, on the other hand (34), suggests that the combination of the preposition *ta'* and the definite article *il-*, which occurs commonly in binominals, is neither a separate word nor a prefix, but rather a clitic. This, again, lies somewhere between **prp** and **gen**.

(34) Maltese *mitħna tar-riħ* [mill OF:DEF-wind] WINDMILL

Sometimes grammatical descriptions analyse equivalent constructions in closely related languages in rather different ways. This applies to possessive constructions in Hindi and Nepali. Whereas in Hindi (35a) the possessive morpheme is written, transliterated and referred to as a postposition, in Nepali (35b) it is treated as a suffix. The decision as to which category to assign must be taken in such a way as to minimize any adverse analytical consequences.

(35) a. Hindi मकड़ी का जाला *makṛī **kā** jālā* [spider POSTP web] SPIDER WEB
b. Nepali माकुराको जालो *mākurā.**ko** jālo* [spider.GEN web] SPIDER WEB

4.1.6 Inflection or derivation? (gen ~ adj) ◐

The definitions of **gen** and **adj** in (§3.2.2.2 and §3.2.2.3) do not make reference to the notions of inflection and derivation, but rather to the distinction between transpositional (word-class changing) and non-transpositional affixation. The reason for this is that the traditional distinction between inflection and derivation, whereby derivational affixes change the word-class of their base, while inflectional affixes do not, has been shown to be too simplistic. Haspelmath (1996) uses the example of Slavic possessive adjectives to show that the difference between inflection and derivation is one of degree, with Upper Sorbian being at the inflectional end of the scale and Russian more towards the derivational end. Defining **gen** and **adj** in terms of inflection and derivation would thus result in intermediate forms. Defining them in terms of transposition, on the other hand, results in a more clear-cut distinction.

4.1.7 Head replacement (adj → der) ●

The type **adj** belongs to level 1 in the classification whereas **der** belongs on level 0: the former has three components whereas the latter has just two. An intermediate between these two is represented by the Slovak word *železnica* (36a). The structure of this word parallels that of the Russian *železnaja doroga* (36b) precisely, except for the use of the nominalizing suffix *-ica* instead of a lexical head *doroga*.

(36) a. Slovak *želez.n.ica* [iron.ADJZ.NMLZ] RAILWAY
b. Russian *želez.naja doroga* [iron.ADJZ road] RAILWAY

Thus in one sense the word belongs on level 1 under **adj**. On the other hand, as a derived word it has more in common with other derivations and, indeed, Slovak linguists recognize an alternative synchronic analysis, *želez-nica* [iron-NMLZ], an undoubted instance of the **der** type:

There are two possible starting points for the analysis of the word *železnica*:

> 1. It is derived from *železo (iron)* and can be paraphrased as follows: "the object which is related to iron" (which moves on iron)
> 2. It is derived from *železný* (iron$_{ADJ}$) as univerbization from *železná dráha* ('railway').
>
> (Martina Ivanova, p.c. via Lívia Körtvélyessy)

This form can thus be seen as intermediate between **adj** and **der** and represents a type that occurs rather often in certain Slavic languages, in which the head element of an adjectival binominal is replaced by a more general nominalizing suffix.

4.1.8 Morpheme loss (dbl ➔ con) ❽

The final example of intermediate (gradient) phenomena is that of morpheme loss. Citing data from Hungarian, Kirmandji (KMR), Arbore (ARV) and Maltese, Koptjevskaja-Tamm (2003) shows that "the step between double-marking and head-marking [in PNPs] is not necessarily big":

> Head-marked PNPs in Maltese, similarly to head-marked PNPs in Kirmandji, have developed from earlier double-marked PNPs, partly due to the breakdown of the case system of modern Arabic dialects compared to Classical Arabic, in which the possessor regularly appeared in the genitive case. (p. 647)

The same appears to be the case with binominals, and not just between **dbl** and **con** (the example shown in Figure 4), but also between **dbl** and **gen**, between **prp** and **gen**, and between **gen** and **con** on the one hand and **cmp** on the other. Or more generally, between any strategy involving *n* additional morphemes and one involving *n-1* morphemes.

One particularly striking example is Welsh, in which the dominant type at an earlier stage of the language was **gen** (as it still is in Irish). Following the loss of case marking the dominant types are today **jxt** and **cmp**. Elsewhere in the database there are indications that this process is at work in Galibi Carib, Tarifit and Swahili (37)-(39). In the case of Galibi Carib, examples (37a-c) are **dbl**, **gen** and **con**, respectively. The double-marked pattern (a) may represent an earlier construction from which the others have developed.

(37) Galibi Carib
    a. *emo.li sakila.li* [nose.POSS aperture.POSS] NOSTRIL
    b. *pana.li weti* [ear.POSS dirtiness] EARWAX
    c. *manati poti.li* [breast tip.POSS] NIPPLE OR TEAT

Example (38) is one of three words in the Tarifit sub-vocabulary of Pepper's database in which the preposition *n* is given as optional. With the preposition the construction is considered an instance of **prp**; without it, it is an instance of **gen**.

(38) Tarifit *tisi (n) ufus* [bottom (of) hand:STC] PALM OF HAND

There is also an example in Swahili (39) of a construction in which the associative marker is given as optional. Since it is the only occurrence, it is classified as **prp** by Pepper along with other words that exhibit this marker, but it may also indicate gradience.

(39) Swahili *gari (la) moshi* [car (CON) smoke] TRAIN

4.2 Binominals and adnominal possessives

4.2.1 The modification-reference continuum

Intuitively, as was suggested in §3.1, binominals are closely related to adnominal possessive constructions, and this is demonstrated by the degree of overlap between the typological classification of binominals presented in this chapter and Koptjevskaja-Tamm's classification of possessive noun phrases in Europe. The two are almost identical: seven of Koptjevskaja-Tamm's eight types have been documented for binominals, and the eighth (**prn**), it has been suggested (§3.3.1), is probably out there somewhere, waiting to be discovered. Just two types needed to be added to Koptjevskaja-Tamm's classification (**der** and **cls**) and the former would have to be added to the PNP classification anyway if the analysis were to be extended to include pronominal possessors as well as nominal possessors (40). Whether the latter (**cls**) exists in the PNP domain is a question for further research.

(40) Finnish *ystävä-ni* [friend-1POSS] 'my friend'

Koptjevskaja-Tamm (2002; 2004) distinguishes two types of adnominal possessive: 'anchoring' and 'non-anchoring'. In an anchoring construction (41a), the noun in the genitive case (the possessor) serves as an *anchor*, or reference point, for identifying (or grounding) the head, which is an individual (or set of individuals).

(41)   Lithuanian (Koptjevskaja-Tamm 2004: 155–156)
   a.   *Petr-o namas* [Peter-GEN house] 'Peter's house'
   b.   *auks-o žedas* [gold-GEN ring] 'a gold ring'

In a non-anchoring construction (41b), on the other hand, the noun in the genitive serves as a modifier of the head. The constructions are otherwise identical and Koptjevskaja-Tamm treats them both as adnominal possessives: "The rationale for a similar treatment of anchoring and non-anchoring relations is obvious – both types of adnominal dependents characterize entities via their relations to other entities" (2004: 156). Paraphrasing Koptjevskaja-Tamm (2002: 154), Croft (2022) summarizes the features that differentiate non-anchoring from anchoring constructions as follows:
1. the object modifier is only type identifiable;
2. the modifier-head combination refers to a subclass of a broader class and often functions as a classificatory label for it, suggesting that the modifier and the head together correspond to one concept, but
3. the head cannot be identified via its relation to the modifier.

Croft also generalizes from adnominal possessive to 'nominal modifier construction', a term which covers any construction in which an object is used for modification.[23] The term thus applies to one of the cells in the Scapa Grid of basic cross-linguistic constructions (see Table 2 on page 31).

From this it is clear that binominals, as defined in the present study, are essentially non-anchoring (or 'typifying')[24] nominal modifier constructions, albeit ones in which a diachronic process of lexicalization has proceeded to the point where the binominal is coming to be a unitary lexeme; binominals are basically lexicalized typifying constructions that represent the penultimate stage in a continuum

---

[23] Note that in Croft's terminology, the term 'modification' is used only for modification of an object, never for "modification" of a property or action. The three types of modification are therefore object modification (a.k.a. nominal modification), property modification, and action modification.

[24] Pepper (2020) and Croft (2022) prefer the term 'typifying' to 'non-anchoring', on the grounds that it is better to describe something in terms of what it does, rather than doesn't do: the key thing about typifying constructions is that they denote *types* (or classes, or more precisely subclasses) rather than *individuals*, as is the case with anchoring constructions, cf. *women's magazine* vs. *Peter's magazine*.

of constructions from anchoring object modification to reference, which Croft (2022) calls the 'modification-reference continuum (42).

(42)

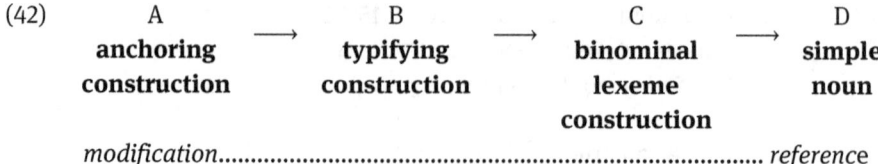

A	→	B	→	C	→	D
anchoring construction		**typifying construction**		**binominal lexeme construction**		**simple noun**

modification.. *reference*

The transition from stage C (binominal form) to stage D (simplex form) is relatively well documented and understood. It was discussed briefly above (§4.1.1) and exemplified with Eng. *lord* and Ger. *Messer* at the endpoint of the continuum, and Eng. *nostril* midway between stages C and D.

The difference between stage B (typifying construction) and stage C is largely based on the degree of lexicalization, which is hard to measure. (One way to do so would be to rely on a comprehensive dictionary of the language and regard lemmas as lexical (hence, binominal) and other typifying constructions as syntactic.

As for the transition from stage A (anchoring construction) to stage B (typifying construction), Koptjevskaja-Tamm (2004) provides a lot of qualitative evidence from European languages. Five cases are distinguished, one of them with two subtypes, as follows:

1. *Identical structures.* The same morphosyntactic strategy is used for both anchoring and typifying constructions. Exemplified by Lithuanian, Georgian, Daghestanian, Russian and Finnish, which use a genitive modifier and inflect nouns for case but lack articles and a grammaticalized definiteness-indefiniteness opposition.
2. *Similar structures.* The same morphosyntactic strategy is used for both anchoring and typifying constructions but articles (markers of definiteness) on the modifier are permitted with the former but not the latter. Exemplified by Italian (prepositional strategy) and Scottish Gaelic (genitival strategy).
3. *Differing morphological complexity.* Typifying constructions are morphologically less complex and/or looser than anchoring constructions Exemplified by (a) Albanian, Rumanian, Turkish and Kirmandji (dependent-marking) and (b) Mordvin and Armenian (head-marking).
4. *Loss of nominal autonomy: compounding.* The relational or indexical marker found in anchoring constructions is lost in typifying constructions, leading to a compound or juxtaposition strategy for the latter. Exemplified by Erzya (Mordvin) and Swedish.

5. *Loss of nominal autonomy: relational adjectives.* Typifying constructions use a derived, adjectival form of the modifying noun instead of case markers (i.e. case affixes or adpositions). Exemplified by Russian.

Koptjevskaja-Tamm's analysis is qualitative. In the next section we discuss how to turn this into a quantitative analysis and, in doing so, present a novel methodology for comparing non-binary constructions. In this way, we arrive at two Greenbergian universals concerning the relationship between adnominal possessives and binominals.

4.2.2 Comparing non-binary typologies

One of the main goals of typology is the discovery of universals, in particular implicational universals. Croft (2003: 53) illustrates the idea with an example drawn from Hawkins (1983: 84), his Universal XI' "If a language has noun before demonstrative, then it has noun before relative clause". This implicational universal covers the following four logically possible types: (i) demonstrative and relative clause both follow the noun (NRel, NDem); (ii) relative clause precedes the noun and demonstrative follows the noun (RelN, NDem); (iii) relative clause follows the noun and demonstrative precedes the noun (NRel, DemN); and (iv) demonstrative and relative clause both precede the noun (RelN, DemN).

The implicational universal restricts language variation to types (i), (iii) and (iv), and excludes type (ii), and can be expressed in the form of a tetrachoric table (Table 5).

Table 5: Tetrachoric table for N+Dem and N+Rel.

	DemN	NDem
RelN	✓	–
NRel	✓	✓

This approach works fine when comparing two binary constructions. i.e., when there are two parameters, each with two possible values, resulting in four logically possible language types. This is the case with the demonstrative modifier construction and the relative clause construction. But if we want to compare binominal constructions with anchoring or typifying constructions, it becomes unmanageable, since Koptjevskaja-Tamm's PNP typology consists of eight types (the six in Figure 1, plus possessive compounds and relational adjectives; see §3.1), and the binominal typology consists of nine. Representing this as an 8x9 table would clearly not be very helpful. Moreover, many languages employ multiple strategies in order to represent attributive possession, just as they do to express binominals (see the discussion of Polish NN.GEN and NA_REL binominals in Cetnarowska, this volume). This complicates the comparison even more.

A different approach is thus required, one that Koptjevskaja-Tamm has already pioneered. Observe that her comparison table and its five primary categories do not focus on the *values* assigned to each language, but on a characterization of the *relationship* between each language's primary anchoring and typifying strategies: for each language the relationship is essentially described as "identical", "similar" or "differing", with the latter amenable to subcategorization such that it encompasses the two cases of "loss of autonomy" in addition to differing morphological complexity. In the following analysis we adopt Koptjevskaja-Tamm's categories, but with a minor adjustment to make them more amenable to statistical analysis.

The five categories listed above may be used as simple nominal variables. However, the adjectives used to describe the first three categories suggest a potential for representation as ordinal variables: *identical → similar → different*.[25] Pepper (2020: 274–275) therefore replaces Koptjevskaja-Tamm's three "orderable" categories with a more fine-grained system of five categories that express the *degree of similarity* between anchoring and binominal constructions. Not surprisingly, since this is about different grades of a property (similarity), a naming system based on adjectives is not very useful, so Pepper proposes one based on adverbs that qualify the adjective 'identical', the Pwav scale[26] (cf. the Likert scale) (43).

(43)   always → mostly → sometimes → rarely → never

Clearly, these categories need to be defined more precisely for the task at hand, but before doing so there is second issue that needs to be addressed: that of mixed languages. As the example of Polish shows (19c, d), languages may have more than one binominal strategy available to them; some have as many as six (and some, like Polish, as many as nine if the order of constituents is taken into account); most have at least four; and only seven of the 106 languages in Pepper's database exhibit only one. The question thus arises which strategy to select

---

[25] Levshina (2015: 17) uses the five-point Likert scale ('strongly disagree' – 'disagree' – 'neither agree nor disagree' – 'agree' – 'strongly agree') as an example of an ordinal variable and points out that "the categories thus differ in order, but we do not know yet by how much.".

[26] Pepper's (2020: 275) name for this scale has been abandoned for one that is less immediately narcissistic.

for the comparison with anchoring constructions. Fortunately, almost every language shows a preference for one type of binominal or another, and 70 of the 106 in Pepper's database can be said to have a dominant type according to Dryer's (2013) criterion for dominance: that a value is either the only one possible or the one that is more frequently used. The comparison to follow is thus based on what Pepper terms the 'primary binominal strategy', defined as the type that occurs most frequently; languages that have no clear preference (Äiwoo, Galibi Carib and Selice Romani) are deemed to have no such strategy. In addition, Pepper employs the term 'secondary binominal strategy' for any non-primary strategy that is 'common' (defined as occurring in at least 10% of the data for any given language). Having defined these terms, the five grades of 'identicality' in (43) can be operationalized as shown in Table 6.

The definitions themselves are, of course, particular to the actual constructions that we are investigating, but the Pwav scale itself has universal validity and could provide an additional tool for typologists, alongside tetrachoric tables and semantic maps, for use when comparing non-binary typologies.

Table 6: The Pwav scale operationalized for the comparison of binominal and anchoring constructions.

grade	description
always	the primary binominal strategy is identical to the primary anchoring strategy and there are no secondary binominal strategies
mostly	the primary binominal strategy is identical to the primary anchoring strategy but there also are secondary binominal strategies
sometimes	a secondary binominal strategy is identical to the primary anchoring strategy, *or* the primary binominal strategy is identical to a secondary anchoring strategy
rarely	a secondary binominal strategy is identical to one of the secondary anchoring strategies
never	binominal strategies and anchoring strategies are quite different

4.2.3 Two universals of nominal modification

Before we proceed with the quantitative analysis of the data, it should be noted that the Pwav scale loses some of the qualitative detail in Koptjevskaja-Tamm's model (for example, differences in complexity and morphological tightness), but it is perfectly possible to add that back in, by subdividing the basic categories, and we do so here with "never" in order to capture grammaticalization. This category has been split in order to highlight cases where the principal binominal strategy is a grammaticalized form of the principal anchoring strategy, following one of eight pathways that involve fusion or loss of a single marker (44). Finally, the rump "never" category contains languages in which no anchoring strategy is the same as any of the binominal strategies.

(44) jxt   gen   gen   con   prn   prn   dbl   dbl
       ↓   ↓   ↓   ↓   ↓   ↓   ↓   ↓
      cmp   cmp   jxt   cmp   jxt   cmp   con   gen

Each pathway in (44) represents a single step: either fusion, as in the case of **jxt** → **cmp**, or loss of a single morpheme, as in **gen** → **cmp**. Other pathways are conceivable (e.g. **prp** → **gen**), but these are not attested in Pepper's data.

In all five categories except "never", binominal constructions can be said to recruit one of the anchoring strategies, sometimes across the board ("always"), sometimes to a lesser degree ("mostly", "sometimes", "rarely"), and sometimes in a more "grammaticalized" form. When the anchoring strategy is not recruited, more often than not, it is compounding (i.e. **jxt** or **cmp**) that fills the void.

Figure 5 plots the numbers for the six categories. We observe that all but 12 of the 105 languages for which data was available (almost 90%) recruit an anchoring strategy for use in the formation of binominals. Of the twelve languages in the sample that do not, the majority (58%) use a compounding strategy, either **jxt** or **cmp**.

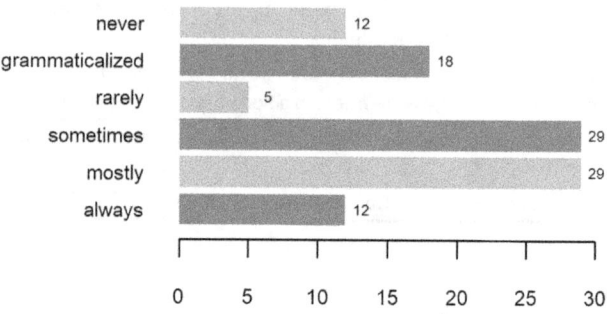

Figure 5: Grades of similarity across anchoring and binominal strategies.

Based on his analysis of the data contained in the binominals database, Pepper posits the following universals:

(45) *With overwhelmingly greater than chance frequency, languages recruit at least one of their binominal strategies from an anchoring nominal modifier construction.*

(46) *If a language does not recruit at least one of its binominal strategies from an anchoring nominal modifier construction, there is a strong tendency for it to use compounding for this purpose.*

5 Conclusion

In this chapter I offered four different definitions of binominal lexeme to complement the informal definition as "noun-noun compounds and their functional equivalents". Although couched in a variety of terms based on different theoretical frameworks, these have essentially identical extensions.

I then presented a nine-way classification of binominals: **jxt, cmp, der, cls; prp, gen, adj, con;** and **dbl**. These are represented on a two-dimensional grid that captures the number of markers, the locus of marking and the degree of fusion. The grid reveals two lacunae or "missing types": **prn** and **nml**. Whereas the first of these probably exists somewhere in the world's languages, the second seems to be a logical impossibility. The chapter also discussed intermediate types and various grammaticalization pathways.

Finally, I examined the relationship between binominal constructions and anchoring nominal modifier constructions and introduced a new methodology, based on the "Pwav scale", for comparing two non-binary constructions. This resulted in two Greenbergian universals concerning the recruitment of binominal strategies from nominal modifier strategies.

References

Adelaar, Alexander. 2009. Malagasy vocabulary. In Martin Haspelmath & Uri Tadmor (eds.), *World Loanword Database*. Leipzig: Max Planck Institute for Evolutionary Anthropology. http://wold.clld.org/vocabulary/28.

Aikhenvald, Alexandra Y. 2000. *Classifiers: A typology of noun categorization devices*. Oxford: Oxford University Press.

Aikhenvald, Alexandra Y. 2017. A typology of noun categorization devices. In Alexandra Y. Aikhenvald & R. M. W. Dixon (eds.), *The Cambridge handbook of linguistic typology*, 361–404. Cambridge: Cambridge University Press. https://doi.org/10.1017/9781316135716.

Allan, Keith. 1977. Classifiers. *Language* 53(2). 285–311.
Bauer, Laurie. 2000. Word. In Geert E. Booij, Christian Lehmann & Joachim Mugdan (eds.), *Morphologie: ein internationales Handbuch zur Flexion und Wortbildung*, vol. 1, 247–257. Berlin: Mouton de Gruyter.
Bauer, Laurie. 2001. Compounding. In Martin Haspelmath, Ekkehard König, Wolfgang Oesterreicher & Wolfgang Raible (eds.), *Language typology and language universals: An international handbook*, 695–707. Berlin: Mouton de Gruyter.
Bauer, Laurie. 2005. The borderline between derivation and compounding. In Wolfgang U. Dressler, Dieter Kastovsky, Oskar E. Pfeiffer & Franz Rainer (eds.), *Morphology and its demarcations: Selected papers from the 11th Morphology meeting, Vienna, February 2004*, 97–108. Amsterdam: John Benjamins.
Bauer, Laurie & Elizaveta Tarasova. 2013. The meaning link in nominal compounds. *SKASE Journal of Theoretical Linguistics* 10(3). 2–18.
Bauer, Winifred. 1993. *Maori*. London: Routledge.
Booij, Geert. 2010. *Construction Morphology*. Oxford: Oxford University Press.
Bybee, Joan L. 1985. *Morphology: A study of the relation between meaning and form*. Amsterdam: John Benjamins.
Corbett, Greville G. 1987. The morphology/syntax interface: Evidence from possessive adjectives in Slavonic. *Language* 63(2). 299–345.
Creissels, Denis. 2009. The construct form of nouns in African languages: A typological approach. In Peter Austin, Oliver Bond, Monik Charette, David Nathan & Peter Sells (eds.), *Proceedings of Conference on Language Documentation & Linguistic Theory 2*, 73–82. London: SOAS.
Creissels, Denis. 2017. Construct forms of nouns in typological perspective. Unpublished paper, SLE 2017. http://www.deniscreissels.fr/public/Creissels-Cstr.pdf.
Croft, William. 1990. *Typology and universals*. Cambridge: Cambridge University Press.
Croft, William. 1991. *Syntactic categories and grammatical relations: The cognitive organization of information*. Chicago: The University of Chicago Press.
Croft, William. 2001. *Radical Construction Grammar: Syntactic theory in typological perspective*. Oxford: Oxford University Press.
Croft, William. 2003. *Typology and universals*. 2nd ed. Cambridge: Cambridge University Press.
Croft, William. 2022. *Morphosyntax: Constructions of the world's languages*. Cambridge: Cambridge University Press.
Dixon, R. M. W. 2010. *Basic linguistic theory. Volume 2: Grammatical topics*. Oxford: Oxford University Press.
Dokulil, Miloš. 1962. *Tvoření slov v češtině. 1: Teorie odvozování slov*. Praha: Československé akademie věd.
Dokulil, Miloš. 1966. Zum wechselseitigen Verhältnis zwischen Wortbildung und Syntax. *Travaux linguistiques de Prague* 1. 215–224.
Dokulil, Miloš. 1994. The Prague School's theoretical and methodological contribution to "word-formation" (derivology). In Philip A. Luelsdorff (ed.), *The Prague School of structural and functional linguistics: A short introduction*, 123–161. Amsterdam: John Benjamins.
Dryer, Matthew S. 2013. Determining dominant word order. In Matthew S. Dryer & Martin Haspelmath (eds.), *The World Atlas of Language Structures Online*. Leipzig: Max Planck Institute for Evolutionary Anthropology. https://wals.info/chapter/s6.

Floricic, Franck. 2016. French. In Peter O. Müller, Ingeborg Ohnheiser, Susan Olsen & Franz Rainer (eds.), *Word-formation: An international handbook of the languages of Europe. Vol. 4*, 2661–2682. Berlin: Mouton de Gruyter.
Haspelmath, Martin. 1996. Word-class-changing inflection and morphological theory. In *Yearbook of Morphology 1995*, 43–66. Springer. http://link.springer.com/chapter/10.1007/978-94-017-3716-6_3.
Haspelmath, Martin. 2009. Terminology of case. In Andrej Malchukov and Andrew Spencer (eds.), *The Oxford handbook of case*, 505–517. Oxford: Oxford University Press.
Haspelmath, Martin. 2010. Comparative concepts and descriptive categories in crosslinguistic studies. *Language* 86(3). 663–687.
Haspelmath, Martin. 2011. The indeterminacy of word segmentation and the nature of morphology and syntax. *Folia Linguistica* 45(1). 31–80. https://doi.org/10.1515/flin.2011.002.
Haspelmath, Martin. 2012. How to compare major word-classes across the world's languages. *UCLA Working Papers in Linguistics, Theories of Everything* 17, Article 16. 109–130.
Haspelmath, Martin. 2020. The morph as a minimal linguistic form. *Morphology* 30(2). 117–134. https://doi.org/10.1007/s11525-020-09355-5.
Hawkins, John A. 1983. *Word order universals*. New York: Academic Press.
Khalilov, Madzhid & Zaira Khalilova. 2016. Bezhta. In Peter O. Müller, Ingeborg Ohnheiser, Susan Olsen & Franz Rainer (eds.), *Word-formation: An international handbook of the languages of Europe. Vol. 5*, 3658–3678. Berlin: Mouton de Gruyter.
Kiefer, Ferenc. 2009. Uralic, Finno-Ugric: Hungarian. In Rochelle Lieber & Pavol Štekauer (eds.), *The Oxford handbook of compounding*, 527–541. Oxford: Oxford University Press.
Koptjevskaja-Tamm, Maria. 2002. Adnominal possession in the European languages: Form and function. *STUF – Language Typology and Universals* 55(2). 141–172.
Koptjevskaja-Tamm, Maria. 2003. Possessive noun phrases in the languages of Europe. In Frans Plank (ed.), *Noun phrase structure in the languages of Europe*, 621–722. Berlin: Mouton de Gruyter.
Koptjevskaja-Tamm, Maria. 2004. Maria's ring of gold: Adnominal possession and non-anchoring relations in the European languages. In Kim Ji-yung, Yury A. Lander & Barbara H. Partee (eds.), *Possessives and beyond: Semantics and syntax*, 155–181. Amherst, MA: GLSA Publications.
Langacker, Ronald W. 2008. *Cognitive Grammar: A basic introduction*. Oxford: Oxford University Press.
Levshina, Natalia. 2015. *How to do linguistics with R: Data exploration and statistical analysis*. Amsterdam: John Benjamins.
Müller, Peter O., Ingeborg Ohnheiser, Susan Olsen & Franz Rainer (eds.). 2015. *Word-formation: An international handbook of the languages of Europe. 5 vols*. Berlin: de Gruyter Mouton.
Nagórko, Alicja. 2016. Polish. In Peter O. Müller, Ingeborg Ohnheiser, Susan Olsen & Franz Rainer (eds.), *Word-formation: An international handbook of the languages of Europe. Vol. 4*, 2831–2852. Berlin: de Gruyter Mouton.
Newman, Paul. 2000. *The Hausa language: An encyclopedic reference grammar*. New Haven: Yale University Press.
Nichols, Johanna. 1992. *Linguistic diversity in space and time*. Chicago: The University of Chicago Press.
Pepper, Steve. 2010. *Nominal compounding in Nizaa: A cognitive perspective*. SOAS University of London Master's thesis.

Pepper, Steve. 2016. Windmills, Nizaa and the typology of binominal compounds. In Lívia Körtvélyessy, Pavol Štekauer & Salvador Valera (eds.), *Word-formation across languages*, 281–310. Newcastle: Cambridge Scholars Publishing.

Pepper, Steve. 2018. Onomasiological types and the typology of binominal lexemes. Paper presented at the *Typology and Universals in Word-Formation IV* conference, Košice 2018. https://www.academia.edu/38060850.

Pepper, Steve. 2020. *The typology and semantics of binominal lexemes: Noun-noun compounds and their functional equivalents*. Oslo: University of Oslo PhD dissertation. https://www.academia.edu/42935602.

Pepper, Steve. in prep. Onomasiological types and the typology of complex nominals.

Ralli, Angela. 2013. *Compounding in Modern Greek*. Dordrecht: Springer.

Russell, Joan. 2003. *Swahili* (Teach Yourself Books). London: Hodder and Stoughton.

Štekauer, Pavol. 1998. *An onomasiological theory of English word-formation*. Amsterdam: John Benjamins.

Štekauer, Pavol. 2005. Onomasiological approach to word-formation. In Pavol Štekauer & Rochelle Lieber (eds.), *Handbook of word-formation*, 207–232. Dordrecht: Springer.

Tuggy, David. 1992. The affix-stem distinction: A Cognitive Grammar analysis of data from Orizaba Nahuatl. *Cognitive Linguistics* 3(3). 237–300.

Uluhanov, Igor' S. 2016. Russian. In Peter O. Müller, Ingeborg Ohnheiser, Susan Olsen & Franz Rainer (eds.), *Word-formation: An international handbook of the languages of Europe, Vol. 4*, 2953–2978. Berlin: Mouton de Gruyter.

Urban, Matthias. 2012. *Analyzability and semantic associations In referring expressions: A study in comparative lexicology*. Leiden University PhD dissertation.

Wälchli, Bernhard. 2005. *Co-compounds and natural coordination*. Oxford: Oxford University Press.

Watson, Rachel. 2015. *Kujireray: morphosyntax, noun classification and verbal nouns*. SOAS University of London PhD dissertation.

Wilkens, Jens. 2016. Turkish. In Peter O. Müller, Ingeborg Ohnheiser, Susan Olsen & Franz Rainer (eds.), *Word-formation: An international handbook of the languages of Europe. Vol. 5*, 3367–3385. Berlin: de Gruyter Mouton.

Yeon, Jaehoon & Lucien Brown. 2011. *Korean: A comprehensive grammar*. London: Routledge.

Denis Creissels
Binominals and construct marking

Abstract: Construct marking, defined as a particular technique of marking the relationships between head nouns and their dependents, is not limited to the few language families (Semitic, Nilotic, and Oceanic) in which the term 'construct' is traditionally used to describe adnominal possession, and construct marking defined in purely formal terms can be used for semantic types of noun modification other than adnominal possession. The use of construct marking is however particularly widespread in adpossessive construction. In the languages that make use of construct marking in their adpossessive construction, it is common that the same markers also have a more or less productive use in the formation of binominals, and if changes affect the adpossessive construction, it may happen that a former construct marker that has ceased to be used in adpossessive construction persists exclusively in binominal formation.

1 Introduction

This paper deals with a particular aspect of the general question of the distinction between binominal formation and adpossessive (adnominal possessive) construction, or neutralization thereof, in the languages of the world. After some general comments on the distinction between binominals and adpossessive construction and the possibility that the same formal elements can be involved in adpossessive construction and binominal formation (section 2), construct marking is defined in section 3 as a particular technique of marking the relationships between head nouns and their dependents in the formation of noun phrases. The illustrations presented in section 3 show that this particular technique of marking the relationships between head nouns and their dependents is widespread in the world's languages, far beyond the few language families (Semitic, Nilotic, and Oceanic) in which the term of 'construct' is traditionally used to describe adnominal possession. Moreover, construct marking defined in purely formal terms can be used for semantic types of noun modification other than adnominal possession. The use of construct marking is however particularly widespread in adpossessive constructions. As developed in section 4, in the languages that make use of construct marking in their adpossessive construction, it is common that the same markers also have a more or less productive use in the formation of binominals, and if changes affect the adpossessive construction, it may happen that a construct

https://doi.org/10.1515/9783110673494-003

marker that was formerly fully productive in adpossessive construction persists mainly, or even exclusively, in binominal formation.[1]

2 Binominal formation and adpossessive construction

As discussed among others by Bally (1932) and Creissels (1979) under the terms of ACTUALIZATION vs. CHARACTERIZATION, and by Koptevskaja-Tamm (2002) under the terms of ANCHORING vs. NON-ANCHORING relations, the adpossessive construction may have uses in which the modifier does not act as a reference point for the identification of the head, and rather delimits a subclass of the class of the potential referents of its head. Binominals are often lexicalized forms of 'characterizing' / 'non-anchoring' possessives.

Whatever its formal characteristics, a binominal as defined in the introduction to this volume (Masini, Mattiola & Pepper, this volume) is a complex nominal lexeme whose formation involves two nominal lexemes. This means that, semantically, a binominal belongs to the same type as underived nominal lexemes. By itself (i.e., before being involved in the determination operations that create noun phrases denoting entities), a binominal only has a potential denotation, and is best defined as denoting a property (or a relation), exactly like underived nominal lexemes: in English (eng), *textbook* denotes a property (or a set a potential referents), in the sense that any object can be characterized as being a textbook or not, exactly like *book*. Adpossessive construction in its prototypical use encodes a different type of semantic operation, since it involves a noun phrase denoting an individual (the possessor) and a nominal lexeme (the possessee) whose set of potential referents is restricted to those considered by the speaker as having some kind of privileged relationship with the possessor: *John's book* does not denote a kind of book, but can be used to denote any particular book considered by the speaker as belonging to the personal sphere of an individual identified as *John*.

An important typological parameter is that, for easily understandable historical reasons, a construction formally identical to adpossessive construction may be recruited, with a variable degree of productivity, as a binominal formation pattern.

---

1 I wish to thank the editors of this volume and the anonymous reviewers, whose insightful comments helped me improve it significantly. Thanks are also due to the audiences to which previous versions of this paper have been presented for their feedback. The usual disclaimers apply.

For example, in English (eng), *teacher's book* is a binominal whose formation involves the same N_1's N_2 pattern as the adpossessive construction *John's book*.

In some languages, the overlap between adpossessive construction and binominal formation is only very marginal. For example, the Mande language Mandinka (mnk) has a handful of binominal lexemes such as *Álá lá sùwôo* [God GEN horse.DEF] 'praying mantis', lit. 'God's horse', but as a rule, the binominal lexemes of Mandinka (mnk) are formed according to a specific compounding pattern involving juxtaposition and special tone rules, and there is no possible ambiguity between for example the binominal *mùsù-sámátòo* [woman-shoe.DEF] 'woman's shoe' and the adpossessive construction *mùsôo lá sàmàtôo* [woman. DEF GEN shoe.DEF] 'the shoe of the woman'.

In other languages, a pattern of binominal formation similar to adpossessive construction is productive. Depending on the determination system of individual languages, the distinction may be marked by determiners. For example, in French (fra), the adpossessive construction involves the preposition *de* 'of', and N_1 *de* N_2 is also a productive way of forming binominals, but the absence of any determiner accompanying the second element of binominals such as *chaussure de femme* lit. 'shoe of woman' marks the distinction with the adpossessive construction, in which the second element is obligatorily determined. By contrast, in languages that do not have a system of obligatory determiners, the ambiguity may be general. For example, in the Bantu language Tswana (tsn), depending on the context, *dì-dʒɔ́ ˈts-á-dí-ɲ̀tʃá* [CL8-food CL8-GEN-CL10-dog] can equally be interpreted as 'the food of the dogs' (where 'dogs' refers to a specific group of dogs) or 'dog food' (binominal denoting a particular kind of food).

Section 4 of the present paper examines the possibility of such overlaps in languages whose adpossessive construction involves a particular type of marking, designated here as 'construct marking', defined and illustrated in section 3.

3 Construct marking in typological perspective

In this section, I propose a notion of *construct form of nouns*, generalizing the notion of *construct state* as traditionally used in Semitic linguistics.

3.1 Definition

In Semitic linguistics, CONSTRUCT STATE applies to nouns immediately followed by another noun in the role of adpossessor, or by a bound pronoun in possessive function. In this context, nouns occur in a form distinct from their free form. For example, in Hebrew (heb), the construct state of *malkah* 'queen' is *malkat*, as in *malkat ha-medina* 'the queen of the country'. Similarly, in Moroccan Arabic (ary), the construct state of *xala* '(paternal) aunt' is *xalt*, as in *xalt l-bənt* 'the aunt of the girl' or *xalt-i* 'my aunt'. In the Ethiosemitic language Ge'ez (gez), the construct state of nouns is straightforwardly formed by the addition of a suffix *-a* to nouns, as in *wald-a nəguś* 'the son of the king'.

Cross-linguistically, it is relatively common that person markers cross-referencing the dependent noun attach to the head of adpossessive constructions. Such person markers are commonly designated as possessive affixes. Morphological marking of nouns licensing the adjunction of modifiers without cross-referencing them at the same time is perhaps less common, but by no means limited to the Semitic languages.

My proposal is to consider the construct state of Semitic nouns as a particular case of a more general notion of CONSTRUCT MARKING OF NOUNS defined as follows. The two essential characteristics of construct marking are that:
- it is obligatory if the noun fulfills the role of head in a given type of noun – modifier construction;
- it does not cross-reference features of the modifier that conditions its use.

This definition is more restrictive than the definition of the morphosyntactic strategy CON in the typology of binominals used in this volume, defined as consisting of "a head and a modifier (both of them independent lexemes), with an additional morpheme attached to the head" (see Pepper, this volume). Like Dixon's notion of 'pertensive' (see section 3.2.4), the definition of the morphosyntactic strategy CON makes no distinction between indexes cross-referencing the adpossessor and construct markers whose only role is to allow the presence of a given type of modifier, whereas according to my definition of construct marking, adpossessor indexation is not an instance of construct marking. Construct marking as I define it is a particular instance of what Nichols (1992: 48–49) calls REGISTRATION (which marks the presence of an argument/dependent but does not agree or copy features such as person, number and/or gender) as opposed to INDEXATION (which copies or otherwise marks features of the argument/dependent).[2] Note however that, as will be discussed below for Hungarian (hun) and

---

[2] In other words, the distinction between adpossessor indexes and construct markers as two possible varieties of head marking in the noun phrase is comparable to the distinction between argument indexes and applicative markers as two possible varieties of head-marking in the clause.

Turkish (tur), the adnominal possession construction of some languages shows particularities that may blur the distinction between construct marking and adpossessor indexation.

Note also that, according to this definition:
- it is essential for a construct form to have its distribution conditioned by the combination with a given type of modifier, but depending on the individual languages, adnominal possessors are not the only type of modifier that may condition the use of a construct form;
- in a language in which nouns have a construct form morphologically distinct from their free form, construct form marking is obligatory when nouns combine with modifiers of a given type (in Semitic languages, NPs in adpossessive function), but does not necessarily imply the presence of such a modifier (in Semitic languages, the construct form is also used with adnominal possessors expressed as possessive suffixes);
- special non-autonomous forms of nouns used exclusively in derivation or (morphological) compounding, are NOT construct forms, at least in a strictly synchronic perspective, since the definition posited above refers to the ability for the construct form to act as the head of a syntactic construction.

Not all languages have noun forms meeting this definition. It is however a crosslinguistically valid definition in the sense that languages whose nominal system includes such forms are not rare, and are not particularly restricted in their distribution across language families and geographical areas. In the remainder of this section, after clarifying some terminological points (3.2), I give an overview of construct forms in the languages of the world (3.3), and conclude with a brief discussion of the cross-linguistic variation observed in construct marking and the possible origins of construct marking (3.4).

3.2 Some terminological clarifications

Apart from Semitic, Nilotic and Oceanic are the only groups of languages in the descriptions of which the term 'construct' is commonly used as a label for inflected forms of nouns meeting the definition formulated above. But conversely, the term 'construct' is sometimes used for other types of forms, which may be a source of confusion. Consequently, a brief discussion of terminological conventions departing from those adopted here is in order.

3.2.1 Construct marking and case

Construct forms of nouns have in common with case forms that they are conditioned by the syntactic status of nouns, but the notion of case, as it is commonly used in grammatical descriptions, encodes the role of NPs as elements of broader constructions, irrespective of their internal structure, whereas construct forms encode information on the internal structure of NPs. In other words, case is a particular variety of DEPENDENT MARKING, whereas construct marking is an instance of HEAD MARKING.

Neglecting this distinction and considering construct forms as cases would imply broadening the definition of case to any morphological variation of nouns carrying syntactic information. My position on this point is that the head *vs.* dependent marking distinction in noun-modifying constructions is crucial, in the description of individual languages as well as in typological perspective. Consequently, I do not regard it as desirable to reformulate the definition of 'case' in order to be able to consider construct forms as a particular type of case.

In this connection, it is important to evoke the problem raised by the use of 'state' in descriptions of Berber languages, which suggests a false analogy between the morphological distinction for which this term is used in Berber grammars, and the states of Semitic nouns.

In Berber languages, nouns have two forms traditionally termed states. One of them is generally termed 'free state', and the other one 'annexed state', but some descriptions use 'construct state' instead of 'annexed state', which favors the confusion even more. The point is that, contrary to Semitic states, the so-called states of Berber nouns are involved in a mechanism of dependent marking, not of head marking: in Berber languages, the choice between the 'free state' and the 'annexed state' is not conditioned by the relation between the noun and its dependents, but by the function of the NP within a broader construction. In a broad typological perspective, the two so-called states of Berber nouns are simply cases – see Arkadiev (2015) for a recent discussion.

3.2.2 Construct marking and adnominalizers

ADNOMINALIZER is the general term I propose for grammatical elements that can be analyzed as marking that a word or phrase at the periphery of which they are located fulfills a noun-modifying function.

Persian-style ezâfe markers, illustrated in (1), constitute a particular type of adnominalizer that can easily be confused with construct marking, although they clearly do not meet the definition of construct marking put forward in the present article.³

(1) Persian (pes) – Pollet Samvelian, pers.com.
(1a) ketâb-e   târix
     book-ADNZ history
     'history book'
(1b) ketâb-e   târix-e   sabz
     book-ADNZ history-ADNZ green
     'green history book'
(1c) ketâb-e   târix-e   sabz-e   bi   arzeš
     book-ADNZ history-ADNZ green-ADNZ without value
     'worthless green history book'
(1d) ketâb-e   târix-e   sabz-e   bi   arzeš-e   Maryam
     book-ADNZ history-ADNZ green-ADNZ without value-ADNZ Maryam
     'Maryam's worthless green history book'

The point is that the ezâfe marker *-e* could be analyzed as a construct marker in (1a), since it is then attached to a noun forming a head-modifier construction with the following word, but this analysis cannot be extended to its other occurrences in (1b-d), in which it attaches to a word that does not form a head-modifier construction with the following word or phrase. The possible confusion between such an adnominalizer and construct marking arises from a morphology-syntax mismatch: Persian-style ezâfe markers mark the syntactic role of the word or phrase to their right, but attach to the word to their left, with which they have no direct syntactic link: *ketâb(-e târix(-e sabz(-e bi arzeš(-e Maryam))))*.

3.2.3 Construct forms and non-autonomous forms of nominal lexemes

As already mentioned, forms of nominal lexemes used exclusively as the input of derivational or compounding operations do not meet the definition of construct form that delimits the scope of this cross-linguistic investigation, although they may be historically related to construct forms, as will be evoked in section 4.3. Attention should therefore be paid to the fact that some authors (for example

---

3 Abbreviations: 1 = 1st person; 2 = 2nd person; 3 = 3rd person; ADNZ = adnominalizer; CL = noun class; CONST = construct marker; DEF = definite; F = feminine; GEN = genitive; H = high (tone); L = low (tone); M = masculine; NAUT = non-autonomous form of nouns; NEG = negation; NMLZ = nominalizer; PL = plural; PRF = perfect; REL = relativizer; SG = singular.

Jacques (2012) on Rgyalrong languages) use the term of construct form (or state) precisely for non-autonomous forms of nominal lexemes that, at least synchronically, do not involve construct marking according to the definition adopted in this paper.

3.2.4 Construct and pertensive

In the last decade, quite a few authors working on languages that have the type of nominal form for which I propose to generalize the label 'construct form' have designated the forms in question by the term 'pertensive' introduced by Dixon (2010: 268). However, 'pertensive' as defined by Dixon and 'construct' as used in this paper are not entirely equivalent:
- in Dixon's terminology, 'pertensive' is restricted to the marking of the possessee in the adpossessive construction, whereas 'construct' as used in this paper extends to forms of nouns whose use may be conditioned by any type of modifier;
- in Dixon's terminology, 'pertensive' includes any type of marking of the possessee in adpossessive construction (including person markers expressing the person of the possessor), whereas according to the definition put forward in this paper, a construct marker is a morphological element which is obligatory in the presence of a given type of modifier, but does not cross-reference features of the modifier it licenses.

3.3 Construct marking in the languages of the world

As already mentioned in section 3.1, construct marking was first recognized in languages belonging to the Semitic family. In this section, I present some illustrations in languages belonging to other language families. This enumeration does not pretend to be exhaustive, it only aims at exemplifying the cross-linguistic variation in forms analyzable as instantiations of the general concept of construct form put forward in this paper.

3.3.1 The languages of Sub-Saharan Africa

3.3.1.1 Construct forms in Nilotic and other East African languages
In African linguistics, the existence of construct forms of nouns is mainly mentioned in descriptions of East African languages belonging to the Nilotic family.

Andersen (2002) on Dinka (din) includes detailed references on previous works dealing with this topic in other Nilotic languages.

Among Nilotic languages, Shilluk (shk) illustrates the case of a language with two distinct forms meeting the definition of construct form (Remijsen & Ayoker 2017). One of them (designated as 'pertensive' by Remijsen and Ayoker) is used when the noun is the head in adpossessive construction, the other one (designated as 'construct form') marks the noun as being modified by most modifiers other than possessors. For example, *gwôk* 'dog' occurs as *gwôook* in *gwôook twɔ́ɔŋ* 'Twong's dog', and as *gwôooŋ* in *gwôooŋ dwɔ̂ɔŋ* 'big dog'.

In the northeastern part of Sub-Saharan African, outside of the Nilotic language family, a construct form of nouns has been identified in Mous' (1993) description of the Cushitic language Iraqw (irk), and in Hellenthal's (2010) description of the Omotic language Sheko (she). The construct form of Sheko nouns is marked by a tonal alternation, a situation relatively common in Sub-Saharan Africa. This tonal change affects nouns modified by a numeral, a relative clause, a noun in adpossessive function, or a possessive prefix (Hellenthal 2010: 252).

3.3.1.2 Construct forms of nouns in Bantu languages

In the Bantu language Tswana, the nouns whose basic tonal contour ends with two successive H tones (which constitute an important proportion of Tswana nouns, perhaps the majority) show a tonal alternation . . .HH ~ . . .HL that must be recognized as morphological, since its conditioning cannot be stated in purely phonological terms. In this alternation, the variant ending with . . .HL must be analyzed as a construct form. Interestingly, Tswana shows that the use of a construct form of the head noun and of an adnominalizer introducing the modifier may combine in the same construction.

For example, in (2a), *sìtswáná* 'Tswana culture, language, etc.' is the head of the NP *sìtswánà sé básìbúàŋ́* 'the Tswana they speak > the way they speak Tswana', and consequently, the contact with the relative clause *sé básìbúàŋ́* triggers the use of the construct form *sìtswánà*. In (2b), *sìtswáná* is also in contact with a relative clause (*sé básìrékílèŋ́*) but this relative clause modifies *sìtílɔ́* 'chair',[4] not *sìtswáná*; in (2b), *sìtswáná* has no dependent, and consequently the construct form *sìtswánà* would not be correct.

---

4 The construct form *sìtílɔ̀* is licensed by the adpossessor *sásìtswáná*.

(2) Tswana (Bantu – pers.doc.)
(2a) χà-kí-rátí   sì-tswánà   s-é   bá-sì-búà:-ŋ́.
     NEG-1SG-like CL7-Tswana.CONST CL7-ADNZ CL2-CL7-speak-REL
     'I do not like the Tswana they speak (the way they speak Tswana).'
(2b) χà-kí-rátí   sì-tílɔ̀   s-á-sì-tswáná   ˈs-é
     NEG-1SG-like CL7-chair.CONST CL7-GEN-CL7-Tswana CL7-ADNZ
     bá-sì-rékílè:-ŋ́.
     CL2-CL7-buy.PRF-REL
     'I do not like the Tswana chair they bought.'

In Tswana, nouns with a basic tonal contour ending with . . .HH must take the construct form characterized by the contour . . .HL when immediately preceding one of the following types of dependents:
– a demonstrative,
– a noun phrase in adpossessive function,
– an adjective or a relative clause introduced by an adnominalizer homonymous with the demonstrative (and historically cognate with it),
– the interrogative determiner -fí,
– the negative determiner -pé,
– the determiner -sìlí 'other'.

In his analysis of relativization in the Bantu language Eton (eto), Van de Velde (2017) argues that, in Eton, the so-called "augment" (a nominal prefix whose original function was admittedly the expression of definiteness distinctions) has only persisted as an obligatory element of the 'noun + relative clause' construction, and consequently fulfills a purely syntactic function of construct marker in the present state of the language.

This situation is interesting to compare to that described by Jenks, Makasso and Hyman (2017) for Basaá (bas). In both languages, a prefix í- analyzable as the reflex of the Bantu augment is found with nouns modified by a relative clause. However, according to Jenks, Makasso and Hyman's description, unlike Eton, this prefix is not obligatory in Basaá, and it encodes definiteness distinctions. Consequently, Basaá and Eton can be analyzed as illustrating successive stages in the same grammaticalization process, with some interesting typological particularities:
– In Basaá, according to Jenks, Makasso and Hyman, the use of the augment to express definiteness distinctions has been restricted to nouns modified by a relative clause. Typologically, definiteness distinctions conditioned by the presence of a given type of noun modifier are not unknown, but the involvement of relative clauses in this phenomenon is not common (in Baltic and

Slavic languages, which are the best-known cases of languages illustrating this kind of situation, the conditioning factor is rather the presence of an adjective).
– As regards Van de Velde's analysis of Eton, head marking (or in other words, the use of a construct form of nouns) in the 'noun + relative clause' construction is rarely mentioned in the literature: quite obviously, construct forms of nouns (i.e., noun forms signaling that the noun combines with a given type of modifier) are more typically found with nouns heading adpossessive construction.

3.3.1.3 Construct forms of nouns in Chadic languages

The Chadic language Hausa (hau) has a construct form of nouns characterized by a suffix -*n* (singular masculine or plural) or -*ř* (singular feminine), commonly called a 'genitive linker'. This suffix occurs when the noun is the head of an adpossessive construction, as in (3a) and (3c). It must also be used when the noun takes a possessive suffix other than first-person singular, see (3e) and (3f). It results from the cliticization of a pronoun *na/ta* resuming the head noun in the synonymous construction illustrated by (3b) and (3d).

(3) Hausa (hau) – pers.doc.
(3a) kàre-n   Daudà   (cf. kàree 'dog')
     dog-CONST.SG.M Dauda
     'Dauda's dog'
(3b) kàree na   Daudà
     dog   that_of.SG.M   Dauda
     'Dauda's dog'
(3c) saanìya-ř   Daudà   (cf. saanìyaa 'cow')
     cow-CONST.SG.F   Dauda
     'Dauda's cow'
(3d) saanìyaa ta   Daudà
     cow   that_of.SG.F   Dauda
     'Dauda's cow'
(3e) kàre-n-sà
     dog-CONST.SG.M-3SG.M
     'his dog'
(3f) saanìya-ř-sà
     cow-CONST.SG.F-3SG.M
     'his cow'

In Hausa, the same suffix -*n* ~ -*ř* is found with attributive adjectives preceding nouns in the construction illustrated by *fari-n kàree* 'white dog' or *fara-ř saanìyaa* 'white cow' (*fari-* and *fara-* are the masculine and feminine forms, respectively, of the adjective 'white'). See Creissels (2009) for a discussion of the possible analyses of this situation.

A construct form of nouns is also found in Wandala (mfi). According to Frajzyngier (2013), in the adpossessive construction of Wandala, 'non-relational' head nouns take an obligatory 'pertensive' suffix *-á*. The distribution of the form of Wandala nouns marked by this suffix is similar to that of Semitic construct forms, since it must be followed either by an NP in the role of adnominal possessor, or by a person marker referring to a possessor.

3.3.1.4 The construct form of Yoruba nouns

In the Western Benue-Congo language Yoruba (yor), nouns have a special form used when they are followed by a noun in adpossessive function beginning with a consonant, or by an enclitic possessive pronoun. This form is marked by the suffixation of a copy of the last vowel, which consequently meets the definition of construct form marker. This vowel copy acting as a construct form marker invariably has a mid tone if it is followed by a noun in adpossessive function (as in *fìlà-ā Túndé* [hat-CONST Tunde] 'Tunde's cap', *ọmọ-ọ Táíwò* [child-CONST Taiwo] 'Taiwo's child', *ílé-ē Bísí* [house-CONST Bisi] 'Bisi's house'), whereas with enclitic possessive pronouns, its tone is low in the 1SG and 2SG (as in *ọmọ-ọ̀ mī* [child-CONST 1SG] 'my child'), mid in the other persons (as in *ílé-ē wá* [house-CONST 1PL] 'our house') – Rowlands 1969: 45–46.

3.3.1.5 The construct form of Wolof nouns

In the Atlantic language Wolof (wol), a construct form of nouns characterized by the suffix *-u* (sg.) / *-i* (pl.) is used exclusively for nouns followed by an adnominal possessor. It occurs with no other type of dependent, and, unlike Semitic construct forms, it does not occur with possessive affixes or determiners either.

The construct form of Wolof nouns shares with Semitic construct forms a constraint of strict contiguity with the dependent noun: other dependents of the head noun in the construct form must follow the possessor, and if the possessor itself has dependents that must precede it, they must be placed to the left of the head noun, as illustrated by (4).

(4) Wolof (wof) – pers.doc.
(4a) *fas w-u ñuul*
horse CLw-ADNZ be_black
'black horse'

(4b) suma   nijaay
      1SG   maternal_uncle
      'my uncle'
(4c) suma | fas-u | nijaay | w-u | ñuul |
      1SG   horse-CONST   maternal_uncle   CLw-ADNZ   be_black
      'the black horse of my uncle' (lit. 'my horse of uncle black')
(4d) *fas-u   suma   nijaay
       horse-CONST   1SG   maternal_uncle

3.3.1.6 Construct forms of nouns in Mande languages

In the South Western Mande language Mende (men), the initial of nouns shows a consonant alternation triggered by the syntactic status of the noun. One of the two forms can be characterized as a construct form, since it is automatically used whenever the noun is immediately preceded by a dependent, whereas the other (the free form) occurs whenever the noun is the first element of an NP, or is not accompanied by any dependent, as illustrated by (5).

(5)   Mende (men) – pers.doc.
(5a) ndopô 'child', tokó 'arm', ngíla 'dog' (free forms)
(5b) ndopó-i   loko-í
      child-DEF   CONST.arm-DEF
      'the child's arm'
(5c) ndopó-i   yilɛ-í
      child-DEF   CONST.dog-DEF
      'the child's dog'

Most accounts of Mende morphology suggest describing the initial of the construct form in terms of 'lenition' of the initial of the free form, but as shown in Creissels (1994: 152–168), the construct form must rather be characterized as lacking an underlying nasal present at the initial of the free form. In Mende, a nasal with exactly the same morphophonological properties but prefixed to verbs is the manifestation of a third-person object pronoun, and comparison with Kpelle (kpe) shows that, before being reanalyzed as the mark of the free form of nouns, the nasal prefixed to nouns was a definite article.

However, this is only part of the story. The construct form of Mende nouns is also marked tonally: as can be seen in (5), Mende nouns used as heads in adpossessive construction, in addition to a change in their initial consonant, show a uniform L tonal contour, regardless of the lexical tone they show in their free form. Interestingly, the historical processes that led to a segmental marking of the construct form of Mende nouns must be relatively recent (since they are easy to reconstitute by comparing Mende with the other South Western Mande languages) whereas the existence of tonally-marked construct forms of nouns must be very ancient in the Mande language family. Construct forms of nouns marked by an L or LH replacive morphotoneme are found in the two major branches of the Mande family (see among others Creissels (2016) on the West Mande language Soninke (snk), Khachaturyan (2015: 53) on the South Mande language Mano (mev)),[5] and a tonally marked construct form of nouns can safely be reconstructed at Proto-Mande level.

3.3.1.7 Construct forms of nouns in Dogon languages

A major typological feature of Dogon languages (Heath 2008; McPherson 2013) is the complexity of the tonal alternations affecting nouns and triggered by the presence of various types of modifiers. For example, in Tommo So (dto), alienably possessed nouns have a L tonal overlay replacing their lexical tones – Ex. (6).

(6)   Tommo So (dto) – McPherson 2013: 183–4
(6a)   gìné 'house', ìsé 'dog' (free forms)
(6b)   Sáná   gìnè
        Sana   house^L
        'Sana's house'
(6c)   Àrámátá   ìsè
        Ramata   dog^L
        'Ramata's dog'

3.3.2 The languages of the Americas

3.3.2.1 Nahuatl

In the variety of the Uto-Aztecan language Nahuatl known as Classical Nahuatl (nci), nominal inflection includes a paradigm of person prefixes encoding the person of a possessor, and these person prefixes attach to a special stem formed by substituting the 'possessive' suffix *-uh* (sg.) / *-huān* (pl.) for the 'absolute'

---

[5] Following the Russian terminological tradition, Khachaturyan calls this construct form 'izafet'. This is etymologically correct, since *'iḍāfah* is the term used in Arabic grammars for the adpossessive construction in which the head noun occurs in the construct form. However, this can be misleading, since for most general linguists, this term rather evokes adnominalizers of the kind found in West Iranian languages and called *ezâfe* in Iranian linguistics – cf. section 3.2.2.

suffix of the free form, as in (7b). Moreover, as illustrated in (7c), in the adpossessive construction, the head noun must take the same suffix, and the modifier is obligatorily cross-referenced by a possessive prefix. According to the definition adopted here, the suffix *-uh* (sg.) / *-huān* (pl.) is therefore a construct form marker.

(7)   Classical Nahuatl (nci) – Launey 1981: 90–92
(7a) *cihuā-tl* 'woman, wife' (free form)
(7b) *no-cihuā-uh*
      1SG-wife-CONST.SG
      'my wife'
(7c) *in   ī-cihuā-uh   Pedro*
      DEF   3SG-wife-CONST.SG   Pedro
      'Pedro's wife'

3.3.2.2 Athabaskan languages

In Slave (den) and other Athabaskan languages, nouns divide into two subclasses. The 'inalienably possessed nouns' imply the overt expression of a possessor (either as a possessive prefix, or as a noun phrase preceding the possessee). With such nouns, the only way to avoid mentioning a specific possessor is the use of an 'unspecified possessor' prefix such as Slave *ʔe-* in *ʔe-ghú* 'a tooth' (Rice 1989: 118), to be compared with *se-ghú* 'my tooth' (Rice 1989: 119), where *se-* is the 1st person singular possessive prefix. By contrast, 'alienably possessed nouns' do not require the expression of a possessor, and in combination with possessive prefixes or noun phrases in the role of adnominal possessor, they obligatorily take a suffix traditionally called 'possessed noun suffix', which in the terminology used in this paper is a construct form marker, as illustrated in (8) and (9).

(8)   Slave (den) – Rice 1989: 39
(8a) *ts'ah* 'hat' (free form)
(8b) *se-ts'ár-é*
      1SG-hat-CONST
      'my hat'

(9)   Dënesųłıné, aka Chipewyan (chp) – Saxon & Wilhelm 2016: 38
(9a) *bes* 'knife' (free form)
(9b) *John   be-bes-é*
      John   3-knife-CONST
      'John's knife'

According to Saxon & Wilhelm (2016), in addition to its use in the alienable possession construction, the construct form of Dënesųłiné / Chipewyan and Tłįchǫ / Dogrib (dgr) is also used when nouns denoting a unit of measurement combine with a numeral to form a measure phrase, and when nouns are preceded by a "characterizing" relative clause, in which the verb takes a nominalizing suffix, as in (10).

(10)   Tłįchǫ, aka Dogrib (dgr) – Saxon & Wilhelm 2016: 42
       behcįį̀   k'èdì-ı   dǫ-ǫ̀
       vehicle drive-NMLZ   person-CONST
       'driver', lit. 'vehicle-driving person'

3.3.2.3 Amazonian languages

In his typological overview of noun phrase structure, Dixon (2010) quotes data from Montserrat's (2010: 162–3) description of the Brasilian isolate Mỹky (irn) and from Derbyshire's (1979: 68–70, 1985: 199–200) description of the Carib language Hixkaryana (hix) showing that these languages have forms meeting the definition of construct form adopted here.

Overall (2007) discusses the possibility of analyzing the adpossessive construction of the Jivaroan language Aguaruna (agr) as involving a construct form marker ('pertensive' in his terminology) distinct from the suffixes encoding the person of the possessor.

3.3.3 The languages of Eurasia

3.3.3.1 Russian (rus) and other Slavic languages

In Russian (rus), in noun phrases including a numeral and fulfilling a syntactic role requiring nominative or accusative case, the head noun takes a special form (sometimes misleadingly called 'paucal', cf. Paperno 2012), which never occurs in nominative or accusative noun phrases that do not include a numeral, and consequently meets the definition of construct form. There are two such forms, one of them is selected by numerals that end in 2, 3 or 4, the other by numerals ending in bigger simple numerals. The former is usually identical to the genitive singular, and the latter to the genitive plural, but some nouns show a contrast, for example *rjad* 'row', gen.sing. *rjáda*, occurs as *rjadá* in combination with numerals ending in 2, 3 and 4, and *čelovék* 'person', gen.pl. *ljudéj*, occurs as *čelovék* (identical to the nom. sing.) in combination with numerals ending in bigger simple numerals.

Among the other Slavic languages, the situation of Bulgarian (bul) is particularly straightforward, since due to the drastic simplification of nominal inflection, there is no possible confusion between the construct form of nouns required after numerals (as in *dva stol-a* [two chair-CONST] 'two chairs') and other inflected forms of nouns.

3.3.3.2 Hungarian (hun)

Recent accounts of Hungarian morphology (among others É. Kiss & al. 2003) agree that the formation of the possessed form of Hungarian nouns, traditionally described as involving stem allomorphy triggered by the addition of possessive suffixes, is better analyzed as involving complex endings consisting of three successive morphemes:

- a 'general possessive marker' (*általános birtokviszonyjel*) with two allomorphs depending on the context: *-(j)a/e* and *-Ø*,
- a number marker with the two possible values *-Ø* (singular) and *-i* (plural), with a plural marker *-i* different from the plural marker *-k* found in non-possessed nominal forms,
- a person marker expressing the person of the possessor, which has a zero form for the 3rd person singular, as illustrated in (11).

In this analysis, the 'general possessive marker' meets the definition of a construct form marker, since it is obligatory in the presence of a noun phrase in adpossessive function – cf. (12).

(11)   Hungarian (hun) – Creissels 2006
       kocsi-ja-i-m   car-CONST-PL.CONST-1SG   'my cars'
       kocsi-ja-i-d   car-CONST-PL.CONST-2SG   'your (sg.) cars'
       kocsi-ja-i   car-CONST-PL.CONST(3SG)   'his/her cars'
       kocsi-ja-i-nk   car-CONST-PL.CONST-1PL   'our cars'
       kocsi-ja-i-tok   car-CONST-PL.CONST-2PL   'your (pl.) cars'
       kocsi-ja-i-k   car-CONST-PL.CONST-3PL   'their cars'

(12)   Hungarian (hun) – Creissels 2006
       a   vendég-ek   kocsi-ja-i
       DEF   guest-PL   car-CONST-PL.CONST
       'the cars of the guests'

This system is however somewhat blurred by the existence of a zero allomorph of the construct form marker, the zero marking of 3SG in the paradigm of the person markers referring to possessors, and the rule according to which, if no noun phrase in adpossessive role is present, a noun form with construct marking but no overt person marker is interpreted as referring to a third person possessor. See Creissels (2006) for a more detailed presentation of the data, and a discussion.

3.3.3.3 Turkish (tur) and other Turkic languages

Turkish nouns are commonly described as having a possessive inflection with a paradigm of possessive suffixes including a 3rd person possessive suffix *-(s)I*. The status of this suffix is, however, problematic, since, in contrast to the 1st and 2nd person possessive suffixes, it does not always imply reference to a possessor. The interpretation of constructions involving this suffix depends on the presence of a modifying noun in the nominative or genitive case:
– if no modifying noun in the nominative or genitive case is present, *-(s)I* implies reference to a possessor whose identity must be retrieved from the context;
– if a modifying noun in the genitive case is present, this noun is interpreted as referring to a possessor;
– if a modifying noun in the nominative case is present, this noun is interpreted as having generic reference, and the construction is interpreted as a binominal in which the modifier in the nominative case restricts the meaning of the head noun.

(13)   Turkish (tur) – pers.doc.
(13a) *müdür* 'manager' (free form)
(13b) *müdür-ü*
       manager-*(s)I*
       'its manager'
(13c) *banka-nın   müdür-ü*
       bank-GEN   manager-*(s)I*
       'the manager of the bank'
(13d) *banka   müdür-ü*
       bank   manager-*(s)I*
       'bank manager'

In the literature on Turkish (tur), there is controversy between supporters of the view that *-(s)I* is the 3rd person possessive suffix in all of its uses, and supporters of a distinction between two homonymous suffixes, the possessive suffix and a 'compound marker' or 'linking element'. None of these two analyses is really satisfying, and my claim is that *-(s)I* is best analyzed as a construct form marker licensing modification by a noun in the nominative or genitive case, with the default interpretation '3rd person possessive' when no modifying noun is present (which can be analyzed as an anaphoric zero, depending on the theoretical framework).

An essentially similar analysis has been proposed by Kunduracı (2013), who doesn't refer to the notion of construct marking, but argues that Turkish *-(s)I* is not a person marker. According to her analysis, the 3rd person marker in possessive constructions is zero, and she explicitly claims that *-(s)I* is functionally similar to 'possessed noun markers' found in Amerindian languages that meet the definition of construct marker put forward in the present article (in particular, the Athabaskan construct markers, cf. section 3.3.2.2). The reader is referred to her paper for a detailed discussion of properties of *-(s)I* that distinguish it from the possessive markers of 1st and 2nd person, and consequently contradict its identification as a 3rd person marker, even in constructions in which its presence implies reference to a 3rd person possessor.

3.3.3.4 Karbi (mjw)

According to Konnerth (2014: 200), the Tibeto-Burman language Karbi (mjw) has a nominal prefix *a-* she calls 'general possessive' or 'modified' prefix, which occurs on nouns that are modified by pre-head elements (but not if modified by post-head elements). This suffix "occurs on a head noun if that head noun is modified by a pre-head demonstrative, content question word, possessor noun, or adverbial, by a pre-head deverbal modifier, or by a pre-head classifier or numeral." Interestingly, the same *a-* prefix can also be found in constructions in which none of the pre-head modifiers that trigger its use is present, in which case it is interpreted as marking third person possession. This might well be its original function, since, as discussed by Konnerth (2014: 201), it seems to be the reflex of a Proto-Tibeto-Burman prefix **ʔa-* / **(ʔ)ə* / **ʔə̃* / **ʔaŋ* / **ʔak* reconstructed by Matisoff (2003: 104) with a range of functions including third person possessive.

3.3.4 The languages of Australia and the Pacific

3.3.4.1 Oceanic languages

The use of the term 'construct' for a morphological mechanism meeting the definition retained here for this term is common in descriptions of Oceanic languages:

> In Micronesian and eastern Melanesian languages, the possessed NP is marked with what is generally referred to as the 'construct' suffix, or some other linking morpheme. The construct suffix sometimes coincides in shape with the third person singular pronominal suffix, but the two are frequently morphologically distinct. (Lynch & al. 2001: 41)

Ex. (14) illustrates the construct form of nouns in the Oceanic language Anejom (aty).

(14) Anejom (aty) – Lynch & al. 2001: 41
      etma-k   *etma-n*   *etma-i*   *natimarid*
      father-1SG   father-3SG   father-CONST   chief
      'my father'   'his/her father'   'the chief's father'

Bril (2013) provides a detailed description of the morphological modification of head nouns in Nêlêmwa (nee) adnominal possession. Here is one of her examples:

(15) Nêlêmwa (nee) – Bril 2013: 76
      pwââdagax-a   *jowo*   *ena*
      NMLZ:be_beautiful-CONST   door_frame   that
      'the beauty of that door-frame'

3.3.4.2 Martuthunira (vma)

According to Dench (2013), the Australian language Martuthunira (vma) has a rare 'pertensive' suffix meeting the definition of construct marker retained in this paper, since it "can be described as the obverse of the source suffix. Where the source suffix attaches to the Possessor and codes this as the parent of the Possessee head, the pertensive attaches to Possessee and codes this as the child of the Possessor head."

3.4 Conclusion to section 3

Inflected forms of nouns meeting the definition of construct form put forward in this paper are found all around the world, in languages that have no close genetic or areal link. They show cross-linguistic variation with respect to the following parameters:
- the types of dependents that require the use of a construct form of their head;
- the possibility of using a construct form without any overt dependent;
- the possibility that construct marking interferes with the expression of some features of the head noun (number, gender);
- the possibility that the distinction between free form and construct form is restricted to a subset of nouns delimitable in either phonological or semantic terms;
- the morphological nature of construct form marking (prefixation, suffixation, or other).

The languages in the sample give an idea of the possible variation in the syntactic distribution of construct forms. However, in the languages that have a single construct form, its distribution almost always includes the role of head in adpossessive construction, and in the languages that have two or more distinct construct forms, one of them is used in the adpossessive construction. Among the languages quoted in this paper, the only exceptions are the Bantu language Eton, where construct marking is only used to license modification by relative clauses, and Slavic languages, where construct marking is only used to license modification by numerals.

As regards the possible interaction between construct marking and the expression of features of the noun marked as construct, some languages in the sample have construct markers that are portmanteau morphs expressing also number and/or gender: Hausa, Wolof, Nahuatl .

As regards the morphological nature of construct form marking, the addition of an affix (either a prefix or a suffix) to the free form is common, but construct form marking may also involve the deletion of a morphological element present in the free form, as in Mende, the replacement of a morphological element present in the free form by the construct marker, as in Nahuatl, or stem-internal alternations, including prosodic alternations, as in Mande languages, Dogon languages, Sheko, Tswana.

In the languages that have a construct form used in adpossessive construction, it variously interferes with possessor indexation. In Semitic languages, person markers representing pronominal possessors are in complementary distribution with possessor NPs, and the construct form is used both with nominal and pronominal possessors. In Wolof, the construct form is used exclusively with nominal possessors. In Nahuatl, construct marking obligatorily combines with possessor indexation. In Hungarian, Turkish, and Karbi, third person possession is the default interpretation of a construct form in the absence of any overt indication of a possessor.

It is also worth noting that there seems to be no correlation between the relative order of nouns and their modifiers and the use of construct marking, since among the languages of the sample, construct forms are equally attested in *noun – modifier* and *modifier – noun* constructions.

Diachronically, not all the construct forms illustrated in this paper are historically transparent. For example, in Semitic linguistics, there is controversy about the possible origin of the Ge'ez construct marker -*a* and its possible relationship with the accusative marker -*a*. The illustrations provided in the previous sections nevertheless suggest a variety of scenarios that may result in the emergence of a construct form of nouns:
– construct marking may result from the morphologization of prosody-driven phonological processes, as proposed for Hebrew by Borer (2008: 492);

- construct marking may result from the morphologization of sandhi processes, either segmental (as in Semitic languages) or tonal (as in Tswana);
- in Mende, the construct form of nouns is marked by the absence of a prefix present in the free form that diachronically can be characterized as a frozen definite article, whereas in Eton, it is the construct form of nouns that is marked by a prefix analyzable as a frozen definite article;
- in Hausa, the construct form of nouns is marked by a suffix resulting from the encliticization of a resumptive pronoun in an adnominal possession construction whose literal equivalent in English would be something like 'the dog that.of the man' for 'the man's dog';
- the construct marker of Karbi seems to result from the reanalysis of a third person possessive, and this is also the probable origin of the construct markers of Hungarian and Turkish.

The scenario illustrated by Hausa is probably a particular case of a more general type of evolution by which, due to prosodic factors, a genitive marker originally attached to the possessor phrase in the adnominal possessive construction is reanalyzed as a construct marker: either $N1_{possessee}$ GEN=$N2_{possessor}$ > $N1_{possessee}$-CONST $N2_{possessor}$, as in Hausa, or $N1_{possessor}$=GEN $N2_{possessee}$ > $N1_{possessor}$ CONST-$N2_{possessee}$. However, in the documentation I have been able to consult, I came across no clear case of construct marking showing particularities that would suggest the latter scenario as its probable origin.

4 Construct marking in the formation of binominals

Languages may have more or less productive patterns of binominal formation formally similar to their adpossessive construction, and this applies in particular to languages whose adpossessive construction involves construct marking.

4.1 Languages in which construct marking is not used productively for the formation of binominals

In some of the languages that make use of construct marking in the adpossessive construction, construct marking is not used productively in the formation of binominals.

This situation can be illustrated by the Mande language Soninke. The adpossessive construction of Soninke follows the order *possessor – possessee* and involves no segmental marking, but a tonal modification of the possessee that must be analyzed as construct marking. The construct form of Soninke nouns is marked by a low-high tone pattern (with high tone on the last syllable only) replacing the lexical tone pattern of the noun. For example, the construct form of *kíttè* 'hand' is *kìtté*. In the adpossessive construction, the possessor undergoes no modification at all, either segmental of tonal.

Soninke also has a very productive pattern of binominal formation in which two nouns are juxtaposed in the order *modifier – head*, but as illustrated in (16), no ambiguity with the adpossessive construction can arise, since in this compounding pattern, it is the first noun (i.e., the modifier) that occurs in a special form (the 'non-autonomous' form), used exclusively when nominal lexemes occur as the first formative of complex lexemes.

(16) Soninke (snk) – pers.doc.
(16a) *yúgò* 'man', *kíttè* 'hand' (free forms)
(16b) *yúgò-n   kìttê*
 man-DEF   hand.CONST.DEF[6]
 'the hand of the man'
(16c) *yúgú-kíttè*
 man.NAUT-hand.DEF[7]
 'man's hand'

Hungarian provides another illustration of a language in which the construct form that characterizes nouns modified by an adnominal possessor is only exceptionally used in the formation of binominals. Hungarian has a very productive compounding pattern in which two nouns are simply juxtaposed in the order *modifier – head*, and precisely, as illustrated in (17), construct marking contributes to the distinction between such binominals and adpossessive constructions involving the same nouns.

(17) Hungarian (hun) – pers.doc.
(17a) *a   férfi   cipő-je*
 DEF man   shoe.CONST
 'the shoe of the man'

---

6 *kìttê* can be decomposed as *kìtté* + ˋ, where *kìtté* is the construct form of 'hand', and the floating low tone is the manifestation of definiteness marking before a pause.
7 In Soninke, nouns are obligatorily quoted in the definite form (hence the low tone on the last syllable – cf. footnote 6).

(17b) férfi-cipő
       man-shoe
       'man's shoe'

There is however in Hungarian a very limited set of binominals whose head exceptionally shows construct marking. For example, *tojás-héj* [egg-shell] 'egg shell' has the regular structure of a compound noun, whereas *tojás-fehér-je* [egg-white-CONST] 'egg white' is among the compound nouns that exceptionally involve construct marking.

4.2 Productive use of construct marking in the formation of binominals

In many languages whose adpossessive construction involves construct marking of the head noun (the possessee), the same construct marking is more or less productively used in the formation of binominals, alongside with other possible formal types of binominals.

A first illustration of the productive use of construct marking in the formation of binominals has already been encountered above (section 3.3.3.3) with Turkish. Further illustrations are given in (18).

(18)   Turkish (tur) – pers.doc.
       para çanta-sı   [money bag-CONST]   'wallet'
       köpek diş-i   [dog tooth-CONST]   'canine tooth'
       baş örtü-sü   [head cover-CONST]   'kerchief'
       diş fırça-sı   [tooth brush-CONST] 'tooth brush'

In Turkish, case-marking of the modifying noun distinguishes such binominals from adpossessive constructions, since nominative marking (i.e., zero marking) of the modifying noun in the formation of binominals whose second formative is in the construct form contrasts with genitive marking of adpossessors (cf. ex. (13) above).

In most languages that make more or less productive use of construct marking in the formation of binominals, there is no systematic morphological distinction between the modifying noun in such binominals and the possessor in adpossessive construction. This is in particular the situation found in Semitic languages.

In such cases, the interpretation of a sequence N_1 N_2.CONST or N_1.CONST N_2 as a binominal or an adpossessive construction depends on the determination system of individual languages – more precisely, on the rules governing definiteness marking in the adpossessive construction and in the formation of binominals. For example, in Arabic (ara), binominals involving construct marking of the head noun, such as *sikkat l-ḥadīd* [road.CONST DEF-iron] 'railway', the modifying noun is obligatorily marked as definite, whereas in the adpossessive construction, the possessor NP can be definite or indefinite. Hebrew also has binominals involving construct marking in which the modifying noun, although semantically generic, is obligatorily marked as definite, such as *beyt ha-yetomim* [house.CONST DEF-orphan.PL] 'orphanage' or *ben ha-melex* [son.CONST DEF-king] 'prince', but this is not the general rule in Hebrew, cf. *beyt sefer* [house.CONST book] 'school' or *beyt xolim* [house.CONST patient.PL] 'hospital' (Borer 2008).

Example (19) provides further illustrations of binominals involving construct marking in the Athabaskan language Dënesųłné / Chipewyan.

(19)   Dënesųłné / Chipewyan (chp) – Saxon & Wilhelm 2016: 60–64
       dechën-tu-é   [wood-water-CONST]   'sap'
       k'es-léz-é   [tree/poplar-dust-CONST]   'ashes'
       la-yú-é   [hand-clothing/equipment-CONST] 'tool'

Like any other formal type of binominals, binominals involving construct marking may develop non-compositional meanings, as illustrated by Hebrew *melaxex pinka* [chewer.CONST bowl] 'toady, sycophant', lit. 'bowl-chewer' (Borer 2008). Example (20) illustrates semantically more or less opaque binominals involving construct marking in the Atlantic language Wolof.

(20)   Wolof (wol) – pers.doc.
       doom-u jàngoro [child-CONST illness]   'microbe'
       doom-u xaj   [child-CONST dog]   'bastard'
       doom-u tubaab   [child-CONST European]   'doll'

4.3 Patterns of binominal formation historically related to construct marking

In the evolution of languages, changes in the shaping of adposssessive construction are not uncommon. In particular, languages whose adpossessive construction involves construct marking of the possessee may develop an alternative construction with unmarked possessee. For example, the adpossessive construction of Semitic can be reconstructed as involving construct marking of the possessee, but the development of adpossessive constructions with unmarked possessee and prepositional marking of the possessor is pervasive across Semitic languages, cf. for example Fabri (1996) on Maltese (mlt), Ech-Charfi (2014) on Moroccan Arabic (ary).

In languages in which construct marking is also productively used in binominal formation, a possible scenario is that the development of an alternative adpossessive construction affects the productivity of construct marking as a way of coding the possessor in the adpossessive construction without affecting its productivity in binominal formation.

The Ethiosemitic language Amharic (amh) illustrates a variant of this scenario, involving also language contact, which has led to a situation in which a marker that was initially productively used as a construct marker in the adpossessive construction persists only in binominal formation.

In the adpossessive construction of Amharic, the Semitic *possessee.CONST possessor* pattern has been completely replaced by the *GEN-possessor possessee* pattern, as in *yä-ləj-u däbtär* [GEN-boy-DEF notebook] 'the boy's notebook'. However, Amharic has a relatively productive pattern of binominal formation N1-*ä* N2 historically related to the Semitic *possessee.CONST possessor* pattern of adpossessive construction. This pattern is particularly productive with *bet* 'house' or *bal* 'master, husband' as the first formative.

(21) Amharic (amh) – Kozicki 2017, Leslau 2005
 bet-ä mängəst   [house-*ä* kingdom]   'palace, parliament'
 bet-ä mädhanit [house-*ä* medicine] 'pharmacy'
 bet-ä krəstiyan [house-*ä* Christian] 'church'
 bal-ä suq   [master-*ä* shop]   'shopkeeper'
 bal-ä qəne   [master-*ä* hymn]   'poet'

Historically, the -*ä* involved in the formation of such compounds is the construct marker of Ge'ez, a now extinct Ethiosemitic language closely related to the ancestor of present-day Amharic, cf. section 3.1. Ge'ez was the official language of the Kingdom of Aksum and Ethiopian imperial court and still is the liturgic language of the Ethiopian Church, and as such exerted considerable influence on Amharic.

5 Conclusion

In this paper, after defining construct marking as a particular technique of marking relationships between head nouns and their dependents, I have first shown that noun modifying constructions involving construct marking in the sense of the definition I propose can be found well beyond the language families in which the term of 'construct' is traditionally used, and I have illustrated the cross-linguistic variation in construct marking.

As regards the relationship with binominal formation, in the languages that make use of construct marking in their adpossessive construction, it is common (although not universal) that construct markers are also used more or less productively in the formation of binominals, resulting in potential ambiguity in the interpretation of N_1.CONST N_2 or N_1 N_2.CONST sequences. In Turkish, any ambiguity is avoided by the contrast between genitive marking of the possessor in the adpossessive construction and nominative/zero marking of the modifying noun in binominal formation, but this kind of strategy is not common cross-linguistically. Most of the time, the distinction between adpossessive construction and binominals whose formation involves construct marking entirely relies on the use of determiners, which means that the possibility of sequences that are ambiguous between these two types of interpretation depends on the details of the determination system of individual languages.

Historically, a possible evolution is that, due to changes affecting the expression of adnominal possession, a construct marker also used in the formation of binominals loses its productivity in adnominal possession while remaining productive in binominal formation, with the possible outcome that a former construct marker persists only as a kind of linking element between the two formatives of binominal lexemes, as attested in Amharic.

References

Andersen, Torben. 2002. Case inflection and nominal head marking in Dinka. *Journal of African Languages and Linguistics* 23(1). 1–30.

Arkadiev, Peter. 2015. The Berber "state" distinction: Dependent marking after all? A commentary on Mettouchi and Frajzyngier (2013). *Linguistic Typology* 19(1). 87–100.

Bally, Charles. 1932. *Linguistique générale et linguistique française*. Paris: E. Leroux.

Borer, Hagit. 2008. Afro-asiatic, Semitic: Hebrew. In Rochelle Lieber & Pavol Štekauer (eds.), *The Oxford handbook of compounding*, 491–511. Oxford: Oxford University Press.

Bril, Isabelle. 2013. Ownership, part-whole, and other possessive-associative relations in Nêlêmwa (New Caledonia). In Alexandra Y. Aikhenvald & Robert M. W. Dixon (eds.), *Possession and ownership: A cross-linguistic typology*, 65–89. Oxford: Oxford University Press.

Creissels, Denis. 1979. *Les constructions dites possessives, étude de linguistique générale et de typologie linguistique*. Habilitation thesis (thèse d'état). University of Paris IV.

Creissels, Denis. 1994. *Aperçu sur les structures phonologiques des langues négro-africaines*, 2nd edn. Grenoble: ELLUG.

Creissels, Denis. 2006. Suffixes casuels et postpositions en hongrois. *Bulletin de la Société de Linguistique de* Paris 101(1). 225–272.

Creissels, Denis. 2009. Construct forms of nouns in African languages. In Peter K. Austin, Oliver Bond, Monik Charette, David Nathan & Peter Sells (eds.), *Proceedings of Conference on Language Documentation & Linguistic Theory 2* (London, November 13–14 2009), 73–82. London: SOAS.

Creissels, Denis. 2016. Phonologie segmentale et tonale du soninké (parler du Kingi). *Mandenkan* 55. 3–174.

Dench, Alan. 2013. Possession in Martuthunira. In Alexandra Y. Aikhenvald & Robert M. W. Dixon (eds.), *Possession and ownership: A cross-linguistic typology*, 126–148. Oxford: Oxford University Press.

Derbyshire, Desmond C. 1979. *Hixkaryana*. Amsterdam: North-Holland Publishing.

Derbyshire, Desmond C. 1985. *Hixkaryana and Linguistic Typology*. Dallas, TX: Summer Institute of Linguistics.

Dixon, Robert M. W. 2010. *Basic linguistic theory – Volume 2: Grammatical Topics*. Oxford: Oxford University Press.

Ech-Charfi, Ahmed. 2014. The genitive in Moroccan Arabic. *International Journal of Linguistics* 6(1). 171–191.

E. Kiss, Katalin, Ferenc Kiefer & Péter Siptár. 2003. *Új magyar nyelvtan* [New Hungarian grammar] (3rd edition). Budapest: Osiris Kiadó.

Fabri, Ray. 1996. The construct state and the pseudo-construct state in Maltese. *Rivista di linguistica* 8(1). 229–244.

Frajzyngier, Zygmunt. 2013. Possession in Wandala. In Alexandra Y. Aikhenvald & Robert M. W. Dixon (eds.), *Possession and ownership: A cross-linguistic typology*, 243–260. Oxford: Oxford University Press.

Heath, Jeffrey. 2008. *A grammar of Jamsay*. Berlin: Mouton de Gruyter.

Hellenthal, Anne-Christie. 2010. *A grammar of Sheko*. Leiden: Leiden University PhD dissertation.

Jacques, Guillaume. 2012. From denominal derivation to incorporation. *Lingua* 122(11). 1207–1231.

Jenks, Peter, Emmanuel-Moselly Makasso & Larry Hyman. 2017. Accessibility and demonstrative operators in Basaá relative clauses. In Gratien Atindogbé & Rébecca Grollemund (eds.), *Relative clauses in cameroonian languages*. Berlin: Mouton de Gruyter.

Keren, Rice. 1989. *A grammar of Slave*. Berlin: Mouton de Gruyter.

Khachaturyan, Maria. 2015. Grammaire du mano. *Mandenkan* 54. 1–252.

Konnerth, Linda Anna. 2014. *A grammar of Karbi*. University of Oregon PhD dissertation.

Koptevskaja-Tamm, Maria. 2002. Adnominal possession in the European languages: Form and function. *STUF – Language Typology and Universals* 55(2). 141–172.

Kozicki, Michal. 2017. Neologism construction in Amharic by compounding various parts of speech. *Studies of the Department of African Languages and Cultures* 51. 53–68.

Kunduracı, Aysun. 2013. Pseudo-3rd person marker and possessive constructions in Turkish. In Shan Luo (ed.), *Actes du congrès annuel de l'Association de linguistique 2013 / Proceedings of the 2013 annual conference of the Canadian Linguistic Association*, 1–14. Canadian Linguistic Association.

Launey, Michel. 1981. *Introduction à la langue et à la littérature aztèques. Tome 1: Grammaire*. Paris: L'Harmattan.

Leslau, Wolf. 2005. *Concise Amharic-English English-Amharic dictionary*. Addis Ababa: Shama books.
Lynch, John, Malcolm Ross & Terry Crowley. 2001. Typological overview. In John Lynch, Malcolm Ross & Terry Crowley (eds.), *The Oceanic languages*, 34–53. London: Routledge.
Masini, Francesca, Simone Mattiola & Steve Pepper. This volume. Exploring complex lexemes cross-linguistically. In Steve Pepper, Francesca Masini & Simone Mattiola (eds.), *Binominal lexemes in cross-linguistic perspective*. Berlin: Mouton de Gruyter.
Matisoff, James A. 2003. *Handbook of Proto-Tibeto-Burman: System and philosophy of Sino-Tibetan reconstruction*. Berkeley, CA: University of California Press.
McPherson, Laura. 2013. *A grammar of Tommo So*. Berlin: Mouton de Gruyter.
Monserrat, Ruth. 2010. *A língua do povo Mỹku*. Campinas: Editora Curt Nimuendajú.
Mous, Maarten. 1993. *A grammar of Iraqw*. Hamburg: Helmut Buske.
Nichols, Johanna. 1992. *Linguistic diversity in space and time*. Chicago: The University of Chicago Press.
Overall, Simon E. 2007. *A grammar of Aguaruna*. La Trobe University PhD dissertation.
Paperno, Denis. 2012. Quantification in Standard Russian. In Edward Keenan & Denis Paperno (eds.), *Handbook of quantifiers in natural language*, 729–780. Cham: Springer.
Pepper, Steve. This volume. Defining and typologizing binominal lexemes. In Steve Pepper, Francesca Masini & Simone Mattiola (eds.), *Binominal lexemes in cross-linguistic perspective*. Berlin: Mouton de Gruyter.
Remijsen, Bert & Otto Gwado Ayoker. 2017. Shilluk noun morphology and noun phrase morphosyntax. Presentation given at the *13th Nilo-Saharan Linguistics Colloquium*. Addis-Ababa, May 2017.
Rowlands, Evan Colyn. 1969. *Yoruba*. Teach Yourself Books. London: English Universities Press.
Saxon, Leslie & Andrea Wilhelm. 2016. The "possessed noun suffix" and possession in two Northern Dene (Athabaskan) languages. *IJAL* 82(1).35–70.
Van de Velde, Mark. 2017. The augment as a construct form marker in Eton relative clause constructions. In Gratien Atindogbé & Rébecca Grollemund (eds.), *Relative clauses in Cameroonian languages*. Berlin: Mouton de Gruyter.

Jakob Lesage
Compounds and other nominal modifier constructions in Pama-Nyungan languages

Abstract: Binominal compounds and binominal phrases are often assumed to be independent categories. In descriptions of lesser-known languages, their distinctions are sometimes taken for granted and their commonalities glossed over. These distinctions and commonalities are not always straightforward, however. In this chapter, I define and compare four types of nominal modifier constructions in Pama-Nyungan languages: binominal compounds, descriptive phrases, generic-specific constructions, and inalienable possession constructions. I argue against using (non-)compositionality and figurativity as a criterion to distinguish between compounds and phrases. I illustrate the different ways in which languages may distinguish these four constructions. Not all categories are easily differentiated in individual languages, based on the available data from grammars. There is morphosyntactic overlap between these constructions in many languages, and some languages appear to make more distinctions than others. Cross-linguistic similarities between these categories hint at potential constructional links between compounds and other syntactic structures.

1 Introduction

1.1 In short

In this chapter,[1,2] I give an overview of binominal lexemes, as defined in this volume, in Pama-Nyungan languages and I relate them to other types of nominal modification constructions. I focus on the following questions:

---

[1] The current chapter is based on research that I did for my MA thesis in Leuven, which was supervised by Jean-Christophe Verstraete. I would like to thank Jean-Christophe for his guidance and support. I am also thankful to Dana Louagie, Heinz Giegerich, Linda MacFarlane, Lora Litvinova and Sasha Vydrina for sharing their thoughts and materials. The comments provided by the editors and series editors, and the detailed feedback by a reviewer made the chapter much stronger. I gratefully acknowledge the financial support of the AdaGram project financed by the "Emergence(s)" programme of the city of Paris.
[2] Where possible, I follow the Leipzig Glossing Rules. I use the following symbols and abbreviations in this chapter (see Figure 1 for the language codes): ( ) = can be omitted; * = ungrammatical or impossible utterance in a language; – = morpheme boundary; . = gloss boundary where there

https://doi.org/10.1515/9783110673494-004

- What properties set apart binominal lexemes from (other) nominal modification constructions across Pama-Nyungan languages?
- To what degree can binominal lexemes be recognized as a distinct construction type across Pama-Nyungan languages?
- To what extent do binominal lexemes and other nominal modification constructions share properties across Pama-Nyungan languages?

I also address how the structure of different binominal constructions may relate to the general structure of noun phrases in these languages.

1.2 Elaboration of the problem

There has been little focus on compounding in the recent typological literature on Pama-Nyungan languages.[3] MacFarlane's (1987) extensive honours thesis, which focuses mostly on semantic analysis, remains the only family-wide treatment of compounds to date. In this chapter, I pay some attention to semantics but focus more on the formal properties of binominal constructions. Specifically, I compare compounds to several types of 'binominal phrases' in Pama-Nyungan languages. Some of these binominal phrases have received considerable attention in the literature on individual languages, either in isolation (Wilkins 2000 on "classifying constructions" in Mparntwe Arrernte [AER]), or in relation to compounds (Kilham 1974 on close-knit phrases and compounds in Wik-Mungkan [WIM]). In this chapter, I attempt to disentangle and relate the binominal constructions found across Pama-Nyungan languages. I take stock of how individual languages distinguish these constructions and how their differences may be more or less apparent across languages. As such, the chapter sheds light on the diversity found among

---

is no morpheme boundary; / in gloss = alternative translation; / in transcription = phonological representation; 1 = first person; 2 = second person; 3 = third person; > indicates that the person index before the symbol refers to an agent-like argument and the person index after the symbol to a patient-like argument; ? = uncertain gloss; ADJ = adjective; ABS = absolutive; CMP = binominal compound; ERG = ergative; GS = generic-specific; IP = inalienable possession; LOC = locative; N = noun; NEUT = neuter noun class; NP = noun phrase; PH = descriptive phrase; PL = plural; PN = proper name; PP = past punctual; SG = singular; VEG = vegetable noun class.

3 There is some work on compounds and word-like phrases in non-Pama-Nyungan language, notably by Baker and colleagues (e.g. Baker & Nordlinger 2008; Baker 2014, 2018). Their work uses a different definition of *compound* than the one used here, however (see §1.3.1), and focuses on the Gunwinyguan languages. I want to thank an anonymous reviewer for referring me to these sources.

Pama-Nyungan languages regarding binominal constructions in general and regarding binominal compounds in specific.

In §1.3, I define the scope of the chapter, both in terms of constructions (§1.3.1, §1.3.2) and languages (§1.3.3). In §1.3.1, I propose a set of comparative concepts for different binominal constructions across Pama-Nyungan languages. In §2, I discuss the semantic (§2.2), phonological (§2.3), morphological and syntactic (§2.4) properties of different binominal constructions. In §3, I explore what distinctions languages make, i.e. which comparative concepts may be grouped together, and which concepts are often distinguished. §4 provides some general observations, relating compound structures to general noun phrase structures across languages.

1.3 Scope of the chapter: Constructions and languages

1.3.1 Nominal modifier constructions and other constructions: Comparative concepts

I define binominal constructions as constructions that are made up of two nominals. My definition is broader than that of *binominals* used elsewhere in this book and differs from it in two ways. (a) Binominal constructions as defined in this chapter may be phrases or lexemes (or both at the same time). The volume focuses on binominal lexemes and does not consider phrases. (b) The nominals considered in this chapter may be nouns or adjectives. The volume generally excludes adjectives. I include adjectives because it is not possible to clearly distinguish nouns and adjectives in various languages of the sample and, where this may be possible, not all grammars provide enough data or analysis to make such a distinction (see Louagie 2020: 66–83 and references therein for a comprehensive overview of this issue).

The binominal constructions I consider in this chapter are (a) binominal compounds, (b) 0 descriptive phrases, 0 generic-specific constructions, and 0 inalienable possession constructions. These terms are operationalized here as comparative concepts (Haspelmath 2010) and I define them as follows.

(a) **Binominal compounds** have a (nominal) modifier with a classifying function rather than a qualifying function (cf. Rijkhoff 2008: 792; cf. McGregor 2002: 3). The modifier in these constructions does not provide a description of the referent but indicates a notion that is associated with it. This notion specifies the kind of the entity that is being referred to (cf. Rijkhoff 2008: 792; Spencer 2011: 500–502).

In a typical English [ENG] compound such as *blackbird*, *black* does not ascribe a property to the bird (it is perfectly possible for *blackbird* to refer to a white blackbird, for example). It indicates a notion, blackness, which is associated with the kind of bird referred to. As already mentioned, the definition of compound in this chapter is broader than the definition in the rest of this volume, and broader than what Giegerich (2015) and Rijkhoff (2008) intend. It encompasses all binominal lexemes, including phrasal lexemes.[4]

As a comparative concept, this definition differs from many traditional definitions of compounds which tend to be language specific. When they do have a cross-linguistic ambition, they often rely on language-specific criteria and categories. The current definition does not rely on a notion of 'lexeme' (Bauer 2001: 695, 2003: 40), 'word' (Fabb 1998: 66; Booij 2005: 75; Bauer 2006: 719; 2017), 'stem/root' (Brinton & Traugott 2005: 34) or 'free form' (Aikhenvald 2007: 24; Crystal 2008: 96). Sometimes, authors provide a disjunctive definition based on a variety of language-specific criteria which may or may not apply in other languages (cf. Bauer 2006, 2009, 2017; Lieber & Štekauer 2009). My definition also differs from that used in some analyses of Non-Pama-Nyungan languages such as the Gunwinyguan family. Baker & Nordlinger (2008) and Baker (2018), for instance, analyze a number of descriptive noun + adjective combinations as compounds based on some phonological and syntactic properties. Since the modifier in these constructions has a qualifying rather than a classifying function (Baker 2018: 261–262) they are functionally quite different from my comparative concept.[5]

Since it is essential to keep apart language-specific analyses of compounds and their typological analysis, I use a lower-case c for the comparative concept (compound) and a capital C for descriptive categories (Compound).

(b) **Descriptive phrases** have a qualifying modifier. This modifier describes an inherent property of the referent (cf. Giegerich 2015: 10–12; Rijkhoff 2008: 794).

The difference between *black bird* (a descriptive phrase) and *blackbird* (a compound), for example, is that in the first instance *black* always indicates an actual property of the entity. While all *blackbirds* belong to the set of birds, and some (most) to the set of things that are black, all *black birds* belong simultaneously to the set of birds and to the set of things that are black. To take a noun phrase

---

4 Phrasal lexemes (e.g. Masini 2009) are a category in between phrases and compounds. See §3.2.2 for some potential candidates in Pama-Nyungan languages.
5 Baker's (2018) *root-level compound* corresponds closely to my definition of compounds.

consisting of two nouns, instead of an adjective-noun combination: a ʹchild doctor, with primary stress on the first element, qualifies as a compound, as this is a type of doctor that is associated with children, whereas a child ʹdoctor, with primary stress on the second element, qualifies as a descriptive phrase, denoting a doctor that is also a child. Another example of a pair, this time with the same pronunciation, is *criminal lawyer* (a lawyer that works on criminal cases – with a classifying modifier[6]) vs. *criminal lawyer* (a lawyer that commits crimes themselves, a descriptive phrase with a qualifying modifier).[7]

(c) **Generic-specific constructions** are a combination of a generic and a specific noun. Their relationship is hyperonymous or hyponymous: the generic noun is a hyperonym of the specific noun; the specific noun a hyponym of the generic noun. An example is Eastern Arrernte [AER] *yerre alkerke* [ant meat.ant] 'meat ant' (Wilkins 2000: 188).

The exact function, grammaticalization, and frequency of occurrence of such constructions varies widely across Australian languages (Louagie 2020). The classic reference on generic-specific constructions is Wilkins (2000) on Mparntwe Arrernte, where they are called *classifying constructions*.

It is often difficult to establish whether the generic or the specific noun is the head of the construction. As a solution, it is sometimes proposed that the generic and the specific nouns jointly occupy a functional head slot in the noun phrase (e.g. Gaby 2006a: 283; Sadler & Nordlinger 2010; Verstraete & Rigsby 2015: 142). The analysis may differ from language to language. In this chapter, analysing the construction as double-headed would obscure the links it has with other constructions. In the remainder of this chapter, I assume that the generic-specific construction in each language follows the general word order pattern for N-N phrases in that language.[8] Interestingly, this principle always selects the generic noun as the modifier and the specific noun as the head. Note that this is a typological analysis, and that it may differ from the language-specific analysis of a

---

[6] In English, this would be a phrasal lexeme (see also footnote 4).
[7] Note that the stress difference does not apply to the two instances of *criminal lawyer*. Other criteria for distinguishing English phrases from compounds *do* work, however: *very criminal lawyer* can only refer to a lawyer that is criminal, as does *he is a criminal lawyer as well as a sneaky one*.
[8] The data never contradicts this type of analysis. For example, when there is a fixed modifier-head order for regular N-N phrases in a language, the order between generic and specific noun is also fixed. When there is *no* fixed modifier-head order for regular N-N phrases, the order between generic and specific nouns is also flexible (cf. §2.4.3). There are no analytical inconsistencies in treating the word order of generic-specific constructions as equivalent to that of other N-N phrases.

language. This does not mean that I disagree with the language-specific analysis. It simply means that I approach the issue from a different perspective and, in line with Haspelmath (2010), using comparative concepts that differ from language-specific categories.

(d) **Inalienable attributive possession constructions** (henceforth simply *inalienable possession constructions*) refer to entities that are inherently associated with or possessed by other entities, such as a kangaroo's tail. The relationship can be conceptualized as a part-whole association. One could speak of a meronymic or holonymic relationship: the part noun is a meronym of the whole noun; the whole noun is a holonym of the part noun.

Inalienable possession constructions have in common with descriptive phrases that the modifier (the possessor) describes something that is *inherently* associated with the referent. They have in common with binominal compounds that the modifier classifies, rather than qualifies, the head: the possessor is not a property of the referent, but another entity that indicates what *kind* of the 'head' it is (e.g. *kangaroo's tail* is a type of tail associated with (a) kangaroo(s)). In this chapter, I am only concerned with contiguous inalienable possession constructions (as opposed to, for instance, external possession).

1.3.2 Excluded binominal constructions

I do not include binominal constructions with a numeral component, although numerals often qualify as nouns or adjectives in Pama-Nyungan languages (Bowern & Zentz 2012: 142, 155, n18). I also exclude constructions including pronominals and proper nouns. Other binominal constructions that I exclude noun phrases with a comitative (*the man with the hat*), a privative (*the man without the hat*) or a spatial modifier (*the hat on the man*). I also exclude alienable possession constructions (*the hat of the man*). I leave these constructions out of the analysis because they are structurally very different from binominal compounds in Pama-Nyungan languages. Pama-Nyungan languages typically mark alienable possession with a genitive suffix on the possessor. Comitative, privative and spatial modifiers are each marked with a dedicated suffix (cf. Dixon 2002a: 138–143; 1980: 293). Compounds, on the other hand, are characterized by simple juxtaposition without marking of the parts (with the exception of a linking morpheme that may occur in between the two nominals, cf. §2.4.2). A more detailed look at these constructions may yield more binominal lexeme formation strategies.[9]

Note that the scope of this chapter is slightly different from the general scope of this book. Types of binominal lexemes that I do not include but do exist in Pama-Nyungan languages are adpositional constructions (**prp**) and genitive constructions (**gen**). It is not clear to me whether adjectival constructions (**adj**), head- and dependent-marked constructions (**dbl**), and derivations (**der**) as targeted in the book exist in Pama-Nyungan languages. There are construct forms (**con**) with a linking element in the Kulin group and in Arabana-Wangganguru. I treat these briefly in §2.4.2. Classifier constructions (**cls**) are represented by generic-specific constructions, but not beyond that, although there are Australian languages with other types of nominal classification (see Louagie 2020 for an overview).

1.3.3 Languages

My sample is primarily a convenience sample, since many grammars of Pama-Nyungan languages provide limited information about compounds. I include twenty-four languages in the analysis, diverse enough genealogically and areally to be representative of Pama-Nyungan languages in general. I had to exclude various lineages because I could not find information on compounds in their grammars. The map in Figure 1 shows the areal and genealogical distribution of the sample.[10] If a language is classified as 'not related at a lower level', this does not mean that a language is a primary branch of the Pama-Nyungan family, but that none of the other languages in the sample is closely related to it. Throughout this chapter, I follow the language names currently used by Glottolog (Hammarström et al. 2021).[11]

---

[9] In one language, Paakantyi [DRL], inalienable possession can also be expressed with a genitive suffix when the possessor is human (Hercus 1982: 75–76). In this case, I choose to only consider inalienable possession constructions with non-human possessors. If human possessors were to be included for this language, this would have minimal consequences for my analysis. It would add a non-compound related construction in the 'inalienable possession' category to Paakantyi in §3, but at the same time it would make the presentation more complex with no apparent benefit to the explanations.

[10] Tindale's map (1974), the AIATSIS map (Horton & Australian Institute of Aboriginal and Torres Strait Islander Studies 2000) and Glottolog (Hammarström et al. 2021) provided the starting point for the map used here. Glottolog was my source for genealogical data.

[11] An anonymous reviewer noted that, since the sample contains descriptions of varying depth and reliability, it may be better to focus on the best sources instead of attempting to be representative. I agree that representativeness is mostly unachievable for Pama-Nyungan lan-

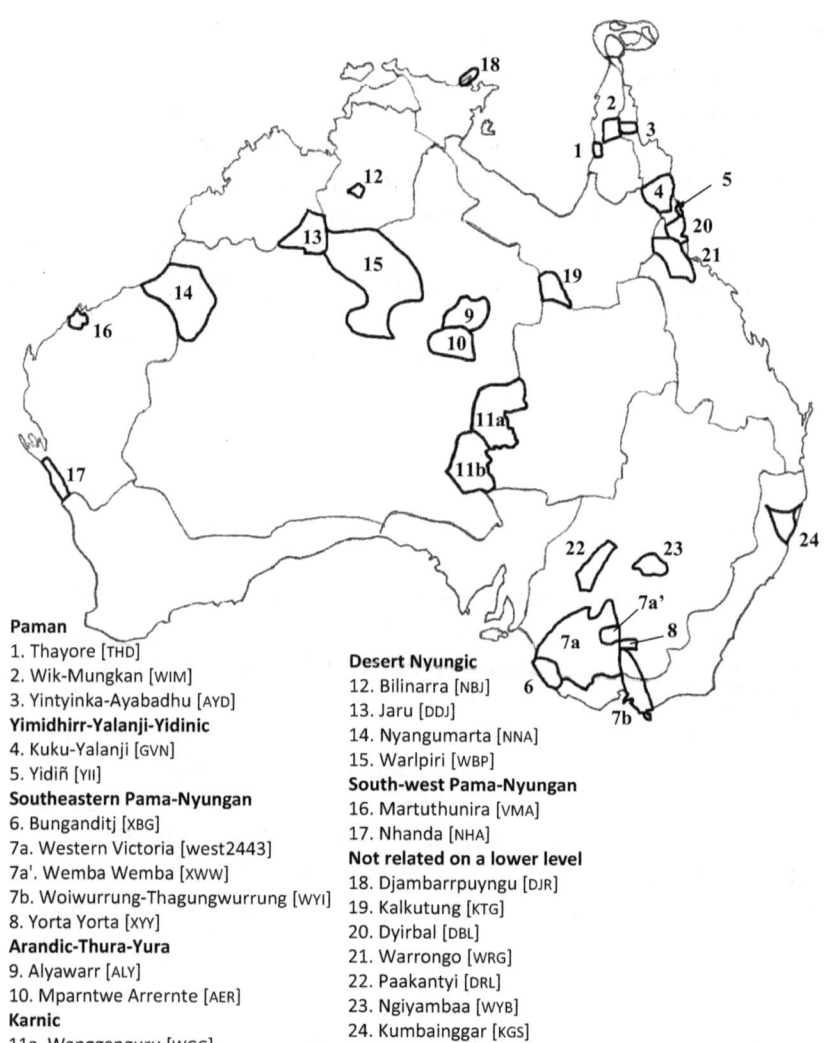

Figure 1: Map of languages in the sample.

---

guages. However, there is a danger in focusing exclusively on those few languages that are best described. One should be cautious of conclusions about Pama-Nyungan languages in general based on a (detailed) study of just a few languages. Binominal constructions in Thayore [THD], for instance, tell us something about binominal constructions in that language only, and have to be compared with binominal constructions in as many other languages as possible before we can even attempt to conclude anything about the nature of binominal constructions in

The main sources used for each language are the following. The sources in (a) contain some analysis of compounds and/or related constructions. The sources in (b) mention a category of compounds – sometimes just in passing – and give a few examples, but they do not provide an explicit analysis of compounds or how they may be different from (binominal) phrases.

a) Arabana-Wangganguru: Arabana [ARD] & Wangganguru [WGG] (Hercus 1994); Paakantyi [DRL] (Hercus 1982); Djambarrpuyngu [DJR] (Wilkinson 1991); Jaru [DDJ] (Tsunoda 1981); Kuku-Yalanji [GVN] (Patz 2002); The Kulin group: Woiwurrung-Thagungwurrung [WYI], Wemba Wemba [XWW] & Western Victoria [glottocode: west2443][12] (Blake 1991, 2011; Hercus 1992); Thayore [THD] (Gaby 2006a); Martuthunira [VMA] (Dench 1994); Mparntwe Arrernte [AER] (Wilkins 1989); Nhanda [NHA] (Blevins 2001); Warlpiri [WBP] (Simpson 2009); Warrongo [WRG] (Tsunoda 2011); Wik-Mungkan [WIM] (Kilham 1974); Yintyinka-Ayabadhu [AYD] (Verstraete & Rigsby 2015).
b) Bunganditj [XBG] (Blake 2003); Dyirbal [DBL] (Dixon 1972); Kumbainggar [KGS] (Eades 1979); Kalkutung [KTG] (Blake 1979); Ngiyambaa [WYB] (Donaldson 1980); Nyangumarta [NNA] (Sharp 1998); Yidiñ [YII] (Dixon 1977); Yorta Yorta [XYY] (Bowe & Morey 1999)

My source for Alyawarr [ALY] (Yallop 1977) mentions the term "compound" several times, with some analysis. But when it does, the description only gives examples of reduplication and verbal compounding: it presents no instances of (bi)nominal compounds. Finally, for Bilinarra [NBJ], Meakins & Nordlinger (2014) do not mention nominal compounding. In Meakins' (2013) Multimedia Database, I did not find any

---

Pama-Nyungan languages in general. An illustration of this danger is the widespread idea that Australian languages have unusually flexible noun phrase structures. A study of just a few well-known striking cases leads to different conclusions from a study of a broader typological sample (cf. Louagie & Verstraete 2016). Where relevant, I mention what data is available and what data is missing for languages in the sample.

12 Western Victoria only has a Glottocode, no ISO-code. It is not listed as a separate language in the ISO 639-3 list. Glottolog and ISO 639-3 make different decisions on whether Western Victoria is a group of dialects (Glottolog's position) or a group of languages (the ISO 639-3 position). The languages ISO 639-3 includes in the Western Victoria group, with their ISO 639-3 codes, are Djabwurrung [TJW], Wergaia [WEG], Ladji Ladji [LLJ], Madhi Madhi [DMD], Nari Nari [RNR], Wadi Wadi [XWD], Barababaraba [RBP], and Wemba Wemba [XWW]. I count them as one language, like Glottolog, because one of my main sources, Blake (2011), treats three varieties of Western Victoria in one, and it was impossible to separate them in my analysis: Jardwadjali (which does not have an ISO 639-3 code or a Glottocode), Djabwurrung [TJW], and Djadjawurrung [DJA] (which is not in Glottolog). I treat Wemba Wemba [XWW] separately, because one source, Hercus (1992), is dedicated solely to that variety.

examples of compounds either. This language was kept in the sample, however, because it may be an example of a language which simply has no formal distinction between compounds and different kinds of nominal modification constructions.

For each language in the sample, I compiled a datasheet summarizing the available information on binominal compounds and other relevant constructions. These datasheets can be found in the appendix of Lesage (2014).[13]

2 Properties of binominal constructions in individual languages

2.1 Overview

Within the sample of Pama-Nyungan languages, different types of binominal constructions can be distinguished and/or grouped together based on phonological, prosodic, morphological, syntactic and semantic properties. All properties recurring in Pama-Nyungan languages also occur as properties of compounds in other languages of the world (cf. Aikhenvald 2007; Bauer 2006, 2009; Lieber & Štekauer 2009; Haspelmath & Sims 2010).

The properties that have received the most attention in the Australianist literature are semantic, viz. exocentricity and non-compositionality (e.g. MacFarlane 1987; Simpson 2009; Baker 2018). In §2.2, I argue that these properties are neither necessary nor sufficient to distinguish compounds from phrases in Pama-Nyungan languages. Both exocentricity and non-compositionality can be reduced to figurativity (e.g. metonymy or metaphoric speech), which is a general characteristic of language and not of any binominal construction in specific. In addition, compositionality is hard to assess, and judgements of compositionality depend on the contextual and cultural knowledge of the observer. Moreover, even if absence of compositionality is a common (but not defining) feature in compounds, which it may well be, this is because compounds often lexicalize and lose their original compositional meaning – not because it is an inherent characteristic of compounds.

After abandoning exocentricity and compositionality as criteria for distinguishing different binominal constructions, I turn to formal properties, which are easier to operationalize. In §2.3, I discuss phonological criteria such as boundary phenomena between two nominals, different stress patterns, and secondary phonological processes triggered by these boundary phenomena and stress pat-

---

13 See https://zenodo.org/record/2447347#.XBtnNM17lPY.

terns. In §2.4, I mention morphosyntactic criteria, viz. the locus of case markers, the presence of linking morphemes and different ordering of modifier and head. In §2.4.4, I briefly discuss other syntactic criteria that could not be used in the sample due to the limits posed by the data.

§2.5 provides an overview of the criteria that could be applied to the sample and how they are distributed across languages. §3 illustrates which constructions can be found across languages, which distinctions are made, and which of the comparative concepts introduced in §1.3.1 may share properties across Pama-Nyungan languages.

2.2 Semantics: Exocentricity, compositionality and figurative speech

2.2.1 Exocentricity

MacFarlane (1987: 159) observes that "[t]he vast majority of compounds in Aboriginal languages are exocentric". Similarly, Simpson (2009: 615) concludes that in Warlpiri, nominal compounds are "overwhelmingly semantically exocentric". Following authors such as Booij (1992), Heyvaert (2009) and Bauer (2016), I argue that exocentricity is not an inherent or exclusive property of (a separate sub-type of) binominal compounds. Exocentric constructions are compounds or phrases that are interpreted figuratively, and although such figurative interpretations may be an interesting characteristic of some binominal compounds, it can hardly be used as a criterion to set apart a separate type of construction in a language.

Traditionally, a compound is considered exocentric if its "semantic head is 'outside' the compound" (Haspelmath and Sims 2010: 40), or more precisely, if the construction "denotes something which is not a sub-class of either of the elements in the compound" (Bauer 2003: 42). Such constructions are found in various languages in the sample, such as Djambarrpuyngu [DJR] (Wilkinson 1991: 528). (1) is not a 'song' or a 'big (one)', (2) is not a 'word' or a 'big (one)', and (3) is not a 'path'.

(1) DJR *manikay-ḏumurr* [song-big] 'someone who likes to sing'

(2) DJR *dhäruk-ḏumurr* [words-big] 'someone who likes to talk'

(3) DJR *dhuwurr-yätjkurr* [path-bad] 'sinner'

Such constructions also occur in other languages, usually referring to humans, animals or plants. In (4)–(7), *Jina-baji* does not refer to some sort of *jina* 'foot'; it refers to a *person* who *has* bad feet; *guṇḍu-jambi* is not a type of penis, but *someone who has* a long penis; *kuna-maju* refers to an emu, not to 'bad excrements'.

(4)   GVN *Jina-baji* [foot-sore] 'Sorefoot (nickname)' (Patz 2002: 11)

(5)   DDJ *guṇḍu-jambi* [penis-long] 'one who has a big penis' (Tsunoda 1981: 236)

(6)   WBP *kuna-maju* [anus/shit-bad] 'emu' (Simpson 2009: 611)

(7)   AER *alknge-therrke* [eye-green] 'cat' (Wilkins 1989: 146)

It is also possible to analyze these examples without exocentricity, however. In an overview of compounding in Dutch [NLD], Booij (1992: 39) presents the argument that apparently exocentric nominal compounds such as Dutch *bleekneus* [pale-nose] 'pale-nosed person' are simply cases of metonymically interpreted noun phrases: a person part term is used to refer to the person as a whole. They are not a separate morphosyntactic category. This analysis can be applied to the examples in (1)–(7) and to many alleged exocentric compounds in the sample. There is no need to interpret constructions such as (5) as being headless: a "long-penis person" could just be metonymically named after his long penis, and a cat, as in (7), after its "green eyes". It is not necessary to assume ellipsis of a head element. Other examples of compounds that are considered exocentric are not interpreted metonymically but metaphorically. (8) is an oyster that looks like a 'dog ear', in (9), the mainland is metaphorically depicted as a 'big thigh', and in (10), a barge is like a 'flat nose' (Wilkinson 1991: 528).

(8)   DJR *buthuru-wuŋgan* [ear-dog] 'hammer oyster'

(9)   DJR *makarr-yindi* [thigh-big] 'mainland'

(10) DJR *ŋurru-bilkpilk* [nose-flat] 'barge

2.2.2 Non-compositionality

MacFarlane (1987: 155–156) defines a compound as a unit with a "meaning which is not just the sum of the meanings of the components", thus setting it apart from close-knit phrases and generic-specific constructions. Baker (2018: 262, 267–268) distinguishes 'true', lexicalized (or Root-level) Compounds from incorporation constructions (which he calls Word-level compounds) in Gunwinyguan, partly based on their non-compositionality. When applied to the sample, this criterion is problematic for four reasons.

Firstly, many descriptions and much of the general literature contradict the observation that compounds are non-compositional. For Djambarrpuyngu, Wilkinson (1991: 547), for example, says that the meaning of a compound is usually transparent. Verstraete & Rigsby (2015: 143) find it easy to derive the meaning of suspected compounds in Yintyingka-Ayabadhu from their parts, even when they are conventionalized. Jackendoff (2009: 115) says that compounds, when newly formed, should be compositional to be interpretable. And Booij (2009) proposes a constructional schema that compositionally relates the structure of a compound to its meaning (cf. Baker 2014: 241–242).

Secondly, other constructions than compounds are sometimes called non-compositional, and it is not clear what kinds of meaningful distinctions a criterion of non-compositionality would allow us to make between constructions. Gaby (2006a: 84, 208) says that the meaning of some generic-specific constructions in Thayore is not compositional, which she also says about some (but not all) Compounds (Gaby 2006a: 205). Classifier constructions in some other languages are not always obviously compositional (Louagie 2020: 58). For more examples of non-compositional constructions that are not compounds, see Haspelmath & Sims (2010: 191).

Thirdly, and this is an underlying issue in many discussions of non-compositionality of compounds, there is no way to define compositionality in a way that accurately captures the distinction between compounds and other constructions. Compositionality can be defined in different ways. The most rigid definitions say that compositionality requires a mathematical formula that completely derives the meaning of an expression from the meaning of the parts and the way in which they are combined:

(11) "the meaning of a complex expression is fully determined by its structure and the meanings of its constituents – once we fix what the parts mean and how they are put together we have no more leeway regarding the meaning of the whole." (Szabó 2017)

This definition leaves no room for the many different meanings a newly created compound could have out of context: is a meat stone a stone made of meat, a stone used to grind meat, a stone in the shape of meat? In principle, it could be ambiguous between these meanings (and more, see Pepper, this volume). The context in which a compound occurs usually resolves such ambiguity. Neither ambiguity nor context-dependence are directly covered by the definition in (11). So we may be tempted to say that compounds are non-compositional. However, the same can be said of many other constructions, such as noun incorporation in

Wubuy, where the relationship between the noun and the verb may be one of a number of options (Baker 2014).[14] Or possessive constructions in English, where many possible relationships may hold between possessor and possessee (Spencer 2011: 500).[15] Even basic locational predication clauses such as *the ball is under the table* need information outside of the actual syntactic structure before their specific meaning is known (Langacker 1999: 63–64). It is not clear how this definition helps us delimit one construction from another in a meaningful manner.

Another perspective on compositionality incorporates pragmatic information into the definition of a construction. One could say that the meaning of a compound is a result of the meaning of the parts and a relation between them that is arbitrarily, contextually or pragmatically determined (Spencer 2011: 490, citing Downing 1977). This is how many authors implicitly use the concept (e.g. Booij 2009, cited in Spencer 2011: 498). But, given the broad scope of the possible relation between the parts, which may even be arbitrarily determined, almost any compound could be considered compositional. It is difficult to establish what would count as a non-compositional expression under this definition, beyond those expressions where one of the constituents is a cranberry morph and has no clear meaning of its own.[16] Gaby (2006a: 205–206) gives some examples of compounds in Thayore which are not clearly compositional, but also not clearly non-compositional. In *thaa-porpr* [mouth-soft] 'kind', one could argue that softness is associated with kindness or that the softness of one's mouth may be folklorically linked to kindness. *Kun-yangkar* [bum-calf] 'sibling' reflects a link between shins and siblings that has a cultural parallel in grieving rituals, where women gash their shins to lament their dead siblings. And *meer-pork* [eye-big] 'star' may be a metaphorical description of stars like big eyes. It is reasonable to assume that at their inception all compounds are compositional in a broad sense, and that it is only after repeated usage that the link between the form and the meaning of the parts may fade. But at what point does the meaning become non-transparent? And who decides whether this is the case? A speaker? A linguistic community as a whole? The fieldworker?[17] The reader of a grammar?

---

14 For example, *numba-mung-gujugujang* [2SG>1-hair-tickle] can mean both 'You tickled me in the hair.' or 'You tickled me with your hair.'
15 For example, *Lora's apartment* can mean 'the apartment Lora owns', 'the apartment Lora rents', 'the apartment Lora drew/described/likes/painted', and the like.
16 Cranberry morphs violate the Domain Condition for compositionality, which requires that the parts should have a meaning by themselves (cf. Salo & Sandu 2006: 717).
17 During field work on Kam [KDX], a Niger-Congo language of Nigeria, some of my consultants rejected my analysis of *màn àlíb* [fat head] 'brain' as 'fat of the head', although the meaning seemed completely transparent to me.

This brings us to the fourth reason (non-)compositionality is a problematic criterion. Even if we allow a broad, culturally and contextually enriched definition in our compositionality judgements, there is never enough contextual or cultural information available in a grammar (or in any source, for that matter) to know whether the meaning of a seemingly non-transparent compound is compositional or not. As a result, we may never be able to determine whether some compounds are compositional.[18]

To conclude, there is no current definition of compositionality that captures the semantic difference between compounds and other constructions. Under a rigid definition, all language in natural interaction could be considered non-compositional. Under a more lenient definition, considering context and all sorts of cultural knowledge, any compound with meaningful parts may be compositional, depending on who is the judge. When non-compositionality unambiguously applies, e.g. when one item of the compound is no longer meaningful or when a metaphor has become opaque, this is an artefact of lexicalization. While some authors suggest that a binominal construction has to be lexicalized to be considered a "true" compound (e.g. Baker 2014: 253), lexicalized compounds are not necessarily indicative of how compounding in general works in a language (cf. Spencer 2011, citing Ricca 2010: 249–253). When we study derivational processes such as causatives or nominalization, we do not limit ourselves to lexicalized cases, so I see no reason we should consider a lexicalized compound as more prototypical than a productively formed compound.

2.2.3 Figurativity in compounds

I have argued why I do not distinguish between endocentric and exocentric constructions in this chapter, and why I do not buy into (non-)compositionality. An issue that came up a few times is figurativity, i.e. metaphorical and metonymic reference to things. For several languages, all the compounds I could identify made use of figurative speech. This is the case for Djambarrpuyngu, Jaru, Dyir-

---

18 It is interesting to note that in formal semantics, logic and related fields, compositionality is accepted as a methodology but not frequently considered as a principle that can be empirically tested. Montague (1973), for example, did not treat it as a hypothesis that was open to discussion but as a starting point for his analysis. Once a phenomenon needs contextual or pragmatic information, logicians and formal semanticists will easily accept non-compositional methods (Janssen 2012). In the same way, one could say that it is interesting to see how compositional methods may be applied to compounds, but less interesting to test whether there is a given definition of compositionality that may or may not apply as a criterion for compoundhood.

bal,[19] Kuku-Yalanji and Nhanda (see §2.2.1 for examples). In these languages, compounding may be inextricably linked with figurativity, even if compounds are not otherwise different from nominal modification constructions. I briefly come back to the potential significance of this in §4.2.

2.2.4 Compound-specific cranberry morphs

In §2.2.2, I briefly mentioned cranberry morphs, as well as bound non-phonological allomorphs of lexical elements that only occur in compounds (cf. Aikhenvald 2007: 26). In this section, I give an overview of such elements in the sample.

In Mparntwe Arrernte, there are at least three bound morphs that only occur in compounds. *ake-* 'head', *akwe-* 'hand/arm' and *arre-* 'mouth' frequently occur as the first member of compounds (Wilkins 1989: 145–146). When these meanings are expressed in isolation, the free forms *(a)kaperte*, *iltye/amwelte* and *arrekerte* are used.

(12) AER *ake-ngkwerne* [head-bone] 'skull' (Wilkins 1989: 146)

(13) AER *akwe-alyenge* /akwalyenge/ [hand/arm-left.hand/arm] 'left hand/arm' (Wilkins 1989: 146)

(14) AER *arre-urrperle* /arrurrperle/ [mouth-black] 'black-mouth snake' (Wilkins 1989: 146)

Bound lexical stems of this kind often correspond to free forms in neighbouring languages. Wilkins (1989: 146) reports that Kaytetye [GBB], a language that is closely related to Mparntwe Arrernte, has *ake*, *akwe* and *arre* as free forms. In most cases, the compound-specific lexemes are more conservative forms than their free counterparts. For Arabana-Wangganguru, Hercus (1994: 28–29) shows that the difference between the regular and the compound-specific term for a concept may be the result of a sound change. In (15), the compound form of *pitha* shows the archaic use of a palatal *ty* instead of the modern dental *th*.

(15) ARD & WGG *pitya-murru* [box.tree-bark?] 'box bark' (Hercus 1994: 29) (expected: **pitha-murru*)

---

19 For Dyirbal, Dixon (1972) gives only one example of a compound.

Although the evidence suggests that processes of lexicalization may lead to the retention of these compound-specific elements, it is not entirely clear from the description whether elements like Mparntwe Arrernte *ake*, *akwe* and *arre* may still be used productively to form compounds.

Cranberry morphs are found in Arabana-Wangganguru (15), Mparntwe Arrernte (12)–(14), Djambarrpuyngu (16), the Kulin group (17) and Thayore (18). I expect this feature to be more widespread.

(16) DJR *mel-parrambarr* [eye-?] 'eyebrow' (Wilkinson 1991: 129)

(17) Western Victoria, Wemba Wemba variety [xww]
mirri-kar [?-leg] 'tree frog' (Hercus 1992: 29)

(18) THD *pil-perrk* [hip-?] 'hipbone' (Gaby 2006a: 206)

2.3 Phonological criteria

2.3.1 Boundary phenomena

If two stems combine, something may happen to the final sounds of the first stem or the initial sounds of the second element. The result is that the two parts become more fused. Generally, a process of simplification is involved. There are several ways in which sounds may be simplified. Sometimes, a phoneme or consonant cluster is elided. This may happen either to stem-initial syllables or consonants, or to stem-final syllables or vowels. Alternatively, a second stem's onset may be lenited (weakened to a semivowel or fricated). Table 1 summarizes the boundary phenomena found in the sample.

Three languages show elision of stem-final central vowels: low-central /a/ for Paakantyi and Yorta Yorta, mid-central /ə/ for Mparntwe Arrernte.[20] As Table 1 shows, lenition of word-initial stops occurs in three languages (Paakantyi, Djambarrpuyngu and Thayore).

---

[20] For Yorta-Yorta, the relevant examples may be due to hiatus resolution, where a stem-final *a* is dropped if it is followed by a vowel. The main source does not discussed this, however, so it may still be a compound-specific phenomenon (Bowe & Morey 1999). For Arabana-Wangganguru, Paakantyi, and Mparntwe Arrernte, however, examples are also found where one would not expect hiatus resolution. I would like to thank an anonymous reviewer for pointing out the potential relevance of hiatus resolution to this analysis.

It is not clear to what extent boundary phenomena are the result of compounding or of lexicalization accompanied by attrition. Do nonce-compounds, created on the spot, exhibit the same simplification processes, or are boundaries simply eroded due to routinized co-occurrence of two adjacent nominals (cf. Brinton and Traugott 2005: 54)? For the data under consideration this is hard to tell since the grammars do not describe differences between newly created and lexicalized compounds. However, boundary phenomena that distinguish different types of binominal constructions are by no means cross-linguistically exceptional, so they will be treated as a synchronic means of distinguishing different binominal constructions here.[21]

2.3.2 Stress patterns

In several languages, stress can distinguish between different types of binominal constructions. This distinction works in different ways. In some languages, compounds are characterized by a reversed order of stress. In the following minimal pair from Wik-Mungkan, (19) exhibits the phrasal stress pattern, where primary stress falls on the second part, the adjective. In (20), however, the first element – a noun – receives main stress. This identifies (20) as a compound in Kilham's (1974) analysis of Wik-Mungkan.

(19) WIM ɲaŋk ˈway [heart bad] 'bad heart' (constructed for illustrative purposes)

(20) WIM ˈɲaŋk-way [heart-bad] 'out of breath' (Kilham 1974: 50, my stress indication)

In Warrongo, the stress pattern is not reversed. Rather, the main difference is that a certain construction has only one clear prosodic peak where other constructions may have two main peaks (Tsunoda 2011: 135).[22]

---

[21] See, for example, compounds and possessive constructions in Slave [DEN] (Athabaskan, Rice 2009).
[22] In Thayore, this criterion distinguishes verbal compounds from phrasal N-V combinations (Gaby 2006a: 146n). It cannot distinguish binominal compounds from phrases since noun phrases, just like compounds, always have exactly one prosodic peak (Gaby 2006a: 278).

Table 1: Boundary phenomena in the sample.

Language	Construction	Rule	Examples
Alyawarr	Compound?[23]	Elision of stem-initial /gh/	*agharta-agharta* → /aghartarta/ [aggressive-aggressive] 'cheeky, a nuisance' (Yallop 1977: 20)
Arabana	Compound	Elision of stem-initial /k/	*pantya-kardi* → /pantyaardi/ [knee-fruit/clitoris] 'kneecap' (Hercus 1994: 101)
Arabana-Wangkangurru	Compound	Elision of CV syllables	*maka-wimpa* → /makampa/ [fire-track] 'Macumba' (Hercus 1994: 57)
Djambarrpuyngu	Compound	Lenition of stem-initial peripheral/laminal stops	*mel-porum* → /mi:lwu:rum/ [eye/seed-edible fruit/ripe, cooked] 'boy ready to be circumcised' (Wilkinson 1991: 75)[24]
Mparntwe Arrernte	Compound	Elision of stem-final /ə/	*arre-yenpe* → /arryenpe/ [mouth-skin] 'lips' (Wilkins 1989: 145)
Paakantyi	Compound	Elision of stem-final /a/	*duḷaga-ŋugu* → /dulagŋugu/ [bad-water] 'alcohol' (Hercus 1982: 283, 305)
Thayore	Compound	Frication of onset	*meer-punk* → /me:ɹβuŋk/ [eye-knee] 'eyebrow' (Gaby 2006a: 34, 140) *riing-ka:l* → /ɻɪ:nɣa:l/ [?-ear] 'leaf' (Gaby 2006a: 34)
Yorta Yorta	Compound	Elision of CV syllables	*dungudja-wala* → /dungula/ [big-water] 'the Murray River' (Bowe & Morey 1999: 38) *galnya-buga* → /galnyoga/ [good-head] 'bald' (Bowe & Morey 1999: 167)
Yorta Yorta	Compound	Elision of stem-final /a/	*nayga-idjiga* → /naygidjiga/ [duck-little] 'little duck' (Bowe & Morey 1999: 38, 182)

In the sample, nine languages have specialized stress patterns for (a sub-type of) Compounds (summarized in Table 2). Arabana-Wangganguru distinguishes yet another category, *prefixed nouns*, based on a third stress pattern (only one stress accent, falling on the second element).

---

[23] Yallop does not give examples of binominal compounds. In fact, this example (reduplication) is the only one he mentions (1977: 20). I include Alyawarr in this table because the grammar describes this elision as a general feature of compounds, so I assume that it also occurs in binominal compounds, if there are any such constructions.

[24] *o* in *porum* is an orthographic representation of /u:/. I would like to thank an anonymous reviewer for pointing this out.

Table 2: Stress patterns in different binominal constructions.

Language	Construction	Stress pattern
Arabana-Wangganguru	Compound	Primary stress on first stem
	Prefixed noun (generic-specific)	Primary stress on second stem
Wik-Mungkan	Close-knit phrase	Primary stress on second stem
	Compound	Primary stress on first stem
Djambarrpuyngu Jaru Kuku-Yalanji Martuthunira Nhanda	Compound	Primary stress on first stem
Warrongo	Compound	Stress on second stem (only one peak)

2.3.3 Secondary phonological processes

Across the sample, a few secondary phonological processes are found. They are called secondary because they are all caused by one of the phonological phenomena in §2.3.1 and §2.3.2.

A first example is found in Arabana-Wangganguru. Because the second member of a compound nominal is not fully stressed, pre-stopping of laterals and nasals is blocked (Hercus 1994: 40–41). Something similar occurs in Alyawarr: when two stems are compounded, a nasally released plosive (e.g. kŋ, pm) may shift to a non-initial position, which results in simplification to a nasal (Yallop 1977: 18), as shown in (21). Yallop does not explicitly associate this with changing stress. He says that this applies to compounds in general, but he does not provide any examples of nominal compounds, only verbal ones.

(21) ALY *aylpura-akngima* /aylpuraɲima/ [carry-shoulder] 'carry on the shoulder' (Yallop 1977: 18)

Another secondary phonological process associated with compounding is found in Paakantyi. Paakantyi words usually do not end in consonants (Hercus 1982: 15) or begin with consonant clusters (Hercus 1982: 48). In compounds, a final low-central vowel /a/ can be lost, which may result in uncommon consonant clusters at morpheme boundaries.

(22) DRL *duḷaga-wada* /duḷagwada/ [bad-heel] 'evil-smelling' (Hercus 1982: 42, my glosses)

2.4 Morphological and syntactic criteria

2.4.1 Locus of case marking

In most languages in the sample, compounds are inflected as a whole, and case markers attach to the right edge of the construction. This property of compounds, observed in languages around the world (cf. Aikhenvald 2007: 26; Bauer 2009: 346; Haspelmath and Sims 2010: 193), contrasts with case marking on nominal modification constructions: in some languages in the sample, case markers may attach to both nominals in the phrase simultaneously, or they may be inserted in between the two nominals as a suffix on the first stem.

Ngiyambaa allows case markers on either member of a nominal modification construction. In the following examples, (23) could be assigned potential compound status (at least if 'long' is a classifying modifier, and (23) is a name for a kind of grass, which is not clear from the source). For (24), a nominal modification construction, an interpretation as compound is not possible since the ergative case suffix comes on the first element.

(23) WYB (Ngiyambaa)
 guṟun   ba:mir-a
 grass   long-LOC
 'among the long grass' (Donaldson 1980: 232)

(24) WYB (Ngiyambaa)
 mugabangay-gu   miri
 skinny-ERG   dog
 'skinny dog' (Donaldson 1980: 232)

This is an interesting criterion for two reasons. Firstly, because it raises the question how different (or similar) binominal compounds are from zero-marked nominal modification constructions. And secondly, because it has different implications for compounds (and their relationship to phrases) in phrase-marking and word-marking languages.

Some argument functions have a zero-case form for nominals across Australian languages, specifically the absolutive ones (marking intransitive subject and transitive object) (Dixon 2002a: 153). A sequence of nominals that agree in absolutive case is thus, in isolation, formally indistinguishable from a sequence of nominals that is inflected on the last element only. For instance, it is impossible to tell whether the following examples in Ngiyambaa are marked as a whole or on each individual noun (Donaldson 1980: 230–231).

(25) WYB (Ngiyambaa)
 gugugun ŋamu
 cow(.ABS?) breast/milk(.ABS?)
 'cow's udder/cow's milk (when it is still inside the cow)'

(26) WYB (Ngiyambaa)
 dhagar malda
 ice(.ABS?) lump(.ABS?)
 'lump of ice'

Donaldson analyses them as phrases but says that "[s]ometimes collocations of this kind become fixed as compound nominals" (1980: 230). She cites (27) as an example of such a compound.

(27) WYB *wi:m-bara:n* [fire-rib] 'fire's rib/the smokeless area of ground around a fire'

Lexicalization, however, is not a part of my definition of compound (cf. §2.2.2). Even if (25) and (26) are not lexicalized, they may be interpreted as compounds created on the spot (i.e. as on-line compounds). In Ngiyambaa and other languages that have zero case marking of some phrases and no other formal differences to set them apart from binominal compounds, there may be a tight link between binominal compounds and zero-marked descriptive phrases. This point applies to many languages in the sample. It raises the question whether compounds in some languages may be recruited from absolutive noun phrases. Note in this context that many compounds denote inanimate or non-human animate entities, which are typically low on an animacy hierarchy and which often occur in an unmarked patient function.[25]

The second interesting issue concerns this criterion's different consequences for phrase-marking and word-marking languages. Australian languages can be divided into those that carry case marking on the noun phrase as a whole (i.e. phrase-marking), those that have case markers on each individual word in the noun phrase (i.e. word-marking), and those that allow both.[26] To give some examples, Thayore and Mparntwe Arrernte always have case marking at the end of the noun phrase (Gaby 2006a: 12, 277; Wilkins 1989: 102); Nyangumarta has case marking on each individual element of the noun phrase (Sharp 1998: 391), and

---

[25] Although it speaks against this suggestion that these entities may just as well, or possibly more frequently occur in oblique functions (as instruments, locations, . . .) where they *are* typically marked overtly. In addition, human names may also be compounds.
[26] This presentation simplifies the issue. See Louagie & Verstraete (2016) for a more elaborate discussion of the phrase-marking vs. word-marking typology.

while Warlpiri and Ngiyambaa usually feature word marking, NP-final phrase-marking also regularly occurs (Simpson 1983: 215; Donaldson 1980: 232). Table 3 summarizes word-marking and phrase-marking in the sample.

In phrase-marking languages, binominal compounds are more like descriptive phrases in terms of case marking. In the languages where phrase-marking is optional, there is a formal overlap between descriptive phrases that are only marked at the end of the noun phrase and binominal compounds. In these cases binominal compounds may be considered a subcategory of regular syntactic phrases (cf. Simpson 2009 and see §4.2 below).

Table 3: Phrase marking vs. word marking languages in the sample.

Strictly word-marking [N-CASE + N-CASE . . .]$_{NP}$ 11 languages	Bilinarra Djambarrpuyngu Dyirbal Kumbainggar Kalkutung Kuku-Yalanji[27] Martuthunira Nyangumarta Yidiñ Yorta Yorta[28] Warrongo
Phrase marking[29] [[N + N . . .]-CASE]$_{NP}$ 7 languages	Alyawarr[30] Arabana-Wangganguru[31] Mparntwe Arrernte Paakantyi Thayore Wik-Mungkan Yintyinka-Ayabadhu

---

27 Patz (2002: 119) claims that possessive constructions do not require case-marking on the possessive form if they appear contiguously. However, she does not give any examples.
28 The data cited by Bowe and Morey (1999) suggest this type for Yorta Yorta. It cannot be claimed with absolute certainty, however, as there is little reliable data.
29 In the sample, languages of this category always mark case on the right edge of the noun phrase. In other Australian languages, only the head may be marked, or only the first word of a noun phrase, or any word may be inflected for case (Dixon 2002a: 144).
30 If all noun phrase members are marked for case, the noun phrase structure is not rendered ungrammatical (Yallop 1977: 116). Whether this changes the function or turns the elements into individual apposed noun phrases is unclear, but it does not appear to be not the default option.
31 If the final noun phrase member is an adjective modifying a preceding noun, this noun may also carry case marking (Hercus 1994: 282–283). In this case, one could argue that the adjective forms an apposed noun phrase of its own.

Table 3 (continued)

Not strictly word-marking[32] [N(-CASE)...N(-CASE)]_NP 4 languages	Jaru Ngiyambaa Nhanda Warlpiri
Not clear from sources 2 languages	Bunganditj Kulin group

2.4.2 Linking morphemes

In Arabana-Wangganguru, a nasal with the same point of articulation as the following consonant may be inserted at the juncture between compound members, e.g. in (28). Hercus (1994: 56) suggests that this nasal links the parts of a compound noun. It occurs without phonological motivation.[33]

(28) ARD & WGG *Midlha-n-thupu-nha* [face-n-smoke-PN] 'Smokey Face (name)' (Hercus 1994: 56)

In the Kulin group, a linker *-i-* is often found connecting members of whole-part compounds.[34]

(29) Western Victoria (glottocode: west2443)
purrp-i-lar [head-*i*-hut] 'roof' (Blake 2011: 33)

(30) Western Victoria (glottocode: west2443)
kalk-i purrp [bone-*i* head] 'skull'
(Blake 2011: 50)

As in Arabana-Wangganguru, insertion of this element is not phonologically motivated. Blake (2011: 33) translates *-i-* as a possessive affix or possessive index,

---

[32] At least one of two adjacent noun phrase elements has to be marked.
[33] An anonymous reviewer suggested that this section be moved to §2.3 on phonological criteria. I consider this a morphological argument, however, since these linking morphemes are (a) not phonologically motivated and (b) markers of a specific construction, and thus arguably morphosyntactic. Cross-linguistically, these morphemes are often related to genitive markers or other inflectional material (cf. Bauer 2009: 346 – see also Creissels, this volume).
[34] Blake (2011: 33) simply calls them "compounds". However, they have a different word order from (other) compounds in Kulin, which is why I mention them as a separate category.

meaning 'its', e.g. for (29) 'head-its-roof'. Elsewhere he suggests that it may in fact be the locative marker -*i* (e.g. head-in-hut) (2011: 50). Here, I prefer to analyze it as a semantically empty element, the sole function of which is to indicate the connection between two parts of a compound.[35]

2.4.3 Order of modifier and head

Verstraete and Rigsby (2015: 143) analyze Yintyingka-Ayabadhu whole-part constructions as compounds. One of their arguments is the modifier-head word order of these constructions, which differs from the canonical head-modifier order in descriptive noun phrases. So, in Yintyingka-Ayabadhu, there may not be a clear formal difference between binominal compounds and contiguous inalienable possession constructions (cf. §4.2). In the sample, eleven languages display word order differences across different binominal constructions, viz. Alyawarr, Arabana-Wangkangurru, Djambarrpuyngu, Jaru, Nhanda, the Kulin group, Mparntwe Arrernte, Thayore, Warlpiri, Wik-Mungkan and Yintyingka-Ayabadhu. The word order differences can be of two kinds: word order may be either free or fixed, and constructions with fixed word order may be head-modifier or modifier-head.

Sometimes one construction (e.g. a compound) follows a strict word order pattern whereas in other constructions (e.g. a descriptive phrase) the order of modifier and head is free. This is the case in Djambarrpuyngu and in Nhanda, where compounds always exhibit head-modifier order but other binominal constructions have no clear word order restrictions (Wilkinson 1991: 528–529). In Jaru, compounds have a head-modifier order, inalienable possession constructions have a modifier-head order, but the order in other constructions is free. The same may apply to the Kulin group (although with reversed order: Compounds have a modifier-head order and inalienable constructions have head-modifier order). However, syntactic data for the Kulin languages is particularly scarce, so it is not possible to say for certain how restricted N-Adj noun phrases are. Table 4 summarizes the data for the languages that distinguish free vs. fixed word orders.

---

[35] Bauer (2009: 346) mentions that Kuku-Yalanji also has linking morphemes in compounds. Upon closer investigation, these linking elements only occur in a specific type of verbal compounds, i.e. "Action-causative compounds with -*mani-l*" (Patz 2002: 99–100). They are not relevant to a discussion of nominal compounds.

Table 4: Word order in different binominal constructions: free vs. fixed.[36]

Language	Construction	Word order
Djambarrpuyngu	N-Adj phrase	No restriction
	Generic-specific	No restriction
	Inalienable possession	No restriction
	Compound	**head-modifier**
Nhanda	N-Adj phrase	No restriction
	(Generic-specific)	(Not attested)
	Inalienable possession	No restriction
	Compound	**head-modifier**
Jaru	N-Adj phrase	No restriction
	Generic-specific	No restriction
	Inalienable possession	**modifier-head**
	Compound	**head-modifier**
Kulin group	N-Adj phrase (?)	No restriction?[37]
	(Generic-specific)	(Not attested)
	Inalienable possession	**head-modifier**
	Adj-N Compound	**modifier-head**

In other languages, the (main) difference is not that one construction has a free order and another construction has a fixed order. Instead, there is (also) a difference between constructions that have modifier- head order and constructions that have head-modifier order. This is the case in nine languages, as summarized in Table 5. The following generalizations can be made:

In most languages, a distinction exists between N-Adj phrases (descriptive phrases) and N-N phrases (inalienable possession + generic-specific constructions).

In two languages (viz. Arabana-Wangganguru and Mparntwe Arrernte), this distinction is mirrored in compounds, where there is a split between N-Adj compounds (which reflect the N-Adj phrase order) and N-N Compounds (which reflect the N-N phrase order).

Jaru and the Kulin group were already mentioned with Table 4: these show a split between constructions with and without a fixed order. In both cases, the constructions with a fixed order are (1) inalienable possession constructions and (2) Compounds.

---

36 I thank an anonymous reviewer for suggestions on how to structure these tables.
37 Most of the primary data was collected in the late 19th century. It is not clear whether there was a preferred order of modifier and head. An early 20th century author claims that adjectives usually come after nouns, although according to Blake (2011: 33) this is not consistent with the data, which also shows adjectives preceding nouns.

For Kumbainggar, Eades (1979: 335) cites the following minimal pair differing only in meaning and word order. These differences could indicate two different construction types or they may be instances of the same construction with a free word order. Since Eades (1979) does not go in further detail, not much else can be said.[38]

(31) KGS *ŋaːlgan-yuːŋgu* [ear-bad] 'someone who is slow to learn a language'

(32) KGS *yuːŋgu-ŋaːlgan* [bad-ear] 'stupid'

2.4.4 Other syntactic criteria

Other morphosyntactic criteria that are often used to distinguish different binominal constructions could unfortunately not be applied to the sample. They include i) the possibility to modify a modifier, ii) syntactic paraphrases with the modifier in predicative position, iii) the *pro-one* test and iv) the possibility of a binominal construction to occupy a single functional slot in the noun phrase.

2.4.4.1 The possibility to modify the modifier

In English, the adjective of an adjective-noun phrase can be modified by an adverb (e.g. *very black bird*). In compounds, this is not possible (**a very blackbird*). Baker (2014: 251, 2018: 263–264, cf. Evans 2003: 329) applies such tests to compounds in Gunwinyguan languages, a Non-Pama-Nyungan family, showing that incorporated nouns and modifiers in N-Adj compounds cannot be modified by numerals, demonstratives and other modifiers (degree adverbs are generally absent in Australian languages). It was impossible to perform such tests on the examples in the sample, since I use secondary data. In the grammars, syntactic tests of this kind are never described for compounds.[39]

---

38 A reviewer suggested that one of these is a compound and the other is a phrase since one has a compositional meaning but the other does not. It is not clear to me how any of the two examples is fully compositional. Is the meaning 'stupid' predictable from the meanings of 'bad' and 'ear'? To a speaker of a language where verbs for 'hearing' may be extended to mean 'knowing' (Evans & Wilkins 2000), maybe, but then it still requires a semantic leap from a thing, a 'bad ear', to a property, 'stupid', or a person/thing, 'stupid person/thing'. The meaning 'slow language learner' is also partly compositional – it is easy to see how someone with 'bad ears' may not be a good listener or learner – but also arguably non-compositional: a *ŋaːlgan-yuːŋgu* is not an ear, but a person who is metonymically referred to by their bad ears. See §2.2 for more on compositionality and figurativity.
39 They are mentioned in some cases for possessive noun phrases that may be cases of external possession (e.g. Wilkins 1989: 437–438).

If such modification could be tested, it may well turn out to be a robust cross-linguistic difference between compounds as defined in this chapter (i.e. where the modifier is a classifying modifier) and descriptive phrases (i.e. where the modifier is a qualifying modifier, cf. Rijkhoff 2008: 793–794). On the other hand, one could argue that this seemingly robust difference is logically dependent on the definition of compound I apply in this chapter. My definition holds that compounds have classifying modifiers. Since classifying modifiers are not descriptive and may sometimes even be seen as "meaningless tags" (Spencer 2011: 502), it is hard to see how they could be modified.[40]

Table 5: Word order in different binominal constructions: modifier-head vs. head-modifier.

Language	Construction	Word order
Alyawarr & Yintyingka-Ayabadhu	N-Adj phrase	head-modifier
	Generic-specific	modifier-head
	Inalienable possession	modifier-head
	(Compound)	(all are equivalent to inalienable possession phrases)
Arabana-Wangganguru	N-Adj phrase	head-modifier
	Generic-specific (prefixed noun)	modifier-head
	Inalienable possession	modifier-head
	N-N Compound	modifier-head
	N-Adj Compound	head-modifier
Jaru	N-Adj phrase	No restriction
	Generic-specific	No restriction
	Inalienable possession	modifier-head
	Compound	head-modifier
Kulin group	N-Adj phrase	No restriction?
	(Generic-specific)	(Not attested)
	Inalienable possession	head-modifier
	Compound	modifier-head
Mparntwe Arrernte	N-Adj phrase	head-modifier
	Generic-specific	modifier-head
	Inalienable possession	modifier-head
	N-N Compound	modifier-head
	N-Adj Compound	head-modifier

---

40 See also Giegerich's (2015) discussions of intersectiveness, subsectiveness and ascriptiveness of adjectives in English.

Table 5 (Continued)

Language	Construction	Word order
Thayore	N-Adj phrase	head-modifier
	Generic-specific	modifier-head
	Inalienable possession	modifier-head[41]
	N-N Compound	modifier-head
	N-Adj Compound	head-modifier
Warlpiri	N-Adj phrase	head-modifier
	(Generic-specific)	(Not attested)
	Inalienable possession	modifier-head
	(Compound)	(all are equivalent to N-Adj phrases)
Wik-Mungkan	N-Adj phrase	head-modifier
	Generic-specific construction	modifier-head
	Inalienable possession	modifier-head
	N-Adj Compound	head-modifier

2.4.4.2 Syntactic paraphrases with the modifier in predicative position

In English and in other languages, the meaning of adjective-noun phrases may be paraphrased by a copula clause with the head noun as (definite) copula subject and the adjective in predicate position: *a green house* → *the house is green*. This is not possible with compounds: *a greenhouse* → **the house is green*. As with the previous criterion, this property of compounds is directly linked with the classifying nature of the modifier in compounds: classifying modifiers cannot occur in a predicative position (Rijkhoff 2008: 473–474). This test is not mentioned in any of the sources used for the sample, though Baker (2014: 252–253; 2018: 262–263) discusses it for verbal compounds in a few non-Pama-Nyungan languages.

2.4.4.3 The pro-one test

Giegerich (2015: 103) describes the *pro-one* test for phrasal status in English, i.e. "the replacement of the head of a noun phrase by the pro-form *one*." *A black cupboard and a white one* is a valid English sentence. This test fails for many compounds: **a greenhouse and a white one*. There are some issues with this test, even in English (dis-

---

41 The analysis of Thayore inalienable possession constructions requires some justification. In the main reference for Thayore, I did not find inalienable possession constructions that were in line with the definition in the current chapter. The only examples in the relevant sections involve possessive pronominals or possessors referred to with proper nouns (Gaby 2006a: 325–333). Those examples, and the general analysis in this source, indicate a head-modifier order. In another source, I *did* find analogous examples (*kuta kaal* 'dog's ear', *meer panjr* 'eye's hairs') (Gaby 2006b: 204–205). I based the analysis in this chapter on the data from the second source.

cussed in Giegerich 2015). It would nonetheless be interesting to see how helpful it is for distinguishing different types of binominal constructions in Pama-Nyungan languages. It is not mentioned in any of the sources used for the sample in this study.[42]

2.4.4.4 Filling a single functional slot in the noun phrase

Some binominal constructions can function as a 'complex head' in the noun phrase, as a complex 'specific noun' in generic-specific constructions, or in a specific 'entity' slot in the noun phrase. Others cannot.

When a binominal construction functions as a complex nominal head, it can be modified as a whole by an adjective. When a binominal compound 'dog bone' is modified with the adjective 'big' in English (i.e. 'big dog bone'), then it is the 'dog bone' that is big, not necessarily the dog; the adjective qualifies the whole construction. When a possessive phrase 'dog's bone' is modified by 'big' (i.e. 'big dog's bone'), it may apply to the 'dog', but not to the bone. In this sense, the compound is a complex head while the possessive phrase is not. For Yintyinka-Ayabadhu, Verstraete & Rigsby (2015: 142, 144) propose an analysis of the generic-specific construction as a complex head in the noun phrase, where the generic and specific noun jointly fill the head slot. This head can then be modified by another noun or adjective, like the 'big dog bone' example.[43]

In some languages, the noun phrase can be analysed as a functional template where prenominal and postnominal modifiers are interpreted as respectively classifiers or qualifiers of the head nominal (e.g. McGregor 1990: 253). I will not go in further detail explaining this type of analysis and I refer the reader to McGregor (1990, 2004) and Louagie (2020: 35–38, 135–137) for more information. In such languages, a distinction could be made between binominal constructions that occupy the slot of the head nominal, and those that occupy two slots, as classifier + entity or as entity + qualifier. This criterion is difficult to operationalize because such tests cannot be applied to secondary data and because the understanding of functional slots appears to be quite different across languages.

In Pama-Nyungan languages with a generic-specific construction, some binominal constructions may fill the 'specific' slot, forming a complex specific noun. In Yintyingka-Ayabadhu, part-whole constructions can function as a specific noun in generic-specific constructions. The same appears to be true for Dyirbal and

---

42 A test that is related to *pro-one* is the possibility to coordinate incorporated nouns with external nouns, which has been described for Gunwinyguan languages (e.g. Wubuy: *wiri-wutu-miɲ, mari aṉṯiḻi, mari pakaḻaŋ wiri-ma-ŋarkiwaɲ* [3PL>NEUT-liver-get.PP and heart and eye 3PL-VEG-cut.out.PP] 'They got the liver, and heart, and the eye they cut out.' (Baker 2018: 264).
43 The authors do not illustrate this analysis further.

Yidiñ. In Thayore, some generic-specific constructions can be repurposed as specific nouns in larger generic-specific constructions. *minh patp* [MEAT hawk] 'hawk' can be preceded by the generic noun *ngat* to form a new generic-specific construction with a new meaning, *ngat minh patp* [FISH MEAT hawk] 'spotted eagle-ray' (Gaby 2006a: 84). Such recursive behaviour is described for some languages, but not for all languages. This may be a gap in descriptions, or it may indicate fundamental differences in generic-specific constructions in different languages. For Mparntwe Arrernte, Wilkins (2000: 198–200) describes the possibility of using two generics with just one specific noun. This construction may be similar to the Thayore construction, or it may be very different (e.g. *kere thipe ilentye* [meat bird galah] 'galah'). For other languages (and other constructions in the languages I just mentioned), not enough data is available to investigate this issue.

2.5 Useful criteria in the sample

Table 6 provides an overview of the criteria that can be used to distinguish different binominal constructions across the sample. Some general comments are the following:
- Based on these criteria, two languages show no formal distinctions between different binominal constructions at all, viz. Bilinarra and Bunganditj. The other languages distinguish at least two constructions.
- There is some uncertainty about the use of the case locus criterion in six languages. This concerns the languages where (a) noun phrases are not obligatorily phrase-marked or (b) where not enough evidence is available to say whether there is phrase- or word-marking (cf. §2.4.1).
- Word order is the most widely available criterion.

3 How do languages divide the domain?

3.1 Overview

§2 illustrated how Pama-Nyungan languages may distinguish different binominal constructions. In this section, I show how languages divide the conceptual map of binominal constructions in different ways. Table 7 lists the languages in the sample, classified according to three parameters:
1. whether or not a morphosyntactically distinct binominal compound construction is recognized based on the criteria in Table 6;

2. what other binominal constructions may cluster together with binominal compounds based on these criteria, and
3. how many distinct binominal constructions are found in a language.

Table 6: Useful criteria in the sample.

Group	Language	boundary	stress	case	loc	link	order	# of criteria
Arandic-Thura-Yura	Alyawarr	?	0	0	0		1	1 (2?)
	Mparntwe Arrernte	1	0	0	0		1	2
Desert Nyungic	Nyangumarta	0	0	1	0		0	1
	Bilinarra	0	0	0	0		0	0
	Jaru	0	1	?	0		1	2 (3?)
	Warlpiri	0	0	?	0		1	1 (2?)
Greater Maric	Warrongo	0	1	1	0		0	2
Kalkatungic	Kalkutung	0	0	1	0		0	1
Karnic	Arabana-Wangganguru	1	1	0	1		1	4
/	Dyirbal	0	0	1	0		0	1
Paman	Yintyinka-Ayabadhu	0	0	0	0		1	1
	Wik-Mungkan	0	1	0	0		1	2
	Thayore	1	0	0	0		1	2
Southeastern Pama-Nyungan	Kumbainggar	0	0	1	0		0	1
	Yorta Yorta	1	0	1	0		0	2
	Kulin	0	0	?	1		1	2 (3?)
	Bunganditj	0	0	0	0		0	0
	Ngiyambaa	0	0	?	0		0	0 (1?)
South-West Pama-Nyungan	Nhanda	0	1	?	0		1	2 (3?)
	Martuthunira	0	1	1	0		0	2
Yarli-Baagandji	Paakantyi	1	0	0	0		0	1
Yimidhirr-Yalanji-Yidinic	Kuku-Yalanji	0	1	1	0		1	3
	Yidiñ	0	0	1	0		1	2
Yuulngu	Djambarrpuyngu	1	1	1	0		1	4
Number of languages	24	6 (7?)	8	9 (15?)	2	13		21 (22?)

In Table 7, the numbers between brackets in the first three columns are language counts. If the third column (*N of constr.*), reads "2 (4)", this means that there are four languages with two different constructions. Note that I use abbreviations for different comparative concepts here (see section 1.3 above): PH stands for

Table 7: Distinguishing binominal constructions.

Specialized compound constr.?	Clusters together with	N of constr.	Language	PH	CMP	IP	GS	Names of categories (legend)
No (6)	PH & IP (3)	2 (4)	Ngiyambaa	1	1	2	2	N/A	1 N-Adj phrase
			Warlpiri					2 Part-whole construction
			Kulin[44]					
	IP & GS (1)		Yintyingka-Ayabadhu	1	2	2	2	1 N-Adj phrase
								2 Part-whole/generic-specific[45]
	All (2)	1 (2)	Bunganditj	1	1	1	N/A	1 Phrase
			Bilinarra				1	
yes (14)	IP (5)	4 (2)	Arabana-Wangganguru	1	2	3	3	4	1 N-Adj phrase
			Mparntwe Arrernte					2 N-Adj compound
								3 N-N Compound (incl. part-whole)
								4 Generic-specific (Arabana: *prefixed noun*)
		3 (3)	Wik-Mungkan	1	2	3	3	3	1 N-Adj phrase
			Thayore					2 N-Adj compound
								3 Part-whole/generic-specific (Wik-Mungkan: *close-knit phrase*)
		2 (9)	Paakantyi	1	2	1	1	N/A	1 Phrase
								2 Compound
	None (12)	3 (3)	Yidiñ	1	2	3	3	1 N-Adj phrase
								2 N-Adj compound
								3 Part-whole/generic-specific

---

[44] In this table, I disregard the potential word order difference in Kulin between 'flexible' phrases and 'fixed' Compounds (cf. §2.4.3).
[45] Verstraete & Rigsby (2015) suggest that these may be analysed as compounds.

Table 7 (continued)

Specialized compound constr.?	Clusters together with	N of constr.	Language	PH	CMP	IP	GS	Names of categories (legend)
yes? (3)		2 (9)	Yorta Yorta					1 Phrase
			Dyirbal	1	2	1	N/A	2 Compound
			Kalkutung					
			Jaru					
			Djambarrpuyngu					
			Martuthunira	1	2	1	1	
			Nyangumarta					
			Warrongo					
		2? (2)	Kumbainggar	1	2	1?	N/A	1 Phrase 1? Phrase = inalienable possession?
			Nhanda					2 Compound
		3? (1)	Kuku-Yalanji	1	2	3?	3	1 N-Adj phrase 2 N-Adj compound 3? Part-whole = generic-specific? 3 Generic-specific
no? (1)	N/A (1)	2? (1)	Alyawarr	1	N/A?	2	2	1 N-Adj phrase 2 N-N phrase

descriptive phrases, CMP stands for binominal compounds, IP stands for inalienable possession and GS stands for generic-specific.

Table 7 also shows which language-specific constructions exist in each language. For each language, in columns PH, CMP, IP, and GS, each number (1, 2, 3, 4) indicates a formally different construction. Each number also has an associated colour. If the same number/colour occurs in the IP column as in the GS column, like for example in Wik-Mungkan, where both are coloured green, this means that a single language-specific construction covers both inalienable possession and generic specific concepts in that language (e.g., in Wik-Mungkan, they are expressed with close-knit phrases). If there are two different numbers in the CMP column, this means that there are two formally different constructions representing the binominal compound concept. This is the case in Mparntwe Arrernte, for instance, where there is a distinction between N-N compounds and N-Adj compounds. N/A indicates that I could not find instances of a construction in the sources. I could not find instances of generic-specific constructions in Ngiyambaa, for example.

The final column provides a legend for each language, giving the language-specific category that corresponds to each number/colour in the table.

3.2 Languages with a dedicated binominal compound construction

Over half of the languages (14 out of 24) have a dedicated binominal compound construction, that is, a construction specific to binominal lexemes. Three more languages may also belong to this group, but this cannot be assessed due to a lack of data.

In nine of these languages, the distinction is two-way: they set apart a general category of nominal modification constructions (including PH, IP and sometimes GS) from dedicated compounds (§3.2.1). Kumbainggar and Nhanda may also belong to this group, but there is not enough data to be sure. In Paakantyi, inalienable possession constructions may also function as binominal lexemes.

In three languages (Wik-Mungkan, Thayore and Yidiñ), there is a three-way distinction between N-Adj phrases, N-Adj compounds and a joint category of part-whole/generic-specific constructions that can also be used as a type of compound (§3.2.2). Kuku-Yalanji may also belong to this group, but there is not enough data to be sure.

Two languages (Arabana-Wangganguru and Mparntwe Arrernte) feature a four-way distinction, this time between N-Adj phrases, N-Adj compounds, generic-specific constructions, and a joint category of part-whole constructions and N-N Compounds (§3.2.3).

3.2.1 A two-way distinction: Phrases and compounds

The nine languages that make a two-way distinction, between phrases and compounds, are Paakantyi, Yorta Yorta, Dyirbal, Kalkutung, Jaru, Djambarrpuyngu, Martuthunira, Nyangumarta and Warrongo. Two other languages, Kumbainggar and Nhanda, may also be of this type, but there is not enough data on these languages to make a clear case. The languages of this type are areally and genealogically diverse.

Table 6 shows that the distinction between compounds and phrases in these languages is made in different ways:
- In seven languages, there is a different placement of case markers (case markers attach to compounds as a whole but may attach to the individual elements of a phrase).

- In four languages, stress patterns are different.
- Three languages have boundary phenomena for compounds.
- In two languages, word order is different for compounds and phrases.
- In five languages, a combination of these criteria is available.

In these languages, only the place of case markers and boundary phenomena may occur as independent criteria without additional support from other properties. Stress or word order never distinguish compounds from phrases by themselves.[46] Inflecting as a single unit and phonological reduction of stem boundaries both indicate a higher degree of cohesion or unity of the parts, which may be an explanation for the criterial significance of these properties: across languages, compounds tend to exhibit a higher degree of fusion or cohesion than phrases (Haspelmath & Sims 2010: 192). Word order differences or different stress patterns do not necessarily indicate more cohesion (unless the difference is between two prosodic peaks and one prosodic peak, which is only relevant for Warrongo).

In Paakantyi, inalienable possession constructions may function as binominal lexemes. The main formal difference between inalienable possession constructions and dedicated compounds is that the latter show boundary phenomena. (33) shows three inalienable possession constructions (Hercus 1982: 76).

(33) a. DRL *ḓalḓa balḓa* [kangaroo skin] 'kangaroo skin'
 b. DRL *baṉḏu birṉa* [fish bone] 'fish bones'
 c. DRL *bāga walbiri* [river bank] 'river bank'

3.2.2 A three-way distinction: Adjective-noun phrases, [generic-specific constructions + inalienable possession constructions] and compounds

In three languages, Wik-Mungkan, Thayore and Yidiñ, there is a three-way distinction between N-Adj phrases, N-Adj compounds, and a joint category of part-whole/generic-specific constructions. These languages are all geographically close, spoken on Cape York peninsula. Wik-Mungkan and Thayore are both Paman languages. In Wik-Mungkan and Thayore, part-whole/generic-specific constructions can also be used as compounds. When they are used as compounds, they are still distinct from N-Adj compounds in that (a) they have a different word order, (b) in the case of Wik-Mungkan, in that their stress is phrasal, and (c) in the case of Thayore in that not all whole-part constructions and generic-specific construc-

---

46 In Jaru they may do so together, however.

tions show a fricated onset.[47] The generic-specific constructions and whole-part constructions that are used as compounds in these languages resemble so-called *phrasal lexemes* that have been identified in other languages (e.g. Masini 2009). (34) and (35) are examples of Wik-Mungkan (a) phrasal lexemes compared with (b) Compounds and (c) nominal modification constructions (my stress marking). Kilham (1974) calls such phrasal lexemes *close-knit phrases*.

(34) a. WIM *maʔ ˈʔek* [hand shell] 'fingernail' (Kilham 1974: 46)
      b. WIM *ˈmaʔ-tayan* [hand-firm] 'trustworthy' (Kilham 1974: 46)
      c. WIM *maʔ ˈtayan* [hand firm] 'a firm hand' (constructed for illustration)

(35) a. WIM *tu:t ˈme:ʔ* [breast eye] 'nipple' (Kilham 1974: 49)
      b. WIM *ˈme:ʔ ʔeɲkan* [eye clear] 'clear place' (Kilham 1974: 49)
      c. WIM *me:ʔ ˈʔeɲkan* [eye clear] 'a clear eye' (constructed for illustration)

(36) are examples of a Thayore (a) phrasal lexeme compared with (b) a compound and (c) a nominal modification construction. The specific noun *minh patp* 'meat hawk' in (36) is an example of a generic-specific phrasal lexeme. Gaby (2006a) calls all these phrasal lexemes compounds.

(36) a. THD *meer-punk* /meːɻβuŋk/ [eye-knee] 'eyebrow' (Gaby 2006a: 34, 140)
      b. THD *meer-pork* /meːɻβoɻk/ [eye-big] 'star' (Gaby 2006a: 205)
      c. THD *meer pork* [eye big] 'a big eye' (constructed for illustration)

(37) THD *ngat minh patp* /ngat miɲβatp/ [fish meat hawk] 'stingray, sp.' (Gaby 2006a: 282)

In Yidiñ and Thayore the formal distinction between compounds and other binominal constructions can be captured, again, in terms of fusion or cohesion. In Yidiñ, compounds are marked for case as if they were a single noun, not as a phrase consisting of multiple nouns. Thayore features boundary phenomena in compounds: the second component of a compound may have a fricated onset. Compounds can also occur in the 'specific' slot of a generic-specific construction,

---

[47] Gaby (2006b: 205) mentions that inalienable possession constructions and complex body part compounds may *sometimes* be distinguished by phonological reduction. It is not clear what 'sometimes' implies here. It may mean that not all compounds feature such frication and, as such, that there are compounds that phonologically resemble phrases. Or it may mean that some phrases also feature frication and that some phrases phonologically resemble compounds. In any case, it may indicate a category in between compounds and phrases, which is the relevant point here.

while phrases cannot (cf. §2.4.4). In Wik-Mungkan, none of the constructions appears as more fused than the others – the main differences between constructions are stress and word order.

3.2.3 A four-way distinction

Two languages, Arabana-Wangganguru and Mparntwe Arrernte, distinguish N-Adj compounds from descriptive phrases and generic-specific constructions, and have an additional N-N compound construction that is formally identical to inalienable possession constructions. These languages are not closely related genealogically, but they are areally close and there was regular interaction between the Arabana, Wangganguru and Arrernte communities (e.g. Hercus 1994: 11–12, 16–18). What is interesting about these languages is that not only compounds can show a higher degree of fusion, but so can inalienable possession constructions and generic-specific constructions. In Arabana-Wangganguru, both compounds and generic-specific constructions (called *prefixed nouns*[48] in Hercus 1994) feature just one stress peak, while phrases may have stress on each individual word.[49] In Mparntwe Arrernte, both compounds and generic-specific constructions can occur in the specific slot of a(nother) generic-specific construction, which is not possible for descriptive phrases (cf. §2.4.4).

(38) and (39) provide examples of (a) phrases, (b) generic-specific constructions, (c) N-Adj compounds, (d) N-N compounds and (e) contiguous inalienable possession constructions (which are formally similar to N-N compounds).[50]

(38) a. ARD/WGG ′ngura ′madla [camp bad] 'bad camp' (constructed for illustration)
b. ARD/WGG kathi-′kungarra [meat-kangaroo] 'meat kangaroo' (Hercus 1994: 102)
c. ARD/WGG ′ngura-madla /′nguramala/ [camp-bad] 'place of a deceased' (Hercus 1994: 41)
d. ARD/WGG ′maka-wimpa /′makampa/ [fire-track] 'Macamba', a place name (Hercus 1994: 57)
e. ARD/WGG karla-thidli /′karlathidli/ [creek-branch] 'branch of a creek' (Hercus 1994: 74)

---

48 It may be interesting to compare such *prefixed* nouns to generic-specific incorporation constructions in Non-Pama-Nyungan languages (Nordlinger & Sadler 2008).
49 I infer this from Hercus (1994: 47–48). Hercus does not mention this explicitly.
50 My stress marking.

(39) a. AER *artwe kngerre* [man big] 'a big man' (Wilkins 1989: 103)
　　b. AER *ngkwarle untyetye* [nectar/honey corkwood] 'corkwood nectar' (Wilkins 1989: 102)
　　c. AER *arre-urrperle* /arurperle/ [mouth-black] 'black mouth snake' (Wilkins 1989: 146)
　　d. AER *lyeke-kaperte* [thorn-head] 'caltrop' (Wilkins 1989: 146)
　　e. AER *kngwelve ingke* [dog foot] 'dog foot' (Wilkins 1989: 412)

3.3 Languages without a dedicated binominal compound

Six languages do not have a dedicated binominal compound. Alyawarr may also belong to this group, but there is not enough data to be sure. In two of these, Bunganditj and Bilinarra, all attested binominal constructions are identical. In three languages, Ngiyambaa, Warlpiri, and Kulin, there is a word order difference between descriptive phrases and inalienable possession constructions. Either of these constructions can also be used as binominal lexemes. Alyawarr may also belong to this group, but there is not enough data to assess this.

In Yintyinka-Ayabadhu, binominal lexemes are never identical to descriptive phrases, but they are formally like other binominal constructions, particularly in terms of word order (generic-specific and inalienable possession). In Ngiyambaa, Warlpiri and Kulin, noun phrases can be marked for case either as a whole or on each individual nominal (cf. §2.4.1). This makes it more difficult to distinguish compounds from nominal modification constructions, since case locus cannot be applied as a consistent criterion.

4 Concluding discussion

This chapter has provided an overview of the properties of binominal constructions across Pama-Nyungan languages. It shows which data is available to make distinctions between binominal constructions and in particular compounds vs. phrases. I questioned the importance of exocentricity and non-compositionality, which can be reduced to figurativity and lexicalization (§2.2). Formal properties that allow us to make distinctions are illustrated in the remainder of §2 and summarized in Table 6. §3 discusses the distinctions that the languages in the sample make based on these properties. In what follows, I summarize and develop topics that I touched on throughout the chapter: degrees of fusion and links between compounds and phrases.

4.1 Degrees of fusion

In various languages, compounds have a higher degree of fusion than phrasal constructions. Depending on the language, constructions other than compounds can also show fusion. I consider binominal constructions as more "cohesive" or "fused" than other constructions if they have one or more of the following properties:
- case markers at the right edge of the construction (vs. after each individual nominal);
- boundary phenomena, weakened stem boundaries;
- a limit of one prosodic peak as opposed to multiple prosodic peaks;
- a fixed order of modifier and head (as opposed to a flexible order of modifier and head);
- they fill a single functional slot in the noun phrase, as opposed to taking up two slots simultaneously (see §2.4.4)

Not all these properties could be consistently tested in the dataset.

In §3.2.1, I noted that in the sample case locus and boundary phenomena have a higher functional load than other criteria to distinguish compounds from phrases. Either case locus or boundary phenomena may be the sole formal property of a dedicated compound construction in a language.

Other characteristics may also set apart binominal constructions, without making them more or less fused. Examples are word order, the order of primary and secondary stress and linking morphemes (which may be interpreted either as linking the two nominals or also as reinforcing the boundary between two nominals). Such characteristics are less often the sole formal property of a dedicated compound construction. In other words, the properties relating to fusion are more closely linked to compounding than other characteristics.

Compounds are not always associated with a higher degree of cohesion, however. In Wik-Mungkan, for example, the main differences between different kinds of compounds and phrases are the location of stress and the order of modifier and head.

Apart from compounds, other constructions may also show a higher degree of fusion than regular phrases. In Mparntwe Arrernte, Arabana-Wangganguru, Yintyinka-Ayabadhu, Wik-Mungkan and Thayore, inalienable possession constructions and generic-specific constructions sometimes show signs of higher cohesion than regular N-Adj phrases. Just like compounds, these constructions may for example be used as a new specific noun in a generic-specific constructions (§2.4.4). Therefore, fusion or cohesion may be a general characteristic of some types of phrases, rather than a defining property of compounds.

Mparntwe Arrernte, Arabana-Wangganguru, Yintyinka-Ayabadhu, Wik-Mungkan and Thayore are languages with various cohesive phrases. Notably, these are also languages with a general noun phrase structure that is arguably more close-knit than in other Pama-Nyungan languages. For example, their noun phrases are marked for case at the right edge (§2.4.1) and the order of noun phrase elements is fixed (§2.4.3). The next section explores the links between compound structure and the structure of phrases or clauses in individual languages.

4.2 Links between compounds and phrases/clauses

In some languages, it is difficult to distinguish compounds from certain types of phrases based on the available criteria. Here, I discuss possible structural links between compounds and phrasal (or even clausal) constructions.

Noun phrase structure is a much-debated issue in Australianist literature: some authors have argued for or against its flexibility or even the existence of a clear noun phrase (e.g. Blake 1983, Heath 1986, Evans 2003: 227–233; Nordlinger 2014: 237–241). Irrespective of flexibility, there is a lot of variation in the way nominal expressions may be construed (Louagie & Verstraete 2016). Some languages allow discontinuous nominal expressions, others allow various orders of head noun and various types of modifiers; some languages allow or require word marking of case, others only or primarily phrase marking. If there is a relationship between compounds and noun phrases, we could also expect that compounds are different in languages with different noun phrase structures. And in the sample, this appears to be the case.

In some languages, there is a tight link between compounds and inalienable possession constructions. In other languages, there is no such link. Whether there is a link or not appears to correlate with phrase marking vs. word marking preferences. Languages with phrase marking have inalienable possession compounds. Strictly word marking languages do not have inalienable possession compounds.[51] To explain this pattern, we could speculate that phrase marking simplifies the use of a whole-part construction as a compound. This is partly because of the semantic similarity between compounds and possessive constructions: in both, the association between modifier and head can be very broad, since the modifier has a classifying rather than a qualifying function (see §1.3.1 and §2.2.2). Another reason is that, in phrase-marking languages, it is impossible for

---

[51] Interestingly, some compounds with cranberry morphs in these languages may derive from historical part-whole compounds or inalienable possession phrases (see §2.2.4).

both continuous inalienable possession constructions and other noun phrases to have case markers intervening between the modifier and the head. This makes it possible for inalienable possession constructions to operate as a single lexeme. Donaldson (1980: 230) and Gaby (2006b: 204–205) make the similar suggestion that part-whole compounds in Ngiyambaa and in Thayore directly lexicalized from inalienable possession constructions.

What, then, can we say about word-marking languages? An interesting observation is that figurative compounds (or 'exocentric compounds') are dominant in some of these languages (cf. MacFarlane 1987). The only compounds I found in Djambarrpuyngu, Jaru, Dyirbal, Kuku-Yalanji and Nhanda are figurative (§2.2). Figurative compounds also occur in other languages, including phrase-marking languages, but their frequency is unclear.

I see two possible links between phrase/clause types and compounds in these languages, which may also apply to Pama-Nyungan languages more generally. I already suggested these links in §2.4.1.

a) Compounds may derive from unmarked noun phrases (cf. Dunkel 1999 for Indo-European).

Like compounds, absolutive noun phrases are often unmarked (or zero-marked) across Australian languages. On the surface, this makes the two indistinguishable. To solidify any link between compounds and unmarked noun phrases, one could investigate the typical meaning of unmarked noun phrases versus compounds, and how much they overlap. The names of inanimate and nonhuman entities, for example, may be compounds, and nonhuman entities may often be patients or intransitive subjects in a clause (rather than agents). Another suggestion for further investigation is to test other properties of absolutive noun phrases and compounds that may happen to coincide, such as word order.

b) Compounds may be related to verbless nominal predication clauses with a topic-comment order (e.g. '(the) nose (is) big', '(the) eye (is) green')

Like absolutive noun phrases, copula subjects and copula complements have no overt case marking in Australian languages (Dixon 2002b). On the surface, this makes a binominal verbless clause indistinguishable from a binominal compound. Notably, clauses becoming lexemes are not unheard of in other languages. English *forget-me-not* and German *Rühr-mich-nicht-an* are both plant names deriving from imperative clauses (Kastovsky 2009: 336). Names deriving from clauses have a figurative meaning, which fits with the figurative/exocentric analysis of many compounds in Pama-Nyungan languages.[52]

4.3 Summary and conclusions

In summary, compound structures may be related to phrase or clause structure. There are several potential links depending on noun phrase structure:
a) with inalienable possession phrases and descriptive N-Adj phrases in phrase-marking languages;
b) with absolutive noun phrases;
c) with verbless clauses.

Links between compounding and phrasal structures have been suggested earlier in the literature on Australian languages, for example by Baker & Nordlinger (2008) and Baker (2014, 2018).

If compounds are essentially a subtype of phrases, this implies that they are not purely lexical objects. Compounds are as much a subject of syntax as they are of morphology or the lexicon. Though some theoretical work posits separate modules for a language's lexicon and syntax (and morphology), the same work has acknowledged that the distinction between compounds and phrases is not straightforward: compounds can only be modelled with processes originating in different modules (e.g. lexicon + syntax) operating within one construction type (e.g. Giegerich 2015). Other models have approached compounds from a syntactic perspective, such as Jackendoff's Parallel Architecture (2009). Masini (2009: 268) states, from a constructionist perspective, that phrases and compound-like constructions may share structure even if they do not share the same function. In Indo-European historical linguistics, it is accepted that prototypes of the first compounds were lexicalized phrases (cf. Schindler 1997; Clackson 2002; Kastovsky 2009). Such lexicalized phrases were re-analysed as templates for the

---

[52] Some authors have shown that figurative/exocentric compounds were predominant in early Indo-European languages, while non-figurative/endocentric compounds were fairly rare (e.g. Meissner & Tribulato 2002). In terms of noun phrase and clause structure, there are curious parallels between word-marking languages in Australia and early Indo-European languages, which had a looser word order, higher reliance on case marking, and an arguably looser noun phrase structure than some present-day Indo-European languages. Both may be characterized as non-configurational (Van de Velde 2009; Van de Velde & Lamiroy 2016). These shared patterns may indicate similar relationships between noun phrases, clauses and compounds in early Indo-European languages and some branches of Pama-Nyungan.

formation of new compounds. This scenario is not unlikely for Pama-Nyungan languages.

From theoretical, descriptive and historical perspectives, the relationship between compounds and phrases is an important subject for further analysis. However, grammars of individual languages rarely specify the distinction or the relationship between compounds and phrases. They treat compounds as lexical objects to be studied from dictionaries, not as morphosyntactic objects considered among a language's phrasal constructions. And phrasal constructions are rarely considered as potential templates for new lexemes (see Masini 2019 and Masini, Mattiola & Pepper, this volume). Beyond investigating distinctions between compounds and phrases, one might address further questions:

How are compounds similar to other constructions?

How are phrases and compounds (diachronically and synchronically) related?

This chapter has approached these questions for a sample of Pama-Nyungan languages. I focused on similarities between compounds and phrases, though there are certainly important differences that may be highlighted in future work (e.g. by investigating underexplored criteria in §2.4.4). The goal of this chapter is to contribute to (and be challenged by) future descriptions of the languages in this sample and in Pama-Nyungan languages more generally.

References

Aikhenvald, Alexandra Y. 2007. Typological distinctions in word-formation. In Timothy Shopen, (ed.), *Language typology and syntactic description, Volume 3: Grammatical categories and the lexicon*, 1–65. 2nd edition. Cambridge: Cambridge University Press.

Baker, Brett. 2014. Incorporation in Wubuy. In Lauren Gawne, & Jill Vaughan (eds.), *Selected papers from the 44th conference of the Australian Linguistic Society, 2013*, 231–260. Melbourne: University of Melbourne.

Baker, Brett. 2018. Super-complexity and the status of 'word' in Gunwinyguan languages of Australia. In Geert Booij (ed.), *The construction of words* Advances in Construction Morphology, 255–286. Cham: Springer.

Baker, Brett & Rachel Nordlinger. 2008. Noun-adjective compounds in Gunwinyguan languages. In Miriam Butt & Tracy Holloway King (eds.), *Proceedings of the LFG08 (Lexical Functional Grammar) Conference*, 109–218. Stanford: CSLI Publications.

Bauer, Laurie. 2001. Compounding. In Martin Haspelmath (ed.), *Language typology and language universals: An international handbook*, vol. 1, 695–707. Berlin: Mouton de Gruyter.

Bauer, Laurie. 2003. *Introducing linguistic morphology*. Second edition. Washington, D.C.: Georgetown University Press.

Bauer, Laurie. 2006. Compound. In Keith Brown (ed.), *Encyclopedia of language and linguistics*. Volume 2, 719–726. Second edition. Oxford: Elsevier.

Bauer, Laurie. 2009. Typology of compounds. In Rochelle Lieber & Pavol Štekauer (eds.), *The Oxford handbook of compounding*, 343–356. Oxford: Oxford University Press.

Bauer, Laurie. 2016. Re-evaluating exocentricity in word-formation. In Daniel Siddiqi & Heidi Harley (eds.), *Morphological Metatheory*, 461–478. Amsterdam: John Benjamins.

Bauer, Laurie. 2017. *Compounds and compounding*. Cambridge: Cambridge University Press.

Blake, Barry J. 1979. *A Kalkatungu grammar*. Canberra: Department of Linguistics, Australian National University.

Blake, Barry J. 1983. Structure and word order in Kalkatungu: The anatomy of a flat language. *Australian Journal of Linguistics* 3(2). 143–175.

Blake, Barry J. 1991. Woiwurrung (Wuy Wurrung): The Melbourne language. In R.M.W. Dixon, Malcolm Ward & Barry J. Blake (eds.), *Handbook of Australian languages, Volume 4*, 30–122. Oxford: Oxford University Press.

Blake, Barry J. 2003. *The Bunganditj (Buwandik) language of the Mount Gambier region*. Canberra: Pacific Linguistics, Research School of Pacific and Asian Studies, Australian National University.

Blake, Barry J. 2011. *Dialects of Western Kulin, Western Victoria – Yartwatjali, Tjapwurrug, Djadjawurrung*. Melbourne, Victoria: La Trobe University. (http://www.vcaa.vic.edu.au/Documents/alcv/DialectsofWesternKulin-WesternVictoria.pdf) (Accessed April 15, 2014.)

Blevins, Juliette. 2001. *Nhanda: An Aboriginal language of Western Australia*. Honolulu: University of Hawai'i Press.

Booij, Geert E. 1992. Compounding in Dutch. *Rivista di Linguistica* 4(1). 37–60.

Booij, Geert E. 2005. *The grammar of words: An introduction to linguistic morphology*. Oxford: Oxford University Press.

Booij, Geert E. 2009. Compounding and Construction Morphology. In Rochelle Lieber & Pavol Štekauer (eds.), *The Oxford handbook of compounding*, 201–216. Oxford: Oxford University Press.

Bowe, Heather J. & Stephen Morey. 1999. *The Yorta Yorta (Bangerang) language of the Murray Goulburn – Including Yabula Yabula*. Canberra: Pacific Linguistics, Research School of Pacific and Asian Studies, the Australian National University.

Bowern, Claire & Jason Zentz. 2012. Diversity in the numeral systems of Australian languages. *Anthropological Linguistics* 54(2). 133–160.

Brinton, Laurel J. & Elizabeth Closs Traugott. 2005. *Lexicalization and language change*. Cambridge: Cambridge University Press.

Clackson, James. 2002. Composition in Indo-European languages. *Transactions of the Philological Society* 100(2). 163–167.

Creissels, Denis. This volume. Binominals and construct marking. In Steve Pepper, Francesca Masini & Simone Mattiola (eds.), *Binominal lexemes in cross-linguistic perspective*. Berlin: Mouton de Gruyter.

Crystal, David. 2008. *A dictionary of linguistics and phonetics*. Sixth edition. Malden, MA Blackwell.

Dench, Alan Charles. 1994. *Martuthunira: A language of the Pilbara region of Western Australia*. Canberra: Department of Linguistics, Australian National University.

Dixon, R.M.W. 1972. *The Dyirbal language of North Queensland*. Cambridge: Cambridge University Press.

Dixon, R.M.W. 1977. *A grammar of Yidiɲ*. Cambridge: Cambridge University Press.

Dixon, R.M.W. 1980. *The languages of Australia*. Cambridge: Cambridge University Press.

Dixon, R.M.W. 2002a. *Australian languages: Their nature and development*. Cambridge: Cambridge University Press.
Dixon, R.M.W. 2002b. Copula clauses in Australian languages: A typological perspective. *Anthropological Linguistics* 44(1). 1–36.
Donaldson, Tamsin. 1980. *Ngiyambaa: The language of the Wangaaybuwan*. Cambridge: Cambridge University Press.
Downing, Pamela A. 1977. On the creation and use of English nominal compounds. *Language* 53(4). 810–842.
Dunkel, George E. 1999. On the origins of nominal composition in Indo-European. In Heiner Eichner, Hans Christian Luschützky & Velizar Sadovski (eds.), *Compositiones Indogermanicae in memoriam Jochem Schindler*, 47–68. Prague: Enigma.
Eades, Diana. 1979. Gumbaynggir. In R.M.W. Dixon & Barry J. Blake (eds.), *Handbook of Australian languages, Volume 1*, 245–361. Amsterdam: John Benjamins.
Evans, Nicholas. 2003. *Bininj Gun-wok: a pan-dialectical grammar of Mayali, Kunwinjku and Kune*. Canberra: Pacific Linguistics, Research School of Pacific and Asian Studies, The Australian National Univ.
Evans, Nicholas & David Wilkins. 2000. In the mind's ear: The semantic extensions of perception verbs in Australian languages. *Language* 76(3). 546–592.
Fabb, Nigel. 1998. Compounding. In Andrew Spencer & Arnold M. Zwicky (eds.), *The handbook of morphology*, 66–83. Oxford: Blackwell.
Gaby, Alice Rose. 2006a. *A grammar of Kuuk Thaayorre*. University of Melbourne PhD dissertation.
Gaby, Alice Rose. 2006b. The Thaayorre 'true man': Lexicon of the human body in an Australian language. *Language Sciences* 28(2–3). 201–220.
Giegerich, Heinz J. 2015. *Lexical structures: Compounding and the modules of grammar*. Edinburgh: Edinburgh University Press.
Hammarström, Harald & Robert Forkel, Martin Haspelmath Sebastian & Bank. 2021. *Glottolog 4.5*. Jena: Max Planck Institute for the Science of Human History. (http://glottolog.org)
Haspelmath, Martin. 2010. Comparative concepts and descriptive categories in crosslinguistic studies. *Language* 86(3). 663–687.
Haspelmath, Martin & Andrea D. Sims. 2010. *Understanding morphology*. Second edition. London: Hodder Education.
Heath, Jeffrey. 1986. Syntactic and lexical aspects of nonconfigurationality in Nunggubuyu (Australia). *Natural Language and Linguistic Theory* 4(3). 375–408.
Hercus, Luise Anna. 1982. *The Bāgandji language*. Canberra: Department of Linguistics, Australian National University.
Hercus, Luise Anna. 1992. *Wembawemba dictionary*. Canberra: Institute of Aboriginal and Torres Strait Islander Studies.
Hercus, Luise Anna. 1994. *A grammar of the Arabana-Wangkangurru language, Lake Eyre Basin, South Australia*. Canberra: Department of Linguistics, Australian National University.
Heyvaert, Liesbet. 2009. Compounding in Cognitive Linguistics. In Rochelle Lieber & Pavol Štekauer (eds.), *The Oxford handbook of compounding*, 233–254. Oxford: Oxford University Press.
Horton, David R. & Australian Institute of Aboriginal and Torres Strait Islander Studies. 2000. *Aboriginal Australia*. Canberra: Geoscience Australia and Aboriginal Studies Press.

Jackendoff, Ray. 2009. Compounding in the Parallel Architecture and Conceptual Semantics. In Rochelle Lieber & Pavol Štekauer (eds.), *The Oxford handbook of compounding*, 105–128. Oxford: Oxford University Press.

Janssen, Theo. 2012. Compositionality: Its historic context. In Markus Werning, Wolfram. Hinzen & Edouard. Machery (eds.), *The Oxford handbook of compositionality*, 19–46. Oxford: Oxford University Press. (Accessed May 11, 2020.)

Kastovsky, Dieter. 2009. Diachronic perspectives. In Rochelle Lieber & Pavol Štekauer (eds.), *The Oxford handbook of compounding*, 323–340. Oxford: Oxford University Press.

Kilham, Christine A. 1974. Compound words and close-knit phrases in Wik-Munkan. In *Papers in Australian linguistics 7*, 45–73. Canberra: Department of Linguistics, Australian National University.

Kilham, Christine A., Mabel Pamulkan, Jennifer Pootchemunka & Topsy Wolmby (eds.). 1989. *Dictionary and source book of the Wik-Mungkan language*. Darwin: Summer Institute of Linguistics, Australian Aborigines Branch.

Langacker, Ronald W. 1999. Correspondences, compositionality, and grammar. *MANUSYA* 2(2). 61–76.

Lesage, Jakob. 2014. *Nominal compounds and other N-N combinations: A typological study of a sample of Pama-Nyungan languages*. University of Leuven MA Thesis.

Lieber, Rochelle & Štekauer, Pavol. 2009. Introduction: Status and definition of compounding. In Rochelle Lieber & Pavol Štekauer (eds.), *The Oxford handbook of compounding*, 3–18. Oxford: Oxford University Press.

Louagie, Dana. 2020. *Noun phrases in Australian languages: A typological study*. Berlin: Mouton De Gruyter.

Louagie, Dana & Jean-Christophe Verstraete. 2016. Noun phrase constituency in Australian languages: A typological study. *Linguistic Typology* 20(1). 25–80.

MacFarlane, Linda. 1987. *Compound nominals in Australian Aboriginal languages*. Canberra: Australian National University Honours Thesis.

Masini, Francesca. 2009. Phrasal lexemes, compounds and phrases: A constructionist perspective. *Word Structure* 2(2). 254–271.

Masini, Francesca. 2019. Competition between morphological words and multiword expressions. In Franz Rainer, Francesco Gardani, Wolfgang U. Dressler & Hans Christian Luschützky (eds.), *Competition in inflection and word-formation*, 281–305. Cham: Springer.

Masini, Francesca, Simone Mattiola & Steve Pepper. This volume. Exploring complex lexemes cross-linguistically. In Steve Pepper, Francesca Masini & Simone Mattiola (eds.), *Binominal lexemes in cross-linguistic perspective*. Berlin: Mouton de Gruyter.

McGregor, William B. 1990. *A functional grammar of Gooniyandi*. Amsterdam: John Benjamins.

McGregor, William. 2002. *Verb classification in Australian languages*. Berlin: New York: Mouton de Gruyter.

McGregor, William B. 2004. *The languages of the Kimberley, Western Australia*. New York: Routledge Curzon.

Meakins, Felicity. 2013. *Bilinarra multimedia database*. Darwin: Australian Society for Indigenous Languages. (http://ausil.org/Dictionary/Bilinarra/index.html)

Meakins, Felicity & Rachel Nordlinger. 2014. *A grammar of Bilinarra: An Australian Aboriginal language of the Northern Territory*. Berlin: Mouton De Gruyter.

Meissner, Torsten & Olga Tribulato. 2002. Nominal composition in Mycenaean Greek. *Transactions of the Philological Society* 100(3). 289–330.

Montague, Richard. 1973. The proper treatment of quantification in ordinary English. In Jaakko Hintikka, Julius Moravcsik,. & Patrick Suppes (eds.), *Approaches to natural language*, 221–242. Dordrecht: Springer.

Nordlinger, Rachel. 2014. Constituency and grammatical relations. In Harold Koch & Rachel Nordlinger (eds.), *The languages and linguistics of Australia: A comprehensive guide*, 215–262. Berlin: Mouton de Gruyter.

Nordlinger, Rachel & Louisa Sadler. 2008. From juxtaposition to incorporation: An approach to Generic-Specific constructions. In Miriam Butt & Tracy Holloway King (eds.), *Proceedings of the LFG08 (Lexical Functional Grammar) Conference*, 394–412. Stanford: CSLI Publications.

Patz, Elisabeth. 2002. *A grammar of the Kuku Yalanji language of north Queensland*. Canberra: Research School of Pacific and Asian Studies, Australian National University.

Pepper, Steve. This volume. Hatcher-Bourque: Towards a reusable classification of semantic relations. In Steve Pepper, Francesca Masini & Simone Mattiola (eds.), *Binominal lexemes in cross-linguistic perspective*. Berlin: Mouton de Gruyter.

Ricca, Davide. 2010. Corpus data and theoretical implications: With special reference to Italian VN compounds. In Sergio Scalise & Irene Vogel (eds.), *Cross-disciplinary issues in compounding*, 237–254. Amsterdam: John Benjamins.

Rice, Keren D. 2009. Athapaskan: Slave. In Rochelle Lieber & Pavol Štekauer (eds.), *The Oxford handbook of compounding*, 542–563. Oxford: Oxford University Press.

Rijkhoff, Jan. 2008. Descriptive and discourse-referential modifiers in a layered model of the noun phrase. *Linguistics* 46(4). 789–829.

Sadler, Louisa & Rachel Nordlinger. 2010. Nominal juxtaposition in Australian languages: An LFG analysis. *Journal of Linguistics* 46(2). 415–452.

Salo, Pauli & Gabriel Sandu. 2006. Compositionality: Semantic aspects. In Keith Brown (ed.), *Encyclopedia of Language and Linguistics*, 716–719. Elsevier.

Schindler, Jochem. 1997. Zur internen Syntax der indogermanischen Nominalkomposition. In Emilio Crespo & José L. García-Ramón (eds.), *Berthold Delbrück y la sintaxis indoeuropea hoy. Actas del Coloquio de la Indogermanische Gesellschaft, Madrid, 21–24 septiembre de 1994*, 537–540. Madrid/Wiesbaden: Ediciones de la Universidad Autónoma de Madrid/Reichert.

Sharp, Janet. 1998. *A grammar of the Nyangumarta language of the Pilbara*. Perth: University of Western Australia PhD dissertation.

Simpson, Jane Helen. 1983. *Aspects of Warlpiri morphology and syntax*. Cambridge, MA Massachusetts: Massachusetts Institute of Technology PhD dissertation.

Simpson, Jane Helen. 2009. Pama-Nyungan: Warlpiri. In Pavol Štekauer & Rochelle Lieber (eds.), *The Oxford handbook of compounding*, 609–622. Oxford: Oxford University Press.

Spencer, Andrew. 2011. What's in a compound? *Journal of Linguistics* 47(2). 481–507.

Szabó, Zoltán Gendler. 2017. Compositionality. In Zalta, Edward N. (ed.), *The Stanford Encyclopedia of Philosophy (Summer 2017 Edition)*. (https://plato.stanford.edu/archives/sum2017/entries/compositionality/)

Tindale, Norman B. 1974. *Aboriginal tribes of Australia*. Berkeley: University of California Press.

Tsunoda, Tasaku. 1981. *The Djaru language of Kimberley, Western Australia*. Canberra: Department of Linguistics, Australian National University.

Tsunoda, Tasaku. 2011. *A grammar of Warrongo*. Berlin: Mouton de Gruyter.

Van de Velde, Freek. 2009. *De nominale constituent: Structuur en geschiedenis*. Leuven: Universitaire Pers Leuven.
Van de Velde, Freek & Béatrice Lamiroy. 2016. External possessors in West Germanic and Romance: Differential speed in the drift towards NP configurationality. In Hubert Cuyckens, Lobke Ghesquière & Daniël Van Olmen (eds.), *Aspects of grammaticalization: (Inter)subjectification, analogy and unidirectionality*, 353–400. Berlin: Mouton de Gruyter.
Verstraete, Jean-Christophe & Bruce Rigsby. 2015. *A grammar and lexicon of Yintyingka*. Berlin: Mouton de Gruyter.
Wilkins, David P. 1989. *Mparntwe Arrernte (Aranda): Studies in the structure and semantics of grammar*. Canberra: Australian National University PhD dissertation
Wilkins, David P. 2000. Ants, ancestors and medicine: A semantic and pragmatic account of classifier constructions in Arrernte (Central Australia). In Gunter Senft (ed.), *Systems of nominal classification*, 147–216. Cambridge: Cambridge University Press.
Wilkinson, Melanie P. 1991. *Djambarrpuyŋu: A Yolŋu variety of Northern Australia*. Sydney: University of Sydney PhD dissertation.
Yallop, Colin. 1977. *Alyawarra: An Aboriginal language of Central Australia*. Canberra: Australian Institute of Aboriginal Studies.

Marie-Elaine van Egmond
New types of binominal lexeme in Anindilyakwa (Australia)

Abstract: This chapter describes four types of binominal lexeme in Anindilyakwa, a polysynthetic language of Northern Australia. In this language, two nouns cannot be simply juxtaposed to create a binominal, because modifiers have to agree in noun class with their heads. Noun class harmony is realised by one of the two components of the binominal taking a derivational prefix that allows it to match the noun class of the independently occurring noun. Depending on the construction, this derivational prefix can occur on either the head or the modifier of the binominal. This noun class harmony presents a challenge for the typology of binominals that is the theme of this book: (i) there are more morphs involved than in Pepper's typology, some of which are non-consecutive; (ii) when the derivational prefix occurs on the head, this may represent one of the missing, "logically impossible", types in the typology.[1]

1 Introduction

This chapter discusses four different types of binominal lexeme that are used to express complex concepts in Anindilyakwa (ISO 639-3: AOI), an Australian Aboriginal language spoken by over 1500 people living on Groote Eylandt in the Gulf of Carpentaria, Northern Territory. It is one of the few Aboriginal languages that is still acquired by children, and it belongs to the Gunwinyguan family (van Egmond 2012, van Egmond & Baker 2020). Like many other Northern Australian languages, Anindilyakwa is polysynthetic, thus making extensive use of morphology to identify grammatical relations, with agreement throughout the clause. As a result, simply putting two nominals together to build a compound noun – as in noun-noun compounds like English *railway* and German *Eisenbahn* [iron.way] 'railway', or the French prepositional compound *chemin de fer* [way of iron] 'railway'- is not an available strategy in this language. This is because in

---

[1] I would like to thank Steve Pepper for inviting me to contribute to this exciting volume, and for brainstorming about the puzzling Anindilyakwa data. I also wish to thank the editors and anonymous reviewer for their useful feedback. My work was supported by the THEORIA Scientific Programme for the Humanities of the Ministry of Education, Science and Culture, Mecklenburg-Vorpommern, Germany, for which I am also most grateful.

https://doi.org/10.1515/9783110673494-005

Anindilyakwa, modifiers need to agree with their heads. Four different derivational affixes are used to achieve this agreement; in all cases, the nominal taking the derivational affix forsakes its intrinsic noun class to match the noun class of an independently occurring noun.

The constructions involved are two possession constructions, one expressing inalienable possession (INALP) and one indicating alienable possession (ALP), plus a proprietive suffix (PROP) which has a 'having, being equipped with' meaning, and a privative (PRIV) construction that contributes a meaning of 'without'. The complex concepts involved denote a permanent and inherent association between the possessed and the possessor, or part and whole, for the INALP construction (e.g. *it*-INALP-*skin it.eye* 'eyelid'), relationships of a less permanent and inherent type for the ALP construction (e.g. *it*-ALP-*bush it.food* 'bush tucker'), one item having the property of another for the PROP suffix (e.g. *it.truck it.house*-PROP 'caravan'), and one item being without the other for the PRIV construction (e.g. *she*-ALP-*man*-PRIV 'widow').

From a typological perspective, the Anindilyakwa binominals are interesting for a number of reasons: firstly, the strategy of noun class harmony is extremely uncommon in Australia, and to my knowledge only occurs in Wubuy, its closest genetic neighbour. And secondly, the Anindilyakwa binominals do not easily fit into Pepper's description of binominals, for the following reasons:

(i) In Anindilyakwa, the relationship between the two combining concepts is clearly stated by the derivational affix (e.g. a part-whole relationship, or one item having the property of another). This specified relationship does not fully conform to Pepper's formal definition of binominals (this volume: section 2.3), which states: "A binominal lexeme is a naming unit that consists primarily of two thing-morphs, and possibly additional grammatical material, formed by combining two concepts *between which there is an unstated (or underspecified) relation of modification*" (italics mine)

(ii) The Anindilyakwa binominal constructions are generally very productive, morphologically and semantically transparent, and an available strategy to coin new words for introduced complex concepts. In this sense, they do not always follow Pepper's (this volume, section 2.4) typological definition of binominals, which states that a "binominal lexeme is an instance of a *lexicalized* nominal modification construction" (italics mine)

(iii) The Anindilyakwa constructions can consist of up to five distinct productive morphemes, some of which may be *non-consecutive*. In other words, any typology of this domain needs to include rules to account for multiple, non-consecutive markers on either the head or the modifier. (See further Pepper, this volume: section 3.1)

(iv) Finally, in the INALP construction, the derivational prefix occurs on the semantic *head*, and thus may instantiate one of the missing types in the typology (though see Pepper, this volume, for an alternative view).

The Anindilyakwa data thus show us once again the value of exploring typologically lesser-known 'exotic' languages, as this can result in a certain progress in typology: access to new data may broaden the scope of the typological generalizations that we can achieve.

This chapter first introduces the features of the Anindilyakwa language that are necessary to understand the binominal lexemes in section 2. Then I will outline the structures and functions of the various binominal lexemes in section 3, and why they do not comfortably fit into Pepper's typology: the inalienable possession construction (section 3.1), alienable possession construction (section 3.2), and the proprietive/privative construction (section 3.3). The semantic differences between these constructions are addressed in section 4, while section 5 explores derived nouns in Wubuy (NUY), a closely related language, that are very similar to the INALP in Anindilyakwa. Section 6 then sums up what can be learned from less well-described languages and makes suggestions as to how to expand the typology of binominal lexemes of the world's languages.

2 Anindilyakwa

In order to understand the various binominal lexeme constructions in Anindilyakwa, it is necessary to provide some background on the nominal morphology of the language. As is common in Australian languages, nominals are one of two major word classes that can be identified in Anindilyakwa along the lines of the affixational potential of the individual lexemes, the other class being verbs (e.g. Dixon 1980). These two classes are differentiated by taking distinct sets of inflectional and derivational affixes. The class of nominal words includes at least six subclasses: nouns, adjectives, pronouns, demonstratives, kinship terms, and adverbs. They are grouped together under the label 'nominals' based on their morphological properties: they all take noun class prefixes, albeit with varying flexibility, and they take case and number suffixes. Moreover, all but the adverb subclass can function as 'thing-roots' that denote physical objects (animate and inanimate), as illustrated in (1). Unless indicated otherwise, all examples in this chapter come from published and unpublished Anindilyakwa dictionaries and stories, and my PhD thesis (van Egmond 2012).[2]

(1) a. *mangma* [VEG.crab] 'crab' — noun
    b. *m-arvma* [VEG-big] 'the big one (e.g., *mangma* 'VEG.crab')' — adjective
    c. *nungkuwa* 'you(SG)' — pronoun
    d. *wurrvng-akina* [3FDU-that] 'those two females' — demonstrative
    e. *nu-ngw-arrka* [3MSG-father-1SG.KIN] 'my father' — kinship term

Table 1 presents the structure of the nominal word, with optional elements in parentheses. Plus and minus signs before the slot number indicate the direction with respect to the stem. Slots marked * may be reduplicated, to express plurality or intensification.

Table 1: Structure of the nominal word.

−6	(−5)	(−4)*	(−3)	(−2)	(−1)*	0*	(+1)	(+2)	(+3)
Pronominal / gender / noun class prefix	Trial number	Quantifier	Inner gender	Inalienable / alienable possession	Body part / generic nominal	Stem	Number	Adnominal case	Semantic case

The only obligatory elements in the nominal word are the noun class/gender/pronominal prefix in slot [−6], and the stem in [0]. Synchronically, however, the overt marking of nouns for noun class is defunct, as loanwords no longer take an overt class marker. Not every element in this template occurs in every nominal

---

[2] The letter *v* in the orthography represents the phoneme /ə/.
 Abbreviations used in the glosses: 1 'first person exclusive', 2 'second person', 3 'third person', ABL 'ablative case', ALP 'alienable possession', COLL 'collective noun class', DU 'dual', EPEN 'epenthetic morph', F 'feminine gender', FEM 'feminine noun class', FEM$_{der}$ 'feminine derivational noun class', INALP 'inalienable possession', INCL 'inclusive', KIN 'kinship', LOC 'locative case', M 'masculine gender', MASC 'masculine noun class', MASC$_{der}$ 'masculine derivational noun class', NEUT 'neuter noun class', O 'object (general)', PL 'plural', POSS 'possessive case', PRG 'pergressive', PRIV 'privative case', PRO 'pronoun', PROP 'proprietive case', PST 'past', RDP 'reduplication', S 'subject (general)', SG 'singular', VEG 'vegetable noun class', XTD 'extended action'.
 Further glossing conventions: a synchronic (active) morpheme boundary is indicated with a dash (-), and a frozen morpheme boundary with a full stop (.), which is not indicated on the lexeme. The plus sign (+) indicates a bound form, e.g. one that cannot occur without the INALP prefix.

subclass: body parts and generics, for instance, can only be incorporated into adjectives (including numerals) and adverbs, but not into nouns, demonstratives, pronouns or kinship terms. The latter three subclasses do not take derivational prefixes either. And the inner gender prefixes in slot [(–3)] only co-occur with the inalienable and alienable possession derivational prefixes in slot [(–2)].

Slot [–6] is occupied by five noun class prefixes that classify non-humans (MASculine, FEMinine, COLLective, VEGetable, NEUTer) and three gender prefixes that classify humans (Male, Female, PLural). For nouns, the class prefix is lexicalized: it cannot be removed from the noun root nor can it be substituted. For the other nominal subclasses, the noun class prefix is flexible and can be varied to agree with the head noun, as illustrated in (2). Human referents take flexible gender prefixes, as shown in (3).

(2) a. *y-akina y-arvma yaraja* [MASC-that MASC-big MASC.goanna] 'that big goanna'
 b. *dh-akina dh-arvma dhuwalya* [FEM-that FEM-big FEM.curlew'] 'that big curlew'
 c. *wurr-akina wurr-arvma wurrendhindha* [COLL-that COLL-big COLL.rat] 'that big rat'
 d. *m-akina m-arvma memvrrerra* [VEG-that VEG-big VEG.flathead] 'that big flathead'
 e. *akina arvma akwalya* [NEUT.that NEUT.big NEUT.fish] 'that big fish'

(3) a. *nv-bungkawa*   [3MSG-boss] 'male boss'
 b. *dhv-bungkawa*   [3FSG-boss] 'female boss'
 c. *wurrv-bungkawa* [3PL-boss] 'bosses'

Not only do modifiers agree in noun class and gender with their heads, as in (2), but the head nouns are also represented on the verb as argument prefixes. In other words, there is obligatory agreement throughout the clause:

(4) *wurr-akina wurru-wilyaba-manja narrv-nga-mvrndak-ararika*
 COLL-that COLL-one-LOC COLL.**O**-FEM.**S**-all-coil.around.PST
 dh-akina dhvngarna
 FEM-that FEM.snake
 'The snake was coiled all around one (*wurruwarda* 'COLL.dog').'

Both the subject (*dhvngarna* 'FEM.snake') and the object (*wurruwarda* 'COLL.dog') are cross-referenced on the verb by the pronominal prefixes. The normal order for the argument prefixes is for the subject to precede the object, but this order is reversed when the object is a higher on the person-animacy scale. In (4), the COLLective class of the object outranks the FEMinine class of the subject, so we get reversed order.

Other relevant features for this chapter are the two distinct derivational prefixes, inalienable possession (INALP) *m(a)-* and alienable possession (ALP) *ng(w)-*, in slot [(–2)] and the two inner gender prefixes (Male *en-* and Female *adh-*) in slot [(–3)] that accompany them. The inner gender prefixes are combined with the possession prefixes in the following way: the INALP prefix takes a gender prefix when the referent of the derived nominal is human or belongs to one of the three 'animate' noun classes (MASC, FEM, COLL), as shown in (5a) for a MASC possessor. The inner gender prefix is absent when the referent belongs to one of the two 'inanimate' noun classes (VEG, NEUT), as shown in (5b) for a NEUT class possessor.

(5) a. *yi-nv-m+adhangkwa*
　　　　MASC-**M**-INALP+flesh
　　　　'flesh of MASC class animal' (e.g. *yimendha* 'MASC.turtle')
　　b. *a-m+adhangkwa*
　　　　NEUT-INALP+flesh
　　　　'flesh of NEUT class animal' (e.g. *alkvrra* 'NEUT.herring')

The ALP prefix, on the other hand, always takes an inner gender prefix, regardless of the referent of the derived noun: FEM class derived nouns take the Female inner gender prefix (6c), whereas all other classes take the Male inner gender prefix (6a,b):

(6) a. *envngv-makarda   akwalya*
　　　　NEUT.**M**.ALP-VEG.sea   NEUT.fish
　　　　'saltwater fish'
　　b. *m-envng-angwinyamba   malhamukwa*
　　　　VEG-**M**.ALP-NEUT.anger   VEG.canoe
　　　　'war canoe'
　　c. *dh-adhvng-arrawa   dhvmbala*
　　　　FEM-**F**.ALP-below   clothing(FEM)
　　　　'underclothes'

The INALP construction (5) is more flexible than the frozen ALP construction (6): in the former, the presence of the inner gender prefix is determined by the noun class of the derived noun, whereas in the latter, the ALP+inner gender prefixes have become synchronically inseparable.

The final relevant nominal feature for this chapter is the adnominal case suffix slot [(+2)] of the template, as this is the slot where the proprietive/privative derivational case suffix occurs, as illustrated in (6b) above for the PRIV suffix.

3 Anindilyakwa binominal lexemes

One frequently used strategy in the world's languages to form binominals is by juxtaposing two 'thing-roots', which may or may not involve an additional marker, as in the English (ENG) noun-noun compound *eyelid*, Dutch (NLD) *vis.boer* [fish. farmer] 'fishmonger', or Turkish (TUR) *demir.yol.u* [iron.road.iz] 'railway'. In Australian languages, too, two thing-roots can be combined to express complex concepts, as in the following Pama-Nyungan (7) and non-Pama-Nyungan (8) examples.[3] Unless indicated otherwise, the Pama-Nyungan examples are from Lesage (2014).

(7) a. *arruta alta* [chin hair] 'beard' Alyawarra (ALY)
    b. *murndal-mraat* [thunder-ground] 'earthquake' Bunganditj (XBG)
    c. *meer-pancr* [eye-body.hair] 'eyelash' Kuuk Thaayorre (THD)
    d. *jamana ngamayi* [foot mother] 'toe' Gurindji (GUE) (Pepper 2016)

(8) a. *gun-denge-bok* [iv-foot-print] 'foot print' Gun-djeihmi (GUP) (Evans 2003: 175)
    b. *nguwah djirru* [guts/shit trouble/harm] 'policeman' Rembarrnga (RMB) (McGregor 2000: 13)
    c. *jalig garrij-ngarna* [child school-ASSOC] 'school kid' Jaminjung (DJD) (Schultze-Berndt 2000)
    d. *ngunga pelpith* [sun head] 'midday' Murrinh Patha (MWF) (Walsh 1996: 376)

However, simply juxtaposing two nominals to form a binominal is not an available strategy in Anindilyakwa. This is because, as already mentioned, there is

---

3 The Pama-Nyungan languages constitute the biggest family in Australia, covering about seven-eighths of the continent and including up to 300 languages. The non-Pama-Nyungan languages in Northern Australia contain perhaps 90% of Australia's linguo-genetic diversity in an eighth of its land area (Evans 2003: 3); they do not form a genetic unit but consist of over 20 language families and about 120 languages. Today, of the over 400 different languages (not to mention dialects) that were spoken at the time of European colonization in 1788, only about 25 are still learned by children, Anindilyakwa being one of them.

obligatory agreement throughout the clause. In Anindilyakwa, this agreement can be achieved by the derivational affixes introduced above: the inalienable possession (INALP) and alienable possession (ALP) prefixes and the proprietive/privative (PROP/PRIV) suffix. These affixes allow noun class harmony between the modifier and the head: they convert a nominal root into a derived nominal of a specific target noun class, which agrees with that of an external noun.

The four constructions each name a subset of complex concepts: nominals derived with the INALP prefix express the part-whole relationship or some other indissoluble connection (9); nominals marked for ALP have a looser sense of 'belonging to' or 'associated with' (10); those marked with the PROP suffix mean 'having, being equipped with' (11a); and those with the PRIV suffix mean 'not having, without' (11b).

(9) a. *ma-ma+kulya*[4]   *menba*
 VEG-INALP+skin   VEG.eye
 'eyelid' (Lit: 'skin belonging to VEG class item, eye')
 b. *yi-nv-m-eminda*   *yikarba*
 MASC-M-INALP-NEUT.nose   MASC.woomera
 'woomera hook' (Lit: 'nose belonging to MASC class item, woomera')[5]

(10) a. *envngv-menba*
 NEUT.M.ALP-VEG.eye
 'glasses, spectacles' (Lit.: 'NEUT class item associated with the eye')
 b. *envngv-makarda-lhangwa*   *angalya*
 NEUT.M.ALP-VEG.sea-POSS   NEUT.country
 'sea country' (Lit.: 'country belonging to the sea')

(11) a. *nvng-adharrvngka-ma*
 1SG-wife-PROP
 'I have a wife'
 b. *nvng-enungu-dharrvngka-ma*
 1SG-M.ALP-wife-PRIV
 'I don't have a wife'

---

4 In Anindilyakwa, +*kulya* is a bound form, as indicated by the plus sign (+), but cognate forms in genetically related languages show that in the language ancestral to the Gunwinyguan family, this word was an independent form, which has been reconstructed for proto-Gunwinyguan as **kurlak* 'skin' (Harvey 2003). The shift of pGN **rl* to *ly* in Anindilyakwa is a regular one (van Egmond 2012, van Egmond & Baker 2020).
5 A woomera is a spear-throwing device.

The nominals derived with the INALP prefix refer to components of body parts (9a) or parts of inanimate objects (9b), where the noun class of the derived noun denoting the part agrees with that of the independent noun expressing the whole. In the ALP construction (10), the derived noun agrees in noun class with the hypernym (introduced objects apart from vehicles are usually NEUT noun class). Likewise, the PROP suffix (11a) enables the noun it attaches to to have a flexible prefix that represents the semantic head. And the PRIV suffix (11b) is added to the ALP construction. Apart from some lexicalized instances, all constructions are very productive, as we will see in the following sections.

3.1 Alienable possession prefix *ng(w)-*

Alienable possession denotes "a variety of rather freely made associations between two referents, that is, relationships of a less permanent and inherent type" (Chappell & McGregor 1996: 4). In Anindilyakwa, the nominal marked for alienable possession is 'associated with' or 'belongs to' the independent noun (which does not need to be present in the clause, depending on the context). The derived nominal agrees in noun class with the independent noun. The ALP prefix can derive a nominal from a noun (12, 13), clan or place name (14), adverb (15a,b), or adjective (15c) (the latter two are not considered to be binominals according to the definition employed in this volume). The ALP prefix is always preceded by a gender morpheme, and the gender+ALP sequence is synchronically unsegmentable: *invng-* 'M.ALP', *adhvng-* 'F.ALP'. The /a/ vowels of the NEUT and VEG noun class prefixes merge with the initial /i/ of *invng-* and become /e/: NEUT *a-* + *invng-* > *envng-*; VEG *ma-* + *invng-* > *menvng-*. The noun marked for ALP retains its intrinsic noun class prefix, as this is frozen to the stem.

(12) a. *envng-erriberriba*   *anhvnga*
    NEUT.M.ALP-NEUT.bush   NEUT.vegetable.food
    'bush tucker'
 b. *envng-erriberriba*   *alyelyikba*
    NEUT.M.ALP-NEUT.bush   NEUT.tongue
    'bush tongue (i.e. traditional language)'
 c. *y-invng-erriberriba*   *yinungwangba=murriya*
    MASC-M.ALP-NEUT.bush   MASC.land.animal=etc.
    'bush animals'

(13) a. *m-envng-akwalya*   *mukayuwa*
      VEG-M.ALP-NEUT.fish   VEG.dillybag
      'fish net'
   b. *m-envng-alhvdha*
      VEG-M.ALP-NEUT.colour/paint/bark
      'daytime' (Lit: 'colour associated with the sun' (*mamawura* 'VEG.sun'))

(14) a. *warnung-amagula*
      3PL.M.ALP-Amagula
      'the Amagula clan people'
   b. *dh-adhvngi-yirrkala*
      3FSG-F.ALP-Yirrkala
      'female from Yirrkala'

(15) a. *dh-adhvng-arrawa*   *dhvmbala*
      FEM-F.ALP-below   clothing(FEM)
      'underclothes'   (Leeding 1996: 221)
   b. *envng-adhuwaba*
      NEUT.M.ALP-today
      'NEUT class item belonging to today, modern'
   c. *envng-arvmvrvma*   *ayakwa*
      NEUT.M.ALP-RDP.big   NEUT.word
      'law, commandments, covenant'

The derived nominal behaves like an adjective in that it is now flexible and can take any pronominal/gender/noun class prefix to agree with the independent noun, which may or may not be present in the clause or discourse. The independent noun belongs to, comes from, or is associated with the nominal marked for ALP. Thus, *envng-erriberriba anhvnga* 'bush tucker' in (12a) literally means 'something of NEUT class, vegetable food, belonging to the bush'.

The ALP construction is very productive. It can be used to coin new words for introduced complex concepts, such as 'glasses' in (10a) above, and the following:

(16) a. *N-envngv-karrawara*
      3MSG-M.ALP-above
      'God' (Lit: 'he belonging to above')
   b. *n-envngi-jebija*
      3MSG-M.ALP-church
      'minister, priest' (Lit: 'he belonging to the church')

c. *envng-arrvrra*
NEUT.M.ALP-NEUT.wind
'tire pump, fan' (Lit: 'NEUT class item associated with wind')

Some ALP constructions have lexicalized to become proper nouns.

(17) a. *dh-adhvngv-mamawuru-manja*[6]
FEM-F.ALP-VEG.sun-LOC
'brown tree snake' (Lit: 'she associated with in the sun') (Leeding 1996: 219)
b. *envngv-mukumuku-manja*
NEUT.M.ALP-VEG.deep.sea-LOC
'octopus' (Lit: 'NEUT class item associated with in the deep sea') (Leeding 1996: 219)
c. *y-invng-akarda*
MASC-M.ALP-sea
'sea eagle' (Lit: 'MASC class item associated with the sea')

In the last example, the traditional noun *makarda* 'VEG.sea' seems to have lost its VEG noun class prefix *m-*, which is unusual for nouns marked for ALP. I take this to be evidence of the lexicalized status of the derived nominal: it is an ancient form, which may have been created at a time when the noun class prefixes were still flexible and could be omitted (as they can in other languages of the Gunwinyguan family); or the noun class marker *m-* may simply have eroded over time.

3.1.1 Structure of the ALP and its place in the binominals typology

In the ALP construction, there is noun class harmony between the modifier and the head, where the derived nominal is the modifier and the independent noun the semantic head. For example, *m-ening-akwalya mukayuwa* [VEG-M.ALP-NEUT.fish VEG.dillybag] 'fish net' in (13a) above is a type of dillybag (a traditional Aboriginal basket made from woven grass), not a type of fish. The structure of the ALP can be represented as follows:

(18) [NCx-G.ALP-NCy.Mod (NCx.Head)]

---

[6] The LOC case in this and the following example presumably is present to denote the animal's preferred place of residing: e.g., the brown tree snake is associated with being in the sun.

where G represents the inner gender prefix and NC the noun classes of the nouns involved. The brackets on the head noun indicate that it can be omitted if the context is clear, as in several examples above. Moreover, it is the semantic head of the construction that is represented on the verb by the argument prefixes:

(19) yingv-m-arrka   m-envng-akwalya   mukayuwa
     3FSG-**VEG**-pull.PST   **VEG**-M.ALP-NEUT.fish   **VEG**.dillybag
     'she pulled in the fishing net'

The VEG object prefix on the verb represents the noun class of *mukayuwa* 'VEG.dillybag' (and not of *akwalya* 'NEUT.fish'), so the semantic head is also the syntactic head.

The ALP appears to be a bit of an outlier in terms of Pepper's typology. On the one hand, the construction seems to be what Pepper calls an adjectival construction (**adj**), where the modifier is marked with an adjectivizer affix. The ALP prefix functions as an adjectivizer, because it allows a noun stem with a frozen class prefix to take a variety of class or person prefixes in agreement with its head – in other words, it behaves like an Adjective. On the other hand, it has more active elements than the typical **adj** structure: (i) the independent noun, which is the head of the construction, (ii) the noun taking the ALP prefix, which is the modifier, (iii) the gender+ALP composite prefix, and (iv) the outer inflectional prefix. The only binominal that consists of four components in Pepper's typology is the double-marked construction (**dbl**), where both the head and the dependent are marked (e.g., TBC *ŋdu.n awa.n* [nose.3SG mouth.3SG] 'nostril'). However, the Anindilyakwa ALP is not an instance of double marking, because only the dependent is marked (not counting the frozen noun class prefix on the head noun). Pepper (this volume, section 3.1, and 2020: 142) handles cases in which multiple morphemes occur on one of the two main constituents by counting them as a single morph, "in order not to complicate the typology unnecessarily". I will follow this concession for now, leaving a more detailed analysis of the Anindilyakwa cases consisting of more than one affix on the modifier for future work.

3.2 Inalienable possession prefix *ma-*

The second type of binominal lexeme in Anindilyakwa are nominals derived with the INALP prefix *ma-*. These refer to parts of inanimate objects, plants, animals, and to components of body parts. The 'part' noun is marked for INALP and maintains its intrinsic noun class prefix, as this is frozen to the stem. The derived nominal behaves like an adjective in that it is now flexible and can take any pronominal/gender/noun class prefix to agree with the independent noun that represents the 'whole'. The INALP prefix is preceded by an additional masculine or feminine gender prefix when the 'whole' refers to a human or belongs to one of the animate classes (20), but not the inanimate classes (e.g., 21a,b). When the noun root starts with a vowel, the final vowel *a* of the INALP prefix is deleted.

(20) a. warnv-m+akvrnda   wurrayangkurra
        COLL.M-INALP+stem   COLL.waterlily
        'stem of waterlily'
    b. yi-nv-m-amamuwa   yi-nv-m-anhvnga
        MASC-M-INALP-round   MASC-M-INALP-NEUT.vegetable.food
        'fruit of MASC class tree' (e.g. yawurdarra 'MASC.red jungle berry')
    c. yukudhukudha   y-inv-m-adhvdhvra
        MASC.chest   MASC-M-INALP-NEUT.bone
        'chest bone'
    d. yi-nv-ma+kulya   kalkwa
        MASC-M-INALP+skin   coconut(MASC)[7]
        'coconut husk' (Lit: 'skin belonging to MASC class item, coconut')
    e. dh-adhv-m-amarda
        FEM-F-INALP-NEUT.leaves
        'leaves of FEM plant' (e.g. dhvrvra 'FEM.holly leaved pea flower')

The INALP conveys the part-whole relation, where the nominal marked for INALP refers to the part and the independent noun to the whole. The part can be part of a body part (e.g., 21a,c) or other inanimate item (21b), or the leaves or fruit of trees (20b,e). The nominal root in the INALP construction is frequently a body part noun, which has shifted its meaning to refer to an item that resembles the body part, such as 'nose' > 'hook' in (9b) above, 'mouth' > 'hole' in (21), 'hand' > 'handle' in (22c), and 'ankle' > 'knot' in (22d).

(21) a. e-m-edhvrra   emindha
        NEUT-INALP-NEUT.mouth   NEUT.nose
        'nose hole' (Lit: 'mouth belonging to NEUT class item, nose')
    b. e-m-edhvrra   akungwa
        NEUT-INALP-NEUT.mouth   NEUT.water
        'water hole' (Lit: 'mouth belonging to NEUT class item, water')

---

[7] *Kalkwa* is not overtly marked for noun class because it is a Macassan loanword, and loanwords do not take noun class prefixes. See footnote 9 for more details about who the Macassans were.

c. *yi-nv-m-edhvrra*   *yuwarra-lhangwa*
MASC-M-INALP-NEUT.mouth   MASC.womb-POSS
'vagina' (Lit: 'mouth belonging to MASC class item, womb')

(22) a. *ma-m-ayama*   *menba*
VEG-INALP-NEUT.body.hair   VEG.eye
'eyebrow' (Lit: 'body hair belonging to VEG class item, eye')
b. *dh-adhv-m-arvngka*   *dhvrija*
FEM-F-INALP-NEUT.head   dress(FEM)
'dress bodice' (Lit: 'head belonging to FEM class item, dress')
c. *ma-m-ayarrka*   *mukayuwa*
VEG-INALP-NEUT.hand   VEG.dillybag
'handle of dillybag'
d. *ma-m-angurnda*   *merra*
VEG-INALP-NEUT.ankle   VEG.rope
'knot in rope'

As in the ALP construction, the independent noun can be omitted when the context is clear:

(23) a. *ma-m-alyelyikba*
VEG-INALP-NEUT.lips
'eyelid, foreskin' (Lit: 'lips belonging to VEG class item, e.g. *menba* 'VEG.eye', *marrkwa* 'VEG.penis'')
b. *yi-nv-m-alyelyikba*
MASC-M-INALP-NEUT.lips
'sternum' (Lit: 'lips belonging to MASC class item, e.g. *yukudhukudha* 'MASC.chest')
c. *ma-m-alhvka*
VEG-INALP-NEUT.foot
'tire, wheel, wheel track, tracks of VEG class animal' (Lit: 'foot belonging to VEG class item or animal, e.g. *dhvraka* 'truck(veg)')
d. *warnv-m+alyirra*
COLL.M-INALP+liquid
'liquid of COLL plant' (e.g. *wurruwarduwarda* 'COLL.spinifex grass')

When the referent is human, the body part refers to something inextricably linked to, or inalienably possessed by, the person, such as the following.

(24) a. nvng-env-m-alhvka
       1SG-M-INALP-NEUT.foot
       'my footprints, my tracks' (Lit: 'something linked to foot belonging to me')
    b. ngarnv-m-adhvdhvra
       1INCLPL.M-INALP-NEUT.bone
       'our skeletons'
    c. dh-adhv-m-ebinga
       3FSG-F-INALP-NEUT.body
       'her body'

These examples suggest that the INALP construction was once used in the past to refer to possessed body parts, which later changed its meaning to refer to items resembling the body part. Indeed, some (older) speakers still accept the readings in (25) (Leeding 1996):

(25) a. nvng-env-m-arvngka
       1SG-M-INALP-NEUT.head
       'my head'
    b. n-env-m-alhakba
       3MSG-M-INALP-NEUT.leg
       'his leg'

However, speakers now say that this is 'how the old people used to say it', and that it is no longer used today. Body parts marked for INALP possession now refer to parts of inanimate items, where the body part resembles this part, or is inextricably linked to it. Human body parts are currently expressed with a possessive pronoun, similar to English:

(26) a. nganyangwa   arvngka
       1SG.PRO.POSS   NEUT.head
       'my head'
    b. env-lhangwa   alhakba
       3MSG.PRO.POSS NEUT.leg
       'his leg'

Body part nouns marked for INALP refer to a range of items that somehow resemble the body part, as illustrated in (27) for *alhakba* 'NEUT.leg'.

(27) a. *ma-m-alhakba*
       VEG-INALP-NEUT.leg
       'tail of shark' (*mangiyuwanga* 'VEG.shark')
   b. *ma-m-alhakba   dingki*
       VEG-INALP-NEUT.leg   dinghy(VEG)
       'back of the dinghy'
   c. *dh-adhv-m-alhakba*
       FEM-F-INALP-NEUT.leg
       'skirt of dress' (*dhvrija* 'dress(FEM)')

These examples show the semantic associations that Anindilyakwa people have with the body part 'leg', which can be used to refer to parts of animals or things that do not have legs. Body part nouns are very important in the Anindilyakwa language and permeate the entire grammar. They occur in numerous environments other than the INALP and they are one of the principal ways to express shape (van Egmond 2012, Leeding 1996).

Nominals derived with the INALP can also be lexicalized:

(28) a. *yi-nv-m-anhvnga*
       MASC-M-INALP-NEUT.vegetable.food
       'wild apple'
   b. *e-m-enungkwa*
       NEUT-INALP-NEUT.spear
       'stringybark tree'
   c. *warnv-m-alhvdha*
       COLL.M-INALP-NEUT.colour/paint/bark
       'bark parcel containing bones of dead child'

These forms are lexicalized because they are proper names that are no longer semantically transparent or decomposable.

3.2.1 Structure of the INALP construction and its place in the typology

The semantic head of the construction is the noun marked with the INALP prefix: for example, *ma-m-ayama menba* [VEG-INALP-NEUT.body.hair VEG.eye] 'eyebrow' is a type of body hair, not a type of eye. This may a bit harder to see in those instances where the body part noun has changed its meaning, such as *ma-m-ayarrka mukayuwa* [VEG-INALP-NEUT.hand VEG.dillybag] 'handle of dillybag' in (22c), where the noun *ayarrka* no longer refers to a body part but to an item related to it (hand > handle). Nonetheless, the head is the derived 'part' noun, not the independent 'whole' noun.

The structure of the INALP can be represented as follows:

(29) [NCx-(G-)INALP-NCy.Head (NCx.Mod)]

where NC_x stands for noun class/pronominal prefix of the syntactic head, and NC_y for the noun class of the semantic head, which is the body part. G is the inner gender prefix that is only present when NC_x belongs to one of the animate noun classes or refers to a human. The noun class of the noun to which the INALP prefix attaches is frozen, but the derived noun behaves like an Adjective, in that it can take any noun class prefix in agreement with the modifier.

Even though the order of the head preceding the modifier is by far the most common in my data, it can be reversed as well, as in 'chest bone' in (20c) above. This is because word order in Anindilyakwa is free: as all grammatical information is captured by the morphology, syntax plays no role whatsoever. This syntactically free, pragmatically determined word order is common property of Australian languages, first identified by Hale (1983). For the INALP it means that there is no fixed head – modifier word order.

Interestingly, it is the independent noun denoting the 'whole' that is represented on the verb as the subject or object argument:

(30) a. *warnvmamalya   narrv-ma-ma-ngv-ma   ma-m-amarda...*
       3PL.people   3PL-**VEG**-take-PST-*ma*   **VEG**-INALP-NEUT.leaves
       'people took the leaves of the *mabalba* ['VEG.peanut tree'] . . .'
    b. *nanga-lhuku-lhukwa-mvrrkaju-wa   dh-adhv-m-alhvka-lhangwiyu...wa*
       3MSG/**3FSG**-RDP-track-follow-PST   **3FSG**-F-INALP-NEUT.foot-ABL.PRG...XTD
       'he kept on following her tracks'

This means that the semantic head of the construction is not the syntactic head: in (30a), the 'part' noun *amarda* 'leaves' is the semantic head of the construction, but the 'whole', the *mabalba* tree, is cross-referenced on the verb as the direct object. Similarly, in (b), the possessor of the tracks, rather than the tracks themselves, is the direct object of the verb.

As argued for the ALP, placing the INALP into Pepper's binominal typology is again problematic, for two reasons. Firstly, like the ALP construction described in the previous section, the INALP construction has potentially *five* active elements. Consider for example *yukudhukudha y-inv-m-adhvdhvra* [MASC.chest MASC-M-INALP-NEUT.bone] 'chest bone' in (20c) above, which includes: (i) the independent noun, (ii) the noun taking the INALP prefix, (iii) the INALP prefix itself, (iv) the inner gender prefix, and (v) the outer inflectional prefix that agrees with the noun class of the independent noun. Again, I will follow Pepper's stipulation (this volume: section 3.1) that two or more consecutive morphs attached to either the modifier or the head are counted as a single morph. Future work must uncover whether the typology needs to be expanded to allow more than one affix on the head of the binominal.

The second, more important, reason why the INALP poses a challenge for Pepper's analysis is that the derivational affix occurs on the semantic *head* of the construction, rather than on the modifier. This means that the INALP is the head-marked correlate of **adj**, which is one of the two missing, "logically impossible", types in Pepper's typology: **nml**. The Anindilyakwa data show that it *is* possible for a transpositional (subclass-changing) affix to occur on the head of a binominal lexeme, and for the head still to be a nominal: the INALP prefix is attached to a noun with an inflexible noun class marker, so that this noun can now agree with an independent noun, thus creating a binominal. Hence, the INALP is a possible candidate for one of the missing types in Pepper's typology of binominal lexemes.

However, Pepper (this volume: section 3.3.2) argues against analysing the INALP as **nml**. Since the form of the head varies according to the properties of the dependent, he suggests, the Anindilyakwa INALP construction must be classified as **con** in his binominal typology. I think this difference in analysis has to do with the definition of noun and the definition of (non-)transpositional. I consider all derivational prefixes discussed here to be transpositional, as they change the subclass of the word they attach to: a noun with a fixed noun class becomes an Adjective with a flexible noun class. Admittedly, this is not a change in word class, but rather in subclass (in Anindilyakwa, and in Australian languages in general (see section2), nouns and adjectives have similar morphological properties and are commonly grouped together under the label 'nominals'). In contrast, Pepper assumes the INALP derivational prefix to be non-transpositional and this leads him to classify this construction as an example of the **con** type. But since all the INALP marker does is change the subclass of the nominal it attaches to, I do not see why this is non-transpositional. Therefore, I treat it parallel to the ALP marker, the only difference being that the latter attaches to the modifier (and is thus classified as **adj**), whereas the former attaches to the head (and may thus be a candidate for **nml**).

3.2.2 The changing structure of the INALP

The INALP is very productive and can be used to coin terms for introduced items, which may be based on loanwords. However, these newly coined examples appear to have a different structure from that of the traditional examples in (30) above. Recall that loanwords do not receive an overt noun class marker and that introduced items (apart from vehicles) are usually assigned NEUT class.

(31) a. *a-mi-jurra*   *angwarnda*[8]
NEUT-INALP-paper NEUT.stone
'paper money' (Lit: 'NEUT class item, money, belonging to / resembling paper')
b. *a-mi-lyelyinga*
NEUT-INALP-knife
'metal' (Lit: 'NEUT class item belonging to / resembling knife')
c. *a-ma-dhvngvra*
NEUT-INALP-FEM.white.clay
'flour' (Lit: 'NEUT class item belonging to / resembling white clay')

(32) *a-ma-bulkwa*   *engeemina*
NEUT-INALP-cattle NEUT.breast.milk
'cow's milk' (Lit: 'NEUT class item, breast milk, belonging to cattle')

The nouns *jurra* 'paper, book' in (31a) and *lyelyinga* 'knife' in (31b) are Macassan loans,[9] while *bulkwa* 'cow, cattle' in (32) comes from English 'bullock'.

These newly coined examples are interesting because they differ from those with traditional nouns. Firstly, they do not involve body parts. Secondly, whereas in the earlier examples the noun marked for INALP is the semantic head of the construction, this appears to be the reverse for these more recently coined examples. Here, the independent noun is the semantic head (as [NEUT-INALP-cattle NEUT.breast.milk] 'cow's milk' is a type of milk). If this pattern is consistent for recent loans, it suggests that the INALP construction may recently have reversed its semantic head, resulting in a reading similar to the ALP construction:

(33) [NCx-(G-)INALP-NCy.Mod (NCx.Head)]

---

8 The noun *angwarnda* traditionally meant 'stone', but this meaning was extended to refer to coins as well. The meaning of 'coin' was then further extended to refer to money in general.
9 The Macassans were fishermen coming from the port of Makassar in Sulawesi to the shores of Northern Australia in search for shells, pearls and trepang. Their visits started in the late 17th century and ended in 1906 when the White Australia policy was enforced (MacKnight 1972, 1976). There are many Macassan loanwords in the languages of Northern Australia, and especially so in Anindilyakwa, where the contact with the Macassans appears to have been particularly intense (Evans 1992).

This in turn could imply that the head-marked type identified in the previous section is highly vulnerable: given that it is rare or perhaps even absent in the rest of the world's languages, and that in Anindilyakwa it appears to have changed its structure from a head-marked to a modifier-marked binominal, this may suggest that this type of construction is particularly susceptible to change.

3.3 Proprietive/privative suffix -ma ~ -mvrra

The remaining two binominal lexemes in Anindilyakwa involve the proprietive/privative derivational suffix. This suffix either co-occurs with the ALP prefix, in which case it contributes a meaning of 'without', or without the ALP prefix, in which case it means 'having, being equipped with, with the property of'. The examples in (34) illustrate the privative meaning of the suffix *-ma* (the longer alternant *-mvrra* is used less frequently), and those in (35) the proprietive meaning.

(34) a. *dh-adhvngv-nungkwarbv-ma*
       3FSG-F.ALP-man-PRIV
       'widow' (Lit: 'she not having a man') (Leeding 1996: 222)
   b. *nvng-enungu-dharrvngka-ma*
       1SG-M.ALP-wife-PRIV
       'I don't have a wife'
   c. *akwalya   envng-amalya-ma*
       NEUT.fish NEUT.M.ALP-NEUT.fat-PRIV
       'fish without fat'
   d. *envng-akwalya-ma   adhvdhvra*
       NEUT.M.ALP-NEUT.fish-PRIV NEUT.bone
       'fish bones without meat'

Here, the complex concept is one of one thing being without another thing. Just like the ALP construction, this concept is expressed as a binominal lexeme where the modifier receives the ALP prefix (in addition to the PRIV suffix). And just like the ALP construction, the order of the modifier and the head is free (compare for instance 34 c and d).

The PROPrietive construction uses the same *-ma ~ -mvrra* suffix but without a derivational prefix:

(35) a. *dhvraka   m-alhvkvra-ma*
       truck(VEG)   VEG-NEUT.house-PROP
       'caravan'

b. *wurr-awinyamba-mvrra*
   3PL-NEUT.anger-PROP
   'quick-tempered people' (Leeding 1989: 296)
c. *ni-jinabv-mvrra   n-akina*
   3MSG-gun-PROP   3MSG-that
   'he has a gun' (Stokes 1982: 101)

The PROP suffix functions in a way similar to the possession derivational prefixes, in that it allows a noun to agree in noun class with a specific external noun. As for the ALP, it is the modifier that is marked with the derivational suffix, while the head noun, which may or may not be present in the clause, is represented by the inflectional prefix on the derived nominal.

3.3.1 Structure of the PROP/PRIV constructions and their place in the typology

Apart from the presence of the GENDER+ALP prefix, the structure of the privative and proprietive constructions is identical:

(36) [NCx-(G.ALP-)NCy.Mod-PRIV/PROP (NCx.Head)]

Apart from the PRIV suffix itself, the structure of the PRIV binominal is identical to the one of the ALP, with the derivational affixes occurring on the modifier: *akwalya envng-amalya-ma* [NEUT.fish NEUT.M.ALP-NEUT.fat-PRIV] 'fish without fat' is a type of fish, not a type of fat. Similarly, for the PROP construction, the modifier receives the derivational suffix: *ni-jinabv-mvrra n-akina* [3msg-gun-prop 3msg-that] 'he has a gun' (Lit: 'he with gun').Again, fitting the construction into Pepper's typology is problematic, because the morphs involved are *non-consecutive*: a noun class prefix is combined with a PROP/PRIV suffix. Whereas in the previous sections, I have followed Pepper (this volume: section 3.1) in counting two or more consecutive morphs as a single morph, but this is not a possible strategy when the morphs are non-consecutive. This may call for an expansion of the typology in order to accommodate the Anindilyakwa data.

4 Competition between the four constructions

The semantic difference between the four constructions in Anindilyakwa is the degree of alienability or separateness: whereas the INALP (37a) expresses *i*nalienability (such as part-whole or other permanent indissoluble connections between the possessor and the possessum), the ALP (37b) conveys looser associations between the possessor and the possessum. In the PROP construction (37c), the connection is even looser, because the possessum is mere property and can thus can also be lost; in the PRIV (37d), the possessor is without the possessum.

(37) a. *a-m-alyelyikba*   *bajikala*
       NEUT-INALP-NEUT.lips   tin(NEUT)
       'tin lid' (Lit: 'lips belonging to NEUT class item, tin')
   b. *envng-alhvkvra*
       NEUT.M.ALP-NEUT.house
       'furniture' (Lit: 'NEUT class item associated with a house')
   c. *wurr-amvrndakijika-mvrra,   wurrv-mani-mvrra* . . .
       3PL-NEUT.things-PROP   3PL-money-PROP
       'they [whitefellas] have things, they have money. . .'
   d. *nvngk-envng-angbilyuwa-ngv-ma   nvngk-envngv-mijawara-ma*
       2SG-M.ALP-NEUT.sickness-?-PRIV   2SG-M.ALP-VEG.sadness-PRIV
       'you will be without sickness and without sadness'

Hence while in the INALP construction one item is a part of another, this is not the case for the other three constructions. Regarding the ALP, this denotes that the external noun "has something to do with" the nominal marked for ALP. This difference is especially clear when the same noun occurs in both constructions, such as the following.

(38) a. *envngv-menba*
       NEUT.M.ALP-VEG.eye
       'glasses, spectacles'
   b. *ma-m-ayama*   *menba*
       VEG-INALP-NEUT.body.hair VEG.eye
       'eyebrow'

(39) a. *envng-alhvka*
       NEUT.M.ALP-NEUT.foot
       'shoe' (Lit: 'NEUT class item associated with the foot')
   b. *n-env-m-alhvka*
       3MSG-M-INALP-NEUT.foot
       'his tracks'

The ALP constructions in the (a) examples denote an item that is associated with the body part marked for ALP, but it is not an inherent part of it: the two can be separated and the body part is not a part of an external whole (which may only be represented by a prefix). The body parts marked for INALP in the (b) examples, by contrast, are an indissoluble part of the external noun.

5 Other languages

The type of construction discussed here, where a noun root of any noun class is converted into a derived noun of a specific target noun class that matches that of an independently occurring noun, is extremely rare in Australia. To my knowledge, noun class harmony only occurs in Wubuy, which is the closest geographical and genetic neighbour of Anindilyakwa. In Wubuy, too, a body part noun can take a derivational noun class prefix (NC_{der}) that allows noun class harmony with an independent noun (Heath 1984). Compare the Anindilyakwa examples in (40) with the Wubuy ones in (41).

(40) Anindilyakwa
    a. *y-inv-ma+dhangkwa*
       MASC-M-INALP+flesh
       'flesh of MASC class animal' (e.g. *yimadhuwaya* 'MASC.stingray')
    b. *ma-ma+dhangkwa*
       VEG-INALP+flesh
       'flesh of VEG class animal' (e.g. *mangma* 'VEG.crab')

(41) Wubuy
    a. *yi:-ni-dhangku*
       MASC- $MASC_{der}$-flesh
       'flesh of masc class animal' (e.g. *yimadhuwayu* 'stingray(MASC)')
    b. *ama-ma-dhangku*
       VEG- VEG_{der}-flesh
       'flesh of VEG class animal' (e.g. *murradi* 'crab(veg)') (see Heath 1984: 160–1)

Although Wubuy lacks a unique INALP prefix *ma-*, the constructions in the two languages are very similar: the outer 'inflectional' set (identical to the regular prefixes) agrees with the whole, while the inner 'derivational' set is distinct.[10] And in Wubuy, too, nouns derived from body parts can refer to parts of inanimate objects, plants and animals. For example, *kulmung* 'belly' is used to refer to the roundish fruits and nuts of plants, as in the following examples (*-ngu-* is a meaningless EPENthetic element that is inserted between two stops at a morpheme boundary):

(42) a. *na-ni-ngu-kulmung*
MASC-MASC$_{der}$-EPEN-belly
'fruit of MASC class tree'
b. *ngarra-ngarri-ngu-kulmung*
FEM-FEM$_{der}$-EPEN-belly
'fruit of FEM class tree' (Heath 1984: 173)

As in Anindilyakwa, the Wubuy derived nominals show whole-to-part noun class harmony: as most body part nouns have a lexically specified intrinsic noun class (e.g. *kulmung* 'belly' belongs to what Heath 1984 labels MANA class, which is the Wubuy correspondence of the Anindilyakwa VEG class), the derivational prefix is used to make the noun class of the derived noun match that of an independently occurring noun (which, as in Anindilyakwa, does not need to be present in the same clause). Unlike in Anindilyakwa, however, the intrinsic noun class of the part noun does not need to be marked overtly on the noun and can thus be omitted, as it is in these examples.

Other examples of meaning extensions include forms based on *lhaany* 'tongue', from which we get derived forms meaning 'blade of spear' or 'clitoris', and derived forms of *ngakara* 'bone' can mean 'hard part' (such as a tough membrane) (Heath 1984: 173–7). However, this meaning extension of body part nouns does not appear to be as widespread in Wubuy as it is in Anindilyakwa.

One reason for why this type of construction is so rare in Australia may have to do with what Evans (1994) describes as problems associated with the assignment of noun class to body parts and other inalienably possessed items in Australian languages. Languages may choose the noun class/gender of the possessor for the body part, resulting in forms like 'he-buttock' and 'she-buttock' (Evans 1994: 1). In other languages, the body part may have an intrinsic gender, giving forms like 'it-buttock'. Or languages may compromise between the two and manage to mark both genders on the body part, such as 'it-he-buttock'. Alternatively, a language

---

[10] Such double noun class marking is rare in the world's languages, and in Australia is otherwise only found in Nungali, Gurr-goni and Yanyuwa (Aikhenvald 2003: 66).

may mark the gender of the possessor on the body part noun but let the body part's gender appear on agreeing adjectives, such as 'he-buttock it-large' for 'his large buttock'. Adding a separate prefix that allows the body part to maintain its intrinsic noun class but at the same time enables the body part noun to agree with its possessor appears to be a fourth strategy restricted to Anindilyakwa and Wubuy.

6 Conclusions

The various derivational affixes in Anindilyakwa described in this chapter are four strategies to create binominal lexemes. All constructions do not straightforwardly fit into Pepper's typology, as they all involve: (i) multiple morphemes occurring on one of the two main constituents, which is not specifically accounted for in his typology, and (ii) noun class harmony, where the derivational prefix allows the noun class of the noun it attaches to to agree with that of an independent noun. So far, the concept of noun class harmony has not received specific attention in Pepper's typology.

Three of the Anindilyakwa constructions – alienable possession, proprietive and privative – are similar to Pepper's adjectival construction (**adj**), where the modifier of the binominal is marked with an adjectivizer prefix. The Anindilyakwa prefixes function like adjectivizers because they change a noun that otherwise has a fixed noun class into an Adjective that agrees in noun class with an independent noun. The fact that these constructions consist of more components than does Pepper's **adj** can be resolved by counting multiple morphemes occurring on the same constituents as a single morph. However, this lumping together of morphs is not possible for the PROP/PRIV construction, where some of the morphs are non-consecutive. Any typology of this domain needs to include rules to account for multiple, non-consecutive markers on either the head or the modifier.

The Anindilyakwa INALP construction is different from the other three in that the adjectivizer prefix does not occur on the modifier but on the head of the binominal. The INALP construction therefore appears to be the head-marking equivalent of **adj** and thus may fill a gap in the typology. This would mean that binominals consisting of two thing-roots and a transpositional morpheme attached to the head are not a logical impossibility.

This chapter has shown that the study of lesser-known languages may shed new light on the issue under investigation and result in progress in typology, as the access to new data broadens the scope of the typological generalizations that we can achieve.

References

Aikhenvald, Alexandra. 2003. *Classifiers: A typology of noun categorization devices*. New York: Oxford University Press.

Chappell, Hillary & William McGregor. 1996. Prolegomenon to a theory of inalienability. In Hillary Chappell & William McGregor (eds.), *The grammar of inalienability: A typological perspective on body part terms and the whole-part relation*, 3–30. Berlin: Mouton de Gruyter.

Dixon, R. M. W. 1980. *The languages of Australia*. Cambridge: Cambridge University Press.

Evans, Nicholas. 1992. Macassan loanwords in Top End languages. *Australian Journal of Linguistics* 12. 45–91.

Evans, Nicholas. 1994. The problem of body parts and noun class membership in Australian languages. *University of Melbourne working papers in linguistics* 14. 1–8.

Evans, Nicholas. 2003. *Bininj Gun-Wok: A pan-dialectal grammar of Mayali, Kunwinjku and Kune*. Vol. 1 and 2. Canberra: Pacific Linguistics.

Hale, Kenneth. 1983. Warlpiri and the grammar of non-configurational languages. *Natural Language and Linguistic Theory* 1 (1). 5–47.

Harvey, Mark. 2003. An initial reconstruction of Proto Gunwinyguan phonology. In Nicholas Evans (ed.), *The non-Pama-Nyungan languages of Northern Australia: Comparative studies of the continent's most linguistically complex region*, 205–268. Canberra: Pacific Linguistics.

Heath, Jeffrey. 1984. *Functional grammar of Nunggubuyu*. Canberra: AIAS.

Leeding, Velma. 1989. *Anindilyakwa phonology and morphology*. Sydney: University of Sydney PhD dissertation.

Leeding, Velma. 1996. Body parts and possession in Anindilyakwa. In Hillary Chappell & William McGregor (eds.), *The grammar of inalienability: A typological perspective on body part terms and the whole-part relation*, 193–250. Berlin: Mouton de Gruyter.

Lesage, Jakob. 2014. *Nominal compounds and other N-N combinations: A typological study of a sample of Pama-Nyungan languages*. Leuven: Katholieke Universiteit Leuven MA thesis.

MacKnight, Campbell. 1972. Macassans and Aborigines. *Oceania* XLII. 283–319.

MacKnight, Campbell. 1976. *The voyage to Marege'. Macassan trepangers in Northern Australia*. Melbourne: Melbourne University Press.

McGregor, William B. 2000. Cockatoos, Chaining-Horsemen, and Mud-Eaters – Terms for "Policeman" in Australian Aboriginal languages. *Anthropos* 95 (1). 3–22.

Pepper, Steve. 2016. Noun-noun compounds and their functional equivalents: The case of Gurindji. Paper presented at the 8th Australianists in Europe workshop, SOAS, London. http://folk.uio.no/stevepe/euroz2016.pdf

Pepper, Steve. 2018. The typology of binominal lexemes. Paper presented at NoSlip, Oslo. http://folk.uio.no/stevepe/NoSLiP18.pdf

Pepper, Steve. This volume. Defining and typologizing binominal lexemes. In Steve Pepper, Francesca Masini & Simone Mattiola (eds.), *Binominal lexemes in cross-linguistic perspective*. Berlin: Mouton de Gruyter.

Schultze-Berndt, Eva. 2000. *Simple and complex verbs in Jaminjung: A study of event categorization in an Australian language*. Nijmegen: Katholieke Universiteit Nijmegen PhD dissertation.

Stokes, Judith. 1982. A description of the mathematical concepts of Groote Eylandt Aborigines. In Susanne Hargrave (ed.), *Work Papers of SIL-AAB Series B volume 8. Language and Culture*, 33–152. Darwin: SIL.
Van Egmond, Marie-Elaine. 2012. *Enindhilyakwa phonology, morphosyntax and genetic position*. Sydney: University of Sydney PhD dissertation.
Van Egmond, Marie-Elaine & Brett Baker. 2020. The genetic position of Anindilyakwa. *Australian Journal of Linguistics* 40(4). 492–527. https://doi.org/10.1080/07268602.2020.1848796
Walsh, Michael. 1996. Body parts in Murrinh-Patha: Incorporation, grammar and metaphor. In Hillary Chappell & William McGregor (eds.), *The grammar of inalienability: A typological perspective on body part terms and the whole-part relation*, 327–380. Berlin: Mouton de Gruyter.

Åshild Næss
Binominals in Äiwoo: Compounds, possessive constructions, and transitional cases

Abstract: This paper discusses the strategies used for the formation of binominal lexemes in the Oceanic language Äiwoo, and the semantic properties associated with the different strategies. The strategies include compounds in which the elements may be independent or bound, as well as various constructions involving possessive marking; the semantic principles differentiating between the various available constructions include relationality, control over the relation, and animacy of the possessor. Moreover, the paper shows how reanalysis of certain constructions may lead to new types or transitional cases, such as bound nouns in compounds acquiring classifier-like properties, or person-marked prepositions being accreted onto nouns as bound possessive marking. The paper also discusses the status of so-called indirect possessive constructions within a typology of binominal constructions and suggests that there may be more to learn about binominal typology by examining in greater detail cases where possessor indexing plays a central role in the formation of binominals.

1 Introduction

This paper describes the different formal constructions available to form binominal lexemes in the Oceanic language Äiwoo [NFL][1], and the semantic relations that characterise the different construction types. Binominals are defined in accordance with the Editors' Introduction as being naming units (roughly, lexical items, see Štekauer 2005) consisting of two "thing-morphs"; including both "thing-roots", defined by Haspelmath (2012) as roots that denote physical objects, and "thing-affixes" with similar meanings (typically described as nominalising affixes). This excludes complex forms where one of the elements is a verb, as in e.g., *teach-er*.

---

[1] The analysis presented in this paper builds on fieldwork funded by the Norwegian Research Council, grant no. 148717, and by the Endangered Languages Documentation Program, grant no. SG0308. I gratefully acknowledge this support. I would like to thank participants in the workshop 'When "noun" meets "noun"' at the 50th Annual Meeting of the Societas Linguistica Europaea, Francesca Masini, and an anonymous reviewer for helpful comments on previous versions.

https://doi.org/10.1515/9783110673494-006

While Äiwoo does have compounds, described in 3.1, a significant number of binominals are formed with various types of possessive constructions, a common pattern in Oceanic languages (Ross 1998). Possession is a complex domain in Äiwoo, and in order to accurately classify the different types of binominals, it is necessary to describe the system of possessive marking in some detail; this is relevant both for the semantics of each construction type and for the discussion of how the Äiwoo facts fit into the binominal typology proposed by Pepper (this volume) (section 5).

Certain types of complex nominal forms are excluded from the discussion below, as they do not clearly fall under the definition of binominals cited above. Many complex nominals in Äiwoo are formed by processes which may be characterised as nominalisation from a verbal root. This includes action nominalisations of the type *nyi-tei-na* [NMLZ-line.fish-NMLZ] 'line fishing', but also more complex constructions such as (1):[2]

(1) *lââsuu   mi-ki-mele*
    ship   BN-IPFV-fly
    'airplane'

mi- is a bound noun with a general meaning 'the one who/which Xs', i.e. 'ship which flies'.[3] Given that the complex form *mikimele* 'the flying one' is itself nominal, *lââsuu mikimele* must be understood as an N-N construction. However, there is no principled way of formally distinguishing such forms from nouns modified by relative clauses (Næss 2018a), and so they are excluded from the discussion in this paper.

Distinguishing clearly between different formal types of binominals in Äiwoo turns out in many cases to be a complex matter. In this paper, I will first present some basic properties of the Äiwoo language, and specifically of nominals (section 2), before moving on to a discussion of binominals. I will start with relatively straightforward cases of compounds (3.1), while constructions arguably showing both compound-like and possessive-like properties will be dealt with in the section on possessive constructions (3.2). I then summarise the formal properties of the various constructions (3.3) and discuss the semantic relations encoded

---

[2] Abbreviations used in glosses follow the Leipzig Glossing Rules where these apply. Additional abbreviations: AUG augmented number, BN bound noun, DIR directional, MIN minimal number, PLAC pluractional, PREF prefix with unclear function, REL relational preposition, UA unit-augmented, UV undergoer voice.

[3] For arguments for analysing *mi-* as a bound noun rather than a nominalising prefix or a relativiser, see Næss (2006, 2018a).

within each type (section 4). Finally, I discuss in more detail the problems of classification both within Äiwoo as such, and in relation to the typology of binominals as presented in Pepper (this volume) (section 5). I round off the paper with a comment on the role played by possessor indexing and how this is pertinent to the typology of binominals (section 6).

2 The Äiwoo language

Äiwoo is spoken by around 7–8,000 people in Temotu Province, the easternmost province of Solomon Islands in the southwest Pacific. It is classified as belonging to the Temotu subgroup of Oceanic, itself a subgroup of the Austronesian language family (Ross and Næss 2007).

Nouns in Äiwoo carry little grammatical marking. There is no case, no gender and no inflectional plural marking (for an account of plural-marking strategies, see Næss 2018b). There are no articles, though demonstratives and deictic clitics may function as determiners. The only obligatory bound marking on nouns is the direct possessive marking discussed in 3.2.2.

Pronouns and possessive marking in Äiwoo follow a so-called minimal-augmented pattern, which treats the 'you and I' category as a "person" in its own right with distinct 'dual' and 'plural' forms. Consider the paradigm in Table 1:

Table 1: Äiwoo independent pronouns.

	Minimal	Unit-augmented	Augmented
1	*iu* 'I'	*iungole* 'I and another'	*iungo(pu)* 'I and others'
1+2	*iuji* 'you and I'	*iudele* 'you and I and another'	*iude* 'you and I and others'
2	*iumu* 'you'	*imile* 'you and another'	*imi* 'you and others'
3	*inâ* 'he/she/it'	*ijiile* 'he/she/it and another'	*ijii* 'he/she/it and others'

Note that each of the person categories have a 'minimal', a 'unit-augmented' and an 'augmented' form, where the unit-augmented indicates the number referred to by the minimal form plus one additional individual and is consistently formed by adding the suffix -*le* to the augmented forms. This is not a dual, because while the 1st, 2nd and 3rd person unit-augmented all refer to two individuals, the 1st+2nd person unit-augmented refers to three – 'you and I plus one'. Similarly, the minimal number is not a singular because the 1+2 minimal refers to two individuals, while the other minimal forms refer to one. The terms 'minimal number' for the category corresponding to the singular in a three-person system, 'unit-augmented' for the category referring to minimal number plus one, and 'augmented' for the category corresponding to the plural in three-person systems, were first introduced by McKay (1978) and have become standard in describing pronoun systems of this kind.

With the exception of two attested forms which appear to premodify nouns,[4] Äiwoo consistently shows noun-modifier order, meaning that all constructions discussed in this paper are head-initial.

The analysis in this paper builds on data collected with native speakers in Honiara and the Reef Islands in 2004, 2005 and 2015. The data consists mainly of narratives of different types, as well as some stimulus descriptions and other elicited materials. No elicitation has been carried out targeting binominals specifically, and the description below is therefore restricted to the forms that can be found in the available materials.

3 Noun-noun constructions in Äiwoo

3.1 Compounds

I use the term 'compounds' for complex forms which consist of two nominal roots without any possessive morphology or any other indication of the relation between them. In Äiwoo, this spans a range of constructions which vary in the degree of cohesion between the elements. On the one hand, the complex kinship terms discussed in 3.1.3 consist of two bound roots neither of which can occur on its own, and the whole form takes stress in the same way as a monomorphemic word. On the other, forms like *nuwopa nyibei* 'hospital' (lit. house sickness) consist of two independent nouns which can and do occur on their own; each element takes penultimate stress as per the stress rules in Äiwoo, though heavier on the final element. In between are forms consisting of one bound and one independent root, where the bound root is a reduced form of an independent noun with the initial syllable dropped: *nupo* 'fishing net', but *po-nebi* 'type of fishing net attached to bamboo sticks' (*nebi* 'bamboo'); such forms take a single main stress on the second noun.

A fourth type of compound-like construction are those involving a bound noun which morphologically and phonologically looks like an independent noun (e.g. *nugo* 'leaf'), but only occurs in construction with another noun (e.g. *nugo*

---

4 These apparent premodifiers likely originate in nouns and may, in fact, be the heads of their constructions; see Næss (2018b: 38–39).

nyenaa 'leaf [of] tree'). Because such constructions have properties in common with direct possessive constructions, they will be discussed in section 3.2.

In the present section, I will thus deal with three types of compounds: one where both nouns retain their full form, one where one of the component nouns takes a distinct, reduced form only found in complex expressions, and one where both elements are bound and do not have independent equivalents. Given the difference in cohesion between the elements in these constructions, one might consider the former to be a case of juxtaposition and the latter two of compounding. However, as Pepper (this volume) points out, the distinction is vague and to a significant extent dependent on "local tradition", and I do not believe that it adds any insights to the analysis of Äiwoo. The core distinction is rather between constructions using some form of possessive marking and constructions showing no such marking; within the latter category, which I will refer to as compounds, there are varying degrees of cohesion between the elements.

As far as the nouns which do have an independent form is concerned, individual nouns tend to a large extent towards one or the other behaviour in compounds, i.e. maintaining their full form or showing a reduced form; but there are cases where one and the same noun occurs in both types, meaning that the nominal lexicon cannot be neatly divided into classes based on the behaviour of words in compounds.

3.1.1 Compounds with one reduced noun

A large proportion of nouns in Äiwoo have an initial syllable *n*V-, historically an accreted article (< Proto Oceanic *na). It is common for a *n*V-initial noun to lose the article reflex when functioning as the head of a compound, as seen in (2):

(2) a. *nupo* 'net' + *nebi* 'bamboo' > *po-nebi* 'type of fishing net attached to bamboo sticks'
    b. *nyengi* 'wind' + *bwää* 'open ocean' > *ngi-bwää* 'season of westerly winds'

Some nouns show further changes in their compounding form, e.g. *nyibä* 'basket' > *be-*, *nubââ* 'shark' > *bo-*, *nyibälo* 'breadfruit' > *bulo-*.

There are also cases where the modifying noun, or both nouns, are reduced, but these are much less common. Reduced modifying nouns occur in a few body-part terms, where the second element is a reduced form of *nede* 'mouth' and *nyike* 'foot, leg' respectively: *nuwote-de* 'tooth', *nubule-de* 'lip, *nubule-ke* 'knee', *nupaa-ke* 'foot sole'. With the exception of *nupaa* 'top, end', the initial elements of these compounds are not attested outside of these complex forms, and their meaning is not clear; note that *nubule-* recurs in both the terms for 'lip' and 'knee' and is defined by Wurm et al. (1985) as denoting a 'round protruding part of something'. Compare *nupaake* 'foot sole' to *nupaa nyimä* 'palm of hand', where both components are independent nouns; the form *nupaa nyike* is also possible, and it is not clear whether there is any difference in usage or meaning. Another example where the modifying noun is reduced is *läge wâdâ* [skin mollusc] 'seashell', where the independent form of the second noun is *nuwâdâ*, discussed further in 3.2.4 below.

Given the rarity of structures with reduced modifying nouns, the status of the N1 is difficult to establish. The only N1s attested outside of this construction are *nupaa* 'top, end' and *läge* 'skin, bark, shell'; both are bound nouns in the sense discussed in 3.2.4 below. If this is the case for this construction type in general, this type differs from the complex kinship terms discussed in 3.1.3 below mainly in that the N1 is disyllabic and thus phonologically free and able to take stress, whereas the N1 in the complex kinship terms are monosyllabic and do not take independent stress.

There are also a limited number of structures with two reduced forms. Apart from the complex kinship terms described in 3.1.3 below, the components of which do not have any corresponding independent nouns, the only examples I have denote varieties of pana (lesser yam, *Dioscorea esculenta*), for which the full noun is *nulie*; in addition to showing the reduced form *ulie*, several terms for pana varieties show a reduced form of the second noun, as in (3):

(3) a. *ulie-bälo*
pana-breadfruit
'variety of pana'
cf. *nyibälo* 'breadfruit'

b. *ulie-gago*
pana-digit
'variety of pana'
cf. *nagago* 'digit'

Not all terms for pana varieties follow this pattern, however: compare *ulie-nälenga*, where the full form *nälenga* 'turmeric' is retained.

As to the main category of reduced forms, the loss of initial *n*V- when a noun occurs as the head of a compound appears largely productive, and on this basis these forms may be categorised as lexical nouns which undergo a predictable change in form when they occur in compounds. However, they clearly have properties in common with what Grinevald (2000) calls 'class terms': "classifying morphemes of clear lexical origin [that] show varying degrees of productivity in the lexicon of a language" (Grinevald 2000: 59; for further discussion see Næss 2006). The fact that some nouns undergo further changes beyond simply the loss of *n*V- in this position may be an indication that they are undergoing a process of grammaticalisation towards class terms or classifiers; such forms typically grammaticalise from nouns (Aikhenvald 2000, Grinevald 2000). It is interesting to note that *nyibälo* 'breadfruit' shows two different reduced forms depending on their position in the compound: *bulo* in initial position, i.e. as head, and *bälo* in second position, cf. (3a). This is likely an effect of the higher frequency of reduced forms in initial position, so that *bulo* may now be seen as a conventionalised form used for varieties of breadfruit, whereas *bälo* in instances like (3a) is simply formed by omitting the article reflex. *bulo* could thus be considered to be closer to a grammaticalised class term than the productively formed *bälo*. In general, these forms might be said to illustrate the transitional stage from the **cmp** to the **cls** type in the binominal typology, cf. 5.6.1 below.

The alternation between full and reduced forms only occurs with nouns which show the initial accreted article; other nouns retain their full form in compounds, cf. 3.1.2 below.

Semantically, nouns in reduced form are mainly found in binominals denoting, firstly, classes of artifacts, as in *be-nupo* [basket-net] 'string basket', *be-tekie* [basket-pandanus.sp] 'pandanus basket', *be-talâu* [basket-meal] 'food basket', cf. *nyibä* 'basket'; secondly, species and subspecies, as in *ulie-bälo* [pana-breadfruit], *ulie-gago* [pana-digit], *ulie-nälenga* [pana-turmeric] 'varieties of pana/lesser yam', cf. *nulie* 'pana', *bu-tepekâ* [triggerfish-flying.fox], *bu-nyibeu* [triggerfish-?] 'species of triggerfish', cf. *nobu* 'triggerfish'; and thirdly, natural phenomena such as terms for different directions or seasons of wind, cf. (2b). As can be seen from these examples, the precise semantic relation between the components varies. For example, a *be-tekie* is a basket (*nyibä*) made from pandanus (*tekie*), a *be-talâu* is a basket used for the purpose of serving a meal (*talâu*), while an *ulie-gago* presumably is a variety of pana whose tuber resembles a finger (*nagago* 'digit').

3.1.2 Compounds with two independent nouns

Compounds may also be formed through juxtaposition of two forms which each occurs as an independent noun on its own. This is not a very frequent construction in my data; the relations encoded in this way include purpose (*nuwopa nyibei* 'house sickness = hospital'[5]), material (*tou nyiivä* 'stone anchor') and some hyponymic species terms (*lâpu nyimema* 'mouse', cf. *lâpu* 'mouse, rat'; *nyimema* is not attested outside of this complex form, though the initial *nyi-* suggests that it should be analysed as a noun).

---

[5] The form *nuwopa eä nyibei*, with the relational preposition *eä* (3.2.5) is also attested, illustrating a possible path from **prp** to **cmp** through loss of the preposition.

Some nouns occur in compounds both in independent and reduced form. The reduced form of *nuwopa* 'house' is *opo*, which occurs in compounds such as *opo nugono* [house areca.leaf] 'leaf shelter', *opo nää* [house spirit] 'traditional cult house'; but as noted above, the term for 'hospital' is *nuwopa nyibei* 'sickness house', with the independent form *nuwopa*. This may be due to the latter being a more recent coinage. In general, constructions with reduced nouns are highly productive, but traditionally there were a rather limited number of types of house; it is possible that speakers here perceive a distinction between traditional and more modern types of house, with only the former referred to with *opo*. The term *opo nâgulo* [house be.dark] 'prison' might be considered a counterexample to this; there may be some degree of free variation, and more research is needed to establish whether terms for new types of houses can be coined with the reduced form *opo*.

3.1.3 Compounds with two bound nouns

Compounds where both elements are bound noun roots are only attested for certain kinship terms. These differ from the constructions discussed in 3.1.1 in that no corresponding independent noun is attested; hence I am using the term 'bound' rather than 'reduced' nouns, because no 'unreduced' forms of these roots exist. The forms in question constitute a small, closed set, and are not productively formed, unlike the compounds discussed in 3.1.1.

In these forms, the initial root is typically *gi-* 'man, male' or *si-* 'woman, female', which also occur in a range of other contexts and show clearly nominal behaviour (Næss 2006, 2018a). They combine with such forms as *-te* 'same-sex sibling'[6] (*gite* 'man's brother', *site* 'woman's sister'), *-bo* 'sibling's or child's child, maternal grandparent' (*gibo* 'nephew, grandson', *sibo* 'niece, granddaughter'), *-piä* 'sibling-in-law' (*gipiä* 'brother-in-law', *sipiä* 'sister-in-law'), etc., to form binominal stems. Note that the second root takes direct possessive marking

---

6 As is common in Oceanic languages, Äiwoo distinguishes between sibling relationships where the siblings are of the same sex and relationships where the siblings are of opposite sex. The complex nature of the Äiwoo sibling terms means that the sex of the ego can be inferred from the combination of the sex of the sibling as indicated by the first root (*gi-* for a man, *si-* for a woman) and the semantics of the second root: since *-te* refers to a sibling of the same sex as ego, *gi-te* necessarily refers to the brother of a man, since the referent is male and the relationship is that of a same-sex sibling. Similarly, *si-te* necessarily refers to the sister of a woman. The corresponding root for opposite-sex siblings is (in the 3MIN) *(nu)we*: *gi-nuwe* 'brother of a woman', *si-we* 'sister of a man'.

(3.2.2), indexing the ego for the kinship relation; the forms given are 3MIN (cf. *gisi/sisi* 'my brother/sister', *gibu/sibu* 'my nephew/niece', *gipio/sipio* 'my brother-in-law/sister-in-law'). The semantic relation between the two elements is one of coordination: a *gi-te* is a same-sex sibling who is also a man, etc.

It is worth noting that these complex kinship nouns form plurals in an unusual way. They take a plural marker *peliva(li)-*, which is likely to be morphologically complex at least from a diachronic perspective. Interestingly, however, this plural marker is not added to the compound as a whole, but replaces the N1; thus the plural of both *gite* 'his brother' and *site* 'her sister' is *pelivalite* 'his/her same-sex siblings'. This could be understood as a type of suppletion, in that a form with singular reference is replaced by a different form with plural reference; but it is unusual in that the suppletion affects only part of a complex stem (Næss 2018b: 39–41).

3.2 Possessives and possessive-like constructions

3.2.1 Possessives in Oceanic

Possessive marking in Oceanic languages typically distinguishes between what is known in the Oceanist literature as direct possessives, where possessor indexing attaches directly to the possessed noun, and indirect possessives, where possessor indexing attaches instead to an independent morpheme, typically described as a possessive classifier (e.g. Lichtenberk 1983, 2009). This formal distinction corresponds roughly to a distinction between inalienable and alienable possession, with directly possessed nouns typically including kinship and body-part terms, although the precise boundaries between the classes vary between languages. Many Oceanic languages further distinguish between different indirect possessive markers, where the choice depends on the precise nature of the possessive relationship, specifically the intended use of the possessed item; a common distinction is between food, drink, and other possessions (Lichtenberk 2009: 268).

Ross (1998: 248) distinguishes between specific and nonspecific possessors, where nonspecific possessors "are often not really possessors at all but generic nouns used indefinitely", as in e.g. *pig's tail*, which does not refer to the tail of a specific pig but a type of animal appendage. Nonspecific possessor constructions are thus binominals, whereas specific possessor constructions are not. This corresponds to the distinction drawn by Koptjevskaja-Tamm (2004) between nonanchoring and anchoring relations, where a typical possessor acts as an "anchor" for the identification of the referent of the possessed nouns, whereas in nonanchoring uses of possessive constructions,

1. the dependent is not individualized; 2. the dependent-head combination refers to a subclass of a broader class and often functions as a classificatory label for it, suggesting that the dependent and the head together correspond to one concept; 3. the head cannot be identified via its relation to the dependent (Koptjevskaja-Tamm 2004: 156).

Koptjevskaja-Tamm's nonanchoring possessives thus correspond to Ross's nonspecific possessor constructions, and constitute the subset of possessive constructions that count as binominals in the sense of being naming units.

As Ross points out, in many Oceanic languages such nonspecific possessor constructions "employ possessive morphosyntax and syntactically are an integral part of the possession system" (Ross 1998: 248). This also holds for Äiwoo, meaning that it is necessary to embed the discussion of binominals in a fairly detailed analysis of the various constructions available for the marking of possession. While some of the constructions to be discussed below are more frequently used to encode anchoring relations, at least some binominals are found within all the types, and so in order to understand the properties of binominals it is necessary to understand the properties of possessive marking more generally.

3.2.2 Direct possession

As stated above, directly possessed nouns are those which indicate possession by means of marking directly on the noun. Most directly possessed nouns in Äiwoo are also obligatorily possessed, in that they do not occur without possessive marking. In general, they distinguish between a 1MIN and a 3MIN stem, with the remaining forms constructed by affixes added to the 1MIN stem, except for the 3AUG and 3UA which are formed by affixation to the 3MIN stem.

(4) a. *tumo*
      father.1MIN
      'my father'
   b. *tumo-mu*
      father-2MIN
      'your father'
   c. *tumwä*
      father.3MIN
      'his/her father'
   d. *tumwä-i*
      father-3AUG
      'their father'

However, some directly possessed nouns have only a 3MIN stem and form the 1MIN by the suffix *-u*, e.g. *gino* 'his/her son' – *gino-u* 'my son', *sipe* 'his/her daughter' – *sipe-u* 'my daughter'.

Directly possessed nouns in Äiwoo include most kinship terms and other terms for human relations such as *ibete* '(his/her) friend', as well as what, following Schokkin (2020: 64), I will call primary body part terms, i.e. the most obvious and prominent body parts such as *nuwotaa* 'head', *nyime* 'arm, hand', *nyike* 'leg, foot', *nuwosä* 'stomach', *numângä* 'back', etc.

These nouns do not have an unpossessed form, which means that 3MIN direct possessive marking is obligatory even when a noun specifying the possessor is present:

(5) a. *tumwä   John*   b. *nyimä   singedâ*
       father.3MIN John   hand.3MIN   woman
       'John's father'   'the woman's hand'

However, two attested body-part nouns take optional suffixed possessive marking: *nyii* 'breast' – *nyiiä* 'her breast', and *delâ* 'blood' – *delaa* 'his/her/its blood'. A plausible analysis of the latter form is that it arises from *delâ+ä*, in which case both these nouns take a 3MIN marker *-ä*. They differ, however, in their 1MIN forms: *nyii-o* 'my breast', but *delaa-u* 'my blood'. That is, *delâ* patterns like the kinship terms mentioned above which add a suffix *-u* to their 3MIN form, whereas *nyii* adds suffixes in both 1MIN and 3MIN. A parallel case in the kinship domain is *singedâ* 'woman', which has a possessed form *singedaa* 'his woman, his wife'; for this noun I have attested both *singedaau* and *singedâu* as 1MIN forms. The status of these forms will be further discussed in 4.1.

A few binominals involve directly possessed nouns. In the case of *ibe tumwä* [old.man father.3MIN] 'paternal grandfather', we see a binominal kinship term in which both components also have an independent use. This is the only example of this that I am aware of where the head (*ibe*) is not itself a directly possessed noun (cf. the discussion of *isä pelivano* 'wife' and *tumwä pelivano* 'husband' below). Other 'grandparent' terms are formed with bound kinship roots: *ibebo* 'maternal grandfather' ~ *ipebo* 'maternal grandmother', as well as as *ipetä* 'paternal grandmother'. In all these cases the first element is an independent noun (*ibe* and *ipe* are respectful terms meaning 'old man' and 'old woman' respectively), while the second element is a bound kinship root, cf. 3.1.3 above.

Some binominals also involve directly possessed nouns as their head, and in some cases also as their dependent. The latter includes the conventionalised terms *isä pelivano* [mother.3MIN children.3MIN] '(his) wife (lit. mother of his children)' and *tumwä pelivano* [father.3MIN children.3MIN] '(her) husband (lit. father of her children)',[7] which are the polite and most frequent way of referring

---

7 The head noun here appears in the 3MIN stem; the 3AUG suffix *-i* does not cooccur with a coreferential plural possessor noun phrase. That is, the options are *isä-i* 'their mother' or *isä pelivano* 'his children's mother', but not **isä-i pelivano*.

to spouses, even for couples who have no children. In these cases, the resulting binominal is itself directly possessed, i.e. *isä pelivano* and *tumwä pelivano* strictly speaking translate as 'his wife' and 'her husband' respectively. *isä pelivano* is lexicalised to the point of starting to undergo phonological reduction; a common pronunciation is [sæpelvano].

An example where the second component is not directly possessed is binominals formed with the directly possessed noun *melo* 'animal young', e.g. *melo kuli* [young.3MIN dog] 'puppy', *melo poi* [young.3MIN pig] 'piglet'. A number of species names are formed with *melo*, e.g. *melo taapi* [young.3MIN cooking.leaf] 'stick insect', *melo tolomane* [young.3MIN sea.anemone] 'clownfish, anemonefish'. With these binominals, the referent is metaphorically construed as the offspring of some item in nature: a leaf for the stick insect and a sea anemone for the anemonefish.

3.2.3 Indirect possession

The core function of the indirect possessive construction is to indicate possession in the sense of ownership. The precise relationship between possessor and possessed is specified by one of six possessive classifiers, which indicate the "purpose of the possession" (Chappell and McGregor 1996: 4): they distinguish forms for food (and items used in catching, growing or preparing food), drink, betelnut and paraphernalia associated with betel chewing, tools and household utensils, houses and land property, and a general class encompassing all possessive relations not covered by one of the other five. The classifiers are given in Table 2 in their 1MIN and 3MIN form; as with direct possessives, the general tendency is for there to be distinct 1MIN and 3MIN stems, but note that the betel and general classes form the 1MIN by suffixation to the 3MIN, and that the food class derives all except the 1st person forms by suffixation to the 3MIN.

Table 2: Possessive classifiers.

Class	1MIN	3MIN
food	*nugo*	*na*
drink	*numo*	*numwä*
betel	*dano*	*da*
tools	*nugu*	*nogo*
house/land	*to*	*tä*
general	*nou*	*no*

The possessive classifiers classify the possessive relationship rather than the possessed noun itself; thus it is possible for a noun to occur with different possessive classifiers if it can be construed as possessed for different purposes, as illustrated with *nenu* 'coconut' in (6):

(6) a. *nenu   nugo*   b. *nenu   numo*
       coconut   POSS:FOOD.1MIN   coconut   POSS:DRINK.1MIN
       'my coconut (to eat)'   'my coconut (to drink)'
   c. *nenu   no-u*
       coconut   POSS:GEN-1MIN
       'my coconut (as a general possession)'

In addition to expressing ownership, the indirect possessive construction is also used for a number of other types of relation. Firstly, it is used for kinship in cases where the kinship noun itself is not inherently relational, such as *tememe* 'baby' or *dowâlili* 'child' (in the sense of 'young human' rather than 'offspring'); these take the general possessive classifier *no*. The exception is *singedâ* 'woman', which when possessed (in the meaning of 'wife') takes direct marking, cf. 3.2.2.

Secondly, certain personal characteristics take the 'tool' possessive classifier; this is attested with such forms as *nubanulou* 'character', *tevelu* 'behaviour, practice', *saliki* 'generosity'.

Thirdly, the tool possessive is also used to indicate the agent or source of an object or action: *pole nogo* 'his/her work', *täpeva nogo* 'his/her gift (that s/he gives)', *lopâ nogo* 'his/her speech, talk', *tepolâu nogo* 'his/her sea journey'. This is the same strategy used to mark the agent of action nominalisations formed with the nominalising circumfix *nyi- -na*, e.g. *nyi-wo-na nogo* (NMLZ-go-NMLZ POSS:TOOL.3MIN) 'his/her going'.

As with direct possession, indirect possession is most commonly used for anchoring relations rather than binominals proper. However, a few binominals are formed with indirect possessives. Those I have attested include, firstly, *nabe na nubââ* [bait POSS:FOOD.3MIN shark] 'shark bait', where the semantic relation can be said to be one of purpose (bait for the shark to eat), and secondly, some complex terms for species, as in *numou na nää* [octopus POSS:FOOD.3MIN spirit] 'species of octopus (lit spirit-food octopus)', *tukule nogo nubââ* [headrest POSS:TOOL.3MIN shark] 'blue sea star, Linckia laevigata (lit. shark's headrest)'. In some of these forms the possessor noun is a reduced form (cf. 3.1.1), e.g. *u-na Deved* [banana-POSS:FOOD.3MIN David] 'variety of banana (lit. David's banana)', compare *nou* 'banana'.

3.2.4 Bound nouns

It is common for Oceanic languages to distinguish several categories of bound nouns, in the sense of nouns which cannot occur without some indication of a possessor. Directly possessed nouns are a subtype of this, but there are also nouns which do not appear to take direct possessive marking, but nevertheless obligatorily occur with a specification of an entity that they belong to in the sense of being a part of (see e.g. von Prince 2016: 73 for Daakaka [BPA] or Early ms. 125–126 for Lewo [LWW]).

The boundary between bound nouns in this sense, and directly possessed nouns, is not easy to draw in Äiwoo. There are a few indisputable cases which a) cannot take direct possessive marking and b) necessarily cooccur with a noun specifying the whole of which they are a part. These include e.g. *nyiluu* 'hair, feather', *nagago* 'digit', and *läge* 'skin, bark, shell'. These are secondary body-part terms which require specification of the larger body part to which they attach: *nyiluu nuwotaa* [hair head.3MIN] 'hair of head', *läge nyisi* [skin body.3MIN] 'skin of body', *nagago nyime* [digit hand.3MIN] 'finger', *nagago nyike* [digit leg.3MIN] 'toe'. Note that the second noun in these constructions is a directly possessed noun, and the only way of indicating possession of the secondary body part is through possessive marking on the noun denoting the larger whole, e.g. *nyiluu nuwotaau* [hair head.1MIN] 'my hair', etc.

The majority of plant-part terms are more difficult to classify as either directly possessed or bound nouns. In general, such nouns must combine with a noun referring to the type of plant or tree that the part belongs to. If general reference to e.g. 'leaf', 'branch', 'fruit' is intended, the default noun is *nyenaa* 'tree': *nula nyenaa* [branch tree] 'branch', *nugo nyenaa* [leaf tree] 'leaf', *nuwa nyenaa* [fruit tree] 'fruit' etc. As such, they resemble the secondary body-part nouns described above in that their most frequent occurrence is in construction with a noun denoting the whole of which they are a part. Plant-part terms occur as bound nouns in a number of other Oceanic languages such as Lewo of Vanuatu (Early ms: 126–127) and Nemi [NEM] of New Caledonia (Ozanne-Rivierre 1991: 335), as well as elsewhere in the world, e.g., in Hup [JUP] of Brazil (Epps 2008: 246–250).

There is, however, some evidence that the Äiwoo plant-part nouns take suffixed possessive marking, and as such may be better classified as directly possessed. My data on this is extremely limited, but (7) shows *nula* 'branch' with a 1MIN suffix -*u*, cf. the subset of directly possessed nouns that take 1MIN -*u* (3.2.2):

(7) Ngaa   iki   läki-lâ-mu=dä=to=wâ   nula-u.
    so   be.suitable   chop-out-2MIN=some=now=DIST   branch-1MIN
    'So you should chop off some of my branches.' (spoken by a bamboo plant)

The same noun is attested without a directly following noun in a context where the possessor is clearly retrievable:

(8) (We cut down the tree and take it to the edge of the garden,)
i-labu-woli-ngopu   eä   nula
PFV-chop-down-1AUG   CONJ   branch
i-le-laki-oli-ngopu.
PFV-PREF-chop-down-1AUG
'we chop it up and cut off its branches.'

This suggests that *nula* may in fact be properly understood as a 3MIN form, in which case *nula nyenaa* 'branch of tree' would seem largely parallel to a direct possessive construction such as *tumwä John* 'John's father'.

It is interesting to note that *läge* 'skin, bark, shell', which can refer both to a human body part and a plant part, is attested in a similar context as *nula* in (8), notably in its use as a plant-part term:

(9) *Ile   nyenaa   läge   ki-e-luwa-kä-i   ku-nupo=kâ*
    PROX   tree   skin   IPFV-PLAC-take-DIR:3-3AUG   IPFV-net=DIST
'That tree whose bark they take to make into a net . . .'

To the best of my knowledge, this is not possible with the 'skin' sense; that is, the only way to say 'his/her/its skin' is with the complex form *läge nyisi* 'skin of his/her/its body', though I lack the data to definitely confirm this.

There are further contexts in which complex forms with *läge* seem to pattern variously as compounds or as possessive constructions. Consider (10):

(10) *I-wâ-pu-ee=nâ   be-tepu   nogo   ä*
     PFV-CAUS-go-up=DIST basket-cup   POSS:TOOL.3MIN   CONJ
     de-läge   wâdâ.
     thing-skin   mollusc
'He pulled up her basket and seashell things (i.e. shell jewellery).'

The independent noun for 'mollusc' is *nuwâdâ*; the fact that the initial *nV-* is lost in the complex form *läge wâdâ* parallels the compound constructions discussed in 3.1.1. Contrast (11):

(11) *Lâto i-te-kä toponu=kâ, mo läge vesi-i.*
thus PFV-see-DIR:3 turtle=DIST CONJ skin still-UV
'And Turtle looked at [the object thrown down from the banana tree by his friend Rat], but it was still a skin [not the banana he had asked for].'

The modifier *vesi* 'still' is more commonly found modifying verbs. The most readily available explanation for the presence of the suffix *-i*, which otherwise attaches to intransitive verbs and adverbs when they modify a verb in the undergoer voice, is that *läge* is possessive-marked; possessive nouns pattern morphologically like undergoer-voice verbs in certain respects and take the suffix *-i* or *-nyii*[8] when modified by certain forms, cf. *gino mole-nyii* [son.3MIN exactly-UV] 'his true son'.

Läge 'skin, bark, shell', then, appears in both compound-like and possessive-like binominals, and presently available data is not sufficient to determine whether these properties vary between individual binominals or whether all the forms in fact display both types of properties. More generally, we have seen in this section that the line between nouns which are bound in the sense of obligatorily forming a compound with another noun, and directly possessed nouns, is difficult to draw conclusively. It should be noted, however, that while the directly possessed nouns described in 3.2.2 are used mainly for anchoring relations, the plant-part terms discussed here are binominals proper: *nula nyenaa* is generally used to mean 'tree branch' rather than identifying a specific branch of a specific tree. The secondary body-part terms function as directly possessed binominals: there is no way to say, e.g., 'hair' without using a complex construction, but these forms differ from the plant-part terms in that the second noun in the construction takes obligatory possessive marking anchoring the whole complex form to a possessor referent.

3.2.5 Relational prepositions

A number of binominals are formed with what I will call relational prepositions, as in e.g. *touto eä poi* (fat REL.3MIN pig) 'pig fat', *nupo eä nubââ* (net REL.3MIN shark) 'shark net'. The forms of the relational prepositions are *eä/wä, lä, nä,* and *ngä*; the choice between forms seems to be largely lexically determined, as no systematic semantic or phonological criteria can be identified. Compare, for instance, semantically similar forms like *nyidebo nä* 'remedy for it [a given disease]' and

---

8 The choice appears to be lexically determined.

nuwoi lä 'remedy [lit. water] for it' and phonologically similar ones like *nyige nä* 'its kernels' and *nyibe lä* 'its wrapping'.

Relational prepositions are person-marked; the forms in *-ä* are the 3MIN forms (compare e.g. *eä* with *eou* '1MIN', *eomu* '2MIN'). Person-marked prepositions are not uncommon in Oceanic languages (Pawley 1973, Lichtenberk 1985). This construction thus shares with direct possession the property of obligatory possessor indexing, even when the possessor is also overtly expressed by an independent noun. The implications of this for the classification of this construction type will be discussed in 5.4–5.5.

Relational prepositions have a fairly general meaning and are used to indicate a variety of relations between nouns; the English preposition *of* is often a suitable translation. This is in contrast to the indirect possessive markers which specify a particular subtype of possessive relation.

I analyse these forms as prepositions rather than suffixes to the possessed noun mainly on the basis of examples like (12):

(12) Mo   käsä   [ngângo mana nä]   kode   nyidâbu eve.
     CONJ be.like   be.strong very REL.3MIN maybe   day   three
     'But it was like really strong for maybe three days (lit. the [being] really strong of it [lasted] maybe three days).'

In most contexts, *ngângo* functions as a verb meaning 'to be strong'. The criteria for distinguishing nouns from verbs in Äiwoo are complex; in examples like *päko eä* 'its good (side), its benefit' one might argue that the stative verb *päko* 'be good' has undergone zero-conversion into a noun meaning 'goodness, benefit', in which case a nominal possessive suffix would plausibly apply to it. However, in (12) the entire phrase *ngângo mana* 'being very strong' is modified by *nä* 'its'; this is clearly not a case of lexical conversion of a verb to a noun, but rather of a complex verbal expression showing a referential function. Detailed questions of analysis aside, a possessive suffix would be expected to select for nouns as a lexical class, which is clearly not the case here.

There is some evidence, however, that relational prepositions may be a diachronic source of possessor marking in some nouns, which can make the two hard to distinguish. This is the case, for instance, for a number of nouns which require the expression of a possessor, and appear to have a basic 3MIN form, as with the plant-part nouns discussed in 3.2.4. This goes for forms such as *nubolä* 'materials/component parts of', *nuulä* 'juice of', *nuuwä* 'flesh of', *numaluwä* 'middle of', *numadongä* 'crust of', where the final syllable has the same form as the relational prepositions, but where the nouns are not attested without *-lä/-wä/-ngä*. It may also be the case for a number of nouns with final *-aa*, such as *daa* 'bottom of', *naa* 'end of', *nataa* 'thorn of' (cf. the plant-part nouns discussed in 3.2.4), *nupaa* 'top of', *nyimaa* 'nest of', *numoleaa* 'middle of'. As noted for *delâ* 'blood' in 3.2.2, such forms ending in *–aa* might plausibly involve an underlying *-ä* or *eä* attached to an *–â*-final stem, although no unpossessed *-â*-final form is attested for the nouns discussed here. If this is indeed a case of accretion, it is difficult to determine whether the underlying form is a 3MIN possessive suffix *-ä* or a relational preposition *eä*, but on analogy with the forms listed above ending in *-lä, -wä, -ngä* etc., one might assume that accretion of *eä* is equally plausible.

Tâulâ 'anchor' has a 3MIN form *tâulaa* 'its (the canoe's) anchor', thus patterning like *delâ* 'blood' and *singedâ* 'woman' (3.2.2). Unlike the latter nouns, however, it can also occur with an indirect possessive: *tâulâ nogo* 'his/her anchor'. In general, Äiwoo nouns do not alternate between direct and indirect possession,[9] and this, in conjunction with the fact that *tâulaa* encodes a part-whole relation, leads me to suspect that this form is the result of an accreted relational preposition; the semantic argument holds equally for the other forms discussed in this section. It must be admitted, however, that the distinction between these and directly possessed nouns is fairly tentative. Note that a development similar to that suggested here is attested in certain Oceanic languages of New Caledonia, where nouns tend to show an accreted possessive marker when the possessor is inanimate, e.g. Drehu [DHV] *im* 'arm', *ime-n* 'sleeve', *mek* 'eye', *meke-n* 'point, foremost part' (Ozanne-Rivierre 1991:324); this will be discussed further in 4.5.

Relational prepositions are used, firstly, to indicate part-whole relations involving inanimate entities, e.g. *daalâu wä nuwopa* 'eaves of house', *nadu nä pot* 'lid of pot', *nubu eä nyibälo* 'core of breadfruit'.

Secondly, they are used for certain kinds of body parts. These include bones and internal organs (*nupe eä* 'his/her kidney', *temenge eä* 'his/her skull'), most nouns for genitals (*bâu wä* 'his penis', *tuvili eä* 'his testicles'), as well as some secondary body parts (cf. 3.2.4 above), e.g. *likupo nä nyike* [calf REL leg] 'calf', *numolou wä nede* [gums REL mouth] 'gums'. It is not unusual in Oceanic languages for internal organs to be encoded differently from external body parts; for example, internal organs are indirectly possessed in Paamese (Crowley 1996: 397–399), while in Daakaka nouns for internal organs have to take a derivational morpheme in order to accept a possessor, while external body parts are directly possessed (von Prince 2016). For nouns referring to genitals to be treated differently from other body parts is not unheard of either; Harvey (1996: 119) notes that

---

[9] This is possible in many Oceanic languages, as discussed by Lichtenberk (2009: 273–276). In Äiwoo, however, a meaning such as 'my head (detached from my body, e.g. a fish head)' would have to be expressed as e.g. *nuwotaa sii nugo* [head.3MIN fish POSS:FOOD.1MIN] 'my fish head'; i.e. both the direct and the indirect possessor must be expressed.

Australian languages often assign nouns for genitals to a different noun class than other body-part nouns.

Moreover, relational prepositions are used for source relations, as in (13), purpose relations, as in (14), as well as for quantity expressions such as those in (15):

(13) a. näbä   eä   toponu
        shell REL.3MIN turtle
        'turtle shell'
     b. touto eä   poi
        fat   REL.3MIN pig
        'pig fat'
     c. nuwoli eä   nugou
        egg   REL.3MIN ant
        'ant eggs; rice'

(14) a. nupo   eä   nubââ
        net   REL.3MIN shark
        'shark net'
     b. ulivängâ eä   nyi-bei
        remedy   REL.3MIN NMLZ-ill
        'remedy for an illness'

(15) a. nakabu wä   nyuu
        lot   REL.3MIN star
        'a lot of stars'
     b. nuwo   wä   sii
        heap   REL.3MIN fish
        'a school of fish'

The classification of relations outlined above is far from clear-cut; for example, one may question whether 'turtle shell' or 'pig fat' should be considered a source relation or a part-whole relation. However, since body parts are generally encoded with direct possession, I consider it plausible that these are rather viewed as relations of source. The semantic relationship between relational prepositions and indirect possession will be discussed in 4.2 below.

While some of the examples given above again clearly refer to anchoring relations, many are clearly binominals. This goes for many of the secondary body-part terms, which require a specification of the larger body part to which they attach, cf. the secondary body-part terms discussed in 3.2.4; and for terms relating to source and purpose such as 'pig fat', 'shark net' etc. Part-whole terms like *daalâu wä nuwopa* 'eaves of house', *nubu eä nyibälo* 'core of breadfruit' etc. probably have both anchoring and nonanchoring uses; that is, *nubu eä nyibälo* could be used for 'the core of the breadfruit' (anchoring), but also for 'breadfruit core' as a general concept (nonanchoring).

3.3 Summary of formal properties

Above, I have outlined the formal properties of seven grammatical constructions which may be used to form binominals in Äiwoo: three types of compounds, with varying properties, direct and indirect possessives, bound noun constructions and relational prepositions. These constructions are summarised in Table 3 below.

Table 3: Summary of noun-noun constructions in Äiwoo.

Construction type	Example	N1	N2	Possessor indexing
1a Compound with reduced N1	*po-nebi* 'net attached to bamboo sticks'	Reduced	Free	No
1b Compound with reduced N2	*nubule-ke* 'knee'	Bound?*[10]	Reduced	No
1c Compound with reduced N1+N2	*ulie-bälo* 'variety of pana (lit. breadfruit pana)'	Reduced	Reduced	No
2 Compound with two bound roots	*si-te* 'sister of a woman'	Bound	Bound	No**[11]
3 Full-noun compound	*nuwopa nyibei* 'hospital'	Free	Free	No
4 Direct possessive	*isä pelivano* '(his) wife'	Bound	Bound or free	On N1
5 Bound noun construction	*nugo nyenaa* 'leaf'	Bound	Free	?
6 Indirect possessive	*nabe na nubââ* 'shark bait'	Free	Free	On possessive classifier
7 Relational preposition	*näbä eä toponu* 'turtle shell'	Free	Free	On relational preposition

---

[10] See 3.1.1.
[11] No possessive marking indicating the relation between the two nouns in the compound, although since this class consists entirely of directly possessed kinship terms, the N2 is marked for the 'possessor' of the kinship relation.

I distinguish here between construction where one or both nouns are **reduced**, in the sense that a corresponding noun incorporating the article reflex *nV-* exists (e.g. *po ~ nupo* 'net') and constructions where one or both nouns are **bound**, in the sense of not occurring outside a complex construction, but where no corresponding independent noun exists. Directly possessed nouns are classified here as bound in the sense that they do not occur without possessive marking. Nouns which do occur independently are referred to in the table as **free**.

The second parameter included in the table is whether or not the construction involves possessor indexing, and if so, on which element this occurs. As should be clear from the discussion in 3.2.4, the status of bound noun constructions of the type *nugo nyenaa* 'leaf (of tree)' is indeterminate with respect to this parameter.

4 Semantic parameters

In this section I will attempt to formulate some generalisations across constructions regarding the types of semantic relations found between the two nouns in each type of binominal. As should be clear from the discussion in section 3, the boundaries between many of the formal construction types are far from clear, and thus the generalisations must be understood as glossing over a fair amount of variation and borderline cases. Even so, some clear tendencies can be observed, and many of the exceptions can be attributed to a tendency of drift towards direct possessive marking, discussed in 4.5 below.

4.1 Relational vs nonrelational nouns

The first major distinction to be drawn is that between nouns which are inherently relational and nouns which are not (Lichtenberk 2009: 262). Inherently relational nouns include body-part terms, which by definition stand in a relation to the entity whose body they are a part of, and kinship terms which identify a person's relation to another; one cannot, for example, be a sister without being **someone's** sister. These are the nouns which form the core of the directly possessed class in Äiwoo. Note that nouns which are not inherently relational but can be used as kinship terms generally do not take direct possession (3.2.3); an apparent exception is *singedâ* 'woman, wife', with the 3MIN form *singedaa* 'his wife' which could perhaps be attributed to an accreted relational preposition, cf. *sigiläi eä* [man REL] 'her husband' (3.2.5, 4.5). There is a similar pattern for *delâ* 'blood', although in general, internal body parts take relational prepositions; this could be understood either as indicating that blood has a different status from other internal body parts, perhaps because people's blood is more frequently encountered than e.g. their hearts or their livers, or that the direct marking on *delâ* similarly originates from an accreted relational preposition.

4.2 Controlled vs uncontrolled relations

What distinguishes the indirect possessive construction from the relational preposition construction is mainly the distinction between a relation that is controlled by the possessor and one that is not. This is a common distinction in Oceanic possessive systems (e.g. von Prince 2016: 84–85), although generally construed in terms of the distinction between inalienable-type, directly marked relations as being uncontrolled vs. alienable-type, indirectly marked relations as being controlled. In Äiwoo, the system is better described as involving, in the first instance, a distinction between those nouns which are inherently relational and those which are not, as mentioned in the previous section; the former are directly possessed, whereas the latter in turn distinguish those relations which are controlled from those which are not. The difference can be seen in (16) (recall that *eou* is the 1MIN form of the relational preposition that has the 3MIN form *eä*):

(16) a. *totokale no-u* b. *totokale eou*
  picture POSS:GEN-1MIN   picture REL.1MIN
  'my picture (which I own)'   'a picture of me'

In (16a), the possessor is the owner of the picture, and could presumably get rid of it if he or she wanted; it is a relation controlled by the possessor. In (16b), on the other hand, the possessor is the subject matter of the picture, and this is not a relation that can be changed once the picture is taken or painted.

Turning to binominals, this distinction explains why some purpose relations are encoded by direct possessives, while other, superficially similar relations take a relational preposition. Compare e.g. *nabe na nubââ* [bait POSS:FOOD.3MIN shark] 'shark bait' and *nupo eä nubââ* [net REL shark] 'shark net'. These two terms appear to be semantically parallel in that both describe objects used for catching sharks; yet the first takes the possessive classifier for food, while the second takes a relational preposition. The difference lies in the way the shark interacts with the object in question: the bait is to be eaten by the shark, i.e. the shark in a sense "uses" the bait and is in control of whether to eat it or not. The net, on the other hand, is not used by the shark, and the shark is not in control of the interaction. In this case, an indirect possessive would mean that the shark owned the net and used it as a tool. The food possessive used for 'shark bait' would be infelicitous here since a net is not eaten; the appropriate form would be the 'tools and utensils' possessive *nogo*. *Nupo nogo nubââ*, however, can only mean 'the shark's net' (i.e. owned by the shark), not 'net used for catching sharks'.

That the indirect possessive construction indicates relationships of control also explains why it is found with agent relations such as *pole nogo* 'his/her work'; an agent is in the typical case a controlling participant.

4.3 Animate/human vs inanimate possessor

The third major distinction of relevance is that between human and animate possessors on the one hand and inanimate possessors on the other. Animate possession is, as a rule, encoded either by direct or indirect possessive marking; direct possessive marking for kinship and primary body-part terms and indirect possession for relations of ownership.

With inanimate possessors, which is where most binominals are found, the picture is more complex. We saw that plant-part nouns showed characteristics both of bound nouns and of directly possessed nouns. Secondary body parts, on the other hand, are either bound nouns, i.e. occur obligatorily in construction with another noun (*nyiluu nuwotaa* 'hair of head') or constructed with a relational preposition (*numolou wä nede* 'gums of mouth'). In both cases, since the noun they are in construction with is always a directly possessed noun, their semantics can be construed as a two-step relation: they are parts of a larger whole, but that whole is a primary body part, which in turn is directly possessed.

It is not unusual for Oceanic languages to distinguish formally between body parts of humans and animals on the one hand and parts of inanimate objects on the other; this is described e.g. for Nêlêmwa [NEE] by Bril (2013) and for Tolai [KSD] by Mosel (1984). Plant parts appear to be in a somewhat intermediate position in Äiwoo, as discussed above, while parts of unambiguously inanimate entities are generally encoded with relational prepositions (*nadu nä pot* 'lid of pot'), though note the drift towards accretion which will be discussed in 4.5.

4.4 Interactions between parameters

The three parameters of relational vs. nonrelational, animate vs. inanimate possessor and controlled vs. uncontrolled relations interact in the following way. The basic distinction is between relational and nonrelational nouns. Within the relational nouns, there is a further subdivision into constructions with animate vs inanimate possessors, and within the animate possessors a further distinction between kinship terms, which are directly possessed, and body-part terms, which are directly possessed if they are external and primary but are either bound nouns or take a relational preposition if they are internal or secondary. Inanimate possessors are typically encoded with relational prepositions, though note the aforementioned exceptional behaviour of plant-part nouns.

Nonrelational nouns can be further subdivided into controlled and uncontrolled relations, where the controlled relations take indirect possessives. The nonrelational, uncontrolled forms could be considered the 'elsewhere' category and do not show a single consistent marking strategy, although some patterns appear to be discernible.

One type of semantic relation found in this category are source relations (fat from pig, shell from turtle), which appear to take relational prepositions fairly consistently, perhaps because source relations can be construed as a type of part-whole relation where the part has been separated from the whole. Content relations in the sense of the content of speech or visual representations similarly take relational prepositions, as do many quantity expressions. The latter can be viewed as semantically linked to part-whole relations, in that a certain quantity of something can be understood as a part of the total number or amount of the entity in question that exists. Finally, forms denoting species/subspecies or types of artifacts are generally compounds, which may vary in their structural properties.

Figure 1 below summarises the semantic distinctions discussed in 4.1–4.3, and the main formal strategies used to encode them. It can be seen that the strategies to a certain extent form a cline, with direct possessives on the left, indirect possessives on the right, and various other strategies in between the two. However, a tendency for drift towards direct possession, to be discussed in 4.5. below, means that there is a tendency for the types marked with relational prepositions to increasingly share properties with those taking direct possessive marking.

4.5 The drift towards direct possession

Above I have outlined a number of general tendencies regarding correlations between formal constructions and the semantics of the noun-noun relation that the constructions encode. While these hold on an overarching level, we see a general drift in the system towards direct possessive marking. A number of problematic cases were discussed above, all of which involved determining whether or not a particular form should be analysed as direct possessive marking, as opposed to either unmarked bound nouns (plant parts, 3.2.4) or relational prepositions (3.2.5). In the latter case, it was suggested that an original relational preposition

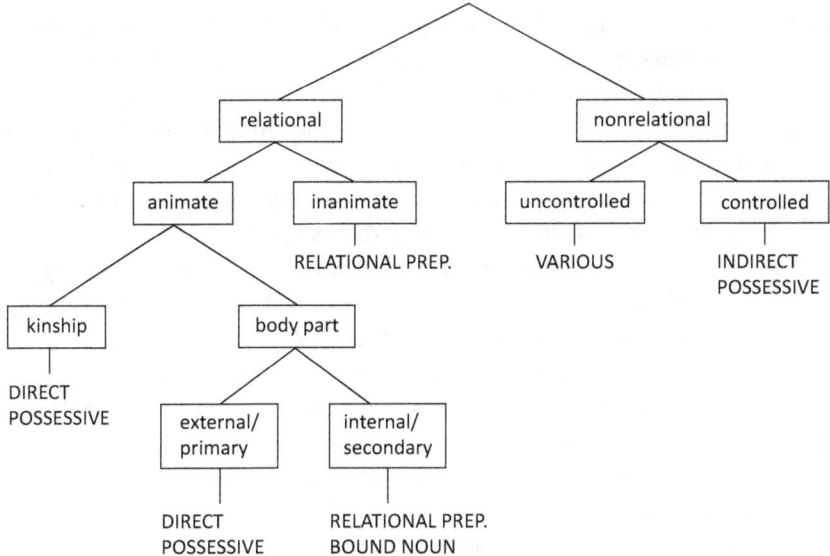

Figure 1: Main semantic distinctions and their formal encoding.

may have accreted to certain nouns, resulting in forms which are indistinguishable in practice from direct possessives, given that the relational prepositions are themselves possessive-marked.

A similar process of accretion is discussed by Ozanne-Rivierre (1991) for a number of Oceanic languages of New Caledonia, where what she refers to as genitive markers have accreted to the root, a process which "mainly affects bound nouns associated with inanimate possessors (parts of a whole, names of parts of plants, anatomical metaphors, etc.)" (Ozanne-Rivierre 1991: 321). There thus seems to be a tendency in at least some Oceanic languages for part-whole and plant-part terms to move towards direct possessive marking. This illustrates one way in which binominals can be formally classified as intermediate between the categories posited in the binominal typology, in the sense of showing properties that do not clearly fall into one or the other type.

5 Typological categories

5.1 Preliminary remarks

The typology presented in Pepper (this volume) assumes nine types of binominals: juxtapositions (**jxt**), compounds (**cmp**), derivations, i.e. forms consisting of a noun root and some form of nominaliser (**der**), constructions consisting of a noun root plus a classifier (**cls**); two types of bound dependent-marking strategies where the dependent noun takes an adjectivizing affix (**adj**) or some form of case-marker (**gen**), as well as a strategy where an adposition forms a constituent with the head (**prp**); a head-marking strategy where the head is marked by some form of 'construct' morpheme (**con**); and finally a double-marking strategy (**dbl**) where both the head and the dependent are formally marked.

The Äiwoo data shows examples of the **cmp**, **con**, and perhaps **prp** types (for the latter, see discussion in 5.4–5.5). While the directly possessed binominals with a directly possessed head, such as *isä pelivano* [mother.3MIN children.3MIN] 'wife' might on the face of it look like a double-marked construction, the marking on the dependent is independent of the binominal construction as such; *pelivano* 'children' is obligatorily possessive-marked whether it occurs as part of a binominal or not. I therefore consider these to be instances of the **con** type, and discuss them under 5.2 below.

One might argue that Äiwoo also shows forms of the **adj** type; this would pertain to forms such as *lââsuu mi-ki-mele* [ship BN-IPFV-fly] 'airplane' in example (1) above, in the sense that the bound noun *mi-* is commonly used to form attributive modifiers to nouns (Næss 2006: 277–278). However, as mentioned above, *mi-* is in itself nominal, and the construction as a whole is best analysed as a case of apposition ('ship, the flying one'). Moreover, the forms to which *mi-* are added are in most cases verbal, which would exclude such constructions from the category of binominals as defined in this volume; and, as noted above, there is no principled way of distinguishing such constructions from nouns modified by relative clauses. On these grounds I do not consider Äiwoo to have binominals of the **adj** type. Below, I will discuss in turn each type that the language can be uncontroversially shown to have, as well as some intermediate cases showing possible pathways of transition between types. I will also discuss the status of the relational prepositions and indirect possessive markers, which prove somewhat challenging to classify according to the typology.

5.2 Construct (con) binominals

con-type binominals in Äiwoo are the cases where a directly possessed noun combines with another noun to form a lexicalised expression. This includes the kinship terms *isä pelivano* 'mother', *tumwä pelivano* 'father', as well as the terms for animal young and animal species formed with *melo* 'animal young' (3.2.2). At least some plant-part terms may also be considered to fall into this type; see discussion in 5.6.3 below.

5.3 Compound (cmp) binominals

Äiwoo shows a number of subtypes of compounds. One is the complex kinship terms such as *gi-te* [man-same.sex.sibling] 'brother of a man', *si-te* [woman-same.sex.sibling] 'sister of a woman' etc., where neither component has an independent use, and where the final component is directly possessed (3.1.3). Another is the construction where one element, typically the head, loses the reflex of the Proto Oceanic article *na, and sometimes undergoes further changes compared to the independent form of the noun (3.1.1). This type will be discussed further in 5.6.1 below. A third type, relatively rare in my material, consists of two nouns taking the same form that each would have when used independently (3.1.2).

I count the bound nouns discussed in 3.2.4 (*nyiluu* 'hair', *nugo* 'leaf' etc.) as compounds to the extent that there is no evidence that the head noun can take suffixed possessive marking. In this, I follow the distinction made by Chappell and McGregor (1989) between inalienable possession expressed by juxtaposition, where an inalienable possessive construction may have a pronominal possessor, and compounds, where pronominal possession is not possible. On this definition, the secondary body-part terms discussed in 3.2.4 count as compounds, as they can only be possessed through possessive marking on the dependent, not on the head; whereas the plant-part terms, which appear to have 3MIN marking on the head, would count as the **con** type (cf. 5.2). The plant-part terms will be discussed further in 5.6.3 below.

5.4 Preposition-marked (prp) binominals

The relational preposition construction (3.2.5) forms binominals which appear to be of the **prp** type. This is the "elsewhere" construction in the sense that it covers a range of relations not expressed by any of the other types, and as such it is very frequent in my data.

I have analysed these forms as prepositions based on the arguments given in 3.2.5, but they differ from canonical prepositions in that they take person indexing, and this in turn affects the compatibility of this construction with the **prp** category as defined in the binominal typology of Pepper (this volume). Specifically, this typology takes adpositions to form a constituent with the modifier, but it is far from clear that this holds for the relational prepositions, which may themselves function as modifiers of a nominal head, without the need for an additional nominal modifier; e.g. *talâu wä* 'a meal/feast for it (a particular occasion)', cf. *talâu wä nuu pevaio* [meal REL place morning] 'breakfast', *nenu wä* 'coconut of/for it (e.g. a dish)', cf. *nenu wä nuwoli* [coconut REL egg] 'egg white'. Thus the status of this construction as falling under **prp** depends on one's exact criteria for identifying prepositions. An alternative possibility will be proposed in 5.5 below.

5.5 The indirect possessive

The problems in reconciling what I have called relational prepositions in Äiwoo with the **prp** class carry over to the indirect possessive construction. Recall that this construction is formed with an independent possessive marker indicating the type of possession – food, drink, betel, tools, land, and other – and that the person and number of the possessor is indexed on this marker rather than on either the possessor or the possessee, as in *tukule nogo nubââ* [headrest POSS:TOOL.3MIN shark] 'blue sea star (lit. shark's headrest)'.

While such indirect possessive markers are common in Oceanic languages, it is not clear how to classify them. As noted, they are often referred to as possessive classifiers, but this is clearly not a **cls** construction, which is defined as a classifier combining with a nominal base to form a binominal expression. As with the relational prepositions, they can modify the head directly, without the need for a nominal modifier; e.g. *tukule nogo* 'his headrest' is a perfectly well-formed expression.

Moreover, indirect possessive markers are frequently found in predicative function:

(17) a. *Lâto ny-ââ lâto tä=jo=wâ.*
 thus place-DEM:DIST thus POSS:LOC.3MIN=PROG=DIST
 'So the place gradually became his.'
 b. *Eâmo iie eopu lâ dä no-eopu-mu=wâ?*
 then who also DIST some POSS:GEN-also-2MIN=DIST
 'And who else is yours (= children)?'

From the data available to me, this does not appear to be the case for the relational prepositions, further supporting the argument that while the latter may be analysed as prepositions of a non-canonical type, indirect possessive markers are a distinct class. The question is then how to categorise this construction within the binominal typology. It could perhaps be considered an instance of the unattested type which would be a head-marking correlate of **prp**, on the assumption that the noun and the possessive classifier form a constituent of which the noun is the head.[12] If this analysis is accepted, the relational prepositions would presumably fall into the same class on the same grounds, although their grammatical behaviour does appear more preposition-like than that of the indirect possessive markers.

5.6 Transitional cases

5.6.1 cmp > cls

As already mentioned in 3.1.1, the construction where the head noun loses its initial *nV-* in compounds might be considered to be transitional between a compound and a classifier or class term construction. This is supported by the fact that a number of nouns show changes beyond simply the loss of their initial syllable in this construction, e.g. *nubââ* 'shark' > *bo-*, *nuduwo* 'yam' > *du-*.

5.6.2 prp > con

As was discussed in 4.5, there is a tendency for relational prepositions to become accreted to the head noun in a number of cases. This constitutes a transition from the **prp** to the **con** type, assuming the relational prepositions are classified as **prp** (5.4–5.5). More data on possible non-3MIN forms of these nouns might help clarify the exact relation between the two types in Äiwoo.

5.6.3 cmp > con

The plant-part terms discussed in 3.2.4 could be considered to be intermediate between the **cmp** and the **con** types. This is because the form of the head noun does not in any way indicate the presence of overt 3MIN marking, and so when a modifying noun is present, the resulting construction looks like a compound.

---

12 Cf. the claim in Palmer and Brown (2007) that indirect possessor-indexing hosts in Oceanic have a tighter syntactic relationship with the possessum noun than the possessor NP. Palmer and Brown in fact argue for analysing the indirect possessive marker itself as the head of the construction; not all their arguments apply to the Äiwoo construction, though note the predicate use of the indirect possessive markers exemplified in (17).

However, the head noun may be used on its own when a possessor is identifiable from the context, and this suggests the presence of possessive marking, since these nouns normally require some overt indication of a possessor; moreover, they accept suffixed possessive marking in other persons.

As was noted in 3.2.4, *läge* 'skin, bark, shell' in particular seems to vacillate between the two types, showing formal properties both of compounds and of direct possessive constructions. More research is needed to determine whether this is a consequence of the particular polysemy found with *läge*, which can refer to both a body part and a plant part, or whether these are properties of plant-part or secondary body-part nouns more generally.

6 Concluding remarks: The role of possessor indexing

As will be evident from the above discussion, possessor indexing plays an important role in all but the unambiguous compounding constructions. It is found on the head in the direct possessive construction, on the possessive classifier in the indirect possessive construction, and on the relational prepositions; and in most of the ambiguous or transitional cases, the key question is whether possessor indexing is present and where it is located.

The binominal typology presented in this volume assumes that such indexing may be present either on the head (**con**) or on the dependent (**gen**); but Äiwoo shows a more complex picture where relational morphemes such as possessive classifiers and relational prepositions may also carry possessive marking, and it is in these cases that problems arise in assigning the Äiwoo constructions to appropriate types. While a typological classification must necessarily gloss over a range of language-specific or family-specific subtypes, it is clear that the use of possessor indexing is pervasive in the formation of binominals in Äiwoo, ranging across a number of different subtypes. This appears to be a characteristic of Oceanic languages more generally, as noted by Ross (1998); an interesting question for future research might be exactly how possessor indexing is employed in the formation of different types of binominals in languages beyond the Oceanic family.

References

Aikhenvald, Alexandra Y. 2000. *Classifiers: A typology of noun categorization devices*. Oxford: Oxford University Press.
Bril, Isabelle. 2013. Ownership, part-whole, and other possessive-associative relations in Nêlêmwa (New Caledonia). In Alexandra Y. Aikhenvald & R.M.W. Dixon (eds.), *Possession and ownership*, 65–89. Oxford: Oxford University Press.
Chappell, Hilary & William McGregor. 1989. Alienability, inalienability and nominal classification. *Proceedings of the Fifteenth Annual Meeting of the Berkeley Linguistics Society*, 24–36.
Chappell, Hilary & William McGregor. 1996. Prolegomena to a theory of inalienability. In Hilary Chappell & William McGregor (eds.), *The grammar of inalienability: A typological perspective on body part terms and the part-whole relation*, 3–30. Berlin: Mouton de Gruyter.
Chappell, Hilary & William McGregor (eds.) 1996. *The grammar of inalienability: A typological perspective on body part terms and the part-whole relation*. Berlin: Mouton de Gruyter.
Crowley, Terry. 1996. Inalienable possession in Paamese grammar. In Hilary Chappell & William McGregor (eds.), *The grammar of inalienability: A typological perspective on body part terms and the part-whole relation*, 383–438. Berlin: Mouton de Gruyter.
Early, Robert. *A grammar of Lewo*. Unpublished manuscript.
Epps, Patience. 2008. *A grammar of Hup*. Berlin: Mouton de Gruyter.
Grinevald, Colette. 2000. A morphosyntactic typology of classifiers. In Gunter Senft (ed.), *Systems of nominal classification*, 50–92. Cambridge: Cambridge University Press.
Harvey, Mark. 1996. Body parts in Warray. In Hilary Chappell & William McGregor (eds.), *The grammar of inalienability: A typological perspective on body part terms and the part-whole relation*, 111–153. Berlin: Mouton de Gruyter.
Haspelmath, Martin. 2012. How to compare major word-classes across the world's languages. In Thomas Graf, Denis Paperno, Anna Szabolcsi & Jos Tellings (eds.), *Theories of everything: In honor of Edward Keenan*, 109–130 (UCLA Working Papers in Linguistics, 17). Los Angeles: UCLA.
Koptjevskaja-Tamm, Maria. 2004. Maria's ring of gold: adnominal possession and non-anchoring relations in European languages. In Ji-yung Kim, Yury A. Lander & Barbara H. Partee (eds.), *Possessives and beyond: Semantics and syntax*, 155–181. Amherst, MA: GLSA Publications.
Lichtenberk, Frantisek. 1983. Relational classifiers. *Lingua* 60. 147–176.
Lichtenberk, Frantisek. 1985. Syntactic category change in Oceanic languages. *Oceanic Linguistics* 24(1/2). 1–84.
Lichtenberk, Frantisek. 2009. Attributive possessive constructions in Oceanic. In William McGregor (ed.), *The expression of possession*, 249–291. Berlin: de Gruyter Mouton.
McKay, Graham R. 1978. Pronominal person and number nategories in Rembarrnga and Djeebbana. *Oceanic Linguistics* 17(1). 27–37.
Mosel, Ulrike. 1984. *Tolai syntax and its historical development*. Canberra: Pacific Linguistics.
Næss, Åshild. 2006. Bound nominal elements in Äiwoo: A reappraisal of the "multiple noun class systems". *Oceanic Linguistics* 45(2). 269–296.
Næss, Åshild. 2018a. Beyond roots and affixes: Äiwoo deverbal nominals and the typology of bound lexical morphemes. *Studies in Language* 41(4). 914–955.

Næss, Åshild. 2018b. Plural-marking strategies in Äiwoo. *Oceanic Linguistics* 57(1). 31–62.
Ozanne-Rivierre, Françoise. 1991. Incorporation of genitive relators in the languages of New Caledonia and the Loyalty Islands. In Robert Blust (ed.), *Currents in Pacific linguistics: Papers on Austronesian languages and ethnolinguistics in honour of George W. Grace*, 321.338. Canberra: Pacific Linguistics.
Palmer, Bill & Dunstan Brown. 2007. Heads in Oceanic direct possession. *Oceanic Linguistics* 46(1). 199–209.
Pawley, Andrew. 1973. Some problems in Proto-Oceanic grammar. *Oceanic Linguistics* 12(1/2). 103–188.
Pepper, Steve. This volume. Defining and typologizing binominal lexemes. In Steve Pepper, Francesca Masini & Simone Mattiola (eds.), *Binominal lexemes in cross-linguistic perspective*. Berlin: Mouton de Gruyter.
Ross, Malcolm. 1998. Possessive-like attribute constructions in the Oceanic languages of Northwest Melanesia. *Oceanic Linguistics* 37(2). 234–276.
Ross, Malcolm, and Åshild Næss. 2007. An Oceanic origin for Äiwoo, the language of the Reef Islands? *Oceanic Linguistics* 46(2). 456–498.
Schokkin, Dineke. 2020. A grammar of Paluai, the language of Baluan Island, Papua New Guinea. Berlin: Mouton de Gruyter.
Štekauer, Pavel. 2005. Onomasiological approach to word-formation. In Pavel Štekauer & Rochelle Lieber (eds.), *Handbook of word-formation*, 207–232. Dordrecht: Springer.
von Prince, Kilu. 2016. Alienability as control: The case of Daakaka. *Lingua* 182. 69–87.
Wurm, Stephen, Patrick Bwakolo & Martin Moŷiŷa. 1985. Work in progress towards a dictionary of the Reef Islands Aŷiwo language. Bound computer printout.

Bożena Cetnarowska
NN.GEN and NAREL juxtapositions in Polish: Syntactic schemas employed in building phrasal nouns

Abstract: Phrasal construction schemas (postulated within the framework of Construction Morphology) can be instantiated either by free syntactic combinations or by compound-like phrasal nouns in Polish (traditionally referred to as "juxtapositions"). Two types of Polish phrasal nouns are discussed in this chapter: NN.GEN juxtapositions consisting of a head noun and a postmodifying noun in the genitive case, and NAREL juxtapositions, in which a head noun is followed by a relational adjective. Juxtapositions resemble morphological compounds in being able to motivate (semantically) suffixal derivatives as well as compound nouns or compound adjectives. Phrasal nouns exhibit other features of lexical units since their constituents (in spite of being independently inflected) are shown to be syntactically minimal and non-referential. It is emphasized that phrasal nouns function as naming units that can fill the gaps for non-existing morphological compounds. In the case of pairs consisting of phrasal nouns and compound nouns which contain the same stems, their semantic interpretation is compared. Brief comments are offered on the coexistence of synonymous NN.GEN and NAREL juxtapositions.

1 Introduction

The aim of this chapter is to analyse selected types of multiword units in Polish [POL].[1] I also intend to show how syntactic schemas, which account for the structure of noun phrases in Polish, are used to analyse and to build multiword lexemes. Such lexemes are traditionally referred to by Polish morphologists (Grzegorczykowa 1982; Szymanek 2010; Nagórko 2016) as "juxtapositions" (Pol. *zestawienia*). Within the framework of Construction Morphology (Booij 2010; Masini 2009), they are treated as phrasal nouns, i.e., as combinations which show phrasal internal structure, but which function as naming units.

---

[1] I am grateful to the anonymous reviewers and to the editors of the volume (especially to Francesca Masini) for comments and suggestions concerning both the content and form of my chapter.

The focus will be on juxtapositions which can be regarded as binominal lexemes, since they involve a combination of two thing-morphs. Pepper (2020) defines a thing-morph as "a morph that profiles a thing (prototypically a physical object)", extending Haspelmath's (2012) notion of a "thing-root" (i.e., a root that denotes an animate or inanimate physical object).

Two types of Polish juxtapositions will be discussed, namely those consisting of a head noun followed by a dependent noun in the genitive case (NN.GEN),[2] e.g. *dom dziecka* [house child.GEN] 'orphanage', and those consisting of a head noun followed by a relational adjective (NAREL), e.g. *dom studencki* [house student-ADJZ] 'dormitory'. In the typology of binominal lexemes proposed by Pepper (2020), the first type belongs to genitive constructions (**gen**), while the second one represents adjectival constructions (**adj**). Both types of juxtapositions involve dependent marking (cf. Pepper 2020; Koptjevskaja-Tamm 2002). They will be compared to Polish morphological compounds, such as *parowóz* [steam-LV-wagon] 'steam locomotive', which are treated by Pepper (2020) as yet another kind of binominal (abbreviated as **cmp**).

There are further kinds of binominals in Polish which will not be discussed in detail here. They include, among others, juxtapositions in which the head noun is preceded by an adjective, e.g. *wełniany płaszcz* [wool-ADJZ coat] 'woollen coat', which are discussed by, among others, Cetnarowska (2014) and Clasmeier (2020).[3] Some attention will be given to the occurrence of binominals whose internal structure can be represented as noun-ADJZ-NMLZ, and which are treated as denominal derivations (**der**) by Pepper (2020).

This chapter is organized as follows. In section 2 features of morphological compounds and juxtapositions are contrasted, while section 3 deals with similarities in the behaviour of juxtapositions and compounds. In section 4 I will illustrate competition (as well as complementarity) between morphological compounds and NN.GEN or NAREL binominals. Section 5 will focus on the status of juxtapositions as syntactic or lexical units, and the notion of construction schemas. In sections 6 and 7 I identify differences between free syntactic combinations and NN.GEN or NAREL binominals: juxtapositions show syntactic

---

[2] The following abbreviations are used: 1 first person, 2 second person, 3 third person, AREL relational adjective, ACC accusative, ADJZ adjectivizer, AN adjective-noun (combinations), DIM diminutive, F feminine, GEN genitive, INS instrumental, LV linking vowel, M masculine, N neuter, NA noun-adjective (combination), NKJP National Corpus of Polish, NMLZ nominalizer, NN.GEN noun+genitive attribute, NOM nominative, PL plural, PASS.PTCP passive participle, PST past tense, SEM semantic interpretation, SG singular, VOC vocative.
[3] See also Cetnarowska (2019) for a discussion of coordinate NN constructions in Polish.

restrictedness and their non-head constituents are non-referential. Conclusions are stated in section 8.

2 Morphological compounds vs. juxtapositions in Polish

Before investigating different types of juxtapositions in Polish, it is useful to explain the notion of "compounds proper" (Pol. *złożenia właściwe*), which is commonly used by Polish morphologists (e.g. Grzegorczykowa 1982; Szymanek 2010).

The so-called compounds proper exhibit properties which are cross-linguistically attributed to morphological compounds (as discussed by, among others, Lieber and Štekauer 2009; Ralli 2013). They consist of two stems[4] connected by a linking vowel (LV), which is usually *-o-*, e.g. *ostr-o-słup* [sharp-LV-pole] 'pyramid', *cukr-o-mocz* [sugar-LV-urine] 'glycosuria'.

Polish compounds proper are written as single orthographic words. This is shown in (1–3) for morphological compounds which consist of two thing-roots. They exhibit the stress pattern of words and receive the main lexical stress on the penultimate syllable. The inflectional ending is attached to the right-hand stem,[5] which determines the grammatical gender of the compound lexeme.

(1) *ręk-o-dzieł-o* [hand-LV-work-NOM.SG] 'handicraft'

(2) *cukr-o-mocz* [sugar-LV-urine] 'glycosuria'

(3) *kilowat-o-godzin-a* [kilowatt-LV-hour-NOM.SG] 'kilowatt hour (kWh)'

---

[4] In the case of some compounds proper, such as *cudz-o-ziemi-ec* [foreign-LV-land-suff] 'foreigner' and *nos-o-roż-ec* [nose-LV-horn-suff] 'rhinoceros', the constituent that follows the linking vowel, i.e., ?*ziemiec* or ?*rożec*, does not occur as (a stem of) an independent word. Such compounds proper are often described as involving the addition of two co-formatives, i.e., both a linking vowel and a suffix, and they are referred to as "interfixal-suffixal formations" by Polish morphologists (Szymanek 2010; Nagórko 2016). Bisetto and Melloni (2008: 233) use the term "parasynthetic compounds" with respect to complex lexemes (such as the above-mentioned compound *cudzoziemiec* 'foreigner') which result from the simultaneous occurrence of compounding and derivation.

[5] Alternatively, it can be assumed that the stem of the whole compound receives the appropriate inflectional ending, as in the case of *głowonóg* 'cephalopod'.

Juxtapositions do not exhibit features of morphological compounds. They contain no linking vowels and are represented with separate orthographic words, each of which receives its own lexical stress. Each constituent of a juxtaposition is a locus of inflection, but only one of them (usually the left-hand one) determines the grammatical gender of the whole multiword unit. The juxtaposition in (4) represents the GEN subtype of binominals. The left-hand constituent is the head. The noun *prawo* 'right, law' is of neuter gender and determines the grammatical gender of the whole juxtaposition.

(4) *praw-o jazd-y* [right-N.NOM.SG driving-F.GEN.SG] 'driving licence'

The binominal lexeme in (5) consists of the head noun *poczta* 'mail' (of feminine gender) and the relational adjective *dyplomatyczna* 'diplomatic', which agrees in its inflectional specification (F.NOM.SG) with the head noun.

(5) *poczt-a dyplomat-yczn-a* [mail-F.NOM.SG diplomat-ADJZ-F.GEN.SG] 'diplomatic mail'

Relational adjectives are denominal derivatives with a fairly general meaning 'relating to N', e.g. *dyplomatyczny* (from the noun *dyplomata* 'diplomat') 'relating to a diplomat or diplomats'. The speaker/listener has to be aware of a possible relationship between the head noun and the nominal base of the relational adjective in order to determine an appropriate interpretation of NAREL combinations. For instance, the adjective *dyplomatyczny* can be roughly paraphrased as 'consisting of diplomats' in the Polish juxtaposition *korpus dyplomatyczny* 'diplomatic corps, i.e., the body of diplomats accredited to a given country', and as 'granted to diplomats' in *immunitet dyplomatyczny* 'diplomatic immunity'. Relational adjectives in Polish are regularly derived by means of several adjectivizing suffixes, such as *-ow(y), -n(y), -ck(i)/-sk(i), -n(y), -iczn(y)/ -yczn(y), -aln(y)*[6] (see Szymanek 2010: 85–97 for details). Relational adjectives cross-linguistically are treated as "pseudo-adjectives" (Levi 1976; Fábregas 2007; Rainer 2013) and as transpositional derivatives (Spencer 1999, 2013). They show inflectional properties of adjectives (e.g. in Slavic languages) but differ from canonical adjectives in being non-predicative and non-gradable (see Szymanek 2010: 79–84 and Cetnarowska 2015 on properties of relational adjectives in Polish.) In this sense, they

---

[6] The suffix-final element placed in round brackets is the inflectional ending, i.e., the vowel *-y* which is the marker of M.NOM.SG.

are semantically similar to nouns; hence combinations of nouns and relational adjectives are treated as a subtype of binominal lexemes (i.e., **adj** in Pepper 2020).

3 Compound-like properties of juxtapositions

Although juxtapositions do not show the characteristic properties of morphological compounds, in certain respects their behaviour is similar to that of compounds proper.

Like morphological compounds and affixal derivatives, juxtapositions have a naming function, which can be defined as "a fixed link between a composite expression ad a complex concept" (Bücking 2010: 253). Consequently, Polish multiword units (especially NN.GEN and NAREL binominals) are often translation equivalents of morphological compounds[7] in Germanic languages, as is observed by, among others, ten Hacken (2013). This type of equivalence is further exemplified in (6).

(6) Polish NAREL juxtapositions as translation equivalents of Germanic compounds
   a. POL *prawo morskie* [law sea-ADJZ]
      ENG *maritime law*
      DEU *Seerecht*
   b. POL *prawo kościelne* [law church-ADJZ]
      ENG *canon law*
      DEU *Kirchenrecht*

(7) Polish NN.GEN juxtapositions as translation equivalents of Germanic compounds
   a. POL *prawo umów* [law contract.GEN.PL]
      ENG *contract law*
      DEU *Vertragsrecht*
   b. POL *prawo pracy* [law labour.GEN.SG]
      ENG *employment legislation*
      DEU *Arbeitsrecht*

---

7 Polish NAREL juxtapositions can also occur as translation equivalents of AN combinations in English which contain associative adjectives, e.g. *prawo karne* 'criminal law', *prawo krajowe* 'domestic law'. The status of such English multiword expressions is ambiguous between compounds and phrasal units (see Giegerich 2005).

Morphologically complex words in Polish, such as compounds proper and affixal derivatives, are likely to become semantically lexicalized. The meaning of the compound noun *żółtodziób* [yellow-LV-beak] 'greenhorn' does not transparently relate to the meaning of its constituents. The compound noun *głowonóg* [head-LV-leg] 'cephalopod' is not fully semantically compositional either. It does not denote a type of leg (or a combination of a head and a leg) but a class of marine animals.

Since juxtapositions have a naming function (as compounds proper do), they are also likely to undergo semantic drift and exhibit 'surplus semantic information' (which does not follow directly from the meaning of their constituents). The NAREL binominal *Droga Mleczna* [road milk-ADJZ] 'Milky Way' is not a name of a road but of the galaxy which contains our solar system. The NN.GEN juxtaposition *pies ogrodnika* [dog gardener.GEN] 'dog in the manger' is not compositional, either. It denotes someone who prevents others from using what he/she does not need and has no use for. The semantic paraphrase of NN.GEN juxtaposition *Noc Muzeów* [night museum.GEN.PL] 'Long Night of Museums' contains surplus semantic information. During this special night museums stay open late into the night, admission is free and special programmes are prepared for visitors.

The interpretation of juxtapositions frequently involves extralinguistic and specialist knowledge. For instance, the NAREL juxtaposition *rzut karny* [throw penalty-ADJZ] 'penalty throw, penalty kick, penalty shot' may receive different interpretations depending on whether it appears as a term in football, ice hockey, volleyball, or other sports disciplines. In the case of football (i.e., soccer) *rzut karny* 'penalty kick' describes a shot taken from the penalty mark (11 meters from the goal line). In ice hockey during a penalty shot the puck is dropped at the centre ice and the player is allowed to attempt to score a goal (unobstructed), with no other players on ice (except the goaltender).

Compound nouns proper may function as bases for the formation of compound adjectives. The compound nouns *rękodzieło* [hand-LV-work] 'handicraft' and *ślinotok* [saliva-LV-course] 'excessive salivation' give rise to the compound adjectives *rękodzielniczy* 'relating to handicraft' and *ślinotokowy* 'relating to excessive salivation'.

Some compound adjectives[8] are motivated semantically by juxtapositions. The compound adjectives in (8) are related (formally and semantically) to NAREL binominals, i.e., to the juxtapositions *prawo administracyjne* [law administration-ADJZ] 'administrative law' and *autobus nocny* [bus night-ADJZ] 'night bus'.

---

[8] Juxtapositions also seem to function as input to compound noun formation (with the suffix -*ist(a)* attached). The compound noun *żelaznogwardzista* [iron-ADJZ-LV-guard-NMLZ] 'member of the Iron Guard (in Romania)' is related semantically to the AN juxtaposition *Żelazna Gwardia* [iron-ADJZ guard] 'Iron Guard'.

(8) a. *administracyj-n-o-praw-n-y*
administration-ADJZ-LV-law-ADJZ-NOM.SG
'relating to administrative law'
b. *noc-n-o-autobus-ow-y*[9]
night-ADJZ-LV-bus-ADJZ-NOM.SG
'relating to a night bus'

Moreover, certain suffixal formations appear to be semantically related to NAREL binominals, as shown in (9). The derivatives in (9a) and (9c) have the same denotation as the NAREL juxtapositions in (9b) and (9d), though they may differ in their degree of formality (the suffixal noun in 9a being more informal than the NArel binominal in 9b).

(9) a. *kabl-ów-k-a* [cable-ADJZ-NMLZ-NOM.SG] 'cable television'
b. *telewizj-a kabl-ow-a* [television-NOM.SG cable-ADJZ-NOM.SG] 'cable television'
c. *odrzut-ow-iec* [recoil-ADJZ-NMLZ] 'jet airplane'
d. *samolot odrzut-ow-y* [plane jet-ADJZ-NOM.SG] 'jet airplane'

The suffixal formations in (9a) and (9c) can be treated as resulting from the process of "morphological condensation" (see Masini and Benigni 2012 on Russian [RUS]), which is usually termed "univerbation" by Slavists (e.g. Martincová 2015).[10]

4 Competition between compounds proper and juxtapositions

In this section, it will be demonstrated that some juxtapositions and compounds proper have identical (or synonymous) stems as their constituents. The data in (10–13) exemplify juxtapositions and compounds proper that have the same basic denotation. The lexemes in (10a), (11a) and (12a) are compounds proper. The examples in (10b), (11b) and (12b) are NAREL juxtapositions. Even if they use different stems than the corresponding compounds proper (i.e., *lokomotywa* 'loco-

---

[9] This neologism appears in a title of the song "Nocnoautobusowa" (its lyrics being available online at https://www.tekstowo.pl/piosenka,orkiestra_na_zdrowie,nocnoautobusowa.html).
[10] Within the framework of Construction Morphology, the paradigmatic relation between suffixal derivatives and parallel NAREL juxtapositions can be stated by means of second order schemas (Booij and Masini 2015; Cetnarowska 2019).

motive', instead of *wóz* 'wagon'), the expressions in (11a) and (11b), or those in (12a) and (12b), denote the same type of objects, i.e., a steam locomotive in (11) and an electric locomotive in (12). The compound noun in (12a) contains the bound (shortened) stem *elektr-* 'electric'. There is a difference in the level of formality between the items in each pair in (10), (11) and (12): the NAREL juxtapositions are perceived as more formal expressions, belonging to specialist (technical) terminology. They have fewer attestations in the National Corpus of Polish (NKJP) than the corresponding compounds proper.[11] As shown by the data from NKJP, the compounds proper in (11a) and (12a) appeared earlier[12] than the equivalent juxtapositions.

(10) a. *mebl-o-wóz* [furniture-LV-wagon] 'removal van'
 b. *wóz mebl-ow-y* [wagon-NOM.SG furniture-ADJZ-NOM.SG] 'removal van'

(11) a. *par-o-wóz* [steam-LV-wagon] 'steam locomotive'
 b. *lokomotyw-a par-ow-a* [locomotive-NOM.SG steam-ADJZ-NOM.SG] 'steam locomotive'

(12) a. *elektr-o-wóz* [electr-LV-wagon] 'electric locomotive'
 b. *lokomotyw-a elektr-yczn-a* [locomotive-NOM.SG electr-ADJZ-NOM.SG] 'electric locomotive'

Moreover, in some cases there is "a division of labour" between juxtapositions and compounds proper. Juxtapositions tend to be endocentric: they are hyponyms of their semantic head, which is the left-hand constituent in the case of Polish NN.GEN and NAREL binominals. The NN.GEN juxtaposition *grzmot pioruna* 'thunderclap' in (13a) describes a type of a noise. By contrast, the compound proper in (13b) is exocentric, with its semantic head not being expressed overtly (or being 'outside' of the compound, cf. Plag 2003: 145). It does not denote a

---

11 The NKJP corpus is available online at http://nkjp.pl. The compound *meblowóz* 'removal van' occurs 38 times (in its NOM.SG form) in the full NKJP corpus, while there are 15 occurrences of the synonymous NAREL juxtaposition *wóz meblowy* (NOM.SG). The morphological compound *parowóz* 'steam locomotive' has 1,114 attestations (in its NOM.SG form) in NKJP as compared to 65 instances of *lokomotywa parowa* 'steam locomotive' (NOM.SG). The compound noun *elektrowóz* 'electric locomotive' shows 177 attestations (NOM.SG) vs. 35 occurrences of *lokomotywa elektryczna* 'electric locomotive' (NOM.SG) in NKJP.
12 The dates of the first examples in the NKJP corpus are as follows: *parowóz* (1923), *lokomotywa parowa* (1960); *elektrowóz* (1968), *lokomotywa elektryczna* (2001).

type of a clap or boom, but occurs (rather rarely) in poetic language as a lexeme meaning 'waterfall'.

(13) a. *grzmot piorun-a* [rumble thunder.GEN] 'thunderclap'
     b. *wod-o-grzmot* [water-LV-rumble] (poetic) 'waterfall'

The comparison of the NAREL binominals in (14) with the compounds proper in (15) shows the same pattern. The NAREL expressions in (14) are hyponyms of their head constituent (which is the polysemous noun *róg* 'horn, corner, angle, ventricle'). They denote a type of a musical instrument (in 14a-b) or a part of the ventricular system of the brain (in 14c-d). For endocentric compounds, the semantic head is the right-hand constituent, such as *meblowóz* 'removal van' in (10a) above. The compounds proper in (15), by contrast, are exocentric. They can be treated as possessive compounds in the compound typology employed by Plag (2003: 146). Instead of acting as names for a particular type of a horn (a corner, an angle or a ventricle), they denote an entity that is characterized (sometimes metaphorically) by a given property expressed by the compound. The interpretation of possessive compounds in (15) involves metonymy (in addition to metaphor). There is a metonymic relation between the attribute (e.g. the part of the body) described by the compound constituents and the animate entity which characteristically possesses such an attribute. *Widłoróg* 'pronghorn' in (15a) is the name of a species of American hoofed mammals with black branched horns which resemble a pitchfork in their shape. *Księżycoróg* in (15b) is a genus of dung beetles (*Copris lunaris*) the male of which has a characteristic horn on its head. *Dzioboróg* in (15c) denotes a type of large birds with long down-curved bills.[13]

(14) a. *róg alp-ejsk-i* [horn Alps-ADJZ-NOM.SG] 'alpine horn'
     b. *róg baryton-ow-y* [horn baritone-ADJZ-NOM.SG] 'baritone horn'
     c. *róg czoł-ow-y* [horn forehead-ADJZ-NOM.SG] 'frontal horn'
     d. *róg bocz-n-y* [horn side-ADJZ-NOM.SG] 'lateral horn'

(15) a. *widł-o-róg* [pitchfork-LV-horn] 'pronghorn'
     b. *księżyc-o-róg* [moon-LV-horn] 'horned dung beetle'
     c. *dziob-o-róg* [bill-LV-horn] 'hornbill'

---

[13] Some possessive compounds are parasynthetic, e.g. *nosorożec* 'rhinoceros' mentioned in footnote 4.

Further examples of the availability of the exocentric interpretation for compounds proper, in contrast to endocentric NAREL binominals, are provided in (16). The NAREL juxtaposition in (16a) describes a type of stimulus, whereas the morphological compound in (16b) denotes a kind of machine that converts electrical energy into mechanical one. While the NAREL juxtaposition in (16c) denotes a type of filter, i.e., a circuit which removes unwanted frequency components from the electronic signal, the compound proper in (16d) refers to a more complex filtration device that removes dust or smoke from a flowing gas.

(16) a. *bodziec elektr-yczn-y* [stimulus electr-ADJZ-NOM.SG] 'electric stimulus'
 b. *elektr-o-bodziec* [electr-LV-stimulus] 'electromotor'
 c. *filtr elektr-yczn-y* [filter electr-ADJZ-NOM.SG] 'electronic filter'
 d. *elektr-o-filtr* [electr-LV-filter] 'electrostatic precipitator'

Juxtapositions can be used to provide names for concepts when the process of compounding cannot be employed. Compounding in Polish is not as productive as in German [DEU] or English [ENG] (as is observed by, among others, Szymanek 2010). For instance, in the PWN dictionary of Polish, which contains over 100 thousand words, there is only one compound proper headed by the noun *miód* 'honey' or by the noun *lód* 'ice', i.e., *zioł-o-miód* [herb-LV-honey] 'herbal honey' and *ląd-o-lód* [ground-LV-ice] 'continental glacier'. Instead, names of various kinds of honey and types of ice are coined by means of NAREL juxtaposition, as is shown in (17). Hypothetical NN morphological compounds, such as ??*malin-o-miód* [raspberry-LV-honey] 'raspberry honey' (corresponding to 17a), or ??*łusk-o-lód* [scale-LV-ice] 'scale ice' (corresponding to 17c), are not attested in the NKJP corpus or in the PWN dictionary of Polish.

(17) a. *miód malin-ow-y* [honey raspberry-ADJZ-NOM.SG] 'raspberry honey'
 b. *miód spadzi-ow-y* [honey honeydew-ADJZ-NOM.SG] 'honeydew honey'
 c. *lód łusk-ow-y* [ice scale-ADJZ-NOM.SG] 'scale ice'
 d. *lód den-n-y* [ice bottom-ADJZ-NOM.SG] 'anchor ice'

Moreover, morphological compound formation in Polish is not a recursive process, hence compounds consisting of three of more noun stems are rare, such as *człekozwierzoupiór* [human-LV-beast-LV-spectre] 'the Anthropos-Spectre-Beast' (which occurs as a title of a novel by Tadeusz Konwicki). By contrast, juxtapositions containing a nominal head accompanied by two (or more) denominal adjectives, such as those in (18), can be formed in Polish.

(18) a. *miód malin-ow-y leś-n-y* [honey raspberry-ADJZ-NOM.SG forest-ADJZ-NOM.SG] 'forest raspberry honey'
  b. *miód spadzi-ow-y sosn-ow-y* [honey honeydew-ADJZ-NOM.SG pine-ADJZ-NOM.SG] 'pine honeydew honey'

5 Juxtapositions as the subject matter of morphology or syntax

In traditional accounts of Polish morphology (e.g. Szober 1923) juxtapositions are a subtype of composites (i.e., compounds in a wider sense of the term).[14] The class of composites is divided into three subtypes. Apart from compounds proper and juxtapositions (discussed in the previous sections), it includes a group of so-called solid compounds, defined by Nagórko (2016: 2834) as "the merger of syntactic structures without any linking material", e.g. *czcigodny* (esteem.GEN worthy.NOM) 'esteemed'.

In later accounts (couched within the frameworks of structuralist linguistics or generative grammar), juxtapositions are treated as syntactic units (see, among others, Kallas 1980; Willim 2001; Rutkowski and Progovac 2005). Consequently, there is no (or little) discussion of juxtapositions in the descriptions of Polish morphology by Grzegorczykowa and Puzynina (1999), Szymanek (2010), or Nagórko (2016). Only semantically opaque juxtapositions, such as *pies ogrodnika* [dog gardener.GEN] 'dog in the manger' or *pięta achillesowa* [heel Achilles-ADJZ] 'Achilles' heel', are treated as lexical items, within the domain of lexicology or phraseology (see Nagórko 1997).

A different position is taken by, among others, ten Hacken (2013), who advocates treating Polish juxtapositions as (regular) compounds, on the basis of their functional equivalence to compounds in Germanic languages (as exemplified in the previous section).

The framework of Construction Morphology (Booij 2010; Hüning 2010; Masini 2009) allows for the recognition of multiword units, such as Polish juxtapositions, as complex lexemes in between syntax and the lexicon. These multiword units, referred to also as phrasal lexemes, follow the syntactic patterns of a given language but have a naming function. One of the assumptions made in the model

---

14 Grzegorczykowa and Puzynina (1999: 363) employ the Polish term *wyraz złożony* to refer to composite lexemes (such as juxtapositions, compounds proper or solid compounds). Handke (1976) uses the Latin term *compositum* (pl. *composita*).

of Construction Grammar (Goldberg 2006) is that, instead of rules, construction schemas are posited. Constructions are viewed as conventionalized associations of form and meaning. They are stored in the mental lexicon of the speaker as more or less abstract templates.

As argued by Booij (2015: 189), construction schemas can express the parallelism between morphological and syntactic constructs. Consequently, a general syntactic template, e.g. [N N.GEN]$_N$, can be instantiated by the more specific syntactic schema in (19)[15] which accounts for free syntactic combinations (such as (21a)), or by the schema in (20), which accounts for the formation (and analysis) of phrasal lexemes (e.g. (21b)).

(19) [N$_i$ NP$_j$.GEN]$_{NPk}$ ⟷ [SEM$_i$ with some relation R[16] to SEM$_j$]$_k$

(20) [N^0_i N^0_j.GEN]$_k$ ⟷ [NAME for SEM$_i$ with some relation R to SEM$_j$]$_k$

(21) a. *dom naszego wujka* [house our.GEN uncle.GEN] 'our uncle's house'
     b. *dom studenta* [house student.GEN] 'dormitory'

The schema in (20) specifies the naming function of phrasal nouns. It also indicates that the non-head constituent of a [N N.GEN] phrasal lexeme is a non-projecting category (N^0), i.e., a category which is syntactically minimal.[17] The genitive postmodifier in a noun phrase need not be syntactically minimal and can be accompanied by its own premodifiers or postmodifiers, e.g. the possessive adjective *naszego* 'our.GEN.SG' in (21a).

Along the same lines, the abstract template [N A]$_N$ can be instantiated either by the syntactic schema in (22), which accounts for free syntactic combination

---

15 I follow, among others, Goldberg (2006) and Booij (2010) in assuming that constructions always consist of a statement of their formal complexity and a statement of their semantic interpretation (even if the latter is fairly general and abstract). A slightly different position is taken by Jackendoff (2013) in his theory of Parallel Architecture. Jackendoff (2013:79) assumes that apart from meaningful constructions (which are pairings of form and meaning, e.g. the *Time-away* construction), the grammar of a language stores independent principles of semantic structure (with no syntactic effect) as well as independent principles of syntactic form, such as [$_{VP}$V NP] and [$_{NP}$Det N]. If Jackendoff's position were adopted, the syntactic construction schemas in (19) and (22) would include no statement of semantic interpretation.
16 Relations expressed by means of genitive modifiers include, among others, Possession, Origin, Subject, Object, Relation, Measure.
17 A non-projecting category, e.g. N^0 and A^0, does not project a phrase of its own and therefore it does not occur with complements or specifiers (Booij 2010: 176).

(such as those in 24a), or by the schema in (23), which accounts for phrasal lexemes like those in (24b-c).

(22) $[N_i \; AP_j]_{NPk} \longleftrightarrow$ [SEM$_i$ with the property described by AP$_j$]$_k$

(23) $[N^0{}_i \; A^0{}_j]_k \longleftrightarrow$ [NAME for SEM$_i$ with some relation R to SEM$_j$]$_k$

(24) a. *list niezwykle spokojny* [letter extremely peace-ADJZ] 'an extremely calm letter'
b. *Ocean Spokojny* [ocean peace-ADJZ] 'the Pacific Ocean'
c. *lisek pustynny* [fox-DIM desert-ADJZ] 'fennec fox'

An adjective (or AP) in Polish typically comes before the head noun, as in (25):

(25) *bardzo spokojny dzień* [very peaceful day] 'a very calm day'

However, the N+AP word order is found when AP is a reduced relative (as in (24a) above and (26a) below). The N+AP order is also used for stylistic effect, e.g. in elevated style (26b) or in emotionally laden expressions such as curses (in 26c) (see Topolińska 1984 and Linde-Usiekniewicz 2013 for more discussion).]

(26) a. *bagaż schowany pod fotelem* [luggage hidden under armchair] 'luggage stored under the seat'
b. *Ojcze nasz* [father-VOC our-VOC] 'Our Father' (in the Lord's prayer)
c. *profesorek kopany* [professor-DIM kicked-PASS.PTCP] 'the bloody (little) professor'

The abstract construction schema [N A], although relatively rarely used for free syntactic combinations, is instantiated regularly by phrasal lexemes in Polish.

Since the discussion in this chapter focuses on binominal lexemes, i.e., NA juxtapositions which contain relational adjectives, the schema for phrasal nouns in (23) can be made more specific, as shown in (27). The part of the schema in (27) following the double-headed arrow predicts the semantic interpretation of NAREL binominals. It refers to the entity E that is the nominal base of the relational adjective in question, e.g. the noun *kultura* 'culture' from which the transpositional (relational) adjective *kulturalny* 'relating to culture' is derived.

(27) $[N^0{}_i \; A^0{}_j]_k \longleftrightarrow$ [NAME for SEM$_i$ with some relation R to entity E of SEM$_j$]$_k$

(28) *attaché kultur-aln-y* [attaché culture-ADJZ-NOM.SG] 'cultural attaché'

Constituents of NAREL juxtapositions are predicted to be syntactically minimal by the constructional schema in (27), as will be discussed in the next section.

6 Syntactic minimality, recursiveness and non-reversibility

Phrasal lexemes are expected to be syntactically restricted, in comparison to free syntactic combinations (see Masini 2009; Booij 2010).

One of the manifestations of syntactic restrictedness is the syntactic minimality of constituents of phrasal nouns. The genitive postmodifier which follows its head in the NN.GEN juxtaposition cannot be itself modified (as indicated by the schema in (20) above). The addition of a premodifying adjective to the genitive constituent *studenta* 'student.GEN' in (29a) changes the interpretation: (29b) is no longer a naming unit but a free syntactic combination.

(29) a. *dom studenta* [house student.GEN] 'dormitory'
b. *dom bardzo sympatycznego studenta* [house very.GEN likeable.GEN student.GEN] 'a house of (some) very likeable student'

A similar example is provided in (30) to show that the addition of a degree adverb before the relational adjective changes the NAREL juxtaposition in (30a) into a free syntactic combination with a descriptive function in (30b). Moreover, the adjective *dyplomatyczny* changes its interpretation from that of a classifying modifier (in 30a) to a qualifying[18] modifier in (30b) paraphrasable as 'tactful, politic'.

(30) a. *kurier dyplomatyczny* [courier diplomatic] 'diplomatic courier'
b. *kurier niezwykle dyplomatyczny* [courier extremely diplomatic] 'a courier who is extremely tactful'

The multiword units in (31), (32) and (33) seem to invalidate the requirement of the syntactic minimality of constituents of phrasal lexemes. The genitive constit-

---

18 The term "qualifying" describes here the function of the adjective and can be contrasted with the classifying function (see Rutkowski and Progovac 2005; Cetnarowska, Pysz and Trugman 2011). Qualitative adjectives usually have a qualifying function, e.g. the denominal adjective *olbrzymi* 'giant' is a qualifying modifier in the free syntactic combination *olbrzymi kłopot* 'enormous trouble'. However, they have a classifying function in NA juxtapositions, such as *pancernik olbrzymi* [armadillo giant-ADJZ] 'giant armadillo (*Priodontes maximus*)'.

uent of those juxtapositions takes a postmodifying adjective in (31) while in (32) it occurs with a premodifying adjective. In (33) the NAREL juxtaposition *przewozy towarowe* 'freight transportation' is accompanied by the adjectival premodifier *kolejowe* 'relating to railway'.

(31) *dom studenta zaocznego* [house student.GEN extramural.GEN] 'dormitory for extramural students'

(32) *dom małego dziecka* [house small.GEN child.GEN] 'orphanage for infants'[19]

(33) *kolejowe przewozy towarowe* [railway-ADJZ transport.PL goods-ADJZ] 'railway freight transportation'

However, such structures are not a violation of the syntactic minimality principle. As was demonstrated in (18) in section 4 for NAREL binominals, the formation of juxtapositions in Polish is recursive, as is the process of compounding in Germanic languages, including German and English. This is shown by the translation of the example in (33) into English, and by its German equivalent *Bahnfrachtverkehr* (rail-freight-traffic) 'transport of goods by rail'. The genitive constituent of the juxtapositions in (31) and (32) is itself a juxtaposition (of the NA or AN type). The internal structure of the binominal in (31) can be therefore represented as [N^0 [N^0 A^0].GEN], i.e., [dom [studenta zaocznego]], while the structure of (32) as [N^0 [A^0 N^0].GEN], i.e., [dom [małego dziecka]]. Both *student zaoczny* [student extramural] 'extramural student' and *małe dziecko* [small child] 'infant' are naming units.

The juxtaposition in (33) can be divided into the following constituents: [A^0 [N^0 A^0]]. It is an example of a [ARELN] binominal, whose head is itself a NAREL binominal, i.e., *przewozy towarowe* 'freight transportation'. One can also have a double application of the construction schema in (27), as exemplified by the juxtaposition in (34), whose internal structure may be represented as [[N^0 A^0] A^0].

(34) *przewozy towarowe kolejowe* [transport.PL goods-ADJZ railway-ADJZ] 'railway freight transportation'

Another manifestation of syntactic restrictedness (apart from syntactic minimality) of phrasal lexemes is the fixed order of constituents (as stated by, among others, Nagórko 2016).

---

19 *Małe dziecko* (lit. little child) functions as a name for a fixed concept in (32). Orphanages for infants usually accept babies between one month and one year of age.

The genitive constituent of the NN.GEN binominal in (35) cannot be shifted to the pre-head position, as the resulting combination is unacceptable.

(35) a. *mąż stan-u* [man state.GEN] 'statesman'
     b. * *stanu mąż* [state.GEN man]

In the case of NAREL binominals, e.g. (36a), the shifting of the denominal adjective to the pre-head position may lead to its reinterpretation as a qualifying adjective, and then the resulting AN combination has a descriptive function. (36b) is a syntactic phrase, not a naming unit.

(36) a. *attaché kulturalny* [attaché cultural] 'cultural attaché'
     b. *kulturalny attaché* [cultural attaché] 'a/the polite attaché'

In the case of some denominal adjectives there is no change in meaning related to prenominal versus postnominal position, e.g. *zimowa kurtka* [winter-ADJZ jacket] and *kurtka zimowa* [jacket winter-ADJZ], both paraphrasable as 'winter jacket'. This notwithstanding, such instances of ARELN units as *zimowa kurtka* [winter-ADJZ jacket] are not free syntactic combinations but juxtapositions. Some reasons for the availability of pre- or post-head position in noun+adjective constructions are mentioned by Cetnarowska, Pysz and Trugman (2011), Cetnarowska (2014) and Clasmeier (2020). For instance, when there is another classifying relational adjective, a genitive attribute or a PP modifier following the head noun, the classifying adjective (which usually follows the noun) can be placed before the noun, cf. *struktura molekularna* [structure molecular] 'molecular structure' vs. *molekularna struktura wody* [molecular structure water.GEN] 'molecular structure of water'. The speaker's decision to place a classifying adjective in the pre-head or the post-head position may also result from stylistic factors, prosodic (rhythmic) factors or information structure requirements (see Cetnarowska 2014). Both in the AN and NA combinations *zimowa kurtka* and *kurtka zimowa* 'winter jacket', the denominal adjective *zimowa* 'relating to winter' has a classifying function and the whole combination is interpreted as a name for a fixed concept (as can be expected of compounds and compound-like expressions).[20]

---

[20] Moreover, although the requirement of fixed word order is often cited as one of the defining features of juxtapositions (e.g. by Nagórko 2016), it is possible to encounter variable word order in the NKJP corpus even in the case of idiomatic NA or AN juxtapositions, e.g. *pięta achillesowa* [heel Achilles-ADJZ] 'Achilles' heel, a weak spot' (NA word order – 245 occurrences, AN word order – 4 occurrences), *niebieski ptak* [blue bird] 'loafer, sponger' (AN – 88 hits, NA – 8 hits), *kro-*

7 Non-referentiality

The nominal genitive modifier, as well as the nominal base of a relational adjective in a binominal lexeme, can be regarded as nouns (or noun phrases) which are not referential.

Referential nouns and noun phrases refer to some particular individual (or entity) in the external world or in the mental world of the discourse participants, e.g. *the man in a black hat*. Nouns which are constituents of morphological compounds or constituents of juxtapositions do not refer to any individual (as is observed by Bücking 2010 for German). They have a 'kind' reading, i.e., they denote a kind (or a class) of individuals. In the case of NN.GEN binominals in Polish, it can be shown that the genitive modifier is non-referential. It cannot be pronominalized (see (37)). It cannot be accompanied by a relative clause, either (as in (39)). When the NN.GEN sequence is a free syntactic combination, by contrast, the noun (or noun phrase) in the genitive case can be pronominalized and relativized (as in (38) and (40)).

(37) a. *Zburzyliście   cztery   domy   studenta.*
       demolish.PST.2PL four.ACC.PL house.ACC.PL student.GEN.SG
       'You demolished four dormitories.'
   b. *#Zburzyliście   cztery   jego domy*
       demolish.PST.2PL four.ACC.PL his   house.ACC.PL
       Acceptable only in the reading:
       'You demolished four houses which belong(ed) to him.'
       Unacceptable in the reading: 'You demolished four dormitories.'

(38) a. *Zburzyliście   domy   moich   sąsiadów.*
       demolish.PST.2PL house.ACC.PL my.GEN.PL neighbour.GEN.PL
       'You demolished my neighbours' houses.'
   b. *Zburzyliście   ich   domy.*
       demolish.PST.2PL their house.ACC.PL
       'You demolished their houses.'

---

kodyle łzy [crocodile-ADJZ tears] 'crocodile tears; false and insincere display of emotions' (AN – 358 hits, NA – 11 hits).

(39) *Kupiłam   mundur   strażaka,   który*
    buy.PST.1SG.F uniform.ACC.SG firefighter.GEN.sg which.NOM.SG
    na syna   nie pasował.
    on son.ACC.SG not fit.PST.3SG
    'I bought a firefighter uniform which didn't fit (my) son.'
    (*Który* 'which, who' does not refer to a firefighter but to a uniform.)

(40) *Rozmawialiśmy z   żoną   strażaka,   który*
    talk.PST.1PL   with wife.INS.SG firefighter.GEN.sg which.NOM.SG
    był   prawdziwym bohaterem.
    be.PST.3SG real.INS.SG hero.INS.SG
    'We talked to the wife of the firefighter, who was a real hero.'
    (*który* 'who, which' does not refer to the wife, but to the firefighter.)

Syntactic operations (such as pronominalization and relativization) do not (normally) access constituents of morphologically complex words. This follows from the Lexicalist Hypothesis, as formulated (in its strong version) by Anderson (1992).[21]

Consequently, constituents of morphological compounds and of relational adjectives are not visible to anaphoric expressions (such as pronouns). This can be shown for the stem *głow-* 'head' (feminine gender), which is the non-head constituent in the previously discussed compound proper *głowonóg* [head-LV-leg] 'cephalopod'. *Głowa* 'head' is not visible as a potential antecedent to the pronoun *ona* 'she', as is shown by the infelicity of the pair of Polish sentences in (41b).[22]

(41) a. *Złapaliśmy dziwnego głowonoga. Jego głowa była w kształcie młotka.*
       'We caught a strange cephalopod. Its head was in the shape of a hammer.'
    b. #*Złapaliśmy dziwnego głowonoga. (Ona) była w kształcie młotka.*
       'We caught a strange cephalopod. It was in the shape of a hammer.'

In the case of the NAREL juxtaposition *mundur strażacki*, the relative pronoun *który* 'which, who' cannot take the noun *strażak* 'firefighter' (which is the derivational base of the relational adjective) as its antecedent. Moreover, *strażak* 'firefighter' cannot be coreferential with the pronoun *niego* 'him.ACC.SG' in (42).

---

[21] Anderson (1992: 84) states that "[t]he syntax neither manipulates nor has access to the internal form of words."
[22] The pronoun *ona* 'she' cannot be coreferential with the cephalopod itself since the whole compound *głowonóg* 'cephalopod' is of masculine gender.

(42) *Kupiłam   mundur   strażacki,   który*
     buy.PST.1SG.F uniform.ACC.SG firefighter-ADJZ-GEN.sg which.NOM.SG
     na niego   nie pasował.
     on him.ACC.SG not fit.PST.3SG
     'I bought a firefighter uniform which didn't fit him (*który* 'which, who' does not refer to a firefighter but to a uniform).

An interesting issue which can only be discussed briefly are parallel NAREL and NN.GEN binominals, such as those in (43).

(43) a.   *dom studenta* [house student.GEN] 'dormitory'
     a.' *dom studencki* [house student-ADJZ] 'dormitory'
     b.   *hotel asystenta* [hotel assistant.GEN] 'dormitory for university teachers'
     b.' *hotel asystencki* [hotel assistant-ADJZ] 'dormitory for university teachers'
     c.   *dział finansów* [department finance.GEN.PL] 'financial department'
     c.' *dział finansowy* [department financial] 'financial department'
     d.   *czapka górnika* [cap miner.GEN] 'miner's cap, i.e., miner's shako'
     d.' *czapka górnicza* [cap miner-ADJZ] 'miner's cap, i.e., miner's shako'

The binominals in each pair (e.g. 43a and 43a') are propositionally synonymous and they show no marked difference in their stylistic value. Burska (2016) analyses Polish NN.GEN and NAREL juxtapositions in a corpus of contemporary press articles and concludes that both types of nominal juxtapositions are common among phrasal nouns attested in this text type.[23]

This does not mean that a NN.GEN juxtaposition can always be replaced by a parallel NAREL juxtaposition, or vice versa. When the non-head genitive constituent is itself complex, it cannot be replaced by an adjectival attribute (see Cetnarowska, Pysz and Trugman 2011). For instance, the non-head *student zaoczny* [student extramural] in the NN.GEN juxtaposition *dom studenta zaocznego* [house student.GEN extramural.GEN] 'dormitory for extramural students', given in (31) in section 6, consists of a noun and a relational adjective. A hypothetical parallel juxtaposition containing two adjectival modifiers would not be synonymous

---

[23] A search in the NKJP corpus for the NN.GEN juxtaposition *dom studenta* 'dormitory'(NOM. SG+GEN.SG) returns 94 hits while the search for the NAREL *dom studencki* (NOM.SG) yields 244 hits. There are 13 occurrences of the NN.GEN binominal *hotel asystenta* 'dormitory for university teachers' and 18 occurrences of the NAREL binominal *hotel asystencki*. The NN.GEN juxtaposition *dział finansów* 'financial department' occurs 11 times in the corpus while its NAREL equivalent *dział finansowy* is found 41 times. The search for the juxtapositions in (43d) and (43d') in NKJP yields no results when the head noun is in the NOM.SG form.

to (31) since each of the adjectives would have to be interpreted as expressing a property of the head noun (i.e., a property of the house). Therefore, both (44a) and (44b) are semantically odd and unacceptable.

(44) a. *dom studencki zaoczny* [house student-ADJZ extramural]
     b. *zaoczny dom studencki* [extramural student-ADJZ house]

Rainer (2013) and Ohnheiser (2015) observe that specific semantic relations between the head of a juxtaposition and its genitive or adjectival attribute may be more commonly expressed either by NN.GEN binominals or by NAREL binominals. For instance, the direct object of a deverbal action noun typically corresponds to the genitive attribute, and not to a relational adjective. This is shown in (45).

(45) a. *zbier-ani-e truskaw-ek* [pick-NMLZ-NOM.SG strawberry-GEN.PL] 'strawberry picking'
     b. **zbier-ani-e truskaw-ow-e* [pick-NMLZ-NOM.SG strawberry-ADJZ-NOM.SG] 'strawberry picking'

By contrast, the semantic relation of POSSESSION (Bourque 2014; Pepper 2020, this volume) can hold between the constituents of NN.GEN as well as NAREL binominals (such as 43d and 43d'). The relation of PURPOSE, i.e., 'a Head intended for a Modifier', obtains between the components of the NN.GEN juxtaposition in (43a-b) as well as between the components of the NAREL juxtaposition in (43a'-b'). The semantic link between the constituents of both (43c) and (43c') can be stated as TOPIC, i.e., 'a Head concerned with a Modifier'.[24] The acceptability of particular NN.GEN and NAREL binominals is ultimately a matter of speakers' usage, as certain potential juxtapositions do not become conventionalized,[25] e.g. ?*dział płacowy* [department salary-ADJZ] vs. *dział płac* [department salary.GEN.PL].[26]

---

[24] I would like to thank Steve Pepper for discussing with me the identification of semantic relations postulated by Bourque (2014) and by Pepper (2020; this volume). I am also grateful to him for pointing my attention to semantic promiscuity of binominals (analysed by Jackendoff 2010 on the basis of English compound nouns).

[25] See Bauer (1983: 42) on the notion of institutionalization of lexemes, and Schmid (2011: 72) on the notion of conventionalization.

[26] There are no occurrences of ?*dział płacowy* in the NKJP corpus. However, a search in NKJP yields some examples of a similar NAREL juxtaposition containing a coordinate (morphological) compound adjective, i.e., *dział kadrowo-płacowy* [department personnel-ADJZ-LV-salary-ADJZ], which is synonymous to the NN.GEN juxtaposition *dział kadr i płac* [department personnel.GEN.PL and salary.GEN.PL] 'human resources and payroll department'.

8 Conclusions

This chapter investigated different ways of combining two thing-morphs in Polish, focusing on juxtapositions containing a head noun postmodified by another noun in the genitive case (NN.GEN) as well as on juxtapositions where a head noun is followed by a denominal relational adjective (NAREL). Such binominals consist of fully inflected lexemes, which means they are regarded by some researchers as regular syntactic phrases, i.e., as free syntactic combinations. However, within the framework of Construction Morphology, they are treated as phrasal nouns, i.e., as multiword lexical units. Compound-like properties of juxtapositions were emphasized, such as their tendency to undergo semantic lexicalization, and their ability to motivate semantically suffixal derivatives, such as *kablówka* [cable-ADJZ-NMLZ] 'cable TV', and morphological compounds, e.g. the compound adjective *administracyjnoprawny* [administration-ADJZ-LV-law-ADJZ] 'relating to administrative law'. Competition between juxtapositions and compounds proper was illustrated, e.g. *lokomotywa parowa* [locomotive steam-ADJZ] 'steam locomotive' and *parowóz* [steam-LV-wagon] 'steam locomotive'. Examples were provided of pairs of morphological compounds and juxtapositions which are not semantically equivalent, because the compound proper is exocentric while an NN or NAREL binominal with the same noun stems is endocentric. Moreover, the process of forming NAREL or NN.GEN juxtapositions complements the compounding process in cases when restrictions on compounding prevent the formation of NN compounds.

It was argued that abstract construction schemas postulated within the framework of Construction Morphology, such as [NN.GEN] and [NA], can be instantiated either by more specific syntactic schemas for regular noun phrases, or by schemas which represent multiword lexemes (i.e., juxtapositions). Differences between both types of (lower level) schemas were highlighted, among them the syntactic minimality and the non-referentiality of non-head constituents of juxtapositions.

References

Anderson, Stephen R.A. 1992. *A-morphous morphology*. Cambridge: Cambridge University Press.
Bauer, Laurie. 1983. *English word formation*. Cambridge: Cambridge University Press.
Bisetto, Antonietta & Chiara Melloni. 2008. Parasynthetic compounding. *Lingue e linguaggio* VII(2). 233–260.
Booij, Geert. 2010. *Construction Morphology*. Oxford: Oxford University Press.
Booij, Geert. 2015. Word formation in construction grammar. In Peter O. Müller, Ingeborg Ohnheiser, Susan Olsen & Franz Rainer (eds.), *Word-formation. An international handbook of the languages of Europe*, vol. 1, 188–202. Berlin, München, Boston: Mouton de Gruyter.

Booij, Geert & Francesca Masini. 2015. The role of second order schemas in the construction of complex words. In Laurie Bauer, Livia Kőrtvélyessy & Pavol Štekauer (eds.), *Semantics of complex words*, 47–66. Cham: Springer.

Bourque, Yves. 2014. *Towards a typology of semantic transparency: The case of French compounds*. Toronto: University of Toronto PhD dissertation.

Burska, Katarzyna. 2016. *Analityzmy leksykalne i ich syntetyczne odpowiedniki w prasie* [Analytical lexical constructions and their synthetic equivalents in the press]. Łódź: Wydawnictwo Uniwersytetu Łódzkiego.

Bücking, Sebastian. 2010. German nominal compounds as underspecified names for kinds. In Susan Olsen (ed.), *New impulses in word formation*, 253–281. Hamburg: Helmut Buske Verlag.

Cetnarowska, Bożena. 2014. On pre-nominal classifying adjectives in Polish. In Anna Bondaruk, Gréte Dalmi & Alexander Grosu (eds.), *Topics in the syntax of DPs and agreement*, 100–127. Amsterdam: John Benjamins.

Cetnarowska, Bożena. 2015. Categorial ambiguities within the noun phrase: Relational adjectives in Polish. In Joanna Błaszczak, Dorota Klimek-Jankowska & Krzysztof Migdalski (eds.), *How categorical are categories? New approaches to the old questions of noun, verb, and adjective*, 115–153. Berlin: Mouton de Gruyter.

Cetnarowska, Bożena. 2019. Compounds and multi-word expressions in Polish. In Barbara Schlücker (ed.), *Complex lexical units*, 279–306. Berlin: Mouton de Gruyter.

Cetnarowska, Bożena, Agnieszka Pysz & Helen Trugman. 2011. Distribution of classificatory adjectives and genitives in Polish NPs. In Kamila Dębowska-Kozłowska & Katarzyna Dziubalska-Kołaczyk (eds.), *On words and sounds: A selection of papers from the 40th PLM, 2009*, 273–303. Newcastle upon Tyne: Cambridge Scholars Publishing.

Clasmeier, Christina. 2020. *Niebieski ptak* und *cukier biały* – Eine Klassifikation und Korpusanalyse der Funktion und Wortfolge polnischer Farbadjektive. *Zeitschrift für Slawistik* 65(1). 96–133.

Fábregas, Antonio. 2007. The internal syntactic structure of relational adjectives. *Probus* 19 (1). 135–170.

Giegerich, Heinz J. 2005. Associative adjectives in English and the lexicon-syntax interface. *Journal of Linguistics* 41 (3). 571–591.

Goldberg, Adele. 2006. *Constructions at work. The nature of generalization in language*. Oxford: Oxford University Press.

Grzegorczykowa, Renata. 1982. *Zarys słowotwórstwa polskiego* (5th edn.) [Outline of Polish word-formation]. Warszawa: Państwowe Wydawnictwo Naukowe.

Grzegorczykowa, Renata & Jadwiga Puzynina 1999. Rzeczownik [Noun]. In Renata Grzegorczykowa, Roman Laskowski & Henryk Wróbel (eds.), *Gramatyka współczesnego języka polskiego. Morfologia* [Grammar of contemporary Polish. Morphology], 389–464. 3rd edn. Warszawa: Wydawnictwo Naukowe PWN.

ten Hacken, Pius. 2013. Compounds in English, in French, in Polish, and in general. *SKASE Journal of Theoretical Linguistics* 10(1). 97–113. http://www.skase.sk/Volumes/JTL22/.

Handke, Kwiryna. 1976. *Budowa morfologiczna i funkcje compositów polskich (z uwzględnieniem innych języków zachodniosłowiańskich)* [Morphological structure and functions of Polish composites (taking into consideration other West Slavic languages)]. Wrocław: Polska Akademia Nauk.

Haspelmath, Martin. 2012. How to compare major word-classes across the world's languages. *UCLA Working Papers in Linguistics, Theories of Everything 17*, Article 16, 109–130.

Hüning, Matthias. 2010. Adjective + Noun constructions between syntax and word formation in Dutch and German. In Alexander Onysko & Sascha Michel (eds.), *Cognitive perspectives on word formation*, 195–215. Berlin: Mouton de Gruyter.
Jackendoff, Ray. 2010. *Meaning and the lexicon: The Parallel Architecture 1975–2010*. Oxford: Oxford University Press.
Jackendoff, Ray. 2013. Constructions in the Parallel Architecture. In Thomas Hoffmann & Graeme Trousdale (eds.), *The Oxford handbook of Construction Grammar*, 70–92. Oxford: Oxford University Press.
Kallas, Krystyna. 1980. *Grupy apozycyjne we współczesnym języku polskim* [Appositional groups in contemporary Polish]. Toruń: Uniwersytet Mikołaja Kopernika.
Koptjevskaja-Tamm, Maria. 2002. Adnominal possession in the European languages: Form and function. *STUF – Language Typology and Universals* 55(2). 141–172.
Levi, Judith N. 1976. *The syntax and semantics of nonpredicating adjectives in English*. Bloomington: Indiana University Linguistics Club.
Lieber, Rochelle & Pavol Štekauer. 2009. Introduction: Status and definition of compounding. In Rochelle Lieber & Pavol Štekauer (eds.), *The Oxford handbook of compounding*, 3–18. Oxford: Oxford University Press.
Linde-Usiekniewicz, Jadwiga. 2013. A position on classificatory adjectives in Polish. *Studies in Polish Linguistics* 8(3). 103–126.
Martincová, Olga. 2015. Multi-word expressions and univerbation in Slavic. In Peter O. Müller, Ingeborg Ohnheiser, Susan Olsen & Franz Rainer (eds.), *Word-formation: An international handbook of the languages of Europe*, vol.1, 742–757. Berlin: Mouton de Gruyter.
Masini, Francesca. 2009. Phrasal lexemes, compounds and phrases: A constructionist perspective. *Word Structure* 2(2). 254–271.
Masini, Francesca & Valentina Benigni. 2012. Phrasal lexemes and shortening strategies in Russian: The case for constructions. *Morphology* 22(3). 417–451.
Nagórko, Alicja. 1997. *Zarys gramatyki polskiej* [Outline of the grammar of Polish]. 2nd edn. Warszawa: PWN.
Nagórko, Alicja. 2016. Polish. In Peter O. Müller, Ingeborg Ohnheiser, Susan Olsen & Franz Rainer (eds.), *Word-formation: An international handbook of the languages of Europe*, vol. 4, 2831–2852. Berlin, München, Boston: De Gruyter.
Ohnheiser, Ingeborg. 2015. Compounds and multi-word expressions in Slavic. In Peter O. Müller, Ingeborg Ohnheiser, Susan Olsen & Franz Rainer (eds.), *Word-formation. An international handbook of the languages of Europe*, vol. 1, 757–779. Berlin: Mouton de Gruyter.
Pepper, Steve. 2020. *The typology and semantics of binominal lexemes: Noun-noun compounds and their functional equivalents*. Oslo: University of Oslo PhD dissertation.
Pepper, Steve. This volume. Hatcher-Bourque: Towards a reusable classification of semantic relations. In Steve Pepper, Francesca Masini & Simone Mattiola (eds.), *Binominal lexemes in cross-linguistic perspective*. Berlin: Mouton de Gruyter.
Plag, Ingo. 2003. *Word-formation in English*. Cambridge: Cambridge University Press.
Rainer, Franz. 2013. Can relational adjectives really express any relation? An onomasiological perspective. *SKASE Journal of Theoretical Linguistics* 10(1). 12–40. http://www.skase.sk/Volumes/JTL22/.
Ralli, Angela. 2013. *Compounding in Modern Greek*. Dordrecht: Springer.

Rutkowski, Paweł & Ljiljana Progovac. 2005. Classification Projection in Polish and Serbian: The position and shape of classifying adjectives. In Steven Franks, Frank Y. Gladney & Mila Tasseva-Kurktchieva (eds.), *Formal approaches to Slavic linguistics: The South Carolina meeting*, 289–299. Ann Arbor, MI: Michigan Slavic Publications.

Schmid, Hans-Jörg. 2011. *English morphology and word-formation. An introduction*. 2nd edn. Berlin: Erich Schmid Verlag.

Spencer, Andrew. 1999. Transpositions and argument structure. In Geert Booij & Jaap van Marle (eds.), *Yearbook of Morphology 1998*, 73–101. Springer: Dordrecht.

Spencer, Andrew. 2013. *Lexical relatedness: A paradigm-based model*. Oxford: Oxford University Press.

Szober, Stanisław. 1923. *Gramatyka języka polskiego. Nauka o znaczeniu i budowie wyrazów* [Grammar of Polish. The study of meaning and structure of words]. Lwów–Warszawa: Książnica Polska. Tow. Naucz. Szkół Wyższych.

Szymanek, Bogdan. 2010. *A panorama of Polish word-formation*. Lublin: Wydawnictwo Katolickiego Uniwersytetu Lubelskiego.

Topolińska, Zuzanna. 1984. Składnia grupy imiennej [The syntax of a nominal group]. In Maciej Grochowski, Stanisław Karolak & Zuzanna Topolińska (eds.), *Gramatyka współczesnego języka polskiego. Składnia* [Grammar of contemporary Polish. Syntax], 301–393. Warszawa: Państwowe Wydawnictwo Naukowe.

Willim, Ewa. 2001. On NP-internal agreement: A study of some adjectival and nominal modifiers in Polish. In Gerhild Zybatow, Uwe Junghanns, Grit Mehlhorn & Luka Szucsich (eds.), *Current Issues in formal Slavic linguistics*, 80–95. Frankfurt/Main: Peter Lang.

Corpora

NKJP = Przepiórkowski, Adam, Mirosław Bańko, Robert Górski & Barbara Lewandowska-Tomaszczyk (eds.), 2012. *Narodowy Korpus Języka Polskiego* [The national corpus of the Polish language]. Warszawa: Wydawnictwo Naukowe PWN.

Dictionaries

The PWN dictionary of Polish = *Wielki Słownik Języka Polskiego PWN ze słownikiem wyrazów bliskoznacznych (Pendrive)*. 2018. Warszawa: Wydawnictwo Naukowe PWN.

Françoise Rose and An Van linden
The derivational use of classifiers in Western Amazonia

Abstract: Western Amazonian languages stand out in having classifiers that – in addition to the well-established classifier environments – also appear as derivational devices on nouns. Since classifiers are commonly assumed to originate in nouns, classifier languages confront us with an analytical problem in the domain of binominals, i.e. how to distinguish between the derivational use of classifiers on nouns, and noun-noun compounds. The present paper addresses this problem on the basis of primary data from Harakmbut (isolate, Peru) and Mojeño Trinitario (Arawak, Bolivia), two unrelated Western Amazonian languages. As a factor bearing on this problem, we show that in both languages the noun/classifier distinction is blurred by the fact that there is a class of nouns that share many features with the canonical classifiers, i.e. that of bound nouns. In this paper, we discuss how noun-classifier derivation differs from noun-noun compounding, or classifiers from bound nouns for that matter, at the phonological, semantic and syntactic levels in both languages.

1 Introduction

Amazonian nominal categorization systems are known for challenging the traditional view of the distinction between noun classes and classifiers (Payne 1987; Grinevald and Seifart 2004). Among these, Western Amazonian classifiers are particularly interesting for two reasons. First, they typically form multiple-classifier systems (Aikhenvald 2000), with the same set of classifiers occurring in different syntactic environments. Second, their classifiers are multifunctional (Krasnoukhova 2012), in having the three functions of categorization, derivation and, less importantly, agreement. This paper focuses on the derivational use of classifiers in Western Amazonian languages, previously noted in the literature (Payne 1987; Aikhenvald 2000: 220; Seifart and Payne 2007; Petersen de Piñeros 2007; Krasnoukhova 2012: 209; Brandão 2016; Wojtylak 2016), but not yet extensively described, neither in individual languages nor cross-linguistically.[1] It will deal more specifi-

---

[1] But see Seifart (2005: 106–122) for a discussion of the derivational uses of noun classes on nouns in Miraña.

cally with the derivational use of classifiers on nominal roots,² which is functionally equivalent to noun-noun compounding, and thus participates in the formation of binominal lexemes, i.e. "lexical items that consist primarily of two nominal constituents and whose function is to name a (complex) concept that involves an unstated (or underspecified) relation between two entities" following the definition of Pepper (2020: 1, see also Masini, Mattiola & Pepper, this volume). The functional resemblance of classifiers on nouns and binominal compounds is illustrated in (1)-(2) from Harakmbut (AMR, see below), with classifier-derived nouns (hereafter N-CLF) in (1), and noun-noun compounds (N-N) in (2).³

Harakmbut
(1) a. *siro-pi* [metal-CLF:stick] 'knife' (cf. Hart 1963: 1)   N-CLF
     b. *siro-puʔ* [metal-CLF:cylindrical;hollow] 'metal tube'   N-CLF
         (cf. Hart 1963: 1)

(2) a. *ndumba-kuwa* [forest-dog] 'bush dog' (Helberg 1984: 252;   N-N
         Tripp 1995: 194)
     b. *ãwĩt-ku* [giant.otter-head] 'giant otter's head' (Hart 1963: 3)   N-N

The constructional approach to binominal lexemes that sees roots and affixes as end-points on a continuum (Pepper 2020: 15) is particularly useful to investigate the use of classifiers in binominal lexeme formation. Indeed, since classifiers are commonly assumed to originate in nouns (Mithun 1986: 395; Aikhenvald 2000), more specifically in compounds (cf. Seifart 2010), and are often difficult to distinguish in a straightforward manner (Dixon 1986: 106), classifier languages confront us with an analytical problem in the domain of binominals: how can we distinguish between the derivational use of classifiers on nouns, and noun-noun compounds? This boils down to discussing the empirical realization of the types **cls** "classifier" and **cmp** "compounding" of Pepper's (2020: 145–169) typology of binominals (see Section 2). The nominal roots found in compounds are also

---

2 Classifiers can also be used as nominalizing devices on verbs, see Krasnoukhova (2012: 210).
3 Abbreviations: 1: first person; 2: second person; 3: third person; ACC: accusative; AN: animate; ACT: active; ART: article; CLF: classifier; DEM: demonstrative; DERIV: derivative; DEP: dependent verb form; DIM: diminutive; DIST: distal; DIST.PST : distant past; F: feminine; FAN: addictive; GEN: genitive; GRN: general relational noun; HAB.A: habitual actor; IMP: imperative; IND: indicative; INS: instrumental; IRR: irrealis; LOC: locative; M: masculine; NH: non-human; NOM: nominative; NPF: noun prefix; NPOSD: non-possessed; NVOL: non-volitional; PFV: perfective; PL: plural; PLURACT: pluractional; PREP: preposition; PSD: possessed; REC.PST: recent past; SG: singular; SOC: sociative causative; SPAT: spatial; SP.P.NZ: specific patient nominalizer; SUBST: substitutive; TRNS: transitiviser; VPL: verbal plural.

themselves considered to be on the continuum between affixes and canonical nominal roots. Addressing this empirical question therefore results in studying the language-internal competition between classifier-derived nouns (N-CLF) and noun-noun compounds (N-N), and involves tackling more general and theoretical questions like the definition of classifiers, and the distinction between derivational affixes and bound roots (Lieber and Štekauer 2009).

The present paper addresses the competition between two binominal constructions (N-CLF and N-N) through the comparison of two Western Amazonian languages: Mojeño Trinitario and Harakmbut. These languages are genetically unrelated and not in contact and are being studied by the authors on the basis of primary data collected in the field. Mojeño Trinitario (TRN) is an Arawak language spoken in the lowlands of Bolivia, in and around the old missionary town of Trinidad and in the Isiboro-Sécure territory. It is spoken by around 3000 speakers (Crevels and Muysken 2009) and is endangered by the gradual loss of inter-generational transmission. Investigation on Mojeño benefits from previous work on the language (Gill 1957), on its sister language Mojeño Ignaciano (IGN, especially Olza et al. 2002), on a variety spoken in the 17th century in Jesuit missions (Marbán 1702), and on historical work on the Arawak family (Payne 1991a inter alia). A basic introduction to Mojeño Trinitario is Rose (2015). Harakmbut is a Peruvian Amazonian language spoken in the departamentos of Cusco and Madre de Dios. It is considered an isolate (Tovar 1961; Loukotka 1968; Lyon 1975; Helberg 1984; Wise 1999: 307), as Adelaar's (2000, 2007) proposal of a genetic link with the Brazilian Katukina family still awaits further corroboration. Earlier work on Harakmbut has mainly focused on the most vital dialect, i.e. Amarakaeri[4] (AMR) (Hart 1963; Helberg 1984, 1990; Tripp 1976, 1995), as does the present paper; Van linden (2022) presents a basic description. With about 1000 speakers left (Moore 2007: 46), the language is highly endangered, also aggravated by parents' reluctance to pass on the language to their children.

Because the boundary between classifiers and nouns is not straightforward in these two languages, we will compare classifiers and nouns within and beyond binominal lexemes in order to distinguish compounding and derivation through classifiers in binominals. In general terms, classifiers are morphemes providing an overt categorization of nominals (Grinevald Craig 2004: 1016). They encode "some salient perceived or imputed characteristics of the entity to which an associated noun refers" (Allan 1977: 285). The two classifier systems differ in

---

4 Speakers of the Amarakaeri variety regard the label 'Amarakaeri' as a derogatory term, as it means '(fierce) murderer', going back to an ancient story about the origin of the different ethnolinguistic groups of the Harakmbut people. They prefer to call their variety 'Arakmbut'.

that Mojeño Trinitario is a multiple and multifunctional classifier language with an extensive set of classifiers formally rather distinct from nouns, but showing almost the exact same syntactic distribution, while Harakmbut has a small set of classifiers that are formally identical to nominal roots but show a distribution distinct from that of nouns. In this language, classifiers are mainly used as verbal classifiers;[5] they are hardly used as categorizing devices on nouns. Yet, both languages show patterns of word formation in which classifiers function as derivational affixes, which are at first sight not easy to distinguish from noun-noun compounds.

In this paper,[6] we will first present the different types of nouns and binominals found in the two languages (Section 2). Importantly, we will introduce the class of bound nouns (Section 2.1), which contribute significantly to the analytical problem focused on here. In Section 3, we will compare classifiers and bound nouns in the two languages at different levels of analysis, thus proposing a methodology to distinguish between N-CLF and N-N in any classifier language. We will start with the result of our analyses, providing an inventory of the sets of classifiers and bound nouns in the languages studied, and describe their form and meaning (Section 3.1). We will then discuss how classifier-derived nominals compare to noun-noun compounds, or classifiers to bound nouns for that matter, at several levels, viz. phonological/prosodic, syntactic and semantic (Sections 3.2 to 3.4). In the process, we will also discuss the theoretical question of whether classifiers are thing-morphs, i.e. morphs that denote a thing (Pepper 2020: 12), a concept extended from that of thing-roots, i.e. roots that denote an (animate or inanimate) physical object (Haspelmath 2012). Thing-morphs themselves cover both thing-roots and thing-affixes. Finally, we will summarize our findings, and elaborate on their diachronic implications (Section 4).

---

[5] Or, following Passer (2016: 17), "verb" classifiers rather than "verbal" ones (e.g. Aikhenvald 2000: chap. 6).

[6] Authorship of this paper is shared jointly. Work on Mojeño Trinitario has been supported by the ASLAN Laboratoire d'excellence, Lyon, France. Work on Harakmbut has been made possible by mobility grants and postdoctoral grants from the Research Foundation, Flanders (FWO) (2009–2014) and the Fund for Scientific Research (FNRS) (2015–2016), as well as research grants from the research council of the KU Leuven (GOA/12/007 & C14/18/034). The paper was revised during Van linden's research stay in Lyon, supported by the Collegium de Lyon and the ASLAN Laboratoire d'excellence. We thank Olga Krasnoukhova, as well as the editors and referee for helpful comments on earlier drafts.

2 Nouns and binominals

This section presents the different types of binominal lexemes (or constructions) found in Mojeño Trinitario and Harakmbut. After presenting the two classes of simple nouns (Section 2.1), we list the different types of binominals (Sections 2.2 to 2.7), with special attention to N-N compounds (Section 2.5) and classifier-derived nouns, the phenomenon central to this paper (Section 2.7). Section 2.8 elaborates why classifier-derived nouns deserve closer attention. Section 3 will then focus on word formation, i.e. the creation of one-word lexemes, restricting the discussion to the **cmp** and **cls** constructions of Pepper's (2020) typology.

First we give a preliminary quantitative account of the different types of binominals attested in the two languages, on the basis of the list of 100 complex concepts designed by Pepper (2020: 391–392). We classified the data collected with this list into Pepper's nine types of binominals (Pepper 2020: 145–169), listed below with simplified definitions:

- **jxt**: juxtaposition of two separate thing-roots without any additional element
- **cmp**: compounding of two thing-roots in a single word
- **der**: derivation from a thing-root with a thing-affix that contributes some semantic content
- **cls**: thing-root with a classifier, where the denotatum of the binominal is different from that of the base (the classifier is used to derive a new meaning rather than for classification)
- **prp**: head and modifier are independent lexemes, and an additional lexeme forms a constituent with the modifier
- **gen**: head and modifier are independent lexemes, with an additional word-class preserving morpheme attached to the modifier
- **adj**: head and modifier are independent lexemes, with an additional word-class changing morpheme attached to the modifier
- **con**: head and modifier are independent lexemes, with an additional word-class preserving morpheme attached to the head
- **dbl**: head and modifier are independent lexemes, with additional morphemes attached to both.

For Mojeño Trinitario, 90 items have been collected for 88 concepts. Out of these, 27 items are binominals, instantiating five types (**con, der, cmp, cls, jxt**) of Pepper's nine types (Pepper 2020: 145–169), as detailed in Table 1.[7] Most notable is

---

[7] Section 2.4 discusses a marginal construction of the **prp** type, which was not illustrated in the Mojeño Trinitario translations of the list of 100 complex concepts.

the fact that 10 of the 27 binominals involve the derivational use of a classifier: it is the most common binominal structure, and the topic of the present paper. The items that are not binominals are either simple forms (often borrowings) or deverbal nominalizations, not counting as binominals.[8]

Out of the 78 Harakmbut data items collected for 72 entries of Pepper's (2020: 391–392) list, 29 are binominals. These instantiate four of the nine types, as presented in Table 1; there are no examples of **jxt**, **prp**, **adj**, **con** and **dbl**. The predominant type is **cmp** (15 out of 29 items), while **cls** and **gen** are instantiated 6 times each.[9] It should be noted, however, that a few **cmp** and **gen** examples also involve classifiers, which – if ranged with **cls** – would yield a 28% share of **cls** (8 out of 29 binominals). Non-binominal items include 19 simple forms, two descriptive phrases, and 28 verb-based items. Taken together, therefore, noun-noun compounds and classifier-derived nouns constitute two major devices to form binominals in these two Western Amazonian languages.

Table 1: Mojeño Trinitario and Harakmbut's binominals in Pepper's list of 100 complex concepts.

	jxt	cmp	der	cls	gen	con
TRN (27)	11%	19%	22%	37%	0%	11%
AMR (29)	0%	52%	7%	21%	21%	0%

Before presenting the various types of binominals found in Mojeño Trinitario and Harakmbut, it is important to distinguish two classes of simple nouns, bound and independent nouns.

2.1 Simple nouns: Bound nouns and independent nouns

In both languages, noun roots are easily distinguished from verb roots or other words classes, mainly on the basis of their morphological potential. As in many Amazonian languages (Krasnoukhova 2012), there is a crucial distinction between

---

8 Interestingly, among the 20 simple native forms, five suspiciously show final syllables homophonous with classifiers (without being synchronically segmentable), and out of the 28 deverbal nominalizations, 12 involve classifiers as a derivational device. These additional uses of classifiers go beyond the topic of this paper.
9 Note that these numbers are different from the counts in Pepper (2020: 441, 479). For instance, Pepper overlooked some spatial markers in his analysis, which inflated his **cmp** type (19 items) at the expense of his **gen** type (3 items).

two classes of nominal roots, i.e. bound nouns and independent nouns.[10] This is a morphological distinction, in that bound nouns require some morphology to constitute a word, unlike independent nouns.[11] The former category is illustrated in (4) and (6); the latter in (3) and (5).

Trinitario
(3) a. *wiye* [ox] 'ox' independent noun
    b. *n-wiye-ra* [1SG-ox-PSD] 'my ox'

(4) a. *n-juma* [1SG-sickness] 'my sickness' bound noun
    b. *jma-re* [sickness-NPOSD] 'sickness'

Harakmbut
(5) a. *pagŋ* [father] 'father' independent noun
    b. *ndoʔ-edn pagŋ* [1SG-GEN father] 'my father'

(6) a. *ndoʔ-edn-ndik* [1SG-GEN-name] 'my name' bound noun
    b. *wa-ndik* [NPF-name] 'name'

Independent nouns may occur as nominal heads without affixes, cf. *wiye* in (3) and *pagŋ* in (5). Bound nouns, by contrast, never occur as nominal heads without affixes, cf. *-juma* in (4) and *-ndik* in (6). In Mojeño Trinitario, bound nouns take possession-related affixes to reach wordhood status (Rose 2020). Typically they take a person prefix for their possessor, cf. (4a), but a sub-class of bound nouns, including *-juma* in (4), instead take some derivational affix, e.g. the non-possession suffix *-re* in (4b), when no possessor is specified. Independent nouns, in turn, do not need extra affixes when unpossessed (3a). But when they are possessed, a sub-class of them, including *wiye* in (3b), require a derivational suffix (such as *-ra*) in order to take person prefixes. The situation is somewhat different in Harakmbut, where bound nouns require a noun prefix, *wa-* or *e-*, to obtain independent nominal status, cf. (6b).[12] Unlike independent nouns (5b), they can also attach to adnominal modifiers to form one prosodic word, as in (6a) with a genitive-marked pronoun (cf. Van linden 2021, 2022).

This paper will show that bound nouns are more often found in compounds and incorporated in verb forms than independent nouns, thus showing a distri-

---

10 These classes are sometimes called obligatorily vs. non-obligatorily possessed nouns, or inalienable vs. alienable nouns.
11 This is why, in this paper, bound nouns cited within the text are preceded by a hyphen.
12 These noun prefixes have been analysed as nominalizing prefixes in Van linden (2022).

bution roughly similar to that of classifiers. Classifiers constitute yet a different category; they are morphologically bound elements, but not nouns. They will be systematically compared to bound nouns in Section 3.

2.2 Adnominal possession construction

Mojeño Trinitario and Harakmbut have rather different adnominal possession constructions, exemplified in (7) and (8) respectively. In terms of Pepper's typology of binominals, Mojeño Trinitario adnominal possession instantiates the **con** type, because it has an additional marker on the head, whereas the Harakmbut construction exemplifies the **gen** type, because it has an additional marker on the modifier.

(7) TRN to   t(a)-og'e   to   kwoyu
         ART.NH   3NH-body   ART.NH   horse
    'the body of the horse'

(8) AMR apetpet-en   hak
         jaguar-GEN   house
    'the jaguar's den'

In Mojeño Trinitario (7), the adnominal possession construction is made up of two noun phrases (NPs), each consisting minimally of a noun preceded by an article, indicating that the noun is specific. N1 expresses the possessee and takes a person prefix referring to the possessor expressed by N2.[13] In Harakmbut (8), in which NPs minimally consist of a noun only, the order in adnominal possession constructions is that of possessor – possessee, and genitive case is marked on the possessor noun (cf. Tripp 1995: 195).

In addition to structures with a genitive marker in Harakmbut, Pepper (2020: 441, 479) also analyses one-word structures including a spatial element linking two noun roots as instances of the **gen** type. An example is given in (9).

(9) AMR wa-mbaʔ-taʔ-meh [NPF-hand-SPAT:base-hump] 'wrist'

In (9), the spatial affix -taʔ- links two thing-roots: a wrist is a hump at the base of the hand. As the first noun root semantically modifies the second noun root and

---

[13] A sub-class of independent nouns, viz. those that cannot take a possessive prefix, use a juxtaposed generic bound noun -ye'e that carries the possessive prefix (Rose 2015). This sub-class is labelled "non-directly possessible nouns" in Rose (2020).

as the spatial affix does not change the word class of the modifier noun, structures like (9) are indeed similar to genitive constructions like (8). Other spatial linking elements in Harakmbut, like -(o)k- and -ti-, point to different spatial configurations of the component elements (cf. Hart 1963).

2.3 Nouns with derivation suffixes

Both languages have the **der** type of binominals, made of a nominal root and a derivational morpheme. Mojeño Trinitario uses a number of derivational suffixes, five of which are exemplified in Pepper's (2020) list. They are the diminutive -gira (10), the substitutive -ra'o (11) (also used to derive 'step-father' from 'father'), the addictive -more ~-mre 'fan of' (12), the 'habitual actor' -eru (13), and the non-possessed -re (normally used to allow a bound noun to occur without a person prefix, cf. (4b) in Section 2.1) resulting in a non-compositional meaning in (14).

Trinitario
(10) kwoy-gira [horse-DIM] 'foal'

(11) viya-ra'o [Lord-SUBST] 'chieftain'[14]

(12) 'san-ti-mre [field-NPOSD-FAN] 'farmer (lit. fan of field)'

(13) tyuraj-eru [mud-HAB.A] 'potter'

(14) chut-re [head-NPOSD] 'skull'

Harakmbut also has a number of derivational suffixes, like -eri in (15); nominal bases suffixed by -eri refer to animate entities living in or coming from the place denoted by the nominal base. The two examples of the **der** type in Pepper's (2020) list involve the diminutive suffix -si?po as in (16).

Harakmbut
(15) Porto-lus-eri [Puerto-Luz-AN] 'people living in/coming from Puerto Luz'

(16) wa-mbo-si?po [NPF-youngster-DIM] 'boy'

---

14 Viya is a noun lexicalized from vi- 1PL and iya 'father' meaning both 'Sir' and 'Lord' (to refer to Christian god).

2.4 Binominals with a preposition

Binominals of the **prp** type, i.e. with an additional lexeme forming a constituent with the modifier, are found in Mojeño Trinitario only. This infrequent construction uses the preposition *te* (with very broad semantics), linking the head element in initial position to the modifying noun that follows. It should be noted that the first noun is always an independent noun borrowed from Spanish, such as *manteka* and *eskina* in (17).[15]

Trinitario
(17) a. *manteka te jimo* [butter PREP fish] 'fish grease'
      b. *j-mu-ena eskina-no te plasa* [DEM-NH.PL-DIST corner-PL PREP square] 'those corners of the square'

2.5 N-N compounds

Both languages allow compounding of two nominal roots in a complex nominal word (**cmp** type). It is striking that the two noun classes (bound and independent) are not distributed evenly across N1 and N2 in N(1)-N(2) compounds, but rather show the same skewed distribution. In Table 2, we have split the **cmp** type of Table 1 according to different noun classes in N1 and N2 positions. Independent nouns (I in Table 2) are only rarely found as N2, whereas bound nouns (B in Table 2) frequently occur as N2.

Table 2: Types of N-N compounds according to morphological class of N1 and N2 in Pepper's list of 100 complex concepts.

	I-I	I-B	B-B	B-I
Mojeño Trinitario (5)	0	1	4	0
Harakmbut (15)	0	5	9	1

In both languages, most typical N-N compounds, such as (18) and (19), are endocentric compounds in which N2 is the semantic head and N1 is semantically subordinate. The semantic head of a compound is identified on the basis that the concept expressed by the compound is a sub-class of the concept denoted by the

---

15 This construction, unattested in Old Mojeño, most likely emerged due to contact, facilitated by the formal resemblance between Spanish and Mojeño Trinitario prepositions *de* and *te*.

head: "the whole compound must be a hyponym of its head" (Scalise and Fábregas 2010: 111).

(18) TRN *kasiki-yeno* [cacique-wife] 'cacique's wife'

(19) AMR *kaymãri-mbogŋ* [zungaro-lip] 'lip of a zungaro fish'

In both languages, N2 is more rarely an independent noun; examples are given in (20) and (21). In Trinitario, N1 is the semantic head in such cases.

(20) TRN *'nuuku-mari* [hole-stone] 'cave'

(21) AMR *wa-taʔpi-widn* [NPF-spine-stone] 'kidney' (Tripp 1995: 130b)

In Mojeño Trinitario, the selection of the gender value of the article (non-human, human plural, masculine singular or feminine singular) signals the morphological head of the compound, i.e. the element of the binominal which defines the formal properties of the compound as a lexical item (Scalise & Fábregas 2010: 124).[16] Either N1 or N2 can be the morphological head. In (18), the compound *kasikiyeno* triggers a feminine singular form of the article, like *yeno* does, even though *kasiki* is masculine. However, in other endocentric compounds, it is N1 that determines the form of the article. In Harakmbut, there is no such way of determining the morphological head of N-N compounds.

In addition, we have also documented some exocentric compounds, i.e. compounds which are not hyponyms of any of their components (cf. Bauer 2001: 700), as in (22).

(22) TRN *ñi paku-miro* [ART.M dog-face] 'a (male) being with a human body and a dog head'

In (22), neither *paku* 'dog' nor *miro* 'face' can be considered the semantic head of the compound, as the compound refers neither to a type of dog nor to a type of face, but – through metonymy – to a type of human being. That is, the semantic head 'lies outside' the component elements of the compound. This compound has no morphological head either: while both *paku* and *miro* trigger non-human agreement, *pakumiro* instead takes human agreement (see the singular mascu-

---

16 Note that the morphological head of a binominal is by definition a sub-part of a lexeme and should not be confused with the syntactic head of a noun phrase, which is a full word.

line article *ñi* in (22)). The Harakmbut example (19) can also be used as an exocentric compound. In that case, it refers to a person whose lips resemble these of a zungaro fish. In fact, metonymy based on animal body part nouns like (19) produces great nicknames among the Harakmbut community. Several aspects of N-N compounds will be described more in-depth in Section 3.

2.6 N N juxtaposition

Mojeño Trinitario also has a binominal construction of the **jxt** type, with two nominal words and without additional material, e.g. (23)-(24).

(23) TRN *ñi*   *'chane* *'jiro*
             ART.M person   man
             'the man'

(24) TRN *no*   *n-jañono-no*   *trinrano-no*
             ART.PL 1SG-relative-PL Trinitario-Pl
             'my Trinitario relatives'

This construction differs from N-N compounds in that the two nominal roots do not form a single word, but are simply juxtaposed. Both nouns are separate phonological and morphological words, as shown by the plural marking on both N1 and N2 in (24). Moreover, unlike in most N-N compounds, N1 is the head, and N2 the modifier (N2 is not the head of a separate noun phrase as it lacks an article).[17] This construction also differs from the adnominal possession construction both semantically and formally. Semantically, it does not involve a relation of possession between two nouns, but codes a variety of other relations between N1 and N2. For instance, N2 can be a hyponym (23), a synonym, a noun expressing substance or material, or a noun qualifying N1 (24); N1 can be a measure term with the countized element in N2, or N1 can be a title used with the proper name in N2. Formally, N1 is not possessed, unlike in the adnominal possession construction (see Section 2.2).

---

17 There are examples of N2 preceded by an article in the semantic subtypes where either N2 expresses substance/material, or N1 is a measure term.

2.7 N-CLF derived nouns

Both languages have binominals based on a nominal root plus a classifier that does not 'classify' this root, but rather derives a new stem with a different meaning (see Section 3.4.1 for contrasting examples). We have analysed these examples as denominals based on a classifier (**cls**). The derivational use of classifiers is not characteristic of prototypical classifier systems (Krasnoukhova 2012: 209), but has been mentioned before for some classifier languages (Payne 1987: 28–29; Aikhenvald 2003: 84, 225). The classifier immediately follows the noun root to form a complex noun stem in both languages, cf. (25)-(26), and thus occupies the same slot as N2 in N-N compounds. In Mojeño Trinitario, some nouns derived with a classifier additionally take the derivational suffix *-rV* (with vowel harmony) between the root and the classifier, as in (27).[18]

(25) TRN a. *to yuk-pi* [ART.NH fire-CLF:fili] 'a candle'
         b. *to giore-pi* [ART.NH snake-CLF:fili] 'a worm'
         c. *to 'o'e-pi* [ART.NH rainbow-CLF:fili] 'an eel'

(26) AMR a. *peraʔ-po* [rubber-CLF:sphere] 'plastic ball' (Hart 1963: 5)
         b. *siro-po* [metal-CLF:sphere] 'tin can' (Hart 1963: 1)
         c. *aymõrõ-po* [honey-CLF:sphere] 'bee'

(27) TRN a. *n-iypé-re-ku* [1SG-foot-DERIV-CLF:path] 'my footprint'
         b. *v-emtone-re-pi* [1PL-labor-DERIV-CLF:fili] 'our way/process of working'

Semantically, the addition of the classifiers on these noun roots causes substantial changes of meaning, e.g. from 'fire' to 'candle' in (25a). Nevertheless, the semantic import of classifiers in N-CLF derived nouns is typically less specific than that of nouns in N-N compounds, whether independent or morphologically bound. In both languages, and presumably across languages, classifiers tend to have more general semantics than nouns, as they denote shapes, qualities or substances (see Aikhenvald (2000: 271–305) for an overview of the semantics of classifiers).[19] This is in line with Lieber and Štekauer's (2009: 5) semantic criterion to

---

[18] The derivational suffix *-rV*, although it can surface as *-re*, differs from *-re* NPOSD in that it applies to any noun class, while *-re* NPOSD only applies to a lexically determined subset of bound nouns when they are used without a possessive person prefix.

[19] This is not true of Mojeño Trinitario unique classifiers, which have the same meaning as that of a lexical noun, from which they differ in form, see classifier *-pewo* 'CLF:foot' vs *-iype* 'foot'.

distinguish bound roots from derivational affixes, i.e. that "roots in some sense have more semantic substance than affixes." At the same time, as is apparent from examples (25)-(26), in both languages classifiers have a semantic effect on nouns that is far less abstract than that of the – clearly derivational – diminutive suffixes in (10) and (16) or the 'habitual actor' suffix in (13) above; a candle in (25a) is an instance of a long flexible object related to fire. We will elaborate on the semantic import of classifiers in Section 3.4 and relate this to the question of whether classifiers are thing-affixes.

2.8 Why N-CLF formations deserve closer attention

In the previous sections, we have presented two classes of simple nouns and seven binominal constructions in Mojeño Trinitario and Harakmbut, following Pepper's (2020) typology. Although it is the least frequent binominal type in Pepper's (2020) cross-linguistic study, the **cls** type is not marginal in South America, unlike in other macro areas (2020: 170). More specifically, it is found in three of the ten South American languages of the sample, viz. in Mojeño Trinitario, Harakmbut and Murui Huitoto [HUU] (Wojtylak 2016), all spoken in Western Amazonia. Krasnoukhova (2012: 209) also states that the derivational function of classifiers "is very prominent among languages with a multifunctional classifier system" in South America. This type of binominal construction thus deserves closer examination, as it is cross-linguistically rare but at the same time areally pervasive.

The constructional approach to binominal lexemes adopted here is a fruitful way of pursuing this goal because it facilitates the comparison of classifier-derived nouns with N-N compounds. The previous discussion has indicated two reasons why comparing these two phenomena is key. One is that the semantic contribution of classifiers to binominals is not very different from that of nouns in N-N compounds, and the other is that classifiers take up the same position in N-CLF formations as N2 in N-N compounds.

Section 3 will investigate the similarities and differences between classifiers and bound nouns in greater detail. It will show that the distinction between classifier-derived nouns and N-N compounds is difficult to make in the two languages studied for different reasons: in Mojeño Trinitario because classifiers and bound nouns show a very similar distribution also beyond binominal constructions, and in Harakmbut because all classifiers are formally identical to bound nouns, some of which have a very general, abstract meaning.

3 Classifiers vs. bound nouns

In this section we distinguish classifiers from bound nouns. Section 3.1 presents the inventories of the two categories in Mojeño Trinitario and Harakmbut, and the criteria underlying them regarding form/meaning mapping. In addition, the inventories result from meticulously comparing the behaviour of classifiers and bound nouns in larger morpho-syntactic units. Specifically, we will compare classifiers and bound nouns in terms of their phonological and prosodic integration in morphologically complex nouns (Section 3.2), their syntactic distribution within and beyond the noun phrase (Section 3.3), and finally their functions when occurring on nouns and in verb forms (Section 3.4). We posit that, in any classifier language, classifiers and bound nouns will differ along at least one of these dimensions of analysis.

3.1 Inventories, form and meaning

Distinguishing classifiers from bound noun roots is not straightforward. This section will spell out some considerations used in each language to identify elements as belonging to one or the other category.

Mojeño Trinitario has 31 classifier suffixes, listed in the appendix of Rose (2019a). Most of these are of a CV form and lack any obvious relationship to a noun (28). Some have a long history; *-pi* 'CLF:filiform' (28a), for instance, has been reconstructed for proto-Arawak, along with its lexical source **pi* 'snake' (Payne 1991b: 248) (note that (28b) is not the reflex of **pi*). Others show a formal and semantic resemblance to a noun (29). Finally, some have the same form as and a meaning related to that of a noun (30). When a classifier is formally related to or similar to a noun, its meaning is more abstract and general, often denoting shape or localization. A subset of classifiers have allomorphs depending on whether they are stem-final (on nouns, numerals and stative verbs), or stem-internal in active verbs, such as *-mo~-me* 'CLF:fabric' in (31a) and (31b) respectively.

Trinitario
(28) a. *-pi* 'CLF:fili' (for thin, long, flexible items)
b. *giore* 'snake'

(29) a. *-ju'e~-je* 'CLF:interior'
b. *-ju'e* 'stomach'

(30) a. *-miro* 'CLF:face' (referring to either faces or places in front of a ground)
    b. *-miro* 'face'

(31) a. *t-jitu-mo* [3-be_thick-CLF:fabric] 'it is thick (of a fabric, for ex.)'
    b. *s-oktáya-me-ko* [3F-step_on-CLF:fabric-ACT] 'she is stepping on the blanket (for ex.)'

Bound nouns form a large sub-class of the Mojeño Trinitario nouns (32)-(33), with two morphological sub-classes (Rose 2020). Bound nouns of the first class obligatorily take a possessive prefix when used as the head of a noun phrase (32). Bound nouns of the second class generally take a possessive prefix when used as the head of a noun phrase (33a), except when they carry a derivational suffix for non-possession, like *-ti* in (33b) or *-re* in (4b).[20] Semantically, these nouns denote parts of wholes and kinship relationships, as well as items of clothing and personal accessories, some bodily excretions, personal attributes and a few artefacts. Nominal roots are at least (underlyingly) disyllabic in Mojeño Trinitario. They do not show allomorphy, although their form with or without a prefix can have a different surface realization, due to rhythmic syncope (33) (see Section 3.2).

Trinitario
(32) a. *n-amri* [1SG-grandchild] 'my grandchild'
    b. **amri* 'grandchild'

(33) a. *n-yowo* [1SG-axe] 'my axe'
    b. *ywo-ti* [axe-NPOSD] 'axe'

To distinguish classifiers from bound roots in a consistent way, we have used the following methodology for Mojeño Trinitario. If a 'suspect' item used in word formation is formally and/or semantically distinct from a similar element that is used as the head of a noun phrase, it is considered a classifier. This is the case for the classifier *-mu'i* (~*-m'i*) used to refer to various aspects of the environment (e.g. time, looks) (34a), the underlying form of which differs from that of its lexical nominal source *-imu'i* (~*-im'i*) 'physical property' (34b). This means that, conversely, if the suspect element shows neither a formal nor a semantic distinction between its use in word formation and as the head of a noun phrase, it is considered a noun. This is the case with *-chupu* (~*-chpu*) 'trunk' in (35a) and (35b)).

---

[20] The distribution of these suffixes is lexically determined.

Trinitario
(34) a. to   n-ijare-**m'i**
        ART.NH 1SG-name-**CLF:setting**
        'my birthday'
    b. to   ta-**em'i**   ma   'chane (taem'i < ta+ imu'i)
        ART.NH 3NH-**physical_property** ART.M[21] person
        'the shape of a man'

(35) a. to   manka-**chpu**
        ART.NH mango-**trunk**
        'the mango tree trunk'
    b. to   ta-**chupu**   (to)   manka
        ART.NH 3NH-**trunk**   ART.NH   mango
        'the trunk of a mango tree'

Harakmbut has a much smaller inventory of classifiers, about 13, all of which are formally identical to a bound noun. They are monosyllabic, mostly of a CV form, which is not distinctive of bound nouns nor classifiers, as there are a few independent nouns with the same syllabic structure, e.g. *ho* 'peach palm'. Examples are given in (36) to (43), with the (a)-examples representing the classifiers, and the (b)-examples their formally identical bound nouns.

Harakmbut
(36) a. -*mba?*   CLF:hand;leaf   b. -*mba?* 'hand', 'leaf'; 'hand/leaf-shape'

(37) a. -*pe*   CLF:disk   b. -*pe* 'jaw, chin, cheek'; 'sth disk-like'

(38) a. -*pa*   CLF:rod   b. -*pa* 'penis'; 'rod'

(39) a. -*pu?*   CLF:cylindrical;hollow   b. -*pu?* 'bamboo'; 'tube'

(40) a. -*nda*   CLF:fruit   b. -*nda* 'fruit'; 'fruit shape (e.g. grapefruit)'

---

21 Note that the masculine singular human article shows two forms, depending on the gender of the speaker (i.e. genderlects, see Rose 2013). The form *ñi* in examples (22), (23), (53) and (58b) is uttered by a woman, whereas the form *ma* in example (34b) is uttered by a man (Rose 2013).

(41) a. *-po*   CLF:sphere   b. *-po* 'something round'

(42) a. *-pi*   CLF:stick   b. *-pi* 'something stick-like'

(43) a. *-wẽ*   CLF:liquid   b. *-wẽ* 'river; liquid'

This formal identity of classifiers and bound nouns bears heavily on the analytical problem of distinguishing between N-N compounds and N-CLF formations in Harakmbut. As items like (36) to (43) show two different types of semantic extensions in different syntactic environments, we analysed the same form as instantiating two different morphological categories, classifier and noun. For a number of items (about half), e.g. in (36) to (39), the bound noun has a more specific meaning referring to a body or plant part in addition to a more abstract meaning referring to a shape identical to their classifier counterparts. Whenever these items in binominals involve their more specific meaning, they are analysed as bound nouns. For the other half, including (40) to (43), however, there is no difference in meaning between the two categories. The meaning of the bound nouns is somewhat atypical for nouns, as they refer in a general way to entities with the shape or substance denoted by the classifier. Items like (40) to (43) and items like (36) to (39) when carrying an abstract meaning are attributed categorial status depending on their syntactic distribution and function in comparison to other – less ambiguous – items of the sets of classifiers and bound nouns. However, as these two categories share the function of word formation when occurring on nouns (see Section 3.4), even this paradigmatic approach cannot guarantee the correct analysis. Consider the difference between (44) and (45), for example.

Harakmbut
(44)   *wã-õh-wẽ* [NPF-nose-liquid] 'nostril'

(45)   *kumo-k-wẽ* [barbasco-SPAT:separation-(CLF:)liquid] 'barbasco juice'

In (44), the binominal can be analysed as an exocentric compound, as 'nostril' refers to neither a type of nose, nor a type of liquid, but to the place where liquid (mucus) leaves the nose. As the N-CLF formations in Harakmbut are never semantically exocentric, unlike N-N compounds, *-wẽ* is analysed as a bound noun in (44). In (45), by contrast, either analysis for *-wẽ* is acceptable, as spatial linkers are found between two nominal roots in **gen** binominals (like (9)) as well as between a nominal root and a classifier in **cls** binominals (see Pepper 2020: 479).

Bound nouns form a large sub-class of the Harakmbut nouns, referring to inalienably possessed entities, such as body parts, plant parts, and landscape parts, as well as basic shapes or qualities of entities (Van linden 2021). They also include kinship terms. The 73 items identified as "shape morphemes" by Hart (1963), 45 to 50 of which Payne (1987: 36) analyses as classifiers, are all bound nouns but they do not exhaust the class (kinship terms, for instance, are not included by either author). However, in our analysis, only a small subset of these also function as classifiers, specifically verb classifiers (see Section 3.4).

We now move on to comparing N-N compounds and N-CLF derived nouns, or bound nouns and classifiers, at different levels of analysis. Phonology and prosody do not provide clear criteria for distinguishing bound nouns and classifiers for the two languages examined here (Section 3.2), but the study of the syntactic distribution of classifiers and bound nouns (Section 3.3) as well as their functions in some of these syntactic environments (Section 3.4) does.

3.2 Phonology and prosody

Phonology and prosody are not instrumental in distinguishing classifier-derived nouns from nominal compounds in the two languages under study.

In Mojeño Trinitario, classifiers and bound nouns in compounds behave identically as part of the word for phonotactics and rhythmic syncope (Rose 2019b). Phonotactics in Mojeño Trinitario resolves hiatus at morpheme boundaries within the word by several processes (diphthongization, or deletion of one of the vowels, accompanied by palatalization or labio-velarization of the preceding consonant in some environments). These processes apply in all words to solve hiatus, including between a noun and its classifier (46) as well as between the two nominal roots of a compound noun (47).

Trinitario
(46) a. *vtseramo*   vi-tsera+omo [1PL-tear-CLF:liquid] 'our tears'   N-CLF
     b. *sawariomo* sawar**e**+**o**mo [tobacco-CLF:liquid] 'tobacco juice'   N-CLF

(47) a. *kwoyichko*   kVwoy**u**+**i**chVko [horse-excrement] 'horse excrement'   N-N
     b. *wakaechkopa* wak**a**+**i**chVko-pa [cow-excrement-CLF:mass] 'cow dung'   N-N

Metrical parsing in Mojeño Trinitario is iambic for most word classes, and applies iteratively from left to right, with stress falling on the final foot of the word (Rose

2019b). A rather pervasive process of rhythmic syncope makes each vowel in a weak metrical position subject to deletion (except the final vowel, which is always maintained). This process applies in all words, and thus forms evidence that classifier-derived nouns (48) and binominal compounds (49) are single words. Stressed syllables have been underlined, and the syncopated vowels are in bold in the underlying representation.

Trinitario
(48) a. *spo<u>nj</u>i*   sV**po**n**i**+ji [corn-CLF:amorph] 'corn field'   N-CLF
    b. *Trin<u>ra</u>m'i* Trin**ra**+m**u**'i [Trinidad-CLF:setting] 'the festival of Trinidad'   N-CLF

(49) a. *swoto<u>ne</u>pgi* sV-woto**ne**+p**i**gi [3F-button-ankle] 'malleolus (outer ankle)'   N-N
    b. *kwoy<u>su</u>mu*   kVwoy**u**-**su**mu [horse-snout] 'mounting ox'   N-N

In Harakmbut, classifiers and bound nouns also behave identically as part of the prosodic word for stress placement. (There are no specific phonotactic processes to be mentioned here, and Harakmbut does not show rhythmic syncope.) Examples are in (50) and (51), in which the stressed syllables have been underlined.

Harakmbut
(50) a. *<u>si</u>ro* [metal] 'metal; machete'
    b. *si<u>ro</u>-pi* [metal-CLF:stick] 'knife' (cf. Hart 1963: 1)   N-CLF

(51) a. *<u>ta</u>re* [manioc] 'manioc'
    b. *ta<u>re</u>-mbaʔ* [manioc-hand;leaf] 'manioc leaf'   N-N

While in the morphologically simple nouns in (50a) and (51a), the stress falls on the first syllable, in the complex nouns (50b) and (51b) the stress falls on the last syllable of these disyllabic noun roots. Examples (50) and (51) provide evidence that both compounds and nouns derived with a classifier form single prosodic words, with the main stress falling on the penultimate syllable (cf. Van linden 2022: 443-444).

3.3 Syntax

The syntactic distribution of classifiers and bound nouns in Mojeño Trinitario and Harakmbut is compared in Table 3. In both languages, bound nouns are found in at least the same syntactic environments as classifiers (however, sometimes with distinct functions, as laid out in Section 3.4). The crucial difference in their distribution is that classifiers are not accepted as the head of a noun phrase. This is in line with the idea that "bound roots can be distinguished from affixes only by virtue of also occurring as free forms" (Lieber and Štekauer 2009: 5). The distribution of classifiers in Harakmbut is much more restricted than has been claimed in earlier work, which was typically not based on primary data but on Hart's (1963) paper about "shape morphemes".[22] It is certainly more restricted than in Mojeño Trinitario, whose system clearly corresponds to what Aikhenvald (2000) labels a 'multiple classifier system'.

Table 3: The syntactic distribution of classifiers and bound nouns in Mojeño Trinitario and Harakmbut.

Syntactic environment	Mojeño Trinitario		Harakmbut	
	CLF	bound N	CLF	bound N
as NP head	✗	✓	✗	✓
on nouns	✓	✓	✓	✓
on numerals	✓	✓	✗	✓
on adjectives	✓	✓	✓	✓
in verbs	✓	✓	✓	✓

In Mojeño Trinitario, classifiers cannot be used as the head of a noun phrase (52). For instance, the classifier -*pi*, which prototypically classifies 'filiform' objects like ropes, belts, or snakes, can be defined as classifying "long, thin, flexible items" (25a). It cannot refer by itself to a long, thin and flexible item (52). By contrast, bound nouns can be used as the head of a noun phrase, like *yeno* in (53), also illustrated in a compound in (18).

Trinitario
(52) *to   ta-pi   (to)   yuku   *ART CLF
       ART.NH   3NH-CLF:fili   ART.NH   fire
       'a long, thin and flexible piece of fire'

---

22 For example, Derbyshire and Payne (1990: 246, 260) mistakenly state that the classifier system in Amarakaeri/Harambut is a primarily verb-incorporated system that has developed non-gender concordial functions, and that classifiers have a nominalizing function (1990: 267). Aikhenvald (2000: 123), in turn, wrongly mentions languages of the "Harakmbet" family as examples of languages with large sets of numeral classifiers (without giving a reference).

(53) su ñi-yeno ñi kasiki ART N
     ART.F 3M-wife ART.M cacique
     'the wife of the cacique'

The situation in Harakmbut is different due to the formal identity of classifiers and bound nouns. The form *-pa* in (54a) can be analysed as a classifier or as a bound noun occurring on a noun; in (54b) it is a noun and can hence function as the head of a noun phrase in a clause. It thus behaves in the same way as the unequivocal bound noun *-ayʔ* in (55). That is, on nouns the difference between classifiers and bound nouns is almost impossible to make in Harakmbut (see also Section 3.1).

Harakmbut
(54) a. *hak-pa* [house-(CLF:)rod] 'rafter' (cf. Hart 1963: 3)   N-CLF /= N-N
     b. *wa-pa* [NPF-penis;rod] 'penis; rod'   N

(55) a. *wa-kuʔ-ayʔ* [NPF-head-bone] 'skull'   N-N
     b. *wa-ayʔ* [NPF-bone] 'bone'   N

In both languages, bound nouns can attach to the right of numerals (56a) and (57a), but only Mojeño Trinitario numerals can take classifiers (56b). In the examples, the stressed syllables have been underlined to support the identification of prosodic words.

Trinitario
(56) a. *api-pgienu* api+**pigienu** [two-**neck**] 'two necks'   NUM-N
     b. no   api-**na**-no   ('chañ-ono')   NUM-CLF
        ART.PL two-**CLF:human**-PL person-PL
        'two persons'

Harakmbut
(57) a. *ĩh-tõ-ẽ-ỹ*   *mbottaʔ-**mbaʔ***   NUM-N
        1SG.IND-SOC-be-1.IND two-**hand**
        'I have two hands'
     b. *ĩh-tõ-ẽ-ỹ*   *mbottaʔ* wa-**mbaʔ**   NUM N
        1SG.IND-SOC-be-1.IND two   NPF-**hand**
        'I have two hands'

Numerals in Mojeño Trinitario are bound roots: they obligatorily combine with a classifier, an independent or bound noun or a multiplicative. Classifiers are found much more frequently on numerals than bound nouns; and while in elicitation, all classifiers can be affixed to numerals, in the texts collected in the field the classifier -*na* for humans is almost exclusively found, irrespective of the semantic features of the participant it classifies. Therefore, -*na* can be considered a default classifier on numerals. If the classifier is semantically specific enough, the head noun can be omitted as in (56b). This possibility is typical of multifunctional classifiers, which have been noted to occur on modifiers to form an NP on their own, that is, without a nominal root (Krasnoukhova 2012: 211). By contrast, Harakmbut numerals are free morphemes, and are never suffixed with classifiers. It should be noted that the construction involving fusion of the numeral and a bound noun (57a) is not obligatory; bound nouns may equally attach to a noun prefix to obtain independent nominal status, with the numeral occurring as a distinct prosodic word, cf. (57b).[23]

Adjectives do not require the presence of classifiers or bound nouns in either language, as exemplified in (58a) and (59). They nevertheless can combine with a nominal root or a classifier to form a single prosodic word in both languages. The rare Mojeño Trinitario examples all involve bound nouns, which lose their possessive prefix in this combination (58b). Classifiers also are (rather rarely) found on adjectives, either for 'agreement' (58c) or for word-class changing derivation resulting in a lexical nominalization (58d).

Trinitario
(58) a. *to   'chope   smeno*   ADJ N
         ART.NH   big   forest
         'the big forest'
    b. *ñi   'moperu   'chope-**chuti** t-kowo   te   tajunorokku* ADJ-N=ADJ
         ART.M   youngster big-**head**   3-bathe PREP creek
         'the big-headed boy bathes in the creek' (Ibáñez Noza et al. 2007: 181)
    c. *to   'chope-**gie**   wkugi*   ADJ-CLF=ADJ
         ART.NH big-**CLF:CYL** tree
         'the big trunk'
    d. *to   'chope-'e*   ADJ-CLF=N
         ART.NH big-**CLF:convex**
         'a drum'

---

23 Numeral constructions with independent nouns show only one structural type, i.e. that with numeral and head noun forming two distinct words (cf. Van linden 2022: 451-453).

Harakmbut adjectives do not obligatorily take classifiers or bound nouns, but they are nevertheless bound roots in that they either need suffix -*nda* or prefix *wa-* to constitute words, as in (59). The examples in (60) illustrate the use of nouns and classifiers on adjectives; again stressed syllables have been underlined to assess wordhood.

Harakmbut
(59) a. <u>ku</u>wa <u>u</u>ru-nda   N ADJ
         dog   beautiful-NDA
         'a/the beautiful dog'
    b. mbi?igŋ wa-<u>mbo</u>ro   N ADJ
         fish   WA-big
         'a/the/some big fish'

(60) a. a-<u>yok</u>-i   sal   <u>u</u>ru-**wet<u>to</u>ne**-ta-nda   ADJ-N=N
         1SG.IMP-give-1.IMP salt beautiful-**woman**-ACC-NDA
         'I (should) give salt to the beautiful woman.'
    b. ndo? ĩh-ẽ-ỹ̃   <u>mbo</u>ro-**?i**-nda   ADJ-N=ADJ
         1SG   1SG.IND-be-1.IND big-**foot**-NDA[24]
         'I am big-footed'
    c. ĩh-tõ-ẽ-ỹ̃   <u>wa</u>-?i   <u>mbo</u>ro-nda   N ADJ=NP
         1SG.IND-SOC-be-1.IND   NPF-foot   big-NDA
         'I have big feet.'
    d. <u>mbo</u>ro-**po**-nda [big-**CLF:sphere**-NDA] 'fat, big'   ADJ-CLF=ADJ

In Harakmbut, adjectives combine with both independent (60a) and bound nouns (60b), but the result is quite different. Combinations with independent nouns, like *wettone* 'woman' in (60a), result in a nominal word form.[25] Combinations with bound nouns, by contrast, result in an adjectival word form, like 'big-footed' in (60b). Crucially, bound nouns that function as a nominal head, as in (60c), cannot fuse with the adjective root. Very rarely, classifiers are also found on adjectives (60d), which yields complex adjectives, similarly to the pattern with bound nouns illustrated in (60b). That is, unlike in Mojeño Trinitario, classifiers on adjectives are not used for agreement or for deadjectival nominalization.

---

24 The analysis of the suffix -*nda* remains unclear; this is why the gloss just repeats the form itself.
25 Note also that adjectives do not obligatorily fuse with independent nouns. The distribution of constructions might relate to the referential properties of the NP (see Van linden 2022: 453-454). More research is needed here.

Finally, in both languages bound nouns and classifiers are incorporated in verb forms. In Mojeño Trinitario, they both attach either to stative verbs or to active verbs immediately after the root, as in (61a) and (61b). Classifiers are associated with nominal expressions of different grammatical roles: the unique argument of intransitive verbs, the patient of transitive verbs, or obliques as in (61a) (Rose 2019a). Incorporated bound nouns also correspond – in the counterpart clause without incorporation – to the unique argument of an intransitive root, to an oblique, or to the patient argument of a transitive root (61b). In Harakmbut, classifiers (62a) and bound nouns (62b) also share the same slot in the morphological template of the verb, but they precede the verb root in that language. Both types of incorporated elements are associated with the unique argument of an intransitive root, as in (62a), or the patient argument of a transitive root, as in (62b).

(61) TRN a. *n-semo-**pi**-ko* [1SG-be_angry-**CLF:fili**-ACT] 'I am angry at these words.'
 b. *t-vi-**o'i**-ri-ko* [3-take_out-**fruit**-PLURACT-ACT] '(s)he collects fruits.'

(62) AMR a. *o-**poʔ**-sak-on* [3SG.IND-**CLF:sphere**-break-PFV.NVOL] 'it (the pot) has broken.'
 b. *ih-**mbaʔ**-tegŋ-me-y* [1SG-**hand**-cut-REC.PST-1.IND] 'I cut my hand.'

In conclusion, classifiers and bound nouns have a very similar syntactic distribution in Mojeño Trinitario, with just one environment restricted to nouns, i.e. that of head of a noun phrase. In Harakmbut, classifiers share fewer syntactic environments with bound nouns. Both categories are frequently found on nouns and incorporated in verbs in the two languages under study, which is why we turn to the functions they have in these environments in the next section.

3.4 Functions

In both languages studied here, classifiers and bound nouns share the syntactic environments of occurring on nouns (Section 3.4.1) and being incorporated in verb forms (Section 3.4.2). Focusing on how their functions in these environments differ, we will contribute to the debate on whether classifiers constitute thing-affixes, a question we link up with headedness.

3.4.1 Functions on nouns

Table 4 compares the functions of classifiers and bound nouns when appended to nouns in Mojeño Trinitario and Harakmbut. While both can be used to create new lexical items, classifiers have an additional function of qualification (or property-assignment), especially in Mojeño Trinitario. This is why Mojeño Trinitario classifiers can be described as multifunctional classifiers (Krasnoukhova 2012): the same set is used for qualification, derivation (and some agreement).

Table 4: The functions of classifiers and bound nouns on nouns in Mojeño Trinitario and Harakmbut.

Functions on N	Mojeño Trinitario		Harakmbut	
	CLF	bound N	CLF	bound N
word formation	✓	✓	✓	✓
qualification	✓	✗	(✓)	✗

The literature on classifiers on nouns does not usually tease apart different functions of classifiers on nouns. Instead, the functions of classifiers on nouns are either vaguely referred to collectively as "classification/ categorization" (Seifart 2010: 725) or subsumed under the cover term "derivation" (Payne 2007, Wojtylak 2016, Aikhenvald 2000). Only a few authors briefly mention distinct functions of classifiers on nouns. For instance, Contini-Morava and Kilarski (2013: 268–269) distinguish between two major semantic functions of nominal classification: "The first, 'expansion of the lexicon', involves the use of nominal classification markers to create nouns. [...] The second type [is] 'differentiating referents'". In the same vein, Brandão (2016: 279) mentions that in Paresi [PAB], classifiers on nouns either derive new nouns or not. Interestingly, Pepper (2020: 148–154) also explicitly distinguishes two functions of classifiers on nouns and only includes the derivational use of classifiers on nouns in his typology of binominals, i.e. structures where the denotatum of the binominal is different from that of the base (see Section 2). In the present paper, the following semantic criteria are used to distinguish the two major functions of classifiers: if N-CLF designates an instance of the type denoted by the nominal root, we are dealing with qualification; if N-CLF denotes an entity (or type) different from that denoted by the nominal root, we are dealing with derivation, subsumed under word formation in Table 4, so as to include the process of compounding observed for bound nouns.

Mojeño Trinitario examples of classifiers on nouns are presented in (63)-(64). When classifiers are used on nominal roots for derivation, they serve to derive a complex concept in a generally semantically transparent way (63a). However, they can also be used on nominal roots to categorize the referent of the root, in terms of shape or material (64).

Trinitario
(63) a. *yuk-pi* [fire-CLF:fili] 'candle'   derivation
 b. *gióre-pi* [snake-CLF:fili] 'worm'   derivation

(64) a. *mári-si* [stone-CLF:sphere] 'round stone'   qualification
 b. *tsera-(o)mo* [tear-CLF:liquid] 'tear'   qualification

Example (63) shows the use of the classifier *-pi* 'CLF:filiform' for derivation. In (63a), 'candle' is not a type of fire: the classifier-derived word refers to some entity distinct from that referred to by the nominal root. In (63b), the derivation is not compositional, as the referent of the root ('snake') already belongs to the shape class expressed by the classifier: the resultant meaning is lexicalized. Example (64) shows the use of classifiers for qualification. In (64a), the use of *-si* on *mari* 'stone' does not change the meaning of the word but highlights physical characteristics of the referent (shape/material). The use for qualification is less crucial to the overall meaning of N-CLF; it often seems redundant, as in (64b). Senft discusses this use as follows: "The classifier that refers to a nominal referent may [...] highlight a special (shade of) meaning which then extracts one special referent out of the sum of possible extralinguistic referents the noun can refer to if it is not specified by this classifier" (Senft 2000: 36).

It should be noted that some Mojeño Trinitario roots are obligatorily classified: they cannot stand by themselves without a classifier, such as **mopo*, **wayo*, and **tére* shown in (65d) and (66b, e).

Trinitario
(65) a. *mópo-si* [bee_related-CLF:sphere] 'bee'   derivation
 b. *mop-ji* [bee_related-CLF:amorph] 'beeswax'   derivation
 c. *mop-omo* [bee_related-CLF:liquid] 'honey'   derivation
 d. **mopo*

(66) a. *wáyo-si* [deer_fly-CLF:sphere] 'deer fly'   qualification
 b. **wayo*
 c. *tére-pi* [belt-CLF:fili] 'belt'   qualification
 d. *tére-mo* [belt-CLF:fabric] 'woven belt'   qualification
 e. **tére*

Yet, the same criteria apply for distinguishing between derivation and qualification; N-CLF in (65) yields lexemes with meanings distinct from that of the root, while N-CLF in (66) refers to an element of the type expressed by the root itself. Note that in the case of *mopo, which can be combined with distinct classifiers (65) (unlike *wayo), the gloss used is general enough to accommodate the different derivatives.[26] In contrast with these two uses of Mojeño Trinitario classifiers on nominal roots, bound nouns in N-N compounds are only used for word formation (see Section 2.5).

In Harakmbut, classifiers are generally used on nouns for derivation (67a), but there is a marginal use of classifiers on proper names that arguably rates as qualification. Specifically, the second author noted that members of the family hosting her referred to her as *Anpi* as in (67b).

Harakmbut
(67)   a.   *wã-õh-pi* [NPF-nose-CLF:stick] 'beak (of a bird)' (cf. Hart 1963: 2)
       b.   *An-pi* [An-CLF:stick] 'An, who is slender (or stick-shaped) (and whom we hold dear)'

It turned out that uses like (67b) are only acceptable in contexts of knowing the person well and having a good relationship with them. They highlight the overall physical appearance of that person, and function as terms of endearment at the same time. Insofar as the criterion proposed above to distinguish between the two functions of classifiers on nouns concerns denotation only (and not connotation as well), this classifier use on proper names instantiates qualification. While this use is highly socially constrained, the derivational use of classifiers, illustrated in (67a) with the same classifier -pi, is not; it constitutes a productive process of word formation. Bound nouns in compounds, in turn, are only used for word formation (see Section 2.5).

The Mojeño Trinitario data allow us to look into the notion of headedness in N-CLF formations. The examples in (68) suggest that the specific function of the classifier is crucial in that domain.

Trinitario
(68)   a.   *to wayo-si* [ART.NH deer_fly$_{NH}$-CLF:sphere] 'the deer fly'   qualification

---

[26] In cases of obligatorily classified roots like *mopo* 'bee-related', it could be questioned to what extent the nominal root still is a thing-root, as it does not really denote a physical object (Haspelmath 2012: 115), but rather a semantic domain.

b. *su choka-si* [ART.F blond_haired_F-CLF:sphere] 'the blond woman'   qualification

c. *to Peru-pa'i* [ART.NH Pedro_M-CLF:ground] 'Pedro's land'   derivation

In (68a) and (68b), in which the classifier *-si* is used for qualification, it is the nominal root that functions as the morphological head, as it triggers the appropriate gender value on the article, i.e. non-human for (68a) vs. feminine for (68b). The classifier *-si* for spherical items only highlights some aspect of the referent, i.e. by classifying it as an insect in (68a) or by focusing on its most relevant body part, the head, in (68b). In (68c), in which the classifier *-pa'i* is used for derivation, by contrast, the classifier is the morphological head as it determines the gender value of the article (if the nominal root were the head, the article would show masculine gender, agreeing with *Pedro*). Note that this morphological headedness does not imply that classifiers can function as the syntactic head of NPs; in (68c), the classifier *-pa'i* is the morphological head of the word *Perupa'i*, and it is the complex word form *Peru-pa'i* that is the head of the NP, not just the classifier *-pa'i*.

This formal evidence of headedness in Mojeño Trinitario also informs the discussion of whether classifiers rate as thing-affixes. When used for derivation, we tend to follow Pepper's (2020: 10–12) onomasiological approach (after Štekauer 2000) and analyse classifiers as heads – and hence thing-affixes – in N-CLF formations, with the nominal root as semantically subordinate, which squares with the paraphrases we provided for classifier-derived nouns above and in Section 2.7. This analysis meshes well with the nominalizing function of classifiers on adjectives, as in (58d), and verbs, as in (69) (compare with (65c)).

(69) TRN *to t-ijr-omo* [ART.NH 3-be_hot-CLF:liquid] 'breakfast/dinner, lit. hot liquid'

When used for qualification, by contrast, we argue that classifiers do not function as heads and are not thing-affixes. They clearly have a modifying function (cf. Mithun 1986), and we propose to term them "property-affixes", as they assign a (temporary or inherent) property to the referent of the nominal root, or to the type denoted by the root, characterizing it in terms of shape, quality or substance, in a way that is formally different from the prototypical property-roots in these languages, i.e. adjectives. This analysis fits with the agreement function of classifiers on modifiers (58c) and the classifying function of classifiers in verbs (see next section). We can thus conclude that the categorial status of classifiers as thing-affixes depends on the function they have on nominal roots.

The status of the classifier as semantic and morphological head in N-CLF words where the classifier plays a derivational role does not prevent the nominal root (semantically a modifier) to remain referential. This is illustrated in (70), where the nominalization *to nnujre* '(the thing) that I chewed' modifies the nominal root *saware* 'tobacco', which is in turn the modifier part of the classifier-derived word *sawariomo* 'tobacco juice' (it is obviously not the juice that was chewed, as the juice precisely results from the process of chewing leaves).

Trinitario
(70) *n-es-cho   to   sawari-omo,   éto-na*
     1SG-give_drink-ACT ART.NH tobacco-CLF:liquid   one-CLF:GEN
     kchara to   sawari-omo   to
     spoon   ART.NH   tobacco-CLF:liquid   ART.NH
     n-nu-j-re
     1SG-chew-CLF:amorph-SP.P.NZ
     'I gave her the tobacco (juice), one spoon of tobacco juice that I had chewed.'

3.4.2 Functions in verb forms

Moving on to the syntactic environment of incorporation in verbs, Table 5 shows that the uses of classifiers and bound nouns are not functionally equivalent. That is, classifiers and bound nouns do not participate in the same functional types of noun incorporation as defined by Mithun (1984). In both Mojeño Trinitario and Harakmbut, classificatory noun incorporation (Type IV) is exclusively found with classifiers, while lexical compounding (Type I) is restricted to incorporation of nouns. Type II and Type III incorporation show variation between the languages studied. This section discusses these four types of noun incorporation, and their availability in the two languages examined.

Table 5: The functions of classifiers and bound nouns in verbs.

Types of noun incorporation (Mithun 1984)	Mojeño Trinitario		Harakmbut	
	CLF	bound N	CLF	bound N
Type I: lexical compounding	✗	✓	✗	✓
Type II: manipulation of case	✓	✓	✗	✓
Type III: backgrounding in discourse	✓	✗	✓	✓
Type IV: classifying with 'coreferential' NP	✓	✗	✓	✗

In both languages, Type I noun incorporation, which serves to create new lexemes for "name-worthy" activities (Mithun 1984: 848) and derives intransitive predicates from transitive ones, is found exclusively with nouns (71)-(72).

(71) TRN *t-vi-**o'i**-ri-ko* [3-take_out-**fruit**-PLURACT-ACT] '(S)he collects fruits.'
Type I with N

(72) AMR *oʔ-**ndagŋ**-ka* [3SG.IND-**path**-make] '(S)he is making a path.'
Type I with N

In (71), the transitive verb stem *-vi* 'take out' is combined with the bound noun *-o'i* 'fruit' to yield an intransitive verb that denotes an "institutionalized" activity (Mithun 1984: 849), i.e. fruit-picking. The incorporated noun bears the semantic relationship of patient to its host verb. In (72), the bound noun *-ndagŋ* 'path' is incorporated into the transitive verb stem *-ka* 'make;do' to form the intransitive verb 'path-make'.

Type II noun incorporation, which affects the valency structure of the whole clause (Mithun 1984: 856), is found with both classifiers (73) and bound nouns (74) in Mojeño Trinitario, while it is restricted to the latter category in Harakmbut (75).

Trinitario
(73) n-eja-**j**-ko   to   tyuraji
     1SG-sit-**CLF:amorph**-ACT   ART.NH   mud
     'I am (heap)-sitting in the mud.'   Type II with CLF

(74) na-ech-**kute**-cho-po   eto   povre   sorare
     3PL-cut-**hindleg**-ACT-PFV 3NH   poor   animal
     'They cut off the hind leg of the poor animal.'   Type II with N

Harakmbut
(75) mbe-**ku**-ti-kot-uy-ne   apoareʔ-a   taʔmba-ya
     3SG>1/2SG-**head**-SPAT:up-fall-DIST.PST-IND   papaya-NOM   swidden-LOC
     'A papaya fell on my head in the swidden long ago.' Type II with N

The examples with nouns, (74) and (75), involve possessors being advanced to object status, which position is vacated by the incorporated body part (cf. Mithun 1984: 857–858). The construction with the classifier in (73) is somewhat different, and not discussed in Mithun (1984). Specifically, the classifier functions as an applicative marker (Rose 2019a), which promotes in (73) the locative argument of an intransitive verb to object position; the resulting construction is formally transitive.

Type III noun incorporation is used to background known or incidental participants in discourse (Mithun 1984: 859). It is restricted to classifiers in Mojeño Trinitario (76). In Harakmbut it is found with both classifiers (77) and bound nouns (78).

Trinitario
(76) p-eja-**pue**-gi-a [2SG-sit-**CLF:ground**-ACT-IRR] '(Please) sit down (on the floor).'
Type III with CLF

Harakmbut
(77) pera   o-n-ka   ãñĩ,   o-mbewik-po   eskalera-te,
      pear   3SG.IND-SPAT:on-do FILLER 3SG.IND-go.up-DEP   ladder-LOC
      ãñĩ   o-**ma**-nda-e-a   ãñĩ,   kanasta-yo [...]
      FILLER 3SG.IND-VPL-**CLF:fruit**-get-TRNS FILLER basket-LOC
      'He is picking pears, eh, going up on a ladder, eh, he is taking/collecting them (the fruits), eh, in a basket.' (spontaneous speech)
Type III with CLF

(78) apetpet-ʔidn   ih-waway-me-y   ndumba-yo.   ken   ndoʔ-edn
      jaguar-tooth   1SG.IND-find-REC.PST-1.IND   forest-LOC   then 1SG-GEN
      wa-mambuy-ta   ih-**ʔidn**-yok-me-y
      NPF-same_sex_sibling-ACC   1SG.IND-**tooth**-give-REC.PST-1.IND
      'I found a jaguar's tooth in the forest. Then I gave it (the tooth) to my sister.'
Type III with N

In (76), the incorporated classifier -*pue* introduces a non-topical participant (cf. the "absolute" function of classifiers in Grinevald and Seifart 2004) which is immediately retrievable from the context of the speech event (exophoric retrieval). In (77), the first clause contains a full NP introducing the topical argument *pera* 'pear'; in the second one, anaphoric reference to the pears is realized by the classifier -*nda* for fruit (prototypically grapefruit). In (78), the bound noun -*ʔidn* 'tooth' likewise anaphorically refers to the full NP *apetpetʔidn* 'jaguar's tooth' in the previous clause. It should be noted that the use of the incorporated items in (77)-(78) is not literally anaphoric, since they are non-referential, but they "retain the entity in question within the arena of discourse", because "incorporated nouns, not salient constituents in themselves, do not obstruct the flow of information, yet their presence is sufficient to narrow the scope of the verb" (Mithun 1986: 381–382).

Finally, Type IV noun incorporation, also termed classificatory noun incorporation because the incorporated element classifies a more specific external NP present in the clause (Mithun 1984: 863), is restricted to classifiers in both languages. Examples are given in (79) and (80).

Trinitario
(79) t-eja-**me**-re-ko te pjo ñi-ye'e estera
3-sit-**CLF:fabric**-PLURACT-ACT PREP DEM 3M-GRN mat
'He is (fabric-) sitting on a mat.' Type IV with CLF

Harakmbut
(80) idn-pa-a i-ma-**nda**-kot-a-y palta
tooth-CLF:rod-INS 1SG.IND-VPL-**CLF:fruit**-fall-TRNS-1.IND avocado
'I am making the avocados fall with a hook-shaped rod.'
Type IV with CLF

Example (79) contains the verb -*eja* 'sit' and the classifier -*me*, which specifies the shape of the locative argument (*estera*). (Note that (79) is syntactically different from (73) in that the locative argument is coded as a prepositional phrase, while in (73) it is coded as an object noun phrase. The classifier in (79) has no effect on the valency of the verb.) Similarly, in (80) -*nda* characterizes the O-argument of the verb in terms of shape, expressed by the external NP *palta*. In both languages, classificatory noun incorporation constructions are typically used to introduce new topics, or re-activate aforementioned ones.

In conclusion, looking at the functional types of incorporated classifiers and bound nouns has enabled us to describe these two categories with greater precision. The two languages allow only bound nouns in Type I noun incorporation[27] (lexical compounding) and only classifiers in Type IV (classificatory noun incorporation). The data also corroborate two diachronic hypotheses proposed by Mithun: (i) Types I to IV form an implicational hierarchy for the development of noun incorporation (1984: 874), and (ii) classifiers originate in nouns (1986: 395). Type II for Mojeño Trinitario and Type III for Harakmbut form truly transitional stages, in which both bound nouns and classifiers are allowed.

The differential availability of classifiers and bound nouns for the different types of noun incorporation also bears on the question of whether classifiers are

---

27 There are a few exceptions here; the independent noun *hak* 'house' also occurs in Type I noun incorporation in Harakmbut.

thing-affixes. Type I most clearly involves thing-morphs, analogously to N-N compounding, but is restricted to nouns in both languages.[28] Type IV, in turn, most clearly involves what we have called "property-affixes", and is restricted to classifiers. Indeed, their use in Type IV is semantically analogous to their qualifying use on nouns. Taking into account these most clear-cut types, the data suggest that incorporated in verb forms, classifiers are more likely property-affixes than thing-affixes.

4 Conclusions and diachronic implications

This paper has focused on binominal lexemes in two Western Amazonian languages, Mojeño Trinitario and Harakmbut, and has tackled the analytical problem of distinguishing between classifier-derived nouns and noun-noun compounds, that is, the types **cls** and **cmp** in Pepper's (2020) typology of binominals. This entailed scrutinizing the distinction between classifiers and bound nouns in the two languages, as these elements have a similar semantic effect on the noun root they combine with in the binominal types studied and occupy the same (rightmost) slot in them. This in turn required us to look far beyond complex nouns.

Methodologically, our analysis has benefitted from our comparative approach, systematically searching for paradigmatic oppositions both across and within the languages under investigation. While our phonological and prosodic analyses highlighted the similarity between the two binominal types studied (both forming single word forms, Section 3.2), looking at the form and meaning of 'suspect' items (Section 3.1) as well as comparing the syntactic distribution of classifiers and bound nouns (Section 3.3), and their functions on nouns and when incorporated in verb forms (Section 3.4) proved crucial in drawing the boundary between classifiers and bound nouns. The criteria that emerged from our study as most important to this distinction are summarized in Table 6. We are confident that our methodology can be applied to other Western Amazonian languages as well, where derivational use of classifiers abounds (Section 2.8). In particular, it could be useful in clarifying the status of so-called "repeaters" (Grinevald Craig 2004: 1026), i.e. bound forms formally similar to some nouns and used with the same morphosyntactic distribu-

---

[28] Note that nouns in Type I noun incorporation are analysed here as thing-morphs in spite of being non-referential (cf. Mithun 1984: 849). This is by analogy with noun-noun compounds, like *apple juice*, in which *apple* is non-referential as well, but still a thing-morph. In our discussion on the categorial status of classifiers, we thus abstract away from referentiality.

tion as classifiers. Repeaters are not prototypical classifiers in that, sharing their semantics with a single noun, they are too specific to be truly used for categorization. Instead of analysing repeaters as a special type of classifiers, we would consider them simply as (bound) nouns.

Table 6: Criteria to distinguish between classifiers and bound nouns in Mojeño Trinitario and Harakmbut.

	Mojeño Trinitario	Harakmbut
CLF formally or semantically distinct from N	✓	✗
CLF have a qualifying function on N; bound nouns do not	✓	(✓)
CLF cannot function as NP head; bound nouns can	✓	✓
CLF have a categorizing function when incorporated in verbs; bound nouns do not	✓	✓

For Mojeño Trinitario, a multiple and multifunctional classifier language with an extensive set of classifiers that has almost the exact same syntactic distribution as bound nouns, the impossibility for classifiers to function as head of a noun phrase together with the formal distinctness of classifiers and bound nouns allowed us to distinguish between classifier-derived nouns and noun-noun compounds. Our findings thus challenge Gill's (1957) claim that in Mojeño Trinitario some bound nouns are used as classifiers. They are also more precise than what Admiraal and Danielsen (2014) and Facundes and Freitas (2015) concluded for two other Arawak languages, Baure and Apuriña, i.e. that classifiers or classificatory nouns are a sub-type of bound nominal roots. For Harakmbut, a verbal classifier language with a small set of classifiers, the binominals studied turned out to be one of the few syntactic environments/functions for which classifiers and bound nouns are not in complementary distribution. As Harakmbut classifiers are formally identical to bound nouns, it proved at times impossible to distinguish between classifier-derived nouns and noun-noun compounds. Typically, items with very general semantics, merely referring to a shape, quality or substance, like *-pi* in (1a), were analysed as classifiers in binominals.

Our study has also reflected on the status of classifiers as thing-affixes. Not surprisingly, our functional approach suggests a nuanced answer. The Mojeño Trinitario data provided formal evidence that in classifier-derived nouns classifiers are the morphological head, determining gender agreement on the article. In classifier-qualified nouns, by contrast, it is the noun that is the morphological head. Taking into account the semantic and formal similarity between classifier-derived nouns and noun-noun compounds (in which N2 is the head) in the two languages studied, this extra piece of formal evidence of headedness convinced us that, in their derivational use, classifiers are thing-affixes, which is in line with the onomasiological approach taken in Pepper (2020: 10–12), inspired in turn by Štekauer (2000). Additional evidence comes from nominalization in Mojeño Trinitario, where (unlike in Harakmbut) classifiers are used to derive nouns from verbs (69). However, in all other syntactic environments and functions studied, classifiers are more aptly analysed as what we labelled "property-affixes". This holds especially for their qualifying use on nouns (Section 3.4.1) and their use in Type IV 'noun' incorporation (cf. Mithun 1984) (Section 3.4.2), functions that are excluded for bound nouns. Arguably, it also holds for their agreement uses on numerals and adjectives in Mojeño Trinitario, where they categorize the head noun rather than nominalize their host, while bound nouns on the same host types always yield nominals (Section 3.3). We can thus conclude that classifiers are prototypically property-morphs and only rate as thing-morphs when they share the same position and function as other prototypical thing-morphs, i.e. nouns, as in binominals.

Finally, we turn to the diachronic implications of our study. Our data corroborate the hypothesis that classifiers originate in nouns (Mithun 1986: 395; Aikhenvald 2000: 353–361), more specifically bound nouns in both languages. This development is in line with the general direction of grammaticalization from roots into affixes. In addition, our data suggest that bound nouns developed the types of noun incorporation I to IV proposed in Mithun (1984) in that same order (Section 3.4.2). The origin of classifiers is still visible in synchrony in Harakmbut, with pervasive polyfunctionality of the classifiers/bound nouns. We hypothesize that the classifiers merely referring to shapes or substances (like -*pi* 'CLF:stick' in (1a)) have gone further down the grammaticalization pathway than those whose corresponding bound noun still has a more specific meaning (like -*puʔ* 'CLF:cylindrical;hollow' in (1b)). The idea is that items like -*pi* lost their more specific meaning (semantic bleaching), with only the more schematic classifier meaning remaining. Harakmbut classifiers do not include any item (anymore) for which the more specific meaning is the only one available when used as a bound noun; that is, they have already undergone semantic generalization. Unfortunately, there is little material available for further diachronic or comparative work on this. In Mojeño Trinitario, the noun-to-classifier pathway is confirmed by cases of classifier/noun homonymy (e.g. -*miro* in (30)) and cases showing phonetic erosion and semantic bleaching of the classifier vis-à-vis its corresponding bound noun (e.g. -*ju'e~-je* in (29)). For other cases, recourse must be made to reconstructions of the nominal sources of classifiers (e.g. -*pi* 'CLF:fili' (Section 3.1)). It remains to be investigated whether more nominal sources of classifiers can be reconstructed on the basis of comparison with sister languages. Comparing the two languages, we seem to be dealing with a different historical depth of the emergence of classifiers, with Mojeño Trinitario showing an 'older' system including also some more recently integrated classifiers.

Our data also support the diachronic hypothesis that the development of nouns into classifiers took place in morphologically complex forms. Admiraal and Danielsen (2014: 90) and Croft (2017: 427) have pointed to noun-noun compounding as source constructions for classifiers, Mithun (1984, 1986) to noun incorporation, and Payne (2007: 472) and Seifart (2010: 729) to both. This paper suggests that the locus of change for the languages examined is the syntactic environments shared by classifiers and nouns, i.e. mainly noun-noun compounding and noun incorporation, but also combinations with numerals and adjectives. These latter two types of structures are generally underdescribed (Admiraal and Danielsen 2014 is an exception to this), and have therefore been overlooked as possible source environments for classifiers. We believe that these four morphologically complex structures instantiate a general template consisting of a host root and an element to its right. In the languages studied here, the elements attached to the different types of host are predominantly bound nouns and classifiers. This is why we conclude that classifiers developed from bound nouns in Mojeño Trinitario and Harakmbut in a general morphologically complex source template. Our data thus nicely fit Seifart's (2010: 729) generalization that "classifiers of different types seem to diachronically 'piggyback' on existing constructions although the details of how this might generalize both within and across different classifier types remain still unclear."

References

Adelaar, Willem. 2000. Propuesta de un nuevo vínculo genético entre dos grupos lingüísticos indígenas de la Amazonía occidental: Harakmbut y Katukina. In Luis Miranda Esquerre (ed.), *Actas del I Congreso de Lenguas Indígenas de Sudamérica*, vol. 2, 219–236. Lima: U. Ricardo Palma.

Adelaar, Willem. 2007. Ensayo de clasificación del katawixí dentro del conjunto harakmbut-katukina. In Andres Romero-Figueroa, Ana Fernández Garay & Angel Corbera Mori (eds.), *Lenguas indígenas de América del Sur: Estudios descriptivo-tipológicos y sus contribuciones para la lingüística teórica*, 159–169. Caracas: Universidad Católica Andrés Bello.

Admiraal, Femmy & Danielsen, Swintha. 2014. Productive Compounding in Baure (Arawakan). In Swintha Danielsen, Katja Hannß & Fernando Zúñiga (eds.), *Word formation in South American languages*, 79–122. Amsterdam: John Benjamins.

Aikhenvald, Alexandra. 2000. *Classifiers: A typology of noun categorization devices*. Oxford: Oxford University Press.

Allan, Keith. 1977. Classifiers. *Language* 53(2). 285–311.
Bauer, Laurie. 2001. Compounding. In Martin Haspelmath, Ekkehard König, Wulf Oesterreicher & Wolfgang Raible (eds.), *Language typology and language universals*, Vol. I, 695–707. Berlin: Mouton de Gruyter.
Brandão, Ana Paula. 2016. A Incorporação de Nomes e Classificadores Em Paresi-Haliti (Aruák). *Liames* 16(2). 271–283.
Contini-Morava, Ellen & Marcin Kilarski. 2013. Functions of nominal classification. *Language Sciences* 40. 263–299.
Crevels, Mily & Pieter Muysken. 2009. Lenguas de Bolivia: presentación y antecedentes. In Mily Crevels & Pieter Muysken (eds.), *Lenguas de Bolivia*, 13–26. La Paz: Plural Editores.
Croft, William. 2017. Classifier constructions and their evolution: A commentary on Kemmerer. *Language, Cognition and Neuroscience* 32(4). 425–427.
Derbyshire, Desmond C. & Doris L. Payne. 1990. Noun classification systems of Amazonian languages. In Doris Payne (ed.), *Amazonian linguistics: Studies in lowland South American languages*, 243–271. Austin: University of Texas Press.
Dixon, R.M.W. 1986. Noun classes and noun classification in typological perspective. In Colette Craig (ed.), *Noun classes and categorization*, 105–112. Amsterdam: John Benjamins.
Facundes, Sidney & Marilia Fernandez Pereira de Freitas. 2015. De compostos nominais produtivos a um sistema incipiente de classificação nominal em Apurinã (Aruák) [From productive noun compounding to an incipient noun classification system in Apurinã (Arawak)]. *Moara* 43(2). 23–50.
Gill, Wayne. 1957. *Trinitario grammar*. San Lorenzo de Mojos: Misión Nuevas Tribus.
Grinevald, Colette & Frank Seifart. 2004. Noun classes in African and Amazonian languages: Towards a comparison. *Linguistic Typology* 8(2). 243–285.
Hart, Raymond. 1963. Semantic components of shape in Amarakaeri Grammar. *Anthropological Linguistics* 5(9). 1–7.
Haspelmath, Martin. 2012. How to compare major word-classes across the world's languages. *UCLA Working Papers in Linguistics, Theories of Everything 17*, Article 16. 109–130.
Helberg Chávez & Heinrich Albert. 1984. *Skizze einer Grammatik des Amarakaeri*. Tübingen: Tübingen University PhD dissertation.
Helberg Chávez & Heinrich Albert. 1990. Análisis funcional del verbo amarakaeri. In Rodolfo Cerrón Palomino & Gustavo Solís Fonseca (eds.), *Temas de lingüística amerindia*, 227–249. Lima: Concytec.
Ibáñez Noza, Eulogio, Pedro Fabricano Noe, Marcelo Guaji Noe, Claudio Guaji Jare, Bartola Guaji Jare & Nemecio Yuco Parada. 2007. *Gramática Mojeña Trinitaria*. Tomo I. Trinidad, Beni: Centro Social y Comunitario "Ipeno Imutu", Cabildo Indigenal de Trinidad.
Krasnoukhova, Olga. 2012. *The noun phrase in the languages of South America*. Utrecht: LOT.
Lieber, Rochelle & Pavol Štekauer. 2009. Introduction: Status and definition of compounding. In Rochelle Lieber & Pavol Štekauer (eds.), *The Oxford handbook of compounding*, 3–18. Oxford: Oxford University Press.
Loukotka, Cestmír. 1968. *Classification of South American Indian languages*. Los Angeles: Latin American Center, UCLA.
Lyon, Patricia Jean. 1975. Dislocación tribal y clasificaciones lingüísticas en la zona del río Madre de Dios. In *XXXIX Congreso Internacional de Americanistas, Lima 1970. Actas y Memorias, Vol. 5.*, 185–207. Lima: Instituto de Estudios Peruanos.
Marbán, Pedro. 1702. *Arte de la lengua Moxa, con su Vocabulario, y Cathecismo*. Lima: Imprenta Real de Joseph de Contreras.

Masini, Francesca, Simone Mattiola & Steve Pepper. This volume. Exploring complex lexemes cross-linguistically. In Steve Pepper, Francesca Masini & Simone Mattiola (eds.), *Binominal lexemes in cross-linguistic perspective*. Berlin: Mouton de Gruyter.
Mithun, Marianne. 1984. The evolution of noun incorporation. *Language* 60(4). 847–879.
Mithun, Marianne. 1986. The convergence of noun classification systems. In Colette Craig (ed.), *Noun classes and categorization*, 379–397. Amsterdam: John Benjamins.
Moore, Denny. 2007. Endangered languages of lowland tropical South America. In Matthias Brenzinger (ed.), *Language diversity endangered*, 29–58. The Hague: Mouton.
Olza Zubiri, Jesús, Conchita Nuni de Chapi & Juan Tube. 2002. *Gramática Moja Ignaciana*. Caracas: Universidad Católica Andres Bello.
Passer, Matthias Benjamin. 2016. (What) Do verb classifiers classify? *Lingua* 174. 16–44.
Payne, Doris L. 1987. Noun classification in the Western Amazon. *Language Sciences* 9(1). 21–44.
Payne, David. 1991a. A classification of Maipuran (Arawakan) languages based on shared lexical retentions. In Desmond Derbyshire & Geoffrey Pullum (eds.), *Handbook of Amazonian Languages*, Vol. 3, 355–499. Berlin: Mouton de Gruyter.
Payne, David. 1991b. Clasificadores nominales: La interacción de la fonología, la gramática y el léxico en la investigación comparativa del Maipuran. *Revista Latinoamericana de Estudios Etnolingüísticos* 6. 241–257.
Pepper, Steve. 2020. *The typology and semantics of binominal lexemes. Noun-noun compounds and their functional equivalents*. Oslo: University of Oslo PhD dissertation.
Petersen de Piñeros, Gabriele. 2007. Nominal Classification in Uitoto. *International Journal of American Linguistics* 73(4). 389–409.
Rose, Françoise. 2013. Los Generolectos Del Mojeño. *Liames* 13. 115–34.
Rose, Françoise. 2015. Mojeño Trinitario. In Mily Crevels & Pieter Muysken (eds.), *Lenguas de Bolivia*, vol 3, *Oriente*, 59–97. La Paz: Plural Editores.
Rose, Françoise. 2019a. From classifiers to applicatives in Mojeño Trinitario: A new source for applicative markers. *Linguistic Typology* 23(3). 435–66. https://doi.org/10.1515/lingty-2019-0024
Rose, Françoise. 2019b. Rhythmic syncope and opacity in Mojeño Trinitario. *Phonological Data and Analysis* 1(2). 1–25.
Rose, Françoise. 2020. The possessive noun classes of Mojeño Trinitario. Presented at the *Atelier Morphosyntaxe*, laboratoire Dynamique du Langage, Lyon, France, October 20.
Scalise, Sergio & Antonio Fábregas. 2010. The head in compounding. In Sergio Scalise & Irene Vogel (eds.), *Cross-disciplinary issues in compounding*, 109–126. Amsterdam: John Benjamins.
Seifart, Frank. 2005. *The structure and use of shape-based noun classes in Miraña (North West Amazon)*. Nijmegen: Max Planck Institute for Psycholinguistics PhD dissertation.
Seifart, Frank & Payne, Doris. 2007. Nominal classification in the North West Amazon: Issues in areal diffusion and typological characteristics. *International Journal of American Linguistics* 73. 281–287.
Seifart, Frank. 2010. Nominal classification. *Language & Linguistics Compass* 4(8). 719–736.
Senft, Gunter. 2000. What do we really know about nominal classification systems. In Gunter Senft (ed.), *Systems of nominal classification*, 11–49. Cambridge: Cambridge University Press.
Štekauer, Pavol. 2000. Beheading the word? Please, stop the execution. *Folia Linguistica* 34(3–4). 333–356.

Tovar, Antonio. 1961. *Catálogo de las lenguas de América del Sur*. Buenos Aires: Editorial Sudamericana.
Tripp, Robert. 1976. *Los verbos Amarakaeri. Datos Etno-Lingüísticos: Colección de los archivos del ILV 33*. Lima: Instituto Lingüístico de Verano.
Tripp, Robert. 1995. *Diccionario amarakaeri-castellano*. Yarinacocha: Ministerio de Educación & Instituto Lingüístico de Verano.
Van linden, An. 2021. Where alienability accounts fall short: bound nouns in Harakmbut. Paper presented at the 54th Annual Meeting of the Societas Linguistica Europaea (SLE54), Online conference. https://doi.org/10.17605/OSF.IO/UDVEW.
Van linden, An. 2022. Harakmbut. In Patience Epps & Lev Michael (eds.), *Amazonian languages, An international handbook. Language Isolates*, Volume 1: Aikanã to Kandozi-Shapra, 437–477. Berlin: Mouton de Gruyter.
Wise, Mary R. 1999. Small language families and isolates in Peru. In R. M. W. Dixon & Alexandra Y. Aikhenvald (eds.), *The Amazonian languages*, 307–340. Cambridge: Cambridge University Press.
Wojtylak, Katarzyna I. 2016. Classifiers as Derivational Markers in Murui (Northwest Amazonia). In Lívia Körtvélyessy, Pavol Štekauer & Salvador Valera (eds.), *Word-formation across languages*, 393–425. Newcastle-upon-Tyne: Cambridge Scholars Publishing.

Chiara Naccarato and Shanshan Huang
Binominals denoting instruments: A contrastive perspective

Abstract: This chapter presents a contrastive analysis of complex nominals denoting instruments within the semantic field of COOKING in four languages: Italian, Russian, Mandarin Chinese, and Japanese. The study takes an onomasiological perspective to word formation with an aim to detect the morphosyntactic strategies adopted by the four languages to express the same concepts. Based on data from a corpus of cooking recipes created *ad hoc* for this investigation, we classify complex nominals denoting instruments by employing the analytical tools of the onomasiological theory of word formation. The results of our analysis show that there is a correlation between onomasiological type and type of cooking instrument. The onomasiological type to which binominals belong is most frequently associated with instruments for serving food, in which the semantic relation between the two constituents is one of PURPOSE. As for the morphosyntactic strategies employed, we found that Italian and Russian binominals are the result of derivation and adjectival or prepositional constructions, whereas Mandarin Chinese and Japanese use noun-noun compounding. Japanese frequently employs loanwords, which sometimes compete with compounds based on native or hybrid material.[1]

1 Introduction

The paper investigates complex nominals denoting instruments – with a particular focus on binominal constructions – in a novel sample of Italian (ISO 639-3: ITA), Russian (RUS), Mandarin Chinese (CMN), and Japanese (JPN). The choice of languages was motivated by a combination of factors. On the one hand, we wanted to compare languages that are typologically distant from one another. On the other hand, we chose to include only languages in which we are proficient, with an aim to be as accurate as possible in our analysis.

The analysis is restricted to the semantic domain of COOKING and focuses on binominals denoting instruments within this domain. Thus, instruments are

---

1 We thank the editors and the anonymous reviewers for their helpful comments on earlier versions of this paper. Any errors or inaccuracies in the paper are sole responsibility of the authors. Chiara Naccarato gratefully acknowledges the support from the Basic Research Program of the National Research University Higher School of Economics.

https://doi.org/10.1515/9783110673494-009

intended here as any type of kitchenware that can be used to handle, prepare, cook, serve, or store food.

In order to identify "patterns apt to express one and the same function" (Rainer 2013: 27), we conduct our analysis in a meaning-to-form fashion and adopt the onomasiological approach to word formation developed by Štekauer (1998, 2005a, 2005b) to find out how the same concepts are formally realized in the languages examined. Thus, unlike other chapters in the volume, we do not focus on a specific construction type, neither investigate the whole binominal domain of a specific language. Our study is onomasiologically designed and takes a specific semantic domain as the starting point to look at constructions apt to express the same function in different languages.

In this chapter, we discuss: i) what word-formation strategies are common for binominal constructions in the four languages; ii) what instrument types are more commonly denoted by binominal constructions; iii) the semantic relation between the two nominal constituents in such constructions; and iv) the degree of conceptual variation among the four languages. As we will show, binominal constructions in Italian and Russian are typically denominal derivatives and adjectival or prepositional constructions, whereas Mandarin Chinese and Japanese consistently employ noun-noun compounding. We will also show that binominals are strongly associated with a specific type of instruments, i.e., instruments for serving food, and typically express PURPOSE relations. Conceptual variation among the four languages is not pervasive, and only emerges in a few items displaying a certain degree of cultural specificity.

The chapter is structured as follows. In Section 2, we give a brief overview of our theoretical framework, i.e., the onomasiological approach to word formation. Section 3 explains our methodological choices. More specifically, we discuss how the data were collected, processed, and ultimately organized in a database. In Section 4, we show how the data were classified, and present the results of our analysis. Finally, Section 5 summarizes and discusses the results of this study.

2 The onomasiological approach to word formation

Our comparative study on complex nominals adopts an onomasiological perspective on word formation.

First, the process of data selection, which will be further discussed in Section 3, is onomasiological by its very nature, as the first step of our selection process consisted in retrieving all terms denoting instruments in a corpus of cooking recipes, independently of the formal features of such terms (see Section 3).

Second, we employ the analytical tools of the onomasiological theory of word formation to classify our data (see Section 4.1).

Specifically, we follow the onomasiological approach to word formation as developed by Pavol Štekauer in a number of studies (cf., among others, Štekauer 1998, 2005a, 2005b, 2016). As highlighted by Štekauer himself, this theory "emphasizes the triadic aspect of word formation existing between extra-linguistic reality (object to be named), speech-community (coiner) and word formation, in order to emphasize the active role and cognitive capacity of a coiner" (Štekauer 2005b: 44). Thus, within this approach, word formation is intended as a dynamic process that emerges whenever an individual speaker needs to name an object of the extra-linguistic reality.

The process of coining a new naming unit is described by Štekauer as a multilevel structure (cf. Štekauer 2005b: 45–46) which emphasizes "the important interconnections between extra-linguistic reality, speech community, the conceptual level as a supralinguistic level, and the relations between the individual components of grammar as well as inside the Word-formation Component itself" (Štekauer 2005b: 44).

The formal structure of a naming unit can be defined based on whether the constituents of the onomasiological structure are linguistically expressed or not. Such constituents are the onomasiological base and the onomasiological mark (cf. also Pepper, this volume, a). The onomasiological base is the element that identifies the conceptual class to which a certain entity belongs. For instance, in the word *piano player*, the suffix *-er* is the onomasiological base which determines the conceptual class to which the entity denoted by the word *piano player* belongs, i.e., that of Agent. The onomasiological base is then determined by an onomasiological mark, which "'entrenches' the object named with regard to all the other members of the class" (Štekauer 2005b: 52) and can be either simple or complex. When it is complex, it includes both the determining constituent (sometimes distinguishing between a specifying and a specified element) and the determined (i.e., actional) constituent. Thus, the onomasiological structure of the word *piano player* can be described as follows:

– the suffix *-er* is the onomasiological base which determines that the word belongs to the Agent class;
– the noun *piano* constitutes the determining constituent of the onomasiological mark;
– the verb *play* constitutes the determined (i.e., actional) constituent of the onomasiological mark.

Depending on whether the constituents of the onomasiological structure are linguistically expressed or not, we can distinguish different onomasiological types. In the latest classification by Štekauer (2016), several changes were proposed to the original model. However, in what follows, we will stick to the original classification in five onomasiological types (Štekauer 1998) with the addition of a sixth onomasiological type, as proposed in the revised classification by Pepper (2018); cf. also (Pepper, this volume, a).

In Onomasiological Type 1 (OT1), all constituents (i.e., onomasiological base, determining constituent, and determined constituent) are linguistically expressed, as in the above-mentioned example *piano player*.

In Onomasiological Type 2 (OT2), the determining constituent is left unexpressed, as in *player*, where we find the onomasiological base *-er* and the determined constituent *play*, but we do not find the object of the action *play* (as *piano* in *piano player*).

Conversely, in Onomasiological Type 3 (OT3), it is the determined constituent that is left unexpressed. An example of OT3 is represented by the word *pianist*, in which the onomasiological base is constituted by the suffix *-ist*, which attributes the conceptual class Agent to the word, and the determining constituent of the onomasiological mark is expressed by the noun *piano*.

In Onomasiological Type 4 (OT4), the onomasiological mark cannot be analyzed into a determining and a determined constituent. In a word such as *blue-eyed*, for instance, we find the onomasiological base *-ed* and the onomasiological mark *blue eye*.

Onomasiological Type 5 (OT5) includes all instances of what is traditionally called conversion, e.g., *play* (V) → *play* (N), in which a process of recategorization takes place at the conceptual level. In this case, the onomasiological level is unstructured, i.e., there is no onomasiological base and no onomasiological mark.

Finally, following Pepper (2018), we include in Onomasiological Type 6 (OT6) all cases in which both the determining and the determined constituent are linguistically expressed, but the base is not, e.g., *pickpocket*.

One of the advantages of the onomasiological approach is that it allows addressing the conceptual sides of word formation, rather than its formal aspects (Grzega 2009: 217). Thus, we can do without the traditional categorization of word-formation processes: one onomasiological type can encompass various word-formation strategies, and the same word-formation strategy can fall within various onomasiological types (Körtvélyessy et al. 2015: 94).

In Section 4, we will focus particularly on instances of Onomasiological Type 3, i.e., binominals as defined in this volume (see Masini, Mattiola & Pepper, this volume). Binominals, which are the result of a combination of two thing-morphs (cf. Haspelmath 2012: 115), are formally realized in our database as derived nouns, noun-noun compounds, adjectival[2] or prepositional constructions in which the relation between the two nominal constituents[3] is unstated, which results in "low semantic transparency" and "poor meaning predictability" (Körtvélyessy et al. 2015: 96). A *pianist* is defined as one who plays the piano, but this word could in principle be used to denote a person who has some other relation with pianos, e.g., one who produces pianos.

In our study, we use the classification in onomasiological types to find binominals denoting instruments in the COOKING domain. Then, we look at the word-formation features of such binominals to see what strategies are common for the four languages being compared.

3 Retrieving the data and building the corpus

The analysis presented in Section 4 is based on data extracted from a corpus of recipes created *ad hoc* for this study. For each language, we created a subcorpus that contains recipes from online magazines and recipe websites, including texts from open transcriptions of video recipes, for a total of approximately 50,000 words per subcorpus.

From each subcorpus we extracted terms denoting instruments, i.e., any type of kitchenware used to handle, prepare, cook, serve, or store food. To do this, we used the corpus analysis toolkit AntConc (Anthony 2018). This tool allows one to upload and visualize lists of words contained in such texts.[4] The function "Word List" creates a list of word types (i.e., lemmas) in the uploaded texts. These word-lists can be sorted by frequency, by alphabetical order, or by reverse alphabetical order, depending on the aim of the research. In this case, we chose the alphabetical order, and went through such lists of word types for each language to select all terms denoting instruments. To collect all instrument nouns, including terms made up of more than one word, we checked the list of collocates for each term, which is another function provided by AntConc. For instance, we found the

---

2 By "adjectival constructions" we mean constructions constituted by a head noun and a modifying relational adjective, e.g., RUS *želez-naja doroga* [iron-ADJZ road] 'railway'. (Note that in similar examples in Russian, we do not mark the presence of inflectional morphology, e.g., the nominative feminine singular ending *-aja* in *želez-n-aja*.)
3 In the case of derived nouns, the two nominal constituents are the base noun and the suffix.
4 In the case of Chinese and Japanese, raw texts are tokenized in a preliminary step by using SegmentAnt (Anthony 2017), which yields a tokenized .txt file that is then used to obtain the wordlist in AntConc.

Russian term *ložka* 'spoon' in the wordlist developed by AntConc. The function "Collocates" allows for visualization of a list of words which frequently co-occur with this term. In this way, we were able to collect the terms in (1).

(1) RUS a. *stolovaja ložka*   'table spoon'
       b. *čajnaja ložka*   'tea spoon'
       c. *desertnaja ložka* 'dessert spoon'

Then, we compared the lists of terms collected for the four languages, and filled the gaps, i.e., empty spaces for a certain term in one or more languages, by looking for appropriate translations. The complete list of instrument nouns at this point consisted of 127 terms for each language.

Subsequently, we went through the wordlists in each language and looked for complex terms, i.e., terms that arise as the result of a word-formation operation, be it derivation (e.g., RUS *blin-nica* [pancake-NMLZ] 'crêpe griddle'), compounding (e.g., CMN *cài-băn* [vegetable-board] 'cutting board'), prepositional constructions (e.g., ITA *pentola a pressione* [pot PRP pressure] 'pressure cooker'), or adjectival constructions (e.g., RUS *konserv-nyj nož* [canned_food-ADJZ knife] 'can opener').[5]

Given the comparative nature of the study, we then selected 50 terms that were complex in, at least, three of the four languages. Thus, we included in the analysis terms such as *gravy boat*, because this term is complex in three of the four languages (ITA *sals-iera* [sauce-NMLZ], RUS *sous-nica* [sauce-NMLZ], CMN *ròu-zhī-pán* [meat-juice-plate]), whereas in Japanese the same concept is expressed through a loanword: *gurēbībōto* (cf. ENG *gravy boat*), which is conceived as simplex. Conversely, we did not include in the analysis terms which turned out to be simplex in two or more languages. For instance, we excluded the term *fork*, which is simplex in all languages: ITA *forchetta*, RUS *vilka*, CMN *chāzi*, JPN *fooku*.

Note that the selected terms are not necessarily binominals. In fact, only rarely did we find binominal constructions for the same concept in all four languages (see further example (2) and the Appendix). However, in the analysis presented in Section 4.2, we focus specifically on binominals.

---

[5] Abbreviations: A adjective; ADJZ adjectivizer; LV linking vowel; N noun; NMLZ nominalizer; PRP preposition; V verb.

4 Complex instrument nouns from a contrastive perspective

4.1 Classifying and analysing complex instrument nouns

The terms selected through the procedure described in Section 3 were classified according to the following parameters:
- the type of instrument, i.e., instrument for handling, preparing, cooking, serving, or storing food;[6]
- the type of word-formation process according to Pepper's (this volume, a) classification;
- the onomasiological type (see Section 2).

For instance, the instrument *cutting board* is classified as an instrument for preparing food, and the corresponding terms found in the four languages are classified as shown in (2).

(2) a. ITA   *tagli-ere*   **dev**[7]   OT2
           [cut-NMLZ]   V-NMLZ
    b. RUS   *kuchon-naja doska*   **adj**   OT3
           [kitchen-ADJZ board]   N-ADJZ N
    c. CMN   *cài-bǎn*   **cmp**   OT3
           [vegetable-board]   N-N
    d. JPN   *mana-ita*   **cmp**   OT3
           [fish-board]   N-N

Thus, for the instrument *cutting board*, we found three word-formation strategies (deverbal derivation in Italian, a construction with a relational adjective in Russian, and noun-noun compounding in Mandarin Chinese and Japanese) and two onomasiological types (OT2 in Italian and OT3 in the other languages).

The same classification was applied to all 50 instruments selected, as shown in the Appendix. The terms are grouped according to the type of instrument that they denote. Then, for each term, we indicate the onomasiological type instantiated and the word-formation strategy employed in each language. For OT3 we

---

[6] The set of instrument types was defined inductively.
[7] The abbreviation "dev" is used to distinguish cases of deverbal derivation (OT2) from cases of denominal derivation ("der", OT3).

also report the binominal type according to Pepper's (2020) classification; cf. also (Pepper, this volume, a).

4.2 A comparison of binominals denoting cooking instruments

In the present section, we present the results of our analysis according to the parameters discussed in Section 4.1. First, we provide a contrastive picture comparing the four languages, and then we focus on the results in each language. Since binominals are the main focus of our research, we will only briefly discuss the general results and devote more space to examining binominals (i.e., OT3).

The graph in Figure 1 displays the distribution of onomasiological types in the four languages. In Italian, Russian and Mandarin Chinese most instrument nouns are instantiations of OT3. OT1 is also quite frequent in Russian and Mandarin Chinese, while in Italian and Japanese this onomasiological type is not represented. In most cases OT1 in Russian and Mandarin Chinese corresponds to OT6 in Italian (cf., for instance, ITA *trita-carne* [grind-meat] vs. RUS *mjas-o-rub-ka* [meat-LV-grind-NMLZ] and CMN *jiǎo-ròu-jī* [[grind-meat]$_V$-NMLZ] 'mincer'). This is not surprising, given that OT6 is represented by VN compounds, which are highly productive in Romance, but much less so in Slavic languages, as well as in Chinese. In both Russian and Mandarin Chinese, synthetic compounds including a nominalizing affix are much more productive, which explains the higher frequency of OT1 in these languages. Note, however, a prominent difference between Russian and Mandarin Chinese: whereas in Russian the nominal element precedes the verbal stem in such compounds, the opposite order is usually found in Mandarin Chinese. OT2 and OT4 are less frequent in all languages. Japanese stands out for its abundance of simplex terms, which in most cases are loanwords, as will be discussed in Section 4.2.4. However, it should be noted that, if we do not consider loanwords, the distribution of onomasiological types is rather similar to the other languages, with OT3 dominating over the others.

The occurrence of certain onomasiological types appears to be correlated with the type of instrument that the terms denote. The pie diagrams in Figure 2 show the percentage of instrument type for each onomasiological type (OT5 is absent because we did not find any instances of this onomasiological type in our data). Percentages do not refer to a specific language, but to the total number of nouns denoting a certain type of instrument in Italian, Russian, Mandarin Chinese and Japanese. In other words, for each onomasiological type, we counted how many terms instantiating a certain instrument type we found in the four languages. For instance, OT3 covers a total of 90 terms (22 in ITA, 27 in RUS, 25 in CMN, and 16 in JPN). Out of these 90 terms, 42 are instantiations of instruments for serving (13 in ITA, 13 in RUS, 12 in

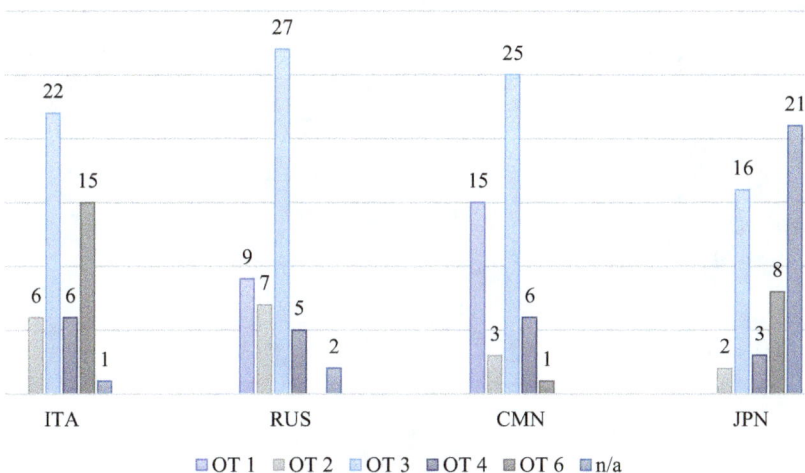

Figure 1: Onomasiological types' distribution in ITA, RUS, CMN, JPN.

CMN, and 4 in JPN), which corresponds to 46 percent of the total; 15 are instantiations of instruments for handling (4 in ITA, 5 in RUS, 4 in CMN, and 2 in JPN), which corresponds to 17 percent of the total, and so on.

Interestingly, OT1, OT2 and OT6 show higher percentages of instruments used to prepare or cook food. These onomasiological types differ from the others in that they include the determined (i.e., actional) constituent, as in *coffee grinder* (OT1, determined constituent *grind*) or *grater* (OT2, determined constituent *grate*). This correlation between instrument types and onomasiological types can be simply explained in terms of the actional constituent being more salient in such nominals, i.e., it is relevant to express what kind of action can be carried out with such instruments. Conversely, OT3 is more often associated with other instrument types, particularly instruments for serving food, as *salad bowl*. Here, what seems to be more relevant is the determining rather than the determined constituent (which is not expressed): it is the type of food the instrument is used for that is more salient. OT4, which is far less frequent in our database (instantiated by a total of 20 terms across the four languages), shows a more balanced distribution of different instrument types. Figure 3 shows the distribution of onomasiological types by instrument type and gives the mirror image of the correlations just discussed. Instruments to cook or prepare food show higher percentages of onomasiological types including the determined constituent (OT1, OT2 and OT6), whereas instruments to handle, store, and – particularly – serve food are most often realized as OT3.

Let us now focus on OT3, which constitutes the main object of this research. As we discussed earlier (see Section 2), OT3 covers binominals, i.e., lexemes com-

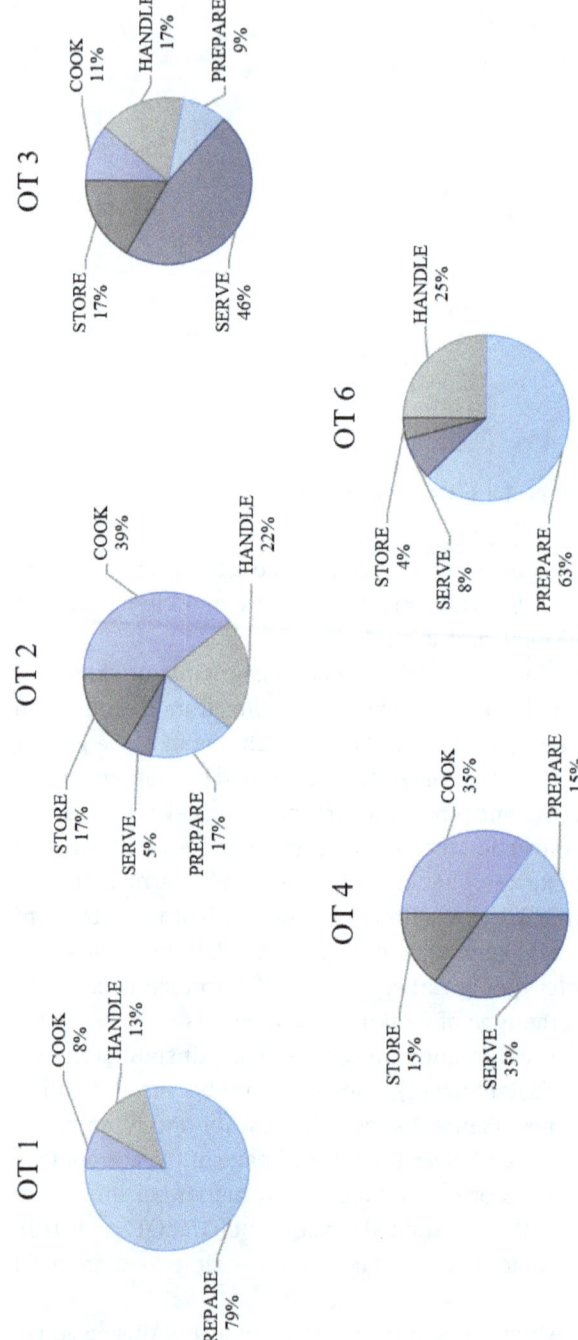

Figure 2: Instrument type by onomasiological type.

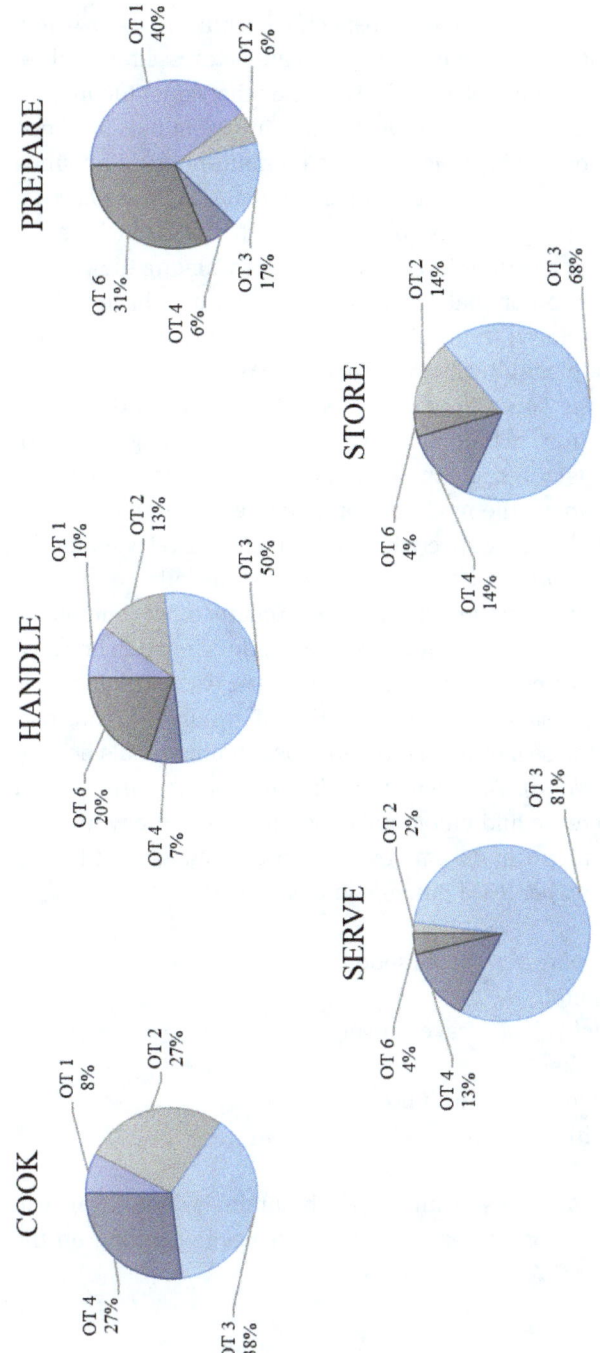

Figure 3: Onomasiological types by instrument type.

bining two nouny elements whose relation is unspecified. Unlike in cases where the determined (i.e., actional) constituent is linguistically expressed, OT3 does not include a verbal element stating the relation with the other constituent(s).

The semantic relation between the two constituents in binominals has been investigated in previous studies, which mostly focus on noun-noun compounds (cf. Levi 1978; Warren 1978; Ryder 1994; Jackendoff 2010; Bauer & Tarasova 2013; Bourque 2014; Eiesland 2016; Pepper, this volume, b). Such studies include different attempts to account for a certain level of systematicity among the various types of semantic relations in binominals. Although such attempts have yielded classifications with higher or lower levels of specificity, some semantic relations have been recognized by almost all scholars, such as PART-WHOLE (e.g., *armchair*), RESEMBLANCE (e.g., *sunflower*), LOCATION (e.g., *sea port*), etc. One of the most common semantic relations in binominals is that of PURPOSE (e.g., *ball bat*). As Eiesland (2016: 121) points out for noun-noun compounds in Norwegian, the PURPOSE relation is found when "the modifier noun denotes the purpose of the head noun, sometimes in the sense of specifying the realm that is relevant for the purpose of the head noun": a *ball bat* is a bat used to strike the ball.

PURPOSE is also the semantic relation that appears to characterize binominals denoting cooking instruments. Our data show that the semantic relation between the two nominal constituents is consistently that of PURPOSE, e.g., a *salad bowl* is a bowl for salad, used to serve salad (cf. also Pepper's (this volume, b) considerations on the frequency of the semantic relation PURPOSE in binominals belonging to the domain *Modern World*). This semantic relation is particularly explicit in Italian and Russian, where we find binominal constructions of the type N PRP N (**prp**). In such cases, the prepositions employed in both languages are typical purpose prepositions: *da*[8] and *per* in Italian, *dlja* in Russian (3).

(3) a. ITA *cucchiaio da minestra* 'table spoon'
 [spoon PRP soup]
 b. ITA *paletta per dolci* 'cake shovel'
 [shovel PRP cake]
 c. RUS *vaza dlja fruktov* 'fruit bowl'
 [vase PRP fruit]

Turning to the word-formation processes underlying binominals denoting instruments, we found that OT3 encompasses different strategies depending on the

---

[8] On the telic function of *da* see also Busa & Johnston (1996).

language. To classify the word-formation type for each term in the database, we resorted to Pepper's (2020) typology.

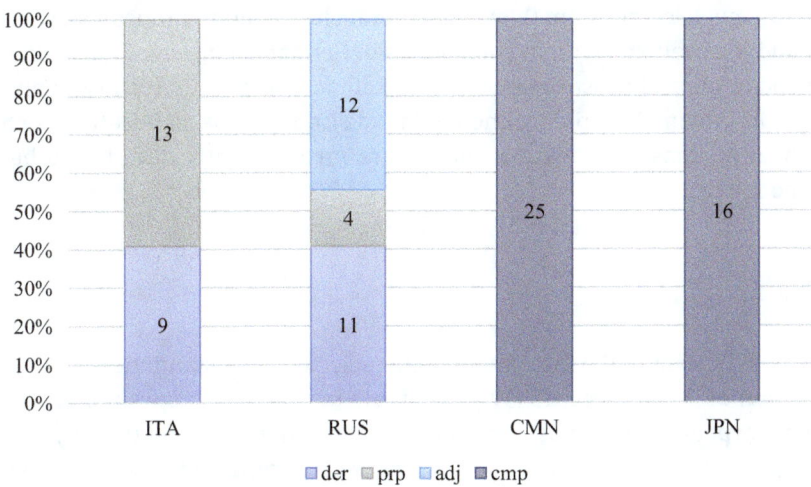

Figure 4: OT3 and word-formation strategies.

As shown in Figure 4, whereas Italian and Russian employ derivation and prepositional or adjectival constructions, Mandarin Chinese and Japanese consistently employ noun-noun compounding, **cmp** (see also Sections 4.2.1, 4.2.2, 4.2.3, and 4.2.4). Compounding is widely attested in Italian and Russian for other onomasiological types, especially when the actional constituent is also expressed, that is when the compounding process is verb-based, as in ITA OT6 *tritacarne* and RUS OT1 *ovoščerezka* (4).

(4) a. ITA *trita-carne*   'mincer'
           [mince-meat]
    b. RUS *ovošč-e-rez-ka*   'vegetable slicer'
           [vegetable-LV-cut-NMLZ]

In Mandarin Chinese and Japanese, instead, compounding is the only word-formation strategy employed, also when other onomasiological types are at play.[9] These results are not surprising and depend on the typological features of the languages examined. In a highly isolating language like Mandarin Chinese, compounding is by far the most productive word-formation strategy. As noted by Xing

---

[9] In Japanese, compounding alternates with borrowing, as will be discussed in Section 4.2.4.

(2006: 117), about 80% of the Chinese lexicon is constituted by compounds. By contrast, Italian and Russian feature rich derivational systems, especially in the nominal area of word formation. Compounding is productive in these languages too, but to a much lesser extent than in other branches of Indo-European like Germanic, and it is well known that compounds in Germanic languages most often correspond to phrasal constructions in both Romance and Slavic (cf. also (Cetnarowska, this volume) on phrasal nouns in Polish). Japanese also features rich derivational systems, but nominalizations are predominantly deverbal rather than denominal.

4.2.1 Italian

In Italian, 44 percent of the instrument nouns selected are instantiations of OT3, that is 22 out of 50. Of these, 13 (59 percent) are instances of prepositional constructions, **prp**, and the prepositions employed are either *da* or *per* (5), *da* being more frequent than *per* (10 vs. 3 cases), which is consistent with Masini's (2009) findings about phrasal lexemes of this type.

(5) ITA a. *carta da forno*   'baking paper'
            [paper PRP oven]
         b. *coppa per gelato*   'ice cream cup'
            [cup PRP ice cream]

The remaining 9 nouns (41 percent) instantiating OT3 are the result of denominal derivation, and in all cases we find the feminine instrument suffix *-iera*, as shown in (6).

(6) ITA a. *insalat-iera*   'salad bowl'
            [salad-NMLZ]
         b. *te-iera*   'tea pot'
            [tea-NMLZ]
         c. *sals-iera*   'gravy boat'
            [sauce-NMLZ]

4.2.2 Russian

In Russian, the general picture is quite similar to Italian. 54 percent of the instrument nouns selected are instantiations of OT3, i.e., 27 out of 50. Binominals denoting instruments are realized as adjectival constructions, **adj** (12 binominals out of 27, i.e., 44 percent of the cases), denominal nouns, **der** (11 nouns out of 27, i.e., 41 percent of the cases), or prepositional constructions, **prp** (4 binominals out of 27, i.e., 15 percent of the cases). Relational adjectives are almost always formed with the adjectivizing suffix -*n*- (with the only exception of the adjective *stolovaja* 'related to the table' in *stolovaja ložka* 'table spoon', in which the adjectivizing suffix is -*ov*-), while prepositional constructions only show the preposition *dlja* 'for' (7).

(7) RUS a. *desert-naja tarelka* 'dessert plate'
            [dessert-ADJZ plate]
        b. *lopatka dlja torta* 'cake shovel'
            [shovel PRP cake]

As regards cases of denominal derivation, **der**, in Russian we found slightly more variation with respect to Italian, as three suffixes are represented in the database: -*nica*, -*nik*, and -*onka* (8).

(8) RUS a. *chleb-nica* 'bread box'
            [bread-NMLZ]
        b. *čaj-nik* 'kettle, teapot'
            [tea-NMLZ]
        c. *sol-onka* 'salt shaker'
            [salt-NMLZ]

4.2.3 Mandarin Chinese

In Mandarin Chinese, OT3 is found in 25 cases out of 50, that is, 50 percent of the total. As already mentioned, in Mandarin Chinese, compounding is the only word-formation process represented in our database regardless of the onomasiological type. All 25 instantiations of OT3 are realized as noun-noun compounds, **cmp**, in which the onomasiological base and the determining constituent of the onomasiological mark are free or bound roots.[10] For example, in (9), *kāfēi* 'coffee' is a free root because it can occur as an independent word (it is in fact a loan-

---

[10] For the analysis of the data in Mandarin Chinese, we adopted the definition of compound by Liao (2014: 8–9), i.e., "a morphological word is a compound if it consists of two or more (free or bound) roots".

word), whereas *bēi* 'cup' is considered as a bound root because it does not normally occur as an independent word with the meaning of 'cup, glass'. Normally, it occurs together with *-zi*, a derivational affix which frequently combines with monosyllabic roots (Liao 2014: 6).

(9)   *kāfēi-bēi*   'coffee cup'
       [coffee-cup]

4.2.4 Japanese

As already mentioned, the situation in Japanese is quite peculiar compared to the other languages in our sample. Indeed, we found that 42 percent of the Japanese terms in our database are loanwords, mainly from English.

We did not assign an onomasiological type to loanwords that are directly borrowed from another language, as we consider them as simplex terms. Nevertheless, we did regard compounds with a partial or total use of borrowed linguistic material as complex terms. For instance, a compound such as *ōbun-pēpā* [oven-paper] 'baking paper' was classified as a complex term because it is coined from two separate borrowings that are used independently in the languages. Our data show three possible situations:

- competition between a native compound (10a) and a direct borrowing (10b);
- competition between a direct borrowing (11a) and compounds based on two independent loanwords (11b and 11c);
- competition between hybrid compounds, that is, compounds in which the constituents belong to two different lexical strata, i.e., a loanword and a native word (12a), or two loanwords from different languages (12b) (cf. Irwin 2011; Kageyama & Saito 2016).

(10) JPN a. *sen-nuki*   [cork$_{JPN}$-pull$_{JPN}$]   'bottle opener'
            b. *botoru-opunnā*   [bottle$_{EN}$-opener$_{EN}$]

(11) JPN a. *bēkingu-pēpā*   [baking$_{EN}$-paper$_{EN}$]   'baking paper'
            b. *bēkingu-shīto*   [baking$_{EN}$-sheet$_{EN}$]
            c. *ōbun-pēpā*   [oven$_{EN}$-paper$_{EN}$]

(12) JPN a. *pan-ire*   [bread$_{POR}$-holder$_{JAP}$]   'bread box'
            b. *pan-kēsu*   [bread$_{POR}$-case$_{EN}$]

OT3 is instantiated by 16 cases in our corpus, all of which are the result of noun-noun compounding, such as *cha-saji* [tea_JPN-spoon_JPN] 'teaspoon' or *mana-ita* [fish_JPN-board_JPN] 'cutting board'. As just discussed, the nominal constituents in such compounds are frequently constituted by loanwords, e.g. *dezāto-sara* [dessert_JPN-plate_JPN] 'dessert plate' or examples in (10b), (11a-c), (12b).

4.3 Conceptual variation

The comparison of complex instrument nouns in different languages also allowed us to detect some degree of conceptual variation across languages. Specifically, we found three possible situations:
- identical conceptualization, i.e., the onomasiological type coincides and the two constituents are identical in all languages (13);
- slightly different conceptualization, i.e., the onomasiological type coincides but one of the constituents varies (14);
- different conceptualizations (15).

(13) a. ITA *piatto da dessert* [plate PRP dessert] 'dessert plate'
    b. RUS *desert-naja tarelka* [dessert-ADJZ plate]
    c. CMN *tiánpǐn-pán* [dessert-plate]
    d. JPN *dezāto-sara* [dessert-plate]

(14) a. ITA *piatto piano* [plate **flat**] 'dinner plate'
    b. RUS *melkaja tarelka* [**flat** plate]
    c. CMN *dà-pán* [**big**-plate]
    d. JPN *oo-zara* [**big**-plate]

(15) a. ITA *tagl-iere* [**cut**-NMLZ] 'cutting board'
    b. RUS *kuchon-naja doska* [**kitchen**-ADJZ board]
    c. CMN *cài-bǎn* [**vegetable**[11]-board]
    d. JPN *mana-ita*[12] [**fish**-board]

Example (15) is an interesting case of different conceptualizations which seem to depend on cultural reasons. While *cutting board* in Italian is simply an 'instru-

---

11 *cài* indicates vegetables or any non-staple food, including eggs, meat, or fish, that accompany the main staple food of a meal.
12 The internal structure of this term may be perceived as synchronically opaque, as *mana* is an archaic term for 'fish', whereas in modern Japanese we find the term *sakana*.

ment for cutting' and in Russian a 'kitchen board', in Mandarin Chinese it is conceptualized as a 'board for vegetables' and in Japanese as a 'board for fish'. Such cases are not so frequent, but sometimes cultural specificity does emerge. Another example is constituted by the terms for *crêpe griddle*, which are based on the French word *crêpe* in all languages except for Russian *blinnica*, which is based on the word *blin*, denoting the traditional Russian pancake made from wheat.

5 Discussion and conclusions

In this chapter we investigated binominals denoting cooking instruments in a contrastive perspective, comparing Italian, Russian, Mandarin Chinese, and Japanese.

The onomasiological classification of the data allowed us to select and analyze binominal lexemes, i.e., OT3, in the four languages.

First, we noticed that there seems to be a correlation between the onomasiological type at play and the type of instrument denoted. Specifically, while OT1, OT2 and OT6 are more strictly associated with instruments for preparing or cooking food (in which the actional part of the phenomenon named is particularly salient), OT3 is more frequently associated with instruments for serving food, in which it is the determining constituent that is particularly relevant. The determining constituent in binominals, indeed, expresses the purpose for which the instrument is used, which is the salient piece of information.

Second, we compared the word-formation strategies employed in the four languages to form binominals. Whereas we found derivation and adjectival or prepositional constructions in Italian and Russian, noun-noun compounding was found to be the only option for Mandarin Chinese and Japanese. Overall, these results are not surprising. In an isolating language like Mandarin Chinese, compounding is extremely productive and covers most of the word-formation domain. Compounding is a productive process in Italian and Russian too, but to a much lesser extent as compared to Mandarin Chinese, and phrasal constructions are often employed instead. Italian and Russian also abound with derivatives, which is obviously not the case for Mandarin Chinese. Japanese stands out from the other languages for employing a high percentage of loanwords, which sometimes compete with compounds based on native or hybrid material.

Although the languages in the sample show a general tendency to conceptualize complex instruments in the same way, i.e., the two constituents in binominals often coincide, in a few cases we found conceptualizations showing some degree of cultural specificity.

Appendix: Complex instrument nouns in ITA, RUS, CMN, and JPN (the database)

Instrument	Type	ITA	OT	WF	RUS	OT	WF	CMN	OT	WF	JPN[13]	OT	WF
crêpe griddle	COOK	Crepiera	3	N-NMLZ der	blinnica	3	N-NMLZ der	kělìbǐngkǎopán	1	N-[V-N]$_{IN}$	kurepupan	n/a[14]	LW
kettle	COOK	Bollitore	2	V-NMLZ	čajnik	3	N-NMLZ der	shāoshuǐhú	1	[V-N]v-N	kama	n/a	simplex
baking paper	COOK	carta da forno	3	N PRP N prp	pergamentnaja bumaga	4	N-ADJZ N	hóngbèizhǐ	2	[V-V]v-N	bēkingushīto	3	N-N cmp
											obunpēpā	3	N-N cmp
											bēkingupēpā	n/a	LW
deep fryer	COOK	friggitrice	2	V-NMLZ	fritjurnica	3	N-NMLZ der	yóuzháguō	2	[N-V]v-N	agenabe	2	V-N
cake pan	COOK	Tortiera	3	N-NMLZ der	forma dlja vypečki	2	N PRP V-NMLZ	dàngāomújù	3	N-N	kēkikkatā	3	N-N cmp
pressure cooker	COOK	pentola a pressione	4	N PRP N	skorovarka	2	A-V-NMLZ	gāoyāguō	4	[A-N]$_{IN}$-N	atsuryoku-nabe	3	N-N cmp
microwave	COOK	forno a microonde	4	N PRP N	mikrovolnovka	4	A-NMLZ	wēibōlú	4	[A-N]$_{IN}$-N	denshirenji	4	A-N
bottle opener	HANDLE	apribottiglie	6	V-N	otkryvalka	2	V-NMLZ	kāipíngqì	1	[V-N] v-NMLZ	sennuki	6	N-V
											botoruopuna	n/a	LW

(continued)

---

13 Words highlighted in grey are variants of the same concept that were not taken into account for the quantitative analysis in Section 4.2.
14 The abbreviation n/a is used for lexemes which cannot be attributed an onomasiological type, such as simplex lexemes and direct borrowings (LW).

(continued)

Instrument	Type	ITA	OT	WF	RUS	OT	WF	CMN	OT	WF	JPN	OT	WF
can opener	HANDLE	apriscatole	6	V-N	konservnyj nož	3	N-ADJ|Z N adj	kāiguànqì	1	[V-N] v-NMLZ	kankiri	6	N-V
corkscrew	HANDLE	cavatappi	6	V-N	štopor	n/a	LW	kāipíngqì	1	[V-N] v-NMLZ	corukunuki	6	N-V
skimmer	HANDLE	schiumarola	2	V-NMLZ	šumovka	2	V-NMLZ	lòusháo	2	V-N	sukimaa	n/a	LW
tablespoon	HANDLE	cucchiaio da minestra	3	N PRP N prp	stolovaja ložka	3	N-ADJ|Z N adj	tāngsháo	3	N-N cmp	teburusupūn	n/a	LW
teaspoon	HANDLE	cucchiaino da caffè	3	N PRP N prp	kofejnaja ložka	3	N-ADJ|Z N adj	kāfēishí	3	N-N cmp	kōhī supūn	n/a	LW
dessert spoon	HANDLE	cucchiaino da dessert	3	N PRP N prp	desertnaja ložka	3	N-ADJ|Z N adj	tiánpǐnchí	3	N-N cmp	dezātosupūn	3	N-N cmp
teaspoon	HANDLE	cucchiaino da tè	3	N PRP N prp	čajnaja ložka	3	N-ADJ|Z N adj	chásháo	3	N-N cmp	chasaji	3	N-N cmp
coffee grinder	PREPARE	macinacaffè	6	V-N	kofemolka	1	N-V-NMLZ	mòfēnjī	1	[V-N] v-NMLZ	kōhīmiru	n/a	LW
egg cutter	PREPARE	affetta uovo	6	V N	jajcerezka	1	N-V-NMLZ	qiēdànqì	1	[V-N] v-NMLZ	eggusuraisā	n/a	LW
food processor	PREPARE	tritatutto	6	V-N	kuchonnyj kombajn	3	N-ADJ|Z N adj	shípǐnjiāgōngjī	1	[V-N] v-NMLZ	fūdo-purosesā	n/a	LW
juicer	PREPARE	spremiagrumi	6	V-N	sokovyžimalka	1	N-V-NMLZ	zhàzhījī	1	[V-N] v-NMLZ	jūsā	n/a	LW
mincer	PREPARE	tritacarne	6	V-N	mjasorubka	1	N-V-NMLZ	jiǎoròujī	1	[V-N] v-NMLZ	minsā	n/a	LW

Binominals denoting instruments: A contrastive perspective — 297

peeler	PREPARE	pelapatate	6	V-N	kartofelečistka	1	N-V-NMLZ	qūpíqí	1	[V-N] v-NMLZ	pīrā	n/a	LW
vegetable slicer	PREPARE	tagliaverdure	6	V-N	ovoščerezka	1	N-V-NMLZ	qiēpiànjī	1	[V-N] v-NMLZ	kawamukiki	1	N-V-NMLZ
grater	PREPARE	grattugia	2	V-NMLZ	terka	2	V-NMLZ	Nǎilàopàosīqì	1	N [V-N] v-NMLZ	suraisā	n/a	LW
nutcracker	PREPARE	schiaccianoci	6	V-N	ščipcy dlja orechov	3	N PRP N prp	hútáojiāzi	1	N-N	chízuoroshi	6	N-V
salad washer	PREPARE	lavainsalata	6	V-N	sušilka dlja salata	1	V-NMLZ PRP N	shūcàituōshuǐjī	1	N [V-N] v-NMLZ	kurumiwari	6	N-V
bread knife	PREPARE	coltello a seghetto	4	N PRP N	nož-pilka	4	N-N	miànbāodāo	3	N-N cmp	sarada mizukiri	6	N N-V
toothpick	PREPARE	stuzzicadenti	6	V-N	zubočistka	1	N-V-NMLZ	yáqiān	3	N-N cmp	buredo-naifu	n/a	LW
cutting board	PREPARE	tagliere	2	V-NMLZ	kuchonnaja doska	3	N-ADJZ N adj	càibǎn	3	N-N cmp	tsumayōji	3	N-N cmp
meat mallet	PREPARE	batticarne	6	V-N	molotok dlja otbivanija mjasa	1	N PRP V-NMLZ N	mùchuí	4	N-N	manaita	3	N-N cmp
saucer	SERVE	piattino da tè	3	N PRP N prp	čajnoe bljudce	3	N-ADJZ N prp	chátuō	6	N-V	nikutataki	6	N-V
caviar cup	SERVE	coppa per caviale	3	N PRP N prp	ikornica	3	N-NMLZ der	yúzǐjiāngwǎn	3	N-N cmp	chataku	6	N-V
coffee cup	SERVE	tazza da caffè	3	N PRP N prp	kofejnaja kružka	3	N-ADJZ N adj	kāfēibēi	3	N-N cmp	kyabiya kappu	n/a	LW
gravy boat	SERVE	salsiera	3	N-NMLZ der	sousnica	3	N-NMLZ der	ròuzhīpán	3	N-N cmp	kōhīikappu	n/a	LW
											gurēbibōto	n/a	LW

(continued)

(continued)

	Instrument Type	ITA	OT	WF	RUS	OT	WF	CMN	OT	WF	JPN	OT	WF
ice cream cup	SERVE	coppa per gelato	3	N PRP N prp	kremanka dlja moroženogo	3	N PRP N prp	bīngqílínbēi	3	N-N cmp	aisukappu	n/a	LW
milk pitcher	SERVE	lattiera	3	N-NMLZ der	moločnik	3	N-NMLZ der	niúnǎi hú	3	N-N cmp	mirukupichā	n/a	LW
salad bowl	SERVE	insalatiera	3	N-NMLZ der	salatnik, salatnica	3	N-NMLZ der	shālawǎn	3	N-N cmp	saradabōru	n/a	LW
teacup	SERVE	tazza da tè	3	N PRP N prp	čajnaja kružka	3	N-ADJZ N adj	chábēi	3	N-N cmp	tīkappu	n/a	LW
tea pot	SERVE	teiera	3	N-NMLZ der	čajnik	3	N-NMLZ der	cháhú	3	N-N cmp	tīpotto	n/a	LW
dessert plate	SERVE	piatto da dessert	3	N PRP N prp	desertnaja tarelka	3	N-ADJZ N adj	tiánpǐnpán	3	N-N cmp	dezātosara	3	N-N cmp
fruit bowl	SERVE	fruttiera	3	N-NMLZ der	vaza dlja fruktov	3	N PRP N prp	guǒpán	3	N-N cmp	furutsusara	3	N-N cmp
soup plate	SERVE	piatto fondo	4	N A	glubokaja tarelka	4	A N	tāngpán	3	N-N cmp	sūpusara	3	N-N cmp
cake shovel	SERVE	paletta per dolci	3	N PRP N prp	lopatka dlja torta	3	N PRP N prp	dàngāochǎn	3	N-N cmp	kēkisābā	3	N-N cmp
serving plate	SERVE	piatto da portata	3	N PRP N prp	servirovočnoe bljudo	3	N-ADJZ N adj	dàpán	4	A-N	morizara	2	N-V
dinner plate	SERVE	piatto piano	4	N A	melkaja tarelka	4	A N	dàpán	4	A-N	ōzara	4	A-N

freezer	STORE	*congelatore*	2	V-NMLZ	*morozil'nik, morozilka*	2	V-NMLZ	*bīngxiāng*	3	N-N	*reitōko*	3	N-N cmp
fridge	STORE	*frigorifero*	n/a	simplex	*cholodil'nik*	2	V-NMLZ	*bīngxiāng*	3	N-N	*reizōko*	3	N-N cmp
saltshaker	STORE	*saliera*	3	N-NMLZ der	*solonka*	3	N-NMLZ der	*yánguàn*	3	N-N	*shioire*	3	N-N cmp
sugar bowl	STORE	*zuccheriera*	3	N-NMLZ der	*sacharnica*	3	N-NMLZ der	*tángguàn*	3	N-N	*satoire*	3	N-N cmp
bread box	STORE	*portapane*	6	V-N	*chlebnica*	3	N-NMLZ der	*miànbāohé*	3	N-N	*pan'ire* / *pankēsu*	3 / 3	N-N cmp / N-N cmp
aluminium foil	STORE	*carta stagnola*	4	NA	*fol'ga*	n/a	LW	*lǔbózhǐ*	4	N-N	*arumifoiru*	4	A-N

References

Anthony, Laurence. 2017. SegmentAnt (Version 1.1.3). Tokyo: Waseda University. See https://www.laurenceanthony.net/software.
Anthony, Laurence. 2018. AntConc (Version 3.5.7). Tokyo: Waseda University. See https://www.laurenceanthony.net/software.
Bauer, Laurie & Elizaveta Tarasova. 2013. The meaning link in nominal compounds. *SKASE Journal of Theoretical Linguistics* 10(3). 2–18.
Bourque, Yves Stephen. 2014. *Toward a typology of semantic transparency: The case of French compounds*. Toronto: University of Toronto PhD dissertation.
Busa, Federica & Michael J. G. Johnston. 1996. Cross-linguistic semantics for complex nominals in the Generative Lexicon. In *Proceedings of the AISB Workshop on Multilinguality in the Lexicon*. Brighton (England): University of Sussex.
Cetnarowska, Bożena. This volume. NN.GEN and NAREL juxtapositions in Polish: Syntactic schemas employed in building phrasal nouns. In Steve Pepper, Francesca Masini & Simone Mattiola (eds.), *Binominal lexemes in cross-linguistic perspective*. Berlin: Mouton de Gruyter.
Eiesland, Eli-Anne. 2016. *The semantics of Norwegian noun-noun compounds: A corpus based study*. Oslo: University of Oslo PhD dissertation.
Grzega, Joachim. 2009. Compounding from an onomasiological perspective. In Rochelle Lieber & Pavol Štekauer (eds.), *The Oxford handbook of compounding*, 217–232. Oxford: Oxford University Press.
Haspelmath, Martin. 2012. How to compare major word-classes across the world's languages. *UCLA Working Papers in Linguistics, Theories of Everything* 17, Article 16. 109–130.
Irwin, Mark. 2011. *Loanwords in Japanese*. Amsterdam: John Benjamins.
Jackendoff, Ray. 2010. *Meaning and the lexicon: The parallel architecture 1975–2010*. Oxford: Oxford University Press.
Kageyama, Taro & Michiaki Saito. 2016. Vocabulary strata and word formation processes. In Taro Kageyama & Hideki Kishimoto (eds.), *Handbook of Japanese Lexicon and Word Formation*, 11–50. Berlin: Mouton de Gruyter.
Körtvélyessy, Lívia, Pavol Štekauer & Július Zimmermann. 2015. Word-formation strategies: Semantic transparency vs. formal economy. In Laurie Bauer, Lívia Körtvélyessy & Pavol Štekauer (eds.), *Semantics of complex words*, 85–114. Dordrecht: Springer.
Levi, Judith N. 1978. *The syntax and semantics of complex nominals*. New York: Academic Press.
Liao, Wei-Wen Roger. 2014. Morphology. In C.-T. James Huang, Yen-Hui Audrei Li & Andrew Simpson (eds.), *The handbook of Chinese linguistics*, 3–25. Oxford: Wiley-Blackwell.
Masini, Francesca. 2009. Phrasal lexemes, compounds and phrases: A constructionist perspective. *Word Structure* 2(2). 254–271.
Masini, Francesca, Simone Mattiola & Steve Pepper. This volume. Exploring complex lexemes cross-linguistically. In Steve Pepper, Francesca Masini & Simone Mattiola (eds.), Binominal lexemes in cross-linguistic perspective. Berlin: Mouton de Gruyter.
Pepper, Steve. 2010. *Nominal compounding in Nizaa: A cognitive perspective*. School of Oriental and African Studies. London: University of London MA thesis.
Pepper, Steve. 2016. Windmills, Nizaa and the typology of binominal compounds. In Lívia Körtvélyessy, Pavol Štekauer & Salvador Valera (eds.), *Word-formation across languages*, 281–310. Newcastle: Cambridge Scholars Publishing.

Pepper, Steve. 2018. Onomasiological types and the typology of binominal lexemes. Paper presented at the *Typology and Universals in Word-Formation IV* conference, Košice, 28 June 2018. See http://folk.uio.no/stevepe/WFT18.pdf.

Pepper, Steve. 2020. *The typology and semantics of binominal lexemes: Noun-noun compounds and their functional equivalents*. Oslo: University of Oslo PhD dissertation.

Pepper, Steve. This volume, a. Defining and typologizing binominal lexemes. In Steve Pepper, Francesca Masini & Simone Mattiola (eds.), *Binominal lexemes in cross-linguistic perspective*. Berlin: Mouton de Gruyter.

Pepper, Steve. This volume, b. Hatcher-Bourque: Towards a reusable classification of semantic relations. In Steve Pepper, Francesca Masini & Simone Mattiola (eds.), *Binominal lexemes in cross-linguistic perspective*. Berlin: Mouton de Gruyter.

Rainer, Franz. 2013. Can relational adjectives really express any relation? An onomasiological perspective. *SKASE Journal of Theoretical Linguistics* 10(1). 12–40.

Ryder, Mary Ellen. 1994. *Ordered chaos: The interpretation of English noun-noun compounds*. Berkeley, CA: University of California Press.

Štekauer, Pavol. 1998. *An onomasiological theory of English word-formation*. Amsterdam: John Benjamins.

Štekauer, Pavol. 2005a. Onomasiological approach to word-formation. In Pavol Štekauer & Rochelle Lieber (eds.), *Handbook of word-formation*, 207–232. Dordrecht: Springer.

Štekauer, Pavol. 2005b. *Meaning predictability in word formation. Novel, context-free naming units*. Amsterdam: John Benjamins.

Štekauer, Pavol. 2016. Compounding from an onomasiological perspective. In Pius ten Hacken (ed.), *The semantics of compounding*, 54–68. Cambridge: Cambridge University Press.

Warren, Beatrice. 1978. Semantic patterns of noun-noun compounds. *Acta Universitatis Gothoburgensis* 41. 1–266.

Xing, Janet Zhiqun. 2006. *Teaching and learning Chinese as a foreign language: A pedagogical grammar*. Hong Kong: Hong Kong University Press.

Part 2: **Meaning (semantic relations)**

Steve Pepper
Hatcher-Bourque: Towards a reusable classification of semantic relations

Abstract: A key feature of binominal lexemes is the unstated (or underspecified) relation, ℜ, that pertains between the two major constituents. The nature of ℜ – the kinds of relations – has been the topic of considerable research during recent decades. While early studies focused almost exclusively on English, the last few years have seen a spate of work on other languages. Unfortunately, this work has been uncoordinated and each researcher entering the field has tended to devise their own classification, making it difficult to compare results and advance our understanding of the phenomenon. This is a pity, because such an understanding has the potential to provide insights into the nature of concept combination and the associative character of human thought. The purpose of this chapter is to present a well-documented, systematic classification of semantic relations that operates at multiple levels of granularity and is suitable for reuse across languages. Hatcher-Bourque is based on revisions of two earlier classifications, those of Anna Granville Hatcher and Yves Bourque, which operate at different levels of granularity. These are integrated into a single, coherent system, with automatic mapping from one level to the other. The classification is applied to a set of 3,650 binominals from 106 languages, and an analysis is presented of the frequency and distribution of semantic relations at both a highly abstract level and a more granular level. The Hatcher-Bourque classification, and an accompanying, Excel-based tool, the *Bourquifier*, are offered to the research community in order to encourage collaboration, and researchers are invited to participate in the Hatcher-Bourque Cake Challenge.

1 Introduction

1.1 Background

The unstated (or underspecified) semantic relation, ℜ, is a defining feature of binominals (see *Introduction*). Jackendoff (2016) provides a nice set of examples to show that the kind of semantic relation can be "hugely varied", even across binominals that share a common head, such as *cake*.

Note: This chapter has been made Open Access *in memoriam* my parents Harry Pepper (1926–1996) and Edna Pepper (1932–2022).

Open Access. © 2023 Steve Pepper, published by De Gruyter. This work is licensed under the Creative Commons Attribution-NonCommercial-NoDerivatives 4.0 International License.
https://doi.org/10.1515/9783110673494-010

> *chocolate cake* 'a cake made with chocolate in it'
> *birthday cake* 'a cake to be eaten as part of celebrating a birthday'
> *coffee cake* 'a cake made to be eaten along with coffee and the like'
> *marble cake* 'a cake that resembles marble'
> *layer cake* 'a cake formed in multiple layers'
> *cupcake* 'a little cake made in a cup'
> *urinal cake* 'a (nonedible) cake to be placed in a urinal'

The nature of ℜ has been a perennial topic of interest in the study of compounding that can be traced back to the Sanskrit grammarians. Modern treatment of the topic can be said to originate with Jespersen's (1942) discussion in Volume 6 of his *Modern English Grammar on Historical Principles*.[1] The year 1960 saw the publication of three seminal works by Marchand, Lees and Hatcher that inspired further work in a number of different directions. In the years that followed there were important contributions by Adams (1973), Downing (1977), Levi (1978), Warren (1978), Ryder (1994), Jackendoff (2009; 2010; 2016) and Schäfer (2018), all of which focused on English [ENG]. More recently the topic of semantic relations has been explored in other languages, including French [FRA] (Arnaud 2003; 2016; Bourque 2014), Nizaa [SGI] (Pepper 2010), Danish [DAN] (Szubert 2012), Norwegian [NOR] (Eiesland 2016) and Spanish [SPA] (Toquero 2018). The matter has also received considerable attention in computational and corpus linguistics (e.g. Vanderwende 1994; Moldovan et al. 2004; Girju et al. 2005; Ó Séaghdha 2008; Tratz & Hovy 2010; Nakov 2013; Schäfer 2018) and was the focus of an NAACL-HLT Workshop on Semantic Evaluations task on "the interpretation of noun compounds using paraphrasing verbs and prepositions" (Butnariu et al. 2009).

1.2 Towards a reusable classification

The point of departure for the present chapter is three observations regarding this previous work. *The first observation* is that opinions differ as to whether the set of semantic relations found in binominals is finite or infinite. Jespersen (1942: 143) asserted that "the number of possible logical relations between the two elements [of a noun-noun compound] is endless" and Downing (1977: 810) concluded that "the semantic relations that hold between the members of [novel] compounds cannot be characterized in terms of a finite list of 'appropriate compounding relationships'." However, most researchers have had enough faith in the useful-

---

[1] But see also Grimm (1826), Mätzner (1860), Bergsten (1911) and Carr (1939).

ness of a finite list that they have taken the trouble to develop one. The position taken in the present research accords with that of Tratz & Hovy (2010: 679), who contend that "the vast majority of noun compounds fits within a relatively small set of categories." Furthermore, it seems likely that, while the interpretation of novel compounds depends greatly on context, established compounds do so to a lesser degree and are more likely to exhibit a fixed set of basic relations.

The second observation is that among authors who have attempted to enumerate a list of relations, the number of relations varies considerably from four (in the case of Hatcher), to upwards of 40 or 50 (depending on whether or not subtypes are included). The position taken in the present paper is that the number of relations one identifies should be a function of the degree of granularity required by the investigation in question. It can therefore be anything the researcher desires, from one (as suggested by Bauer 1979) to unlimited (as opined by Jespersen). We further claim that any relation can be subdivided into more specific relations, if the need arises and – concomitantly – that any two arbitrary relations can be combined into a single, more general relation.

For some investigations, a small number of (high-level) relations will suffice; for others, a larger number of (low-level) relations is required. The advantage of a granular, low-level classification is that it is more concrete, and thus much easier to apply in practice; its disadvantage is that it results in a rather fragmentary picture from which it can be difficult to generalize. The advantage of a more abstract, high-level classification is that the generalizations are built into the scheme; its disadvantage is that the high level of abstraction makes it extremely hard to apply consistently.

This suggests that a classification scheme that operates at more than one level of granularity – with automatic mapping from lower to higher levels – may prove beneficial. Such a scheme, if based on sound principles, would enjoy both of the advantages outlined above, and suffer from neither of the disadvantages.

The third observation that is relevant here is that each researcher tends to construct their own scheme instead of reusing an existing one. That is the case in almost every one of the studies listed above, and one might legitimately ask why this should be so. Three possible reasons might be put forward. The first is simply that the material in question is notoriously slippery. Meaning only exists in our minds and is therefore hard to pin down. Getting inside someone else's head is not easy, and it is made more difficult by the fact that many systems are rather poorly documented. The second reason is that judgements regarding the nature of a semantic relation are subjective and dependent on the level of granularity one aspires to: some might regard a system of 12 relations (such as Levi's) as too vague, while others (Hatcher, no doubt) would find it too low-level (and too unsystematic). The third reason is that no system is perfect. It is easy to spot inconsistencies and errors in others' work, and when we encounter such errors, there is a tendency to think that we can do a better job ourselves.

Whatever the reasons may be, the practice of discarding the work of others and starting from scratch does not seem conducive to the advancement of science. The position taken in this paper is that a better approach is to build on the work of earlier researchers, to reuse existing schemes, testing and refining them as necessary, and working incrementally towards the goal of a robust, flexible and easily reusable system that has been tested against different kinds of data from a large range of languages. The Hatcher-Bourque classification presented here is such a system. It is hereby offered to the research community as a basis for further collaborative work, together with an Excel-based tool for the computer-assisted analysis of semantic relations, the *Bourquifier* (Pepper 2021).

1.3 A note on terminology

Before proceeding, it is worth spending time to understand the structure of a semantic relation and the terminology to be used in this chapter.

The **relation** ℜ that pertains between the two major **constituents** of a binominal lexeme, such as *honey bee*, is by definition **binary**. It involves two **participants**, *honey* and *bee*, each of which plays a particular **role** in the relation. We can characterize the relation here as one of PRODUCTION: a honey bee is a bee that *produces* honey; the bee plays the role of producer and the honey plays the role of product.

It is important to distinguish between the role of a participant in a particular relation and its **type**, the class to which it belongs and that reflects its essential being. A bee is primarily an insect, not a producer, and honey is a kind of sweet fluid rather than just a product. Roles vary depending on the relation in question, whereas types are constant: the bee in *beehive* is playing a quite different role from the bee in *honey bee*, but it is still a bee.

All binary relations are **bidirectional**, in the sense that if A is related to B, then B is perforce related to A. In a **symmetric** relation, such as that of COORDINATION, B is related to A *in the same way* as A is related to B (if A is coordinate with B, then B is coordinate with A). In such relations, the role is the same for both participants. In an **asymmetric** relation, such as that of PRODUCTION, B is related to A *in a different way* from how A is related to B, and there are two distinct roles.

When a relation is asymmetric, it can take two forms depending on how the relation is profiled: in *honey bee*, the constituent denoting the producer (*bee*) is the semantic **head** and the constituent denoting the product (*honey*) is the **modifier**. By contrast, in *beeswax*, the constituent denoting the product is the head and the constituent denoting the producer is the modifier. Because it is asymmetric, the PRODUCTION relation can be said to consist of two "**sub-relations**", which we might label "producer of" and "produced by". When both sub-relations are employed in binominal word-formation, the relation is said to be **reversible**, and the terms **basic** and **reversed** may be employed to distinguished between the two. Note that a relation may be asymmetric without necessarily being reversible.

In the following discussion, RELATIONS are shown in small caps and roles are underlined.

1.4 Structure of this chapter

This chapter is structured as follows: Following this introduction, §2 presents the low-level classification of 25 relations developed by Bourque (2014) that was chosen as the starting point for the present study; it also details the minor adjustments and extensions that were made to it, resulting in the Bourque29 component (29 refers to the number of relations) of the Hatcher-Bourque classification. §3 describes Hatcher's (1960) high-level classification of four relations and how it was extended by the addition of one more relation in order to cover appositional as well as non-appositional binominals, resulting in the Hatcher5 component of the Hatcher-Bourque classification.

§4 describes the two-tiered Hatcher-Bourque system that results from the integration of Bourque29 with Hatcher5, and how this system relates to Aristotle's three principles of remembering. §5 then presents the *Bourquifier* application and its use as a computer-assisted tool to expedite the analysis of semantic relations and ensure more consistent results.

§6 contains a statistical analysis, showing the frequency of various low- and high-level relations in a sample of 3,650 binominals from 106 languages, and §7 provides a conclusion and a challenge. Documentation for the complete Hatcher-Bourque classification is to be found in the appendix, in the form of detailed summaries of each relation and a one-page at-a-glance table.

2 Bourque's low-level classification

2.1 Description of Bourque25

Out of the dozens of classification schemes to be found in the literature, the one selected for the present study is the one developed by Yves Bourque in his 2014 dissertation *Toward a typology of semantic transparency: The case of French com-*

pounds (Bourque 2014). This choice was dictated by a number of considerations, in particular the quality of Bourque's documentation, which includes templates, linking material, examples and extensive discussion of overlaps between relations. A further reason was that the scheme avoids the Anglocentrism of many earlier studies, for example by providing examples in both English and French, employing descriptive labels (e.g. PURPOSE instead of Levi's FOR), and using the terms 'non-head' (or 'modifier') and 'head' instead of the word order dependent 'A' and 'B' of Jespersen and Hatcher, or 'N1' and 'N2' of Levi and Jackendoff. In addition, a study involving nearly 4,000 binominals (Pepper 2020) shows that this classification operates at a level of granularity that is both *manageable*, in terms of the number of relations (25), and *precise*, in terms of expressing the nature of the various relations.

Bourque's classification is furthermore based explicitly on a synthesis of 16 earlier classifications.[2] Whereas all but one of these are based on data from English, Bourque himself tested the system using a large database of French compounds, thus increasing the chance of cross-linguistic coverage.

From the 16 earlier classifications, Bourque synthesizes a set of "retained relations", 15 in all, shown in Table 1. Of these 15, ten are considered to be reversible and are indicated by [R].

Table 1: Bourque's (2014:170) retained relations.

COORDINATION	COMPOSITION[R]	TIME[R]
HYPERNYMY[R]	SOURCE[R]	TOPIC
SIMILARITY	PART[R]	FUNCTION
PRODUCTION[R]	LOCATION[R]	PURPOSE
CAUSE[R]	POSSESSION[R]	USE[R]

Each relation is introduced by a summary table such as that exemplified for PRODUCTION in Figure 1. For reversible relations like PRODUCTION, the summary table consists of two rows, one for each of the (directed) 'sub-relations'; these are labelled Basic and Reversed. Each row then contains a "structure template" in both English and French, examples (in the form of compounds, i.e. binominals of type **cmp** or **jxt**) from each language, and "linking material". For non-reversible relations the second row is empty.

---

[2] Those of Jespersen (1942), Hatcher (1960), Adams (1973), Levi (1978), Downing (1977), Warren (1978), Shoben (1991), Vanderwende (1994), Lauer (1995), Rosario and Hearst (2001), Arnaud (2003), Moldovan & al (2004), Girju & al (2005), Girju & al (2009), Séaghdha (2008), Jackendoff (2010).

The structure template consists of a test frame with slots for the head (H) and modifier (M), respectively. Populating these slots with the constituents of a binominal results in a paraphrase of the relation that helps the analyst judge whether that relation is appropriate to the binominal in question. Thus we see that the paraphrase of *honey bee* as "a bee that makes honey' (the Basic form of PRODUCTION) provides a satisfactory reading, whereas that of the Reversed form, "a bee that honey makes", does not. Conversely, *beeswax* is "a wax that bees make" and not "a wax that makes bees".

PRODUCTION			
Relation Type	Structure Template	Examples	Linking Material
Basic	an H that makes M	honey bee	makes, produces
	un T qui fait M	appareil photo	fait, produit
Reversed	an H that M makes	beeswax	
	un T que M fait	jazz manouche	

Figure 1: Bourque's template for PRODUCTION.

The linking material "is meant to draw parallels between the retained relation and those proposed elsewhere in the literature and may include such items as verbs (e.g. *have*, *cause*, *make*, etc.), prepositions (e.g. *for*, *from*, *of*, etc.), and even nouns (e.g. *kind*, *type*)" (Bourque 2014: 178).

In addition to the summary table, each relation is accompanied by a lengthy discussion that can run to several pages. This covers the precise nature of the relation, the ways in which it has been treated by earlier researchers, overlaps with other relations, and any other issues. The complete classification is summarized in Table 2.

Bourque's system of 15 relations (of which 10 are reversible, for a total of 25 "sub-relations") was sufficient to cater for the varied sample of nearly 4,000 binominals that will be described in §5. However, a few infelicities were discovered in the process, and when it came time to map the system to that of Hatcher, certain extensions were deemed necessary. The following section (§2.2) describes the non-substantive changes that were made to the original system, and §2.3 describes the substantive extensions that resulted in the Bourque29 component of the Hatcher-Bourque classification.

2.2 Non-substantive changes to Bourque

The non-substantive changes to Bourque's classification involved renaming some relations, rewording some templates, and changing some examples. They are presented in the following sections. (Refer to Table 2 for the original formulations and Table 7, in the Appendix, for the revised version.)

Table 2: The original Bourque25 classification.

Label	Type	Template	Linking material	Example
HYPERNYMY	Basic	an H of kind M	kind of, type of	oak tree
	Rev.	an H that M is a kind of		bear cub
COORDINATION		a C is an H and an M	is also, is both / and	boy king
SIMILARITY		an H that is similar to M	similar to, like	ant lion
FUNCTION		an H that serves as M	functions, serves as	buffer state
POSSESSION	Basic	an H that possesses M	possess (have / of)	career girl
	Rev.	an H that M possesses		family estate
PART	Basic	an H that is part of M	part of (have / of)	table leg
	Rev.	an H that M is part of		wheelchair
LOCATION	Basic	an H located at/near/in M	at, near, in, etc.	window seat
	Rev.	an H that M is located at/near/in		bedroom
COMPOSITION	Basic	an H made of M	composed/ made of	sugar cube
	Rev.	an H that M is made of		sheet metal
SOURCE	Basic	an H (made) from M	(made) from	cane sugar
	Rev.	an H that M is (made) from		sugar cane
CAUSE	Basic	an H that causes M	causes	sunburn
	Rev.	an H that M causes		motion sickness
PRODUCTION	Basic	an H that makes M	makes, produces	honey bee
	Rev.	an H that M makes		beeswax
TOPIC		an H about M	about	history conference
TIME	Basic	an H that occurs at/during M	during, at, in, before, etc.	summer job
	Rev.	an H at/during which M occurs		golf season
USE	Basic	an H that uses M	use / with, by	steamboat
	Rev.	an H that M uses		hand brake
PURPOSE AND PROPER FUNCTION		an H intended for M	for	animal doctor

Changes to names of relations

Previous researchers have employed a variety of strategies for naming relations. Levi used a mixture of verbs (BE, HAVE, MAKE, CAUSE, USE) and prepositions (IN, FOR, FROM, ABOUT); Warren preferred to use role pairings (SOURCE-RESULT, WHOLE-PART, PART-WHOLE, SIZE-WHOLE, GOAL-OBJ, PLACE-OBJ, TIME-OBJ, ACTIVITY-ACTOR), but had recourse to other means for symmetric and non-reversible relations (COPULA, RESEMBLANCE, PURPOSE); Jackendoff's "basic functions" employ a verb-based naming system for the most part, but with the odd adjective, role or abbreviation thrown in (CLASSIFY, BE, BE AT/IN/ON, MADE FROM, CAUSE, MAKE, SERVES AS, HAVE, PROTECT (FROM), but also SIMILAR, KIND, PART, COMP).

Bourque's system is more consistent, but not entirely so. As Table 1 shows, all 15 relations are named by nouns. Of these, six are nominalizations of the verb or adjective typically used to express the relation, e.g. PRODUCTION < *produce* (the others are COORDINATION, COMPOSITION, POSSESSION, LOCATION and SIMILARITY). HYPERNYMY also denotes a relation, but one that is lexical rather than conceptual. PART, CAUSE, SOURCE, TIME and TOPIC, on the other hand, all denote one of the roles in the relation, while FUNCTION, USE and PURPOSE[3] can denote either a role or a relation.

For the Hatcher-Bourque classification, it was considered desirable that names should denote relations rather than roles or linguistic means of expression, preferably using nominalizations of relevant verbs. Where this was not possible, a role-pair was preferred to a single role, but the latter was considered acceptable for symmetric and non-reversible relations. While it was not possible to achieve complete consistency, the following improvements were made:

- HYPERNYMY (lexical relation) > TAXONOMY (conceptual relation)
- PART (role) > PARTONOMY (relation)
- CAUSE (role) > CAUSATION (relation)
- TIME (role) > TEMPORALITY (relation)
- SOURCE (role) > SOURCE-RESULT (relation)
- USE (conversion) > USAGE (nominalization)

---

[3] Bourque actually uses the name PURPOSE AND PROPER FUNCTION for this relation, but since his system already includes a relation called FUNCTION the name has been shortened. Considerations relating to having been designed to (or supposed to) perform a certain function (Millikan 1984: 17, cited in Jackendoff 2016: 23) are thus relegated to the description of the relation instead of its name.

The names TOPIC, FUNCTION and PURPOSE, on the other hand, were retained. Since these appear to be non-reversible, this is not a major issue, especially since the latter two can denote relations as well as roles.

Changes to templates

Changes made to Bourque's templates were motivated by the desire for greater transparency and/or consistency. The template for Reversed HYPERNYMY is actually incorrect, generating "a bear cub is a cub that bear is a kind of" for Bourque's example *bear cub*. A bear is a kind of animal, and not a kind of (bear) cub. One way to correct this error would be to adapt Jackendoff's "an N_2 that is a kind of N_1" (i.e. "an H that is a kind of M"), but a simpler solution was to replace both HYPERNYMY templates with the more transparent "(an) M is a kind of H" and "(an) H is a kind of M". Thus, an oak is a kind of tree (whereas a tree is not a kind of oak), and a cub is a kind of bear (whereas a bear is not a kind of cub).

In addition, Bourque's templates for COMPOSITION, PRODUCTION and SOURCE (all of which employ the verb 'make') were modified to use the verbs 'compose' and 'produce' and the noun 'source', respectively, thereby tying the templates more closely to the name of the relation. For example, the template for Basic PRODUCTION (e.g. *honey bee*) was changed from "an H that makes M" to "an H that produces M", and that for Basic COMPOSITION (e.g. *sugar cube*) was changed from "an H made of M" to "an H composed of M".

Changes to examples

Most of the changes to Bourque's examples were motivated by pedagogical and, in a couple of cases, aesthetic considerations. Only one of his 25 examples is actually erroneous: the use of *sunburn* to exemplify Basic CAUSE, paraphrased as "an H that causes M". It is, of course, the sun (M) that causes the burn (H), not the other way round, so this example properly belongs under Reversed CAUSE, with the paraphrase "(a) burn that (a) sun causes". A better example for Basic CAUSE is *tear gas:* "(a) gas that causes (a) tear".

It is arguable that the example provided by Bourque for SIMILARITY is not incorrect, but it is certainly suboptimal. An *ant lion* (or antlion) is not a lion that is similar to an ant, it is a kind of insect, albeit not exactly an ant. The name appears to be a left-headed calque from Latin *formicaleo*, which means that the paraphrase "an ant that is similar to a lion" does in fact work. However, as a highly exceptional left-headed compound it is unsuitable in an English context for pedagogical reasons (it works fine as Fr. *fourmi-lion*, which may be how Bourque got to choose it as his example). It is replaced by *kidney bean* (a bean shaped like a kidney), an example taken from Hatcher (1960).

Conservation of space is the main consideration for choosing *history book* instead of *history conference* for TOPIC, and *sunburn* instead of *motion sickness* for Reversed CAUSE; real estate is at a premium not only on paper, but also in the *Bourquifier* (see §4.2).

Finally, a number of changes were motivated by the desire to use what David-Antoine Williams[4] has dubbed "boathouse words" wherever possible, for pedagogical reasons. These are pairs of words that have the pleasing property of consisting of the same two constituents in reverse order, like Bourque's examples for SOURCE, *cane sugar* and *sugar cane*. For COMPOSITION Bourque already has *sugar cube*, which is complemented nicely by *cube sugar*. In addition, *song bird* and *bird song* work well for PRODUCTION, as do *oil lamp* and *lamp oil* for USE, and *car motor* and *motor car* for PART. Finding a suitable boathouse pair for LOCATION is more difficult (the closest I have come is *house music* and *music hall*), and candidates are still being sought for POSSESSION, TIME, CAUSE and DIRECTION.

2.3 Substantive changes to Bourque's classification

The more extensive changes to Bourque25 involved the addition of codes for relations, the provision of names for roles, the enforcement of consistency when distinguishing between Basic and Reversed forms, and the addition of two new relations. These changes are described and justified in the following sections.

Addition of codes

In order to represent the data in a database and perform the quantitative study described in §5, unique identifiers were needed for each relation. Bourque will have encountered the same need, but he did not publish his codes, so new ones were created. These take the form of three- or four-letter mnemonic codes for Basic relations, and the same codes suffixed with -R for reversed relations, thus POSS for Basic POSSESSION, POSS-R for Reversed POSSESSION, etc. These codes are included in the documentation in the Appendix, in order to promote interoperability and to save other users the trouble of devising their own codes.

---

4 https://thelifeofwords.uwaterloo.ca/boathouse-words/ (accessed 2021-02-10).

Addition of explicit roles

A more substantive change is the introduction of explicit names for the roles played by the participants in each relation, as described in §1.2. Thus, the PRODUCTION relation is supplied with the roles product and producer, the POSSESSION relation with the roles possessor and possessum, etc. Every asymmetric relation (reversible or not) involves two distinct roles, as here. The two symmetric relations, on the other hand, each involve a single role which is played by both participants in the relation. For COORDINATION that role is named coordinand, and for SIMILARITY it is named likeness.

These names serve as an aid in conceptualizing asymmetric relations, in understanding the difference between a Basic and its corresponding Reversed relation, and in describing and communicating about individual relations. If one adopts the convention of using the role played by the modifier to characterize a (directed) 'sub-relation', every one of the 29 sub-relations of the revised Bourque29 system can be referred to simply as the 'X relation'. Thus, 'possessor relation' and 'possessum relation' can be used instead of the unwieldy terms Basic POSSESSION relation and Reversed POSSESSION relation for *family estate* and *career girl*, respectively. The reason why this works is because it proved possible to ensure that every role was unique – except for the use of entity as one of the roles in the TOPIC, FUNCTION and PURPOSE relations. Since these relations are non-reversible, there will seldom be a collision between multiple, homonymous *-entity relations.[5]

Alignment of Basic and Reversed relations

Asymmetric relations, as already noted, can take two forms, which work in opposite directions to one another (and incidentally are often paraphrased using active and passive sentences, respectively). As we have seen, Bourque labels these two forms Basic and Reversed, respectively, but he does not provide any rationale for choosing one form rather than the other to designate as Basic. It seems that the choice was essentially arbitrary. While this clearly did not matter to Bourque for the purpose of his investigation, such arbitrariness is unnecessary, leads to a less logically consistent result, and may prove confusing.

---

5 If at some point Reversed forms of TOPIC, FUNCTION and PURPOSE are found, the classification (including the relevant role names) will have to be revised.

Consider the relations PART, LOCATION and COMPOSITION in Table 2. All of these are in some sense specializations of a more general relation CONTAINMENT. If we now focus on the three Reversed examples of these relations (*wheelchair*, *bedroom* and *sheet metal*), we see that a part (*wheel*) is in some sense "contained in" its whole (*chair*), that a thing located (*bed*) is "contained in" its location (*room*), and that a material (*metal*) is "contained in" the object of which it is made (*sheet*). The wheel, the bed and the metal are thus all "containees" (in a very general sense), whereas the chair, the room and the sheet are all "containers". However, while wheel and bed are denoted by modifiers, metal is denoted by the head constituent. If we now consider the POSSESSION relation (exemplified by *family estate*), in which the possessor somehow "contains" the thing possessed, we see that the containee *estate*, like *metal* (but unlike *wheel* and *chair*), is denoted by the head constituent.

This inconsistency can be removed by simply inverting Bourque's POSSESSION and COMPOSITION relations such that the containees are denoted by the modifier instead of the head. Thus, the original pair of POSSESSION (sub-)relations *(before)* becomes the revised pair of (sub-)relations *(after)*.

before:
POSSESSION   Basic   an H that possesses M   possess   *career girl*
             Rev.   an H that M possesses   (have / of)   *family estate*
after:
POSSESSION   Basic   an H that M possesses   possess   *family estate*
             Rev.   an H that possesses M   (have / of)   *career girl*

The same applies to COMPOSITION (and TAXONOMY) where Basic and Reversed are likewise inverted.

Similar considerations apply to Bourque's SOURCE and USE, which are incompatible with CAUSE and PRODUCTION. Focusing again on the Reversed relations, we see that in the latter two relations, the participant that constitutes the point of origin (the motion in *motion sickness* and the bee in *beeswax*) is expressed by the modifier, whereas in the SOURCE and USE examples, the point of origin (the cane of *sugar cane* and the brake in *hand brake*) is expressed by the head. In the revised Bourque classification, the sub-relations of SOURCE and USE are therefore also inverted.

For consistency with other containment-related relations, forms such as *history book* are deemed to embody the Reversed form of the TOPIC relation rather than the (unattested) Basic form. Of the two paraphrases available for the CONTAINMENT relation, the Reversed form is clearly the most felicitous: cf. "a book that contains history" vs. the Basic form "*a book that is contained in (a) history".

The attested forms of the other non-reversible relations, PURPOSE and FUNCTION, embody the Basic forms of the relation.

Addition of new relations

Although Bourque's set of 15 relations was sufficient to cater for the 3,650 binominals examined for the study on which this work is based, two more relations were added for the sake of completeness, and to facilitate the integration with Hatcher's system (described below). These were CONTAINMENT and DIRECTION.

The first of these was prompted by consideration of the Hawaiian binominal *pahu meli* [box honey] BEEHIVE. Is a beehive "a box that honey is part of" (Bourque's Reversed PART) or "a box that honey is located at/near/in" (his Reversed LOCATION)? Of course, location is involved, and one could also (at a pinch) say that honey is part of the beehive, but it would be more felicitous to say that the box *contains* honey. Now, although CONTAINMENT is not one of Bourque's relations, he does not ignore the matter. He discusses it in depth in the context of the overlap between PART and LOCATION, using the example of *toolbox*. His discussion is quoted here at some length in order to convey the detail of his discussions in general:

> Another issue to consider is that some compounds might be analysed as either PART or LOCATION. This dual analysis is related to the fact that LOCATION may subsume PART: if something is a part of something else, then it is located at/on/in that thing (cf. Baron & Herslund 2001). One possible solution is to reserve location for only those compounds that actually involve a locative noun, as does Adams (1973). The problem, of course, is that one must treat combinations such as *toolbox* or *treehouse* using some other relation, as they do not, in the strictest sense, involve places. The key distinction that will be used here is one that views the PART relation as a reference to an integral component of the whole, without which it would either be incomplete, defective, or non-functional. Thus, a negation test may be used to determine whether the modifier denotes an essential part of the compound. The formulation in (105) below shows how such a test might apply to compounds in which the head denotes the whole (cf. 104 above):
>
> (105) a. a C without an M is still a C
> b. un C sans M est toujours un C
>
> A positive response to the above sentence would indicate that the modifying noun is not an essential component of the object denoted by the compound, but instead a distinguishing feature. Thus, a toolbox without tools is still a toolbox, which indicates that tools is connected to box via **some other relationship (i.e. container-contained)**. This result is the same for the French *boîte à outils* (i.e. *une boîte à outils sans outils est toujours une boîte à outils*). When applied to compounds that denote a part-whole association, the test produces defective or incomplete readings. (pp. 196–197, emphasis added)

The case of "honey box" (*beehive*) is parallel to *toolbox*: a beehive without honey is indubitably still a beehive. The distinction Bourque makes is useful, but his conclusion to treat *toolbox* (and thus also "honey box") as (mere) location seems inadequate. It seems better to bite the bullet and add the relation CONTAINMENT (which even Bourque recognizes as "some other relationship") to his system, on the grounds that the ability to perceive containment is a fundamental part of our cognitive endowment. The relation is reversible and may be exemplified, following Hatcher (1960: 364), by *orange seed* and *seed orange*.

The other addition made to Bourque's set of relations was motivated by one of Jespersen's examples: *sun worship*. Strictly speaking this is not a binominal since *worship* denotes an action, not a thing. However, the scope of Bourque's classification is noun-noun compounds in general and therefore it should be able to accommodate *sun worship*. It turns out that none of Bourque's relations are appropriate. Clearly the notion of the sun as some kind of goal is involved, so one might think that Bourque's SOURCE would do the job, but no amount of tweaking of either the Basic or the Reversed template produces a paraphrase that is acceptable for both *sun worship* and *cane sugar*. This seems to be because goal as a complement of source is not compatible with result. It seems that a new relation is unavoidable, but what to call it, and how to make it sufficiently distinct from SOURCE? The answer is provided by Hatcher, who includes *sun worship* in her category A←B (to be discussed below), pointing out that "the sun is that toward which the worship is *directed*" (see Figure 2; emphasis added). Now, as we have seen, it is frequently the case that the verb used to express the paraphrase can serve in nominalized form as the name of the relation itself (recall 'possess' > POSSESSION). The solution to the problem of how to name the new relation is thus given: 'direct' > DIRECTION, understood as an asymmetric relation which relates a starting point or origin and an endpoint or goal, and exemplified by *sun worship* and *sales target*, respectively.

Adding such a relation to Bourque's scheme can be justified on two grounds (over and above the desire to accommodate *sun worship*): firstly, it is very general, and secondly, the ability to conceptualize direction is an important part of the human cognitive endowment. Further research may show that DIRECTION is rarely encountered in binominals, but it may turn out to be more important when synthetic compounds and other complex nominals containing an action-root are considered (as in *sun worship*).

The classification resulting from the modifications to Bourque's system described in the preceding sections consists of 17 relations, two of them symmetric, and three non-reversible, for a total of 29 (directed) 'sub-relations', hence the name "Bourque29". Documentation for each of these is provided in the Appendix, together with an at-a-glance summary. In the following section we turn to the high-level classification developed by Anna Granville Hatcher to which Bourque29 will be mapped in §4.

3 Hatcher's high-level classification

3.1 The critique of Jespersen

Hatcher presents her (1960) four-way classification of non-appositional compounds in the form of a critique of Jespersen's (1942) attempt to classify semantic relations. Jespersen concedes that his analysis is incomplete and that there are many compounds which "do not fit in anywhere", but he claims that his failure is simply due to the inherent unclassifiability of his material: "the number of possible logical relations between the two elements is endless" (p. 138); "the analysis of the possible sense-relations can never be exhaustive" (p. 143).

But, says Hatcher,

> it all too often happens that scholars in linguistics proclaim a given problem to be insoluble, when they themselves have not worked out the categories necessary for its solution; we should, then, examine the outline offered by Jespersen to see if some of the difficulty he encountered may not be explained by his method of classification. For example, was his set of categories constructed with logical rigor: and, before surrendering to the "difficult" types that he mentions, had he been able, at least, to account for all the "easy" compounds, subdividing these as carefully as his patience and his talent permitted? The subdivision of the obvious may lead to greater understanding of the less obvious, if one is guided by logically consistent criteria. (p. 356)

Thereupon, Hatcher sets about dissecting and reordering Jespersen's system. She starts by listing seven of Jespersen's types, omitting one of the original eight (Similarity) on the grounds that it more properly belongs to "apposition", which she wants to keep separate. Examining each of these in turn, Hatcher notes a lack of careful subdivisions, an absence of any principle of symmetry, and the mixing of two basic criteria, Reference and Relation. Her rearrangement of Jespersen's scheme is depicted in Figure 2.

Hatcher chooses to avoid Reference and to base her new scheme exclusively on Relation, so she starts by separating the first three of Jespersen's types **1–3** (Subject/Object, Place and Time) – all of which are either based on reference or mixed – from types **4–7** (Purpose, Means, Characterizing Feature and Material), all of which are relational. The former are set to one side, and to the latter she adds two relational types found in Mätzner (1860) but absent in Jespersen (α *broomstick* and β *castor oil*). She then proceeds to reorganize these six relational types into four abstract classes:

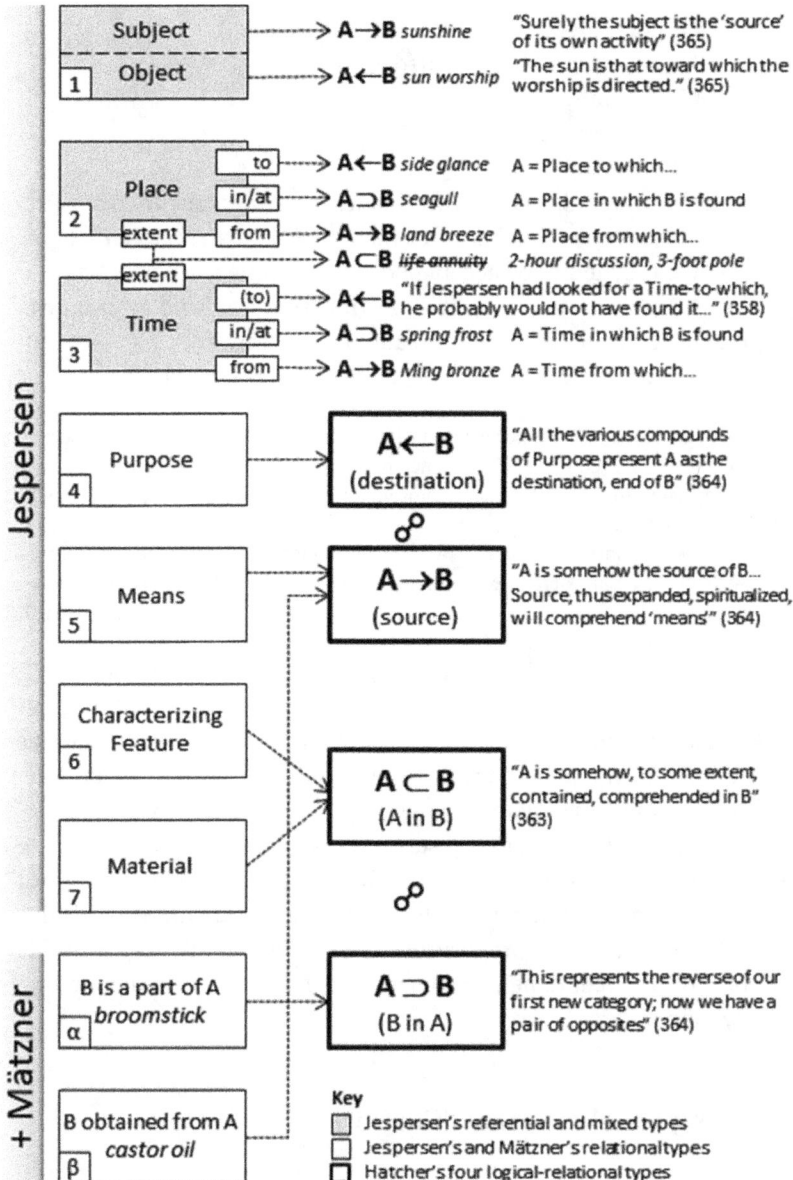

Figure 2: Hatcher's reworking of Jespersen's classification.

(a) A ⊂ B   "A is contained in B" (notated Ⓐ by Hatcher)
(b) A ⊃ B   "B is contained in A" (notated Ⓑ by Hatcher)
(c) A→B   "A is the source of B"
(d) A←B   "A is the destination of B"

Having reduced the six relational categories of Jespersen/Mätzner to two pairs of mutually exclusive concepts, Hatcher turns her attention to the referential types, in order to see how they might be accommodated in her new scheme. She starts with (2) Place, (3) Time and their subdivisions (*to*, *in/at*, *from* and *extent*), which map neatly into her scheme, as (d), (b), (c) and (a), respectively.

Finally, the two verbal types (**1**) Subject and (**2**) Object are "easy":

> *Sunshine* and *sun worship*, these perfect opposites, fall under A→B and A←B, respectively. Surely the subject is the "source" of its own activity (in putting *sunshine* under A→B, we are merely adding Agent to Agency); and in *sun-worship* (A←B), the sun is that toward which the worship is directed.
>
> Thus we see that both the referential and the relational types of Matzner-Jespersen can be included in our two pairs of relational criteria: the static Ⓐ and Ⓑ, and the dynamic A→B and A←B. (p. 365)

Hatcher concludes this part of her analysis by pointing out that the scheme she has developed has two advantages over the one she has just "torn to pieces". Firstly, it is logically conceived, and therefore neater and more pleasing aesthetically; and secondly, it is far more comprehensive, and thus may "be able to account for all possibilities of determinative, non-appositional compounding in the English language," which she suggests are surely not "endless" (p. 365–366). At the same time she expresses the hope that her work represents not a "result", but rather a beginning, and that it will offer "a more spacious framework" within which research dedicated to the proposition that "all compounds are endowed by their creators with the right to belong somewhere" may proceed more profitably and hopefully than before.

3.2 Extending Hatcher's classification

Hatcher's work is often cited, but usually dismissed, often on less than scientific grounds. For example, Søgaard (2005: 320) writes:

> such an account is by definition both arbitrary (Bauer 1978; van Santen 1979) and incomplete because of the infinite set of compounding relationships. For illustration, try to place a compound such as *car thief* in [Hatcher's] four-way typology. Is a car thief a 'car in a thief', a 'thief in a car', a 'thief as the goal of a car' or a 'thief as the source of a car'?

Unfortunately for Søgaard the last two paraphrases are incorrect: He has muddled up the order of A and B. The head of the construction (B) is *thief*, not *car*, so these two paraphrases should read: a '*car* as the goal of a *thief*' and a '*car* as the source of the *thief*'. With the correct paraphrase, it is obvious that the car is indeed the goal of the thief (i.e. A←B). Søgaard's objection must therefore be rejected.

One researcher who has taken Hatcher seriously is Arnaud (2003; 2016). Arnaud's work on categorizing the modification relations in French subordinative NN_N compounds is full of interesting observations, examples and discussion. However, in the present context it is noteworthy for the fact that Arnaud first develops his own highly granular classification, and then attempts to map it onto Hatcher's four-way scheme (which Noailly 1990, also working on French compounds, had arrived at independently).

Arnaud's classification is based on a database of 949 French binominals of type **cmp** and **jxt,** which he dubs "les composés timbre-poste" (postage stamp compounds). As none of the then-existing taxonomies of semantic relations seemed satisfactory, he decided to start from the data up, applying the principles of cognitive linguistics, "in particular the idea that relations are emergent phenomena which gain psychological existence" (2016: 71). The analysis resulted in a classification with 58 categories, ranging from the highly abstract (e.g. "Non-head is the goal of Head') to the very precise (such as the subtype of the LOCATION relation "Non-head is a secondary activity taking place in Head").

Arnaud now proceeds to map his set of 58 empirically derived (low-level) relations to Noailly and Hatcher's set of four logically derived (high-level) relations. For the most part, this is plain sailing:

> In most cases, the fine-grained categories were easy to group under these [high-level relations]. For example, the description in (18) was classified as an instance of (19).

(18) It is against the effects of Non-head that Head is made/conceived/set up
ex.: *minimum vieillesse* (lit. 'minimum old-age', i.e. basic old-age benefits)

(19) NON-HEAD ← HEAD
Abstract relation (19) represents the fact that in (18) the denotatum of N_2 is, so to say, aimed at that of N_1 (p. 81).[6]

---

6 Arnaud's 'non-head' and 'head' correspond to Hatcher's A and B. The high-level relation in his (19) is therefore equivalent to her A←B. It can be useful to think that A stands for Attribute (= modifier, non-head) and B for Base (= head).

Arnaud's bottom-up deduction thus melds neatly with Hatcher's top-down induction. Or at least, it almost does. Arnaud experienced difficulties with 12 of his 58 low-level categories that did not map straightforwardly to Hatcher's four, and he felt obliged to extended Hatcher's system with four more high-level relations: ANALOG, BE, HEAD SYMB NON-HEAD and NON-HEAD SYMB HEAD.

The frequencies of the four high-level categories are shown in Table 3. Arnaud himself concedes that "[the four new] categories are marginal compared with the initial four," but he believes they "show that Noailly erred on the side of abstraction (and Hatcher, too, as equivalent English compounds are easily found)" (p. 81).

Table 3: Frequencies of high-level relations in Arnaud (2016).

Relation	Equiv.	Freq.	%
NON-HEAD ← HEAD	A←B	428	38.1
((NON-HEAD) HEAD)	A ⊂ B	295	26.3
NON-HEAD → HEAD	A→B	159	14.2
(NON-HEAD (HEAD))	A ⊃ B	126	11.2
ANALOG	–	62	5.5
HEAD SYMB NON-HEAD	–	24	2.1
BE	–	23	2.0
NON-HEAD SYMB HEAD	–	5	0.4

Pepper (2020) examines each of the 12 low-level relations that seemed to Arnaud to justify the creation of his four new high-level relations and shows that all but one of them can in fact be accommodated by Hatcher's four-way system. For example, the first of Arnaud's problematic forms, *régime jockey*, denotes a diet that is typical of jockeys. But if A ('jockey') typifies (or characterizes) B ('diet'), then it is a *characterizing feature* of B and therefore belongs, as Figure 2 shows, under Hatcher's A⊂B, "A is somehow, to some extent, contained, comprehended in B". Thus it turns out, in other words, that Hatcher's system is broad enough to cater for eleven of the twelve low-level relations that prompted Arnaud to add four new high-level categories.

The single exception, one of four subtypes of ANALOG, is exemplified by the form *brasse papillon* [breast_stroke butterfly] 'butterfly stroke', which falls under Arnaud's low-level category "Non-head names analogically a perceptual characteristic of Head". Here there can be no doubt that some kind of analogy is at work. But *brasse papillon* is not a non-appositional compound in Hatcher's terms and therefore falls outside the scope of her 1960 paper.

If we want to extend Hatcher's scheme to cover appositional compounds, then we do indeed need a new high-level relation. However, ANALOGY may not be the best term for that relation. Hatcher's logically defined pair of reversible relations are both based on Contiguity, which is one of Aristotle's "three principles of remembering", the others being Similarity and Contrast. In Pepper (2020) I suggest that the relation underlying the types of appositional compound discussed by Hatcher herself in an earlier paper (Hatcher 1952), i.e. species-genus and cross-classification – as well as Arnaud's *brasse papillon* (and incidentally also coordinative compounds) – is Similarity. This is at about the right level of generality or abstraction as Hatcher's original two pairs. So her four-way system can be extended to a five-way system consisting of two pairs of asymmetric relations (which Hatcher referred to as 'static' and 'dynamic') that account for non-appositional compounds, and a fifth, symmetric relation that accounts for appositional compounds.

The extended system (Hatcher5) is summarized in Table 4. Following Bourque, Hatcher's A and B are replaced with M and H, and machine-readable codes (e.g. *HinM*) have been added as alternatives to notations such as M⊃H or Ⓑ. Furthermore, Hatcher's "static" and "dynamic" have been tentatively recast as CONTAINMENT and DIRECTION, respectively.

Table 4: Revised high-level classification (Hatcher5).

Contiguity-based		
CONTAINMENT ("static")		
M ⊃ H	*HinM*	"H is contained in M" (*orange seed*)
M ⊂ H	*MinH*	"M is contained in H" (*seed orange*)
DIRECTION ("dynamic")		
M ← H	*HtoM*	"M is the destination of H" (*sugar cane*)
M → H	*MtoH*	"M is the source of H" (*cane sugar*)
Similarity-based		
SIMILARITY		
M ≅ H	*MisH*	"H is similar or identical to M"

4 The Hatcher-Bourque classification

4.1 Description

Mapping the revised Bourque classification to the revised Hatcher system was quite straightforward. Three of the 17 relations are based on similarity in one way or another and thus map to the new relation:

- TAXONOMY equates to what Hatcher (1952) terms the "species-genus" type (e.g. *pumice stone*);
- COORDINATION and SIMILARITY correspond to two subtypes of her "cross-classification" type (exemplified by *fuel oil* and *butterfly table*).

The remaining 14 relations map neatly to Hatcher's original two pairs of relations as follows:
- CONTAINMENT, POSSESSION, PARTONOMY, LOCATION, TEMPORALITY, COMPOSITION and TOPIC are subtypes of her "static" relations; Basic forms map consistently to *HinM* ("B is contained in A") and Reversed forms to *MinH* ("A is contained in B")
- DIRECTION, SOURCE-RESULT, CAUSATION, PRODUCTION, USAGE, FUNCTION and PURPOSE are subtypes of her "dynamic" relations; Basic forms map consistently to *HtoM* ("B is the source of A") and Reversed forms to *MtoH* ("A is the source of B").

As Figure 3 shows, the Hatcher-Bourque classification operates at two main levels of granularity, labelled Bourque29 and Hatcher5, respectively. Bourque29 consists of the 17 rather granular, low-level relations, indicated by the codes in the five boxes at the bottom of the diagram. Of these, 12 are reversible, giving a total of 29 (24+5) low-level (directed) 'sub-relations' (hence, Bourque29). The low-level relations map to the three schematic, high-level relations of Hatcher5, labelled SIMILARITY, CONTAINMENT and DIRECTION. Of these, the latter two are reversible, for a total of five high-level (directed) 'sub-relations' (hence Hatcher5).

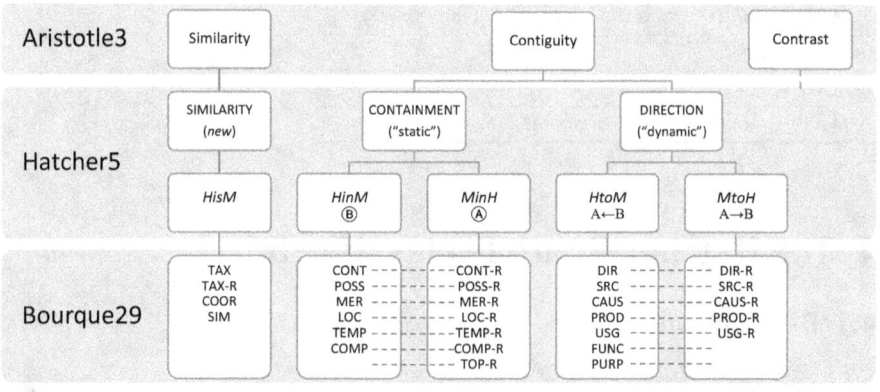

Figure 3: The Hatcher-Bourque classification as a hierarchy.

The relations of CONTAINMENT and DIRECTION are both based on Contiguity, one of Aristotle's three principles of memory, while Similarity constitutes another of those principles (Koch 2001: 1143). The third principle, Contrast, appears to play only a very minor role in binominal word-formation and has not yet been investigated in detail. It is therefore not part of this initial version of Hatcher-Bourque. However, examples do exist, for example Mandarin 东西 *dōng.xī* [east.west] 'thing' (Ceccagno & Scalise 2006: 238). This justifies including a placeholder in Figure 3.

The complete classification is documented in the Appendix in the form of descriptions of each individual low-level relation and an at-a-glance summary table (Table 7).

4.2 The Bourquifier: A piece of cake

Classifying large numbers of binominals can be a daunting and error-prone task, even with a well-documented classification that includes test frames and examples. In order to simplify the task and reduce the risk of errors, an Excel application called the *Bourquifier* has been created (Pepper 2021). This tool is designed to assist the analyst, not to replace her. The way it works is by the analyst typing the head and modifier (and optionally the binominal itself) into the relevant cells, upon which all 29 templates are automatically populated. These can then be scanned in a matter of seconds to find the most appropriate relation.

The interface of the *Bourquifier* (Figure 4) shows the 17 low-level relations of Bourque29 listed under the heading *Relation*, and the roles associated with each of them in the adjoining column. (Note that for the two symmetric relations, COORDINATION and SIMILARITY, the two roles are the same.) These relations are grouped according to the three high-level relations of Hatcher5: SIMILARITY, CONTAINMENT and DIRECTION.

To the right of the column headed *Roles* the interface is divided into two sections, for Basic and Reversed forms of the relation, respectively. Each section consists of four columns: one for the B29 code (e.g. TAX-R), one for the corresponding H5 code (e.g. *MisH*), one for the template (e.g. "(an) M is a kind of H") and one for the example (e.g. *oak tree*). For symmetric and non-reversible relations, one section is blank.

Figure 5 shows how the *Bourquifier* is used to analyse a specific example, here *sunburn*, which it may be recalled from §2.2 was erroneously chosen by Bourque to exemplify his Basic CAUSE relation (see Table 2). The populated templates in the *Bourquifier* make it very clear that *sunburn* actually belongs under the Reversed

Bourquifier 4 (Hatcher-Bourque 29/5/v2)				Binominal (B) B		Modifier (M) M	Head (H) H			Relation ANY
H3	Relation	Roles	B29	H5	Basic template	Example	B29	H5	Reversed template	Example
SIMILARITY	TAXONOMY	SUPERTIPE SUBTYPE	TAX	HisM	(an) H is a kind of M	bear cub	TAX-R	HisM	(an) M is a kind of H	oak tree
	COORDINATION	COORDINATE COORDINATE	COOR		(an) H that is also (an) M	boy king			(symmetric)	
	SIMILARITY	LIKENESS LIKENESS	SIM		(an) H that is similar to (an) M	kidney bean				
CONTAINMENT	CONTAINMENT	CONTAINER CONTENTS	CONT	HisM	(an) H that is contained in (an) M	orange seed	CONT-R	HisM	(an) H that contains (an) M	seed orange
	POSSESSION	POSSESSOR POSSESSUM	POSS		(an) H that is possessed by (an) M	family estate	POSS-R		(an) H that possesses (an) M	career girl
	PARTONOMY	WHOLE PART	PART		(an) H that is part of (an) M	car motor	PART-R		(an) H that (an) M is part of	motor car
	LOCATION	LOCATION LOCATED	LOC		(an) H located at/near/in (an) M	house music	LOC-R		(an) H that (an) M is located at/near/in	music hall
	TEMPORALITY	TIME ACTIVITY	TEMP		(an) H that occurs at/during (an) M	summer job	TEMP-R		(an) H at/during which (an) M occurs	golf season
	COMPOSITION	COMPOSITE MATERIAL	COMP		(an) H that (an) M is composed of	cube sugar	COMP-R		(an) H that is composed of M	sugar cube
	TOPIC	ENTITY TOPIC			(non-reversible)		TOP-R		(an) H that is about (an) M	history book
DIRECTION	DIRECTION	GOAL ORIGIN	DIR		(an) H whose goal is (an) M	sun worship	DIR-R		(an) H that is the goal of (an) M	sales target
	SOURCE-RESULT	RESULT SOURCE	SRC		(an) H that is a source of (an) M	sugar cane	SRC-R		(an) H whose source is (an) M	cane sugar
	CAUSATION	EFFECT CAUSE	CAUS		(an) H that causes (an) M	tear gas	CAUS-R		(an) H that (an) M causes	sunburn
	PRODUCTION	PRODUCT PRODUCER	PROD	HtoM	(an) H that produces (an) M	song bird	PROD-R		(an) H that (an) M produces	birdsong
	USAGE	USER USED	USG		(an) H that (an) M uses	lamp oil	USG-R		(an) H that uses (an) M	oil lamp
	FUNCTION	FUNCTION ENTITY	FUNC		(an) H that serves as (an) M	buffer state			(non-reversible)	
	PURPOSE	PURPOSE ENTITY	PURP		(an) H intended for (an) M	animal doctor				

Figure 4: The Bourquifier interface.

Bourquifier 4 (Hatcher-Bourque 29/5/v2)				Binominal (B) sunburn		Modifier (M) sun	Head (H) burn			Relation CAUS-R
H3	Relation	Roles	B29	H5	Basic template	Example	B29	H5	Reversed template	Example
SIMILARITY	TAXONOMY	SUPERTIPE SUBTYPE	TAX	HisM	(a) burn is a kind of sun	bear cub	TAX-R	HisM	(a) sun is a kind of burn	oak tree
	COORDINATION	COORDINATE COORDINATE	COOR		(a) burn that is also (a) sun	boy king			(symmetric)	
	SIMILARITY	LIKENESS LIKENESS	SIM		(a) burn that is similar to (a) sun	kidney bean				
CONTAINMENT	CONTAINMENT	CONTAINER CONTENTS	CONT	HisM	(a) burn that is contained in (a) sun	orange seed	CONT-R	HisM	(a) burn that contains (a) sun	seed orange
	POSSESSION	POSSESSOR POSSESSUM	POSS		(a) burn that is possessed by (a) sun	family estate	POSS-R		(a) burn that possesses (a) sun	career girl
	PARTONOMY	WHOLE PART	PART		(a) burn that is part of (a) sun	car motor	PART-R		(a) burn that (a) sun is part of	motor car
	LOCATION	LOCATION LOCATED	LOC		(a) burn located at/near/in (a) sun	house music	LOC-R		(a) burn that (a) sun is located at/near/	music hall
	TEMPORALITY	TIME ACTIVITY	TEMP		(a) burn that occurs at/during (a) sun	summer job	TEMP-R		(a) burn at/during which (a) sun occurs	golf season
	COMPOSITION	COMPOSITE MATERIAL	COMP		(a) burn that (a) sun is composed of	cube sugar	COMP-R		(a) burn that is composed of sun	sugar cube
	TOPIC	ENTITY TOPIC			(non-reversible)		TOP-R		(a) burn that is about (a) sun	history book
DIRECTION	DIRECTION	GOAL ORIGIN	DIR		(a) burn whose goal is (a) sun	sun worship	DIR-R		(a) burn that is the goal of (a) sun	sales target
	SOURCE-RESULT	RESULT SOURCE	SRC		(a) burn that is a source of (a) sun	sugar cane	SRC-R		(a) burn whose source is (a) sun	cane sugar
	CAUSATION	EFFECT CAUSE	CAUS		(a) burn that causes (a) sun	tear gas	**CAUS-R**		(a) burn that (a) sun causes	sunburn
	PRODUCTION	PRODUCT PRODUCER	PROD	HtoM	(a) burn that produces (a) sun	song bird	PROD-R		(a) burn that (a) sun produces	birdsong
	USAGE	USER USED	USG		(a) burn that (a) sun uses	lamp oil	USG-R		(a) burn that uses (a) sun	oil lamp
	FUNCTION	FUNCTION ENTITY	FUNC		(a) burn that serves as (a) sun	buffer state			(non-reversible)	
	PURPOSE	PURPOSE ENTITY	PURP		(a) burn intended for (a) sun	animal doctor				

Figure 5: The Bourquifier ('sunburn').

form of the relation, with the paraphrase "(a) burn that (a) sun causes". (Note that the highlighting on CAUS-R is a result of the analyst typing the code into the red box in the top right-hand corner; it does not happen automatically.)

It is worth noting at this point that sometimes more than one paraphrase will apply to a single binominal. For example, *motor car* (Figure 6) may be analysed as
- "a car that contains a motor" (CONT-R: Reversed CONTAINMENT),
- "a car that a motor is part of" (PART-R: Reversed PARTONOMY), or
- "a car that a motor is located at/near/in" (LOC-R: Reversed LOCATION).

Bourquifier 4 (Hatcher-Bourque 29/5/V2)			Binominal (B) motor car			Modifier (M) motor	Head (H) car			Relation PART-R
H3	Relation	Roles	B29	H5	Basic template	Example	B29	H5	Reversed template	Example
SIMILARITY	TAXONOMY	SUPERTYPE SUBTYPE	TAX	HtoM	(a) car is a kind of motor	bear cub	TAX-R	MtoH	(a) motor is a kind of car	oak tree
	COORDINATION	COORDINATE COORDINATE	COOR		(a) car that is also (a) motor	boy king			(symmetric)	
	SIMILARITY	LIKENESS LIKENESS	SIM		(a) car that is similar to (a) motor	kidney bean				
CONTAINMENT	CONTAINMENT	CONTAINER CONTENTS	CONT	HtoM	(a) car that is contained in (a) motor	orange seed	CONT-R	MtoH	(a) car that contains (a) motor	seed orange
	POSSESSION	POSSESSOR POSSESSUM	POSS		(a) car that is possessed by (a) motor	family estate	POSS-R		(a) car that possesses (a) motor	career girl
	PARTONOMY	WHOLE PART	PART		(a) car that is part of (a) motor	car motor	PART-R		(a) car that (a) motor is part of	motor car
	LOCATION	LOCATION LOCATED	LOC		(a) car located at/near/in (a) motor	house music	LOC-R		(a) car that (a) motor is located at/near	music hall
	TEMPORALITY	TIME ACTIVITY	TEMP		(a) car that occurs at/during (a) motor	summer job	TEMP-R		(a) car at/during which (a) motor occurs	golf season
	COMPOSITION	COMPOSITE MATERIAL	COMP		(a) car that (a) motor is composed of	cube sugar	COMP-R		(a) car that is composed of motor	sugar cube
	TOPIC	ENTITY TOPIC			(non-reversible)		TOP-R		(a) car that is about (a) motor	history book
DIRECTION	DIRECTION	GOAL ORIGIN	DIR	HtoM	(a) car whose goal is (a) motor	sun worship	DIR-R	MtoH	(a) car that is the goal of (a) motor	sales target
	SOURCE-RESULT	RESULT SOURCE	SRC		(a) car that is a source of (a) motor	sugar cane	SRC-R		(a) car whose source is (a) motor	cane sugar
	CAUSATION	EFFECT CAUSE	CAUS		(a) car that causes (a) motor	tear gas	CAUS-R		(a) car that (a) motor causes	sunburn
	PRODUCTION	PRODUCT PRODUCER	PROD		(a) car that produces (a) motor	song bird	PROD-R		(a) car that (a) motor produces	birdsong
	USAGE	USER USED	USG		(a) car that (a) motor uses	lamp oil	USG-R		(a) car that uses (a) motor	oil lamp
	FUNCTION	FUNCTION ENTITY	FUNC		(a) car that serves as (a) motor	buffer state			(non-reversible)	
	PURPOSE	PURPOSE ENTITY	PURP		(a) car intended for (a) motor	animal doctor				

Figure 6: The Bourquifier ('motor car').

When every candidate relation maps to the same high-level relation (as is the case here, since all three relations map to *MinH*), we have a simple case of overlap between very similar relations. In such cases, either relation may be used, but the more specific relation (here, PARTONOMY) is usually to be preferred. However, sometimes the candidate relations map to different high-level relations – as would be the case if "a car that uses a motor" (USG-R: Reversed USAGE) were considered an appropriate paraphrase for *motor car* – since this relation maps to *MtoH*. In such cases the combination of concepts can be considered to be "doubly motivated"; i.e. the combination motor + car is motivated both by the PARTONOMY relation and by the USAGE relation. There is nothing untoward about this, since there is no reason to believe that every combination of concepts should be motivated by a single relation.[7]

---

[7] Those that have tried the *Bourquifier* have found it very helpful. Readers can see for themselves that analysing a binominal is a piece of cake by taking part in the Hatcher-Bourque Cake Challenge. Simply download the *Bourquifier* (see the URL in the References) and use it to analyse the seven examples given in §1.1. Send me your results and I will buy you coffee and cake next time we meet. The results of my own analysis are given at the end of this chapter, but don't change your results to fit these. The point of the exercise is to see how much inter-annotator agreement is achieved using the *Bourquifier*.

5 Frequency of semantic relations

The Hatcher-Bourque classification was developed as part of a broader investigation into the typology and semantics of binominal lexemes (Pepper 2020), and it was used to classify 3,738 binominals from 106 languages denoting 100 different concepts.[8] Only 83 of these binominals (2.2%) resisted classification.[9] 79 of them were simply unanalysable, either because of a cranberry morpheme, as in Chakali [CLI] *nebi.kaŋkawal* [finger.??] 'thumb', or because the motivation is veiled by unfamiliar beliefs or cultural practices, as in Takia [TBC] *tamol sos* [man Derris_root] 'widower'. Four binominals use a numeral modifier to denote a day of the week (e.g. Iraqw [IRK] *deelór tám* [day:of three] 'Wednesday'), for which no appropriate relation exists. However, since such cases are more properly regarded as instances of property modification rather than object modification, they are outside the scope of Hatcher-Bourque. The remaining 3,650 binominals were easily analysed using the *Bourquifier*. The resulting data lends itself to an analysis of the relative frequency of semantic relations cross-linguistically.

It is not unreasonable to surmise that the frequency with which different semantic relations are used to motivate the combination of concepts in binominal word-formation could provide insights into the way in which humans conceptualize the world. This is a topic which has hardly been addressed in the typological literature at all; to my knowledge, the only researcher to even approach the question from a cross-linguistic perspective is Bauer (2001), who has the following to say:

> In a detailed survey of just three languages, Bauer (1978: 147) points out that underlying semantic relationships of location appear to be the most common relationships in those languages. The same is true with the sample [of 36 languages] discussed here. Compounds in which the head is the location of the entity denoted in the modifier (e.g. English *furniture store*) or where the head denotes an entity located at the modifier (e.g. English *bone cancer*) are the types most frequently illustrated or commented on for the languages in my sample across all areas. The next most frequent type to be illustrated is the type where the head is made from the material in the modifier (e.g. English *sandcastle*). Other meanings are illustrated or commented on far more sporadically. While this does not show that other meanings are not also in common use, it does suggest that compounds may be used prototypically to indicate location or source (especially if 'made from', 'made by', 'belonging to' and 'coming from' are all interpreted as sources).

---

8 Sources for all material mentioned in this section can be found in Pepper (2020).
9 In addition five entries were considered to be incorrect, in the sense that the form registered in the database does not express the intended meaning. For example, the Yaqui word *muumu jo'ara* [bee house] almost certainly denotes a beehive and not beeswax, as stated in the source. Such cases could have been analysed in their own terms (in this case as Basic POSSESSION), but instead they were simply excluded, in order not to distort the analysis of individual meanings.

With Hatcher-Bourque, Bauer's three examples (*bone cancer*, *furniture store* and *sandcastle*) are classified as Basic LOCATION ("a cancer located at/near/ in a bone"), Reversed LOCATION ("a store that furniture is located at/near/in") and Reversed COMPOSITION ("a castle composed of sand"). We can now use the binominals data to test Bauer's conjecture. The frequencies of the Bourque29 low-level relations are investigated in §5.1, and those of the Hatcher5 high-level relations in §5.2.

5.1 Frequency of low-level relations

The overall frequency of low-level semantic relations in the database, shown in Figure 7, can be summarized in the following scale:

PART >> PURP > COOR > LOC > COMP-R, POSS > USG-R > TEMP > . . .

By far the most frequent relation is one that Bauer does not even mention: PART. This is the Basic PARTONOMY (or whole) relation, in which an entity is modified by the whole of which it is part, as in *car motor*. The quite extreme frequency of this relation may be due to the large number of binominals in the database that denote body parts, which tend to be based on this relation (as in *eyelid*). For this reason, Figure 7 also shows the frequencies when body parts are excluded entirely. Apart from the greatly reduced frequency of PART and a slightly reduced frequency for LOC (the location relation) the differences are minimal. So while it may be the case that the present data overstate the prevalence of PART, it is clearly one of the most important relations, and probably more frequent that LOC and LOC-R combined.

Bauer's suggestion that the next most frequent type is the material relation (Reversed COMPOSITION), e.g. *sandcastle*, is also not supported by the data, which put it at joint fifth in terms of overall frequency. Instead, the next most frequent relation is purpose, also not mentioned by Bauer. As we will see below, this relation is especially prevalent in binominals that belong to the domain *Modern World* and/or denote entities that fall into the semantic type Advanced technology (or concept).

The third most frequent relation is COORDINATION. In the binominals data, it is mostly found in items that denote animates of a certain age (Hawaiian [HAW] *kao keiki* [goat child] KID), gender (Mbyá Guaraní [GUN] *kavaju kunha* [horse woman] MARE), or both (Ket [KET] *qīm.duīl* [woman.child] GIRL). However, it should be borne in mind that the set of meanings on which these data are based was designed to exclude many kinds of coordination relation (such as Vietnam-

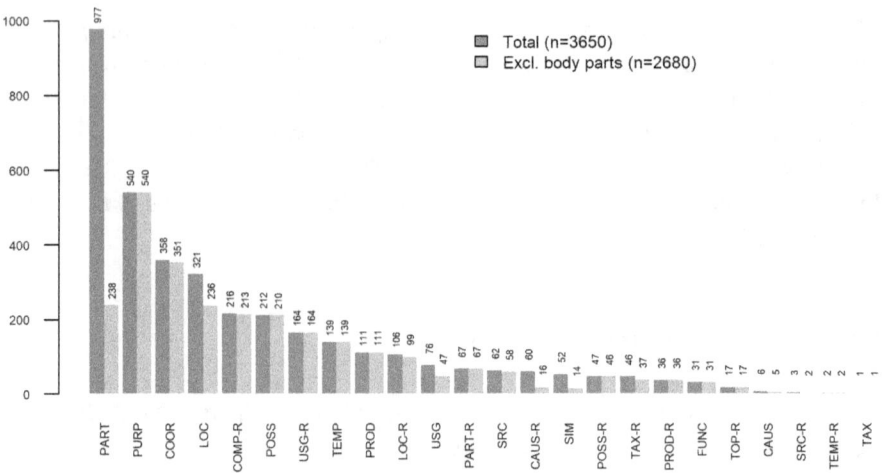

Figure 7: Overall frequency of low-level semantic relations.

ese [VIE] *bố mẹ* [father mother] PARENTS), so the prevalence of species-attribute combinations cannot be taken as fully representative.

The location relation (Basic LOCATION), found when words denoting eye and water are combined to denote TEAR, is only the fourth most frequent. Together with its inverse, the located relation, for example Hupdë [JUP] *yɔ̃ʼh mɔy* [medicine house] HOSPITAL, it is found in 428 binominals, i.e. 12% of the data. Thus Bauer's suggestion that this is the most common kind of relation is clearly unsupported.

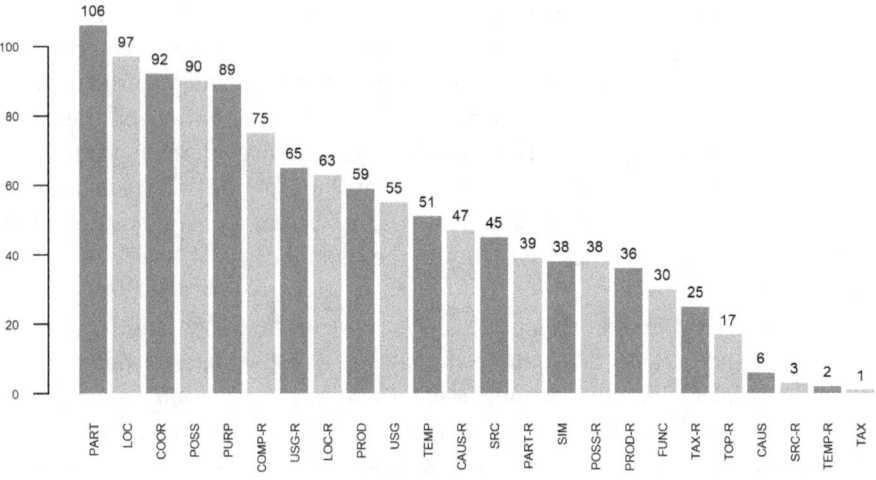

Figure 8: Number of languages that exhibit a particular relation.

We can also look at relations in terms of the number of languages in which each relation is attested (Figure 8). The frequency scale here is:

PART > LOC > COOR, POSS, PURP > COMP-R > USG-R, LOC-R, PROD > ...

The same six relations predominate in both scales, albeit with slightly different rankings. Note that the composite relation (COMP, e.g. *cube sugar*) is not attested at all in the database. Note also the infrequency of a further four – CAUS, SRC-R, TEMP-R and TAX – in which the modifier expresses the effect (*tear gas*), the source (*cane sugar*), the (temporally located) activity (*golf season*) and the supertype (*bear cub*).

The distribution across meanings (Figure 9) shows a generally similar scale, but now with the TAX-R relation displaying far greater prominence. USG now appears among the top six, with COMP-R and POSS relegated to joint 9th and 11th place:

PART > COOR, PURP, TAX-R, LOC > USG, SIM, USG-R, POSS, LOC-R, COMP-R...

This suggests that while the subtype relation, TAX-R (*oak tree*) is not especially common, it is rather versatile in terms of the range of meanings that it can express. Conversely, while the material (COMP-R) and possessor (POSS) relations are rather frequent, their scope of application is relatively limited. It is also worth noting that of the 46 binominals that exhibit the subtype relation (Figure 7), 18 employ the **der** strategy. In many cases, the gloss indicates an (apparently redundant) nominalizer or diminutive affixed to a root whose meaning is the same as that of the derived form, as in Lithuanian [LIT] *spen.elis* [nipple.DIM] NIPPLE OR TEAT.

Overall, the data indicate that the most frequent low-level semantic relations cross-linguistically, at least as far as binominal lexemes are concerned, are as shown in Table 5.

Table 5: Most frequent low-level semantic relations.

Relation	Modifier role	Template	example
PART	whole	(an) H that is part of (an) M	car motor
PURP	purpose	(an) H intended for (an) M	animal doctor
COOR	coordinand	(an) H that is also (an) M	boy king
LOC	location	an H that (an) M is located at/near/in	house music
POSS	possessor	(an) H that (an) M possesses	family estate
COMP-R	material	(an) H composed of (an) M	sugar cube

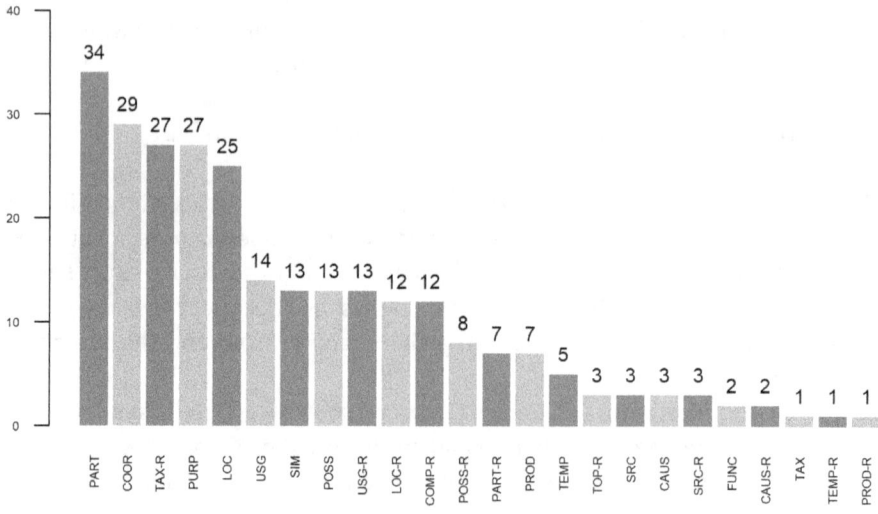

Figure 9: Number of meanings that exhibit a particular relation.

Figure 10 shows how many of the nine morphosyntactic strategies (as defined in the binominal typology described in Pepper, a, this volume) are used to express each kind of relation. Comparison with the overall frequency scale extracted from Figure 7 (above) shows that the most frequent relations can be expressed by any one of the nine binominal types. This very strongly suggests that there is no overall correlation – at the cross-linguistic level – between morphosyntactic strategies and semantic relations. However, this should not be taken to mean that there is no such correlation at the level of individual languages. On the contrary, studies such as Pepper (2010) show that semantic relation can be an important explanatory factor in the study of intra-linguistic competition between binominal strategies.

As the data become sparser, the number of strategies associated with each relation declines; thus, at the lower end of the scale, we find TEMP-R, SRC-R and TAX, each of which is expressed by just one or two strategies. However, since each of these three relations is represented in the database by just two or three exemplars, this does not constitute evidence against the lack of overall correlation.

The frequency of different relations varies according to the semantic type of the referent. Figure 11 shows the proportional distribution of the six most common relations – PART, PURP, COOR, LOC, COMP-R and POSS – across seven semantic types. The results for Animal, Natural phenomenon and Location should be approached with caution, since these semantic types represent only 7, 5 and 12 of the 100 meanings, respectively, but the variation across the other four types is striking.

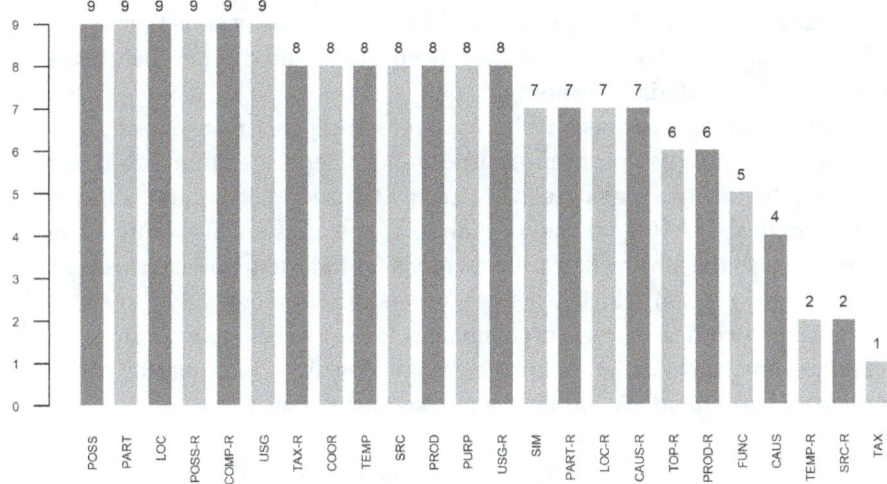

Figure 10: Number of binominal types that exhibit each relation.

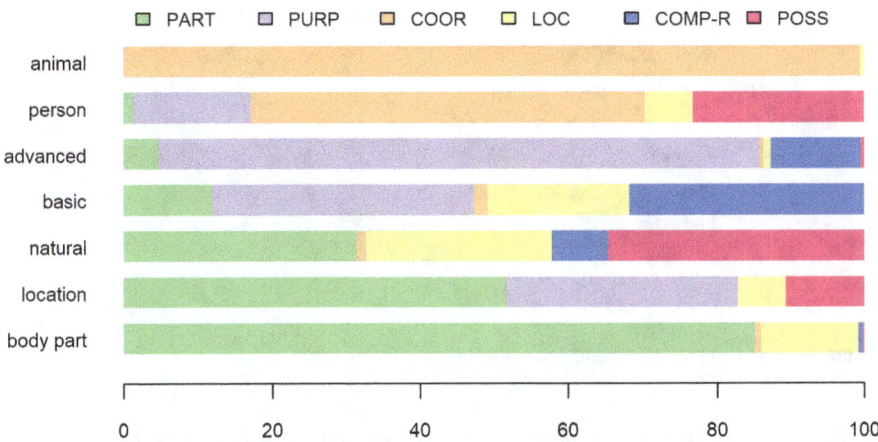

Figure 11: Low-level relations and semantic types.

In binominals denoting Body parts the whole relation (PART) accounts for 85% of the data; the only significant alternative is located (LOC), which is the preferred relation for naming bodily substances, such as EARWAX and TEAR. On the other hand, PART is rarely used to denote an Advanced technology (or concept), such as BICYCLE PUMP, KEYWORD or RAILWAY; instead, the purpose relation predominates, accounting for over 80% of the data, with material (COMP-R) the most frequently used alternative (as in many words for RAILWAY, which is often conceptualised as a road composed of iron). In short, there is a strong tendency to name (secondary) body parts/fluids in terms of the (primary) body parts they are a part of/located at, and to name advanced concepts in terms of either their intended function or the material they are made of.

The semantic type Basic technology (or concept) is more mixed: as with Advanced technology (or concept), purpose and material are the most widespread relations, but the two are now equally frequent; however, in contradistinction to the latter, the whole (PART) and location (LOC) relations are also quite frequent. These are also the most widely used relations for Natural phenomena – together with possessor (POSS), which expresses the relation between a spider and its web, or bees and their hive, as well as phenomena viewed as belonging to some supernatural being, such as Ket *Albara kàŋ* 'Milky Way, lit. Alba's hunting trail' and Assamese [ASM] *ramdhenu* 'rainbow, lit. Lord Rama's bow'.

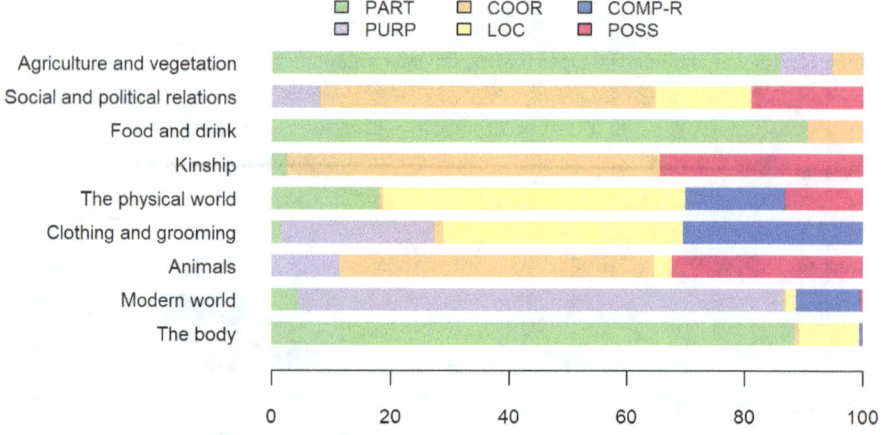

Figure 12: Low-level relations and semantic fields.

A similar variation is found across semantic fields. Figure 12 shows the frequency of the six most common semantic relations across the nine most frequent semantic fields. We note again that PART plays the dominant role in The body, but also in Agriculture and vegetation and Food and drink; and, as expected, Modern world is dominated by the purpose relation. We see also that the patterning in Animals and Kinship is remarkably similar: binominals in these fields have an overwhelming preference for either COOR or POSS. The latter is also widely used in Social and political relations. Finally, the location relation (LOC) that Bauer assumed to be most widespread is in fact largely confined to the fields of The physical world and Clothing and grooming.

5.2 Frequency of high-level relations

We turn now from the low-level semantic relations of Bourque29 to the high-level relations of Hatcher5. For ease of reference, Table 6 provides a summary of the five high-level relations and the 29 low-level relations that map to them. (Note that CONTAINMENT and DIRECTION were not used to annotate the contents of the binominals database and therefore do not figure in the statistics of the preceding section.) As for the low-level relations, the terms in the role column will sometimes be used in the following in order to simplify the discussion. They are in effect shorthand labels for the Hatcher5 'sub-relations'.

Table 6: Summary of mappings from high- and low-level.

Hatcher5	Modifier role	Bourque29
MisH	N/A	TAX-R, TAX, COOR, SIM
HinM	container	CONT, POSS, PART, LOC, TEMP, COMP, TOP
MinH	contents	CONT-R, POSS-R, PART-R, LOC-R, TEMP-R, COMP-R
HtoM	goal	DIR, SRC, CAUS, PROD, USG, FUNC, PURP
MtoH	origin	DIR-R, SRC-R, CAUS-R, PROD-R, USG-R

The first four plots in the previous section showed how the low-level relations distribute across the database as a whole (with and without body parts), and across languages, meanings and morphosyntactic strategies.

Figure 13 provides similar information for the high-level relations. Predictably, the information content is considerably reduced; on the other hand, the categories are much more balanced and therefore more amenable to statistical analysis.

The first thing to note is that every one of the nine morphosyntactic strategies is attested in the data as expressing each of the five high-level relations (plot d); this provides additional evidence that there is no overall, cross-linguistic correlation between morphosyntactic strategies and semantic relations. (Again, this does not mean that such correlations do not exist within individual languages.)

The high-level container relation *HinM* (Hatcher's "B is contained in A") accounts for nearly half of the data (a). This comes as no surprise, given that this relation subsumes PART. If body parts are excluded it has roughly the same frequency as the goal relation *HtoM* (Hatcher's "A is the destination of B"), which subsumes the rather frequent purpose relation, among others. With body parts included, the overall scale is as follows (>> denotes very significantly more frequent than; > denotes significantly more frequent than):

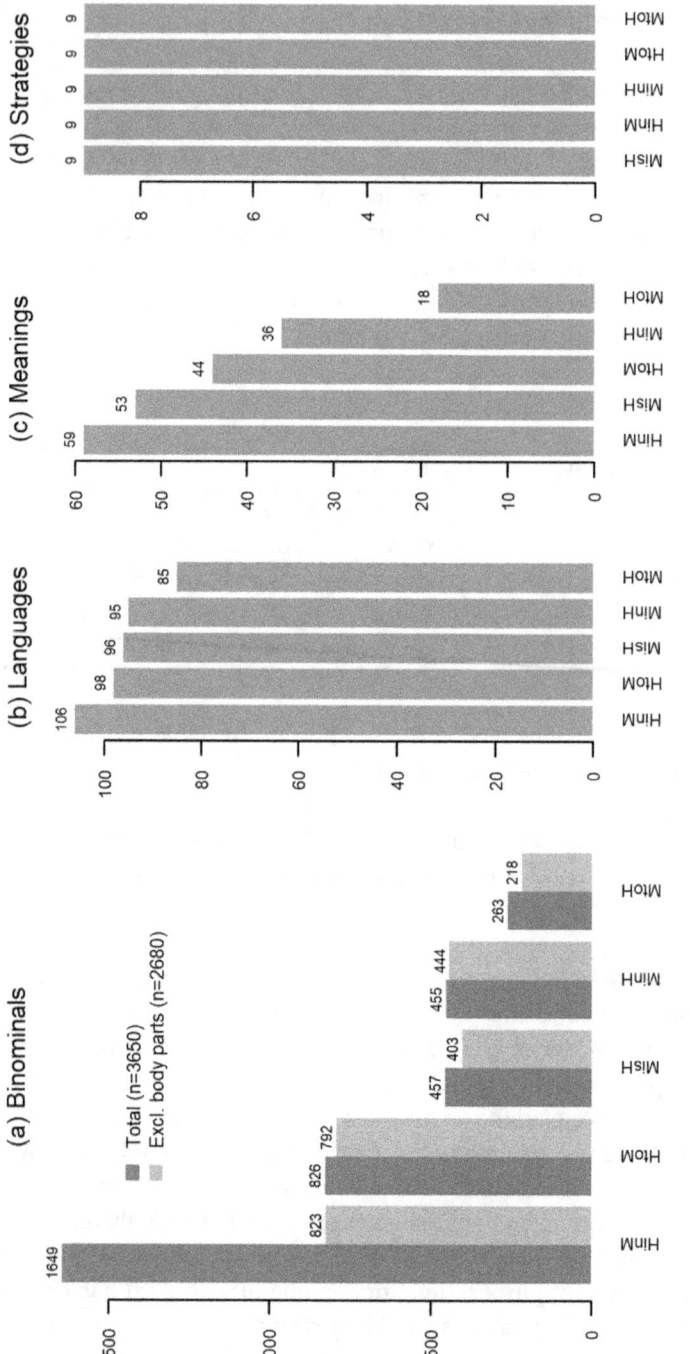

Figure 13: High-level relations across binominals, languages, meanings and strategies.

HinM >> *HtoM* > *MisH MinH* > *MtoH*

With body parts excluded, the scale is

HinM, HtoM > *MisH, MinH* > *MtoH*

The two most frequent low-level relations (*HinM* and *HtoM*) account for two-thirds of the data and thus suggest a pronounced tendency for a complex meaning to be conceptualized in terms of either its container or its goal – both of which should be interpreted in Hatcher's very broad sense.

Plot (b) tells us that *HinM* is ubiquitous, occurring in every language in the sample. However, the other four low-level relations are also widespread across languages and they are probably also ubiquitous. The fact that they are not attested in every language is almost certainly due to the paucity of data for some languages: it would be highly unlikely that a language that is represented by fewer than, say, ten data points[10] would exhibit all five high-level relations.

The distribution of relations across meanings (c) shows a scale similar to the two preceding ones –

HinM > *HtoM* > *MisH* > *MinH* > *MtoH*

– but the values are more spread out: *HinM* is less dominant, while *MisH*, the similarity-based relation added to Hatcher's original four is higher up the scale (in the sense that it is significantly more widespread across meanings than *MinH*). This reflects what was referred to above as the versatility of the subtype relation (TAX-R). More worthy of mention, though, is the fact that none of the high-level relations appears suited for conceptualizing anything like the full range of meanings. Even *HinM*, which is found in every language and accounts for over 45% of all binominals in the database, is used with only just over half of the 100 meanings: in other words, there are limits to the versatility of conceptualizations that are based on how an entity is (in the broadest sense) "contained".

With regard to semantic types, Figure 14 shows clearly that the container relation (*HinM*) is central to the conceptualization of (secondary) Body parts and also important for concepts that express Location or that denote Basic technologies (or concepts) and for entities in the Natural world. On the other hand, it is marginal to the conceptualization of Persons and of almost no use when it comes

---

10 There are five of these in the database: Gurindji [GUE], Puyuma [PYU], Selice Romani [RMC], Datooga [TCC] and Tuwari [TWW].

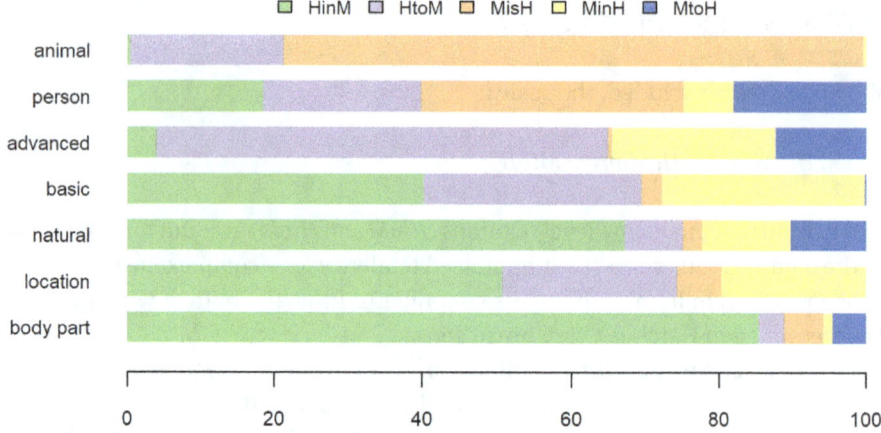

Figure 14: High-level relations and semantic types.

to Animals and Advanced technologies (or concepts). With the semantic types Animal and Person (and only those) the similarity-based *HisM* relation is most important, whereas conceptualizations that are goal-oriented – indicated by the *HtoM* relation – are most frequent with Advanced technologies (and concepts), but also encountered with other semantic types (albeit only rarely with Body parts and Natural phenomena).

Conceptualization of an entity in terms of its contents (*MinH*) is considerably less common than the inverse and never the dominant form; it is found most often with semantic types that denote Basic and Advanced technologies (and concepts) and Locations, rarely with Body parts and never with Animals. As for origin-based conceptualizations, they are mostly found with Persons (in particular, professions), Natural phenomena, and Advanced technologies (and concepts).

Similar patterns emerge with respect to semantic fields (Figure 15, the high-level equivalent of Figure 12). Whereas the low-level plot highlights similarities between Animals and Kinship, the new one reveals additional commonalities, in particular between The body, The physical world and Food and drink. In all of these, the container relation (*HinM*) predominates: there is a tendency for conceptualizations where (to quote Hatcher 1960: 363–364) the target concept, B, "is somehow, to some extent, contained, comprehended in" the modifying concept, A.

In sum, and referring back to the notion of roles, we see that the container (*HinM*) is particularly important for The body, Food and drink and The physical world; the goal (*HtoM*) for the Modern world; similarity (*MisH*) for Kinship and Animals; contents (*MinH*) for Clothing and grooming and for Social and political relations; and origin (*MtoH*) for Agriculture and vegetation.

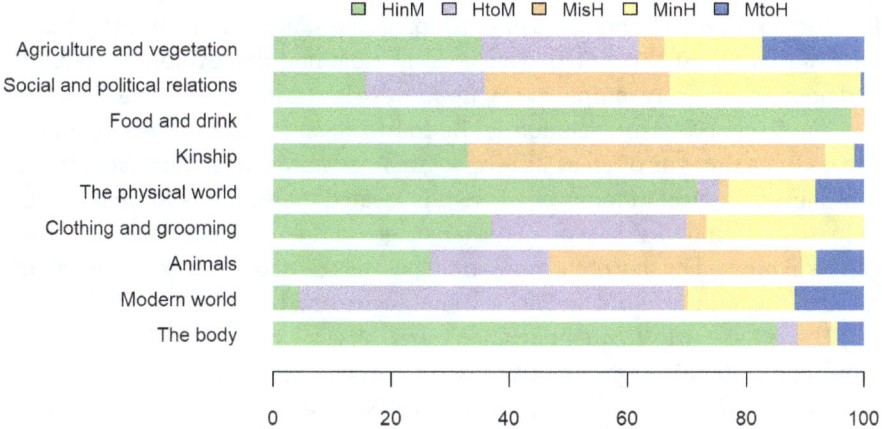

Figure 15: High-level relations and semantic fields.

5.3 Discussion

The analysis of the data provides insights into the ways in which humans tend to conceptualize the world. It suggests, *contra* Bauer, that PARTONOMY and PURPOSE are far more widespread, and thus more important, than the LOCATION relation. Of the two types of PARTONOMY – Basic (PART) and Reversed (PART-R) – the former is far more frequent than the latter, which indicates that the conceptualization of a complex meaning is much more likely to involve modification by the whole (or, more generally, the container) than modification by the parts (or, more generally, the contents). The Basic PARTONOMY relation (PART) occurs most frequently with body parts and in the semantic field of agriculture and vegetation. It can express about one third of the 100 meanings used in this survey; it is found in all 106 languages of the sample; and it can be expressed using any one of the nine nominal modification strategies.

Bauer's suggestion that the next most frequent type is where the head is made from the material in the modifier is also not supported by the data: both PURPOSE and COORDINATION are much more common than COMPOSITION. The purpose relation is most often encountered in the semantic field Modern world to denote advanced technological concepts; it only occurs in 89 of the 106 languages, no doubt because some of the languages in the sample do not have words for concepts of that kind; significantly, the only morphosyntactic strategy that does not occur with this relation is the classifier strategy, **cls**, but this is also the most sparsely populated of all strategies. COORDINATION is used primarily to denote animates of a certain age, gender or both; it is therefore unsurprising that it occurs mostly in the domains of kinship, animals, agriculture and vegetation. Cases such as these account for over 90% of binominals that exhibit this relation, and once again, every morphosyntactic strategy is attested in the data.

The Basic LOCATION relation is the fourth most frequent type overall and occurs three times as often as its reverse; in other words, it is more usual to conceptualize an object in terms of where it is located than what is located at, near or in it. It is found in almost all of the languages of the sample (97 out of 106) and can be expressed by any of the nine strategies. It is most often encountered in the fields of the natural world and basic technologies and concepts.

The other fairly frequent relations are those of possessor (Basic POSSESSION) and material (Reversed COMPOSITION). The range of meanings that can be expressed by these two is limited: only 12% in each case; all the same, they can be expressed by any strategy. On the other hand, the reversed form of POSSESSION is uncommon, and the Basic form of COMPOSITION does not occur in the data at all

Apart from the latter, every one of the 25 relations used for annotation was found in the data, but some were very rare, in particular those involving modification by an effect (e.g. *tear gas*, CAUS), a source (*cane sugar*, SRC-R), a temporal activity (*golf season*, TEMP-R), or a supertype (*bear cub*, TAX). While these are fairly peripheral in binominals, they may be more common in other types of compounds, for example those in which the head or the modifier is an action-morph rather than a thing-morph (see Pepper, this volume, a for the precise definition of binominal used in the present study).

The data for the low-level relations suggests that there is no overall correlation between morphosyntactic strategy and semantic relation: many relations are expressed by every strategy, most are expressed by almost every strategy, and those that are expressed by just a few strategies are those where the data is sparse. This impression is confirmed by the analysis of high-level relations: every one of the five relations of Hatcher5 are attested with every one of the nine morphosyntactic strategies, so we can state quite categorically that there is no such overall correlation. It is thus not the case some strategies are used to express some relations, while other strategies are used for other relations.

However, while this applies cross-linguistically, it does not mean that there are no such correlations within individual languages. In fact, the opposite is the case: As I showed in Pepper (2010), the Cameroonian language Nizaa uses left-headed and right-headed compounds for two distinct sets of relations. Zúñiga (2014) reports something similar for Mapudungun [ARN], as does Atoyebi (2010) for Oko [OKS]. Bourque himself (p. 253) compares N N and N à N binominals in French and shows that the two constructions have very different profiles (for example, PURPOSE and USE account for 48% of all French N à N binominals in his database, but only 13% of his N N binominals). Some of the contributions in this volume start to address this issue for other languages, but there is much work to be done. That work would be much more productive if researchers were to adopt the same classification system, and that is the purpose of Hatcher-Bourque.

6 Summary and further work

In this chapter I started out by providing a brief overview of previous studies on semantic relations in compounding. I then described in some detail the systems developed by Bourque and Hatcher and how they were harnessed in the present study. Bourque's classification was revised and extended with two new relations, CONTAINMENT and DIRECTION, for a total of 29 relations, 12 reversible and five unidirectional. Hatcher's classification was also revised – by the addition of a fifth high-level relation, SIMILARITY – in order to extend its coverage to appositional as well as non-appositional compounds. The two revised classifications were then unified to create the two-tiered Hatcher-Bourque classification, and an Excel-based tool called the *Bourquifier* was developed to assist in the slippery task of classifying individual binominals. Both Hatcher-Bourque and the *Bourquifier* are offered to the research community in order to promote collaboration in the field of semantic relations.[11]

It is important to state that the current version of Hatcher-Bourque (29/5/v1) is a work-in-progress. It needs to be tested against more data from more languages. It may still need refining, through improved examples and templates, and perhaps even the addition of more relations. Certainly CONTRAST needs to be fleshed out, and COORDINATION could be subdivided to better handle the variation currently covered by this category. Perhaps it should be possible to distinguish between partial and full COMPOSITION? If so, this can be done by increasing the granularity. Could one conceive of logical subdivisions between the two layers of Bourque29 and Hatcher5, such as grouping SOURCE-RESULT, CAUSATION and PRODUCTION (on the one hand) and USE, FUNCTION and PURPOSE (on the other) within Hatcher's 'dynamic' pairing of DIRECTION-based relations? And why *exactly* are some asymmetric relations apparently non-reversible?

---

[11] Hatcher-Bourque Cake Challenge (§4.2). The results of my analysis of the seven cake examples in §1.1 are as follows: *chocolate cake:* material (COMP-R); *birthday cake:* purpose (PURP); *coffee cake:* UK material (COMP-R) / US purpose (PURP); *marble cake:* likeness (SIM); *layer cake:* material (COMP-R); *cup cake:* container (CONT); *urinal cake:* location (LOC).

Appendix: Documentation for Hatcher-Bourque 29/5/v1

This appendix documents version 1 of the Hatcher-Bourque 29/5 classification.[12] In the following presentation, the 17 low-level relations are grouped according to the three high-level relations, SIMILARITY, CONTAINMENT and DIRECTION. Reference in square brackets, e.g. [5.2.2.1], are to the extended discussion of the relation (possibly under another name) in Bourque (2014).

1 Similarity-based relations

The similarity-based relations are those found in what Hatcher (1952) calls "appositional" compounds. Hatcher identified two basic types, "species-genus" (e.g. *pumice stone*) and "cross-classification" (e.g. *fuel oil*, *butterfly table*). The former corresponds to TAXONOMY, and the latter to COORDINATION and SIMILARITY, respectively. These all map to the similarity-based high-level relation, *MisH*.

TAXONOMY (supertype / subtype)

Basic	TAX	*MisH*	"an H is a kind of M"	*bear cub*
Reversed	TAX-R	*MisH*	"an M is a kind of H"	*oak tree*

The relation between a type (e.g., *tree*) and one of its subtypes (e.g., *oak*). Both constituents satisfy the ISA test: an oak tree is an oak, and an oak tree is a tree. In addition, and crucially, every oak is a tree. In the Basic form, the superordinate concept is denoted by the modifier (*bear* in *bear cub*), and in the Reversed form by the head (*tree* in *oak tree*). The Reversed form of this relation is sometimes called the species-genus relation, and compounds that exhibit it are sometimes called pleonastic, epexegetic or subsumptive. [5.2.2.1 HYPONYMY; inverted]

---

[12] See Pepper (2020) for the earlier version. Changes between the two are documented in Pepper (2021).

COORDINATION (coordinand)

Symmetric   COOR   *MisH*   "an H that is also an M"   *boy king*

When this relation pertains, both constituents (*boy* and *king*) satisfy the ISA test: a boy king is both a boy and a king. However, there is no type-subtype relation between the two: it is not the case that every boy is a king, and neither is every king a boy. This is the crucial difference between the COORDINATION and TAXONOMY relations. [5.2.2.2]

SIMILARITY (likeness)

Symmetric   SIM   *MisH*   "an H that is similar to an M"   *kidney bean*

In this relation the modifying concept has some characteristic feature in common with the referent. In the case of *kidney bean*, it is shape: a kidney bean is a bean shaped like a kidney. [5.2.2.3]

2 Containment-based relations

The containment-based relations are finer-grained subtypes of Hatcher's high-level relations, "A is somehow, to some extent, contained, comprehended in B" (*MinH*), and its inverse, "B is somehow, to some extent, contained, comprehended in A" (*HinM*).

CONTAINMENT (container / contents)

Basic   CONT   *HinM*   "an H that is contained in an M"   *orange seed*
Reversed   CONT-R   *MinH*   "an H that contains an M"   *seed orange*

The relation between a <u>container</u> and its <u>contents</u>: the seed is contained in the orange and the orange contains the seed. In *orange seed*, the modifier denotes the container, whereas in *seed orange*, the modifier denotes the contents. (See Pepper 2020: 226–227 for further discussion.)

POSSESSION (possessor / possessum)

Basic   POSS   H*in*M   "an H that is possessed by an M"   *family estate*
Reversed   POSS-R   M*in*H   "an H that possesses an M"   *career girl*

The relation between a <u>possessor</u> and a <u>possessum</u>, both in the specific sense of ownership (*family estate*) and the more general sense of belonging (*career girl*). [5.2.2.5; inverted]

PARTONOMY (whole / part)

Basic   PART   H*in*M   "an H that is part of an M"   *car motor*
Reversed   PART-R   M*in*H   "an H that an M is part of"   *motor car*

The relation between a <u>whole</u> and one of its <u>parts</u>. A motor can be specified in terms of the car of which it is a part (*car motor*), and a car can be specified in terms of one of its most salient parts (*motor car*). [5.2.2.6 PART]

LOCATION (location / located)

Basic   LOC   H*in*M   "an H located at/near/in an M"   *house music*
Reversed   LOC-R   M*in*H   "an H that M is located at/near/in"   *music hall*

The relation between an entity or activity (the thing <u>located</u>) and its <u>location</u>. A music hall is a hall in which (a certain kind of) music is (or was) performed. The origin of the term 'house music' is unclear, but it is likely that 'house' refers to the location in which the music was either created or performed. This relation may be restricted to spatial locations; relations involving a temporal location use TEMPORALITY. [5.2.2.7]

TEMPORALITY (time / activity)

Basic   TEMP   H*in*M   "an H that occurs at/during an M"   *summer job*
Reversed   TEMP-R   M*in*H   "an H at/during which M occurs"   *golf season*

The relation between an entity or <u>activity</u> and the <u>time</u> period during which it occurs, i.e. its temporal location. A summer job is something performed during the summer; a golf season is the time period during which golf is pursued. [5.2.2.12 TIME]

COMPOSITION (composite / material)

| Basic | COMP | HinM | "an H that an M is composed of" | cube sugar |
| Reversed | COMP-R | MinH | "an H composed of an M" | sugar cube |

The relation between a composite entity and the material of which it is composed. The relation inherent in *cube sugar* and *sugar cube* is one and the same (the cube is composed of sugar). The difference is that the one denotes the material (sugar), the other, the composite object (cube). [5.2.2.8; inverted]

TOPIC (entity / topic)

| Basic | | | | |
| Reversed | TOP | MinH | "an H that is about an M" | history book |

The relation between an entity or event and the topic that it is "about": a history book is a book that is about history. An alternative template – "an H that is concerned with an M" – may produce a more felicitous paraphrase, as in the case of *history department*: a department that is concerned with history. [5.2.2.11]

3 Direction-based relations

The direction-based relations in this section are finer-grained subtypes of Hatcher's high-level relations "A is somehow the source of B" (*MtoH*) and its inverse "B is somehow the source of A" (*HtoM*).

DIRECTION (goal / origin)

| Basic | DIR | HtoM | "an H whose goal is an M" | sun worship |
| Reversed | DIR-R | MtoH | "an H that is the goal of an M" | sales target |

The relation between a point of origin (usually an activity) and its goal. In *sun worship*, the sun is the goal towards which the worship is directed, and a *sales target* is that towards which a sales activity is directed. (See Pepper 2020: 227–228 for further discussion.)

SOURCE-RESULT (result / source)

Basic	SRC	HtoM	"an H that is a source of an M"	*sugar cane*
Reversed	SRC-R	MtoH	"an H whose source is an M"	*cane sugar*

The relation between a source and a result – in a general sense that does not involve either causation or production; in *sugar cane*, while the cane is the source of the sugar, it cannot felicitously be said to cause or produce it. [5.2.2.9 SOURCE; inverted]

CAUSATION (effect / cause)

Basic	CAUS	HtoM	"an H that causes an M"	*tear gas*
Reversed	CAUS-R	MtoH	"an H that an M causes"	*sunburn*

The relation between a cause and an effect. Tear gas is a gas that causes tears; sunburn is a burn that is caused by the sun. [5.2.2.10 CAUSE]

PRODUCTION (product / producer)

Basic	PROD	HtoM	"an H that produces an M"	*song bird*
Reversed	PROD-R	MtoH	"an H that an M produces"	*birdsong*

The relation between a product and its producer. Both *song bird* and *birdsong* involve the production of song by a bird, but whereas in the former, the modifier denotes the product, in the latter it denotes the producer. [5.2.2.10]

USAGE (used / user)

Basic	USG	HtoM	"an H that an M uses"	*lamp oil*
Reversed	USG-R	MtoH	"an H that uses an M"	*oil lamp*

The relation between something that is "used" and the entity ("user") that uses it. An oil lamp uses oil, and its oil is used by the lamp. In *lamp oil* the modifier denotes the user, while the modifier of *oil lamp* denotes the thing used. [5.2.2.13 USE; inverted]

FUNCTION (function / entity)

Basic   FUNC   *HtoM*   "an H that serves as an M"   *buffer state*
Reversed

The relation between an entity and its function: a buffer state is a state that serves as a buffer. Unlike PURPOSE (below), this relation does not involve any element of intentionality. Despite being asymmetric, it does not appear to be reversible. [5.2.2.4]

PURPOSE (purpose / entity)

Basic   PURP   *HtoM*   "an H that is intended for an M"   *animal doctor*
Reversed

The relation between an entity and its purpose: an animal doctor is a doctor whose skills are directed towards animals. Unlike FUNCTION (above), this relation involves an element of intentionality. Despite being asymmetric, it does not appear to be reversible. [5.2.2.14]

Table 7: The Hatcher-Bourque classification.

Bourque29	B29	H5	Template	Example
TAXONOMY supertype, subtype	TAX-R	MisH	an M is a kind of H	oak tree
	TAX	MisH	an H is a kind of M	bear cub
COORDINATION coordinand, coordinand	COOR	MisH	an H that is also an M	boy king
SIMILARITY likeness, likeness	SIM	MisH	an H that is similar to M	kidney bean
CONTAINMENT container, contents	CONT	HinM	an H that is contained in an M	orange seed
	CONT-R	MinH	an H that contains an M	seed orange
POSSESSION possessor, possessum	POSS	HinM	an H that is possessed by an M	family estate
	POSS-R	MinH	an H that possesses an M	career girl
PARTONOMY whole, part	PART	HinM	an H that is part of an M	car motor
	PART-R	MinH	an H that an M is part of	motor car
LOCATION location, located	LOC	HinM	an H located at/near/in an M	house music
	LOC-R	MinH	an H that M is located at/near/in	music hall
TEMPORALITY time, event	TEMP	HinM	an H that occurs at/during an M	summer job
	TEMP-R	MinH	an H at/during which M occurs	golf season
COMPOSITION composite, material	COMP	HinM	an H that an M is composed of	cube sugar
	COMP-R	MinH	an H composed of an M	sugar cube
TOPIC entity, topic	TOP-R	MinH	an H that is about an M	history book
DIRECTION goal, origin	DIR	HtoM	an H whose goal is an M	sun worship
	DIR-R	MtoH	an H that is the goal of an M	sales target
SOURCE result, source	SRC	HtoM	an H that is a source of an M	sugar cane
	SRC-R	MtoH	an H whose source is an M	cane sugar
CAUSATION effect, cause	CAUS	HtoM	an H that causes an M	tear gas
	CAUS-R	MtoH	an H that an M causes	sunburn
PRODUCTION product, producer	PROD	HtoM	an H that produces an M	song bird
	PROD-R	MtoH	an H that an M produces	birdsong
USAGE user, used	USG	HtoM	an H that an M uses	lamp oil
	USG-R	MtoH	an H that uses an M	oil lamp
FUNCTION function, entity	FUNC	HtoM	an H that serves as an M	buffer state
PURPOSE purpose, entity	PURP	HtoM	an H that is intended for an M	animal doctor

References

Adams, Valerie. 1973. *An introduction to modern English word-formation*. London: Longman.
Arnaud, Pierre J.L. 2003. *Les composés timbre-poste*. Lyon: Presses Universitaires de Lyon.
Arnaud, Pierre J.L. 2016. Categorizing the modification relations in French relational subordinative [NN]$_n$ compounds. In Pius ten Hacken (ed.), *The semantics of compounding*, 71–93. Cambridge: Cambridge University Press.
Atoyebi, Joseph Dele. 2010. *A reference grammar of Oko: A West Benue-Congo language of North-Central Nigeria*. Rüdiger Köppe.
Baron, Irène & Michael Herslund. 2001. Semantics of the verb HAVE. In Irène Baron, Michael Herslund & Finn Sørensen (eds.), *Dimensions of possession*, 85–98. Amsterdam: John Benjamins.
Bauer, Laurie. 1978. *The grammar of nominal compounding: With special reference to Danish, English and French*. Odense: Odense University Press.
Bauer, Laurie. 1979. On the need for pragmatics in the study of nominal compounding. *Journal of Pragmatics* 3(1). 45–50.
Bauer, Laurie. 2001. Compounding. In Martin Haspelmath, Ekkehard König, Wolfgang Oesterreicher & Wolfgang Raible (eds.), *Language typology and language universals: An international handbook*, 695–707. Berlin: Mouton de Gruyter.
Bergsten, Nils. 1911. *A study on compound substantives in English*. Uppsala University PhD dissertation.
Bourque, Yves. 2014. *Toward a typology of semantic transparency: The case of French compounds*. University of Toronto PhD dissertation.
Butnariu, Cristina, Su Nam Kim, Preslav Nakov, Diarmuid Ó Séaghdha, Stan Szpakowicz & Tony Veale. 2009. SemEval-2010 Task 9: The interpretation of noun compounds using paraphrasing verbs and prepositions. In *Proceedings of the Workshop on Semantic Evaluations: Recent Achievements and Future Directions* (DEW '09), 100–105. Stroudsburg, PA: Association for Computational Linguistics. http://dl.acm.org/citation.cfm?id=1621969.1621987.
Carr, Charles Telford. 1939. *Nominal compounds in Germanic*. London: University of Oxford Doctoral dissertation.
Ceccagno, Antonella & Sergio Scalise. 2006. Classification, structure and headedness of Chinese compounds. *Lingue e linguaggio* V(2). 233–260.
Downing, Pamela. 1977. On the creation and use of English compound nouns. *Language* 53(4). 810–842.
Eiesland, Eli-Anne. 2016. *The semantics of Norwegian noun-noun compounds: A corpus-based study*. University of Oslo PhD dissertation.
Girju, Roxana, Dan Moldovan, Marta Tatu & Daniel Antohe. 2005. On the semantics of noun compounds. *Computer Speech & Language* 19(4). 479–496 (Special Issue on Multiword Expression). https://doi.org/10.1016/j.csl.2005.02.006.
Girju, Roxana, Preslav Nakov, Vivi Nastase, Stan Szpakowicz, Peter Turney & Deniz Yuret. 2009. Classification of semantic relations between nominals. *Language Resources and Evaluation* 43(2). 105–121.
Grimm, Jacob. 1826. *Deutsche Grammatik: 2*. Göttingen: Dieterichsche Buchhandlung.
Hatcher, Anna Granville. 1952. Modern appositional compounds of inanimate reference. *American Speech* 27(1). 3–15.

Hatcher, Anna Granville. 1960. An introduction to the analysis of English noun compounds. *Word* 16(3). 356–373.

Jackendoff, Ray. 2009. Compounding in the Parallel Architecture and Conceptual Semantics. In Rochelle Lieber & Pavol Štekauer (eds.), *The Oxford handbook of compounding*, 105–128. Oxford: Oxford University Press.

Jackendoff, Ray. 2010. The ecology of English noun-noun compounds. In Ray Jackendoff, *Meaning and the lexicon: The parallel architecture 1975–2010*, 413–451. Oxford: Oxford University Press.

Jackendoff, Ray. 2016. English noun-noun compounds in Conceptual Semantics. In Pius ten Hacken (ed.), *The semantics of compounding*, 15–53. Cambridge: Cambridge University Press.

Jespersen, Otto. 1942. *A modern English grammar on historical principles. Part 6: Morphology.* London: George Allen and Unwin.

Koch, Peter. 2001. Lexical typology from a cognitive and linguistic point of view. In Martin Haspelmath, Ekkehard König, Wolfgang Oesterreicher & Wolfgang Raible (eds.), *Language typology and language universals: an international handbook*, 1142–1178. Berlin: Mouton de Gruyter.

Lauer, Mark. 1995. *Designing statistical language learners: Experiments on compound nouns.* Macquarie University PhD dissertation.

Lees, Robert B. 1960. *The grammar of English nominalizations.* Bloomington: Indiana University.

Levi, Judith N. 1978. *The syntax and semantics of complex nominals.* New York: Academic Press.

Marchand, Hans. 1960. *The categories and types of present-day English word-formation.* Wiesbaden: Harrassowitz.

Mätzner, Eduard. 1860. *Englische Grammatik. Vol. 1 Die Lehre vom Worte.* Berlin: Weidmannsche Buchhandlung.

Moldovan, Dan, Adriana Badulescu, Marta Tatu, Daniel Antohe & Roxana Girju. 2004. Models for the semantic classification of noun phrases. In *Proceedings of the HLT-NAACL Workshop on Computational Lexical Semantics*, 60–67. Association for Computational Linguistics.

Nakov, Preslav. 2013. On the interpretation of noun compounds: Syntax, semantics, and entailment. *Natural Language Engineering* 19(3). 291–330.

Noailly, Michèle. 1990. *Le substantif épithète.* Paris: Presses Universitaires de France.

Ó Séaghdha, Diarmuid. 2008. *Learning compound noun semantics.* University of Cambridge, Computer Laboratory.

Pepper, Steve. 2010. *Nominal compounding in Nizaa: A cognitive perspective.* SOAS University of London Master's thesis. https://www.academia.edu/4237937.

Pepper, Steve. 2020. *The typology and semantics of binominal lexemes: Noun-noun compounds and their functional equivalents.* Oslo: University of Oslo PhD dissertation. https://www.academia.edu/42935602.

Pepper, Steve. 2021. *The Bourquifier: An application for applying the Hatcher-Bourque classification.* MS Excel. https://www.academia.edu/83122396.

Pepper, Steve. This volume, a. Defining and typologizing binominal lexemes. In Steve Pepper, Francesca Masini & Simone Mattiola (eds.), *Binominal lexemes in cross-linguistic perspective.* Berlin: Mouton de Gruyter.

Rosario, Barbara & Marti A. Hearst. 2001. Classifying the semantic relations in noun compounds via a domain-specific lexical hierarchy. In *Proceedings of the 2001 Conference on Empirical Methods in Natural Language Processing*, 82–90.

Ryder, Mary Ellen. 1994. *Ordered chaos: The interpretation of English noun-noun compounds*. Berkeley: University of California Press.
Santen, A. van. 1979. Een nieuw voorstel voor een transformationelle behandeling van composita en bepaalde adjectief-substantief kombinaties. *Spectator* 9. 240–262.
Schäfer, Martin. 2018. *The semantic transparency of English compound nouns*. Berlin: Language Science Press.
Shoben, Edward J. 1991. Predicating and nonpredicating combinations. In Paula J. Schwanenflugel (ed.), *Psychology of word meanings*, 117–135. Hillsdale, NJ: Psychology Press.
Søgaard, Anders. 2005. Compounding theories and linguistic diversity. In Zygmunt Frajzyngier, Adam Hodges & David S. Rood (eds.), *Linguistic diversity and language theories*, 319–337. Amsterdam: John Benjamins.
Szubert, Andrzej. 2012. *Zur internen Semantik der substantivischen Komposita im Dänischen*. Wydawnictwo Naukowe UAM.
Toquero, Luis Miguel. 2018. *The semantics of Spanish compounding: An analysis of NN compounds in the Parallel Architecture*. West Virginia University MA thesis.
Tratz, Stephen & Eduard Hovy. 2010. A taxonomy, dataset, and classifier for automatic noun compound interpretation. In *48th Annual Meeting of the Association for Computational Linguistics*, 678–687. Uppsala: Association for Computational Linguistics.
Vanderwende, Lucy. 1994. Algorithm for automatic interpretation of noun sequences. In *Proceedings of the 15th conference on Computational linguistics*, vol. 2, 782–788. Association for Computational Linguistics.
Warren, Beatrice. 1978. *Semantic patterns of noun-noun compounds*. Gothenburg: Acta Universitatis Gothoburgensis.
Zúñiga, Fernando. 2014. Nominal compounds in Mapudungun. In Swintha Danielsen, Katja Hannss & Fernando Zúñiga (eds.), *Word formation in South American languages*, 11–31. Amsterdam: John Benjamins.

László Károly
Binominal strategies and semantic correlations in Turkic languages

Abstract: The Turkic languages use both derivation and compounding to form new lexemes. These two different strategies often occur in free variation. Consequently, the same semantic concept can be expressed by using both of them.

In this paper, I discuss (1) endocentric compounds based on two non-derived nouns, and (2) nouns formed on the basis of other non-derived nouns by means of derivational suffixes. I first give an overview and formal classification of the compounding and derivational strategies in the Turkic languages. Then I focus on the question how they are related to each other in terms of their semantics.

1 Introduction

Turkic languages are of the agglutinative type, with rich synthetic morphology both in category-defining and category-changing domains. Bound morphemes, such as those used for derivation and inflection, are typically suffixes. Long and consistently ordered chains of morphemes can be formed by means of suffixation in every Turkic language. Limiting the discussion to derivational morphology, several individual morphemes can be concatenated into a chain,[1] as in examples (1) to (3).

---

[1] Though no statistical data is available, the average number of derivational suffixes in a row is usually two or three in the Turkic languages. Depending on the definition of derivation used in an analysis, the maximum number of concatenable suffixes is not higher than four or five.

Note: An earlier version of this paper was published as Károly (2020). I thank the editors and the anonymous reviewers for their careful reading of the manuscript and their many insightful comments and suggestions. Any of the faulty passages, errors or omissions in the article are entirely my own responsibility.

https://doi.org/10.1515/9783110673494-011

(1) Tatar TAT *kara* 'black' > *kara-la-* 'to blacken' > *kara-la-n-* 'to blacken oneself, to get blackened' > *kara-la-n-dɨr-* [black-VBZ-REFL-CAUS]² 'to blacken'³

(2) Turkish TUR *tanı-* 'to know, recognize' > *tanı-ş-* 'to know one another' > *tanı-ş-tır-* 'to introduce a person' > *tanı-ş-tır-ıl-* [know-RECP-CAUS-PASS] 'to be introduced'

(3) Yakut SAH *atiː* 'sale, trade' > *atiː-laː-* 'to sell' > *atiː-la-s-* 'to buy' > *atiː-la-h-aːččɨ* [sale-VBZ-RECP-AGNR] 'customer'

Apart from bound morphemes, Turkic languages make extensive use of compounding to form new lexical items. Compounding is particularly productive in the domains of noun and verb formation; see (4) to (6).

(4) Uigur UIG *čiray nur-i* [lamp light-POSS] 'lamplight'

(5) Yakut SAH *atax iariː-ta* [leg disease-POSS] 'rheumatism'

(6) Uzbek UZB *adå qil-* [completion make] 'to complete'

Looking at the literature on word-formation in the Turkic languages, one is immediately struck by the overwhelming dominance of research on derivation. Monographic descriptions of derivation, with or without theoretical grounding, are available for both historical and modern Turkic languages; see e.g. Erdal (1991) for Old Turkic, and Korkmaz (2009) for a discussion of Turkish that also deals with compounding. Most of the academic grammars have also devoted special attention to derivation. In addition, Tenishev (1988) provides a historical-comparative overview of derivation in Turkic. The use of compounding as a word-formation strategy, on the other hand, seems to be a rather neglected category in the literature. Systematic analyses and classifications of compounding strategies are exceptionally rare.

---

2 Abbreviations: ABL ablative; ADJZ adjectivizer; AG agentive; AGNR agent nominalizer; CAUS causative; DAT dative; DER derivational suffix; F feminine; GEN genitive; IZ izafet; LOC locative; M masculine; NOM nominative; PASS passive; POSS 3rd person possessive suffix; RECP reciprocal; REFL reflexive; REL relationalizer; VADJ verbal adjective; VBZ verbalizer.

3 According to the available data, Tatar *karala-* and *karalandir-* have the same meaning. Other Turkic languages also show similar cases; see e.g. Turkish *bölümle-* 'to divide into classes, to classify' and *bölümlendir-* id. To determine possible differences in meaning and usage between +lA- and +lAndXr- derivatives in Turkic in general, a detailed look at textual examples is needed.

Researchers often concentrate only on certain patterns or types of compounding instead of providing a complete overview. Ubryatova (1948) and Kaĭdarov (1958) made early attempts to describe compounds (in their terminology, "pair words") in Yakut and Uigur, respectively. Stachowski (1997) provides a cursory description of certain types of compounding in Dolgan. An overview of compounding in Tatar is given by Károly (2016). As always, Turkish is in a significantly better position than the other Turkic languages. Although there is no monographic presentation of compounding in Turkish as a whole, there are detailed surveys of certain subtypes. Göksel and Haznedar (2007) provide a useful overview of the main characteristics of compounds in the three major nominal categories noun, adjective and adverb.[4] Phrasal compounds are analysed by Göksel (2015). Compounds based on nominal constituents or that yield nominals have always enjoyed scholarly attention: Van Schaaik (2002) and Çürük (2017) have produced detailed studies of these types.

An important terminological caveat is appropriate at this point: the very term "compound(ing)" is defined in different ways in the literature (see also Masini, Mattiola & Pepper this volume). A narrower definition, used in this paper, interprets it exclusively as a means of word-formation to form new lexemes. Accordingly, a genuine compound should entail formal stability and certain semantic specialization.[5] A broader definition might also label various phrasal constructions with no or only a marginal relation to the lexicon as cases of compounding. For instance, the Turkish syntactic phrase *bir türlü mutlu olamıyoruz düşüncesi* 'the thought that we can never be happy' in Göksel (2015: 362) is not a compound in the narrow sense of the term. Van Schaaik provides an analogy to establish a link between genuine compounds and syntactic phrases: his higher order compound is "a linguistic structure that resembles a standard compound ... but ... it has a non-first order head" (Van Schaaik 2002: 170).

Comparative analysis of compounding across Turkic languages is still in its infancy. Trips and Kornfilt (2015) have published a study on phrasal compounds[6], including a modest comparison of Turkish and Yakut (Sakha) data.[7]

---

4 Nonetheless, the authors do not pay attention to some of the frequently used compounding strategies, e.g. those of yielding verbs.

5 For a fairly similar understanding, see Moyna (2011), especially her exclusion of syntactic freezes and phrasal constructions in sections 1.5.2 and 1.5.4, respectively.

6 The authors' definition of compounding is similar to that of Göksel and Van Schaaik, i.e. a broad one.

7 The authors provide a stimulating discussion on theoretical aspects, but they unfortunately fail to properly interpret the quoted Yakut data, resulting in unnecessary complications in their analysis. This is primarily because they fail to differentiate between (formally similar) finite and non-finite clauses, and they do not recognize some fundamental differences in agreement marking between Turkish and Yakut.

1.1 Derivation and compounding in Turkic

Derivational and compounding strategies for word formation are not strictly distributed in a complementary way in Turkic, but often occur in free variation. Accordingly, the same semantic concept can be expressed by using both strategies; see examples (7) to (12). Dictionaries also provide compounds as equivalents for derived words, such as (9) and (10) taken from a Turkish explanatory dictionary (Türk Dil Kurumu 2019; a. = entry head, b. = explanation).

(7) Turkish TUR
    a. *kamyoncu* 'lorry driver' ← *kamyon* 'lorry' and agentive +*CX*[8]
    b. *kamyon şoför-ü* [lorry driver-POSS] 'lorry driver'
    c. *kamyon sürücü-sü* [lorry driver-POSS] 'lorry driver'

(8) Kazakh KAZ
    a. *temirši* 'blacksmith' ← *temir* 'iron' and agentive +*šI*
    b. *temir usta-sï* [iron artisan-POSS] 'blacksmith'

(9) Turkish TUR
    a. *dişçi* 'dentist' ← *diş* 'tooth' and agentive +*CX*
    b. *diş hekim-i* [tooth doctor-POSS] 'dentist'

(10) Turkish TUR
    a. *koldaş* 'work fellow' ← *kol* 'arm' and co-agentive +*DAš*
    b. *iş arkadaş-ı* [work friend-POSS] 'work fellow'

(11) Uzbek UZB
    a. *mustahkamla-* 'to strengthen' ← *mustahkam* 'strong' and verbalizer +*lA-*
    b. *mustahkam qil-* [strong make] 'to strengthen'

(12) Turkish TUR
    a. *ütüle-* 'to iron' ← *ütü* 'flat iron' and verbalizer +*lA-*
    b. *ütü yap-* [flat.iron make] 'to iron'

The present paper will focus on the question how derivation and compounding are related to one another in terms of their semantics. The analysis is intended

---

[8] Capital letters indicate the morphophonemes appearing in harmonic suffixes. For example, the letter ‹C› stands for /č/ and /ǰ/, and the ‹X› for /ï/, /i/, /u/, and /ü/.

as a preliminary study, showing some basic tendencies and characteristics of the Turkic languages in general.

In conformity with the theme of the volume (binominal constructions), the scope of the paper is limited to: (1) nouns (nominal concepts)[9] formed on the basis of other non-derived nouns (nominal concepts) by means of derivational suffixes (i.e. denominal nominal suffixes)[10]; (2) endocentric compounds based on two non-derived nouns (nominal concepts).[11]

Due to their complex semantics, resulting from metaphoric or metonymic meaning change, exocentric constructions are not discussed in this paper. Compounds consisting of verbal bases with their arguments are not considered either, as are coordinative compounds, i.e. co-compounds composed of two juxtaposed nouns referring to a unitary concept.

In a first step, the binominal constructions will be classified according to their formal properties. In a second step, they will be divided into categories on the basis of the semantic relation between their head and their derived lexical output. The semantic relation types will then allow for a systematic comparison between compounds and derivatives as two different word-formation strategies. Thirdly, the Onomasiological Theory, as defined by Štekauer (1998), will be used to provide a systematic comparison of derived and compound binominals.

In addition to data collected from various Turkic languages, the analysis will be based on 201 semantic concepts listed in Pepper (2020: 489–490). These have been checked[12] in five Turkic languages representing five branches of the family: Turkish (Oguz branch; see Türk Dil Kurumu 2019), Kazakh (Kipchak branch; see Bektaev 1999 and Shnitnikov 1966), Uigur (Turkestan branch; see Nadzhip 1968 and Schwarz 1992), Khakas (South Siberian branch; see Baskakov & Inkizhekova-Grekul 1953 and Subrakova 2006) and Yakut (Northeast Siberian branch; Pekarskiĭ 1907–1930, Sleptsov 1972 and Sleptsov et al. 2004–2019). The collected data has made it possible to make some family-internal generalizations as well.

In the comparative analysis, special attention will be devoted to two very frequently used derivational suffixes, the multifunctional +*lXk* and the agent-form-

---

[9] In other words, thing-roots; see further in the introduction.
[10] In other words, thing-affixes, prototypically thing-suffixes for Turkic; see further in the introduction.
[11] Often referred to in the literature as primary compounds or N+N root compounds.
[12] Choosing lexemes of a language that express a semantic concept is far from trivial. Sometimes two or more items are available, with no or just a slight semantic difference between them. Sometimes different sources (dictionaries, on-line corpora) provide different lexemes. In such cases, the morphologically simpler item has been preferred according to the following hierarchy: non-derived (root) lexeme > derived lexeme > compound. Thus, non-derived lexemes were always preferred even if derived ones or compounds were also available.

ing +čI, which will be compared with their equivalents in the domain of compounding.

Table 1 shows the different binominal strategies found in the Turkic languages and the corresponding binominal types as defined by Pepper (2020; this volume). The binominal type "construct" (**con**) can be realized in two different ways: (1) by the native possessive construction, or (2) by the borrowed izafet construction (see further below).

Table 1: Binominal types in Turkic.

Binominal type	Abbreviation	Turkic strategy/terminology
juxtaposition	**jxt**	juxtaposition
derivation	**der**	derivation
genitival	**gen**	case-marked construction
adjectival	**adj**	relational construction
construct	**con**	possessive construction, izafet construction

2 Compounding in Turkic

This section provides an overview of the formal characteristics of compounding strategies in the Turkic languages.[13] Compounding is recursive in Turkic, but as already stated in the introduction only examples of the type $[N+N]_N$ will be discussed here.

2.1 Juxtaposition (jxt)

Juxtaposition, or bare compounding, is one of the most frequently used strategies in Turkic; see Johanson (1998: 50) for a general account and Van Schaaik (2002: 21–2) for Turkish in particular. Although no broad-scale study exists of the frequency and productivity of this type, the data collected for this study shows that it is a less frequent and less productive strategy than the possessive type; see below under 2.2. Juxtaposition typically represents an attributive relation, with the non-head accordingly modifying the head but not being one of its complements. The

---

13 For the internal classification of compounds, I use the framework proposed in Bisetto and Scalise (2005) and Scalise and Bisetto (2009). See further Guevara and Scalise (2009).

modifier often describes the material of which a given object is made; see examples (13) and (14):

(13) Kazakh KAZ *tas žol* [stone road] 'a paved highway'

(14) Turkish TUR *yün palto* [wool coat] 'coat made of wool'

It is worth noting that attributive compounds can sometimes be formed by means of the possessive construction; see e.g. Kazakh *tas köpir-i* [stone bridge-POSS] 'stone bridge, a bridge made of stone', as opposed to Turkish *taş köprü* [stone bridge] 'stone bridge, a bridge made of stone'. See further the Turkish compound *demir yol-u* [iron way-POSS] 'railway', which does not refer to a road made of iron, but rather to a broader concept, a means of transportation.

Other types of juxtaposition are also attested in varying degrees. It is relatively rare in Turkish and in North Siberian Turkic, whereas the other Turkic languages seem to use this strategy more frequently; see examples (15) to (19).[14]

(15) Kazakh KAZ *taw teke* [mountain goat] 'wild goat'

(16) Kazakh KAZ *yalam-tor* [universe-net] 'Internet'

(17) Turkmen TUK *ayak gap* [foot sack] 'shoes'

(18) Yakut SAH *oskuola ǰiä* [school house] 'school building'

(19) Kumyk KUM *at yariš* [horse race] 'horse race'

Appositional/copulative compounds are typically formed by juxtaposition; see e.g. Turkish *balık ekmek* [fish bread] 'fried fish roll' and Kazakh *äyel däriger* [female doctor] 'female doctor'.

As example (20) shows, juxtaposition is sometimes in free variation with the possessive construction.

(20) Kazakh KAZ
    a. *žel diyirmen* [wind mill] 'windmill'
    b. *žel diyirmen-i* [wind mill-POSS] 'windmill'

---

[14] It is unclear how this type emerged in some of the Turkic languages. This might be a contact or areal phenomenon, but future research is needed for clarification.

2.2 Possessive construction (con)

The most common strategy for compounding in Turkic is to mark the relation between the constituents by means of the possessive suffix in 3rd person singular on the head of the construction: [non-head/modifier/complement head-POSS]; see Johanson (1998: 50). This is an indexical strategy, according to Croft's (2003: 34–7) terminology.

This type of construction is often referred to as a possessive compound or an (indefinite) izafet construction in the Turcological literature; see Van Schaaik (2002: 22–24) for an overview. The indexer of the construction is sometimes referred to as a compound marker (see e.g. Van Schaaik 2002 and Göksel 2015) or a linking element (see e.g. Göksel and Haznedar 2007). I prefer the term possessive (construction) not only because my intention in this section is to provide a formal/structural account, but also because the indexer is etymologically identical with the possessive suffix, and the construction itself originates from an underlying possessor–possessum relation with various semantic extensions based on some underlying analogy or similarity.

Compounds of the possessive type typically represent a subordinative relation, i.e. a complement relation between head and non-head, as shown in examples (21) and (22):

(21)   Kazakh KAZ *tap žaw-ï* [class enemy-POSS] 'class enemy'

(22)   Uigur UIG *burun töšük-i* [nose hole-POSS] 'nostril'

Possessive constructions have to be distinguished from genitive constructions, which are typically syntactic phrases. They have the structure: [non-head/modifier-GEN head-POSS]. Whereas possessive constructions name general concepts, genitive structures may express specificity or definiteness,[15] as in examples (23) to (25).

(23)   Kazakh KAZ
    a. *bala oyïnšïy-ï* [child toy-POSS] 'child's toy'
    b. *bala-nïŋ oyïnšïy-ï* [child-GEN toy-POSS] '(the) toy of the child'

(24)   Turkish TUR
    a. *ev kapı-sı* [house door-POSS] 'entry door'
    b. *ev-in kapı-sı* [house-GEN door-POSS] '(the) door of the house'

---

15 Since Yakut has lost the genitive case, it can no longer make a distinction between the two types.

(25) Uigur UIG
   a. *čïray nur-i* [lamp light-POSS] 'lamplight'
   b. *čïray-niŋ nur-i* [lamp-GEN light-POSS] '(the) light of the lamp'

2.3 Izafet construction (con)

The term "izafet" (< Arabic *'iḍāfa* 'addition, attachment') refers to a construction borrowed from Persian; see Bodrogligeti (2001: 347–349) for Chagatai, Buğday (1999: 19–20) for Ottoman, and Van Schaaik (2002: 281–282) for Turkish. It differs from the standard Turkic structures because it is head-initial: [head-IZ modifier]. In Croft's terminology (2003: 38–9), this is a linking strategy.

The izafet constructions are most commonly borrowed as fixed lexical units originally having only Persian or Arabic constituents. Therefore they cannot be considered native formations in Turkic:

(26) Turkish TUR *nokta-i nazar* [point-IZ view] 'point of view, viewpoint'

(27) Chagatai CHG *dard-i dil* [pain-IZ heart] 'pain of the heart, heartache'

In rare cases, typically in historical sources, izafet constructions were built with a constituent of Turkic origin, typically as the modifier of the construction; see (28) and (29).

(28) Chagatai CHG *āvāra-i yazï* [vagabond-IZ open.plain] 'the vagabond of the lea'

(29) Ottoman OTA *hararet-i güneş* [heat-IZ sun] 'heat of the sun'

2.4 Relational construction (adj)

The modifier of a relational construction is typically a noun derived either by an adjectivizer or by a relationalizer. The most commonly used element is the adjectivizer +*lXg* (and its cognates in the modern Turkic languages, with minor differences such as Turkish +*lX*) which forms a possessive-like semantic relation. Its counterpart, the privative adjectivizer in +*sXz*, is also used relatively frequently. See for example:

(30) Old Uigur OUI *yayïš-lïy orun* [libation-ADJZ place] 'sacrificial site'

(31) Kazakh KAZ *uya-lï telefon* [cell-ADJZ telephone] 'cell phone'

(32) Turkish TUR *bağım-sız tümce* [dependence-ADJZ clause] 'independent clause'

Although +*lXk* is widespread in the Turkic languages, Yakut and Dolgan do not possess it; instead they use +*LA:x* as a functional equivalent. See for example:

(33) Yakut SAH *ačiki-la:x moyoy* [glasses-ADJZ snake] 'cobra'

As shown in examples (34) to (36), the Siberian Turkic languages often imitate Russian relational constructions due to strong contact influence. In a Russian relational construction, the modifier is a full-fledged adjective derived from a noun (see Naccarato & Huang this volume); see e.g. *serdeč-n-aja bolezn'* [heart-REL-F.NOM disease] 'heart disease' or *det-sk-ij dom* [children-REL-M.NOM house] 'orphanage'. The adjectivizer in +*nAy* is a direct borrowing of Russian +*nyj*:

(34) a. Khakas KJH *parad-nay izĭk* [parade-ADJZ door] 'main entrance'
 b. Russian RUS *parad-n-aja dver'* [parade-REL-F.NOM door] id.

(35) a. Tuva TYV *lakmus-tug sa:zïn* [litmus-ADJZ paper] 'litmus paper'
 b. Russian RUS *lakmus-ov-aja bumaga* [litmus-REL-F.NOM paper] id.

(36) a. Yakut SAH *kalendar-nay jïl* [calendar-ADJZ year] 'calendar year'
 b. Russian RUS *kalendar-n-yj god* [calendar-REL-M.NOM year] id.

2.5 Case-marked construction (gen)

A special construction type is one where the relation between the constituents is expressed by adding a case marker other than the genitive to the modifier. Croft (2003: 33–4) labels this a relational construction, while Johanson (1998: 49) designates this type as "attributive use of adverbials". If the phrase functions as a lexical unit, no element can be inserted between the constituents; see the following Turkish example with the ablative case:

(37) Turkish TUR
 a. *kar-dan adam* [snow-ABL man] 'snowman'
 b. **kar-dan üç adam* [snow-ABL three man]
 c. *üç kar-dan adam* [three snow-ABL man] 'three snowmen'

Such relational compounds can be easily expanded by an additional element that is not expressed overtly. For instance, the Turkish compound *kar-dan adam* can be understood as *kar-dan yapıl-mış adam* [snow-ABL become.made-VADJ man] 'a man(-like creature) made from snow'.

A range of attestations with various case suffixes is available from the oldest written documents up to modern times; see for example:

(38) Old Uigur OUI *ara-dïn ažun* [the.middle.of.something-ABL world]
      'the intermediate world/existence'

(39) Turkish TUR *ırz-a tecavüz* [purity-DAT violence] 'rape'

3 Denominal nominals (der)

Defining the class of derivational suffixes which form nouns (nominal concepts) from other nouns (nominal concepts) causes some complications in the Turkic languages, because (1) many of the relevant suffixes can be added to both nouns and adjectives, and (2) it is not possible to divide the derived forms into distinct groups of adjectives and nouns by using morphological criteria. This morphological ambiguity has led some scholars to group denominal nouns, denominal adjectives, deadjectival nouns and deadjectival adjectives together under the label denominal (derivations of) nominals;[16] see e.g. Erdal's monograph (1991) on Old Turkic. A proper analysis of their semantics makes it possible, however, to define a distinct class of those derivational suffixes which prototypically form nouns from nouns.

This section does not attempt to provide an exhaustive catalogue of available suffixes in Turkic. Instead, it gives a list of prototypical categories with some widely attested examples. See further in Tenishev (1988) for a general overview on derivation in the Turkic languages.

3.1 Agent

One of the most commonly used denominal nominal suffixes in Turkic is *+čI* (and its cognates in the modern Turkic languages with minor differences such as

---

[16] In Turkic studies the term "nominal" most commonly represents a superclass of, or a continuum between, nouns and adjectives.

Turkish +*CX*), which denotes the performer of an activity, including occupations, for example:

(40) Old Turkic OTK *tamgačï* 'an official who bears and uses the *tamga*' ← *tamga* 'seal, mark of ownership'

(41) Kazakh KAZ *änši* 'singer' ← *än* 'song'

(42) Yakut SAH *masčit* 'wood cutter' ← *mas* 'wood'

Due to its morpho-syntactic properties, one might conclude, as Johanson (2006: 74) also proposed, that +*čI* is better described as a denominal adjectivizer; see example (43) from Old Uigur. Most of the data, however, especially from the modern Turkic languages, suggests that derivatives in +*čI* are immediately nominalized and thus can be considered nouns.

(43) Old Uigur OUI *kan-čï kurt* [blood-AG worm] 'blood-sucking worm'

Some of the Turkic languages borrowed other agent nominalizers from neighbouring languages due to intensive language contact; see e.g. the Uzbek suffixes +*šunås*, +*kAr*, and +*våz* of Persian origin. Although they are mostly used with foreign stems, there are derivatives formed from native Turkic stems:

(44) Uzbek UZB *tilšunås* 'linguist' ← *til* 'language'

Agent nouns derived with +*čI* can have semantic equivalents in the domain of compounding; see examples (7) and (9) above.

3.2 Co-participant

The widely used derivational suffix +*dAš* (and its cognates in the modern Turkic languages, with minor differences such as Kazakh +*DAs*) denotes a co-participant who is a follower, sympathizer or companion of X denoted by the base noun; see examples (45) and (46).

(45) Kazakh KAZ *klastas* 'classmate' ← *klas* 'class'

(46) Uzbek UZB *vatandåš* 'compatriot' ← *vatan* 'homeland'

Comitatives derived with +dAš can have compound equivalents; see example (10) above.

3.3 Multifunctional suffixes

There are several multifunctional suffixes in Turkic, especially in the domain of deverbal nominalizers; see various Yakut examples in Károly (2013). In the domain of denominal nominals, the suffix +lXk is one of the most frequently used suffixes, being widely attested in both the older and modern Turkic languages. Among other things, it can denote the semantic categories Instrument (47), Abstract (48), State (49), and Location (50).

(47) Tatar TAT *küzlek* 'eyeglasses' ← *küz* 'eye'

(48) Kazakh KAZ *tiništiq* 'peace' ← *tiniš* 'calm'

(49) Tatar TAT *etlek* 'the state of being a dog' ← *et* 'dog'

(50) Old Turkic OTK *yämišlik* 'fruit orchard' ← *yämiš* 'fruit'

In some cases the suffix +lXk forms relational adjectives; see example (51). Such derivatives are not discussed in this paper.

(51) Turkish TUR *günlük* 'daily' (← *gün* 'day') in *günlük maaş* [daily salary] 'daily salary'

Derivatives in +lXk can also have compound equivalents; see the examples under (52) taken from the Turkish explanatory dictionary (Türk Dil Kurum 2019; a. = entry head, b. = explanation).

(52) Turkish TUR
    a. *elmalık* 'apple orchard' ← *elma* 'apple'
    b. *elma bahçe-si* 'apple orchard' [apple garden-POSS]

4 Selection between derivation and compounding

In the formation of a new lexeme, a speaker can choose either derivation or compounding. Due to the complexity of the question, it is essentially unknown what motivates or constrains the choice between the different word-formation strategies. Rainer (2013) provides data (including statistics) on competition among relational adjectives and noun-noun compounding in German. Scalise, Bisetto and Guevara (2005) address the question of how the selection mechanisms by which the head constituent selects the non-head can mark the boundary between derivation and compounding.

Table 2 presents some statistical data on how 201 semantic concepts listed in Pepper (2020: 489–490) are expressed in five modern Turkic languages. The category "binominal types" includes three structurally different subtypes of compounding plus derivation, which are the typical word-formation strategies used in Turkic to form new binominal lexemes. The term "roots" stands for non-derived (or historically derived, but no longer interpretable by present-day lay speakers) basic lexemes, such as (53). The label "other categories" includes the strategies excluded from the present discussion: lexemes derived on the basis of verbal constituents, such as (54); compounds of the type [A+N]$_N$, such as (55); and co-ordinating compounds, such as (56).

Table 2: 201 Semantic concepts and their realization in five modern Turkic languages.

Language	Binominal types					Roots	Other categories	Total
	Possessive construction (con)	Juxtaposition (jxt)	Relational construction (adj)	Derivation (der)	Sum			
Turkish	58	15	8	17	98	88	15	201
Kazakh	31	26	7	24	85	87	26	201
Uigur	26	29	8	20	83	100	18	201
Khakas	36	16	10	7	69	88	44	201
Yakut	38	8	9	9	64	101	36	201

(53) Kazakh KAZ *qas* 'eyebrow'

(54) Uigur UIG *saylam* 'election' ← *sayla-* 'to elect, to select'

(55) Kazakh KAZ *ašïq xat* [open letter] 'postcard'

(56) Yakut SAH *aya-iyä* [father-mother] 'parents'

The data show that compounding is a fundamental word-formation strategy in the Turkic languages that can surpass derivation in productivity in the domain of binominals: 27 to 40 per cent of the analysed lexemes are found to be compounds, whereas only three to 12 per cent are derived. Consequently, the high proportion of compounds may call for a change in the focus of Turkological research regarding the classical view on word-formation.

5 The semantics of binominals in Turkic

The study of the semantic relation between derivation and compounding has only yielded some preliminary and most-often language- or category-specific results in the general linguistic literature. For instance, Fradin (2005: 178) came to the following conclusion when comparing -*eur* derivation and [V+N] compounding in French: "...derivation puts strong and precise constraints both on its input and output as all derivational rules usually do" and "the difference between derivation and compounding could be summed up saying that the first uses strict conditioning while the latter prefers floating adjustment".

Due to a lack of data regarding compounding in Turkic, the present summary cannot go beyond a general description. It can however provide a picture of some major tendencies and characteristics of binominals in the Turkic languages.

To facilitate a systematic comparison of derived and compound binominals, the following definitions will be employed:
(a) the suffixal constituent of a derived word is considered to be the head of the construction; see the notion of headedness in Štekauer (2005: 156–157);
(b) according to Onomasiological Theory, the noun+noun type of binominal is described as Onomasiological Type 3, in which the "determined constituent of the mark" is hidden; see (57) and Štekauer (2009, 2016) for further details;[17]
(c) only those semantic categories that are prototypical in Turkic and expressed both by derivation and by compounding are covered in the description;
(d) only the primary meaning of a given lexeme is considered.[18]

---

17 Another possibility is to strictly rely on the variable relationship 'Variable R' between the two elements of the binominals, see e.g. Bauer (2009: 353), but the onomasiological approach seemed like a better framework for this sort of comparison.
18 As an example, the primary meaning of the Turkish word *pideci* is 'a person making or selling pita'. Other possible meanings such as 'a place selling pita' or 'a lover of pita' are secondary, and the study of their emergence belongs to a specific domain of semantics. Generally speaking, derivatives are more inclined to undergo such semantic extensions than compounds.

(57) Determining   – Determined   – Onomasiological
      constituent   constituent   base
      of the mark   of the mark
      car   robot
      baby   book

5.1 Agent

Binominals referring to the agent are predictable both in derivation and in compounding. In a prototypical example the onomasiological base (head) is the Agent and the determining constituent (modifier or non-head) is the Patient of the construction. The determined constituent, the Action performed by the Agent on the Patient, remains unmarked. See e.g. the following lexemes meaning 'carpenter':

(58) Patient   (Action)   Agent
      ayas 'tree, wood'   –   *uz-ï* 'master-POSS'   (Khakas KJH)
      mas 'tree, wood'   –   *u:h-a* 'master-POSS'   (Yakut SAH)
      ayaš 'tree, wood'   –   *usta-sï* 'master-POSS'   (Kazakh KAZ)
      yayač 'tree, wood'   –   +či   (Uigur UIG)

Since the same semantic structure and output semantics are manifested in the case of the two different constructions, we argue that they are (near) equivalents in terms of processing and that similar extralinguistic factors therefore determine the independent meaning-prediction processes. As far as the actual meaning of the binominals under (58) is concerned, the 'master of wood/trees' is neither a gardener planting trees, nor a forester, but a carpenter dealing with wood and thus making objects from wood. The same is true of the blacksmith, who is the 'master of iron', and thus makes tools, objects, from this material; see example (59).

(59) Patient   (Action)   Agent
      timĭr 'iron'   –   *uz-ï* 'master-POSS'   (Khakas KJH)
      timir 'iron'   –   *u:h-a* 'master-POSS'   (Yakut SAH)
      temir 'iron'   –   *usta-sï* 'master-POSS'   (Kazakh KAZ)
      temir 'iron'   –   +šI   (Kazakh KAZ)
      tömür 'iron'   –   +či   (Uigur UIG)
      demir 'iron'   –   +CX   (Turkish TUR)

Considering the semantics of the modifier, possible meaning-predictions of agent-expressing binominals are as follows:
- name of a raw material → objects, tools made from the given material → a person making, repairing objects made from this material
- name of a specific object for personal use (e.g. shoe, pot, bread) → a person making, repairing, selling the given object
- name of a specific tool for professional or special use (e.g. fishing net) → a person using the given tool as equipment
- name of a living being or entity (either human or animal) → a person dealing with the given living being or entity in various ways
- name of an abstract idea (e.g. magic) → a person creating, performing something in relation to the given idea

Accordingly, names of craftsmen are easily predictable, and the predictability level is independent of the type of binominal used. See e.g. Uigur *tawaqči* 'potter' ← *tawaq* 'plate, dish', Kazakh *qumïraši* 'potter' ← *qumïra* 'jug, pot', *kebisši* 'shoemaker' ← *kebis* 'sandal', and *yetikši* 'shoemaker' ← *yetik* 'boot', all derived from objects for personal use.

Azeri (AZE) *torču* 'fisherman' ← *tor* '(fishing) net' is a typical example of the use of professional equipment as base of the derivation. Similarly, Turkish *akvaryumcu* (← *akvaryum* 'aquarium') refers to a person (either professional or hobbyist) who keeps or maintains an aquarium.

Regarding the names of animals, Kazakh *malši* 'herdsman' (← *mal* 'livestock, cattle') clearly denotes the keeper, tender of livestock. Turkish *balıkçı* (← *balık* 'fish') is primarily, or rather traditionally, a fish hunter who captures fish from a body of water.[19] The compound *balık avcı-sı* [fish hunter-POSS] 'fish hunter' denotes this primary meaning of *balıkçı* with its strong connotation of a hunter of fish working with modern techniques rather than a traditional fisherman.

5.2 Instrument

Names of instruments, tools and various other objects are often formed by the suffix +*lXk*, meaning that they are created, designed for the purpose of X denoted by the base noun. Turkish *gözlük* 'glasses' (← *göz* 'eye'), *gerdanlık* 'necklace' (← *gerdan*

---

19 Considering the historical development of the word, the meaning 'keeper of fish, e.g. in private lakes or in containers for the purpose of selling; fishwife' is secondary. Younger generations of urban areas might however consider the meaning 'fishwife, seller of fish' to be the default one.

'front of the neck') and *kulaklık* 'earphone' (← *kulak* 'ear') are typical examples of this category. As with agent nouns, many of these concepts can also be expressed by means of compounding; see e.g. Turkish *boyun takı-sı* [neck adornment-POSS] 'necklace' and Yakut *mo:y oɣuruo-ta* [neck glass.beads-POSS] 'necklace'.

The creativity of word-formation can be illustrated by the following derivatives: Uigur *siryiliq* 'earlobe' (← *sirya* 'earring') and Kazakh *sɨryalɨq* 'earlobe' (← *sɨrya* 'earring'). The common semantic relation 'body part' → 'object, tool' illustrated above is reversed here; the body part is derived from an object, or tool closely related to it, and thus the earlobe is chiefly for the purpose of clipping an earring on it.

Many of these binominals typically show a Stative – Patient relation between the constituents; see (60). However, multiple interpretations are also possible. For instance, the Khakas compound *ĭrĭmǰĭk uya-zɨ* [spider nest-POSS] 'spider web' can be understood as 'a nest woven by a spider' which would possibly result in an Agent – Theme relation.

(60) | Stative | (State) | Patient | | |
|---|---|---|---|---|
| *qural* 'tool' | – | *taqta-si* 'board-POSS' | 'toolbar' | (Kazakh KAZ) |
| *äšwab* 'tool' | – | *sanduq-i* 'box-POSS' | 'toolbox' | (Uigur UIG) |
| *ĭrĭmǰĭk* 'spider' | – | *uya-zɨ* 'nest-POSS' | 'spider web' | (Khakas KJH) |
| *sirya* 'earring' | – | +*liq* | 'earlobe' | (Uigur UIG) |
| *kulak* 'ear' | – | +*lXk* | 'earphone' | (Turkish TUR) |
| *yerin* 'lip' | – | *dalab-i* 'pomade-POSS' | 'lipstick' | (Kazakh KAZ) |
| *uos* 'mouth' | – | *pomada-ta* 'pomade-POSS' | 'lipstick' | (Yakut SAH) |

As the examples under (61) show, names of instruments can also represent an Object – Instrument relation. The determined constituent of the mark is hidden in most cases, but the compounds sometimes require an overt actional constituent; see e.g. the Yakut word for toothbrush, as opposed to its equivalents in Turkish and Kazakh.

(61) | Object | (Action) | Instrument | | |
|---|---|---|---|---|
| *ti:s* 'tooth' | *su:n-ar* 'washer' | *suokka* 'brush' | 'toothbrush' | (Yakut SAH) |
| *dış* 'tooth' | – | *fırça-sı* 'brush-POSS' | 'toothbrush' | (Turkish TUR) |
| *tis* 'tooth' | – | *ščotka-si* 'brush-POSS' | 'toothbrush' | (Kazakh KAZ) |

5.3 Location

Derived nouns denoting places are frequent in Turkic. A huge number of derivatives in +*lXk* can be found in the older and modern Turkic languages, such as Old Turkic *borluk* 'vineyard' ← *bor* 'wine', *agılık* 'treasury' ← *agı* 'treasure; silk brocade'. These derivatives in +*lXk* can also have counterparts in the domain of compounding; see e.g. Turkish *elmalık* 'apple orchard' ← *elma* 'apple', *elma bahçe-si* [apple garden-POSS] 'apple orchard' and *armutluk* 'pear orchard' ← *armut* 'pear', *armut bahçe-si* [pear garden-POSS] 'pear orchard'.

Considering the words for vineyard, meaning 'a plantation of grape-bearing vines grown for wine making, raisins or table grapes', we see different realizations of this semantic concept. The modifier of the construction can be a lexeme standing for 'wine', or even for 'vine, grape'. Both choice and meaning-prediction are based on extralinguistic factors; in certain cultures a vineyard is more likely to be associated with wine, as its most relevant product; in others, e.g. in Muslim countries, due to the low consumption of wine, the association is different; see examples (62) and (63).

(62) Turkish TUR *üzüm bağ-ı* [grape garden-POSS] 'vineyard'

(63) Kazakh KAZ
    a. *žüzimdik* 'vineyard' ← *žüzim* 'grape'
    b. *žüzim alqab-i* [grape valley-POSS] 'vineyard'

As with instrument formations, the semantic relation between the constituents of binominals denoting location, in the broadest sense of the word, can be described as a Stative – Patient one:

(64)

Stative	(State)	Patient		
yay 'summer'	–	+*lXk*	'summer residence'	(Old Turkic OTK)
buday 'wheat'	–	+*lXk*	'wheat field'	(Kumyk KUM)
bugday 'wheat'	–	+*lXk*	'wheat field'	(Turkmen TUK)
bugda 'wheat'	–	*zämi-si* 'field-POSS'	'wheat field'	(Azeri AZE)

5.4 Abstract

Although the suffix +*lXk* was not used to form abstract nouns in the beginning of the Old Turkic period (see Erdal 1991: 126), there were innumerable such derivatives from the Karakhanid times, and they remain extremely frequent in the modern Turkic languages; see e.g. *yigitlik* 'youth, the time of youth' ← *yigit* 'a young man' and *yarukluk* 'brightness' ← *yaruk* 'light, gleam' (Old Turkic). According to my data, abstract words cannot be expressed by means of endocentric [N+N]_N compounds if the constituents are non-derived thing nouns. This question needs more thorough investigation in future research.

6 The evolution of derivation

It is a widely held view in historical linguistics that derivational affixes, if not borrowed from other languages, may evolve from lexical items through grammaticalization; see e.g. Joseph (1998) for some examples from Turkish, and Kastovsky (2009) for a more general account. In an ideal case in Turkic or other agglutinative languages, the lexical item becomes a full-fledged suffix with harmonic variants according to the morphophonological rules of the particular language.

Making use of the above-mentioned notion of headedness, according to which a derivational suffix is the head of the derived word, it is straightforward to describe or model the evolution of a derivational suffix as the grammaticalization of the head of the underlying compound. Narrowing down the discussion to binominals, I argue that such derivations may originate from [N+N]_N compounds, typically juxtapositions or relational constructions.

As already suggested in the Turkological literature, the suffix +*dAš*, denoting a co-participant, originates from the construction ⟨ *noun* ⟩-*dA äš* [X-LOC companion] headed by the lexeme *äš* 'companion, comrade'; see for example:

(65) a. *karindaš* 'sibling (by the same mother)' ← *karin* 'belly, abdomen'
 b. **karin-da äš* [belly-LOC companion] 'comrade in the womb' (Old Turkic)[20]

As I have reconstructed in Károly (2006), Yakut words in +*SXt* originate from a compound of the juxtaposed type. The suffix +*SXt*, referred to as *nomen morbosis*, goes back to the lexeme *sit* 'smell, odour; decay, putrefaction' (< Old Turkic

---

20 In this section the asterisk (*) indicates reconstructed forms; otherwise it stands for ill-formed language examples.

yid 'smell'). It primarily denotes diseases causing ulceration or inflammation; see examples (66) and (67). Due to a regular semantic extension, the suffix can denote diseases of various kinds that do not necessarily have the symptom of ulceration; see example (68).

(66) Yakut SAH
    a. *tiŋiraxsit* 'hoof disease' ← *tiŋirax* 'hoof'
    b. *tiŋirax sit 'hoof putrefaction'

(67) a. *bilčarxayjit* 'scrofula' ← *bilčarxay* 'gland'
    b. *bilčarxay sit 'gland ulceration'

(68) a. *süräxsit* 'a painful heart disease' ← *süräx* 'heart'
    b. *süräx sit 'heart inflammation'

In the above-mentioned cases there is a one-to-one semantic correspondence between the reconstructed compounds and the lexemes formed by derivation. However (historical) linguists face difficulties when interpreting polysemic or multifunctional suffixes in diachrony, as shown in Rainer (2014).

As far as the history of the Turkic languages is described, +*lXk* is a polysemic (in other views multifunctional) suffix denoting various semantic categories such as Instrument, State, Location, and Abstract. Erdal (1991: 121) argued that this suffix originally had the approximate meaning 'something for the purpose of X described by the base noun'; thus e.g. Tatar *küzlek* 'spectacles' (← *küz* 'eye') is an instrument for the purpose of (helping) the eyes. Considering the possibility that the suffix +*lXk* has evolved from a lexical item, the following statements can be made:

- Derivatives in +*lXk* are of the type [N-DER]$_N$ or [A-DER]$_N$, and therefore the underlying compounds serving as etymological background of the derivation must be of the type [N+N]$_N$ or [A+N]$_N$.
- The fact that endocentric compounds of the type [N+N]$_N$ do not seem to form abstract nouns in Turkic suggests that abstract derivatives in +*lXk* are secondary. This is corroborated by the slow emergence of such derivatives during the Old Turkic period.
- The emergence of abstract nouns in +*lXk* can therefore be viewed as an instance of semantic broadening. State nouns are possible sources of this type of new derivatives, as the example *yigitlik* 'the state of being young' > 'youth' shows.[21]

---

[21] However, we cannot rule out that this semantic extension is just another example for the well-attested phenomenon of ellipsis.

Coming back to the widespread view in historical linguistics that derivational suffixes may originate from lexemes, the above analysis suggests the grammaticalization process of derivational structures evolving from underlying compounds.

7 Conclusions

The aim of this paper has been to describe the semantic relation between binominals formed by derivation and binominals formed by compounding in the Turkic languages. Since compounding in the Turkic languages remains a marginal area of study, the present analysis only provided a preliminary account of some typical features and phenomena.

A thorough analysis of the data collected from a number of older and modern Turkic languages demonstrated that compounding is a frequently used word-formation strategy in Turkic that can surpass derivation in productivity in certain domains of the lexicon.

Some minimal examples supplied evidence that derivation and compounding can yield new lexemes that are of the same semantic category and express the same semantic concept. This does not, however, mean that derivative-compound pairs can be formed automatically on the basis of some underlying patterns. The availability of pairs for a given semantic concept is strongly constrained by various factors such as the paradigmatic limitation of a given word-formation strategy. This limitation immediately raises a question about the minimal structural and semantic requirements for the existence of such pairs. The answer to this, however, is beyond the scope of the paper and will have to be investigated in future research. As Scalise, Bisetto and Guevara (2005) have already noted, the head-selection differences between compounding and derivation are a possible direction for such investigations.

The Onomasiological Theory of word-formation (used here for the first time in Turkic studies, to my knowledge at least), provides an adequate framework for the systematic comparison of derivation and compounding, as demonstrated in the paper. In relation to this, the principle of headedness in word-formation, as formulated by Štekauer (2005: 156–157), provides a model for better understanding the evolution of some derivational suffixes from underlying compounds.

Much remains to be done, however. In particular, there is a need for in-depth studies on compounding in the individual Turkic languages, which may in the future lead to somewhat more comprehensive comparative studies on compounding in Turkic.

References

Baskakov, Nikolaĭ A. & Anastasiya I. Inkizhekova-Grekul. 1953. *Khakassko-russkiĭ slovar'* [A Khakas-Russian dictionary]. Moscow: GIINS.
Bauer, Laurie. 2009. Typology of compounds. In Rochelle Lieber & Pavol Štekauer (eds.), *The Oxford handbook of compounding*, 343–356. Oxford: Oxford University Press.
Bektaev, Qaldȳbaĭ (ed.) 1999. *Bol'shoĭ kazakhsko-russkiĭ russko-kazakhskiĭ slovar'* [A large Kazakh-Russian Russian-Kazakh dictionary]. Almatȳ: Kazȳna.
Bisetto, Antonietta & Sergio Scalise. 2005. The classification of compounds. *Lingue e linguaggio* 4(2). 319–332.
Bodrogligeti, András J. E. 2001. *A grammar of Chagatay*. Munich: Lincom Europa.
Buğday, Korkut. 1999. *The Routledge introduction to Literary Ottoman*. London & New York: Routledge.
Croft, William. 2003. *Typology and universals*. Cambridge: Cambridge University Press.
Çürük, Yasemin. 2017. *Türkçede birleşik sözcükler (İsimler)* [Compound words in Turkish (Nouns)]. Ankara: T.C. Ankara Üniversitesi Sosyal Bilimler Enstitüsü Türk Dili ve Edebiyatı (Yeni Türk Dili) Anabilim Dalı dissertation.
Erdal, Marcel. 1991. *Old Turkic word formation. A functional approach to the lexicon 1–2*. Wiesbaden: Harrassowitz.
Fradin, Bernard. 2005. On a semantically grounded difference between derivation and compounding. In Wolfgang U. Dressler, Dieter Kastovsky, Oskar E. Pfeiffer & Franz Rainer (eds.), *Morphology and its demarcations: Selected papers from the 11th Morphology meeting, Vienna, February 2004*, 161–182. Amsterdam: John Benjamins.
Göksel, Aslı & Belma Haznedar. 2007. *Remarks on compounding in Turkish* (MorboComp Project, University of Bologna). http://componet.sslmit.unibo.it/download/remarks/TR.pdf (accessed 2 April 2020).
Göksel, Aslı. 2009. Compounds in Turkish. *Lingue e Linguaggio* 8(2). 213–235.
Göksel, Aslı. 2015. Phrasal compounds in Turkish: Distinguishing citations from quotations. *STUF – Language Typology and Universals* 68(3). 359–394.
Guevara, Emiliano & Sergio Scalise. 2009. Searching for universals in compounding. In Sergio Scalise, Elisabetta Magni & Antonietta Bisetto (eds.), *Universals of language today*, 101–128. Amsterdam: Springer.
Johanson, Lars. 1998. The structure of Turkic. In Lars Johanson & Éva Á. Csató (eds.), *The Turkic languages*, 31–66. London: Routledge.
Johanson, Lars. 2006. Nouns and adjectives in South Siberian Turkic. In Marcel Erdal & Irina Nevskaya (eds.), *Exploring the eastern frontiers of Turkic*, 57–78. Wiesbaden: Harrassowitz.
Joseph, Brian D. 1998. Diachronic morphology. In Andrew Spencer & Arnold M. Zwicky (eds.), *The handbook of morphology*, 351–373. Oxford & Madlen, MA: Blackwell.
Kaĭdarov, Abdu-Ali T. 1958. *Parnȳe slova v sovremennom uĭgurskom yazȳke* [Pair words in the modern Uigur language]. Almaty: Izd-vo Akad. nauk KazSSR.
Károly, László. 2006. Some remarks on the Yakut suffix +SXt. *Turkic Languages* 10(2). 187–192.
Károly, László. 2013. *Deverbal nominals in Yakut. A historical approach*. Wiesbaden: Harrassowitz.

Károly, László. 2016. Tatar. In Peter O. Müller, Ingeborg Ohnheiser, Susan Olsen & Franz Rainer (eds.), *Word-formation. An international handbook of the languages of Europe* 5, 3398–3413. Berlin & Boston: Mouton de Gruyter.
Károly, László. 2020. Derived and compound nouns in Turkic. *Kungl. Humanistiska Vetenskaps-Samfundet i Uppsala* 2019–2020. 171–93.
Kastovsky, Dieter. 2009. Diachronic perspectives. In Rochelle Lieber & Pavol Štekauer (eds.), *The Oxford handbook of compounding*, 323–340. Oxford: Oxford University Press.
Korkmaz, Zeynep. 2009. *Türkiye Türkçesi Grameri: Şekil Bilgisi* [A grammar of Turkish. Morphology]. Ankara: Türk Dil Kurumu.
Masini, Francesca, Simone Mattiola & Steve Pepper. This volume. Exploring complex lexemes cross-linguistically. In Steve Pepper, Francesca Masini & Simone Mattiola (eds.), *Binominal lexemes in cross-linguistic perspective*. Berlin: Mouton de Gruyter.
Moyna, María I. 2011. *Compound words in Spanish. Theory and history*. Amsterdam & Philadelphia: John Benjamins.
Naccarato, Chiara & Shanshan Huang. This volume. Binominals denoting instruments: A contrastive perspective. In Steve Pepper, Francesca Masini & Simone Mattiola (eds.), *Binominal lexemes in cross-linguistic perspective*. Berlin: Mouton de Gruyter.
Nadzhip, Émir N. 1968. *Uĭgursko-russkiĭ slovar'* [An Uigur-Russian dictionary]. Moscow: Sovetskaya Éntsiklopediya.
Pekarskiĭ, Éduard K. 1907–1930. *Slovar' yakutskogo yazyka* [A dictionary of the Yakut language], i–iii. St. Petersburg & Leningrad: Nauka.
Pepper, Steve. 2020. *The typology of binominal lexemes: Noun-noun compounds and their functional equivalents*. Oslo: University of Oslo dissertation.
Pepper, Steve. This volume. Defining and typologizing binominal lexemes. In Steve Pepper, Francesca Masini & Simone Mattiola (eds.), *Binominal lexemes in cross-linguistic perspective*. Berlin: Mouton de Gruyter.
Rainer, Franz. 2013. Can relational adjectives really express any relation? An onomasiological perspective. *SKASE Journal of Theoretical Linguistics* 10(1). 12–40. http://www.skase.sk/Volumes/JTL22 (accessed 25 April 2020).
Rainer, Franz. 2014. Polysemy in derivation. In Rochelle Lieber & Pavol Štekauer (eds.), The *Oxford handbook of derivational morphology*, 338–353. Oxford: Oxford University Press.
Scalise, Sergio, Antonietta Bisetto & Emiliano Guevara. 2005. Selection in compounding and derivation. In Wolfgang U. Dressler, Dieter Kastovsky, Oskar E. Pfeiffer & Franz Rainer (eds.), *Morphology and its demarcations: Selected papers from the 11th Morphology meeting, Vienna, February 2004*, 133–150. Amsterdam: John Benjamins.
Scalise, Sergio & Antonietta Bisetto. 2009. The classification of compounds. In Rochelle Lieber & Pavol Štekauer (eds.), *The Oxford handbook of compounding*, 34–53. Oxford: Oxford University Press.
Schaaik, Gerjan van. 2002. *The noun in Turkish: Its argument structure and the compounding straitjacket*. Wiesbaden: Harrassowitz.
Schwarz, Henry G. 1992. *An Uyghur-English dictionary*. Western Washington: Center for East Asian Studies. Western Washington University.
Shnitnikov, Boris. N. 1966. *Kazakh-English dictionary*. London/The Hague, Paris: Mouton.
Sleptsov, Platon A. (ed.) 1972. *Yakutsko-russkiĭ slovar'* [A Yakut-Russian dictionary]. Moscow: Sovetskaya Éntsiklopediya.
Sleptsov, Platon A. et al. (eds.) 2004–2019. *(Bol'shoĭ) tolkovyĭ slovar' yakutskogo yazyka* [A (large) explanatory dictionary of the Yakut language], i–xv. Novosibirsk: Nauka.

Stachowski, Marek 1997. *Dolganische Wortbildung*. Kraków: Księgarnia Akademicka.
Štekauer, Pavol. 1998. *An onomasiological theory of English word-formation*. Amsterdam: John Benjamins.
Štekauer, Pavol. 2005. Compounding and affixation. Any difference? In Wolfgang U. Dressler, Dieter Kastovsky, Oskar E. Pfeiffer & Franz Rainer (eds.), *Morphology and its demarcations: Selected papers from the 11th Morphology meeting, Vienna, February 2004*, 151–159. Amsterdam: John Benjamins.
Štekauer, Pavol. 2009. Meaning predictability of novel context-free compounds. In Rochelle Lieber & Pavol Štekauer (eds.), *The Oxford handbook of compounding*, 272–297. Oxford: Oxford University Press.
Štekauer, Pavol. 2016. Compounding from an onomasiological perspective. In Pius Ten Hacken (ed.) *The semantics of compounding*, 54–68. Cambridge: Cambridge University Press.
Subrakova, Ol'ga V. (ed.) 2006. *Khakassko-russkiĭ slovar'* [A Khakas-Russian dictionary]. Novosibirsk: Nauka.
Tenishev, Édgem R. 1988. *Sravnitel'no-istoricheskaya grammatika tyurkskikh yazȳkov. Morfologiya* [A historical-comparative grammar of the Turkic languages. Morphology]. Moscow: Nauka.
Trips, Carola & Jaklin Kornfilt. 2015. Typological aspects of phrasal compounds in English, German, Turkish and Turkic. *STUF – Language Typology and Universals* 68(3). 281–321.
Türk Dil Kurumu. 2019. *Güncel Türkçe Sözlük* [A contemporary Turkish dictionary]. Ankara: Türk Dil Kurumu. https://sozluk.gov.tr/ (accessed 23 April 2020).
Ubryatova, Elizaveta I. 1948. Parnȳe slova v yakutskom yazȳke [Pair words in the Yakut language]. *Yazȳk i mȳshlenie* 11. 297–328.

Aslı Gürer
A classification of compounds in Karachay-Balkar

Abstract: This study proposes a classification of compound forms in Karachay-Balkar (KRC), an understudied Turkic language from the Kipchak group. The classification of compounds, a type of binominal, is based on three elements: firstly, an analysis of the grammatical relations between the constituents of noun-noun compounds with and without a linking element; secondly, an analysis of the semantic relations between the constituents of noun-noun compounds with and without a linking element; and thirdly, a comparison of compounds with and without a linking element based on a set of morpho-syntactic diagnostics. In line with Gürer (2017), we suggest that the distribution of the linking element is not optional but rather signals an argument relation between the head and the dependent. Analysis indicates further that the presence of a linking element is observed with endocentric subordinate compounds, although not all compounds within this group have one. The comparison of compounds with and without a linking element reveals that the two types show the same morpho-syntactic properties and that the constituents of a compound act as a single atomic unit, in contrast to syntactic phrases.[1]

1 Introduction

As Bauer (2003: 40) explains, compounding is "the formation of a new lexeme by adjoining two or more lexemes." Although the definition of a compound is concise and straightforward, it is not easy to establish a cross-linguistic classification of compounds, or even an uncontroversial classification for a single language, due to the multifaceted nature of compounds. First, the border between a compound and a phrase becomes blurred as there are some compounds with phrasal and lexical properties that can be analyzed as the products of morphol-

---

[1] We would like to thank the audience at the SLE 2017 workshop *When 'noun' meets 'noun'* for their questions and comments. This work was supported by the Scientific and Technological Research Council of Turkey (Project No. #116K692) and İstanbul Bilgi University. We are grateful to Alan Karaketov, Asuman Tavlan, Aytek Yapıcı, Emine Yalçın, Okan Haluk Akbay, Sefer Solmaz, Talha Bağcı, Tokay Delibay and many other Karachay-Balkar native speakers for their native judgments. We would also like to thank the anonymous reviewers for their insightful comments and suggestions. Any errors are, of course, the author's.

https://doi.org/10.1515/9783110673494-012

ogy or syntax. Hence, in the literature, root compounds, compounds with linking elements, verbal/synthetic compounds, phrasal lexemes (Masini 2009), phrasal compounds (Lieber 1992), and higher-order compounds (van Schaaik 2002) have all been suggested as forming a continuum between a lexical item and a syntactic phrase. Additionally, the same compound form can be analyzed as lexical or phrasal in different studies. A further distinction is made based on the semantic or grammatical relation between the two units. This brings a further challenge as each study presents a different classification tool even for well-studied languages: e.g., Spencer (1991), Haspelmath (2002), Booij (2005), and Bisetto and Scalise (2005) among many others. Even when the same terminology is used, different criteria can be in use which makes the classification even more challenging.

Karachay-Balkar (KRC), an understudied Turkic language, uses compounds productively for the naming function. Considering the above-mentioned challenges, the aim of this study is to provide a classification of compounds in Karachay-Balkar, taking form and meaning as the basis. The focus will be on compounds with and without a linking element.

As illustrated in (1)–(2), compounds can be a combination of two nouns. The first element narrows down the meaning of the second element and hence the second element (underlined) serves as the head. The examples in (2) differ from those in (1) with respect to the presence of the linking element $-(s)In$[2] that the head noun bears. Note that the omission of the linking element (LE) leads to ungrammaticality. In terms of the typology used in this volume, therefore, the two types are **jxt** and **con**, respectively.

(1) a. $[[suv]_N \ [b\imath rg\imath]_N]_N$ b. $[[çuruk]_N \ [cav]_N]_N$
       water   pipe   shoe   oil
       'water pipe'   'shoe polish'

(2) a. $[[tengiz]_N \ k\imath y\imath r\text{-}^*(\imath)]_N]_N$ b. $[[cer]_N \ iye\text{-}^*(si)]_N]_N$
       sea   side-LE[3]   earth   owner-LE
       'seaside'   'God of Earth'

---

[2] The basic morpheme for the linking element is $-(s)In$; the first consonant is dropped when the head noun ends in a consonant. Additionally, the final consonant of the morpheme surfaces only in the presence of a vowel or consonant-initial suffix following the linking element. The vowel agrees in backness and rounding with the final vowel of the head.

[3] Abbreviations used in this study are: ABL = ablative; ACC = accusative; ADJV = adjectivizer; AOR = aorist; CM = compound marker; GEN = genitive; LE = linking element; LOC = locative; NOML = nominalizer; PASS = passive; PAST = past tense; PL = plural; POSS = possessive; PROG = progressive; PTCP = participle; SG = singular.

The non-head constituent can be an adjective, modifying the head noun as illustrated in (3) below.

(3)   a.   [[ak]_ADJ [babuş]_N]_N   b.   [[kara]_ADJ [azab]_N]_N
              white   duck   black   nuisance
              'swan'   'torment'

In addition to simplex lexemes as in (1)–(3), derivations can surface as constituents of compounds, forming synthetic compounds. In (4) below, the constituents in the non-head position are deverbal adjectives. In (5), the head nouns are deverbal nouns.

(4)   a.   [[oltur-gan]_ADJ [kız]_N]_N   b.   [[cet-ken]_ADJ [kız]_N]_N
              sit-ADJV   girl   grow up-ADJV   girl
              'spinster'   'grownup girl'

(5)   a.   [[eşik]_N [tut-huç]_N]_N   b.   [[cer]_N [uç-han]_N]_N
              door   handle-NOML   earth   slide-NOML
              'door handle'   'landslide'

Karachay-Balkar also uses repetition compounds, as used in Fabb (1998). The second constituent can be a fully reduplicated or slightly modified form of the first constituent. In (6a)–(6c), the second unit does not have a meaning but is a made-up reduplicated form of the first unit, and the new term has the same word class as the first unit.[4] In (6d), the juxtaposition of reduplicated nouns yields an adverbial; i.e., a categorical change.

(6)   a.   [[sant]_ADJ -[mant]]_ADJ   b.   [[aksak]_ADJ -[tuksak]]_ADJ
              idiot   lame
              'idiot'   'cripple'
      c.   [[agurça]_N -[magurça]]_N   d.   [[közüv]_N -[közüv]_N]_ADV
              cucumber   array   array
              'vegetables'   'one by one'

---

[4] The examples in (5a) and (5c) are similar to these reduplication examples in Turkish: a) *eşya-meşya* ('object'); b) *kalem-malem* ('pen'). The second part does not have a meaning but is a slightly modified form of the first constituent.

The data so far clearly indicates that the non-head in a compound can be a bare form or a derived form. The phrasal compounds in (7) further indicate that in Karachay-Balkar some complex constructions can have the same form as the compounds.

(7) Non-head   Head
  a. *kazavat-ta sabiy-le   öl-e-dile   ayt-ıl-ğan-*(ı)*
     war-LOC   child-PL   die-PROG-PL   say-PASS-NOML-LE
     'The claim that children die in the war.'
  b. *duniya-da ne   zat   işle-y-biz   sor-uv-*(u)*
     world-LOC what   thing   do-PROG-1PL   ask-NOML-LE
     'The question of what we are doing in the world.'

The head noun is a derived abstract nominal, a higher-order noun within the terms of van Schaaik (2002).[5] The non-head unit is a declarative clause (7a), or an interrogative (7b). Note that the structural properties of these phrasal compounds show parallels with simplex forms in (2). In all examples, the non-head unit, be it a simple lexeme or a complex clause, lacks a marker and the head noun bears the linking element. The constructions in (7) can be analyzed as phrasal compounds which are context-dependent and not fully lexicalized. These constructions would be situated towards the syntactic end of the continuum for compound formation.

Although outside the scope of compound formation, we will also focus on genitive-possessive constructions, which take us further to the phrasal end of the continuum in order to obtain a complete view of the noun-noun configurations in Karachay-Balkar. In (8) below, for example, the head noun bears a genitive case marker and the non-head bears a possessive agreement morpheme.

(8) a. *Ayşat-nı   üy-ü*   b. *men-i   tiş-im*
       Ayşe-GEN   house-3SG.POSS   I-GEN   tooth-1SG.POSS
       'Ayşe's house'   'my tooth'

---

[5] For Turkish, van Schaaik (2002) suggests that the head noun can be a first-order term such as 'garden', second-order term such as 'idea', third-order term such as 'claim', or fourth-order term such as 'question', while the complement can be a simple noun phrase or a predicational, propositional, or clausal unit. The following example indicates a third-order term with a propositional unit:

(1) *Her   şey   tamam   ol-duğ-u   iddia-sı*
    everything all   right   be-NOML-3SG.POSS   claim-CM
    'The claim that everything is all right.'

The focus in this study will be on compounds with and without a linking element as exemplified in (1) and (2). These are instances of 'binominal lexemes', defined by Pepper (2020) as "a lexical item that consists primarily of two thing-morphs and whose function is to name a complex concept that involves an unstated (or under-specified) relation between two entities." The verbal or synthetic compounds, coordinate compounds, and compounds composed of a noun and an adjective are not within the boundaries of binominal lexemes as defined above.[6] As stated above, the aim of the present study is to provide a classification of compounds in Karachay-Balkar with a specific focus on compounds with and without a linking element. Hence, at certain points we will give examples that will be outside the scope of this binominal lexeme definition.

Section 2 investigates the grammatical relation between the constituents of compounds in Karachay-Balkar. Section 3 focuses on the semantic relations between the dependent and the head in binominal compounds. Based on the findings of these sections, Section 4 compares the compounds with and without a linking element based on a set of morpho-syntactic diagnostics and provides a structural explanation for the two patterns. Section 5 concludes the study.

2 Grammatical relations in compounds

Different analyses have been proposed in the literature for the classification of compounds (Bloomfield 1933; Marchand 1969; Spencer 1991; Fabb 1998; Olsen 2001; Bauer 2001; Haspelmath 2002; Booij 2005; Bisetto and Scalise 2005; Scalise and Bisetto 2009). As mentioned in Section 1, the classification of compounds is no easy task as different criteria can be used for the classification, or the same terminology can be used with different assumptions.[7] Bisetto and Scalise (2005) propose a three-way classification for compounds as subordinate compounds, attributive compounds, and coordinative compounds.[8] We illustrate each class with examples from Karachay-Balkar.

---

6 Pepper (2020) places verbal compounds outside the scope of binominal lexemes because the relation between the constituents is explicit with these forms. Compounds with a noun and an adjective (unless it is denominal) are excluded because one of the constituents is not a 'thing-morph'. Finally, coordinate compounds are regarded as binominals, but are out of scope in Pepper (2020), which focuses on determinative noun-noun compounds and their functional equivalents.
7 See Scalise and Bisetto (2009) for a detailed discussion of the problems in classifying compounds.
8 In order to capture the semantic relations between the units of a compound, Scalise and Bisetto (2009) propose a further layer. The subordinate compounds are further grouped as 'ground' and 'verbal nexus' while the attributive compounds are grouped as attributive and appositive.

In subordinate compounds a complement relation exists between the head and the dependent, as shown in (9)–(12). With endocentric subordinate compounds, the entire compound denotes a subset of one of the constituents and this unit is the head of the compound. For example, it is possible analyze the subordinate compound in (11a) as "the side of the sea" in which "sea" is the complement of the head "side". With exocentric compounds, there is no such subset relation and the head is outside the entire compound.

(9)   a.   endocentric   b.   exocentric
             ayak kiy-im   *ayak col*
             foot dress-NOML   foot road
             'shoe'   'toilet'

(10)   a.   *avuz suv*   b.   *avuz aç-ık*
             mouth water   mouth open-SPTCP
             'saliva'   'slowpoke'

(11)   a.   *tengiz kıyır-ı*   b.   *baş kes-er*
             sea side-LE   head cut-NOML
             'seaside'   'bandit'

(12)   a.   *keçe ara-sı*   b.   *üy biyçe*
             night middle-LE   house princess
             'midnight'   'wife'

Attributive compounds encode a modifier relation between the head and the dependent. The first constituent modifies or encodes an attribute of the second constituent. Examples (13)–(16) illustrate endocentric and exocentric compounds within this category.

(13)   a.   endocentric   b.   exocentric
             baş erin   *ak sakal*
             head lip   white beard
             'upper lip'   'old (man)'

(14)   a.   *altın tavuk*   b.   *ak süyek*
             gold hen   white bone
             'peacock'   'noble'

(15) a. kart   ana   b. beder   bet
        old   mother   bad   face
        'grandmother'   'barefaced'

(16) a. ara   şahar   b. boş   boyun
        center city   empty   neck
        'capital city'   'lazy'

With coordinative compounds the two lexemes are conjoined. Either both constituents serve as the head or the head is outside the entire compound, as illustrated in (17)–(20).

    endocentric   exocentric
(17) a. cer   kök   b. at   sirke
        earth   sky   horse   young louse
        'earth and sky'   'lichen'

(18) a. katın   kişi   b. ant   toba
        woman   man   oath   penitence
        'woman and man'   'oath'

(19) a. bar-çı   kel-çi   b. ata   baba
        go-NOML   come-NOML   grandfather father
        'errand'   'ancestor'

(20) a. al-ım/al-ış   ber-im/ber-iş
        buy-NOML   give-NOML
        'shopping'

Note that the linking element -(s)In surfaces only with subordinate compounds that encode a complementary relation between the constituents as in (11) and (12). However, this is not the case for all subordinate compounds, as shown by (9) and (10). The next section investigates the semantic relations between the constituents of a compound.

3 Semantic relations in compounds

The semantic relation between the constituents of a compound is predictable to a certain extent. However, the fact that one can easily form a novel compound to denote a concept indicates that the potential semantic relations between the parts of a compound are numerous. For example, in (21a) and (21b), the non-head constituent indicates the source of the oil. In (21c), on the other hand, the non-head constituent does not signal the source but is an attribute of the head noun. In (21d), the non-head constituent marks the function of the oil.

(21) a. *soz   cav*   b. *çöplev   cav*
        mesentery oil   sunflower oil
        'tallow'   'sunflower seed oil'
     c. *suv   cav*   d. *çuruk   cav*
        liquid   oil   shoe   oil
        'oil'   'shoe polish'

The meanings of compounds can be derived based on world knowledge. However, some far-fetched interpretations become possible when an appropriate context is provided. At first glance, a novel compound like *alma cav* 'apple oil' would be interpreted as the oil that you extract from an apple. Although this does not seem to be possible practically, this is the first interpretation that arises. In a specific context, checked with three native speakers of Karachay-Balkar, this compound can be construed as a deictic compound. Now let's assume that there is a barter market where people exchange goods. If you want to exchange your handmade oil for organic apples, then you might label your apples *alma cav* 'apple oil'; i.e., the oil that you use as an instrument to obtain apples. Hence in addition to the lexicalized compounds given in (9)–(12), one can form novel, deictic compounds. As is clear from this example, there does not seem to be a limit to interpretations provided via different contexts. However, there have been attempts to delimit the possible semantic relations between two nouns (Marchand 1969, Levi 1978; see also Pepper, this volume). Levi (1978) proposes a limited set of predicational relations such as CAUSE, HAVE, MAKE, BE, USE, FOR, IN, ABOUT, and FROM. These predicates provide the link between the non-head and the head constituents. Like pragmatic interpretations, however, it is possible to suggest more than one predicational relation between the constituents. In (22) below, some of these predicational relations are illustrated with examples from Karachay-Balkar.

(22) a. CAUSE *darman   darı*   b. HAVE *cer   iye-si*
              cure   medicine   earth   owner-LE
              'medicine'   'God of Earth'
     c. MAKE   *gıbı   av*   d. USE   *cayav   col*
              spider   web   pedestrian road
              'spider web'   'pathway'
     e. BE   *cuvuk-   teng*   f. IN   *avuz   suv*
              relative friend   mouth   water
              'kith and kin'   'saliva'
     g. FOR   *ayak   kiyim*   h. FROM *çın   ayak*
              foot   garment   porcelain bowl
              'shoe'   'cup'
     i. ABOUT *kaygı   söz*
              trouble statement
              'condolences'

Note that only the form in (22b), with the HAVE relation, bears the linking element. However, the presence of *-(s)In* is not necessarily linked to the HAVE predicational relation, as illustrated in (23). Although the same predicational relation exists, the linking element does not surface.

(23) a. *pil   süyek*   b. *kirit   baş*
        elephant bone   lock   head
        'ivory'   'handle of a lock'

Based on the discussions in Sections 2 and 3, the next section takes a closer look at the distribution and function of the linking element.

4 The linking element in Karachay-Balkar

Seegmiller (1996: 15) suggests that compound types with the linking element are rare and that marking some forms with the linking element is optional. However, as illustrated in (2), the absence of the linking element leads to ungrammaticality. Tavkul (2007: 924) labels the forms in (1) as indefinite noun phrases and suggests that, in contrast to Turkish, these phrases do not bear the linking element. Note, however, that these analyses are problematic because in some forms the linking element is obligatory and the forms with the linking element are similar to lexical items but not to syntactic phrases. Gürer (2017), on the other hand, suggests that the distribution of the linking element is predictable and that *-(s)In* surfaces on the head noun when the head noun and the non-head are inherently relational. The head is a transitive noun and the linking element signals the presence of a projection introducing the argument of the head; i.e., the dependent.[9] Before we discuss the arguments of Gürer (2017) with some novel data, first we explain what is meant by transitivity for a noun.

As is well known, an intransitive verb introduces a single argument to the structure whereas two-place predicate terms such as transitive verbs introduce two arguments. Being transitive or intransitive is not restricted to verbs as nouns also have this property (Löbner 1985, 2002; Barker 1995; Vikner and Jensen 2002; Partee and Borschev 2003).[10] Borschev and Partee (2001: 6) suggest that "relational Ns differ from simple sortal Ns in having an additional argument place; they describe their referents not only (and sometimes not primarily) as being of a certain 'sort' but as standing in a certain relation to some other entity or entities." In (24), for example, the noun 'title' is a transitive noun in that, in addition to the referent itself, the term signals the presence of another referent; i.e., 'the book'. It is a dependent part of the whole.

(24)   *The title of the book is catchy.*

The simple, sortal noun 'book', in contrast, is a one-place term in that the referent of the book does not require the existence of another entity. Hence the relation between the elements of a compound can be a head-complement relation. Building on the lexical structure theory of Pustejovsky (1995), Vikner and Jensen (2002: 196, 205) suggest the following lexical relations for genitive constructions:

(25)   a.   Inherent:
            (i)   kinship terms: *the girl's sister/cousin/father*
            (ii)   verb-related nouns: *the girl's aim/death/arrival*
            (iii)   relational nouns: *the girl's age/position/name/number*

---

9 For Turkish, Öztürk and Taylan (2016) suggest that *-sIn* is the spelling out of the functional head nP that introduces the argument to the structure. They further suggest that *-sIn* surfaces even in forms with intransitive head nouns in Turkish, because these heads are actually transitivized via type-shifting operators. Gürer (2017) shows that unlike Turkish Karachay-Balkar is more restrictive in that *-sIn* surfaces only with nouns that are inherently transitive.

10 Leaving aside the details, Vikner and Jensen (2002) suggest that all genitive NPs are arguments of the head nouns. If the head noun is not relational then it is forced to be relational via type-shifters. Partee and Borschev (2003) suggest that not all genitive NPs are arguments but can be modificational in some languages.

b. Part-whole:
   (i)   dependent part-whole: *the girl's nose*
   (ii)   autonomous part-whole: *the car's engine*
c. Agentive: *the girl's poem*
d. Control: *the girl's car/garden/ball*

In contrast to the pragmatic interpretations that were investigated in Section 3, these lexical interpretations are readily available. Out of these four relations, only inherent and dependent part-whole relation terms are transitive. These terms are transitive because their existence is fully dependent on the presence of another term. If there is a 'sister,' there needs to be another person to validate her sisterhood. Following a similar line, one can talk about the form, colour, corner or bottom only in the presence of an entity. In contrast to a dependent part noun, an autonomous part noun can appear in a sentence independently of the whole. Hence one can talk about seeing an engine on the ground, but this is not possible with dependent part nouns.[11]

Gürer (2017) suggests that the presence of the linking element is closely related to the inherently transitive lexical relations as illustrated in (26) with some new examples.

(26) a. cer   baş-ı   b. tengiz   kıyır-ı
      earth   head-LE   sea   side-LE
      'world'   'seaside'
    c. suv   ız-ı   d. keçe   ara-sı
      water   trace-LE   night   middle-LE
      'riverside, riverbed'   'midnight'
    e. cer   iye-si
      earth   owner-LE
      'God of Earth'
    f. kazavat-ta sabiy-le   öl-e-dile   ayt-ıl-ğan-ı
      war-LOC   child-PL   die-PROG-3PL   say-PASS-NOML-LE
      'The claim that children die in the war.'
    g. duniya-da ne   zat   işle-y-biz   sor-uv-u
      world-LE   what   thing   do-PROG-1PL   ask-NOML-LE
      'The question of what we are doing in the world.'

---

11 Note that this head-complement relation is more fine-grained than the head-complement relation in subordinate compounds in that the dependent term requires the presence of another referent.

In (26a)–(26d), the head noun denotes a dependent part-whole relation. In (26e), the head noun 'owner' refers to a relational noun. Finally, in (27f) and (27g), the head is a verb-related noun that is transitive. Hence, in all these cases, the head noun is inherently transitive.

It is now time to compare these forms with compounds without a linking element. The relation between the head and the dependent in (27a)–(27h) denotes an autonomous part-whole relation whereas that in (27i)–(27j) denotes a control relation.

(27) a. *ayak kiyim*
foot garment
'shoe'

b. *üy hapçük*
house goods
'household goods'

c. *iynek orun*
cow place
'stable'

d. *soz cav*
mesentery oil
'tallow'

e. *çöplev cav*
sunflower oil
'sunflower seed oil'

f. *avuz suv*
mouth water
'saliva'

g. *çuruk cav*
shoe oil
'shoepolish'

h. *gıbı av*
spider web
'spider web'

i. *ayak maşina*
foot machine
'bicycle'

j. *cayav col*
pedestrian road
'pathway'

The data clearly indicates that the presence of the linking element is linked to the transitivity of the head. We provide a new test based on Karachay-Balkar genitive-possessive constructions to validate this hypothesis. In a typical genitive-possessive construction, the non-head is marked with a genitive marker while the head bears a possessive agreement marker, as indicated in the following examples. In all the forms in (28), it is clear that the dependent is the possessor and the head is the possessee.[12]

(28) a. *biz-ni üy-übüz*
we-GEN house-1PL.POSS
'our house'

b. *siz-ni arba-gız*
you-GEN car-2PL.POSS
'your car'

---

[12] Vikner and Jensen (2002) suggest that what is generally taken as a possessor-possession relation in a genitive possessive construction is actually a control relation. Hence, we can interpret these constructions as encoding control relations.

c. tengiz-ni kıyır-ı
   sea-GEN side-3SG.POSS
   'the side of the sea'

d. tav-nı baş-ı
   mountain-GEN head-3SG.POSS
   'the top of the mountain'

For Turkish, Öztürk and Taylan (2016) show that when the head noun is intransitive, it is possible to delete the agreement marker on the head noun. The meaning of the construction then changes and there is not necessarily a possession or control relation. However, this is not felicitous with transitive head nouns.

In order to check this hypothesis for Karachay-Balkar, we carried out an online test of grammaticality judgment with some speakers of Karachay-Balkar. In total, 32 speakers of Karachay-Balkar living in Konya completed the online questionnaire. The age span of the participants ranged from 22 to 64 years. They were asked whether the following sentences were acceptable or unacceptable in Karachay-Balkar. In (29), the head nouns are intransitive and encode a control relation whereas those in (30) are transitive.

(29) a. *Biz-ni üy bek aruv-du*
     we-GEN house very beautiful-3SG
     'Our house is very beautiful.'

   b. *Siz-ni arba bek aruv-du*
     you-GEN car very beautiful-3SG
     'Your car is very beautiful.'

(30) a. **Tengiz-ni kıyır bek aruv-du*
     sea-GEN side very beautiful-3SG
     'The seaside is very beautiful.'

   b. **Üy-nü tüb bek aruv-du*
     house-GEN bottom very beautiful-3SG
     'The floor of the house is very beautiful.'

The examples in (29a) and (29b) were found to be acceptable by 82% and 85% of the participants, respectively. The examples in (30a) and (30b) were found to be acceptable by 36% and 25%, respectively. This pattern relates to the fact that the head nouns in (30) are inherently relational with the non-head units.[13] Hence the deletion of the agreement marker on the head noun yields unacceptability in (30).

---

[13] A reviewer points out that the examples in (29) and (30) also differ with respect to the animacy of the non-head constituent. Hence the ungrammatical forms can be suggested to be restricted to 'control' relations. A better contrastive pair is illustrated in these examples: (a) **biz-ni* (we-GEN) – *ana* (mother) ['our mother']; (b) *biz-ni* (we-GEN) – *arba* (car) ['our car']. As the ungram-

Before we move on to linking elements, a word of caution is in order regarding the optionality of linking elements with some compound forms. Seegmiller (1996: 15) makes the following observation on Karachay-Balkar compounds with a linking element:

> The 'izafet' type of compound that is so common in Turkish, in which the second member of a noun is marked with the suffix **I**, is rare in Karachay. A few compounds may occur either with or without the suffix I – both *ana tili* and *ana til* 'mother tongue' are found [...] but in general the izafet type is quite rare.

Seegmiller's (1996) argument is based on some published sources and on research carried out in New Jersey and in unspecified cities in Turkey. Interestingly, Seegmiller (1996) notes optionality for the linking element with certain compounds. As the research is conducted in two different countries, the first hypothesis is that variation may be due to a difference in dialect. However, this optionality is found even within the sources documenting the dialect spoken in Turkey. For example, the compounds in (31) are given with or without the linking element in two different dictionaries. However, note that the meaning of the compounds is not the same in the two cases.

(31) a. oğarı can-ı   b. oğarı can
      upper side-LE   'upper side'
      'south'   (Nevruz 1991: 471)
      (Tavkul 2000: 137)

As a next step, we checked whether optionality is accompanied by a change in meaning. The contrast between (32a) and (32b) indicates that the presence or absence of a linking element does indeed lead to a change in meaning. This is also the case in (33a) and (33b).[14]

---

maticality of (a) indicates, the deletion of the possessive agreement marker is unacceptable even in these examples.

14 We would like to thank an anonymous reviewer for bringing this set of contrastive data to our attention. Although compounding is a productive word formation tool in Karachay-Balkar, there are not many compounds with the linking element listed in the dictionaries of Nevruz (1991) and Tavkul (2000). Note that the environment for the linking element is quite restricted: the head must be transitive in a subordinating compound type. Hence, compounds with the linking element are not widespread.

(32) a. *suv - baş*　　　　　　　　b. *suv　baş-ı*
　　　　water　head　　　　　　　　　water　head-LE
　　　　'idiot'　　　　　　　　　　　　'water outlet'
　　　　(Tavkul 2000: 357; Nevruz 1991: 542)　(Tavkul 2000: 113)

(33) a. *it - burun*　　　　　　　　b. *it　burn-u*
　　　　dog　nose　　　　　　　　　　dog　nose-LE
　　　　'rosehip'　　　　　　　　　　　'dog nose'
　　　　(Tavkul 2000: 231)

To conclude this section, the data discussed above suggest that the linking element signals the transitivity of the head noun. Additionally, there must be a subordinating relation between the head and the non-head constituent which is of endocentric type. Note that the meaning of the whole compound is more predictable from the relation between head and non-head when the head noun bears the linking element.[15] The semantic relation is not compositional in (32a) and (33a), which seem to be more lexicalized than the forms in (32b) and (33b). Hence the linking element may also signal some morpho-syntactic differences.

The next section investigates whether compounds with and without a linking element differ based on any other diagnostics in addition to the transitivity relation.

5 A comparison of compounds with and without the linking element

In the preceding section, we showed that the elements of compounds with a linking element are inherently relational, whereas those without one are not. This is further supported by parallel genitive-possessive constructions which can surface without

---

15 This revised analysis is not without problems either, as illustrated in the following examples:

(1) a. *süt - baş-ı*　　　　　　　　b. *üy - baş*
　　　　milk　head-LE　　　　　　　　house-　head
　　　　'cream'　　　　　　　　　　　'roof'
　　　　(Nevruz 1991: 546; Tavkul 2000: 359)　(Nevruz 1991: 676; Tavkul 2000: 423)

The form in (1b) is more compositional than the form in (1a). Although the head noun is predicted as being inherently transitive and hence requiring the presence of a linking element, it is missing in (1b). In (1a), the linking element is missing in the Balkar dialect, as noted by Nevruz (1991: 546). The semantic denotation of the head noun *baş* can be different in these instances, leading to this unpredictability. This issue needs further investigation.

possessive agreement markers as illustrated in (29) and (30). This raises an obvious question as to the nature of the structural differences between these two types of compound patterns.

In the remainder of this section we will compare compounds with and without a linking element to find out whether they differ from each other based on a set of morpho-syntactic diagnostics. The investigation will shed further light on the internal structure of these compounds.

As part of the online test of grammaticality judgment, we prepared contexts for the following morpho-syntactic diagnostics: (i) modification of the non-head constituent; (ii) modification of the head constituent alone; and (iii) morphological markers on the non-head constituent. These diagnostics are expected to reveal whether the non-head or the head constituent can serve as an independent unit. If a constituent can serve as an independent unit, then the compound is not an atomic unit but is transparent for the morpho-syntactic operations. If these diagnostics are not acceptable, then these compounds are atomic, opaque units, similar to simple lexical items.

The first diagnostic is the modification of the non-head constituent in the presence or absence of a linking element on the head noun, as in (34) and (35) respectively. As it is possible for the informants to interpret the adjective as the modifier of the whole compound, we prepared contexts to make sure that the adjective can only be interpreted as the modifier of the non-head constituent. The informants were asked whether the sentences were acceptable in the following contexts. Additionally, they were asked whether the "calm thing" was the sea or the seaside in (34), and whether the "porcelain thing" was the tooth or the floss in (35).

(34) I love walking along the seaside. However, I cannot walk along the seaside if the sea is wavy.
?*Men [[şoş tengiz] kıyır-ın-da] aylan-ır-ğa süy-e-me.
I calm sea side-LE-LOC walk-NOML-ABL like-PROG-1SG
'I like walking along the seaside if the sea is calm.'

(35) This dental floss is not used for the hygiene of normal teeth. It is used for porcelain teeth. It is porcelain tooth floss.
?*Bu [[çın tiş] cıcım-dı].
this porcelain tooth floss-3SG
'This is porcelain tooth floss.'

The examples in (34) and (35) were found to be acceptable by 49% and 51% of the informants, respectively. The judgments indicate that these are borderline cases. However, no significant difference was observed between the forms with and without a linking element.

The second diagnostic was the insertion of a constituent between the head and the non-head for compounds with and without a linking element. A genitive-possessive phrase was also included.

(36) a. *kol cangı cavluk
       hand new clothing
       Reading: 'a new handkerchief'
    b. cangı [kol cavluk]
       new hand clothing
       'a new handkerchief'

(37) a. *tengiz aruv kıyır-ı
       sea beautiful side-LE
       Reading: 'a beautiful seaside'
    b. aruv [tengiz kıyır-ı]
       beautiful sea side-LE
       'a beautiful seaside'

(38) a. biz-ni cangı üy-übüz
       we-GEN new house-1PL.POSS
       Reading: 'our new house'
    b. *cangı biz-ni üy-übüz
       new we-GEN house-1PL.POSS
       'our new house'

The examples in (36) and (37) were found to be acceptable only by 20% and 15% of the informants, respectively. However, all the informants found (38a) to be acceptable whereas the reverse pattern in (38b) yielded unacceptability. To summarize, compounds with and without a linking element are not on a par with phrases as it is not possible to insert another term between the constituents, or to modify the non-head constituent in the exclusion of the head constituent. The examples in (39) and (40) further support this conclusion. It is not possible to attach inflectional morphemes to the non-head constituent; the head noun is the locus of morphemes, indicating that the whole compound, with and without the linking element, serves as a single unit.

(39) a. *iynek-le orun
       cow-PL place
       Reading: 'a place of cows'
    b. İynek orun-la-nı kör-dü-m.
       cow place-PL-ACC see-PAST-1SG
       'I saw the places of cows.'

(40) a. *tengiz-le kıyır-ı
       sea-PL side-LE
       Reading: 'side of seas'
    b. Tengiz kıyır-lar-ı-nı süy-er-me.
       sea side-PL-LE-ACC like-AOR-1SG
       'I like sea sides.'

All of these examples clearly indicate that the forms with and without the linking element show exactly the same properties regarding the morpho-syntactic diagnostics. Specifically, the diagnostics indicate that the two constituents serve as a single unit. Compounds with and without the linking element differ only with respect to the presence of the linking element. Hence, we suggest that the structures of the two types of compound do not differ except for the presence of the *n*P projection which introduces the linking element. In (41), the head noun is transitive; hence *n*P is projected to introduce the complement to the structure. Note that this is similar to the *v*P analysis of transitive verbs in that the arguments are introduced in the lower domain; i.e., VP and *v*P.

(41) cer üs-ü   (42) at   arba
    earth surface-LE   horse car
    'ground'   'horse-drawn carriage'

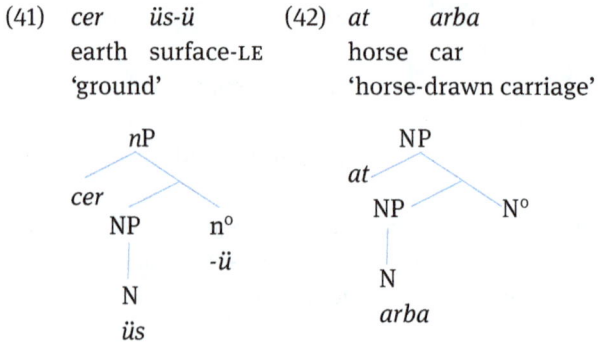

In (42) the head noun is not transitive and hence the *n*P which hosts the valency marker *-(s)In* is missing in the structure. In the absence of an *n*P projection, the dependent is introduced at Spec NP. Hence there is no inherent relation between the head and the dependent. The data in the previous sections also provide evidence for these structures, further indicating that the two compound types do not differ with respect to any other morpho-syntactic diagnostic.

6 Conclusion

This study has proposed a classification of compounds for Karachay-Balkar with a specific focus on compounds with and without a linking element. The discussions of the grammatical and semantic relations between the constituents of compounds revealed that the presence of the linking element is unpredictable. A closer look at the transitivity of the head noun indicated that the distribution of the linking element overlaps with the distribution of transitive head nouns, in line with Gürer (2017). Further evidence for this was based on the deletion of the marker on the head noun in genitive-possessive constructions. Additionally, we found that the linking element surfaces with the endocentric type of subordinate compound. However, compounds with and without the linking element do not differ with respect to any other morpho-syntactic diagnostic.

References

Barker, Chris. 1995. *Possessive descriptions*. Stanford: CSLI Publications.
Bauer, Laurie. 2001. Compounding. In Martin Haspelmath, Ekkehard König, Wulf Oesterreicher, & Wolfgang Raible (Eeds.), *Language typology and language universals,* Vol. 1, 695–707. Berlin: Mouton de Gruyter.
Bauer, Laurie 2003. *Introducing linguistic morphology*. Edinburgh: Edinburgh University Press.
Bisetto, Antonietta and Sergio Scalise. 2005. The classification of compounds. *Lingue e Linguaggio* IV(2). 319–332.
Bloomfield, Leonard. 1933. *Language*. New York: Holt.
Booij, Geert. 2005. *The grammar of words*. Oxford: Oxford University Press.
Borschev, Vladimir & Barbara H. Partee. 2001. Genitive modifiers, sorts, and metonymy. *Nordic Journal of Linguistics* 24(2). 140–160.
Fabb, Nigel. 1998. Compounding. In Andrew Spencer & Arnold M. Zwicky (Eds.), *Handbook of morphology*, 66–83. Oxford: Blackwell.
Gürer, Aslı. 2017. Compound formation in Karachay-Balkar: Implications for the marker –*sI*. *Dilbilim Araştırmaları Dergisi* 28(2). 21–41. https://doi.org/10.18492/dad.301460
Haspelmath, Martin. 2002. *Understanding morphology*. London: Arnold.
Levi, Judith. 1978. *The syntax and semantics of complex nominals*. New York: Academic Press.
Lieber, Rochelle. 1992. *Deconstructing morphology: Word formation in syntactic theory*. Chicago: The University of Chicago Press.
Löbner, Sebastian. 1985. Definites. *Journal of Semantics* 4. 279–326.
Löbner, Sebastian. 2002. *Understanding semantics*. London: Hodder.
Marchand, Hans. 1969. *The categories and types of present-day English word-formation*. München: Verlag C. H. Beck.
Masini, Francesca. 2009. Phrasal lexemes, compounds and phrases: A constructionist perspective. In *Word Structure* 2(2). 254–271.
Nevruz, Yılmaz. 1991. Karaçay-Malkar Türkçesinden Türkiye Türkçesine açıklamalı büyük sözlük. http://static.wpe.au.syrahost.com/var/m_f/fd/fd7/26135/767215-karacay_malkar_-_turkce_sozluk.pdf?download
Olsen, Susan. 2001. Copulative compounds. A closer look at the interface between morphology and syntax. In Geert Booij & Jaap van Marle (Eds.), *Yearbook of morphology 2000*, 279–320. Dordrecht: Kluwer.
Öztürk, Balkız & Taylan, Emine Eser. 2016. Possessive constructions in Turkish. *Lingua* 182. 88–108.
Partee, Barbara & Vladimir Borschev. 2003. Genitives, relational nouns & argument-modifier ambiguity. In Ewald Lang, Claudia Maienborn & Catherine Fabricius-Hansen (Eds.), *Modifying adjuncts*, 67–112. Berlin: Mouton de Gruyter.
Pepper, Steve. 2020. *The typology of binominal lexemes: Noun-noun compounds and their functional equivalents*. University of Oslo PhD dissertation.

Pepper, Steve. This volume. Hatcher-Bourque: Towards a reusable classification of semantic relations. In Steve Pepper, Francesca Masini & Simone Mattiola (eds.), *Binominal lexemes in cross-linguistic perspective*. Berlin: Mouton de Gruyter.
Pustejovsky, James. 1995. *The generative lexicon*. Cambridge, MA: The MIT Press.
Scalise, Sergio & Antonietta Bisetto. 2009. The classification of compounds. In Rochelle Lieber & Pavol Štekauer (eds.), *The Oxford handbook of compounding*, 34–53. Oxford: Oxford University Press.
Seegmiller, Steve. 1996. *Karachay*. Munchen: LINCOM Europa.
Spencer, Andrew. 1991. *Morphological theory*. Oxford: Blackwell.
Tavkul, Ufuk. 2000. *Karaçay-Malkar Türkçesi Sözlüğü*. Ankara: Türk Dil Kurumu Yayınları.
Tavkul, Ufuk. 2007. Karaçay-Malkar Türkçesi. In Ahmet Bican Ercilasun (ed.), *Türk Lehçeleri Grameri*, 883–938. Ankara: Akçağ Yayınları.
van Schaaik, Gerjan. 2002. *The noun in Turkish: Its argument structure and the compounding straitjacket*. Wiesbaden: Harrassowitz Verlag.
Vikner, Carl & Per Anker Jensen. 2002. A semantic analysis of the English genitive: Interaction of lexical and formal semantics. *Studia Linguistica* 56. 191–226.

Polina Pleshak
Binominal lexemes in Moksha and Hill Mari

Abstract: This paper describes the syntax and semantics of binominal lexemes in two Finno-Ugric languages spoken in the Volga Region, Moksha and Hill Mari (Uralic).[1] I will show that Moksha and Hill Mari demonstrate competition between two types of nominal modification construction: (i) juxtaposed (**jxt**), and (ii) genitival constructions (**gen**) that do not express core possessive relations. In addition, I will show that the Finno-Ugric genitive has noncanonical attributive functions in certain contexts, and shares morphosyntactic properties with attributivizers.

1 Binominals in Moksha and Hill Mari

Binominals denote complex concepts that arise from a combination of two other concepts expressed by nouns (or thing-roots). In order to understand how binominals function in a particular language, one should also understand how nominal modification constructions work (cf. Pepper, this volume, a, §4.2). In this paper, I analyse binominals in two Finno-Ugric languages, Moksha and Hill Mari, in the context of other nominal modification constructions. Moksha (ISO 639-3: MDF) is one of the two Mordvin languages, alongside with Erzya (MYV). It is spoken by approximately 130,000 people in the Republic of Mordovia, Russia. Hill Mari (MRJ), also known as Western Mari, is a Mari language, alongside Meadow Mari (MHR, Eastern Mari). It is spoken by approximately 30,000 people in the Mari El Republic, Russia.

---

[1] The research has been supported by Russian Foundation for Basic Research, grant N° 19-012-00627.
    I am grateful to my friends and fieldwork colleagues for insightful discussion of the data and to my language consultants, without who this research could never have happened. I am also grateful to the anonymous reviewer for useful comments and to my friends Isabel Last and Justin Malčić for helping me with English.
    The data for the present research were collected during various field trips. The Moksha data were elicited in the villages of Lesnoje Tsibajevo and Lesnoje Ardashevo in the Temnikovskij district of the Republic of Mordovia between 2015 and 2017. The Hill Mari data come from the villages of Kuznetsovo and Mikrjakovo in the Gornomarijskij district of the Mari El Republic and were elicited between 2016 and 2018. Corpora collected during the same projects were also used. Although most of the phenomena presented in this paper are attested in most of the dialects of these languages, it should be kept in mind that the systems described pertain to the particular dialects investigated.

https://doi.org/10.1515/9783110673494-013

There is a long history of grammatical description of both languages (for Moksha, see Koryakov and Kholodilova 2018: 13 and references therein; for Hill Mari, see Savatkova 2002: 6–7). However, most authors of older descriptive grammars concentrate on the meaning of morphological affixes, with little information about syntax. In Mordvin grammars, we see that nouns in absolute (caseless) forms (1a), as well as in genitive-like adjectival forms (1b) can express properties of objects (Bubrikh 1953; Kolyadenkov and Zavodova 1962; Tsyganov 1964; Tsygankin 1980). Genitive-like affixes are distinguished from genitive case for semantic reasons. However, according to the same grammarians, genitive forms themselves (1c) can also encode attributive relations (Kolyadenkov 1954: 219–222). In section 2, I argue that the two forms can be treated uniformly as genitive.

(1) (Kolyadenkov 1954: 219; 221; 222)
   a. Moksha **al akšə** [egg white] 'an egg white'
   b. Moksha **kev-ən' kud** [stone-ADJ[2] house] 'a stone house'
   c. Erzya **kolxoz-on' paks'a** [collective.farm-GEN field] 'a field of a collective farm'

In most Mari grammars unmarked modifiers that correspond to Mordvin caseless forms are treated as nominative (2). Genitive forms are also reported to have adjectival functions (Savatkova 2002; Pengitov 1961). Abstracting away from terminology, we can conclude that nominal modification constructions in the two languages must be very similar, with an unmarked or genitive form as a modifier.

(2) Mari *kǝrtn'i amasa* [iron door] 'an iron door' (Savatkova 2002: 96)

The distinction between unmarked (**jxt**) and genitive (**gen**) forms is frequently described in terms of (in)definiteness: indefinite modifiers are unmarked, whereas definite ones have genitive marking (Bubrikh 1953: 51 for Mordvin; Anduganov 1990 for Finno-Ugric in general). Kangasmaa-Minn (1966, 1968) points out that in Mari, nominative and genitive in adnominal position are mostly interchangeable,

---

2 Abbreviations: 1–3 – person, ABL – ablative, ACC – accusative, ADJ – adjectivizer, ADV – adverbializer, AOR – aorist, ATR – attributivizer, CAUS – causative, CN – connegative, CVB – converb, DAT – dative, DEF – definiteness, DEST – destinative, DETR – ditransitive, DIM – diminutive, EL – elative, FREQ – frequentative, GEN – genitive, ILL – illative, IMP – imperative, IN/IN2 – inessive, INDEF2 – indefinite, IPFV – imperfective, LAT – lative, MEAS – measure, NEG – negation, NPST – nonpast, O – object, OPT – optative, PASS – passive, PERS – derivational affix denoting humans, PL – plural, POSS – possession, PRET – preterite, PROL – prolative, PRON – pronominal, PROP – proprietive, PRS – present, PST – past, PTCP – participle, RES – resultative, S – subject, SG – singular.

except for canonical animate possessors which are only expressed with the genitive. Some information about binominals can be found in the part of grammar dedicated to word formation; according to their grammars, both Mordvin and Mari use compounding (**cmp**) in order to form new words (Evsevjev 1963: 103; Kolyadenkov 1962: 49–55 for Mordvin, Pengitov 1961: 92–96; Savatkova 2002: 123–128 for Mari).

In terms of the typology of binominal constructions proposed in Pepper (this volume, a), Moksha and Hill Mari exhibit the following types of binominals: juxtaposition, **jxt** (3)–(4); derivation, **der** (5)–(6); adjectival, **adj** (7)–(8); and genitival, **gen** (9)–(10).[3]

(3) Moksha *vir' ki* [forest road] 'forest road'

(4) Mari *šarək miž* [sheep wool] 'sheep wool'

(5) Moksha *pil'ə-ks* [ear-DEST] 'earring'

(6) Mari *kätö-zä* [herd-PERS] 'herdsman'

(7) Moksha *urdaz-u lɛj* [dirt-ATR river] 'dirty river'

(8) Mari *paj-an lem* [meat-PROP soup] 'meat soup'

(9) Moksha *ava-n' panar* [woman-GEN dress] 'women's dress'

(10) Mari *pu-n toma* [wood-GEN house] 'wooden house'

Double-marked structures are also found in these languages (11)–(12), but they only denote canonical possessive relations, which are not binominals as defined above and hence beyond the scope of this paper. For further details on the possessive construction in Finno-Ugric see Pleshak (2018).

(11) Moksha *ava-t' panar-əc* [woman-DEF.SG.GEN dress-3SG.POSS.SG] 'the woman's dress'

(12) Mari *ədərämäš-ən sumka-žə* [woman-GEN bag-POSS.3SG] '(the) women's bag'

---

3 In my examples, I use the transcription that was developed in the corresponding fieldwork projects organized by the Department of Theoretical and Applied Linguistics of Lomonosov Moscow State University. It is similar but not identical to the Uralic Phonetic Alphabet.

The possessive marker on the head noun is optional in some contexts, which results in dependent-marked structures like (11)–(12), which on the surface look like genitival binominals. This suggests that genitival binominals can also express possessive relations in Moksha and Hill Mari (see also the Erzya example (1c) above). In Section 4, I argue that there are two types of genitival constructions in these languages, each with completely distinct semantics and syntactic properties, and that one of them can be regarded as a genitival binominal (**gen**).

The paper is organized as follows. In section 2, I discuss the semantics of binominals in Moksha and Hill Mari. In sections 3 and 4, I describe the morphosyntactic properties of binominals with unmarked modifiers (**jxt**) and genitival binominal constructions (**gen**) respectively. Section 5 provides some conclusions.

2 The semantics of binominals in Moksha and Hill Mari

2.1 Binominals in Moksha

The semantics of binominals in Moksha is discussed by Tsyganov (1964). He notes that complex words (**cmp**) and constructions with absolute forms (**jxt**) compete with genitival binominals (**gen**, constructions with genitival modifiers). My data show a restricted set of semantic relations that can only be encoded by means of compounding or juxtaposition, and not with genitival structures. In this section, I present the data and discuss possible competing forms in the domain of adnominal relations. Koptjevskaja-Tamm (2002, 2004) discusses various adnominal relations, in the context of a study of adnominal genitive constructions in the languages of Europe. These are relations such as predestination (*a women's bag*), material (*wooden spoon*), species (*an avocado tree*) and several quantitative relations like age (*a baby of three months*), among others.[4] For better typological comparability, these relations were taken as a starting point for the present study. Some additional relations were added to fit real distinctions present in the language. The full list of the relations is provided in Table 1 below (as well as Table 2 in the section on Hill Mari).

---

[4] The relation of 'predestination' is subsumed by PURPOSE in the Hatcher-Bourque classification (Pepper, this volume, b); 'material' equates to COMPOSITION and 'species' to TAXONOMY.

Table 1: Relation-construction correspondence in Moksha.

Semantics	NN (cmp)	N N (jxt)	N-GEN N (gen)
Species: kinship terms	OK	n/a	n/a
Species: berries	OK	n/a	OK
Species: mushrooms	OK	OK	n/a
Species: animals	OK	OK	OK
Species: plants	OK	OK	OK
Species: part-whole (+ body parts)	OK	OK	OK
Species: purpose	OK	OK	OK
Natural phenomena (+ inherent properties)	OK	OK	OK
Natural sex of animate beings	n/a	OK	*
Onomastic	n/a	OK	*
Nicknames	n/a	OK	OK
Identification properties	n/a	OK	OK
Substance	n/a	OK	OK
Material	*	*	OK
Predestination	*	*	OK
Quantificational properties	*	*	OK

In the following sections, I discuss the correspondence between semantic relations and morphosyntactic constructions used to encode them in more detail. Binominals with no genitive marker seem to be more restrictive than genitival binominals. Therefore, I start with a discussion of the competition between compounds and genitival binominals, where the term 'compound' will be used as an umbrella term for binominals of type **jxt** as well as for **cmp** (2.1.1). Then I proceed with comparison of **cmp** and **jxt** compounds (2.1.2). Next, I turn to the discussion of the most productive type of binominals in Moksha – **gen** binominals (2.1.3). I conclude the section with an overall evaluation of the Moksha system (2.1.4).

2.1.1 Competition between compounds and genitival binominals

As reported by Tsyganov (1964), expressions denoting the natural sex of animate beings (13) and onomastic expressions such as toponyms (14) are expressed exclusively by compounds.

(13) *ava oftə* [woman bear] 'she-bear'

(14) *s'ɛl'ɛj vel'ə* [Sijali village] 'Sijali village'

According to Tsyganov, there is one further type that is exclusively expressed by compounds rather than genitival constructions, viz. epithets that are used together with nicknames and comparisons, as well as identification properties (see also Feoktistov 1995 for a discussion of three-word compounds, where the first two words constitute a binominal denoting a property). However, the variety of Moksha described in this paper uses another strategy, as shown by the data collected in the field: both juxtaposed and genitival binominals are possible (15)–(16). Moreover, with nicknames the genitive is even preferred.

(15) *prozvišča-c* **sokəl-ən'** / **sokəl s'el'mə**
 nickname-3SG.POSS.sg falcon-GEN falcon eye
 'His nickname is Falcon Eye'.

(16) *per'f-ka-nzə* *las'k-ən'c'* **n'uŗkɛn'ɛ pil'gə** / **pil'gə-n'**
 around-PROL-3SG.POSS run-IPFV.PST.3SG short leg leg-GEN
 id'-n'ɛ
 child-DIM
 'A short-legged child was running around her'.

Part-whole relations with respect to species (17) can be expressed by compounds (as well as by genitival binominals).

(17) **kelu** / **keluv-ən' lopa-n'ɛ-s'** *salavan'ə pra-j*
 birch birch-GEN leaf-DIM-DEF.SG stealthily fall-NPST.3SG
 'The birch leaf is falling slowly'.

Body-parts are represented in Table 1 as a subtype of the part-whole relation, but there is an animacy restriction on the dependent of compound nouns: body parts are ungrammatical in compounds (18) as they have animate "wholes".

(18) **id'-ən'** / **id' kɛd'-s'* *jomla-n'ɛ*
 child-GEN child hand-DEF.SG small-DIM
 'The child's hand is small'.

However, there are two contexts with body parts where compounding is not ruled out. These are animal body parts when used as a concept for comparison (15) or when they have been separated from the main body (19).

Now we can look back at the encoding of nicknames. Even though compounds are not the only means used to express the relation between the two entities in nicknames, this relation is indeed important for the possibility of using compounds.

(19) val'mə-va   n'ɛj-əv-s'   an'c'ək **traks pr'ɛ**
     window-PROL see-PASS-PST.3SG only   cow   head
     'Only a cow's head was seen through the window (the head already separated from cow) (*there was a whole cow, but it was its head that was seen)'.

The other relations that can be encoded not only with genitive structures but also with compounds are species relations with respect to substance (20), place (21) and inherent property relations (22).[5]

(20) mon pid'-an   **sura-n' /   sura   jam**
     I   cook-NPST.1SG millet-GEN millet porridge
     'I'm cooking a millet porridge'.

(21) **paks'ɛ-n' / paks'ɛ pančf-n'ə**   pan'č-s'-t'   n'i
     field-GEN   field   flower-DEF.PL bloom-PST.3-PL already
     'The wild flowers have already finished blooming'.

(22) mon'   s't'a-ft-əman'   **zar'ɛ-n' / zar'ɛ valc'**
     I.GEN wake.up-CAUS-PST.1.O.SG.O.3SG.S dawn-GEN dawn light.DEF.SG
     'I was woken up by the light of dawn'.

Tsyganov also mentions that the purpose relation can be encoded with compounds. My data show that such examples are rather marginal in the dialect being studied, and that genitives are a more natural encoder.

(23) m'in'   **ved'ən' /   ʔved'** vedərkan'əkə   taštəms'
     we.GEN water-GEN water   pail-1PL.POSS get.older-PST.3SG
     'Our water pail has got older'.

---

5 In Hatcher-Bourque, 'part-whole' is termed PARTONOMY, 'substance' is COMPOSITION, and 'place' is LOCATION. The specific "inherent property" in the example (*dawn light*) would be classified as TEMPORALITY.

2.1.2 Two types of compounds: cmp and jxt

Within the category of compounds there is a further distinction between **cmp** and **jxt** compounds, where the former are supposed to be single words formed in the lexicon, while the latter are formed in syntax. The problem is, however, that we see both types represented in the dictionaries. Some of these constructions are written in dictionaries as a single word (**cmp**), whereas others are written as two words (**jxt**). This distinction seems to be supported phonologically: one-word compounds form a single phonological word, whereas other compounds conserve prosodic independence. However, this still requires an accurate phonetic analysis.

The **cmp** compounds that are included in Schankina's (1993) dictionary mostly denote species of animals, plants, and berries (24) or body-part terms (25). **cmp** compounds can also be found that encode species relations with respect to kinship (26) and some natural phenomena (27). However, the same types of meanings can be encoded by genitival binominals as well, as illustrated in (28).

(24) *oftə-mar'* [bear-apple] 'dog-rose'

(25) *prɛ-pakar'* [head-bone] 'skull'

(26) *pɛl'n'ə-rvɛ* [younger.brother-wife] 'younger brother's wife'

(27) *ej-z'urə* [ice-horn] 'icicle'

(28) *ajgər-ən' počka* [stallion-GEN sorrel] 'Russian dock (a plant)'

In (27), one can see a morphophonological process at the boundary between the two roots: *s'urə* 'horn' becomes *z'urə*. Unfortunately, not all words exhibit morphophonological processes; moreover, in speech the initial voiceless consonants of the words are voiced sporadically in other contexts, including the beginning of the sentence (see also Kukhto 2018: 24), which means one cannot rely on morphophonology either to distinguish **cmp** from **jxt**.

An interesting criterion that helps to distinguish **cmp** compound lexemes from **jxt** constructions formed in syntax is proposed by Kolyadenkov (1962). The criterion is compositionality of meaning: only non-compositional binominals are compound lexemes (29). Otherwise, compound words are indistinguishable from compositional **jxt** compounds.

(29) Erzya *ved'-gev* [water-stone] 'mill' (Kolyadenkov 1962: 55)

However, this principle is unidirectional. Entities with a non-compositional meaning are not always expressed with **cmp** compounds. The same concepts may be expressed with **jxt** compounds as well. Consider the examples in (30 a-b) for species of mushroom and for types of body-part (compare (31) with (25)), see also the discussion about irrelevance of types of meanings above.

(30) a. *pičə-pangə* [field-mushroom] 'boletus'
      b. *poju pangə* [aspen mushroom] 'orange-cup boletus'

(31) *ščokə pakar'* [cheek bone] 'cheek-bone'

The distinction seems to depend on the frequency of usage, but this would require a statistical analysis. This is difficult to conduct as all these words are rarely attested in colloquial speech.

Given that some binominals can be more lexicalized than others, the question arises whether they are formed in the syntax or in the lexicon. Most probably, the lexicalized compounds arise from syntactic ones (Kolyadenkov 1962). In Section 4, I will concentrate on the syntactic processes of productive compound formation, but I will not be considering lexicalized one-word compounds.

2.1.3 Genitival binominals

The default structure for expressing adnominal relations in Moksha is the genitival binominal (**gen**). In addition to those relations where we saw competition between compounds and genitival binominals, genitive marking of the modifier is the only option for predestination (32), material (33) or quantificational characteristics of inanimate objects (34) and humans (35).

(32) **ava-n'** /   *ava   panar-s'   povfta-f   lavka-t'
      woman-GEN woman   dress-DEF.SG hang-PTCP.RES   shop-DEF.SG.GEN
      esə
      in.IN
      'The women's dress is hanging in the shop'.

(33) **šuftə-n'** /   *šuftə   s'ec'   pals'
      tree-GEN   tree   bridge.DEF.SG burn.PST.3SG
      'The wooden bridge has burnt'.

(34) **vet'ə kilov-ən'** / *kilo kirɛ-s' t'ejə-n pɛk tožd'ɛ
 five kilo-GEN kilo weight-DEF.SG PRON.DAT-1SG.POSS very light
 'A five-kilo weight is too light for me'.

(35) **kafksəgemən' kizə-n'** / *kizə baba-n'ɛ-s'
 eighty year-GEN year granny-DIM-DEF.SG
 aščəs' skomn'ɛ-n'ɛ-t' lank-sə
 be.situated-PST.3SG bench-DIM-DEF.SG.GEN on-IN
 'The eighty-year-old granny was sitting on the bench'.

It is worth recalling that purposive relations are also expressed by genitive constructions (23), as well as some species of animals and plants: compare genitival (36) with compound (37).

(36) *vir'-ən' saraz* [forest-GEN hen] 'partridge'

(37) *vir' jaks'arga* [forest duck] 'wild duck'

2.1.4 Interim summary

Turning to the overall system of semantic relations, the system of adnominal constructions in Moksha underlines the distinction between material and substance relations, which were not distinguished by Koptjevskaja-Tamm (2004). A comparison of (33), which expresses a relation of material, with (20), which expresses a relation of substance, shows that these two relations must be distinguished since they can have different encodings. The distinction can sometimes be hard to grasp. A relation of material requires a situation with a completely new object as a result. For example, a wooden bridge is no longer simply wood. In a relation of substance, the substance remains while also obtaining a new form. In this case it is either an inherent property of an object or a part of it: in the example above, millet porridge is still millet.

To summarize the expression of semantic relations discussed in this section, the reader can consult Table 1 above, which connects the constructions with the semantics they encode. The table includes all the main types of construction: one-word compounds (NN, **cmp**), two-word compounds (N N, **jxt**) and genitival binominals (NGEN N, **gen**). Some of these data were elicited, and the rest were taken from the dictionary. In the former case the opposition in the table is "OK" vs. "*" as both positive and negative data were collected; in the latter – "OK" vs. "n/a" as there is no negative data in the dictionary. Table 1 shows that there is considerable overlap between the various constructions in the coding of these semantic values.

2.2 Binominals in Hill Mari

Hill Mari has a wide repertoire of attributive suffixes. Because of this, not only caseless and genitival modifiers compete in this domain (giving rise to **gen**, **cmp** and **jxt** binominals), but also nouns with attributivizers (**adj**). The situation with competition between compounds and genitival binominals is the opposite to what we have seen in Moksha. Compounds (mainly **jxt**) serve as the main construction to encode attributive relations (see also Kangasmaa-Minn 1968). Genitive binominals (**gen**), on the other hand, are restricted to encoding of material and origin, which can also be expressed by **jxt**. These two types of binominals differ crucially in their syntactic properties, as will be discussed in Section 4. As in Moksha, genitival structures also encode possessive relations, so **gen** binominals require a closer look. Although Hill Mari, unlike Moksha, does not have different declensions, and there seems to be only one genitive case in its system (without a definite vs. indefinite genitive distinction), genitive constructions in Hill Mari are of two different types. One of these is restricted to the expression of core possessive relations, where the genitival modifier denotes a referent, not a property (see Pepper, this volume, a, §4.2.1); therefore, it is not regarded as a genitival binominal, but rather an anchoring possessive construction. The other type is restricted to the expression of material and origin and is in competition with compounds. The distribution of compounds and genitival binominals is shown in Table 2. Here, again, as in the previous section, asterisks are only given for those examples that were elicited. If the only source was the dictionary, n/a indicates that there were no such examples.

Table 2: Relation-construction correspondence in Hill Mari.

Relation	NN (cmp)	N N (jxt)	N-GEN N (gen)
Species: kinship terms	OK	n/a	*
Species: berries	OK	OK	*
Species: mushrooms	OK	OK	*
Species: animals	OK	OK	*
Species: plants	OK	OK	*
Species: part-whole (+ body parts)	OK	OK	*
Species: purpose	OK	OK	*
Natural phenomena (+ inherent properties)	OK	OK	*
Natural sex of animate beings	n/a	OK	*
Onomastic	n/a	OK	*

Table 2 (continued)

Relation	NN (cmp)	N N (jxt)	N-GEN N (gen)
Nicknames	n/a	OK	*
Identification properties	n/a	OK	*
Substance	n/a	OK	OK
Material	n/a	OK	OK
Predestination	OK	OK	*
Quantificational properties	*	*	*

I start with a discussion of the competition between compounds, genitival binominals, and constructions with attributivizers (2.2.1). Then I compare **cmp** and **jxt** compounds (2.2.2).

2.2.1 Competition between compounds, genitival binominals and constructions with attributivizers

Some relations are expressed in a similar way in Moksha and Hill Mari. Consider the following compounds expressing the natural sex of animate beings (38), onomastic expressions (39) and identification properties (40), comparing them with the ones from Moksha (7), (8) and (15) respectively. Note that identification properties can also be expressed with the proprietive attributivizer and are thus encoded as attributive binominal constructions (**adj**).

(38) ävä möskä [woman bear] 'she-bear'

(39) väkšlap   sola   šajəl-nə   əl-ən   väkš
      Vjakshlap village   back-IN2   be-PRET   mill
      'There was a mill behind the village of Vjakshlap'. (Hill Mari corpus)

(40) šäjək   sənzä-än /   sənzä   moren
      squint   eye-PROP   eye   hare
      'squint-eyed hare'

However, we can see that the use of compounds is much wider in Hill Mari than it is in Moksha. Some relations that have competing genitive forms in Moksha are encoded primarily or even exclusively as compound binominals in Hill Mari. These are part-whole (41), substance (42), place (43) and inherent property relations (44).

(41) **püšängä ukš** kər-əlt-ə
 tree branch tear-DETR-AOR.3SG
 'A tree branch crunched'.

(42) ävä-m **šəl'ə** / ***šəl'ə-n** käšäl-əm šəšer dono šolt-en
 mother-POSS.1SG oat oat-GEN kissel-ACC milk with cook-PRET
 'My mother cooked an oat kissel with milk'.

(43) mən'ə-n t'et'ä-em jažo **sola** / ***sola-n** škol-əš kašt-eš
 I-GEN child-POSS.1SG good village village-GEN school-ILL go-LAT
 'My child goes to a good rural school'.

(44) ängər vəl-nə izi-š **tälzə sotə** kaj-eš
 stream top-IN2 small-ADV moon light be.seen-NPST.3SG
 'The moonlight can be seen above the stream'. (Hill Mari corpus)

Unlike in Moksha, material relations in Hill Mari can be encoded not only with a genitival binominal, but with a compound as well (45). Predestination, which is expressed in Moksha with genitive constructions, is a compound in Hill Mari (a genitive marker on the modifier would switch the meaning from predestination to ownership) (46).

(45) vas'a **kərtn'i** / **kərtn'i-n cep-əm** näl-ən
 Vasja iron iron-GEN chain-ACC take-PRET
 'Vasja bought an iron chain'.

(46) mən' **ədərämäš plat'ə-m** už-a-m
 I woman dress-ACC see-NPST-1SG
 'I see a women's dress'.

Quantificational characteristics of inanimate objects (47) and humans (48) are expressed with a special attributivizer.

(47) **vəclä i-äš** kož-vlä šalg-en ki-ät
 fifty year-ATR.MEAS fir-PL stand-CVB lie-NPST.3PL
 'Fifty-year-old fir-trees stand there'. (Hill Mari corpus)

(48) pr'im'ernə̂ əl-ən   naverno   **ik-tä**   **kändäkš-lu** **i-äš**
    about   be-PRET probably   one-INDEF2   eight-ten   year-ATR.MEAS
    t'ot'a
    grandfather
    'The old man was probably about eighty years old'. (Hill Mari corpus)

Proprietive meanings are expressed in Hill Mari with a proprietive attributivizer (49), see also (Kangasmaa-Minn 1969) for the discussion of the difference between genitive and proprietive adnominal modifiers.

(49) r'ečnoj   kol   **lu-an**   kol   əl-eš
    of.river fish bone-PROP   fish   be-NPST.3SG
    'The fish from the river is bony'. (Hill Mari corpus)

Sometimes the locative relation can be expressed by a combination of a locative case and an attributive suffix (50).

(50) to-nə̂-šə̂ päšä [home-IN2-ATR work] 'housework'

Thus, Hill Mari exhibits a large system of attributivizers which differ in their semantics and their morphosyntactic properties. A noun phrase that bears an attributive suffix can be very complex and denote a referent rather than property (51).

(51) **jažo sola-štə̂-šə̂**   škol-ə̂š   kašt-eš
    good   village-IN-ATR   school-ILL   go-NPST.3SG
    'He goes to the school in a good village'.

The morphosyntax of Hill Mari attributive constructions is a separate topic that merits its own discussion. It is therefore not discussed in the present paper.

2.2.2 Two types of compounds: cmp and jxt

As in Moksha, some compounds in Hill Mari are written as one word and can show morphophonological processes at the boundary between the two roots (**cmp**). For instance, both variants (52a–b) are included in the dictionary (Savatkova 2008). However, there is no evidence that these processes are characteristic only for compounds and not found in other contexts.

(52) a. *jal **parn'a*** [foot finger] 'toe'
      b. *jal-varn'a* [foot-finger] 'toe'

Semantically, **cmp** compounds in Hill Mari follow the same pattern as in Moksha: they denote species in flora and fauna, as well as body-parts (53) and natural phenomena (54). Savatkova (2002) notices that the meaning of **cmp** compounds in Hill Mari is usually hard to derive compositionally, which is very similar to Kolyadenkov's (1962) criterion for compound lexemes in Mordvin. She comments that non-compositionality can arise because of a metaphoric shift of one of the components (usually the second one) (54a) or comparison (metaphor) (54b). This is consistent with the idea that binominals of type **cmp** are more lexicalized than those of type **jxt**, i.e., further along the modification-reference continuum (see Editors' Introduction §3.5.1).

(53) a. *vuj-lu* [head-bone] 'skull'
      b. *ongâlaš lu* [chin bone] 'chinbone'

(54) a. *kečä jal* [sun leg] 'sunbeam'
      b. *kal'a-vač* [mouse-tail] 'braid' (Savatkova 2002: 127–128)

As in Moksha, even non-compositional expressions can be both **cmp** or **jxt** compounds. This complication was also pointed out by Kangasmaa-Minn (1966: 114–117).

2.3 Interim summary: Comparing the semantics of binominals in Moksha and Hill Mari

Moksha and Hill Mari have a similar set of constructions that can encode attributive relations (i.e., object modification), but their distribution is far from equal. Although semantic relations encoded with **cmp** compounds are quite similar, **jxt** compounds seem to have a very different "value" in the two languages. Whereas in Moksha compounds are very restricted semantically, in Hill Mari compounding seems to be the main strategy. The opposite pattern is seen with genitival structures: while this is the main strategy in Moksha, it is only used to encode material and origin semantics in Hill Mari. The systems of attributivizers are also different. While in Moksha the attributivizer encodes only a proprietive meaning, sharing this with adnominal locative dependents, in Hill Mari there are different types of attributivizers. One of them serves to express proprietive meaning, and another one competes with the compounding strategy in encoding locative relations. A special attributivizer is used to encode quantificational characteristics of the object. In some dialects (e.g., in the variant spoken in the village of Mikrjakovo) there is a special attributivizer for purpose and predestination relations.

(55) Mari *t'et'a-lək vərgem* [child-DEST clothes] 'children's clothes'

Table 3 compares the strategies of the two languages.

Table 3: The comparison of relation-construction correspondences in Moksha and Hill Mari.

Relation	Moksha	Hill Mari
Species: kinship terms	cmp	cmp
Species: berries	cmp / gen	cmp / jxt
Species: mushrooms	cmp / jxt	cmp / jxt
Species: animals	cmp / jxt / gen	cmp / jxt
Species: plants	cmp / jxt / gen	cmp / jxt
Species: part-whole (+ body parts)	cmp / jxt / gen	cmp / jxt
Species: purpose	cmp / jxt / gen	cmp / jxt
Natural phenomena (+ inherent properties)	cmp / jxt / gen	cmp / jxt
Natural sex of animate beings	jxt	jxt
Onomastic	jxt	jxt
Nicknames	jxt / gen	jxt
Identification properties	jxt / gen	jxt
Substance	jxt / gen	jxt / gen
Material	gen	jxt / gen
Predestination	gen	cmp / jxt
Quantificational properties	gen	adj

3 Syntactic properties of binominals in Moksha and Hill Mari

As noted by Nakov (2013), phonological, orthographic, morphological and syntactic features of compounds are language-specific. Orthographically, compounds consist of one or two words which may be hyphenated, while morphologically, they may have internal inflection. In the previous sections, I showed that binominals in both Moksha and Hill Mari consist of either one or two words. One-word **cmp** compounds are lexicalized two-word **jxt** compounds. In this section, I describe the morphosyntactic properties of **jxt** compounds in Moksha and Hill Mari, including morphological marking of the dependent, its potential modification, and discontinuity of binominals.

Following Bubrikh (1947), the form of the dependent in binominals in Mordvin is referred to as the absolute. The main property of this absolute form is that it cannot bear any nominal morphology. As both Moksha and Hill Mari have unmarked nominative case, it is hard to prove that the dependent is unmarked rather than nominative. Nevertheless, some arguments can be provided.

Nominative subjects in both languages can bear number or possessive suffixes, whereas in compounds this is strictly prohibited. Consider the example from Moksha in (56), where the subject is marked as singular and having a first singular possessor.

(56) Moksha t'ɛ   kn'iga-**z'ə**   put-f   škaf-t'
              this   book-1SG.POSS.SG   put-PTCP.RES   cupboard-DEF.SG.GEN
              potmə-s
              inside-ILL
              'This book of mine has been put into the bookcase'.

The same is true for Hill Mari: example (57) shows a plural subject with second plural possessor.

(57) Mari šâžar-**da-vlä**   jažo-n   ârg-at
            younger.sister-POSS.2PL-PL   good-ADV   sew-NPST.3PL
            'Your younger sisters sew well'.

This can be contrasted with the compound structures below. In neither language is the plural or possessive suffix grammatical for the non-head noun.

(58) Moksha **kelu** / *****keluf-t**   lopa-n'ɛ-t'n'ə   salavan'ə   pra-j̊-t'
              birch   birch-PL   leaf-DIM-DEF.PL   stealthily   fall-NPST.3-PL
              'The birch leaves (of many birches) fall slowly'.

(59) Mari pazar-âštâ   püergö   **ədərämäš** /   *****ədərämäš-vlä**   kalpak-âm
            market-IN   man   woman   woman-PL   hat-ACC
            vâžal-a
            sell-NPST.3SG
            'A man sells hats for women at the market'.

(60) Moksha *****kelu-z'ə**   lopa-n'ɛ-t'n'ə   salavan'ə   pra-j̊-t'
                birch-1SG.POSS.SG leaf-DIM-DEF.PL   stealthily fall-NPST.3-PL
                Intended: 'The leaves of my birch fall slowly'.

(61) Mari *tengečə mä   **šarə̂k-na**   miž-ə̂m   vâžal-en-nä
            yesterday we   sheep-POSS.1PL   wool-ACC sell-PRET-1PL
            Intended: 'Yesterday we sold our sheep's wool'.

Moreover, Moksha has a morphological marker of definiteness which is broadly present in the subject position (62) but is completely ungrammatical in nominal compounds (63).

(62) Moksha **kn'iga-s'**   put-f   škaf-t'   potmə-s
              book-DEF.SG   put-PTCP.RES   cupboard-DEF.SG.GEN   inside-ILL
              'The book has been put into the bookcase'.

(63) Moksha **kelu** / *****kelu-s'**   lopa-n'ɛ-t'n'ə   salavan'ə   pra-j̊-t'
              birch   birch-DEF.SG   leaf-DIM-DEF.PL   stealthily fall-NPST.3-PL
              'The leaves of the birch fall slowly'.

The second important property is modifying nouns in compounds have many restrictions on their own modification. There is a difference here between the two languages. In Moksha, dependents modified with another unmarked form are not accepted by all speakers (64), and modification with adjectives is extremely marginal (65).

(64) Moksha mon mol'-ən'   (?**pičə**) vir'   ki-va
              I   walk-PST.1SG   pine   forest road-PROL
              'I walked along a (pine) forest road'.

(65) Moksha ??mon af   jarc-s'-an   **sɛngɛr'ɛ** mar'   ked'-tə
              I   NEG eat-FREQ-NPST.1SG   green   apple skin-ABL
              'I don't eat the skin of green apples'.
              (Pleshak and Kholodilova 2018: 285)

In Hill Mari, restrictions are not so strict, in that some dependents can be modified with adjectives.

(66) Mari ᴼᴷ*šongə̂*⁶ **kesä** *miž*   *pižorgə̂-m näl-ə̂n-äm*
         old   goat   wool   mitten-ACC knit-PRET-1SG
    'I've bought a mitten made of an old goat's wool'.

Another set of properties concerns the 'independence' of such dependents. First, no element can be inserted between the two parts of a compound in Moksha.

(67) **paks'ɛ* **mazi**   *pan'čf-n'ə*   *pan'č-s'-t'*   *n'i*
     field   beautiful flower-DEF.PL bloom-PST.3-PL already
     Intended: 'The beautiful wild flowers have already finished blooming'.

(68) **paks'ɛ* **n'i**   *pan'čf-n'ə*   *pan'č-s'-t'*
     field   already flower-DEF.PL bloom-PST.3-PL
     Intended: 'The wild flowers have already finished blooming'.

In Hill Mari, this depends on the semantic relation between the two members of the construction. If a compound encodes the relation of predestination, another unmarked dependent can be inserted between its two parts (69a). Some speakers allow the insertion of lower⁷ adjectives, such as colour, between the material and head noun (70). Higher adjectives, such as subjective evaluation, cannot be inserted (71), nor can unmarked nouns denoting predestination (69b).

(69) Mari a. *pazar-ə̂štə̂* **ə̂dörämäš** *miž*   *noski-m*   *vâžal-at*
              market-IN   woman   wool   sock-ACC   sell-NPST.3PL
         b. **pazar-ə̂štə̂* **miž**   *ə̂dörämäš* *noski-m* *vâžal-at*
              market-IN   wool   woman   sock-ACC sell-NPST.3PL
     'In the market they sell women's woollen socks'.

(70) Mari a. *ävä-m*   **sotə̂** *miž*   *svitər-ə̂m* *pid-en*
              mother-POSS.1SG light   wool   sweater-ACC knit-PRET
         'My mother knitted a light woollen sweater'.
         b. ?*ävä-m*   **miž** *sotə̂* *svitər-ə̂m* *pid-en*
              mother-POSS.1SG wool   light   sweater-ACC knit-PRET
         'My mother knitted a light woollen sweater'.

---

6 The word *šongə̂* – 'old' is used only with animates and trees, so there is no ambiguity in the example.
7 See the scale of adjectival modifiers in Scott (2002), among others.

(71) Mari a. *pazar-ǝštǝ* **jažo miž** noski-m važal-at
market-IN good wool sock-ACC sell-NPST.3PL
b. **pazar-ǝštǝ* **miž jažo** noski-m važal-at
market-IN wool good sock-ACC sell-NPST.3PL
'In the market they sell good woollen socks'.

Unlike Moksha, where recursive compounds seem to be very marginal and left branching occurs only in exceptional cases, Hill Mari admits both types of recursive compounds: left-branching and right-branching (Mukai 2015). Consider the examples (72)–(73) below, representing right-branching and left-branching compounds respectively.

(72) Mari *[ǝdǝrämäš [miž noski]]*
woman wool sock
'woollen socks for women'

(73) Mari *[[kesǝ miž] pižorgǝ]*
goat wool mitten
'goat wool mittens'

Second, the dependents in compounds cannot be postposed in either language.

(74) Moksha a. *son iz'-ǝz'ǝ ker'-ǝ* **mar'** *ked'-t'*
he NEG.PST-3SG.S.3SG.O cut-CN apple peel-DEF.SG.GEN
b. **son iz'-ǝz'ǝ ker'-ǝ ked'-t'* **mar'**
he NEG.PST-3SG.S.3SG.O cut-CN peel-DEF.SG.GEN apple
'He has not cut the apple peel'.

(75) Mari a. *tengečǝ mä* **šarǝk** *miž-öm vǝžal-en-nä*
yesterday we sheep wool-ACC sell-PRET-1PL
b. **tengečǝ mä miž-öm* **šarǝk** *vǝžal-en-nä*
yesterday we sheep wool-ACC sell-PRET-1PL
'Yesterday we sold the sheep wool'.

The last property to be discussed in this section is the potential for the dependent to be part of a nominal predication. As the examples (76)–(77) show, the dependent part of a compound cannot be used predicatively.

(76) Moksha *t'ɛ ki-s' **vir'**
 this road-DEF.SG forest
 Intended: 'This road is a forest road'.

(77) Mari *ti pižorgə̂ **miž**
 this mitten wool
 Intended: 'This mitten is woollen'.

The complete picture of morphosyntactic properties of compounds in Moksha and Hill Mari is shown in Table 4.

Table 4: Morphosyntactic properties of compound binominals in Moksha and Hill Mari.

Properties of the dependent	Moksha	Hill Mari
Nominal morphology	*	*
Postposition	*	*
Occurrence in the nominal predicate	*	*
Modification	?? (restricted)	OK
Discontinuity	*	OK

As the table shows, compounds in the two languages are very similar. They share the absence of any nominal morphology on the dependent, as well as ungrammaticality when the dependent is postposed or used predicatively. However, they differ in that compounds in Hill Mari allow right-branching and left-branching recursion and discontinuity, whereas in Moksha left-branching recursive compounds are only marginally accepted.

4 Competing structures: Morphosyntactic properties of binominal genitival constructions in Moksha and Hill Mari

Section 2 discussed a range of competing forms for compounds, viz. genitival and attributive binominals. In this section, I discuss their morphosyntactic properties.

The difference between the two languages is that the main construction to express attributive relations in Moksha is the genitive construction, and compounding is used only in very specific contexts. In Hill Mari, on the other hand, it is compounding that expresses attributive relations, and genitival binominals are restricted to the relations of material and origin.

Moksha has three declensions: indefinite, definite and possessive (Koljadenkov and Zavodova 1962). The three declensions determine which other nominal categories are expressed together with case (e.g., in the definite declension, these are number and definiteness). The indefinite declension does not distinguish either number or possession – possession is only expressed in the possessive declension.

A noun phrase marked with the genitive of the definite declension (as well as the possessive declension) requires possessive agreement on the head and occurs as the dependent in the (anchoring) possessive construction, which is beyond the scope of this paper (78a). In the absence of an indefinite pronoun or a demonstrative, the indefinite genitive on common nouns cannot denote referential possessors and is similar in its functions to an attributivizer. It does not trigger any agreement on the head (78b).

(78) Moksha a. *ava-t'*   *sumka-c*   *pra-s'*
woman-**DEF.SG.GEN** bag-3SG.POSS.SG fall-PST.3SG
'The woman's bag has fallen'.
b. *ava-n'*   *sumka-s'*   *pra-s'*
woman-**GEN** bag-DEF.SG fall-PST.3SG
'The women's bag (the bag for women) has fallen'.

Hill Mari does not distinguish different declensions, so the genitive in possessive constructions and the attributive genitive have the same marker. But they differ in their syntactic properties. A genitive of material or origin cannot trigger possessive agreement (79), whereas a genitive possessor can (80).

(79) Mari *ävä-m*   *mə̈-läm*   **šarək**   **miž-ən**   *jupkə̂-m* /
mother-POSS.1SG I-DAT.POSS.1SG sheep wool-GEN skirt-ACC
**jupkə̂-žə̂-m*   *näl-ən*
skirt-POSS.3SG-ACC take-PRET
'My mother bought me a skirt of sheep wool'.

(80) Mari *mə̈n'*   *tə̈-škə̈*   *pišt-en-äm*   **vas'a-n**   **ävä-žə̈-n**
I   that-ILL put-PRET-1SG Vasja-GEN mother-POSS.3SG-GEN
sumka-žə̂-m
bag-POSS.3SG-ACC
'I've put Vasja's mother's bag there'.

As compared to dependents in compound constructions, in Moksha dependents in genitives can be modified with adjectives (81) or numerals (82), but not with determiners (83).

(81) Moksha kant-t   kel′mə ved′-ən′   vedərka
              carry-IMP.SG   cold   water-GEN   pail
              'Carry a pail for cold water'.

(82) Moksha kolmə   brad-ən′   kuc′   ašč-i
              three   brother-GEN   house.DEF.SG be.situated-NPST.3SG
              ber′ɛk-t′   tona   bok-sə
              bank-DEF.SG.GEN   that   side-IN
              'The house of the three brothers is situated on that side of the river'.

(83) Moksha #t′ɛ   ava-**n′**   sumka-s′   pra-s′
              this   woman-**GEN** bag-DEF.SG   fall-PST.3SG
              'This bag for women has fallen'.
              *'The bag for this woman'.

In Hill Mari the genitive construction is more complex than the compound construction with which it competes. It is similar to the Moksha genitive construction and can be modified with adjectives (84) or numerals (85) but not with determiners (86).

(84) Mari [**əžar miž-ən**] jupkə-m   näl-ən
            green   wool-GEN   skirt-ACC take-PRET
            'I have taken a skirt of green wool'.

(85) Mari tengečə   pazar-əštə   mən′ **kəm   šarək-ən**   miž-əm
            today   market-IN   I   three   sheep-GEN   wool-ACC
            vəžal-en-äm
            sell-PRET-1SG
            'Today at the market I've sold wool of three sheep'.

(86) Mari #mən′   **ti**   miž-ən   jupkə-m   a-m   či
            I   this   wool-GEN   skirt-ACC   NEG.NPST-1SG   put.on
            'I won't put this woollen skirt'.
            *'I won't put the skirt made of this wool on'.

Unlike compounds, genitival binominals can be discontinuous in both languages (87)–(88). In Moksha genitival dependents can even be postposed (89). In Hill Mari, postposition is impossible for almost all nominal dependents except possessors. Genitival dependents can also be a part of a predicate (90)–(91).

(87) Moksha *bazar-sə   mišən'd'ə-v-i   **l'ɛj-ən'**   urdaz-u   **kal***
     market-IN sell-PASS-PST.3SG river-GEN dirt-ATR fish
     'At the market they sell dirty river fish'.

(88) Mari ^{OK}***kesə̂ miž-ə̂n*** *jažo* ***pižorgə̂-m*** *näl-ə̂n-äm*
     goat wool-GEN good mitten-ACC take-PRET-1SG
     'I've bought a good woollen mitten'.

(89) Moksha *t'ɛči   t'ejə-nək   us'k-s'-t'   lofcə*
     today   PRON.DAT-1PL.POSS   carry-PST.3-PL milk
     pandə   s'ava-n'
     mountain   goat-GEN
     'Today they've carried the mountain goat milk'.

(90) Moksha *mon'   kud-əz'ə   **šuft-ən'**, a *ton'*   **kirpic'-ən'***
     I.GEN   house-1SG.POSS.SG tree-GEN   a you.GEN   brick-GEN
     'My house is wooden, and yours is made of brick'.

(91) Mari *mə̈n'-ə̂n noski **miž-ə̂n***
     I-GEN   sock   wool-GEN
     'My socks are woollen'.

Thus, in both Moksha and Hill Mari genitive case can mark not only referential expressions that are possessors, triggering possessive agreement on the head, but also nouns denoting properties of an object, functioning as an attributivizer. Such genitival modifiers do not trigger agreement on the head. In Moksha, this attributive function has become very productive, and the functions of compounding are very restricted. In Hill Mari, the situation is different: genitival modifiers are very restricted in their functions while compounding is the default means of expressing adnominal relations.

5 Conclusions

In this paper, I described the means of expression of non-possessive adnominal relations in Moksha and Hill Mari, attempting to identify the construction that can be considered default and the constructions competing with them in the domain of binominals. In Moksha, the default binominal construction is the genitival construction (**gen**), whereas in Hill Mari it is compounding (**jxt**). Both languages also have binominal attributive constructions (**adj**), with very different syntactic properties that are beyond the scope of this paper.

Concentrating on the two main types, I tested their syntactic properties. The comparison of these two related languages shows that, although the morphological systems of Moksha and Hill Mari are similar, the presence of the definite-indefinite distinction in Moksha seems to be crucial. The two genitives diverge from each other: the definite genitive marks referential dependents (i.e. anchoring relations) whereas indefinite genitives become attributivizers denoting properties. Having more syntactic flexibility, genitival binominals are the main means to encode attributive relations in Moksha. Genitival binominals in Hill Mari remain restricted, but this is compensated for by the higher complexity of compounds. Another factor that could influence the development of the "genitival attributivizer" in Moksha is the presence of a limited system of attributivizers.

The importance of factors such as the development of the definite declension or the lack of attributivizers can be supported by the fact that in other Finno-Ugric languages, which have no definite marker and a richer system of attributivizers, the links between semantic relations and constructions are similar to the ones found in Hill Mari, rather than to the ones found in Moksha. In Udmurt (ISO 639-3: UDM), for instance, many of the relations discussed here can be encoded with binominals (see Edygarova 2010 for more details). Consider the following examples for species (part-whole) relations and material relations.

(92) Udmurt <...> ***pipu*** kuar kad' en kual'ekja
 aspen leaf like NEG.IMP tremble.NEG.2SG
 '...don't tremble like an aspen leaf'.
 (Perevoschikov 1994: 239 from Edygarova 2010: 193)

(93) Udmurt *zarn'i zundes* [gold ring] 'golden ring' (Edygarova 2010: 189)

A very similar strategy seems to occur in Izhma-Komi (ĸpv, Komi-Zyrian)[8] (94)–(95).

(94) Izhma-Komi **n'ija** vož-jas təə-s'ys vər-enys
larch crotch-PL wind-EL.POSS.3SG move-PRS.3PL
'Larch branches are moving with the wind'.

(95) Izhma-Komi **zələte** čun'kyč us'-is va-e
gold ring fall-PST.3SG water-ILL
'A gold ring fell into the water'.

The final observation to be made here concerns the term *compounding*. This term presupposes only one category for constructions that consist solely of two nominal roots. As mentioned above, some classifications consider the number of orthographic words (one or two) to be one of the features of compounds. However, the fact that binominals that denote similar relations are present in the dictionary as one-word and as two-words compounds suggests that this difference is just a matter of orthographic convention, which is not always based on a thorough linguistic investigation and is not always applied consistently. More relevant are distinctions in morphophonology and syntax. Whereas one-word compounds (**cmp**) are strict lexical units, compounds consisting of two or more words (**jxt**) can have more complex syntactic properties, which have to be taken into consideration in the classification.

References

Anduganov, Jury V. 1990 *K evoljucii zavisimykh častej substantivnykh konstrukcij v finno-ugorskikh jazykakh* [To the evolution of dependent parts of nominal constructions in Finno-Ugric languages]. In *Congressus septimus Internationalis Fenno-Ugristarum. Sessiones sectionum dissertationes: linguistica*, 162–167. Debrecen.

Bubrikh, Dmitry V. 1947. *Erzja-mordovskaja grammatika-minimum* [Erzya-mordvin grammar-minimum]. Saransk: Mordovskoje knižnoje izdateljstvo.

Bubrikh, Dmitry V. 1953. *Istoričeskaja grammatika erzjanskogo jazyka* [Historical grammar of the Erzya language]. Saransk: Mordovskoje knižnoje izdateljstvo.

Edygarova, Svetlana. 2010. *Kategorija posesivnosti v udmurtskom jazyke* [The category of possessiveness in Udmurt]. Tartu: University of Tartu PhD dissertation.

---

[8] The examples are taken from the author's own fieldwork data collected in the village of Samburg (Russia) in winter 2015.

Evsevjev, Makar E. 1963 [1934]. *Osnovy mordovskoj grammatiki. Izbrannye trudy* [Essentials of Mordvin grammar. Selected works]. Vol.3. Saransk: Mordovskoje knizhnoje izdateljstvo.
Feoktistov, Aleksandr P. 1995. Slovo – složnoe slovo – slovosočetanie [Word – complex word –phrase]. In *Uzlovye problem sovremennogo finno-ugrovedenija. Materialy I Vserossijskoj naučnoj konferencii finno-ugrovedov*, 404–406. Joškar-Ola.
Kangasmaa-Minn, Eeva. 1966. *The syntactical distribution of the Cheremis genitive I*. Turku: Kirjapaino Polytypos.
Kangasmaa-Minn, Eeva. 1968. The category of the adnominal genitive in Cheremis. In *Congressus Secundus Internationalis Fenno-Ugristarum. Pars I. Acta Linguistica*, 235–238. Helsinki.
Kangasmaa-Minn, Eeva. 1969. Über die Beziehungen zwischen Genitiv und Possessivadjektiv im Tscheremissischen. *Finnisch-Ugrische Forschungen* 37. 71–90.
Kolyadenkov, Mikhail N. 1954. *Grammatika mordovskikh (mokshanskogo i erzjanskogo) jazykov. Č. II. Sintaksis* [Grammar of the Mordvin (Moksha and Erzya) languages. Part I. Syntax]. Saransk: Mordovskoje knizhnoje izdateljstvo.
Kolyadenkov, Mikhail N. & R A Zavodova (eds.). 1962. *Grammatika mordovskikh (mokshanskogo i erzjanskogo) jazykov. Č. I. Fonetika I morfologija* [Grammar of the Mordvin (Moksha and Erzya) languages. Part I. Phonetics and Morphology]. Saransk: Mordovskoje knizhnoje izdateljstvo.
Koptjevskaja-Tamm, Maria. 2002. Adnominal possession in the European languages: Form and function. *Sprachtypologie und Universalienforschung* 55. 141–172.
Koptjevskaja-Tamm, Maria. 2004. Maria's ring of gold: Adnominal possession and non-anchoring relations in the European languages. In Kim Ji-yung, Yury A. Lander & Barbara H. Partee (eds.), *Possessives and beyond: Semantics and syntax*, 155–181. Amherst, MA: GLSA Publications.
Koryakov Jury B. & Maria A. Kholodilova. 2018. Obschie svedenia o mokshanskom jazyke i issleduemom govore [Basic facts about the Moksha language and the idiom under investigation]. In Svetlana J. Toldova & Maria A. Kholodilova (eds.), *Elementy mokshanskogo jazyka v tipologicheskom osveschenii* [Elements of the Moksha language in typological perspective], 6–18. Moscow: Buki Vedi.
Kukhto, Anton V. 2018. Fonologija [Phonology]. In Svetlana J. Toldova & Maria A. Kholodilova (eds.), *Elementy mokshanskogo jazyka v tipologicheskom osveschenii* [Elements of the Moksha language in typological perspective], 19–37. Moscow: Buki Vedi.
Mukai, Makiko. 2015 Word formation in phase theory. In *The Second Asian and European Linguistic Conference Proceedings*, 84–95.
Nakov, Preslav. 2013. On the interpretation of noun compounds: Syntax, semantics, and entailment. *Natural Language Engineering* 19(3). 291–330.
Pengitov, Nikolay T. (ed.) 1961. *Sovremennyj marijskij jazyk. Č. 2: Morfologija* [The Modern Mari language. Part 2: Morphology]. Yoškar-Ola: Marijskoe knižnoe izdateljstvo.
Pepper, Steve. This volume, a. Defining and typologizing binominal lexemes. In Steve Pepper, Francesca Masini & Simone Mattiola (eds.), *Binominal lexemes in cross-linguistic perspective*. Berlin: Mouton de Gruyter.
Pepper, Steve. This volume, b. Hatcher-Bourque: Towards a reusable classification of semantic relations. In Steve Pepper, Francesca Masini & Simone Mattiola (eds.), *Binominal lexemes in cross-linguistic perspective*. Berlin: Mouton de Gruyter.

Pleshak, Polina. 2018. Adnominal possessive constructions in Mordvin, Mari and Permic. *Eesti ja soome-ugri keeleteaduse ajakiri. Journal of Estonian and Finno-Ugrian Linguistics* 9(1). 139–168.
Pleshak Polina S. & Maria A. Kholodilova. 2018. Imennaja gruppa [Noun phrase.] In Svetlana J. Toldova & Maria A. Kholodilova (eds.), *Elementy mokshanskogo jazyka v tipologicheskom osveschenii* [Elements of the Moksha language in typological perspective], 272–310. Moscow: Buki Vedi.
Pleshak, Polina & Maria Sidorova. 2018. Approksimativnyje kolichestvennyje konstruktsii kak kontekst dlja imennykh grupp maloj struktury v mokshanskom i gornomarijskom jazykakh. [Approximative numeral phrases as a context for small nominals in Moksha and Hill Mari]. In Ekaterina Lyutikova & Anton Zimmerling (eds.), *Typology of morphosyntactic parameters*. Vol. 4. Proceedings of the international conference "Typology of morphosyntactic parameters 2017", 222–239. Moscow: Pushkin State Russian Language Institute.
Savatkova, Anna A. 2002. *Gornoe narečie marijskogo jazyka* [The Hill Mari language]. Savariae: Berzsenyi Dániel Főiskola.
Savatkova, Anna A. 2008. *Slovarj gornomarijskogo jazyka* [Hill Mari dictionary]. Joškar-Ola: Marijskoe knizhnoe izdatelstvo.
Scott, Gary-John. 2002. Stacked adjectival modification and the structure of the nominal phrases. In Guglielmo Cinque (ed.), *Functional structure in DP and IP*, 91–120. New York: Oxford University Press.
Schankina, V. I. 1993. *Mokshenj-ruzonj valks* [Moksha-Russian dictionary]. Saransk: Mordovskjaj knizhnaj izdateljstvasj.
Tsyganov, Nikolay F. 1964. Absoljutnaja (vnepadezhnaja) forma [Absolute (caseless) form]. *Uchenyje zapiski 43*, 179–191. Saransk: Mordovskoje knizhnoje izdateljstvo.
Tsygankin, Dmitry V. (ed.). 1980. *Grammatika mordovskikh jazykov. Fonetika, grafika, orfografija, morfologija* [Grammar of the Mordvin languages. Phonetics, graphic, orthography, morfology]. Saransk: Mordovskij gosudarstvennyj universitet imeni N. P. Ogareva.

Part 3: **Acquisition**

Maria Rosenberg
Binominals and potential competitors in language development: Evidence from Swedish

Abstract: The present study addresses competing binominal types in Swedish language development. It is based on diary data from one child and longitudinal recordings from four children between the ages 1–3. In Swedish, binominal lexemes correspond most often to NN compounding: one of the earliest word-formation patterns acquired by children; and a way to combine concepts to express different semantic relations. Still, other nominal constructions with genitives, adjectives, prepositions, or subordinators can express similar basic semantic relations, thus being competing binominal types in Swedish. In the data, the emergence and later establishment of different binominal types (syntactic or morphological) follow similar developmental paths among the children. NN compounds emerge the first, but once nominal constructions that contain prepositions or subordinators (*som* 'that' or 'as/like') become established, they constitute the strongest competitors to NN compounds, especially for descriptive purposes. The study suggests that Swedish-speaking children's early use of compounding could be a cognitively motivated option, since it implies a rather simple juxtaposition of two nouns, with little semantic specification. Over time, however, children gradually master to express the semantic relation between two concepts also through syntactic means, although NN compounding remains an open and well entrenched pattern for conceptual combination.

1 Introduction

This study investigates competition between types of binominal lexemes (as described in the introduction to this volume, cf. Masini, Mattiola & Pepper this volume) within one language.[1] More specifically, it explores how the emergence and development of novel NN compounds[2] compete – on semantic grounds –

---

[1] I gratefully acknowledge the editors, Francesca Masini in particular, and the anonymous reviewers for valuable comments and suggestions. Remaining errors are mine.
[2] Compounds are defined as "grammatical combinations of words, that is of lexical items or lexemes, to form new words" (Dressler 2006: 24).

https://doi.org/10.1515/9783110673494-014

with other patterns that are used for combining two nominal concepts. The study is based on Swedish production data from five children, followed from ages 1–3 years. Given that binominal lexemes rely on the simple strategy of combining two 'thing' entities (i.e. either two physical entities or one physical entity and one affix that stands for a 'thing') (Croft 2001; Haspelmath 2012; Pepper 2020: 13), NN compounding is the best candidate in Swedish [SWE]. Compounding, being "the most basic morphological technique" (Dressler, Ketrez, and Kilani-Schoch 2017: 287), is one of the first word-formation patterns to emerge in child language, albeit with cross-linguistic and individual differences.

Following Koptjevskaja-Tamm, the present study forms part of a "semantically oriented lexical typology with its core concern in how languages express meanings by words" (2012: 373). It takes compound semantics as its point of departure but broadens the scope to also include other patterns, such as different types of nominal phrases that are able to express similar contents. In this way, the study has an onomasiological perspective: it starts out from concepts (i.e. semantic relations) and examines the forms that can denote these concepts (Grzega 2015: 80). On the other hand, since different kinds of nominal constructions are extracted from the data prior to the semantic analysis, the study also takes a semasiological perspective. Based on the underlying assumption that different patterns of complex nominal constructions gradually find their specific semantic niche within the language system (although free variation is sometimes an option), the overarching research question of the present study is: To what extent is it possible to trace competition, developmentally, between complex nominal constructions that can express similar basic semantic relations?

Considering that lexical typology deals with the issue of how words and vocabularies systematically vary across languages (Koptjevskaja-Tamm 2012: 373), the present study clearly has a narrower scope since it deals with one language. However, by targeting patterns in the interaction between lexicon and grammar in language development, based on a primary data source, it aims to have typological relevance (cf. Koptjevskaja-Tamm 2012). The meta-language chosen for the data analysis corresponds to the logico-semantic relations assumed to underlie NN compounds, binominal lexemes *par excellence*. These relations, though, are to be understood as gradient phenomena with overlap between more central and more peripheral exemplars.

While the volume focuses on binominal lexemes, the present study includes a more extensive range of complex nominal constructions. This is motivated by the fact that the study deals with young children's language development. The young child that seeks a name for two combined, nominal concepts has few clues of whether a simple word, a complex word or a phrase is the most convenient way of expression. Besides, the child can only make use of the morphological patterns and syntactic means that are at their disposal. By extending the view beyond binominals proper, this study aims at exploring the borders between different Swedish nominal constructions, which, can, in fact, function as binominals in other languages (cf. Pepper 2020). This is also suggested by Berman, who argues that different types of binominal constructions are "alternating, apparently 'synonymous' expressive options for combining two nouns in different languages" (2009: 321).

Moreover, it is of interest for the present study to note that Dressler et al. advocate for applying the "methodology of Lexical Typology" to acquisitionist studies in order to "measure morphological richness in terms of wealth of compounding" (2017: 11). The lexical typology methodology applied by Dressler, Ketrez and Kilani-Schoch (eds.) (2017) consists in compiling a list of 52 compound words that occur in German child speech and investigating their translational equivalents from ten further languages under investigation, namely Danish [DAN], Lithuanian [LIT], Russian [RUS], French [FRA], Greek [ELL], Estonian [EST], Finnish [FIN], North Saami [SME], Turkish [TUR] and Hebrew [HEB]. However, the more general focus of Dressler, Ketrez and Kilani-Schoch (eds.) (2017), situated within a usage-based framework, is to explore cross-linguistically the emergence of compounding in parallel to inflection and derivation through quantitative and qualitative analyses of nominal compounds that occur in longitudinal recordings of spontaneous caretaker-child interactions.

The structure of the chapter is as follows: Section 2 accounts for binominal constructions in Swedish and section 3 for how compounding patterns emerge in language development. Section 4 presents theories on conceptual combination and the semantics of compounds. The data are described in section 5. In section 6 follows the analysis of the data, concentrating on different binominal types and how they compete developmentally and on semantic grounds. Finally, a conclusion is given in section 7.

2 Binominal lexemes and potential competitors in Swedish

With respect to word-formation patterns, Swedish, like the other Germanic languages, relies more heavily on compounding than derivation (the inverse of Romance and Slavic languages, see e.g. Clark 1993). Hence, in accordance with the nine binominal types or strategies outlined by Pepper (2020: 142–143), binominal lexemes to be found in Swedish are NN compounds (**cmp**) and different types of [N-NMLZ] derivations (**der**), some examples are shown in (1)–(2) (see e.g. Söderbergh 1968 for a comprehensive overview):[3]

(1) NN compounds
    a. *hand.väska* [hand.bag] 'handbag'
    b. *morot.s.bit* [carrot.LE.piece] 'a piece of carrot'
    c. *blom.blad* [flower.leaf] 'petal' (vs. *en blomma* 'a flower')
    d. *gatu.kök* [street.kitchen] 'snack bar' (vs. *en gata* 'a street')

(2) [N-NMLZ]
    a. *kontor.ist* [office.NMLZ] 'clerk'
    b. *klock.are* [clock.NMLZ] 'sexton, clock ringer'
    c. *musik.ant* [music.NMLZ] 'musician'
    d. *pension.är* [pension.NMLZ] 'retired person'

Swedish compounds are right-headed and written as one word. They are generally prosodically marked by a two-peak intonation. Swedish NN compounding is primarily of the compounding type **cmp** (Pepper 2020: 145–146) with simple concatenation of the two nouns (1a), but liaison forms also occur. The latter are more or less arbitrary from a synchronic point of view (Söderbergh 1968: 15–19). One general tendency is the deletion of the final unstressed vowel of the first compound part (1c). Diachronically, the liaison forms tend to be genitive forms (1b, 1d) (Söderbergh 1968: 15). As Pepper (2020: 165–166) claims, binominals that include linking elements (or liaison forms) are much closer to **cmp** than to genitives (**gen**). Still, Pepper (2020: 166) decides to classify them as **gen** in the Germanic languages in order "to bring out any contrasts that might be relevant" (cf. e.g. Kopf 2018 for German [DEU]). This study takes an alternative decision, by classifying compounds with liaison forms as **cmp**. Assuming that analogy rather than rules are the basis for lexical extension (cf. Blevins and Blevins 2009; Krott 2009; Mattiello 2017), Swedish compounds could be analysed in analogy with Greek compounds where the nouns display stem forms that have to be acquired as a whole or unanalysed by the child (Berman 2009: cf. Stephany and Thomadaki 2017), rather than being decomposed into parts, one of can be an interfix (but cf. Korecky-Kröll, Sommer-Lolei and Dressler 2017: 20).

---

[3] The following abbreviations appear in the glosses: ADJZ = adjectivizer; AGR = agreement; DEF = definite; GEN = genitive; LE = linking element; NMLZ = nominalizer; PL = plural.

Considering that binominals are used to name two combined nominal concepts, other forms that can be used for this purpose in Swedish are genitival as in (3), adjectival as in (4–5), prepositional as in (5–6) (all types featuring in Pepper's 2020 typology of binominals), as well as a noun followed by *som* ('that' or 'as/like') as in (7–8), or two coordinated nouns as in (9):

(3) *hus.et.s vin* [house.DEF.GEN wine] 'the house wine'

(4) *silvr.igt hår* [silver.ADJZ hair]
vs. *silverhår* [silver.hair] 'silvery hair'

(5) *hatt med blomm.or (på)* [hat with flower.PL (on)], *blomm.ig hatt* [flower.ADJZ hat]
vs. *blomhatt* [flower.hat]

(6) *fågel i/av trä* [bird in/of wood]
vs. *träfågel* [wood.bird] 'wooden bird'

(7) *ett hus som ser ut som en svamp* [a house that looks like a mushroom]
vs. *svamphus* [mushroom.house]

(8) *en sko som/till båt* [a shoe as/for boat]
vs. *båtsko* [boat.shoe] or *skobåt* [shoe.boat]

(9) *(både) (en) båt och (en) bil* [(both) (a) boat and (a) car]
vs. *båt.bil* [boat.car] or *bil.båt* [car.boat]

It is, however, important to note that the types of constructions above mostly function as descriptive expressions in Swedish and not as binominal lexemes as intended in this volume. Still, as already mentioned these structures are important in the light of the data that the present study is based on. As Downing (1977) noted, novel NN compounds can have naming and descriptive functions. Berman (2009) equally emphasizes the continuum of compound constructions, ranging from the established end of frozen constructions (e.g. *beeline*) and semantically transparent, colloquial constructions (e.g. *bee sting*) to the more open-ended end, where novel compounds can be used in alternation with phrasal expressions (e.g. *bee wings* vs. *wings of a bee* or *bee garden* vs. *a garden full of bees*). Children likewise produce novel NN compounds with naming and descriptive functions (Rosenberg and Mellenius 2018). For the latter function, syntactic phrases are often more appropriate and idiomatic in Swedish. However, considering that compounds are often used to resume corresponding phrases anaphorically, and thereby introduce a naming function, there is no sharp line between naming and descriptive functions of compounds. Still, this is a case of complex language-internal competition that the child has to resolve.

3 Cross-linguistic evidence about the emergence of compounding patterns

Language development can be seen as gradual, with different processes working in synergy. Children learn approximate representations situated on different linguistic levels simultaneously (e.g. phonology, semantics, morphology). Over time, these representations are refined (Johnson et al. 2010; Ngon et al. 2013). In early acquisition, nouns are often claimed to have an advantage over other grammatical categories, presumably due to their naming function (Waxman et al. 2013). Likewise, items with high token frequency in the input, such as instantiations of particular word-formation patterns, are likely to emerge early (Berman 2009; Elsen and Schlipphak 2015; Dressler et al. 2017: 9).

In compound-prone languages, like the Germanic languages, two-year-old children decompose NN compounds into meaning and form, and soon thereafter they also create novel ones (Becker 1994; Mellenius 1997; Dressler, Lettner, and Korecky-Kröll 2010). Analogical reasoning is an important factor in this process: novel compounds tend to be produced in analogy with acquired compound patterns (Krott 2009; Dressler et al. 2017: 7).

Across languages, compounding, inflection and diminutives are the morphological patterns that emerge first, while derivational morphology tends to appear later (Dressler, Ketrez, and Kilani-Schoch 2017: 288). Since compounds are more transparent morphosemantically compared to derived words, children are said to prefer compounding (Dressler et al. 2017: 8). In Hebrew, however, for children aged 2–8, affixation was preferred for lexical innovations (Berman 2009: 306). In the data of Dressler, Ketrez and Kilani-Schoch (eds.) (2017), the age of earliest emergence of compounding patterns ranges between 1;5 to 2;7 (year;month), and the languages in the study (except for Hebrew, which was studied from ages 2–8) show the following order: Estonian, Turkish, Finnish, German, Danish, Lithuanian, North Saami, French, Russian and Greek (Dressler, Ketrez, and Kilani-Schoch (2017: 288). For German and Danish, compounds emerged at 1;8. The cross-linguistic data also demonstrated a rise of complexity of compound structure, beginning with transparent compounding patterns and moving towards more opaque ones as well as synthetic, phrasal and three-part compounds (Dressler, Ketrez, and Kilani-Schoch 2017: 295–296).

Berman attributes cross-linguistic differences in compound acquisition "to the interplay of target-language typology and usage-based factors of frequency and register variation" (2009: 302), with the factors of structural simplicity and transparency playing a heavier role for its earlier phases. According to Dressler, Ketrez and Kilani-Schoch (2017: 289–290, 299), the most important factor, cross-linguistically, is the morphological wealth of productive compounding patterns in child-directed speech, whereas other factors, such as morphotactic transparency, which facilitates easy detection of the compound parts, and shared morphological typological features, or language family membership, are important to a lesser degree.

An indication of early productivity of compounding is the child's creation of novel compounds (Korecky-Kröll, Sommer-Lolei, and Dressler 2017: 31; Dressler, Ketrez, and Kilani-Schoch 2017: 299–300). Clark's (1993: 146–147) diary data from an English child, ages 1–5, contained nearly 1,000 novel nominal compounds, the majority of which were NN compounds. However, in Dressler, Ketrez and Kilani-Schoch's (eds.) (2017) data of longitudinal recordings, novel compounds were rare and only found in seven of the 12 studied languages. In Danish data from four children (of which half came from CHILDES, MacWhinney 2000), novel compounds were only rarely attested (Kjærbæck and Basbøll 2017). In German data, novel compounds either emerged simultaneously with established compounds or were created much later. Interestingly, a decrease of novel compounds was found after age 3;0 in the German data. The explanation given for this development was that "the creation of neologistic compounds is due to the need of expanding a still 'deficient' lexicon" (Korecky-Kröll, Sommer-Lolei, and Dressler 2017: 27). However, their explanation is contradicted by the diary data of Clark (1993), where the child actually coins most novel compounds between the ages 3;0–3;11.

Finally, considering that, in order to select which morphological patterns to extract from the input, the child must have a critical mass of lexical items to operate on. Thus, "[f]or a more complete view of early first language acquisition, the different developmental aspects of nominal compounding must not only be related to other areas of morphology, but also to the domain of syntax (particularly to noun phrases) and especially to the lexicon" (Dressler et al. 2017: 8). The present study aims to add pieces of the puzzle to complete this view.

4 Conceptual combinations and compound semantics

From a cognitive science perspective, conceptual combinations can be assumed to rely on both linguistic and experiential information and depend on a wider context for their understanding: both head and modifier concepts interact to constrain compound meaning (Lynott and Connell 2010; counter to Gagné and Shoben 1997). Based on previous studies on children's comprehension of novel NN compounds (e.g. Gottfried 1997; Krott, Gagné, and Nicoladis 2010), Lynott and Connell (2010) suggest that young children, age 3 and below, preferentially interpret compounds as combining two intact concepts, with referents that maintain their typical meaning (e.g. *elephant tusk*). Beyond that age, children progressively grasp that one of the two combined concepts expressed by a compound can be extensively reduced in meaning (e.g. *elephant* reduced to big size as in *elephant seal*). This developmental trajectory partly relates to Berman's (2009: 311) argument about whether children's novel compounds express "inherent, permanent" relations between the two parts or rather "more incidental, transient" relations, where she concludes that children's compounds are predominantly contextual and tend to express temporary relations. However, none of these predictions were borne out in Rosenberg and Mellenius (2018), based on spontaneous production data of novel NN compounds from three Swedish children (other than the data used in the present study). Moreover, Mellenius and Rosenberg (2016), applying Jackendoff's (2009) framework of compound semantics, claim that children's novel NN compounds express many different semantic relations from early on.

Neurological evidence suggests that children process semantics and syntax jointly, in the regions that adults recruit for lexical-semantic processing, and that a neural selectivity for syntax processing is not in place before age 10 (Skeide, Brauer, and Friederici 2014). Therefore, the present study assumes that semantic content is the focus for the child that seeks to express two combined concepts. How that content can be expressed, however, will be constrained by the child's linguistic resources evolving over time.

Bauer and Tarasova (2013) (see also Rainer 2013 on relational adjectives) point out that, apart from NN compounds, A N phrases, possessive constructions, neoclassical compounds, and blends can express similar semantic relations. Most studies on compound semantics (e.g. Downing 1977; Levi 1978; Jackendoff 2009) conclude that a rather restricted number of basic relations manages to cover the majority of (NN) compounds (Bourque 2014). Still, because the basic semantic relations often show overlap, any method of compound sub-classification has its controversy (Bauer 1983). For this reason, it is important to strive for a coherent set of relations and to apply these to the data uniformly (Bourque 2014: 168). Furthermore, a classification system with a restricted set of relations, situated at a rather high level of abstraction, is advantageous for cross-linguistic generalization (see also Pepper, this volume).

Hence, the present study makes use of the 15 logico-semantic relations (some of which are reversible, Jackendoff 2009) proposed by Bourque (2014: 170) after a detailed analysis of previous accounts of compound semantics. These relations, along with linking material that can be used to paraphrase a given compound syntactically (see Bourque 2014: 179–210), are shown in Table 1. The relations in bold are those that were attested in the present study.

Still, this classification is not entirely clear-cut. For instance, PURPOSE is more underspecified than most of the other relations, whereas TOPIC is rare and tends to involve specific types of nouns. Moreover, there are always compounds that fall in between two or three relations, depending on how they are interpreted. These complexities, however, will not be dwelled upon since they are of no great concern for this study.

Table 1: Bourque's (2014) proposal of 15 logico-semantic relations for NN compounds.

COORDINATION 'is also, is both/and'	**COMPOSITION** 'composed/made of'	(TIME)[4] 'during, at, in, before, etc.'
HYPERNYMY 'kind of, type of'	**SOURCE** '(made) from'	**TOPIC** 'about'
SIMILARITY 'similar to, like'	**PART** 'part of (have/of)'	FUNCTION 'functions/serves as'
(PRODUCTION) 'makes, produces'	**LOCATION** 'at, near, in, etc.'	**PURPOSE** 'for'
(CAUSE) 'causes'	**POSSESSION** 'possess (have/of)'	**USE** 'use/with, by'

---

4 As Bourque notes (2014: 207–208), TIME is rare and often dependent on the temporal meaning of one of the compound parts. Thus, TIME can be subsumed under LOCATION, as the present study chooses to do. PRODUCTION/CAUSE/SOURCE can also be merged if SOURCE is understood in a broader sense (Bourque 2014: 202–203), as assumed by this study.

5 Data and data analysis

Diary notes were collected from the author's youngest daughter (Anna) between the ages 1;9–3;11. The girl is typically developing and monolingual in Swedish and has three older brothers (five, seven and nine years older). The notes consist of overheard utterances produced on different occasions. The utterances, sorted by age (year;month;day), were written down immediately on paper or computer, mostly regularized to normal spelling. Contextual and semantic information as well as metalinguistic statements (if present) were also reported. The diary data were gathered with a specific interest in novel word formations, but they aimed to obtain a broad, overall picture of the child's language development. Still, it is important to note that, given their fixed semantics and structure, established compounds produced by the child were mostly not regarded to be of special interest when the data were gathered. Therefore, established compounds are mainly attested in the diary data as parts of other utterances.

For early language development, diary data have several strengths: they can capture infrequent items, and they can provide a rich interpretation that connects to the rest of the child's linguistic repertoire and world. Diary data can, in fact, be the only way to gather a sufficient number of examples of children's novel word formations (Elsen and Schlipphak 2015: 2118). Still, the use of diary data also has several obvious weaknesses, such as the impossibility to verify the original notes, the fact that the notes may be biased, and that both input and detailed phonetic information are lacking (cf. Christensen 2010). Hence, although diary data can be reliable (Bretherton & Beeghly 1982), they must be validated through other methods (Wellman et al. 1995). Given these restrictions, this study uses more than half of the longitudinal recordings from Swedish caretaker-child interactions (Strömqvist, Richthoff, and Andersson 1993), available at CHILDES (MacWhinney 2000), as an additional data set. The recordings investigated comprise four Swedish children, namely Bella (22 files, mean length 24 min., ages 1;6;9–3;5;9), Harry (14 files, mean length 30 min., ages 1;8;26–3;11;23), Tea (Harry's younger sister, 14 files, mean length 23 min., ages 1;7;15–3;11;23) and Markus (11 files, mean length 34 min., ages 1;7;25–2;9;29).

The data analysis proceeded in two steps. First, different constructions with two or more nominal concepts in combination, i.e. binominal lexemes or potential competitors, were extracted from the two data sets by a manual search. Second, these constructions were qualitatively analysed for semantic relations and contrasted to other available means for expressing a similar content.

6 Analysis

The diary data had more than 900 utterances with binominal lexemes or potential competitors, and more than 2,000 utterances were extracted from the recordings.

The distribution of the attested binominal lexemes of the NN compound type in relation to three age spans is shown in Table 2. N-NMLZ-derivations were hardly attested and are left out of the analysis. Clearly, the diary data constitute a richer source than the recordings, especially for novel compounds but also for established ones (recall that the diary data are skewed for the benefit of novel compounds). It is noteworthy that Markus, the child whose recordings stopped at age 2;9;29, produced more established and novel compounds compared to the other three recorded children. Otherwise, we see that the children increased their use of both established and novel compounds after age 3. Hence, the idea that novel compounding would be a sign of a 'deficient' lexicon, as proposed by Korecky-Kröll, Sommer-Lolei and Dressler (2017) is not confirmed by the Swedish data.

Table 2: Number of established and novel NN compounds per child and age span in the diary data and the recordings of four Swedish children.

	Established NN cmp (type)				Novel NN cmp (type)			
	1;6–1;11	2;0–2;11	3;0–3;11	n	1;6–1;11	2;0–2;11	3;0–3;11	n
Anna	18	67	76	161	9	75	194	278
Bella	3	20	38	61	0	1	4	5
Harry	0	8	40	48	0	1	9	10
Tea	3	23	34	60	0	1	3	4
Markus	5	32		37	1	9		10

Furthermore, Kjærbæck and Basbøll (2017: 59–60) mention that the low rate of (novel) compounds in the recordings they analysed seems to partly depend on the activity that goes on. The data investigated here lead to a similar conclusion. The arranged settings with puzzles or books that are used as stimuli in the Swedish recordings are not a favourable environment for the creation of novel compounds. This finding confirms that novel compounds are rarely attested in longitudinal recordings (cf. Elsen and Schlipphak 2015), but it does not constitute cross-linguistic evidence of novel compounds being marginal in child speech (cf. Clark 1993; Becker 1994; Rainer 2010; Rosenberg and Mellenius 2018).

6.1 The emergence of binominal lexemes and their potential competitors

In this section, the emergence of binominal lexemes and their potential competitors is traced in the Swedish data sets. The analysis is arranged under sub-headings for each type of nominal construction and also takes into account the semantics of the different constructions.

6.1.1 Established compounds: Various semantic relations

The very first established compounds produced by children can be considered to be learned as wholes (cf. Dressler et al. 2017: 6), thus not necessarily being analysed semantically. Yet, for the first established NN compound in the diary data (that start at 1;9), it is likely to assume that the child recognizes the parts that she already uses as separate words (e.g. *bil* in 10b):

(10) a. *tand.kräm* (1;9;8) [tooth.paste] (PURPOSE)
      b. *en last.bil* (1;9;16) [a load.car] 'a lorry' (PURPOSE)
      c. *inte äta apelsin.skal* (1;9;23) [not eat orange.peel] (PART)

The child early on uses established compounds for cases of parallelism, which suggests that she analyses some of them:

(11) a. *ägg.skal, apelsin.skal, banan.skal* (1;10;10) [egg.shell, orange.peel, banana.peel]
      b. *är det där zink.pasta?* (1;11;28) [is that zink.paste/cream] (she asked about the pasta-package, when I said I would prepare some pasta)

In the recordings, many of the earliest established NN compounds were imitations of caretaker utterances, such as the one by Bella in (12a) (though not the one in (12b)), the ones by Harry in (13), and the ones by Tea in (14):

(12) a. *hals.band* (1;7;28) [neck.lace] (LOCATION)
      b. *hund.mat* (1;10;19) [dog.food] (PURPOSE)

(13) a. *mo.mö, mo.mo* (1;8;26) for the target *mor.mor* [mother.mother] 'maternal grandma' (POSSESSION)
      b. *gock.ack* (2;1;10) for the target *dock.vagn* [doll.wagon] 'doll's carriage' (PURPOSE)

(14) a. *of.fa* (1;7;15) for the target *mor.far* [mother.father] 'maternal grandpa' (POSSESSION)
   b. *lappa* (2;1;17) for the target *hak.lapp* [chin.cloth] 'bib'(PURPOSE)

The opposite was also found. Markus early on produced two established compounds that deviated from the target pronunciation, and then the caretaker, instead, repeated them for reinforcement:

(15) a. *mo.mo* (1;7;25) for the target *mor.mor* [mother.mother] 'grandmother' (POSSESSION)
   b. *siada.s.rumm.et* (1;11;12) for the target *vardag.s.rumm.et* [everyday.LE.room.DEF] 'living room' (PURPOSE)

Children's errors with compounds are briefly discussed by Dressler, Ketrez and Kilani-Schoch (2017: 296–297). In their data from 11 languages, constituent inversion was attested only in Estonian, possibly because this language has both left-headed and right-headed compounds. Since reversal of constituent order would lead to an opaque result, it is sometimes predicted that children, often said to prefer morphotactic and morphosemantic transparency, would not choose this path (Korecky-Kröll, Sommer-Lolei, and Dressler 2017: 31). However, reversal was attested in the German diary data of Rainer (2010); and in the Swedish diary data, eight cases of reversed constituents are found. They were produced between the ages 2;4–3;8, thus rather late in development:

(16) a. *nagel.fingr.ar* (2;4;21) [nail.finger.PL] vs. *finger.nagl.ar* [finger.nail.PL]
   b. *en filt.bebis* (2;5;21) [a blanket.baby] vs. *bebis.filt* [baby.blanket]
   c. *druv.vin.a* (2;11;8) [grape.wine.a] vs. *vin.druva* [wine.grape]
   d. *burk.lins.er* (3;8;7) [case.lense.PL] vs. *lins.burk.ar* [lense.case.PL]

What most of these cases have in common is that they involve words that are new and rather opaque to the child (except 16b). They are thus not well entrenched, and she mostly produces them just after having heard them, which suggests that her memory of these words is unstable. The form in (16c) is interesting, since the child transposes the *-a* ending of the established compound to the last constituent of the reversed compound.

6.1.2 Novel compounds: Various semantic relations

Among the earliest novel NN compounds in the diary data, two parts (*baby*, *dog*) reoccur in several compounds. Some of the novel compounds are formed in analogy with an established compound (in 17f, the first is established, and the last, novel). The earliest novel compounds express different relations, such as PURPOSE, LOCATION, COORDINATION and COMPOSITION:

(17) a. *bebis.hund* (1;9;11) [baby.dog] sees a picture of a 'puppy' HYPERNYMY
 b. *bebis.gröt* (1;10;9, 1;10;15) [baby.porridge] 'porridge' PURPOSE
 c. *bebis.pappa* (1;10;13) [baby.daddy] (I commented a photo by saying "that is daddy when he was a baby") COORDINATION
 d. *hund.blöja* (1;10;20) [dog.diaper] 'diaper with dog-print' LOCATION
 e. *dusch.bad* (1;11;28, 2;0;13) [shower.bath] 'bathtub under the shower' LOCATION
 f. *glass.pinne, vatten.pinne* (2;0;14) [ice-cream.lolly], [water.lolly] COMPOSITION

In the recordings, Markus is the only child who produces a novel compound prior to age 2. Later on, he produces nine novel NN compounds, such as:

(18) a. *bil.båt* (1;10;14) [car.boat] COORDINATION
 b. *jättesten* (2;8;8) [giant.stone] SIMILARITY
 c. *motor.hål.et* (2;9;29) [motor.hole.DEF] LOCATION/PART

The three earliest attested novel NN compounds of the three other children in the recordings were produced after age 2 (Bella's in 19a, Harry's in 19b, and Tea's in 19c):

(19) a. *mus.ost* (2;3;23) [mouse.cheese] PURPOSE
 b. *lykt.buss* (2;6;10) [light.bus] PART
 c. *låtsas.kaffe* (2;6;2) [fake.coffee] HYPERNYMY

Overall, these Swedish production data do not support a development trajectory that assumes that young children find it difficult to combine concepts of which one is reduced or exists potentially (Lynott and Connell 2010), or that are inherently related (Berman 2009). Instead, many of the young children's novel compounds involve one concept that is reduced or has potential existence, or they express inherent relations (e.g. no concrete baby is present in (17a-b), no giant in (18b) and no mouse in (19a)). However, they do lend support to the view that conceptual combination is contextually situated and builds on an interplay between linguistic and experiential information (Lynott and Connell 2010).

6.1.3 N.GEN N constructions: POSSESSION

Berman (2009: 314), as well as Korecky-Kröll, Sommer-Lolei and Dressler (2017: 26), remark that children's early instances of juxtaposition of two nouns are ambiguous between phrase and compound. Still, the earliest N N relation expressed by children, at least for English [ENG] and Hebrew [HEB], is POSSESSION (Berman 2009: 310). In Hebrew, the earliest relations combine an animate possessor with an inanimate possessum, but soon thereafter, periphrastic genitives emerge. This finding is supported by the two Swedish data sets, in which the first N N sequences express POSSESSION, and can therefore be interpreted as emerging genitive constructions.

In the diary data, the child's earliest genitive constructions are of the juxtaposition type, with possessor followed by possessum (20). The possessive pronoun (*min* 'my/mine') emerges simultaneously (21). Soon thereafter, Anna produces target-like Swedish possessive constructions of the synthetic type (22):

(20) a. *mamma tröja* (1;9;8) [mom shirt] (for a shirt of mine) POSSESSION
 b. *Anna hund* (1;9;10) [Anna dog] (for her soft toy dog) POSSESSION

(21) a. *min hund* (1;9;8) [my dog] POSSESSION
 b. *nej inte upp, min chips* (1;9;11) [no not up, my crisp] (she did not want me to eat her potato crisp) POSSESSION

(22) a. *jag sitta mamma.s knä* (1;10;10) [I sit mom.GEN lap] POSSESSION
 b. *Arnold.s nintendo* (1;10;13) [Arnold.GEN nintendo] POSSESSION

In the recordings before age 2, Harry (23a) uses the possessive pronoun *min* 'my', indicating a grasping of POSSESSION, and Markus (23b) produces two N N sequences in a row that express POSSESSION, where the latter indicates an emerging genitive marker:

(23) a. *min bil* (1;10;18) [my car] POSSESSION
 b. *mamma väska* and then *mamma.t väska* (1;11;12) [mom bag], [mom.GEN bag] POSSESSION

The genitive constructions attested for the four children in the recordings show a similar development as the one in the diary data. Markus, who had produced the genitive marker prior to age 2, uses the complete genitive construction beyond that age. In contrast, Bella (24), Harry (25) and Tea (26) first use genitive constructions either with the -s omitted or only the possessor present. Then they move on to a phase where the -s is sometimes left out, sometimes present. Finally, they all produce the complete structure, about two months before or after age 3:

(24) a. *pappa.s (_)* (2;1;28) [daddy.GEN] POSSESSION
 b. *mamma öga* (2;2;13) [mommy eye] POSSESSION
 c. *farfar.s hund* (2;10;17) [grandpa.GEN dog] POSSESSION

(25) a. *nalle.s mage,* (2;4;23) [teddy.GEN tummy] POSSESSION
 b. *morfar bil* (2;8;27) [grandpa car] POSSESSION
 c. *elefant.en.s mage* (3;1;21) [elephant.DEF.GEN tummy] POSSESSION

(26) a. *docka arm.ar* (2;1;17) [doll arm.PL] POSSESSION
 b. *Herman.s ög.on, John pappa* (2;6;2) [Herman.GEN eye.PL], [John daddy] POSSESSION
 c. *Alma.s hund* (3;1;26) [Alma.GEN dog] POSSESSION

In the recordings of Tea, it can be noted that she seems to go through a phase where POSSESSION is expressed by 'have', for instance *dockan ben har* (2;3;27) 'the doll leg has'.

Berman (2009: 310) notes with some surprise that, in Clark and Berman (1985), POSSESSION was not a preferred relation in Hebrew children's comprehension and production of novel NN compounds. The five relations being tested (Possession, Purpose, Container, Material and Location) had similar processing effects, which led to the conclusion that form was more important than semantics for compound processing. The present study could suggest the opposite explanation, namely that since POSSESSION is the default value for genitive constructions and emerges early, its use is downgraded for NN compounding. Independent evidence in favour of this explanation is provided by the fact that POSSESSION is considered to be marginal for English NN compounds (Warren 1978), as well as for French NN compounds (Bourque 2014).

6.1.4 Prepositional phrases: Various semantic relations

In the diary data, precursors to N P N phrases, in which the preposition is omitted, occur simultaneously with novel compounds and precursor genitive constructions:

(27) a. *mamma toa.n* (1;9;11) [mom bathroom.DEF] (mom is in the bathroom) LOCATION
 b. *mjölk matta.n* (1;9;13) [milk carpet.DEF] (milk spilled on the carpet) LOCATION

Within a month later, prepositions that express LOCATION and other relations appear more often, but they often deviate from the target use for some time:

(28) a. *hund under stol* (1;10;3) [dog under chair] LOCATION
 b. *i fot.en* (1;10;20) [in foot.DEF] LOCATION
 c. *på sockan av mamma* (1;10;20) [on sock.DEF of mommy] (she wants to put on mommy's sock on mommy) LOCATION
 d. *salva Arnold* (1;10;20) [ointment Arnold] (ointment for A.) PURPOSE
 e. *Arnold, det är lite salva av mig* (2;3;9) [Arnold, it is some ointment from me] SOURCE
 f. *toast med smör i den* (2;0;4) [toast with butter in it] ('in' instead of 'on') LOCATION

For the N P N phrases in the recordings prior to age 2, Bella produces one P N phrase, *i den* (1;8;23) 'in that', whereas Markus produces quite a lot of (N) (P) N phrases (29a–d). Between the ages 2–3, Markus produces prepositional phrases that express relations such as LOCATION ('in', 'on', 'under', 'behind'), PURPOSE ('for'), Direction ('from', 'out'), TOPIC ('about') (29e) and Instrument ('with').

(29) a. *bajs i blöja.n* (1;11;12) [poop in diaper.DEF] LOCATION
 b. *på arm.en* (1;11;12) [on arm.DEF] LOCATION
 c. *mamma ha den (_) fingr.et* (1;11;12) [mommy have it finger.DEF] (*på* 'on' is missing) LOCATION
 d. *till blomm.or.na* (1;11;12) [for flower.PL.DEF] (fertilizer for the flowers) PURPOSE
 e. *den handlar om en pojke* (2;6;20) [it is about a boy] (a book about a boy) TOPIC

The three other children in the recordings show more or less a similar use of prepositions, but it emerges later. Between the ages 2–3, the attestations from Harry contain 'in' and 'on' expressing LOCATION, although 'on' is often omitted. In the recordings of Bella, a more varied use of prepositions is found, namely LOCATION ('in', 'on'), Direction ('to', 'up') and PART + LOCATION ('with N on') (30a), and SOURCE ('from') (30b), but she often leaves them out before age 2;5. As to the recordings of Tea, prepositions are used sporadically for expressing LOCATION ('in', 'on', 'under'), Direction ('to', 'off') and PURPOSE ('for').

(30) a. *med ost på* (2;3;23) [with cheese on] (a sandwich with cheese) PART+ LOCATION
 b. *den fick jag av tandläkare.n* (2;8;7) [that got I from dentist.DEF] (a toy) SOURCE

After age 3, attestations from Tea (31a) and Harry (31b) show a more complex use of prepositions:

(31) a. *ingen borste till barbie.häst.en* (3;10;22) [no brush for barbie.horse.DEF] PURPOSE
 b. *en jätte.stor zebra med en jätte.lång hals* (3;11;23) [a very.big zebra with a very.long neck] PART

The children's earliest use of prepositional phrases mainly expresses LOCATION, but later on, additional semantic relations are expressed.[5] Given the vast range of semantic relations that can be expressed by prepositional phrases, these are strong competitors to novel NN compounds.

6.1.5 A N phrases: (COORDINATION, HYPERNYMY)

The diary data contain several utterances with single adjectives prior to age 2, but only some A N phrases, such as:

(32) a. *docka grön tröja* (1;10;03) [doll green shirt]
 b. *en grön tröja* (1;10;03) [a green shirt]
 c. *varm spis* (1;10;13) [hot stove]
 d. *stor.a sko.r* (1;10;13) [big.AGR shoe.PL]

---

[5] In the development of syntactic prepositions in Hungarian, children show a strong preference for coding direction (or GOAL) (see Pléh, Vinkler and Kálmán 1997).

In the recordings, two of the four children, Bella and Markus, produce some single adjectives prior to age 2, but no A N sequences are found. In other words, A N phrases seem to be quite rare in the speech of Swedish children younger than 2 years.

Overall, the attestations from the diary data and the recordings show that between the ages 2–3, A N phrases emerge for all children, with agreement as occasionally present (except for Markus, whose adjectives agree with the nouns after age 2). After age 3, A N phrases most often exhibit target agreement. The examples from the diary data serve to illustrate this development:

(33) a. *fin.t hals.band* (2;0;20), *fin.a byx.or* (2;0;23) [nice.AGR neck.lace], [nice.AGR pant.PL]
 b. *kan jag ha *en *lite.n glas* (2;4;30) [can I have a small.AGR glass] (target: *ett lite.t glas* 'a small glass')
 c. *med röd tröja och brun.t hår* (3;5;25) [with red shirt and brown.AGR hair]

According to Krott, Gagné and Nicoladis (2009) A N phrases, with a strong preference for the IS-relation (e.g. a ball IS red), are the syntactic phrases the most similar to NN compounds. However, A N phrases do not combine two 'things' but instead a property and a 'thing'. In Swedish these are rarely binominal lexemes. If we squeeze them into Bourque's (2014) semantics relations, COORDINATON and HYPERNYMY would be the closest match. In the Swedish data, A N phrases emerge later than novel compounds (and prepositional phrases) and they have a more descriptive than labelling function. Four A N compounds are actually attested in the diary data, but they are all non-target like, such as:

(34) *det är en sån liten elak häst, som man brukar kalla . . . . *elakhästen* [it is a such little mean horse that one would call . . . . mean.horse.DEF] (*What would one call such a horse?* She then asks me. She seems to realize that her term was not perfect)

6.1.6 N 'and' N: COORDINATION but not identity

In the diary data, three target-like coordinated phrases with N 'and' N are attested before age 2 (35a–c). Later on, coordinated nouns continue to be used in the same manner (35d), i.e. without combining the two concepts into one single concept (as in compounding):

(35) a. *jag ha smör och ost* (1;10;19) [I have butter and cheese]
 b. *byx.or och tröja* (1;11;26) [pant.PL and shirt]

    c. *jag vill ha gaffel och kniv* (1;11;28) [I will have fork and knife]
    d. *jag kan gå med mjölk.en och rån.en* (2;6;6) [I can go with milk.DEF and wafer.PL:DEF]

In the recordings, the use of a coordinator, 'or', before age 2 is only attested for Markus, who uses it either to coordinate two nouns or as an initial discourse marker:

(36) a. *kula eller kula* (1;11;12) [ball or ball]
      b. *eller sten lägga där* (1;11;12) [or stone put there]

Between the ages 2–3, the attestations from the recordings show an emerging use of 'and' as a co-construction, that is, the conjunction is used initially and clings on to the caretaker's previous utterance (37a), that moves towards the complete N 'and' N construction, which is fully established after age 3. The examples from Bella serve to illustrate this path:

(37) a. *och mjölk* (2;1;28) [and milk]
      b. *socker och morött.er* (2;4;13) [sugar and carrot.PL)
      c. *har han en bok och en teve och en har hals.duk* (3;2;19) [has he a book and a telly and one has neck.cloth] (*halsduk* 'scarf')

Lustigman and Berman (2016) investigate early clause-combining in child-caretaker interactions (three Hebrew children, ages 2;0–3;0). Their data confirm that coordination with 'and' and subordination with 'that' emerge the earliest, simultaneously. The coordinator 'and' (Swedish *och*) is used early on for clause-internal coordination and as an "utterance-initial discourse marker", whereas 'that' (Swedish *som*) "plays a unique role in developing subordination" (Lustigman and Berman 2016: 177). Yet, whereas the earliest use of 'and' and 'that' mostly occur in "autonomously produced contingent clauses", the later use of more advanced and varied clause connectors relies more on "interlocutor-supported contexts", thus being co-constructions rather than autonomously produced constructions (see e.g. 36b, 37a, 39b, 40a, 43a, and 45). An explanation given for this phenomenon (also evidenced for German, Dutch [NLD] and English), is that it decreases the cognitive load for children (Lustigman and Berman 2016: 179). The diary data align with these assumptions, since the earliest uses of 'and' and 'that' occur either in autonomously produced constructions or in co-constructions. The latter are in fact quite prominent in the Swedish production data.

6.1.7 *Som*-constructions: Various semantic relations

Swedish *som* is a multi-functional word that can appear as a conjunction, a preposition, a subordinator, a pronoun initiating a relative clause, or an adverb. Hence, along the lines of Lustigman and Berman (2016: 177), it is a good candidate for serving as a bridging category for clause-combining (cf. also Josefsson and Håkansson 2000, who propose that *som*, with its use as a preposition 'as/like' or as a subordinator 'that', can serve as a lexical bridge for children).

If we start by looking at subordinator *som* 'that' in the diary data, we see that precursor constructions emerge first:

(38) a. *Konrad äter (_) (_) mamma gjort* (1;10;13) [Konrad eats mommy done] (i.e. K. eats <u>sandwiches that</u> mommy done)
b. *det är bä.bä.n (_) äter banan* (1;10;25) [it is baa.baa.DEF eats banana] (i.e. it is the sheep that eats banana)

In the diary data, *som* 'that' is attested from around 2;1 in restricted contexts but continues to be omitted quite often. Its use is not established before age 2;8:

(39) a. *det är jag som ska stänga* (2;1;24) [it is me that shall close]
b. *som man har i näsan* (2;4;3) [that you have in the nose] (i.e. about the nose spray)
c. *ja vill inte ha banan (_) (_) brun* (2;7;27) [I do not want banana brown] (i.e. that is brown)
d. *titta, där är nån som ser på tv* (2;8;3) [look, there is someone that watches telly]

In the recordings, Markus produces a subordinator *som* 'that' prior to age 2 (no precursors were attested). This early attestation is a co-construction that clings on to the mother's previous utterance about a *machine* (*gräsklippare* 'grass-cutter' according to the mother's response). There is also an autonomous production just after age 2:

(40) a. *som klippte gräset* (1;11;12) [that cut the grass]
b. *var det bandspelare.n som snurrade* (2;0;16) [was it tape.recorder.DEF that span]

As to the attestations from the other three recorded children, the subordinator 'that' turns up later. The first attestation found from Bella is (41). In the attestations from Harry, the first one has a dummy item (*ä*) instead of *som* 'that', but the second one indicates that *som* has become established (42a–b). The first attestation from Tea is a co-construction that expands the mother's previous utterance about a horse (43a). In the attestation in (43b), *som* is omitted, but the one in (43c) suggests that *som* is being mastered:

(41) *en ängel som har så lång.t hår* (2;6;17) [an angel that has so long.AGR hair]

(42) a. *jag har min last.bil ä jag fick av Niklas* (3;1;21) [I have my lorry *ä* I got from Niklas]
 b. *dom där bil.ar.na som vi hade förra gång.en* (3;5;20) [those car.PL.DEF that we had last time.DEF]

(43) a. *som är ute* (2;6;2) [that is out]
 b. *vilka vackr.a häst.ar (_) finns i denna* (3;6;7) [what beautiful.AGR horse.PL are in this]
 c. *en fisk som pappa.n har som dom ska äta upp* (3;8;17) [a fish that daddy.DEF has that they will eat up]

If we look at *som* 'as/like' as a preposition (or conjunction), this use, which expresses SIMILARITY, emerges later according to the diary data, around age 2;7:

(44) a. *samma salva som jag* (2;7;8) [same ointment as I] SIMILARITY
 b. *kolla det smakar som godis* (2;8;6) [look it tastes like candy] SIMILARITY
 c. *barbapapp.or är som dock.or men dom ser ut som gubb.ar* (2;10;2) [barbapapa.PL are like doll.PL but they look like oldster.PL] SIMILARITY

In the recordings, *som* 'as/like' is attested later than *som* 'that' for Markus (45: a co-construction) as well as for Bella (46). No attestations of this use are found for Harry, and the first two attestations from Tea's data omit *som* (47a–b), but later on *som* seems to have become established (47c):

(45) *som den röd.a ballong.en är stor* (2;6;20) [like the red.AGR balloon.DEF is big] SIMILARITY

(46) *tavl.or som är rund.a som en ring* (3;4;11) [painting.PL that are round.AGR as a ring/circle] SIMILARITY

(47) a. *ser ut (_) (_) kossa* (2;6;2) [looks cow] (i.e. looks like a cow) SIMILARITY
 b. *det (_) samma tavla (_) vi har där* (2;8;18) [it same painting we have there] (i.e. it is the same painting as we have there) SIMILARITY
 c. *fast det ser ut som en orm* (3;8;17) [but it looks like a snake] SIMILARITY

As we will see below, this use of *som* expressing SIMILARITY becomes, when more firmly established, a strong competitor to the much earlier emerging novel NN compounds.

6.1.8 A developmental trajectory of nominal constructions in Swedish production data

In order to summarize the analysis so far, Table 3 illustrates the time when the different types of nominal constructions attested in the Swedish production data emerged.

Table 3: The emergence of nominal constructions in the Swedish data from five children.

	Anna			Bella			Harry			Tea			Markus	
	>2y	>3y	>4y	>2y	>3y	>4y	>2y	>3y	>4y	>2y	>3y	>4y	>2y	>3y
Establ. NN **cmp**	+	+	+	+	+	+	+	+	+	+	+	+	+	+
Nov. NN **cmp**	+	+	+	–	+	+	–	+	+	–	+	+	+	+
N.GEN N	+	+	+	–	+	+	–	+	+	–	+	+	+	+
Prep. phrases	+	+	+	+	+	+	–	+	+	–	+	+	+	+
A N phrases	+	+	+	–	+	+	–	+	+	–	+	+	–	+
N 'and' N	+	+	+	–	+	+	–	+	+	–	+	+	+	+
som 'that'	–	+	+	–	+	+	–	–	+	–	+	+	+	+
som 'as/like'	–	+	+	–	–	+	–	–	–	–	–	+	–	+

It is noteworthy that established NN compounds, the prototypical binominal lexemes, are the only type that is attested for all five children prior to age 2, and that the constructions containing *som* 'as/like' are the last to emerge.

6.2 Further development and cases of competition

The next part of the analysis concentrates on the novel compounds in the diary data in relation to competing patterns with similar meanings.

6.2.1 Constituent families

The question whether a particular child prefers particular semantic relations in novel NN compounds, can be studied by looking at some compound constituent families, as attested in the diary data. For instance, *dagis* 'kindergarten' and *gunga* 'swing' recur in several compounds, either as head or as modifier. However, as shown by the examples below, they do not express the same relations:

(48) a. *dagis.gung.or* (2;4;19) [kindergarten.swing.PL] (i.e. *dagisets gungor* 'the kindergarten's swings') POSSESSION
 b. *det är dagis.hus där* (2;5;9) [it is kindergarten.houses there] PURPOSE
 c. *barn.gung.or* (2;5;16) [child.swing.PL] PURPOSE
 d. *gung.snöre.t* (2;6;26) [swing.lace.DEF] (i.e. 'the swing's chain') POSSESSION
 e. *mormor.s gung.lek.park* (2;11;7) [grandma.GEN swing.play.ground] LOCATION/PART
 f. *orm.gunga* (3;0;20) [snake.swing] (pretends that her long soft snake is a swing) SIMILARITY

The diary data do not confirm the idea that semantic relations are stored along with particular constituents, nor that a certain child prefers particular relations (Gagné and Shoben 1997; Krott, Gagné, and Nicoladis 2009). Rather, they align with the assumption that concepts can be combined along various parameters (e.g. Estes and Jones 2006; Lynott and Connell 2010).

6.2.2 Recursivity: The rise of complexity

It is clear that most of the nominal constructions under investigation are rather rudimentary when they emerge but gradually become more complex and target-like (cf. Dressler, Ketrez, and Kilani-Schoch 2017: 295–296). Compounds that involve more than two parts are morphologically more complex and semantically more opaque, and they should therefore emerge later (cf. Dressler et al 2017: 2; Korecky-Kröll, Sommer-Lolei, and Dressler 2017: 34). This view fits with the diary data, where the 23 recursive novel NNN compounds were produced between the ages 2;11;3–3;11 (and beyond). Some of them added an extra N to an established compound, mainly as the last part (49a–c) but also first (49d); some of them were completely novel (50a-c):

(49) a. *snö.man.troll* (2;11;3) [snow.man.troll] (LOCATION) + COORDINATION
 b. *snö.dropp.ar.blomm.or* (2;11;21) [snow.drop.PL.flower.PL] (LOCATION) + COORDINATION
 c. *ett stengubbemonster* (3;4;16) (COMPOSITION) + COORDINATION [a stone.oldster.monster]
 d. *min val.pärl.platta* (3;7;26) [my whale.perler.bead] SIMILARITY + (PURPOSE)

(50) a. *luft.båt.anka* (3;4;21) [air.boat.duck] PART + COORDINATION
 b. *metall.kula.ballong.er* (3;9;9) [metal.ball.balloon.PL] COMPOSITION + COORDINATION
 c. **godis.jul.en.käpp.en* (3;9;9) [candy.Christmas.DEF.cane.DEF], which the child immediately reordered to the more target-like *jul.en.godis.käpp.en* [Christmas.DEF.candy.cane.DEF] LOCATION + COORDINATION

Overall, recursive compounds tend to be non-target-like by containing internal inflections (49b and 50c) and not displaying liaison forms. However, structures like (49d), where a first constituent is added to an established compound, are adult-like.

6.2.3 Competition between novel NN compounds and other nominal constructions

Different types of nominal constructions from the recordings can be contrasted to the more target-like novel NN compounds from the diary data, given that they refer to similar entities. Note also that in (51ai), Bella's mother actually reformulates Bella's N 'and' N structure into an NN compound:

(51) ai. Bella *festis och päron är det* (2;8;7) [drink and pear is it], *är det päron. festis?* [is it pear.drink] PART (asks the mother)
 aii. Anna *äpple.juice.dricka* (3;1;5) [apple.juice.drink] PART + COORDINATION
 bi. Markus *pappa öppnade penna.n.s lock.et* (2;210) [daddy opened pen.DEF.GEN cap.DEF] (target *penna.n.s lock*) POSSESSION
 bii. Anna *en pennalock* (2;0;27) [a pen.cap] (target *ett penn.lock*) POSSESSION/PURPOSE
 ci. Tea *kvinna och bagare* (3;11;23) [woman and baker] COORDINATION
 cii. Anna *kvinn.varg.ar* (3;7;18) [woman.wolf.PL] HYPERNYMY

In the recordings, Markus uses an NN compound and a N P N phrase in the same utterance to refer to the same kind of object (52a), and Tea's utterance in (52b) illustrates how easily a novel compound, recursive, can be produced in a context that anchors the constituents:

(52) a. *motor.båt och svart.a båt.en med motor.n* (2;8;8) [motor.boat and black.AGR boat.DEF with motor.DEF] PART
b. *men du har nog inte sett barbie.häst.ar.na.s film.er, vi har barbie.häst.film.ar.na* (3;11;23) [but you have probably not seen the barbie.horse.PL.DEF.GEN film.PL, we have barbie.horse.film.PL.DEF] TOPIC

In the diary data, we find competing patterns for same or similar entities by comparing earlier constructions, mainly NN compounds, with N P N phrases that are produced later (53a–c) (cf. Kilani-Schoch 2017 for French). In (53d), Anna spells out the relation of an NN compound by a preposition:

(53) ai. *jag vill ha te.mjölk* (2;10;1) [I will have tea.milk] LOCATION/PART
aii. *jag vill inte ha kaffe med mjölk i* (2;11;21) [I will not have coffee with milk in] LOCATION/PART
bi. *jag har en tröja med spöke.n på* (3;0;14) [I have a shirt with ghost.PL on] LOCATION/PART
bii. *jag har hittat en blom.klänning, en mask.ros.klänning* (3;0;16) [I have found a flower.dress, a verm.rose.dress] (*maskros* 'dandelion') LOCATION/PART
ci. *morot.torn* (3;4;25) [carrot.tower] COMPOSITION
cii. *jag gjorde ett torn av morött.er.na* (3;6;4) [I made a tower of the carrot.PL.DEF] COMPOSITION
d. *mamma titta, en bebis.flaska, inte för barn, bara för bebis.ar* (3;5;15) [mom look, a baby.bottle, not for children, only for babie.PL] PURPOSE

The later part of the diary data contains cases where prepositional phrases are used as a first option, but where NN compounds would have been equally possible. This is a case of competition between N P N phrases and NN compounds in Swedish, both for children and adults:

(54) a. *jag såg att moln.en var av ost* (3;5;14) [I saw that the cloud.PL:DEF were of cheese] (vs. *ost.moln* [cheese.cloud]) COMPOSITION
b. *de har en lampa till skorsten* (3;6;1) [they have a lamp as chimney] (vs. *skorsten.s.lampa* [chimney.LE.lamp] or *lamp.skorsten* [lamp.chimney]) PURPOSE

c. *jag känner lukt.en av rök* (3;7;3) [I feel smell.DEF of smoke] (vs. *rök.lukt* [smoke.smell]) COMPOSITION

There are few cases of competition between genitive constructions and novel compounds in the diary data, but one example is the following, where Anna first uses a genitive construction but decides to replace it with an NN compound:

(55) *det är hund.ar.s säng, det är en hund.säng* (3;4;22) [it is dog.PL.GEN bed, it is a dog.bed]

Regarding A N phrases in relation to novel NN compounds, there are, likewise, few cases of competition. Occasionally the child coins an NN compound, where A N or N P N phrases would have been more target-like options (recall that A N phrases emerge later):

(56) a. *blom.klänning* (3;0;16) [flower.dress] vs. *blommig klänning* [floral dress] or *klänning med blomm.or (på)* [dress with flower.PL (on)]
b. *jag har *prick.sock och *stjärn.sock* (3;1;7) [I have dot.sock and star.sock] vs. *en prickig sock och en sock med stjärn.or* [a dotty sock and a sock with star.PL]

In the diary data, there are also a few cases where two novel NN compounds compete as a name for an entity:

(57) a. *en sjuk.bil* (3;6;11) [a sick.car] (i.e. ambulance) PURPOSE
b. *en gång såg vi doktor.bil.en* (3;10;13) [one time saw we doctor.car.DEF] (i.e. ambulance) POSSESSION

The diary data confirm the idea that there is no sharp distinction between the naming and descriptive functions of compounds and phrases (cf. Downing 1977). Some of the novel compounds are non-target-like, often just because they tend to be more descriptive than labelling. When prepositional constructions as well as the two types of *som*-constructions ('that' or 'as/like') have become established, they are often used to describe or expand the compound meaning intended by the child. Hence, *som*-constructions strongly compete with novel NN compounds, and in the diary data they can occur as a more explicit reformulation, after the compound has been uttered:

(58) a. *en konstig lampa, en hatt.lampa, det ser ut som en keps, en hatt* (2;10;3) [a funny lamp, a hat.lamp, it looks like a cap, a hat] (for a pendant lamp) SIMILARITY
b. *ett banan.tak, mamma jag såg en banan som var ett tak* (3;3;21) [a banana.roof, mom I saw a banana that was a roof] SIMILARITY
c. *nej, det är en natt.fågel som kommer på natten* (3;4;30) [no, it is a night.bird that comes at night] LOCATION
d. *en sago.rosa.prinsessa, en sago.prinsessa som hade bara rosa kläder* (3;10;18) [a fairytale.pink.princess, a fairytale.princess that had only pink clothes] HYPERNYMY

7 Conclusion

The present study suggests a developmental trajectory for structures (syntactic or morphological) that potentially compete with binominal lexemes in Swedish, based on diary data from one child and longitudinal recordings from four children. The emergence and later establishment of the different nominal constructions seem to follow more or less the same paths, albeit with some age differences. With its focus on novel NN compounds, which combine concepts to express a wide range of semantic relations, this study suggests that adjectival, genitive, and coordinated phrases in Swedish have a narrower semantic scope. There is thus little competition between them and novel NN compounds.

The diary data show that the child mainly uses novel NN compounds for combined concepts, in accordance with the overall preference in Swedish. However, the child also uses novel NN compounds for descriptive cases where syntactic constructions would have been more target-like. In the later part of the diary data, such constructions, containing prepositions or *som* ('that' or 'as/like') turn up – being later acquired than NN compounds. Once established, they constitute the strongest competitors to novel NN compounds for expressions that are more heavily descriptive than labelling.

If we regard compounding as a rather simple concatenative process of combining two forms without specifying the intended meaning, children's early use of compounding – if it is an available and profitable pattern in their language (cf. Corbin 1987) – could be cognitively motivated. This study suggests that it could be a preferred option for young children to start with the juxtaposition of two nouns, very locally, but as their language develops, they gradually learn how to relate two concepts syntactically so as to overtly express their relation. Obviously, NN compounding remains a competitive choice, given that it is a well-entrenched pattern as well as a powerful tool to pack much information in a condensed form.

Future research could explore how the development of competing types of binominals proceeds in interlingual comparison, in order to continue the study of this phenomenon from a typological and a semantic perspective.

References

Bauer, Laurie. 1983. *English word-formation*. Cambridge: Cambridge University Press.
Bauer, Laurie & Elizaveta Tarasova. 2013. The meaning link in nominal compounds. *SKASE Journal of Theoretical Linguistics* 10(3). 2–18.
Becker, Judith A. 1994. "Sneak-shoes", "sworders", and "nose-beards": A case study of lexical innovation. *First Language* 14(41). 195–211.
Berman, Ruth A. 2009. Children's acquisition of compound constructions. In Rochelle Lieber & Pavol Štekauer (eds.), *The Oxford handbook of compounding*, 298–322. Oxford: Oxford University Press.
Blevins, James P. & Juliette Blevins. 2009. Introduction: Analogy in grammar. In James P. Blevins & Juliette Blevins (eds.), *Analogy in grammar: Form and acquisition*, 1–12. Oxford: Oxford University Press.
Bourque, Stephen Y. 2014. *Toward a typology of semantic transparency: The case of French compounds*. Toronto: University of Toronto PhD dissertation.
Bretherton, Inge & Marjorie Beeghly. 1982. Talking about internal states: The acquisition of an explicit theory of mind. *Developmental Psychology* 18(6). 906–921.
Christensen, Lisa. 2010. *Early verbs in child Swedish: A diary study on two boys. Part 1, Verb spurts and the grammar burst*. Media-Tryck: Centre for Languages and Literature, Lund University.
Clark, Eve V. 1993. *The lexicon in acquisition*. Cambridge: Cambridge University Press.
Corbin, Danielle. 1987. *Morphologie dérivationnelle et structuration du lexique*, 2 Vol. Tübingen: Niemeyer.
Croft, William. 2001. *Radical Construction Grammar: Syntactic theory in typological perspective*. Oxford: Oxford University Press.
Downing, Pamela. 1977. On the creation and use of English compound nouns. *Language* 53(4). 810–842.
Dressler, Wolfgang U. 2006. Compound types. In Gary Libben & Gonia Jarema (eds.), *The representation and processing of compound words*, 23–44. Oxford: Oxford University Press.
Dressler, Wolfgang U., Nihan F. Ketrez & Marianne Kilani-Schoch (eds.). 2017. *Nominal compound acquisition*. Amsterdam: John Benjamins.
Dressler, Wolfgang U., Nihan F. Ketrez & Marianne Kilani-Schoch. 2017. Discussion and outlook. In Wolfgang U. Dressler, Nihan F. Ketrez. & Marianne Kilani-Schoch (eds.), *Nominal compound acquisition*, 287–305. Amsterdam: John Benjamins.
Dressler, Wolfgang U., Nihan F. Ketrez, Kilani-Schoch, Marianne & Ursula Stephany. 2017. Introduction. In Wolfgang U. Dressler, Nihan F. Ketrez & Marianne Kilani-Schoch (eds.), *Nominal compound acquisition*, 1–18. Amsterdam: John Benjamins.

Dressler, Wolfgang U., Laura E. Lettner & Katharina Korecky-Kröll. 2010. First language acquisition of compounds: With special emphasis on early German child language. In Sergio Scalise & Irene Vogel (eds.), *Cross-disciplinary issues in compounding*, 323–344. Amsterdam: John Benjamins.

Elsen, Hilke & Karin Schlipphak. 2015. Word-formation in first language acquisition. In Peter O. Müller, Ingeborg Ohnheiser, Susan Olsen & Franz Rainer (eds.), *Word-formation: An international handbook of the languages of Europe*, Vol. 3, 2117–2137. Berlin: Mouton de Gruyter.

Estes, Zachary & Lara L. Jones. 2006. Priming via relational similarity: A COPPER HORSE is faster when seen through a GLASS EYE. *Journal of Memory and Language* 55(1). 89–101.

Gagné, Christina L. & Edward J. Shoben. 1997. Influence of thematic relations on the comprehension of modifier-noun combinations. *Journal of Experimental Psychology: Learning, Memory, and Cognition* 23(1). 71–87.

Gottfried, Gail M. 1997. Using metaphors as modifiers: Children's production of metaphoric compounds. *Journal of Child Language* 24(3). 567–601.

Grzega, Joachim. 2015. Word-formation in onomasiology. In Peter O. Müller, Ingeborg Ohnheiser, Susan Olsen, & Franz Rainer (eds.), *Word-formation: An international handbook of the languages of Europe*, Vol. 1, 79–93. Mouton de Gruyter.

Haspelmath, Martin. 2012. How to compare major word-classes across the world's languages. *UCLA Working Papers in Linguistics, Theories of Everything 17*, Article 16. 109–130.

Johnson, Mark, Katherine Demuth, Michael Frank & Bevan K. Jones. 2010. Synergies in learning words and their referents. *Advances in Neural Information Processing Systems* 23. 1018–1026.

Josefsson, Gunlög & Gisela Håkansson. 2000. The PP-CP parallelism hypothesis and language acquisition: Evidence from Swedish. In Susan M. Powers & Cornelia Hamann (eds.), *The acquisition of scrambling and cliticization*, 397–422. Dordrecht: Kluwer.

Kilani-Schoch, Marianne. 2017. Early development of compounds in two French children's corpora. In Wolfgang U. Dressler, Nihan F. Ketrez & Marianne Kilani-Schoch (eds.), *Nominal compound acquisition*, 91–118. Amsterdam: John Benjamins.

Kjærbæck, Laila & Hans Basbøll. 2017. Compound nouns in Danish child language. In Wolfgang U. Dressler, Nihan F. Ketrez & Marianne Kilani-Schoch (eds.), *Nominal compound acquisition*, 39–62. Amsterdam: John Benjamins.

Kopf, Kristin. 2018. From genitive suffix to linking element: A corpus study on the genesis and productivity of a new compounding pattern in (Early) New High German. In Tanja Ackermann, Horst J. Simon & Christian Zimmer (eds.), *Germanic Genitives*, 91–114. Amsterdam: John Benjamins.

Koptjevskaja-Tamm, Maria. 2012. New directions in lexical typology. *Linguistics* 50(3). 373–394.

Korecky-Kröll, Katharina, Sommer-Lolei, Sabine & Wolfgang U Dressler. 2017. Emergence and early development of German compounds. In Wolfgang U. Dressler, Nihan F. Ketrez & Marianne Kilani-Schoch (eds.), *Nominal compound acquisition*, 19–37. Amsterdam: John Benjamins.

Krott, Andrea. 2009. The role of analogy for compound words. In James P. Blevins & Juliette Blevins (eds.), *Analogy in grammar: Form and acquisition*, 118–136. Oxford: Oxford University Press.

Krott, Andrea, Christina L. Gagné & Elena Nicoladis. 2009. How the parts relate to the whole frequency effects on children's interpretation of novel compounds. *Journal of Child Language* 36(1). 85–112.

Krott, Andrea, Christina L. Gagné & Elena Nicoladis. 2010. Children's preference for HAS and LOCATED relations: A word learning bias for noun–noun compounds. *Journal of Child Language* 37(2). 373–394.

Levi, Judith N. 1978. *The syntax and semantics of complex nominals*. New York: Academic Press.

Lustigman, Lyle & Ruth A. Berman. 2016. Form and function in early clause-combining. *Journal of Child Language* 43(1). 157–185.

Lynott, Dermot & Louise Connell. 2010. Embodied conceptual combination. *Frontiers in Psychology*, Volume 1. Article 212: 1–14.

MacWhinney, Brian. 2000. *The CHILDES project: Tools for analyzing talk*. 3rd ed. Mahwah, NJ: Lawrence Erlbaum.

Masini, Francesca, Simone Mattiola & Steve Pepper. This volume. Exploring complex lexemes cross-linguistically. In Steve Pepper, Francesca Masini & Simone Mattiola (eds.), *Binominal lexemes in cross-linguistic perspective*. Berlin: Mouton de Gruyter.

Mattiello, Elisa. 2017. *Analogy in word-formation: A study of English neologisms and occasionalisms*. Berlin: Mouton de Gruyter.

Mellenius, Ingmarie. 1997. *The acquisition of nominal compounding in Swedish*. Lund: Lund University dissertation.

Mellenius, Ingmarie & Maria Rosenberg. 2016. The semantics of compounds in Swedish child language. In Pius ten Hacken (ed.), *The semantics of compounding*, 110–128. Cambridge: Cambridge University Press.

Ngon, Céline, Andrew Martin, Emmanuel Dupoux, Dominique Cabrol, Michel Dutat & Sharon Peperkamp. 2013. (Non)words, (non)words, (non)words: Evidence for a protolexicon during the first year of life. *Developmental Science* 16 (1). 24–34.

Pepper, Steve. 2020. *The typology and semantics of binominal lexemes: Noun-noun compounds and their functional equivalents*. Oslo: University of Oslo PhD dissertation.

Pepper, Steve. This volume. Hatcher-Bourque: Towards a reusable classification of semantic relations. In Steve Pepper, Francesca Masini & Simone Mattiola (eds.), *Binominal lexemes in cross-linguistic perspective*. Berlin: Mouton de Gruyter.

Pléh, Csaba, Zsuzsanna Vinkler & László Kálmán. 1997. Early morphology of spatial expressions in Hungarian children: A CHILDES study. *Acta Linguistica Hungarica* 44(1–2). 249–260.

Rainer, Franz. 2010. *Carmens Erwerb der deutschen Wortbildung*. Vienna: Verlag der Österreichischen Akademie der Wissenschaften.

Rainer, Franz. 2013. Can relational adjectives really express any relation? An onomasiological perspective. *SKASE Journal of Theoretical Linguistics* 10(1). 12–40.

Rosenberg, Maria & Ingmarie Mellenius. 2018. Children's novel NN compounding in Swedish diary data: Function and form. *Morphology* 28. 229–252. https://doi.org/10.1007/s11525-018-9325-3

Skeide, Michael A., Jens Brauer & Angela D Friederici. 2014. Syntax gradually segregates from semantics in the developing brain. *NeuroImage* 100. 206–111.

Stephany, Ursula & Evangelia Thomadaki. 2017. Compounding in early Greek language acquisition. In Wolfgang U. Dressler, Nihan F. Ketrez & Marianne Kilani-Schoch (eds.), *Nominal compound acquisition*, 119–143. Amsterdam: John Benjamins.

Strömqvist, Sven, Ulla Richthoff & Anders-Börje Andersson. 1993. *Strömqvist's and Richthoff's corpora: A guide to longitudinal data from four Swedish children*. Gothenburg: University of Gothenburg.

Söderbergh, Ragnhild. 1968. *Svensk ordbildning* [Swedish word-formation]. Stockholm: Norstedts.

Warren, Beatrice. 1978. *Semantic patterns of noun-noun compounds*. Gothenburg: University of Gothenburg PhD dissertation.

Waxman, Sandra, Xiaolan Fu, Sudha Arunachalam, Erin Leddon, Kathleen Geraghty & Hyun-joo Song. 2013. Are nouns learned before verbs? Infants provide insight into a long-standing debate. *Child Development Perspectives* 7(3). 155–159.

Wellman, Henry M., Paul L. Harris, Mita Banerjee & Anna Sinclair. 1995. Early understanding of emotion: Evidence from natural language. *Cognition and Emotion* 9(2/3). 117–149.

List of contributors

Bożena Cetnarowska
Institute of Linguistics
Faculty of Humanities
University of Silesia in Katowice
ul. Bankowa 12
40-007 Katowice
Poland
bozena.cetnarowska@us.edu.pl

Denis Creissels
University of Lyon
513 route de la Combette
38410 Saint Martin d'Uriage
France
denis.creissels@univ-lyon2.fr

Marie-Elaine van Egmond
Language Centre
Martin-Luther University Halle-Wittenberg
August-Bebel-Strasse 13c
06108 Halle (Saale)
Germany
marie-elaine.van-egmond@
sprachenzentrum.uni-halle.de

Aslı Gürer
English Language & Literature Department
Istanbul Bilgi University
Kazım Karabekir Cad. No: 2/13
34060 Eyüpsultan İstanbul
Turkey
asli.gurer@bilgi.edu.tr

Francesca Masini
Dipartimento di Lingue, Letterature e Culture Moderne (LILEC)
Alma Mater Studiorum – Università di Bologna
Via Cartoleria 5
40124 Bologna
Italy
francesca.masini@unibo.it

Simone Mattiola
Dipartimento di Filologia Classica e Italianistica (FICLIT)
Alma Mater Studiorum – Università di Bologna
Via Zamboni 32
40126 Bologna
Italy
simone.mattiola@unibo.it

Chiara Naccarato
National Research University
Higher School of Economics
21/4 Staraya Basmannaya Street, Building 5
105066 Moscow
Russian Federation
ch1naccarato@gmail.com

Åshild Næss
University of Oslo
Niels Henrik Abels vei 36
0313 Oslo
Norway
ashild.nass@iln.uio.no

Shanshan Huang
Dipartimento di Lingue, Letterature e Culture Moderne (LILEC)
Alma Mater Studiorum – Università di Bologna
Via Cartoleria 5
40124 Bologna
Italy
shanshan.h@live.com

László Károly
Department of Linguistics and Philology
Uppsala University
Thunbergsvägen 3 H
752 38 Uppsala
Sweden
Laszlo.Karoly@lingfil.uu.se

Jakob Lesage
Institut für Asien- und Afrikawissenschaften
Humboldt-Universität zu Berlin
Unter den Linden 6
10099 Berlin
Germany
jakob.lesage@gmail.com

Steve Pepper
University of Oslo
Frederik Stangs gate 8
0272 Oslo
Norway
pepper.steve@gmail.com

Polina Pleshak
University of Maryland
Marie Mount Hall
7814 Regents Drive
College Park
MD 20742
USA
ppleshak@umd.edu

Françoise Rose
Dynamique du Langage
(CNRS & Université Lyon 2)
14 avenue Berthelot
69363 Lyon Cedex 07
France
Francoise.Rose@cnrs.fr

Maria Rosenberg
Department of Language Studies
Umeå University
SE-901 87 Umeå
Sweden
maria.rosenberg@umu.se

An Van linden
Department of Modern Languages
University of Liège
Place Cockerill 3 - 5
4000 Liège
Belgium
an.vanlinden@uliege.be

Index of Subjects

A N phrase 438, 448, 449, 453, 457
absolute form 402, 404, 417
accretion 203, 205
action nominalization 182, 193
actualization vs. characterization 74
adj (adjectival) 13, 14, 23, 34, 35, 38, 45, 47, 51, 52, 54, 60, 61, 69, 109, 164, 170, 177, 206, 214, 217, 241, 242, 283, 291, 296, 297, 298, 360, 363, 368, 402, 403, 411, 412, 416, 425
adjective 12, 26, 31, 34, 47, 55, 60, 66, 82, 83, 105, 106, 107, 108, 120, 129, 131, 132, 138, 155, 156, 157, 161, 162, 164, 170, 177, 213, 214, 216, 218, 222, 224, 225, 226, 227, 228, 232, 233, 257, 259, 260, 265, 272, 273, 291, 313, 357, 364, 365, 383, 385, 396, 418, 419, 423, 431, 448, 449
adnominalizer 78, 79, 81, 82
adnominal possession 12, 23, 25, 26, 32, 33, 62, 63, 65, 73, 74, 75, 76, 77, 80, 81, 82, 83, 84, 85, 87, 88, 89, 90, 92, 93, 94, 95, 96, 97, 98, 99, 244, 248
adposition 38, 46, 53, 59, 65, 206, 207
affixoid 57
Africa 80, 81
agent role 193, 203, 279, 280, 322, 359, 365, 366, 370, 371, 372
agglutinative 355, 374
agreement 55, 153, 157, 160, 164, 169, 247, 260, 262, 265, 271, 384, 392, 393, 396, 422, 424, 449
alienable possession 12, 88, 108, 155, 156, 157, 158, 160, 161, 177
anchoring construction 62, 63, 64, 67
anchoring vs. non-anchoring 74
animacy hierarchy 124
animate possessor 203, 204, 403, 445
artifacts 204
asymmetric relation 316, 319, 325, 343
attributive relation 360, 402, 411, 415, 421, 425
attributive suffix 411, 414
attributivizer 15, 47, 401, 411, 412, 413, 414, 415, 422, 424, 425

backgrounding 266
binominal lexeme
 – classification of 11, 25, 32, 62, 69
 – definition of 25, 26, 28, 29
binominal strategy 10, 23, 35, 50, 51, 52, 66, 67, 68, 69, 334, 360
binominal type 11, 25, 36, 39, 43, 54, 250, 270, 284, 334, 335, 360, 368, 431, 433
body-part 185, 189, 191, 194, 196, 199, 201, 203, 204, 207, 210, 408, 409, 415
body part term
 – primary 191
bound noun 58, 181, 182, 186, 188, 194, 200, 201, 203, 204, 205, 206, 207, 237, 240, 242, 243, 245, 246, 250, 251, 253, 254, 255, 256, 257, 258, 259, 260, 261, 262, 264, 266, 267, 268, 269, 270, 271, 272, 273
bound pronoun 75
bound root 184, 200, 239, 250, 252, 257, 258, 260, 291
boundary phenomena 112, 119, 120, 138, 139, 142
Bourque25 classification 309, 312, 315
Bourque29 classification 309, 311, 316, 319, 326, 327, 331, 337, 343, 350
Bourquifier 308, 309, 315, 327, 328, 329, 330, 343

caseless form 402
categorization 239, 262, 271, 280
child language 433, 441
classifier 6, 9, 13, 29, 31, 34, 35, 38, 42, 43, 44, 45, 52, 58, 91, 132, 181, 186, 189, 192, 193, 200, 202, 206, 208, 209, 210, 237, 238, 239, 240, 241, 242, 244, 249, 250, 251, 252, 253, 254, 255, 256, 257, 258, 259, 260, 261, 262, 263, 264, 265, 266, 267, 268, 269, 270, 271, 272, 273, 341
classifying construction 104, 107
classifying modifier 107, 123, 130, 131, 226
class term 186, 209
cliticization 53, 83
close-knit phrases 104, 114, 136, 139

cls [classifier] 13, 23, 29, 34, 35, 39, 42, 43, 44, 52, 57, 58, 62, 69, 109, 187, 206, 208, 209, 238, 241, 242, 249, 250, 254, 270, 341
cmp [compounding] 13, 14, 15, 23, 34, 35, 36, 39, 40, 42, 46, 52, 56, 57, 58, 59, 61, 68, 69, 135, 136, 187, 205, 206, 207, 209, 214, 238, 241, 242, 246, 270, 283, 289, 291, 295, 296, 297, 298, 299, 310, 323, 403, 404, 405, 408, 409, 410, 411, 412, 414, 415, 416, 417, 426, 433, 434, 441, 453
competition 10, 15, 214, 239, 292, 334, 368, 401, 405, 409, 411, 412, 432, 436, 453, 456, 457, 458
complex concept 1, 2, 3, 6, 7, 8, 10, 24, 31, 153, 154, 159, 160, 162, 172, 217, 241, 242, 246, 263, 385, 401
complex lexeme 4, 5, 7, 8, 9, 10, 95, 223
complex word 2, 4, 6, 218, 230, 265, 404, 432
compositionality 103, 112, 113, 114, 115, 116, 117, 141, 408, 415
compound 3, 7, 8, 9, 13, 15, 24, 25, 26, 31, 32, 33, 35, 38, 40, 41, 42, 44, 46, 52, 57, 58, 64, 65, 69, 90, 96, 98, 103, 104, 105, 106, 109, 111, 112, 113, 114, 115, 116, 117, 118, 119, 120, 122, 123, 124, 125, 126, 127, 128, 129, 130, 131, 132, 135, 136, 137, 138, 139, 140, 141, 142, 143, 144, 145, 146, 153, 159, 181, 182, 184, 185, 186, 187, 188, 189, 195, 196, 200, 204, 205, 207, 209, 210, 213, 214, 215, 217, 218, 219, 220, 221, 222, 223, 228, 230, 233, 237, 238, 240, 241, 242, 243, 246, 247, 248, 249, 250, 254, 255, 256, 257, 264, 270, 271, 277, 281, 284, 288, 290, 291, 292, 293, 294, 306, 310, 314, 318, 319, 320, 322, 323, 324, 330, 342, 343, 344, 355, 357, 358, 359, 361, 362, 365, 367, 368, 369, 371, 372, 374, 375, 376, 381, 382, 383, 384, 385, 386, 387, 388, 389, 390, 392, 394, 395, 396, 397, 398, 405, 406, 407, 408, 409, 410, 411, 412, 413, 414, 415, 416, 417, 418, 419, 420, 421, 423, 424, 425, 426, 431, 432, 433, 434, 435, 436, 437, 438, 439, 440, 441, 442, 443, 444, 445, 446, 449, 454, 455, 456, 457, 458
− attributive compound 361, 385
− binominal compound 12, 103, 105, 108, 112, 113, 123, 124, 125, 127, 132, 133, 134, 136, 137, 141, 144, 238, 256, 385
− coordinative compound 325, 359, 385, 387
− deictic compound 388
− morphological compound 13, 213, 214, 215, 216, 217, 222, 229, 230, 233
− NN compound 3, 4, 233, 431, 432, 433, 434, 435, 436, 437, 438, 439, 441, 442, 444, 446, 448, 449, 453, 454, 455, 456, 457, 458
− novel compound 307, 388, 435, 436, 437, 438, 441, 444, 447, 449, 453, 456, 457
− phrasal compound 357, 382, 384
− repetition compound 383
− subordinate compound 15, 381, 385, 386, 387, 399
compounding 2, 9, 13, 14, 24, 33, 35, 36, 38, 40, 52, 58, 59, 64, 68, 69, 75, 77, 79, 95, 104, 111, 114, 117, 118, 120, 122, 142, 145, 185, 210, 222, 227, 233, 237, 238, 241, 246, 262, 266, 270, 273, 277, 278, 282, 283, 289, 291, 293, 294, 306, 322, 343, 355, 356, 357, 358, 360, 362, 366, 368, 369, 370, 372, 373, 376, 381, 403, 404, 407, 415, 422, 424, 425, 426, 431, 432, 433, 434, 436, 437, 441, 446, 449, 458
− lexical compounding 266, 269
concept combination 305, 431, 433, 438, 445
conceptual variation 293
con [construct] 8, 12, 13, 14, 15, 23, 35, 38, 45, 46, 47, 48, 49, 50, 51, 52, 53, 56, 61, 62, 68, 69, 109, 170, 206, 207, 209, 210, 241, 242, 244, 316, 360, 362, 363, 368, 382, 426
construct 3, 8, 9, 12, 35, 47, 48, 49, 50, 52, 53, 73, 75, 76, 77, 78, 79, 80, 81, 82, 83, 84, 85, 87, 88, 89, 90, 91, 92, 93, 94, 95, 96, 97, 98, 99, 109, 307, 360
Construction Morphology 4, 213, 233
control 181, 202, 203, 392, 393
coordinated nouns 435
coordination 30, 308, 310, 313, 316, 326, 327, 331, 341, 343, 344, 345, 350, 450
cranberry morph 116, 118, 330

Index of Subjects

dbl [double] 23, 35, 38, 50, 52, 61, 68, 69, 109, 111, 164, 206, 241, 242
definiteness 50, 64, 82, 97, 362, 402, 422
degree of fusion 11, 23, 25, 36, 38, 40, 51, 52, 69, 138, 140, 142
dependent-marking 24, 36, 37, 51, 64, 78, 206, 214
der [derivation] 14, 23, 34, 35, 39, 40, 41, 42, 43, 52, 57, 60, 61, 62, 69, 109, 206, 214, 241, 242, 245, 291, 295, 297, 298, 299, 333, 360, 365, 368, 375, 403, 434
derivation 2, 3, 9, 15, 24, 34, 40, 52, 60, 77, 237, 241, 245, 259, 262, 263, 264, 265, 277, 282, 283, 289, 290, 291, 294, 355, 356, 358, 360, 365, 368, 369, 370, 371, 374, 375, 376, 403, 433
derivational morphology 355, 436
derivational strategy 14, 355
descriptive function 226, 228, 435, 457
descriptive phrase 12, 103, 105, 106, 108, 124, 125, 127, 128, 130, 136, 140, 141, 242
determination 74, 75, 96, 99
direct possessive 13, 183, 185, 188, 189, 191, 192, 194, 195, 201, 202, 203, 204, 205, 210

endocentricity 13, 15, 117, 220, 221, 222, 233, 246, 247, 355, 359, 374, 375, 381, 386, 387, 395, 398
exocentricity 13, 112, 113, 114, 117, 141, 144, 145, 220, 221, 222, 233, 247, 248, 254, 359, 386, 387
ezâfe 78, 79 see also izafet

figurativity 103, 112, 117, 141
formal 5, 6, 9, 14, 73, 74, 96, 97, 104, 112, 124, 125, 127, 133, 138, 139, 142, 154, 181, 182, 189, 200, 201, 204, 205, 210, 220, 247, 251, 252, 254, 258, 265, 271, 279, 280, 355, 357, 359, 360, 362
frequency 69, 107, 144, 222, 281, 284, 288, 305, 309, 330, 331, 332, 333, 334, 336, 337, 360, 409, 436, 437

generic reference 90
generic-specific construction 12, 103, 105, 107, 109, 114, 115, 128, 132, 137, 138, 139, 140, 142
gen [genitival] 8, 13, 14, 15, 23, 24, 33, 34, 35, 36, 38, 45, 46, 47, 50, 51, 52, 53, 58, 59, 60, 61, 62, 63, 66, 68, 69, 88, 109, 193, 202, 206, 208, 210, 213, 214, 216, 217, 218, 220, 221, 223, 224, 226, 227, 228, 229, 230, 231, 232, 233, 241, 242, 243, 244, 254, 266, 268, 314, 360, 362, 363, 364, 401, 402, 403, 404, 405, 406, 407, 408, 409, 410, 411, 413, 416, 417, 418, 420, 422, 423, 424, 425, 434, 435, 445, 446, 454, 455, 456, 457
genitival binominals 404, 405, 406, 408, 409, 410, 411, 412, 422, 424, 425
genitive constructions 109, 245, 362, 390, 404, 410, 411, 445, 446, 447, 457
genitive marker 33, 34, 51, 94, 205, 392, 405, 413, 445, 446
gradient phenomena 40, 56, 432
grammaticalization 11, 23, 25, 33, 38, 67, 69, 82, 107, 186, 374, 376
Greenbergian universal 12, 23, 65, 67, 68, 69

Hatcher5 classification 309, 325, 326, 327, 331, 337, 342, 343
Hatcher-Bourque classification 14, 46, 305, 308, 309, 311, 313, 325, 326, 327, 330, 331, 343, 344, 350
headedness 261, 265, 272, 369, 374, 376
head-marking 24, 37, 49, 51, 54, 61, 64, 78, 83, 177, 206, 208

identification property 406, 412
inalienable possession 12, 103, 105, 108, 127, 128, 130, 136, 137, 138, 140, 141, 142, 143, 145, 155, 158, 160, 207
inanimate possessor 203, 205
independent noun 55, 161, 162, 163, 164, 165, 166, 169, 170, 171, 175, 177, 184, 186, 187, 188, 191, 195, 197, 201, 242, 243, 246, 247, 253, 260
indexation 49, 53, 76, 93
indexer 49, 362

indirect possessive 13, 181, 189, 192, 193, 197, 198, 200, 202, 203, 204, 206, 208, 210
inflection 2, 60, 86, 89, 90, 216, 355, 416, 433, 436
inherently relational 193, 201, 202, 393, 395
inherent property 106, 410, 412
instrument role 14, 26, 221, 373, 375, 388
internal organ 198
izafet 15, 360, 362, 363, 394 see also ezâfe

jxt [juxtaposition] 9, 13, 14, 15, 16, 23, 33, 34, 35, 36, 38, 39, 43, 46, 52, 55, 57, 61, 64, 68, 69, 75, 95, 108, 153, 185, 187, 205, 207, 213, 214, 215, 216, 217, 218, 219, 220, 222, 223, 225, 226, 227, 228, 229, 230, 231, 232, 233, 241, 242, 248, 310, 323, 359, 360, 361, 368, 374, 382, 383, 401, 402, 403, 404, 405, 406, 408, 409, 410, 411, 412, 414, 415, 416, 417, 425, 426, 431, 445, 458

kinship term 155, 157, 184, 186, 188, 190, 191, 201, 204, 206, 207, 255, 390, 405, 411, 416

language acquisition 437
left-branching 420, 421
lexical typology 2, 4, 432, 433
liaison form 434, 455
linker 8, 34, 45, 48, 49, 51, 126, 254
linking element 15, 33, 40, 58, 59, 90, 99, 109, 245, 362, 382, 384, 385, 387, 389, 391, 392, 394, 395, 396, 397, 398, 434
locus of marking 11, 23, 25, 33, 36, 37, 69

manipulation of case 266
material 4, 6, 29, 30, 31, 34, 37, 39, 40, 52, 154, 207, 223, 248, 263, 272, 277, 292, 294, 361, 370, 371, 404, 409, 410, 411, 413, 415, 419, 422, 425, 439
metaphor 112, 117, 221, 359, 415
metonymy 112, 117, 221, 247, 359
modification 10, 12, 23, 27, 30, 31, 32, 62, 63, 64, 67, 73, 91, 92, 93, 95, 123, 130, 154, 323, 330, 341, 342, 396, 401, 415, 417, 418

modification-reference continuum 64, 415
morpheme loss 61
morphological head 247, 265, 266, 271
morphophonological process 414
morphosyntactic criteria 113, 129
multifunctional suffix 367, 375
multiple-classifier system 237

naming function 2, 4, 26, 53, 217, 218, 223, 224, 382, 436
natural sex 412
nickname 114, 248, 406, 407
nml [nominalized] 13, 23, 38, 51, 54, 55, 56, 69, 170
nominal construction 431, 432, 442, 453, 454, 455, 458
nominal modification construction 7, 12, 15, 25, 32, 103, 104, 112, 118, 123, 137, 139, 141, 154, 401, 402
nominal phrase 432
nonanchoring possessive 190
non-autonomous form 77, 79, 80
non-binary typology 65, 67
nonperson indexation 49, 53
nonspecific possessor construction 190
non-transpositional affix 46, 48, 51, 52, 60
noun class harmony 153, 160, 163, 175, 176, 177
noun incorporation 115, 266, 267, 268, 269, 272, 273
– classificatory 266, 269
numerals 88, 89, 93, 108, 129, 157, 251, 257, 259, 272, 273, 423

onomasiological base 27, 28, 29, 32, 279, 280, 291, 370
onomasiological mark 27, 28, 279, 280, 291
onomasiological type 14, 28, 30, 32, 277, 280, 281, 283, 284, 285, 286, 289, 291, 292, 293, 294, 369
– OT1 28, 29, 280, 284, 285, 289, 294
– OT2 28, 29, 280, 283, 284, 285, 294
– OT3 28, 29, 280, 283, 284, 285, 288, 289, 290, 291, 293, 294
– OT4 28, 280, 284, 285
– OT5 28, 280, 284
– OT6 280, 284, 285, 289, 294

onomastic expression 405, 412
order of modifier and head 127, 142

part-whole relation 108, 132, 135, 137, 138,
    144, 154, 160, 165, 174, 198, 199, 204,
    205, 391, 392, 405, 406, 411, 412, 416, 425
patient role 97, 124, 261, 267, 370, 372, 373
person indexation 49, 53
pertensive 48, 80, 92
phonological criteria 112, 196
phonological process 93, 112, 122
phrasal lexeme 2, 3, 4, 106, 139, 223, 224,
    225, 226, 227, 290, 382
place 138, 140, 161, 163, 168, 173, 207, 208,
    228, 245, 254, 273, 280, 363, 390, 392,
    397, 412, 438
plant-part term 194, 196, 205, 206, 207, 209
plural marker 89
polysynthetic 12, 153
possessee 74, 80, 87, 95, 96, 97, 98, 116,
    208, 244
possessive affix 49, 76, 84, 126
possessive construction 32, 33, 49, 53, 54,
    60, 91, 116, 143, 182, 189, 190, 195, 207,
    360, 361, 362, 384, 392, 395, 398, 403,
    422, 438, 445
possessive marking 13, 181, 183, 185, 190,
    191, 194, 196, 201, 204, 207, 210
possessive relation 15, 189, 192, 193, 197,
    401, 403, 404, 411
possessor 13, 33, 61, 63, 74, 80, 84, 86, 87,
    88, 89, 90, 91, 93, 94, 95, 96, 97, 98,
    99, 108, 116, 154, 158, 169, 174, 176, 181,
    183, 189, 191, 192, 193, 194, 195, 196,
    197, 198, 201, 202, 207, 208, 210, 243,
    244, 316, 317, 333, 336, 341, 346, 350,
    362, 417, 422, 445, 446
possessor indexing 13, 181, 183, 197,
    201, 210
postposition 34, 45, 46, 59, 60, 424
predestination 404, 416, 419
predicational relation 388, 389
preposition 9, 13, 14, 16, 24, 29, 33, 34, 36,
    45, 46, 51, 52, 59, 62, 64, 75, 98, 153,
    181, 196, 197, 198, 200, 201, 202, 204,
    207, 208, 209, 246, 269, 277, 278, 281,
    282, 288, 289, 290, 291, 294, 306, 311,
    313, 431, 435, 447, 448, 449, 451, 452,
    456, 457, 458
prepositional phrase 269, 447, 448, 449, 456
privative 12, 108, 155, 159, 160, 172, 173,
    177, 363
prn [pronominal] 23, 38, 51, 53, 54, 62, 68, 69
pronoun 33, 34, 53, 54, 83, 84, 85, 155, 156,
    157, 167, 183, 184, 230, 243, 422, 445, 451
proper name 168, 248, 264
property-affix 265, 270, 272
proprietive 12, 47, 155, 159, 160, 172, 173,
    177, 412, 415
prosodic word 243, 256, 258, 259
prp [prepositional] 14, 23, 34, 35, 38, 45, 46,
    51, 52, 53, 59, 61, 62, 68, 69, 109, 206,
    207, 208, 209, 241, 242, 246, 282, 288,
    290, 291, 293, 295, 296, 297, 298
purpose 187, 192, 193, 199, 202, 232, 371,
    372, 375, 405, 411, 416, 435
Pwav scale 67, 69

qualification 45, 262, 263, 264, 265
qualifying modifier 106, 107, 130
quantity expression 199, 204

referential 197, 213, 215, 229, 268, 322, 422,
    424, 425
registration 76
relational adjective 8, 13, 24, 65, 213, 216,
    225, 226, 228, 229, 230, 231, 232, 233,
    283, 367, 368, 438
relational preposition 13, 196, 197, 198, 199,
    200, 201, 202, 203, 204, 206, 207, 208,
    209, 210
relator 49, 51
repeater 270
resumptive pronoun 94
right-branching 421

Scapa Grid 31, 63
semantic head 113, 155, 161, 163, 164, 168,
    169, 170, 171, 220, 221, 246, 247, 308
semantic relation 5, 8, 10, 11, 13, 14, 15, 28,
    30, 33, 46, 181, 182, 187, 189, 193, 199,
    201, 204, 232, 267, 288, 305, 306, 307,
    308, 309, 320, 323, 330, 331, 332, 333,
    334, 336, 337, 342, 343, 359, 363, 369,

372, 373, 376, 381, 385, 387, 388, 395, 398, 404, 405, 410, 415, 419, 425, 431, 432, 438, 439, 440, 442, 444, 447, 448, 451, 454, 458
- CAUSATION 313, 326, 343, 348, 350
- CAUSE 310, 311, 312, 313, 314, 315, 317, 327, 348, 350
- COMPOSITION 310, 312, 313, 314, 315, 317, 326, 331, 341, 343, 347, 350
- CONTAINMENT 317, 318, 319, 325, 326, 327, 328, 337, 343, 344, 345, 350
- COORDINATION 308, 310, 312, 313, 316, 326, 327, 331, 341, 343, 344, 345, 350
- DIRECTION 315, 318, 319, 325, 326, 327, 337, 343, 344, 347, 350
- FUNCTION 310, 312, 313, 314, 316, 326, 336, 343, 349, 350
- HYPERNYMY 310, 312, 313, 314
- LOCATION 288, 310, 312, 313, 315, 317, 318, 323, 326, 328, 331, 332, 333, 336, 341, 346, 350
- PART 288, 310, 312, 313, 315, 317, 318, 331, 333, 334, 335, 336, 337, 341, 346, 350
- PARTONOMY 313, 326, 328, 329, 331, 341, 346, 350
- POSSESSION 310, 312, 313, 315, 316, 317, 319, 326, 341, 346, 350
- PRODUCTION 308, 309, 310, 311, 312, 313, 314, 315, 316, 317, 326, 343, 348, 350
- PURPOSE 277, 278, 288, 310, 312, 313, 314, 316, 318, 326, 331, 333, 335, 336, 337, 341, 342, 343, 349, 350
- PURPOSE AND PROPER FUNCTION 312
- RESEMBLANCE 288
- SIMILARITY 310, 312, 313, 314, 316, 325, 326, 327, 343, 344, 345, 350
- SOURCE 310, 312, 313, 314, 315, 317, 319, 325, 326, 343, 348, 350
- TAXONOMY 313, 317, 326, 344, 345, 350
- TEMPORALITY 313, 326, 346, 350
- TIME 308, 310, 311, 312, 313, 315, 322, 346, 350
- TOPIC 310, 312, 313, 314, 315, 316, 317, 326, 347, 350
- USAGE 313, 326, 329, 348, 350
- USE 310, 312, 313, 317, 342, 343, 346, 349

South America 13
special form 47, 49, 50, 84, 88, 95
species 27, 187, 192, 193, 204, 206, 221, 325, 326, 332, 344, 404, 407, 408, 409, 410, 415, 425
stress pattern 107, 112, 120, 121, 122, 134, 138, 140, 142, 184, 186, 215, 216, 255, 256
subordinator 451
substance 5, 27, 248, 250, 254, 265, 271, 410, 412
symmetric relation 316, 325, 327
syntactic criteria 113, 123, 129
syntactic minimality 226, 227, 233
synthetic morphology 355

theme 153, 359
thing-affix 30, 40, 41, 42, 52, 57, 181, 241, 250, 261, 265, 270, 271
thing-morph 30, 31, 39, 44, 55, 154, 181, 214, 233, 270, 272, 280, 342, 385
tonal alternation 81, 86
tone rules 75
transitivity 392, 395, 398
transpositional affix 51
typifying construction 63, 64, 65
typology of binominal lexemes 9, 32, 56, 155, 170, 214

unattested strategy 25
univerbation 57, 219

word-formation pattern 431, 432, 433, 436

Index of Languages

Äiwoo 13, 58, 181, 182, 183, 184, 185, 190, 194, 197, 198, 200, 201, 202, 203, 206, 207, 208, 209, 210
Akkadian 50, 51, 52
Arabela 42, 43
Arabic 3, 76, 97, 98, 363
Atlantic-Congo 44

Bandial 29, 43, 44
Barain 45, 49, 50
Berber 78
Bezhta 8, 24, 36, 46, 48
Bora 29, 42, 43, 52

Cambodian 58, 59
Central Yupik 41, 50
Czech 27, 43, 47

Dutch 114, 159, 450

English 3, 33, 35, 54, 57, 74, 75, 94, 106, 116, 129, 131, 132, 144, 153, 159, 167, 171, 197, 222, 227, 292, 305, 306, 310, 314, 322, 324, 330, 437, 445, 446, 450

Finno-Ugric 15, 401, 402, 403, 425
French 3, 8, 24, 33, 45, 46, 52, 75, 153, 294, 306, 309, 310, 318, 323, 342, 369, 433, 436, 446, 456

Galibi Carib 49, 50, 61, 62, 67
Gawwada 41, 44, 45, 46, 52
German 7, 24, 52, 58, 144, 153, 222, 227, 229, 368, 433, 434, 436, 437, 443, 450
Germanic 24, 33, 217, 223, 227, 290, 433, 434, 436
Greek 46, 59, 433, 434, 436

Harakmbut 13, 29, 58, 237, 238, 240, 241, 242, 243, 245, 246, 247, 248, 250, 251, 253, 254, 255, 256, 257, 258, 259, 260, 261, 262, 264, 266, 267, 268, 269, 270, 271, 272, 273
Hausa 48, 49, 53, 55, 83, 93, 94

Hawaiian 318, 331, 332
Hebrew 3, 8, 48, 49, 50, 76, 93, 97, 433, 436, 445, 446, 450
Hill Mari 15, 401, 404, 411, 412, 413, 414, 415, 416, 417, 418, 419, 420, 421, 422, 423, 424, 425
Hindi 46, 60
Hungarian 47, 48, 61, 76, 89, 93, 94, 95, 96

Indo-European 44, 47, 144, 145, 290
Irish 46, 61
Italian 3, 6, 14, 45, 64, 277, 278, 283, 284, 288, 289, 290, 291, 293, 294

Japanese 14, 35, 59, 277, 278, 282, 283, 284, 289, 292, 294

Kalamang 49
Kambaata 46, 51
Kanuri 46
Karachay-Balkar 382, 383, 384, 385, 388, 389, 392, 393, 394, 398
Kazakh 14, 358, 359, 361, 362, 364, 366, 367, 368, 370, 371, 372, 373
Kekchí 48, 50
Ket 331, 336
Khakas 14, 359, 364, 368, 370, 372
Kildin Sami 47
Kirmandji 61, 64
Korean 58, 59
Kupsabiny 48, 49

Lithuanian 41, 63, 64, 433, 436

Malagasy 49, 52
Maltese 45, 50, 51, 59, 61, 98
Maori 58
Mapudungun 7, 342
Minangkabau 43
Mojeño Trinitario 13, 237, 240, 241, 242, 243, 244, 245, 246, 247, 248, 249, 250, 251, 252, 255, 256, 257, 258, 259, 260, 261, 262, 263, 264, 265, 266, 267, 268, 269, 270, 271, 272, 273

https://doi.org/10.1515/9783110673494-017

Moksha 15, 401, 402, 403, 404, 405, 406, 409, 410, 411, 412, 413, 414, 415, 416, 417, 418, 419, 420, 421, 422, 423, 424, 425
Murui Huitoto 250

Nepali 46, 60

Oceanic 12, 13, 73, 77, 91, 92, 181, 182, 183, 185, 189, 190, 194, 197, 198, 202, 203, 205, 207, 208, 210
Oroqen 41, 50

Pama-Nyungan 12, 103, 104, 105, 106, 108, 109, 112, 113, 129, 131, 132, 133, 134, 141, 143, 144, 145, 146, 159
Polish 3, 13, 38, 41, 47, 66, 213, 214, 215, 216, 217, 218, 220, 222, 223, 225, 227, 229, 230, 231, 233, 290
Puyuma 41, 50

Russian 8, 9, 14, 24, 33, 47, 52, 54, 58, 60, 64, 65, 88, 219, 277, 278, 282, 283, 284, 288, 289, 290, 291, 294, 364, 408, 433, 436

Sakha 357
Saramaccan 7, 52
Semitic 12, 48, 51, 73, 75, 76, 77, 78, 80, 84, 93, 94, 96, 97, 98
Slovak 9, 41, 47, 60, 61
Somali 50, 51
Swahili 43, 44, 45, 46, 61, 62

Tagalog 45, 46
Takia 50, 330
Tarifit 45, 47, 62
Trinitario 14, 50, 58, 239, 243, 244, 245, 246, 247, 248, 250, 351, 352, 253, 255, 356, 357, 358, 259, 262, 363, 264, 266, 367, 368, 269, 271, 272, 273
Turkic 14, 15, 90, 355, 356, 357, 358, 359, 360, 361, 362, 363, 364, 365, 366, 367, 368, 369, 373, 374, 375, 376, 381, 382
Turkish 14, 15, 24, 48, 64, 77, 90, 91, 93, 94, 96, 99, 159, 356, 357, 358, 359, 360, 361, 362, 363, 364, 365, 366, 367, 368, 370, 371, 372, 373, 374, 389, 393, 394, 433, 436
Turkmen 361, 373

Uigur 14, 356, 357, 359, 362, 363, 365, 366, 368, 370, 371, 372
Uralic 47
Uzbek 356, 358, 366

Vietnamese 38, 39, 332

Welsh 45, 61
Western Amazonian 13, 58, 237, 239, 242, 270
Western Farsi 48, 50

Yakut 14, 48, 49, 356, 357, 359, 361, 364, 366, 367, 368, 370, 372, 374, 375
Yoruba 59, 84